The
Current
American
Civil
War,

A Global
Perspective

The Current American Civil War,

A Global Perspective

Kern G. Lim

ARCHWAY
PUBLISHING

Archway Publishing books may be ordered through booksellers or by contacting:

Archway Publishing
1663 Liberty Drive
Bloomington, IN 47403
www.archwaypublishing.com
1 (888) 242-5904

Scripture taken from the King James Version of the Bible.

THE HOLY BIBLE, NEW INTERNATIONAL VERSION®, NIV® Copyright © 1973,
1978, 1984, 2011 by Biblica, Inc.® Used by permission. All rights reserved worldwide.

ISBN: 978-1-4808-6400-9 (sc)
ISBN: 978-1-4808-6399-6 (e)

Library of Congress Control Number: 2018951296

Print information available on the last page.

Archway Publishing rev. date: 8/28/2018

Dedication

From my maternal grandmother, I learned the traditional Chinese Values and Ethics. From my Mom, the power of Empathy, and from my Dad, who just passed on this Feb; 学习与生活, 如逆水行舟, 不进则退, Life, as in Learning is always an upstream exercise, if you are not advancing, then you are retreating.

Contents

Introduction

With malice toward none, with charity for all

"This country has been good to me, and I want to pay it back."
William S Knudsen in 1940, when asked why he left as head of
General Motors to serve under President Franklin D Roosevelt

The results of the 2016 General Elections was announced by the major news networks, only in the early dawn of 9th Nov 2016, an unexpected one to many. Since that time, it's been an all-out open Media war against the elected administration, a war of great rhetorical divide in this country, a vicious and hostile Open Civil War! In America, we currently see a great difference in opinions and views that will shape the future of this country and with it, far reaching global effects.

Is this an Ideological War? A War of Information (or mis-information in some cases; of Fake News), War of Values, War of Globalism versus Nationalism, Socialism against Capitalism, the Politically Correct One View of the world against Diversity of Ideas, Progressives at war with Conservatives, subterfuges and sophistries against reason and common sense? At the beginning of the last Civil War in Apr 1861, many had expected it to be over by Christmas, and it finally ended, nearly four years later. Will this War take as long? What will be its outcome? What will be its eventual impact on America, as well as the World? How did it start and what's this current Civil War about?

As I fathomed these questions and watched the cable news; with all the Hate, Wrath, Avarice and Hubris that's tearing America apart, it pains me deeply to see what's happening to my adoptive country. Watching the rhetoric propagated on the Mainstream Media and Social Media on various wide-ranging issues [some I wasn't so familiar with], some arguments sounded counter-intuitive, other familiar sound-bites seemed overly idealistic, while All the politically correct statements seem immune to logic and reason.

I've been most fortunate to have had the opportunity, to live and work in many different cities and countries, to learn various regional cultures, to lead operations across different professional disciplines and Industries. From these experiences, I had come to treasure the great Value of forming an unbiased Independent Perspective; which can only be gained through detailed understanding of relevant facts and agendas of related decision makers. The Genesis of this book stems from the combination of my personal inquisitive curiosity to learn more about the current challenges faced by this country and the desire to contribute back to America; who's been good to me

1998, Settling into Schenectady, NY from Singapore

We had arrived in this country in November of 1998 (Bill Clinton was the President then), as we settled into Schenectady, NY we learned of its past history and how it used to be "the Silicon Valley" of its time when Edison founded the General Electric Company. Despite it being a 'rust belt city', we saw a beautiful country with so much potential, offering great quality of life, full of hope and opportunities (which I still believe in), a land of honest and hardworking people who love their country and extremely proud to be Americans.

Huge space, vast lands, great abundance in natural resources, tremendous amount of freedom, freedom of speech, freedom and diversity in ideas. To each their own, non-judgmental of others, what a great culture and admirable values, so much to see and do, so much to learn. On our first visit to Washington, DC, in the Lincoln Memorial, I saw the Gettysburg address for the first time, "…. Government of the people, by the people and for the People…" that pretty much summed up my view of this beautiful country before the turn of the millennium.

Learnings from Election 2000, the hanging chads

I remembered the 2000 Elections as a close and contentious one, eventually decided by a couple of hundred votes in Florida. The White house passed from Democrat into Republican hands when the dust settled. There was some contention by Al Gore's team after the election and the Media continuously poking fun at President Bush with frequent attempts to ridicule him throughout his Presidency (but nowhere near the sheer anger, hatred and disdain that we see today).

From the 2000 Election, I learned about the government of this country. Whether the Republican or Democrat, both work for the good of this country by different means (shaped by their Ideological leanings). They are two sides of the same coin and the alternating of power shifting between the 2 sides is per design by the founding fathers of this country. This system of governance might be a given to the Americans, inherited from its founders 200 plus years ago (taken for granted by some). To many of the folks in Asia, where a one Dominant party rules and State Authority and Control is widely accepted, this 2-party system seems unnecessary, dangerously High Risk and even Disorienting to some.

To me, the alternating of Power serves as a good check and balance, as per Quote from Lord Acton. "… Power tends to Corrupt and absolute power corrupts absolutely." This power transfer setup also reflects the concept of 道, Taoism in the balance of Yin and Yang 阴阳.

This alternating transition of Power between the parties is not only logical, this great setup also facilitates new perspectives and diversity in ideologies. It allows for renewed dynamism, new growth, prevents Monopoly of Power, and lends transparency into possible corruption. Interestingly, if you look at the symbol of 道, the Yin and Yang are not static in a 2-dimensional diagram. In fact, you are really looking at a 3-dimensional depiction of Dynamic equilibrium. Imagine you are looking straight at the tip of a drill bit, you will see a similar pattern, as the drill bit starts to turn, you can picture the Yin and Yang alternating with each other.

As the 2 parties alternate in peaceful transition of power (both working for the good of the country, the loyal opposition), the country moves forward in a stable way and all citizens benefit. Even without much knowledge of the detailed Economic or other policies, any independent thinking person would be able to understand that Monopoly of power is antithetical to democracy.

Fast Forward, General Election 2016

With the unexpected results (to some fellow travellers) of the last Election, many Progressives began suggesting that Democracy is flawed, or the electoral college process is flawed. Strangely, they didn't seem to think so in 2008 when the same process got President Obama elected with 365 against 173 for McCain. Yet, there is much historical and philosophical evidence that supports their suggestion.

Plato had categorized the various forms of government into; Aristocracy, Monarchy, Oligarchy, Tyranny and Democracy. Yet through bulk of human history, Democracy as form of government was seldom successfully practiced for any extended period of time. In fact, before the American Revolution in 1776, Europe was mostly under Monarchy Rule with some countries under variations of Aristocracy and Oligarchy Rule.

The last experiment on Democratic government had to be traced back nearly 2000 years, to the age of the Greek Polis and early rise of the Republic of Rome, which eventually succumbed to Monarchy/Aristocracy. Even then, that the Greek Polis formed only a tiny fraction of human civilizations in its time, as the rest of the non-Greek world was also under Monarchy rule (Egyptian, Hittites, Persian, China, etc.). The democratic form of government practised by the Greek was viewed as Radical during its time.

In the present day, if we look at the countries in the United Nations, one might have the false impression that many nations are now practising Democracy, this 'mirage' view of the world might prove to be superficial. With the exception of America, a few ex-British Dominions and some countries in Western Europe, the Democratic Rule in all the other countries around the world has been a recent phenomenon, the experience too short and shallow to be judged successful at this stage. The world's most populous country, People's Republic of China is a communist country, most Asian countries' governments are dominated by a single ruling party with a few exceptions, that had western influence (eg. Taiwan, India, Japan & Korea). Still others are communists or quasi-Military Regimes (North Korea, Laos, Cambodia, Myanmar, etc.)

Even for America, after the initial success of the Revolutionary War, it remained a real struggle to get the 'confederation' of the 13 states to work together as a Republic. Many of the founding fathers of this country had become acutely aware of the weaknesses of Democracy in actual practice when they were designing the American form of Government and Constitution back in late 1780s.

James Madison shared his views in Vices of the Political Systems of the United States and later the Federalists Papers: How could a republic bottomed on the principle of popular sovereignty be structured in such a way to manage the inevitable excesses of democracy and best serve the long-term public interests? The realization that political popularity generated a toxic chemistry of appeasement and demagoguery that privileged popular whim and short-term interests at the expense of the long term public interest.

From the experience of the failure of Articles of Confederation to unite the thirteen States; all operating effectively as a coherent entity, comes a practical view grounded in reality : the much vaunted intimacy between elected representatives and their constituents, it turned out, had a quite deplorable downside, as representatives, in order to appease the voters, told them that they did not have to pay taxes, could settle on land promised to the Native Americans, could confiscate loyalists estates regardless of legal prohibitions against doing so, and were perfectly justified in accepting vastly inflated currency, since it permitted debtors to pay their creditors with money that was nearly worthless. The experience of the founding fathers has taught us that Unbridled Democracy was incompatible with the political health of a republic. Jefferson too acknowledged "a choice by the people themselves is not generally distinguished for its wisdom, that the first secretion from them is usually crude and heterogeneous."

So, it seems like the Progressives are correct in pointing out the flaws in the Democratic Process in America, the exact same process that elected President Bill Clinton (twice in 1992, 1996), President George W. Bush 43rd (2000, 2004) and President Obama (2008, 2012). If Democracy and its related process are flawed, then logically, any extension of Democratic Ideals like Human Rights must be flawed too? If people cannot be trusted to voted intelligently for the long term good of the nation, then should they have the right to vote in the first place? Are the progressives suggesting otherwise? Let's explore further.

Clear and Present Danger: Democracy is fragile, unrestrained Abuse will Destroy it

Everything that we see around us is possible because of the very narrow band of EM (Electro Magnetic) Waves known as visible light spectrum, we see it as white light which is a combination of the rainbow colors. We cannot imagine a world without visible light and we easily take it for granted. Democracy in human history is as rare as the visible light in the entire spectrum of EM waves, looking at the wide range of EM Waves stretching from Gamma rays to Radio Waves, the visible light spectrum would only form a razor thin slit (of micrometres), yet our entire earth functions around just that tiny sliver of spectrum, called visible light, isn't that amazing?

Alright, we understand the analogy, Democracy is extremely rare in human history, but why? Is it too unstable? Or too fragile? We'll address Democracy's fragility and its delicate working mechanism in more detail in chapter 2. For now, we can see the danger, that Unrestrained Abuse of 'human rights' as a mere front for furthering one's personal Greedy agenda and short term self-interests; such as Free Welfare Benefits by the Welfare Abusers, puts the Individual Liberty and American Democracy at great risks. This type of abuse is a typical case of Tragedy of the Commons, which we'll explore further in chapter 3.

A global perspective: Abuse of 'Human Rights'

For most living outside America, ideas like demanding for Individual Rights to Free Benefits, Free Healthcare or Government working for the people, sounds 'too good to be true', a luxury disconnected from reality, an 'out of this world' alien concept [who knows, perhaps it works in America?].

Understanding the rhetoric broadcasted endlessly over American Media is easy enough, but intuitively, most thinking folks can understand that unrestrained greed in guise of individual liberty is bad for the society's stability. Thus in other countries, both their government and constituents might conclude that this form of 'free for all, American Democracy' is too risky to experiment with, as it can quickly lead to over-exploitation and eventually into anarchy. Their deep respect for the State's Authority and Power is so ingrained over thousands of years of history that one can best described it as a cultural not a political difference in perspectives.

Or perhaps, looking at it from a different angle, it's the thousand years of wisdom that allows them to understand that the Powerful Ruling class will always exploit the weak individuals, so where does the Human Rights and Power of the weak individual emanates from? The Law? Constitution? After all, laws are just words created by those in power and easily amended accordingly to suit their needs [as we clearly see illustrated in Animal Farm by Orwell and also in the actions of the Activists Judges wishing to amend the Constitution as a 'Living document']. No, the individual rights and liberty as stated in The Constitution comes from the Patriotism of fellow individual Americans that still respects and willing to defend each other's rights, what Ibn Khaldun termed as Asabiyyah [solidarity] in 1377 AD. However, we should remember that Continuous Abuse by fellow travellers, will erode that Alignment with each other as well as to the Nation [as in the case of Globalist's Cult].

To those outside America (whose only view is through CNN, NBC, MSNBC, etc.) what is deemed (even flaunted) as an Entitlement by some Americans would be viewed as a mythical Luxury, one that they have no need for, nor can ill afford. Yet, from a more realistic view with better understanding of the truth, we know that the silent majority of Americans exercise their rights quietly as they go about their daily business. These rights that they exercise are the right to free speech, right to defend themselves when attacked, right to have equal opportunities to education, to jobs, to be treated equality under the law. Any thinking person should be able to understand A right is not a gift of God or nature but a privilege which it is good for the group that the individual should have. By this logic, free benefits like education, healthcare, etc. cannot be Rights as someone else would have to pay for them right? Wanting something for nothing is rooted in Greed and Sloth.

Democracy is great for the individual, great for diversity of ideas which could become the seeds of innovation and growth because it allows for competition, competition of talents, of ideas, of individuals' will power, hard work and strive, innovativeness, etc. To the Americans born in this country, some might take democracy for granted, I hope that this book can help you appreciate the beauty of democracy in America and the danger of unbridled abuse of individual freedom. Just like white light which allows us to see, we might take it for granted until we leave the "thin spectrum", then it's just darkness.

> *"… Vitality springs from diversity – which makes for real progress so long as there's mutual toleration, based on the recognition that worse may come from an attempt to suppress differences than acceptance of them…"*
>
> - quote from B.H. Liddell Hart

Through last year, I was intrigued to observe so many 'so called' celebrities to be chanting the mantras and slogans of "Globalism" when they don't speak another language, have never lived nor worked in other countries for any extended time, let alone had the need to, nor acquired skills to understand other cultures, values or system of governments? Does chanting the incantations of Globalism makes one Global? Obviously not, it just means they joined the Globalist Cult of the Culturally Ignorant.

One does wonder, where did all this anti-American hatred come from? Is there foreign power influence at work here (Russian, Chinese)? Why are the protestors burning the American flag and attacking the very country that protects them and their rights to free speech? Would they ever protest in Iran? Russia? In China? How could someone feel so strongly about issues that they have so little knowledge about or experience in? What happened to Mutual Toleration? Why has there been no outreach for compromise or collaboration? We'll explore the answers and the real strategy behind the protests in chapter 8.

To the outsider, it would appear that in place of the enlightened forefathers, we now see Ignorance, great avarice, lack of values, all translating into Abuse of the Democratic Ideals, Abuse and Exploitation of the Welfare system by Welfare Abusers; equating charity as Entitlements. Instigated and sponsored by the Hordes of Activists' peons, all plundering the America's Public Goods, demanding Healthcare as a right, Greed and Sloth knows no boundaries. We should treasure Democracy while you still have it, we have to stop its Abuse, stop selling away your freedom for Freebies & Welfare Benefits. Please kindly stop thrashing your home, stop being the mouth-piece of the Top 1% sponsored Activists Corporations!

To the more discerning, the key to breaking the vicious cycle of ignorance and Greed, is Self-Restraint and moderation through teaching, inculcating Values, practising Ethos as explained by Aristotle in Nicomachean Ethics, and Awful virtues described by Adam Smith; Discipline, self-restraint, moral rectitude, righteous anger at wrongdoers can help counter Abuse by the Greedy and prevent Democracy from devolving into Anarchy. All of us must do our part in this Civil War to defend Liberty and Democracy, we have to prevent further Corruption of Democracy in this country.

Multiple perspectives, Independent attestation

As I began reading up on the materials and exploring the various issues, it began to dawn on me that what's being presented or discussed in mainstream media or Social media, are only tip of the icebergs, the substantive parts of the real challenges are never properly discussed and seldom mentioned. Surely with all the resources and expertise available to them, the mainstream media and tech workers posting in the internet cannot be that ignorant? Makes one start to wonder if these Media 'journalists' Celebrities are wicked or merely stupid?

From this realization, this book's approach to obtaining the answers to untying the Gordian knot, needs to be disciplined and methodical. First, the due diligence process to accumulate the necessary data, financials and facts, focuses on researching what's required to answer our questions rather than what information's available [helps us avoid the trap of availability].

The resulting analysis and conclusions needs to be supported by logic and reason of related disciplines. To achieve this, we need a multi-discipline base of different fields of knowledge; understanding of organization behaviour in their respective historical and cultural backdrop, the financial benefits, power-relations and political perspectives, economic and legal frameworks, business management leveraging scientific and mathematical knowledge with deep appreciation of human psychology. Grounding in Military Strategies, Religious and philosophies' concepts come in useful too. Knowledge and insights from cross-disciplines will provide us with multiple perspectives to the issues we explore, ensuring we don't have any 'Blind-spots'.

Most importantly, from our personal experiences, we triangulate our findings with the political motivations and agendas of the participants; with their emotional, rational motivations and explore their unstated agendas. We'll also look for independent attestation via third parties or through the actions of other related participants in the events. Next, various Organizational Cultures and Leadership traits are also explored, to better understand the behaviors of participants.

Lastly, through reflection on all the past events; [that cumulates into the causation effects of various currents within the rivers of time], we'll link up all the various derived conclusions, demonstrating to you why many of their causation can be traced back to a few common sources. We'll also share proposals for overcoming the challenges as well as predictions of the future if we don't succeed in solving these issues.

Instead of merely presenting opinions (as in the mainstream media), we'll also provide as much historical empirical evidence, financial numbers, Facts with disciplined analysis needs to be combined with understanding of human psychology to see the 'strategy behind the game', knowing the players and their agenda. We'll jointly do "thought experiments", "what if" scenarios, leverage concepts of scientific evidence in the Natural world, borrow analogies and allegories whenever possible to help elaborate the parallels as well as share with you; management decision-making tools that are data driven.

As we accumulate insights from the past to better understand the present, in hope to steer ourselves towards a better future, we'll be constantly amazed at the serendipity of major events in human history and how interrelated our past was and future will be.

Quick peek at the topics we'll explore and questions we hope to answer

As we sort out the causes of the current Civil War and understand it better, we'll find answers to the questions raised and dive deeper into the various concepts highlighted earlier, the hope is that this book can be of help to both the Patriots and the Progressives. Let's jointly explore the phenomenon of Globalization, the history of Socialism, identify the key players in this Civil War, know their agendas, mindset and understand their strategies.

What are the Ideals of America (both old and new)? We'll address the various Key conflicting Ideologies in the current Civil War, the roots of these Ideologies (Globalism, Socialism, etc.) and their practicality in implementation into effective and efficient policies. The hotly contested issues (the economy, jobs, religious freedom, education, healthcare, environment, global warming, refugees and immigration, borders, etc.) would also be explored, as we start to untie the Gordian knot.

We'll also need to retrace some portions of human history, since we've transitioned away from an agrarian agriculture society, a few events happened that shaped direction of the world as we know it. As a teaser, I'd highlighted 3 events here for discussion:

First, Great Britain, how did a small group of islands control colonies all around the world such that the sun never sets on the British empire? Why did the Industrial Revolution happened in Britain and allowed it to become a major player in World history till end of WWII?

Second, United States of America, how did a country with a fraction [5%] of the world's population come to dominate the World affairs for the last 70 plus years since end of WWII till present?

Thirdly, in more recent history, People's Republic of China, how did China [in 20 years] go from an economy smaller than Brazil, smaller than Italy, of only $730B in 1995, to become the largest world economy in 2015, nearly $20T GDP (PPP) ahead of United States at $18T GDP?

You will get the answers as we jointly explore the modern world history of Mercantilism, protectionism, Free Trade, the major factors that led to Industrial Revolution, even dating back to the Age of the Exploration.

The effects of Crony Capitalism on the American Economy, its interaction with K Street apparatchiks and influence over the Tech Street Giants Monopolies would also be discussed and documented. We'll understand The Islamists' perspective, how the war with the Radical terrorists, led to the Global War on Poverty with the incorporation of the numerous Activists Corporations since turn of the millennium.

We'll look into the effects of the IT Revolution and its subsequent transformation into giant monopolies, to give the readers a "clear and succinct notion of the process by which a particular industry passes from the control of the many to that of the few." [per Tarbell's notes from discussions with McClure to begin Muckraking the Trusts]. The Few that have become too Big to Fail, Too Rich and Corrupt to Jail. As during the age of the Trusts, at the turn of 20th century, we're now also faced with multiple monopolies in the Financial, Technology, Mainstream & Social Media and other Industries. Let's see their combined effects on America and the World.

We'll also see why there is no compromise of ideologies as our fore fathers had been willing to work with their opponents, as President Lincoln had been willing to adopt towards his opposition, and as Rev Martin Luther King Jr. in 60s peaceful civil protests, why do we not see any remote indication of Compromise? Paraphrasing what Tarbell wrote in 1905, "The American public not only has the right to know about the collusion between the Wall Street Crony Capitalists, K Street Apparatchiks, Tech Street Suzerains of Social Media, Mainstream Media sycophants and P.C. Gestapos Activists corporations, their Monopoly of American Political rhetoric and self-serving agendas, it is the duty of the public to know. How else can the American public discharge the most solemn obligation it owes to itself and to the future to keep the springs of its higher life clean?"

With the start of the IT Revolution near end of last century, the current influence of the smart devices, google and internet on the individuals is self-evident, the potential menace it posed [monopoly of thoughts and ideas] to the larger society, also needs to be highlighted and seriously discussed. The pervasive spread of Politically Correct One View (through help of the internet social media) is hurting our society's ability to exercise Reason and apply Common Sense. Its attempt in weeding out any Competition from Diverse Ideas, destroying deep analytical and reflective prowess with proliferation of shallow sound-bites slogans and mantras, all too readily gobbled up, via the mental sloth of the feeble minded and their vainglory to appear as 'in the know'.

For all Americans, let's explore how to bring the country together? Who to reach out to help the country succeed? What we can do to volunteer and help Make this country Great again? As with the approach of the commercial society [negative effects of Industrial Revolution and Capitalism] during the Age of Enlightenment, we should now also be seriously addressing negative effects of IT Revolution, Social Media and Mindless Indoctrination, countering it with Enlightened Education, Revival of Ethos, Traditional American Values and Renaissance of the Growth Culture, Culture of Excellence and Meritocracy.

Finally, despite the difficulties and challenges we currently face, we have hopes for an end to the Civil War, for a smooth transition of Power in K Street back to the American people, the compromise of real ideologies with the loyal opposition, mutual respect for elected leadership of this country (with mutual toleration of diversity in ideas and values, with empathy for thy neighbour Americans).

We also hold hopes for substantial efforts towards a Gaia Equilibrium, Sustainable renewable Energy for Human's future, the Need for Expediting Deep Space exploration, our Solar system colonization to help harness the True Potential of the IT Revolution in support of the Human Telos.

During the 16th century Europe, the conjuncture of a) the invention of the Gutenberg Press needed the combination of b) the Age of Exploration & c) Religious Schism, together they enabled Europe to step out of its medieval shadows into the Age of Enlightenment and subsequently the Industrial Revolution.

Back to the current American Civil War, in similar vein, only the end of the P.C. ONE View Media's Culture of Uniformity will allow growth and spread of new and diverse ideas [as Schism in the Medieval Church], that combined with Space Exploration [Age of Exploration], will finally leverage the untapped potential of the IT Revolution [Gutenberg press] and bring mankind to the next Age of Enlightenment. A better Aligned America and a Better World for all.

Chapter 1

Globalization and end of Nation States

The recent acceleration of Globalization

In 1998, when I attended an Executive Education about Business, Government and International Economy, the Harvard Business School professor provided this material:

Definition of Globalization: A historic process of economic integration across national borders, fostered by significant advances in transportation and communications technologies after WWII; hastened by trade liberalization during the 1950s and 1960s, floating exchange rates during the 1970s, and sovereign lending in the 70s and early 80s. Financial services deregulation and the US-Japanese balance of payments asymmetry accelerated integration on the capital and current accounts. In developing countries, capital account liberalization in the 90s facilitated significant cross-border capital flows – both equity and debt.

It goes on to describe coordinated fiscal and monetary measures; single Europe Act, NAFTA, GATT, etc. this was written in 1998, since then the process of Globalization has accelerated with the advancement of technology, become even more connected and ultimately more uniform. Does this mean the end of Nation States and we all live in one World without borders as some "Globalist slogans and mantras" suggests? Is Nationalism 'Old School' and outdated?

Before we jump on the bandwagon and start chanting the political 'slogans and mantras', let's think a little more deeply and learn a little more. Interestingly, Globalization effects have been around as long as trading has existed, the Phoenicians traded, and before them the Minoans were great sea farers and traders, China traded with the middle East and Europe via the Silk Road.

When the Age of Exploration started, the Portuguese, Spanish followed by the Dutch, English and other European powers also started to have Global impacts too (negative ones for the Latin Americans under the Spanish, similarly for the Native Americans here in North America).

As of End of WWII, the rise of America's dominance also facilitated globalization. So, Globalization is an on-going process; that recently sped up with end of Cold War, allowing the world to becomes more interconnected (not to be confused as a new phenomenon that Celebrity Politicians and their pseudo-intellect lackeys discovered and started marketing in last decade as Globalism).

Next, we'll discuss two types of entities (with their respective interest holders) in this Globalization process; **Economic entities**; like Multinational Corporations (eg. Companies like Apple, Microsoft, Starbucks, McDonald's, Disney, etc.) that does businesses across the world and **Political entities**; USA, China, India, Russia, Britain, etc.) Henry Kissinger pointed this out in his book *World Order* in 2014.

> *"…. The economic managers of globalization have few occasions to engage with its political processes. The managers of the political processes have few incentives to risk their domestic support on anticipating economic or financial problems who complexity eludes the understanding of all but experts…"*
>
> - Henry Kissinger

He goes on to discuss about the government's role to gain national advantage (similar to mercantilism), balancing between the political and economic international orders. According to Kissinger, there needs to be new rules (to be discussed between Governments and leaders of these Economic entities) for the Globalization process as the current rules does not address the inter-relations between economic and political entities well enough. He also mentions a lack of mechanism for the various political and economic leaders to truly address this complex issue.

Let's put this Perspective into charts for easier visualization

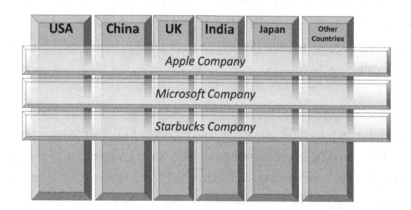

As you can see from the diagram above, the economic and political entities can co-exist, as they have done so for the last 70 years since the Globalization started its acceleration after WWII. The Globalists' mantras and slogans are obviously misleading (Globalism Good, Nationalism Bad), why then are they chanting the slogans? Are they stupid? We'll get to that answer shortly.

For now, let's get back to Henry Kissinger's earlier comments, you'll notice that he indicated twice in 2 consecutive paragraphs that a) The managers of the political processes (ie. Political leaders) have few incentives to risk their domestic support on anticipating economic or financial problems and b) governments are subjected to pressure seeking to tip the process of globalization in the direction of national advantage or mercantilism.

This makes perfect sense as the Political Leaders are beholden to their voters and tax-payers;

as taxes are currently collected from each countries' tax payers, Henry Kissinger therefore assumes the governments will further their voters and tax payers' interests. This is precisely what the China government is doing, furthering their countries' national interests (we'll dive into more details in this chapter). This is also what President Trump campaigned on in Election 2016 furthering the US voters and tax payers' interests over the other political entities. But President Obama has been chanting the Globalists' mantra and slogans for ages, what's going on here? Did Henry Kissinger miss something?

As for the Economic entities, the CEOs of Apple, Microsoft, McDonald's, etc. are beholden to their shareholders, they would like to do business across various countries, increase their Revenue by expanding their market share, thereby serving their shareholders' interests. As sponsors of political campaigns, they would also like to further their shareholders' interests too. Is that the answer? Is President Obama chanting the Globalists slogans to help his campaign sponsors? Perhaps, yet this is only part of the equation.

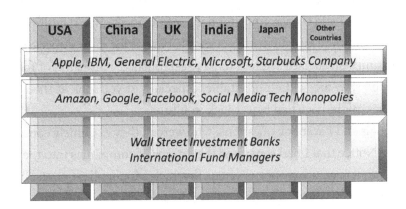

Besides the earlier group of companies we'd discussed, there's two other major groups that's also pushing the Globalists' agenda. There's the Technology Giants / Monopolies in Silicon Valley, theirs are mostly pro-globalists agenda too, but most important of all are the Wall Street Investment Banks and the International Funds.

The Tech giants like Google and Facebook should love the whole world to be using their software and platform and as the world comes together and all live happily ever after in the Google and Facebook's virtual world of bits and bytes, their dream as the world standard would be fulfilled.

But wait a minute, both Google and Facebook are banned in China, in a country of over 1.3 Billion people (official number), the country with the largest internet users in the world. Here in China百度 Baidu, 腾讯Tencent, Alibaba, and 微信 Wechat reigns. With so many internet users at stake wouldn't Google and Facebook be alarmed of the threat to be displaced as the internet standard? Wouldn't they like the Market Share and profits in China?

Chinese Government is doing exactly as Henry Kissinger predicted, they were great at tilting the advantage of Globalization for the betterment of their countrymen. 20 years ago, who would have heard of companies like Huawei华为, Alibaba, Tencent腾讯, Baidu百度, Xiaomi 小米, Haier, TCL, etc. just to name a few. Now these companies are huge, easily rivalling the likes of Apple,

Cisco Systems, Amazon, Google, etc. with all their Technology know-how, all the management expertise, financial resources, economies of scale, etc. How did the Chinese companies grow from 'wannabes' (no Technologies, no Management expertise, etc.) into the Technologies giants with giant market share not only in China but all around the world in less than 2 decades? Here's the answer to one of the questions raised in the Introduction, Rise of China in last 20 plus years, it is State Intervention. The China government has done an absolutely beautiful job (for their countrymen) to allow Technology and Management Expertise to transfer from foreign companies into the local Chinese companies while protecting the China Market for the local companies. It has also helped attract foreign Capital and liquidity to support the early growth stages of these current Tech Giants. A Perfect 10 for the Chinese Government's performance.

Superficially to the inexperienced, it might look like there's a large potential market in China, yet anyone who's worked in China would understand that it was never really a level playing field to start with, besides the obvious barriers like language, cultural, etc. (which can be overcome) there's also the less obvious barriers like skewed, semi-transparent and ever-changing procedural, legal and regional barriers. You add the varying standards of business ethics, multiple layers of people relationships that all combine into an insurmountable barrier for most American companies. To be fair, some companies on surface seemed to have established some kind of foothold in China, but if you dig deeper, they are seldom profitable, especially if you look at their Cashflow. Some European companies might have had better luck in China.

Back to the Google and Facebook questions, why weren't they extremely concerned not having the China Market? Notice that I had separated the groups of companies into the consumer products; Revenue and profit generating ones as versus the Tech Monopolies Giants. In the earlier case, these more traditional companies make and sell products / services for profits. Their share price trades at a multiple of those profits on Wall Street, generally, various industries are valued within a range of multiples of P/Es (Price / Earnings ratio). These traditional companies understand concepts of market segmentation, profit margins and profit pools in the channels of distribution. They will understand that profit margins are usually lower in developing markets (unless you've identified a specific niche) and will protect their higher profit margins regions and largest market share which for USA companies tends to be their home market, thus these 'traditional' companies would like overseas markets to be opened for USA companies but wouldn't be going crazy to open USA market (their domestic high margins market) to overseas competition. They probably would not be getting President Obama to be chanting the 'globalists' borderless slogans'.

But Tech monopolies are a different breed of companies all together, many of them started out as Unicorns; they make no profits. Later, some start to make some profits from advertising (FB), etc. But compared to the 'traditional companies', the profits of these Tech monopolies (google, FB, etc.) are relatively small (this is even more pronounced once you factor in their Share price). Compared to the traditional companies, you will see that the Tech companies' P/E (Price to earnings) ratios are astronomical.

Now we are getting to the last piece of the equation. Since the Tech monopolies are not relying on their users to pay the bills, who is paying the bills, who has major influence on the Share

Price of the Tech monopolies? Their Investors and shareholders; Wall Street Investment Banks, International Funds, Institutional Investors. The 3rd and biggest group in the 'economic entities' that truly wants to push for globalists agenda with no national boundaries and no barriers so that they can move the funds all around the world with no one to check and monitor them. They can easily by-pass Anti-money laundering controls, FCPA (Foreign Corrupt Practices Acts), etc. Do the funds belong to the drug Cartels? To the Terrorists groups? To Foreign governments that wants to see the demise of our country? Do we really know how much of the NYSE and Nasdaq's equities are ultimately held by foreign entities through Investment Banks or Funds?

Case in point to absence of International Financial Governance, in the 90s, a Fund manager made Billions in personal wealth doing just what we just discussed. First in 1992, he betted against the British Pound and came out on top. Next in 1997, he betted against the Developing markets in Asia and caused the Asian Financial Crisis, laughing all the way to the Bank in the process. Many of the Asian economies were set back by decades by his actions. He is George Soros. Seems like the Protest Wall Street movement (Bernie Sanders, Elizabeth Warren) is on to something, except sadly they were all barking up the wrong tree. George Soros is the biggest sponsor of President Obama, Hillary Clinton and the various leftists Activists' corporations, he is the puppet master pulling the strings.

More on George Soros in later chapters, for now suffice to know that he is extremely intelligent, plans Strategically, quick to exploit loop holes in International financial and legal systems. He is also very rich and influential in the financial markets, convicted in his causes and willing to spend to further them. We know that he sponsors most of the activists groups. Why?

Diversion of attention, when the US authorities are distracted by the domestic issues instigated by the activists' corporations, the protests and racial riots, etc. they inevitably pay less attention on regulating the International Funds movements and tracking the large speculative investment funds of International Organizations; possibly Drug Cartels, Terrorists, Foreign Governments opposed to our country that are assisted by International Funds and Investment Houses. Since late 90s, Soros had been able to strongly influence existing International Bureaucracies, helping to "oversee" and "monitor" these International Fund movements, these bureaucratic agencies all report to the International Community (ie. No one) but easily influenced into making unaccountable decisions which are ultimately self-serving in nature.

So, is President Obama merely doing his sponsors' bidding and thus chanting the Globalists' mantras? That's again just part of the answer too, because President Obama is also a smart man. There's two additional reasons, a) it makes him sound smart and look good as he tries to explain this Globalization Phenomenon (to the great celebrity, optics is everything as any marketing guru knows), secondly, as an even more calculated move, b) in a quick sleight of hands, he has relieved himself (at least to his impressionable supporters who bought his line of argument) of his responsibilities to the American voters. Since Globalism is inevitable, jobs leaving this country is also inevitable, then President Obama cannot do much about it, job loss due to globalism is as inevitable as the rising sun each day. Since President is now looking out for the Global interests (the Syrian Refugees must truly appreciate his concern for them), he can no longer be looking out for American Interests anymore, he needs to be more concerned about Global Warming and has no time to be bogged down with the 'minutiae', like job loss or low economic growth.

With no Global Voters to hold him accountable and he has relieved himself of all accountability to the American voters, leaving him only accountable to are his sponsors! What a stroke of genius! (at least to the non sequiturs, that bought this line of 'logic') To the more astute, he is merely shirking his responsibilities to the American voters, having sold the snowflakes a big bag of 'brown stuff'

Now that we know who's pushing the 'Globalists' agenda, let's revisit the factors, conditions leading up to formation of Modern Nation States and their validity in this Global World

> *"A Ruler, any Ruler, must promote and defend the welfare of all those subject to his rule."*
>
> - Aristotle's Politics

A little History: Formation of Modern Nation States

Let's confine our discussion to modern Nation States, otherwise we'll be looking at dates back to the Warring States (475 BC- 221 BC) in China before the consolidation into the Qin dynasty (widely accepted as 1st dynasty of China in year 221 BC) or even earlier (yet the same principles will still hold true). For the western culture nations, a good start would be the time of Peace of Westphalia in 1648 after the 30 years war. For different countries, the establishment into Nations would vary. 1776 for America, 1st French Republic in 1792, German Empire in 1871, Italy in 1861, etc. The roots of idea of Modern Nation States was forming since early 17th century. The Concept of Modern Nation States co-existed with Monarchy rule for couple of hundred years till Revolutions and other movements replaced the Monarchies with Democratic governments in most western countries.

Thomas Hobbes wrote about the "social contract" between the State and Individual in 1651 Leviathan "…. State of Nature .. the absence of Authority produced a "war of all against all". To escape such intolerable insecurity… people delivered their rights to a sovereign power in return for the sovereign's provision of security …" In summary, when there is no State Authority, Chaos and Anarchy prevails, the individuals are constantly under threat of death. By pledging their resources (paying taxes and fighting for the State's army when called upon) to the State, the State in return protects its citizens' safety, properties and other" agreed upon rights. Thomas Hobbes might have penned his views of this "social contract" in 1651, one can imagine the same set of conditions leading to formation of Warring States in China 475 BC or even earlier forms of "Nation States", Jared Diamond in his book, Guns, Germs and Steel discussed this Amalgamation process from Bands, Tribes, Chiefdoms and finally into States. The larger group Size brings about its own challenges like conflict resolutions amongst individuals but once that has been resolved by introduction of Laws*, the advantages far outweigh the disadvantages leading to the inevitable formation of

Nations that we have today. Advantages of the larger States; Increased Food Production through economies of scale, specialization from division of labor, better Law and Order, better quality of life and increased literacy rates.

The actual amalgamation process happened through actual conquests in human history or Threat of Conquests, we understand the 'social contract' concept still holds true but not in the 'literal simplistic sense' of the individuals all signing a contract with their rulers. *Du contrat social ou Principes du droit politique*; 1762 by Jean-Jacques Rousseau also discussed this 'social contract', Rousseau's work contributed to the French Revolution in 1789.

Formation of these Nation States also allowed for pooling of resources that creates competitive advantages; the larger Nation States has access to much more manpower than previous feudal kingdoms and thus a much stronger Military Power to project and use as necessary. Also, the pooling of financial resources which can allow the sponsorship of Expeditions of International Trade and Discoveries which are expensive but highly lucrative. In short, the Larger Nations enjoy economies of scale over the smaller tribes or chiefdoms; also it afforded the ability to specialization in skills leading to increased efficiency and innovativeness.

A new concept had also developed with formation of these new nation states in 17th century. Armand-Jean du Plessis, Cardinal de Richelieu was France's chief minister from 1624 – 1642, clearly envisioned the idea that the State (Nation) was an abstract and permanent entity existing in its own right. It is separate from its rulers (Monarchy) or Religious Duties to the (Roman Catholic) Church. When France (Catholic) supported the Protestant coalition on basis of national-interest calculation, Cardinal du Richelieu was criticized that as a Cardinal he owed his duty to the Catholic Church, this was his reply "…. Man (soul) is immortal, his salvation is hereafter… The State has no immortality, it's salvation is now or never…"

Richelieu was voicing the spirit that was imbued in all the leaders in Europe at that time, this event might seem distant to some readers, these seeds of Nationalism, undeniably contributed to European Enlightenment and subsequently the birth of modern day Nation States including one in 1776 with its Declaration of Independence and establishment of America as a Nation.

This concept has parallels in Finance / Accounting where the Company is its own entity and has interests separate from that of its CEOs, employees, shareholders, creditors, lenders, suppliers, etc. as the Company's interest is cumulation of all its stake holders' interests and even its self-preservation (raison d'être). The legal concept of a legal person / entity leverages the same concept too. In management literature, Alignment of Individuals' Interests to that of the Organization's strengthens it, allowing it to emerge triumph from competitions with other groups. All these concepts should be familiar to Americans, Lincoln summed it up best, "… Government of the people, by the people and for the people…"

As we've witnessed earlier, the State intervention of China's government helped the incredible Rise of China to become the world's Leading Economy (GDP in PPP) in the last 20 years. In the next segment, we'll see that State Intervention also played a critical role in the start of the Industrial Revolution in UK in the mid 19th century.

Free Trade Good, Protectionism Bad and the Evil 3 Little pigs

The Globalists would also like to have you believe that Free Trade is the one and only Politically Correct Answer and protectionism in any way, shape or form is Bad, and the 3 Little Pigs are Evil, Racists, Sexists and Islamophobic because they didn't open the door for the Big Bad (undocumented) Wolf in this borderless world.

In his book Origins of the Modern World, Robert B. Marks used the term Conjuncture to describe a number of events coinciding together that led to a major transformation or shift in human history. In the early 18th century, Britain was running a large trade deficit with India importing high quality cotton from India; which was not only much cheaper but of much finer quality too. To protect its domestic textile industries, UK raised tariffs on imports of Indian Textiles into UK, ie. Implemented *Mercantilist protectionism*.

As Britain Economy grew boosted by its local textile Industry and overseas colonies, it started to run short of natural (land and forest) resources for fuel, as alternative for energy it started to turn to coal & steam power. By 1800 Britain was mining 90% of the World's output for coal. Here again, the UK State intervened again, policies were put in place that encouraged production and transport of coal to London, then Lancashire. Since coal was of strategic importance to Britain, Duties were put in place to discourage export of coal. Heavy tariffs also put on iron imports to protect Britain's emerging Iron Industry.

With the State's intervention, Conjuncture started to happen. Number of Steam powered inventions were getting refined (Thomas Savery, Thomas Newcomen and James Watt), efficiency improved. Spinning and weaving became mechanized, leveraging steam power (burning of coal). With its vast colonies with low costs raw materials cotton and large Markets (America) for Textile products, the productivity of the Lancashire textile surged and outcompeted the Indian textile producers by 1850, capturing the world Textile market. Now, the British abandoned their mercantilist protectionism and became advocates of Free Trade. The Industrial Revolution train has also rolled out of the station, human kind has started to tap into fossil fuel for energy, the constraints of the biological old regime has been broken and the age of Modern world as we know it has started.

Now you also have the answer to part of the question on Great Britain raised in Introduction. In later chapters, you'll also see how President Franklin D. Roosevelt and Harry S. Truman (both Democrat Presidents) also intervened to help shaped USA to become the World Power for the last 70 years since end of WWII. State Intervention allows a higher probability of serendipity and conjunctures of events to happen, this is self-evident logic as the State Leadership performs its role in promoting and defending the welfare of all its subjects. We'll see the same concept in Biology of Life too

Diffusion, Osmosis and Active Transport

There's many parallels in nature, let's turn to biology and science for a change.

Diffusion: The passive movement of molecules or particles along a concentration gradient, or from regions of higher to regions of lower concentration

Osmosis: Diffusion of a solvent (usually water molecules) through a semipermeable membrane, from an area of low solute concentration, to an area of high solute concentration

Active Transport: A kind of transport wherein ions or molecules move against a concentration gradient, which means movement in the direction opposite that of diffusion, or movement from an area of lower concentration to an area of higher concentration. Hence, this process will require expenditure of energy, and the assistance of a type of protein called a carrier protein.

Let's start with Diffusion (the simplest concept), molecules moving from high concentration to low concentration areas if nothing obstructs them. This is a passive process no energy needed just like "…things flow downhill.." Next Osmosis, a semi-permeable membrane .. this allows particles of small enough size (water molecules) to pass through but not the larger particles (solute molecules), since the solute particles cannot diffuse (pass through the semi-permeable membrane), the water particles are able to move across to equalize the concentrations on both sides.

Last but not least, active transport, it moves molecules from lower concentration to higher concentration region. How can that be? This is possible when there's presence of life, when active energy is expended and there's a cellular membrane. The cellular membrane stops the high concentration molecules from flowing out. Energy is expended by the living cell, to pull in the desired molecule in through the cellular membrane. The cellular membrane helps regulates what goes in and out of the cell body, it helps maintains the state of homeostasis (balance) inside the cell and keeps it alive. Without the cellular membrane, in the vastness of early oceans on Earth, how would life have happened? How would single cell organisms have ever evolved without their cellular membranes?

As a parallel analogy, Nation States with their National Identities (complete with clearly marked borders) provided for better opportunities for Conjunctures like Industrial Revolutions to happen as cellular membranes provided the conjunctures for life to happen.

Politicians saying that Jobs will flow from high costs countries to low costs countries is like telling you that diffusion will happen, any genius with half a brain can figure that out. It is like saying s*** flows downhill, our heartfelt Thanks for sharing such valuable insights! The real question is what are we going to do, to make our workforce more competitive in costs, more productive, to be more innovative, provide better service, produce better quality products, introducing new products and services that our competitors do not have, etc.

The British Leaders intervened in the 18th and 19th centuries to make Britain a World Power then, Chinese Leaders also intervened to make China a World Power now. What did the American Politicians do for you? Besides chanting the *Globalists slogans? Is America Dead as a Nation? Such that only passive diffusion happens. Or is it still alive? such that active transport can be observed.

*in later chapters, we'll witness the birth of 'Globalist Pimps' in 60s, when the 'poverty pimps' became infected with the Alinsky Virus.

Earth as one World State?

Looking down at Earth from the International space station or from the moon (when we were last back there, in the 70s… from a time long ago), you see a beautiful blue sphere, you ask the question, Can we become one World? The answer is YES! Biologically, we are and always have been one Earth. Economically and Politically? Yes, It is a Great Idealistic Goal, now let's explore the reality and some of the current challenges and barriers we face to achieving this Great Idealistic Goal.

In the earlier segments, we observed that economic and political entities can co-exists together. We need to search for a better integration of both, we need to manage the Globalization process to manage and secure the interests of all political and economic entities. We should also flush out and bring to justice those abusing the current system too. The Financial systems had become integrated much earlier as wealth can be digitized and moved around Globally at "click of the mouse" [or tap on touchscreens}.

However, we humans are still Physical beings not digital. This seems a rather obvious statement. The same "social contract" penned by Hobbes in 1651 still holds true. People still need the protection of the Nation State (defined by physical boundaries), when you are physically threatened, you need the County's police to protect you, ISIS or ISIL (if you prefer Obama's version better) doesn't come after you in USA soil, because the US Military is protecting you. There is no World Police, no World Military at this time!

Next, there is a Huge Wealth Gap in the world, if you visit rural China, India or even many Latin America countries, you can witness it firsthand. Of course, You can easily google the GDP per capital to quantify the differences in wealth gap but you need to be physically there with them to understand, to empathize the complexities of their government systems, the Power distance between the rich and poor is extremely large in those countries with the corrupted political structures keeping them in poverty.

There's also major Cultural Differences, Religious and Ideological Differences. Just look at the current state of Europe, Germany had admitted refugees (a mere 2% of their population) into their countries in last 5 years, look at the social problems and chaos they face. In fact, look at America, less than 5% of world's population and the huge current disagreement between the opposing two sides. And you wish to have the entire world of 7B people all around the world to have the same Values, similar perceptions? Even the naïve and impressionable cannot be that disconnected from reality?

It's said that God gave human free will, which in turn produces diversity in cultures, in ideologies, in religions, diversity of ideas, etc. Diversity allows for competition which in turn brings about progress of human race. Only mutual toleration of diversity allows for closer integration of Political units.

Interestingly, there was a small window of such opportunity for America to better influence the and shape world in early 90s with the collapse of USSR, with China not yet rising and USA being the dominate World power then, it was then a good time to further the Ideals of Democracy, Freedom, Liberty, Capitalism to as many countries around the world that were willing to embrace it. Instead, President Bush 41st chose to use that dominance to lead the Coalition against Saddam Hussain in 1st Gulf War (setting in motion events that would lead to 9/11). Now we shall see if that opportunity will ever come by again, perhaps it is best to have the world as it is and leave diversity intact?

Lastly but most importantly, why it is not even remotely possible to be one World for a long time to come, the Sharing of Power (rather the refusal to share). The different political groups in power across the various nations (China, Iran, Russia, etc.) all have their own agendas, if you think United Nations has any influence over any countries, you are suffering from *Undifferentiated Goodness (we'll elaborate more in chapter 7). Setting aside cultural, ideological, religious differences, let's just use America as example, one country, yet when the GOP won the 2016 Election, are the Democrats working together for the future of a better America? Power is a very corrupting influence, once you have it, you become addicted to it and choose not to relinquish it. (there are ways to avoid this trap, Lincoln, Washington, MLK and some are able to resist the corrupting influence, we'll discuss how later in this book). So back to Global Power sharing, China, Russia, Iran, North Korea and rest of the world sure didn't get the memo on Globalism, if they did, they probably know it's a silly joke by some dimwitted prankster lying to his own non sequitur Voters. Globalism is just as worthless a façade as *Accord de Paris*. Each government outside America sells their own brand of mindless rhetoric; but few sell the Globalism brand, it is just a slogan for the uninformed egoists and misinformed feeble minded. Even the Globalist Cult leaders themselves know it.

Jared Diamond summed it up Best in his analysis of reasons for Amalgamation of States; there's 2 reasons, Actual Conquest or Very Real Threat of Conquest would force those in Power to be willing to share power! No political leaders in human history ever came together to sign contracts and willingly share their Power, if anything, the contracts of surrender are usually signed in the blood of millions of lives lost.

Remember during the campaign running up to the General Election 2016? Many celebrities (Hollywood, Media, Entertainers, etc.) all claimed and swear that they will move overseas if Donald J. Trump gets elected? Well President Elect Trump and now President Trump did win the Election 2016, where are these celebrities now?

Let's empathize and see it from their perspective. Well as a start, they don't speak other languages, which obviously makes it harder to assimilate into other cultures. They have no real transferable skills, they can't be a celebrity in Iran or China or even Latin America. Being one trick ponies, they cannot learn new skills to make a living abroad. Yet, they are very wealthy, so they can definitely bring their wealth overseas, right?

Yes, that's true, but they would still need to adapt to the new culture, new environment, built new social networks. They would have to face their fear of the unknown and leave their comfort zones. Even Canada is too much of a stretch for them. We will re-visit this mindset again in chapter 3 (Fear of Change, Inability to adapt, fear to step outside their comfort zone, Fear and Insecurity best sums up the Culture of Monopoly)

Chapter 2
Socialism Good, Capitalism Bad

".... Throughout recorded time, and probably since the end of the Neolithic age, there have been three kinds of people in the world, the High, the Middle, and the Low. They have been subdivided in many ways, they have borne countless different names, and their relative numbers, as well as their attitude towards one another, have varied from age to age; but the essential structure of society has never altered. Even after enormous upheavals and seemingly irrevocable changes, the same pattern has always reasserted itself, just as a gyroscope will always return to equilibrium, however far it is pushed one way or the other. The aims of these three groups are entirely irreconcilable. The aim of the High is to remain where they are. The aim of the Middle is to change places with the High. The aim of the Low, when they have an aim - for it is an abiding characteristic of the Low that they are too much crushed by drudgery to be more than intermittently conscious of anything outside their daily lives - to abolish all distinctions and create a society in which all men shall be equal. Thus, throughout history a struggle which is the same in its main outlines recurs over and over again. For long periods the High seem to be securely in power, but sooner or later there always comes a moment when they lose either their belief in themselves, or their capacity to govern efficiently, or both. They are then overthrown by the Middle, who enlist the Low on their side by pretending to them that they are fighting for liberty and justice. As soon as they have reached their objective, the Middle thrust the Low back into their old position of servitude, and themselves become the High. Presently, a new Middle group splits off from one of the other groups, or from both of them, and the struggle begins over again. Of the three groups, only the Low are never even temporarily successful in achieving their aims..."

- 1984 by George Orwell

"Nature smiles at the union of freedom and equality in our utopias. For Freedom and equality are sworn and everlasting enemies, and when one

prevails the other dies. Leave men free, and their natural inequalities will multiply almost geometrically, as in England and America in the nineteenth century under laissez-faire. To check the growth of inequality, liberty must be sacrificed, as in Russia after 1917. Even when repressed, inequality grows; only the man who is below the average in economic ability desires equality; those who are conscious of superior ability desire freedom; and in the end superior ability has its way. Utopias of equality are biologically doomed, and the best that the amiable philosopher can hope for is an approximate equality of legal justice and educational opportunity. A society in which all potential abilities are allowed to develop and function will have a survival advantage in competition of groups."

- Will & Ariel Durant, The Lessons of History

"Four legs good, two legs bag! Four legs good, two legs bad!" as the sheep would bleat in Animal Farm, by George Orwell

革命无罪，造反有理！革命无罪，造反有理！ *as the Red Guards would chant Chairman Mao's slogan during the Cultural Revolution (1966-1976)*

When I first read Animal Farm by George Orwell, I was quite amused by the sheep chanting Four Legs good, Two legs Bad and how towards the end of the story, they were so easily re-educated to chant Four Legs good, Two Legs Better! It was also sad to see that the animals couldn't differentiate between the Pigs and the Humans at the end of the book. Just before my posting to China in 2003, I was bringing myself up to speed on China's recent history and came across the footages of the Cultural Revolution in China with the red guards chanting about the glories of revolution and uprising, it is a state of near Anarchy and this was as recent as 1976! It reminded me of the sheep chanting in Animal Farm.

Present day America, I see similar political slogans and mantras chanting everywhere, not only in the street protests but in the mainstream Media channels, cable-news and social media networks! There is now more Media Propaganda broadcasted here in America than in China. China had risen from its ashes of the Cultural Revolution after Deng Xiaoping took over the helm; allowing Capitalism to work its magic in the China Markets, the China's economy started to take off. China's growing affluence provided majority of the population with better quality of life and education, thus there's less need for Mass Media Propaganda. Third world countries like North Korea relies on Mass Media Propaganda in place of real economic development, as their weak leadership cannot deliver growth in the economy nor add wealth to their people. The last Administration couldn't deliver real growth for the country either, therefore you also get Propaganda like Globalism, Socialism, Climate Change, Racism, Sexism, LGBTQ, etc. in place of economic growth and better quality of life for the people.

The Mythical Social-Welfare Dragon I

In last chapter, we'd witnessed the Leviathan (great sea dragon), when Hobbes discussed the social contract between individual and State. Now we introduce the Social Welfare Dragon. The dragon is a mythical creature, it exists in many different forms across various cultures, each with their own legends about the origins of this creature. But how did the legend of the dragon originate if it was never a real biological creature that lived on this planet? The most logical explanation offered, would be when mixture of fossilized skeletons and bones of different animals were discovered, instead of doing the tedious work of separating out the different animals the Dragon was conjectured up. And why not? when there's already (and still is) a high demand for such a conjecture of mystery and awe; giving the people exactly what they want to believe. The popularity of the dragon myth, till this day and across so many different cultures attest to the demand.

Similarly, the modern day progressive "political paleontologist" looks at various philosophical and social experiments of recent times; Socialism, Communism, Big State Government, Democracy, Capitalism, what does it all mean? We will first explore each ideology and how they really fared in real human societies in recent years. Not as some half-baked, Cut & Paste Sophistry. We'll then understand how and why the progressive "political paleontologists" sell their conjecture of 'Socialism'.

Socialism and Communism

In the last chapter, we discussed briefly the start of the Industrial Revolution. All the advancement in technology and luxuries that we enjoy today; internet, smart-phones, computers, etc. (you get the idea) would not be possible without the Industrial Revolution. Yet Industrialization brought its own set of challenges; a) burning of fossil fuels and releasing so much carbon back into the atmosphere leads to Global warming and climate change (we'll cover that in more details in chapter 7) and b) as people moved from rural farms into cities for work in factories (the society started a transition from agrarian to an industrial one), the working conditions in these factories were appalling and brutal (so graphically captured by Charles Dickens in his novel Oliver Twist published in 1838).

As early as 1768, during the British Age of Enlightenment, a Scottish Intellect wrote the following:

> ".. The boasted refinements, then, of the polished age, are not divested of danger. They open a door, perhaps, to disaster, as wide and accessible as any they have shut. If they build walls and ramparts, they enervate the minds of those who are placed to defend them; if they form disciplined armies, they reduce the military spirit of entire nations; and by placing the sword where they have given a distaste to civil establishments, they prepare for mankind the government of force."

> Adam Ferguson, 1768

Unlike his intellectual counterparts of that period, Ferguson saw the darker side of Commercial Society (effects of Industrialization and Capitalism) leading to government of force, tyranny. His book *Essay on the History of Civil Society* was well received by many especially the leaders of the German Romanticism including Friedrich Schiller and Johann Gottfried Herder (leader of the German Nationalism). Another avid reader of *Essay on History of Civil Society* was Georg Wilhelm Friedrich Hegel whose works went on to influence Karl Marx. Fast forward 80 years into the Industrial Revolution, against the backdrop of harsh miserable factory working conditions, Karl Marx and Friedrich Engels wrote the Communists Manifesto in 1847 and Das Kapital in 1867, 1885, 1894 (3 volumes). This Socialist movement remained a theory or ideology as no country was practicing it at that time. The big break came in 1917 with the Russian Revolution when Lenin and Trotsky orchestrated the birth of Communism, Socialism replacing the rule of the Czars (in place since the 16th century). We'll revisit the other effects of Ferguson's works in chapter 8.

From the Age of Enlightenment, Romanticism branched off in its Idealistic and Uncompromising view of how the Ideal World should look like. The French Revolution in 1789 (much influenced by the works of Jean Jacque Rousseau) and later Russian Revolution, all stemmed from this thread of idealistic (and often times overly simplistic) thinking, both led to Rise of Tyranny, Reign of Terror for French Revolution and Dictatorial rule in Russian till present day's Communism Regime.

Ironically, it was the unassuming and practical approach of acknowledging realities and flaws of Capitalism, Free Markets (understanding both its pros and cons) and compromising with, in order to improve it, that avoided bloodshed and tyranny. The formation of labor Unions to represent the workers' in negotiations with capitalist owners resulted in stability in society and produce the platform for growth of the middle class' wealth. This successful approach in Britain was also adopted in America allowing for Capitalism and Democracy to flourish, driving phenomenal Economic Growth and thus greatly benefiting the lives of Americans for generations.

An interesting sidebar, one of the reasons that contributed to the Russian Revolution (and Birth of Communism, Socialism) was cited as the peasants returning from the front carrying arms. You might notice similar circumstances that also contributed to a) signing of the Magna Carta in 1215 and b) the American Revolution in 1776. The first case of the knights and soldiers returning from crusades that supported the Barons' revolt against King John. The Magna Carta is considered by some a cornerstone of modern democracy. The second event, the American Revolution was greatly facilitated by the fact that the American colonists, militias were already armed at the outbreak of the war.

Arms in the hands of the people gives them power. Your 2nd amendment right. That supports freedom of speech; 1st amendment right, which in turn translates into Diversity of Ideas. Modern democracy and even that of communism / socialism might look very different if arms had not been in the hands of the Russian soldiers or the American Colonists. Interestingly also, in Guns, Germs & Steel by Jared Diamond, the first quoted strategy for the Elite Kleptocrats to stay in power is to Disarm the Populace and arm themselves.

"to disarm the people, was the best and most effectual way to enslave them."
- George Mason,

So now we know the birth of modern day communism, socialism. Next question, which countries had been putting Socialism in practice for last 100 years and how's their outcome look like? After end of WWII, the cold war began, on one side you have USA and its NATO allies, on the other side, you have the USSR and the Eastern Bloc (Warsaw Pact). You might like to see how the various countries allied themselves during the Cold War (1947 – 1991). China is communist but not completely allied with the Russians (esp. after the Sino-Soviet split in 1960).

We have many Communist/Socialist countries that has been exercising Big State Government planned Economies for nearly half a century as against the Capitalists Free Market practitioners. At this juncture, let's clarify the terminologies Democracy and Communism are forms of governments. Capitalism is NOT a form of government; the Capitalists are not interested in running the government, their primary objective is to make money. So how did the Ideology of socialism become Communism in practice? Well, you should remember that Socialism (the Karl Marx version) began as a criticism to Capitalism and all its flaws. Thus, when Socialists took over the government in Russia, Capitalism and free Market economy is naturally frowned upon. Their alternative is big Government State-Controlled Economies. The fifty years period from post WWII till collapse of the USSR provided the best examples for comparison of Free Market Capitalist economies as against the Big Government Planned Economies. Let's look at a few examples:

Planned Economies compared with Free Market Capitalist Economies

United States of America vs USSR, Union of Soviet Socialist Republics

The 2 Super Powers after the Second World War, compare the leader of NATO with the Leader of the Eastern Bloc and Communists States. Great example since all the Allies are Capitalistic Free Market economies and all the Communists (Big State) Government Planned Socialist economies.

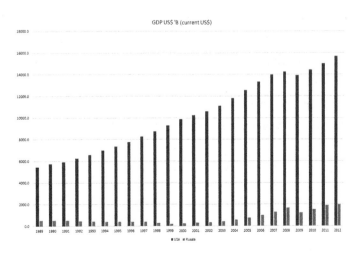

That's total GDP, let's adjust for population size differences. GDP per Capital chart below

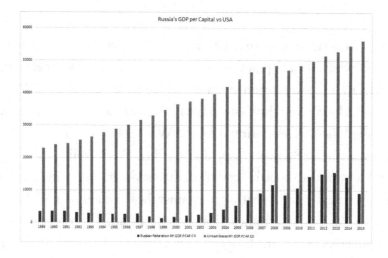

An even easier way of viewing, we express the USSR's GDP per Capital as % of USA's

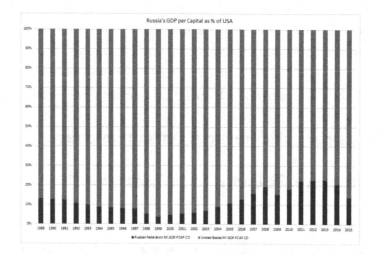

Russia's GDP per capital ranges between 10 – 20% of USA. That tells you the wealth and quality of life of the average citizen in a Big State Government controlled economy, is at best only 20% of what the Capitalistic Market has delivered for the average American! We see the same recurring trends in various countries, different regions of the world, Culturally Similar or otherwise, the same trend holds true.

If we wish to have similar Ethnic and Cultural background comparisons, let's review the Income per individuals in North vs South Korea.

North Korea vs South Korea

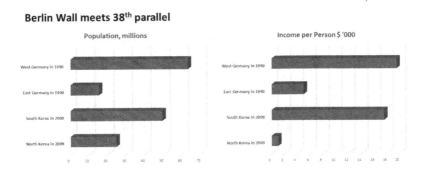

Or East Germany vs West Germany

Better still, let's look at the same Country itself under different Ideological Leaders. Let's take People's Republic of China as an example, 1976 – 78 as the transition of power from Mao to eventually Deng.

China (under Mao, Central Planned Economy) compared with China (under Deng and beyond; Capitalism, Free Market Economy with State protectionism)

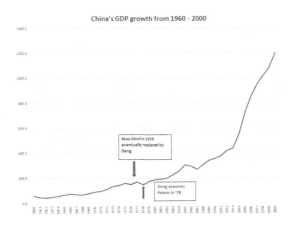

After Deng, all his successors Jiang Zemin ('93 – '03), Hu Jintao ('03 – '13) and now Xi Jinping ('13 – current) adopted similar approach of open market economic policies, encouraging foreign investments and importing, implementing Capitalistic mechanisms, opening Stock markets, Commodity Exchanges, etc. all over cities in China. In 1997, sovereignty of Hong Kong was transferred back to China and the same for Macau in 1999. Taiwan is still Independent as of date. China joined WTO in 2002 and had their remaining trade barriers removed, it's economy continued to soar till the present, averaging 8-9% growth slowing down to 7% for last couple of years.

In the last chapter we saw how the State intervention by the Chinese Government, led to the spurious growth of the Chinese National Brands and Conglomerates, Banks, Tech Giants, Automotive, Electronics, Appliances, Oil and Gas, Power and Utilities, etc..

In every category of Industries, the Chinese have come from State-owned Enterprises or Collective-owned; all technology starved and financial capital starved 'want-to-bes', to become behemoths that now ranks among the Top 10 Globally in Every Category! This achievement is truly a miracle (if you consider all the challenges faced, lack of financial capital, lack of management expertise, financial expertise) only made possible by the superb quality of the political leaders over the last 40 plus years. Their leaders have a strong sense of destiny for their country and cares for the Chinese people, as the Founding Fathers had for this country in its early history. The Chinese leaders also do NOT suffer fools gladly, unlike the last administration of mediocracy and its culture of mediocrity.

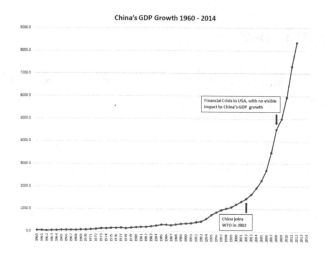

More examples of Successful Economies that adopted the Capitalism & Democracy Model

The economic rise of Japan in 60s & 70s was followed by the Asia 4 Dragon Economies (Taiwan, Korea, Hong Kong and Singapore) from 70s through 90s. What's so unique about these small group of countries, that they were able to adopt Capitalism successfully, while others weren't as stellar in their economic growth? The difference was their embrace of democracy and transparency, paralleled by the rapid rise of their middle-class. Rampant Corruption in the other countries obstructed the workings of the Free Market, not allowing 'Adam Smith's invisible hand' to efficiently allocate the resources to generate best returns for the investors, retarding their economic growth. We will see the stark contrasts below, in the GDP growth of these various Nation Sates.

Dr Goh Keng Swee was the chief architect of Singapore's phenomenal Economic Growth from 1960s – 90s, he retired in 1985 from public office after over 20 years at the helm of Singapore's Financial, National Defense and Educational Ministries, to become Economic advisor to Deng Xiaoping in China.

In Jan 1979, Dr Goh gave a lecture on "Business Morality in Less Developed Countries" at the University of California in Berkeley. In it he contended "in many of the third world countries this process [of modernization, interface between Developed and Developing nations] had been subverted by unethical business practices and corrupt administration, and that unless the situation was changed, less developed countries would not be able to emerge from poverty, no matter how much aid they received from rich nations".

George Rosen's *Peasant Society in a Changing Economy 1975*, was quoted by Dr GKS in 1979 about business morality in less developed countries, with regards to the Patron and Client relationship "in relations with the private sector. All too often the governments have regarded the private industrialist as a client. Controls are seen as a way of enforcing this clientage, and of thereby exchanging a private contribution to the governing group for a permit. When controls have been used in this fashion, they have contributed to the building up of inefficient firms, which in turn require special protection and assistance. .... This incestuous relationship creates an oligarchy of political leaders and industrialists who jointly control the political and industrial system."

Dr Goh saw hope in the successes of Korea and Taiwan then. The competitiveness of the international market helped to eradicate the inefficient companies that were based on the patron-client system. A new breed of entrepreneurs thus emerged "not through patronage but through natural selection in the hard school of competition".

Finally, Dr Goh added "what is required, in addition, is a strong commitment at some stage, to high standards of moral conduct on the part of both government and business leaders. Only then will it be possible for a backward society to go through the prolonged trauma which we call modernization."

Let's review the following 2 charts of GDP $ growth, grouped by Nations with comparable Population sizes (in year 2016). The 1st Chart comprises of Cambodia (16m), Hong Kong (7.3m), Laos (6.8m) and Singapore (5.6m) with the smallest population. The next chart includes Philippines (103m), Vietnam (93m), Thailand (69m), Myanmar (53m), R. Korea (51m) and Malaysia (31m). Looking at the 1st chart, you'll notice the Hong Kong and Singapore dwarfs all the other economies although Cambodia has the largest Population. In fact, if you plot HK and S'pore into the second Chart with much larger population sizes, their economies' size would be between Thailand and Malaysia.

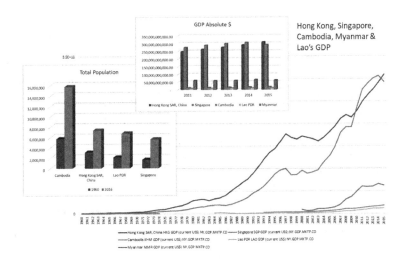

In the 2nd category of larger population size, South Korea (ROK, Republic of Korea) outshines all the other countries despite having a smaller population than Myanmar. The take away is clear, Korea, Hong Kong and Singapore had an earlier head start as Capitalistic Economies, Integration with the Global Economies allowed for their Exponential growth. Their relatively higher degree of transparency in their government, business and commercial environment, together with their embrace of democratic ideals allows for far higher efficiency in allocation of capital and resources to generate highest rate of returns for their investors.

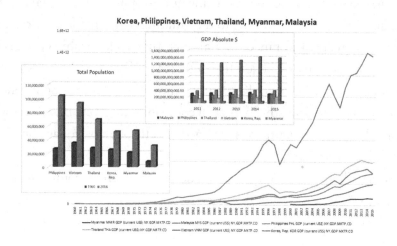

The next category, Thailand, Malaysia and Philippines are also better exposed to International Foreign Investments with a good head-start too. By contrast, the countries in the last category were late to the game, late in adopting Capitalism Model, the last to be open to Foreign Investments, Vietnam, Cambodia, Myanmar, Laos, in that order with varying, degrees of corruption staying as Communists, Military rule regimes (Big State Government) for the longest period.

Now that you've seen for yourself the overwhelming Historical Empirical evidence, what would be your deduction for the most logical causes, that produced these results? Human Motivation. Innovation, personal interests, Adam Smith's "invisible hand" helping to allocate the resources to generate their best and most efficient returns, etc.

> *"The natural effort of every individual to better his own condition.... is so powerful a principle, that it is alone, and without any assistance, not only capable of carrying on the society to wealth and prosperity, but of surmounting a hundred impertinent obstructions with which the folly of human laws too often incumbers its operations."*
>
> - Adam Smith in Wealth of Nations

"It is not from the benevolence of the butcher, the brewer, or the baker, that we expect our dinner," Adam Smith in Wealth of Nations, "but from their regard to their own interests."

Capitalism, Free Market, Perfect Competition

We've discussed the beginnings of modern day Communism, Socialism and witnessed the poor economic performance of their State Planned Economies. We can also trace the roots of Democracy to the Ancient Greece, Roman Republic, with its recent version to the combination of Age of Enlightenment, American Revolution, and various events unfolding in Europe after the Industrial Revolution. Where did Capitalism come from? It is not a form of government, it is not an ideology. Adam Smith wrote about Capitalism, Free Market Laissez-faire but he didn't invent it. No one invented the Free Market, though we can trace the beginnings of banking, aggregation of capital and beginning of stock market in the modern era.

The House of Medici (Casa de' Medici) rose to power in Florence around 14th century, they created the largest banking empire in Europe and was the wealthiest, most influential family for over 3 centuries in Europe. They produced 3 Popes of the Roman Catholic Church and 2 regent queens of France between 16th and early 17th century. As avid patrons and sponsors of arts, they were instrumental in the birth of the Renaissance in Europe. The double entry system for Accounting was also invented during the same time and used by the Medici family to help keep track of their vast wealth and control the growth of their banking empire. If you had not heard of the house of Medici, you would definitely recognize the artists, architects and scientists they had sponsored, names like Michelangelo, Leonardo da Vinci, Raphael, Rubens and Galileo Galilei.

The amassing of capital and wealth by the Medici helped pave the way to Renaissance in Europe; stepping out of the dark ages, and also the birth modern science (Galileo; widely recognized as father of Science, observational Astronomy, modern Physics and the scientific method). Galileo had proposed that Earth and the other planets revolved around the sun (heliocentric), at a time when the conventional wisdom (backed by the Church) then was that the sun revolved around Earth. Galileo was trialed by the Roman Inquisition, found guilty and forced to recant his theories (viewed as heretical and an attack on the Pope). He spent the rest of his remaining years under house arrest.

Another significant moment in aggregation of capital came in 1602 when the Amsterdam Stock Exchange was established by Dutch East India Company (VOC; Verenigde Oostindische Compagnie). Unlike the Portuguese and Spanish whose Expeditions of Discovery and Trade were sponsored by their Monarchy, the Dutch found their answer in stocks and bonds. Through formation of companies' equities contributed by large number of individuals, they were also able to fund the Dutch naval trading expeditions matching the Portuguese and Spanish, thus generating lucrative returns for their investors.

The Industrial Revolution provided more opportunities for investments and capital flowed freely to fund the best investment projects that gives their investors the highest returns, as described by Adam Smith's "invisible hand" in capital allocation. The aggregation of capital merely facilitates, sets up the stage for investment opportunities to get funding. The free market (Laissez-faire) of perfect competition and "Adam Smith's invisible hand" is really a phenomenon analogous to what we can observe in nature like convection currents earth's systems; oceans' currents, wind and even magma that causes plate tectonics. Because Capital is "liquid", it can move like fluids in nature (liquid or gaseous form). This movement or search for new equilibrium in nature, we call wind, ocean currents, etc. The movement of capital in the free market (ideally of perfect competition) can be called Capitalism. In Ancient Chinese philosophy, the search for equilibrium and balance in nature is explained as 道 Dao, Taosim.

As always, in life nothing is perfect, as in nature you don't always experience mild winds and gentle ocean currents, sometimes you get Tsunamis, Earthquakes, hurricanes, tornados, etc. we'll address the short comings of Capitalism in later part of this chapter (forming of large Monopolies will disrupt the natural fluidity and efficiency of resource allocation, thus destroying the free market).

Since the start of the Cold War, USA has been marketing Free Market Capitalism and Democracy as a package to all its allies and pro-west leaning developing economies. The truth is that Democracy as form of government works well with Capitalism, even as they need Not always go together. The two systems complement each other well. Democracy, free speech and flow of ideas, provides 'perfect information' to the Free Market (Laissez-faire) for Capitalism to operate well. The unbridled greed of humans exploiting Free Market Capitalism process [of perfect competition], the aggregation of too much wealth and power in the hands of few can start to impair the Free market, forming monopolies (with barriers to entry). Democracy therefore provides the best check and balance against Monopolies; with free flow of information and ideas to the people, to do (decide for themselves) what's in their best interests and counter the Monopolies.

Beginning in the 60s, Singapore (a small Nation State) started to experiment with a slight variation of Capitalism driven economy but a Single-party controlled government. Thus far, after 50 years, this "new experiment" of State Controlled Capitalism, still seem to serve Singapore well.

After replacing Mao who died in 1976, and having ousting Mao's appointed successor; Hua GuoFeng by 1978, Deng XiaoPing noticed this successful "experiment" in Singapore. This new approach in Singapore was of great significance to Deng as he knew that the State Controlled and Planned economy wasn't working well for China (notice the miniscule China economy in 70s) and the Chinese people. But China wasn't (and still isn't) ready for Democracy.

In 1978, Deng Xiaoping visited Singapore (before his visit to USA in 1979) to learn more about how Big State Control government can also leverage Capitalism to grow their economies. Deng was a pragmatist whose famous quote "不管黑貓白貓能捉老鼠都是好貓" (whether a white or black cat, as long as it can catch mice, it is a good cat), unlike Mao who was big on the Communist & Marx's Socialist Ideologies, the practical Deng believed the ends justify the means, thus China started to open its market adopting Capitalist practices and the economy start to grow. In 1985 (less than 10 years after he took over), China's economy more than doubled in size. By the time of Deng's death in 1997, just before Hong Kong's handover to China (personally negotiated by Deng himself), China's economy had grown over 6 times the size when Deng took over. By year 2015, China's GDP (PPP), adjusted for Purchasing Power Parity has over taken USA's GDP! Capitalism when harnessed well, is a great wealth creator.

Let's try to categorize the various types of governments and economies. In the diagram below, I have scale of Democracy as the y-axis, higher on the y-axis is more democratic government, lower is Socialist Big Government.

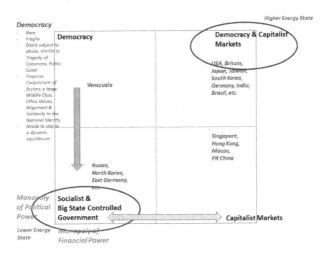

Along the x-axis is the economy, higher along the x-axis are the more Capitalistic economies and lower more Dirigiste, Centrally planned economies. Therefore, on the top right-hand corner are the most democratic and Capitalist economies and lower left-hand corner are the Socialist and Big Govt centrally controlled economies. As mentioned earlier, China has leveraged the Capitalist Market to grow its economy in last 40 years yet able to retain the Communists Party total control of the government. Depending on its leadership, China might move back and forth along a continuum as to how much the government intervenes into its economy.

There have been much sophistries with many fallacious reports listing these below countries as Socialist; China, Denmark, Finland, Netherlands, Canada, Sweden, Norway, Ireland, New Zealand & Belgium. These reports are misleading, the economies of the countries mentioned are fully integrated with the rest of the world, the rules of free market, financial investments, paybacks, floating foreign exchange rates, etc. all apply. They are definitely all Capitalist Economies. If that's the case, why call them Socialist countries? As we'd discussed, China is a Communist country practicing Capitalism with its Economy well integrated globally. As for all the other countries mentioned, their current parties in power (elected via a Democratic process) might be more Liberal leaning and thus Social Welfare is big on their agenda. States having varying degrees of social welfare does NOT make them Socialists states!

The Mythical Social-Welfare Dragon II

Finally, we come back to the progressive "political paleontologists" and the mythical dragon. First, notice they don't sell communism as much. Why? Well, the USSR and Warsaw pact collapsed in 1991. The obvious comparison between the economic performance of the NATO countries and that of their counterparts in the Eastern Bloc speak for itself. So since these Communist,

Socialist countries' track records can be easily verified and they are not stellar by any standards. The progressive "political paleontologists" don't market Communism.

Instead they prefer to market Socialism, just an idea with no track record for anyone to verify against (unless you know your history). The uninformed and the young might not even trace Socialism back to Karl Marx, so the progressive "political paleontologists" pulls another fast one, they call the countries with vibrant Capitalist economies, Socialist countries (because these countries have social welfare programs?). They take all the wealth generated and created by Capitalist economies, put a mask of Social Welfare programs on it and call that Socialism! And Voila, you have your mythical Social Welfare Dragon. Is there a demand for it? You bet there's a demand for this social welfare dragon, some people want all the wealth created by others handed over to them in social welfare benefits (in their minds, very justifiably so too) and yet they fear to compete in the Capitalistic societies, fear of competition, fear of failure.

For such a segment of the population, the social welfare dragon is the perfect answer! Capitalism, along with the need for competition is fearful and thus BAD! But yet, the free goodies from social welfare programs are their rights (as stated in the constitution?), so the social welfare dragon is born => neo-socialism! Via the subterfuge of the Progressive "political paleontologists" you can have your cake and eat it too. The reality now becomes clear, these so call 'social justice warriors' just want their 'freebies', either that or they are the problem profiteers generating the sophistries. Greed and Sloth are the main motivators, there's no ideologies here.

As a quick recap, Karl Marx wrote Das Kapital witnessing the hardworking masses <u>working</u> in factories under the harshest and brutal conditions and paid miserably, thus he attacks Capitalism Ideologically. When Lenin and Trotsky puts Socialism into practice in Russia, it became Communism with Big State Government planned economies (understandable as Capitalism cannot be the solution for them). China and all the Warsaw Pact countries (including Russia) practiced big State planned economies after WWII. Their economies were miniscule by comparison to the NATO allies and other Free Market Capitalist economies (remember that Russia's GDP per Capital hovered between 10 – 20% of the USA). China (under Deng in 1976) started to abandon the State planned economy system and adopted Capitalism to grow their economy. USSR and the Warsaw pact continued till 1991 when they were dissolved. Most of the former Eastern Bloc countries then started to embrace Capitalism too.

You're welcome. Comrade Bernie

We now see clearly that Capitalism has created all the wealth for America till date. Now the Neo-socialist (dangling their "hand-outs") wants a Big Government Socialist economy? Perhaps they had conveniently forgot to tell you that without the Capitalism engine, the present USA economy will shrink (if we look at Russia's experience, to 20% of its current size). They are essentially proposing to kill the goose that lays the golden egg. Empirical evidence has overwhelmingly shown this to be true and the logic behind it is very sound if you study and understand human nature and motivations.

If the Neo-socialist continues their Abuse and breaks the current system, it would first be anarchy (like Venezuela), eventually the Socialist Big Government would rise and control a central planned-Market mechanism. Way before then, the most capable and richest would left America (brought all their Wealth and abilities with them). As we had already witnessed in 1930s, under Nazism and later Communism, many of the most talented people in Europe immigrated into USA and America benefitted tremendously from such immigrant energy, drive and talent.

Unlike the Super Rich Celebrities who fears the unknown, fears change and finds great difficulty adapting to new places. The truly capable and talented overcomes these challenges easily. With their talent and transferable skills, they will also be most welcomed overseas. The rich would also quickly move their wealth out of the Neo-socialist Government reach at the "click of a mouse" or touch screen on their smartphones. As George Soros had already repeatedly demonstrated, the super-Rich Bankers, Fund managers (top 1% in wealth) are always a number of steps in front of the law (in fact in Soros' case, he was a few decades ahead of the IMF, World Bank, SEC or other law enforcement bodies).[1]

As to those that remain, there would be little incentive to invest, innovate or even work hard as all the earnings would be taxed to provide social welfare and benefits for those not working. In fact, unemployment would skyrocket as there would be a rush to collect social welfare and "handouts", since only those minority in power will stand to enjoy the rewards (with some scraps left over for their cronies) in Big-State Government planned Market; while the mass majority will only all be looking at the "standard handout", there'll be no personal incentive to invest for profits or work hard to earn additional income. Naturally, Investments would shrink, workforce would also shrink. Businesses will close down and economies falter to tiny fraction of its current size. Once you remove the incentive for self-advancement in the free market, the loss of human potential for the entire society will be catastrophic. History has demonstrated this time and again in communist economies all around the world. The neo-Socialists want to re-distribute wealth and Tax the Rich. The Rich and talented will disappear, the economy will collapse and that'll be nothing left to distribute, but crimes and corruption.

> *Aristotle's "philosophy of aspiration" – F.M. Cornford. Constantly looking forward, to what we can be rather than what we were, "the universe and everything in it is developing towards something continually better than what came before," including ourselves. To him, the world we make for ourselves continually reflects that constant striving towards improvement.*
> – Arthur Herman, The Cave and the Light

Life is a state of continuous improvement, Capitalism is NOT perfect nor final solution; it can be exploited by the super-rich, forming their monopolies, we will have to constantly address new challenges as they surface and devise new solutions to buffer some of its less desirable con-sequences. Formation of Labor Unions in the factories was one such measure designed in the 19th century to counter the exploitation of labor. Trust Busting the monopolies of Standard Oil,

---

[1] Per The Crisis of Global Capitalism by George Soros 1998, George Soros on Globalization in 2002

etc. in beginning of 20th century was another improvement. We should however, acknowledge that Capitalism in the Free Market (Laissez-faire) is a great engine of economic growth and has contributed significantly to America being the world power it is today.

Instead of telling you the truth, the Neo-Socialists wants to appeal to the greed and selfish side of human weakness, they conjectured up the mythical social-welfare dragon (their version of Socialism) and tries a bait and switch on the uninformed and impressionable youth to vote for Big-Government State Control in return for promise of some miserly social welfare and benefits; which they will never deliver as there will be nothing left to distribute when the economy dissipates. We'll see how this story of Free Welfare and Equality for All is not new and has been sold and re-sold through time (French, Russian Revolutions, as well as all the Communism States)

> "…. Nature smiles at the union of freedom and equality in our utopias. For freedom and equality are sworn and everlasting enemies, and one prevails the other dies. Leave men free, and their natural inequalities will multiple almost geometrically, a in England and America in the 19th century under laissez-faire. To check the growth of inequality, liberty must be sacrificed, as in Russia after 1917. Even when repressed, inequality grows; only the man who is below average in economic ability desires equality; those who are conscious of superior ability desires freedom; and in the end superior ability has its way. Utopias of equality are biologically doomed"
> - The lessons of History by Will and Ariel Durant

This quote best sums up the fate of the Communist economies and why they couldn't ultimately compete with the free market Capitalist economies. Competition has inherent risks for some individuals but the outcome of competition for the society is that the countries, economies become stronger. Choosing not to compete (as the Neo-Socialists' are urging their peons; well-schooled in Greed and Sloth), will set this country on a path of decline into irrelevance.

As the Durants pointed out, "… even when repressed, inequality grows…" this is human nature. A quick reading of Animal Farm might help if you haven't read it.

Before we move on to the short-comings of Capitalism and what we should do to address it. There is one last category of countries; the likes of Venezuela (used to be assets rich) that's Democratic Socialist with a Dirigiste economy, these are unstable entities that are in transition into Big Government Dictatorship. As their economy shrinks under the socialist big government, the people gets frustrated with no accountability (in a democracy as governments keeps changing), as more gets on social welfare, the workforce continues to shrink. The economy is in a death spiral (like a dying star burning up its last remaining hydrogen fuel).

Finally, in a last grasp at straws for Accountability, a Dictator would replace the non-functioning democratic government and the country would become Big State Control Communist country. At least for now, this new state of Dictatorship would be more stable than anarchy.

As Crony Capitalism (which we'll elaborate later) is also a form of Dirigiste economy, if not addressed in time, USA would face the same challenges as Venezuela at the top left hand corner of Chart [Democracy V Capitalism]

> *"There is all the difference in the world between treating people equally and attempting to make them equal"*
>
> – Friedrich August von Hayek

Capitalism Bad, Bernie and Liz Warren are on to something

Capitalism is not perfect. As discussed earlier, one obvious shortcoming at the beginning of Industrial Revolution was the exploitation of labor as entire societies transition from agrarian to Industrial-based. The formation of labor Unions helped counter that exploitation, Free speech and free independent press also contributed to raising awareness of the plight of these abused workers. The Rise in ideology of Socialism was another reaction to exploits of Capitalism and Industrialization. That didn't quite work out after 70 plus years of experimentation. "… Utopias of equality are biologically doomed.." Will and Ariel Durant.

We'll discuss a couple more loopholes that's opened up in the Financial System, leading to the current Crony Capitalism in Wall Street. Some blame this on Capitalism, when it's actually the bureaucrats law-makers who have not kept pace (in the last 30 plus years) with Globalization and technological advances, these 'loop holes' are in fact created by the Washington bureaucrats themselves as we'll see.

As Globalization accelerated, the financial markets around the world became forever integrated and the "digitized wealth" became "borderless". But there's no international financial sheriff to effectively police International activities, for IMF, World Bank have Zero Governance Accountability; Created in 1945, the IMF is governed by, and accountable to the 189 countries that make up its near-global membership.

This is their stated *Corporate Responsibility: The Fund actively promotes good governance within its own organization.* It just means they are accountable to No one (when you are accountable to 189 countries, it means you are not accountable to anyone) with nebulous responsibilities and absolutely none for the Global Finance's governance (read what is not stated, they are only responsible for governance within their own organization, anything else; hear no evil, see no evil). Bureaucracy clouds personal Accountability and Responsibilities, any thinking person can see that Bureaucracies with No Accountability is NOT the solution, however their setup produces funding and resources that can be tapped by individuals for personal benefits, now you might understand the real agenda for politicians that always proposes for more administrative bureaucracies to be funded?

> *"I believe there are more instances of the abridgment of the freedom of the people by gradual and silent encroachments of those in power than by violent and sudden usurpations."*
>
> – James Madison

Abuse of International Financial Markets and Rise of Crony Capitalism in Wall Street

As we'd discussed in last chapter, in 1992 George Soros betted against the British Pounds and started to aggressively short the Pound, the UK Banks tried in vain to defend the Pound. In the end, Soros made Billions and the UK investors, pensioners lost their life savings [Soros became known as the man who broke the Bank of England].

In a speech to Congress on 8th June 1993, Democrat Congressman Henry Gonzalez of Texas; then Chairman of the House of Banking Committee, expressed his concern about Soros speculative activities, stated "recent press accounts state that Mr George Soros, the manager of the Quantum Fund, made over $1 billion betting against the British pound. I am interested in ... the U.S. bank exposure to Mr Soros' fund." As you can see, America's financial watchdogs had started paying attention to such irresponsible speculative 'financial looting' activities then.

The very next day on 9th June 1993, Soros wrote to Times of London commenting that Deutschmark was weak, in the next 24 hours, the German mark went into a tailspin. On 14th July 1998, Soros suggested to Financial Times in London that Russian Rubles was overvalued, the ruble plummeted and the Russian Economy went into depression. Earlier in 1997, Soros also betted against the Asia Developing markets and caused financial capital, [in this case Foreign Investments] to flee these countries. (Thailand, Indonesia, Korea, etc.) Once again, Soros made Billions and many of these countries are still recovering after 2 decades, the Indonesian rupiahs exchange rate never recovered back to its pre-clash value against the US$. Some more resilient economies like Korea has rebounded stronger but others are still hurting from the Asian Financial crisis. Entire generations of these developing countries, economies suffered at the hands of these "bankers" hedge Fund arbitragers.

Soros had noted the loopholes, he exploited them and then very slyly proposed to setup global organizations to regulate and monitor such nefarious activities. He did partially succeeded in doing so, so you can imagine who these bureaucracies owe their allegiance to?

The solution to closing the International Financial loopholes isn't creating more bureaucracies with no accountabilities, especially crony bureaucracies that report to no one but clearly influenced by some to do their personal biddings. This isn't just letting the fox into the henhouse, it is more like having the shepherd and sheepdogs all take instructions from the wolf, so who's protecting the sheep now? In fact, at the point (late 90s), Soros thought that the Financial Crisis would spill into USA and lobbied to setup oversight regulatory bodies under his personal supervision and influence right here in USA too. Luckily, that didn't happen as the panicking investors actually pulled all the funds back into USA as safe haven so Soros didn't get his way in the USA then (but he is tenacious and eventually would get his way when the opportunity comes again).

As you can now see, Bernie Sanders and Liz Warren are correct in a sense, International Finance system is corrupt and not properly regulated. There is much room for improvement and plenty to fix. Sadly, the solutions are way beyond their (Bernie and Warren's) shallow understanding or perhaps that their real hidden agenda? You remember that George Soros is the big sponsor behind President Obama and Hillary Clinton? Soros is also the proud sponsor and brains behind hundreds of Activists and Progressives groups with funds and Assets under management, of over tens of Billions. They are intelligently setup as "Charitable foundations" 501c3, designated as "nonpolitical" by the IRS. Just to give you a feel of their influence, as of 2012, there are 553 progressive Environmental groups with assets over $9.53 Billion (that's right in US$). In that same year, 117 progressive 501c3s that supported Open Borders with over $300 million in funding to spend on advocating open borders, just for that year alone.

George Soros' The Open Society Institute and its global network of Open Society foundations [all activist corporations] are based off the name of Karl Popper's work *The Open Society and its Enemies*, published 1945. Popper, an Austrian Jew who escaped the Nazis, [whom Soros called his 'spiritual mentor'] was criticizing totalitarian regimes like the Communists, Nazis and Fascists as Closed Societies and how Open Societies should be open to new and diverse Ideas. With fall of the Berlin Wall in Nov 1989, Karl Popper did and sensed that the fall of communism hadn't cleared away all the avowed enemies of open society. "Communism is dead," he pointed out "it's left the hatred of capitalism still alive and well." The Big irony is that while Karl Popper was correct, with the demise of Communism, the enemies of Capitalism have not all been vanquished. The new threat to Democracy and Capitalism in America is coming from the Activists Corporations like The Open Society; setup by his student, all pushing towards a Big State Totalitarian Government once again (Soros sees the America system as Totalitarian and thus needs to corrected, leading the charge down the *Road to Serfdom*).

> *"The passion for 'the collective satisfaction of our needs,'" Hayek wrote, was how "the socialists [meaning believers in strong centralized state] have so well prepared the way for totalitarian."*
> - *The Road to Serfdom* 1944, Friedrich August von Hayek

The lists of activists corporations goes on.. we'll look at this more closely in next chapter, suffice to say that the politicians are never going to bite the hand that feeds them. We now know that the shepherd and the sheepdogs all report to the wolf, don't wait for them to protect you or your interests. If you like the social-welfare dragon picture that's been painted for you, that's good to be entertained but remembered that's where it stays, as entertainment. Just like the Hollywood Celebrities, Media Celebrities, Singing Celebrities, etc. the Political Celebrities are just entertainers!

Wall Street and the Bankers, are they all bad? Obviously not, it is the abuse and exploitation of the financial systems for personal enrichment and self-serving purposes is Bad as it breaks down the Free Market Capitalism mechanism. To answer if the current system is being abused, we need to take a step back and ask what is the purpose of the stock market and banking systems? Remember when the Amsterdam Stock Exchange was formed, it early helped to aggregate Capital in support of investment purposes (at that time for Trading Expeditions which were very lucrative then).

This aggregation of capital allowed many good ideas to be funded and eventually become reality. Amazon. Google, Apple, etc. would never exist, if the startups were not supported and funded by venture capitalists. These investment opportunities could be funded in many ways, equities, debt and some form of combination between the two. In a perfect free market; where information is made equally available to all the investors, and the market is made up of numerous small players such that no one can influence the market, it allocates capital most efficiently. Efficient Capital allocation means that (assumption that Capital is limited) the best investment projects (with highest probability of success and gives best returns) gets allocated the most capital while weak projects get zero or no funding. This provides the competition for capital. We should not forget that although all investors have similar information, they might derive different insights from the same information. Best returns doesn't mean purely financial returns, qualitative like more strategic future market share, technologies or even social causes would have value to different investors. Therefore, the most efficient allocation of capital concept also accommodates a wide variety of industries and companies and allow new ones to germinate. I would argue that this fundamental purpose of Stock Exchanges and Banks hasn't changed much. Leveraging the financial, non-financial interests of investors to support and sponsor new business growth creating jobs, innovations and technologies. One can clearly see the evidence of growth in the Internet, Technology Revolution in late 90s and beginning of the new millennial.

When working properly, the Financial System (Wall Street, Stock Market and Banks) supports and reinforce Capitalism (the entire Economy). Sadly, a number of factors has transpired (accelerating in the last decade) that has hurt the Capitalists Free market and now actually hurting the USA economy and retarding meaningful economic growth in recent years. Let's explore a couple of them briefly (for more in depth understanding, you might like to read works from David A. Stockman and James Rickards).

Quantitative Easing (QEs) after 2008 Financial Crisis generated lots of liquidity into the financial system. We can easily see that morally it's NOT the right thing for the Federal Reserve and US Treasury to generate debt for the US Tax payers in order to bail out the "too big to fail" banks, the question is whether is was an effective solution? Obama will tell you it was so. Suffice to say for now, that the QEs money are not Savings generated by household savings. The newly printed QE money coupled with money market interest rates at 0% for the last 7-8 years, distorted the workings of the Capitalist Free Market. Free market doesn't mean free Capital, yet that's the costs of capital to the traders and speculators of the 'Too Big to Fail Banks' [aka Financial Monopolies]. Remember, the QE money never reached the little individual working man, it stayed mainly in the Wall Street Financial systems; Investment Banks, Hedge Funds, Assets Managers, mainly Institutional Investors. Only these large institutions can access the 0% interests and leverage that to fund their zero risk speculations as the Feds had committed to the series of QEs (acquiring US Treasury bonds) ranging from late 2008 through to late 2014. Adam Smith's "invisible hand" hasn't been working in our financial systems for a decade now, in its place rose crony capitalism. Too much Capital at 0% borrowing rate in the hands of few large Institutional Investors, Banks, Funds, Investment companies, etc. the result? DOW at over 24,000 despite the lackluster economy for last 15 years? Astronomical P/Es (Price to Earnings) of Technology companies, look at likes of Amazon, Tesla, Facebook, Google, etc. Renewable Energy contractors starting all sorts of farce projects on federal grants and loans, crazy number of Unicorn companies; unjustifiable valuations with zero earnings.

So, I stand corrected, some of the QEs money did leave Wall street and moved to Tech Street; Silicon Valley, Crony capitalism also made the top "1% Super-Rich" even richer as they leveraged their institutional investors' resources (access to 0% interest, army of traders and speculators, etc.) to increase their already huge wealth Exponentially! Our Financial system has been broken by the irresponsible Monetary Policies practiced by Alan Greenspan and his successor Ben Bernanke, and the Bankers, Traders, speculators all exploiting the failing system. Wall Street and Main Street economy has become unhinged and gone on 2 separate tracks. To help grow the economy, we need to realign the 2 again so that the wall street works as its original intent; ie. Support, reinforce and facilitate the main street activities. The Mega-Banks mergers activities has to be reversed. Smaller and numerous banks would provide more competition and lead the way back to more of a Free Market, Perfect Competition Capitalist approach, we'll revisit the Wall Street challenges and their solutions in chapter 5 & 8.

At a different level, I want to share my 1st glimpse of the Divergence of Wall Street with Main Street at ground level back in 2006. At that time, I was working on an IPO (Initial Public Offering) and thus was spending lots of time with Investment bankers and also Private Equity companies' analysts. After sometime, I made a couple of observations. a) the bankers and analysts were never too interested in the operational details of the companies, they just prefer to "check the boxes", b) they were a little more interested in the financials, mostly how to plug the numbers into their financial models and complete their checklist of questions, c) the PE [Private Equity] Investors have a target to meet on investing their funds, the Due Diligence exercise for some is to "check the box", closing the deals gets them the bonus payouts and d) they loved to talk about financial derivatives like CDO (Collateralized Debt Obligations) setting up the SPEs, selling the MBS (Mortgage Backed Securities) and all these diversifies away the market risks, what a brilliant idea this is (remember, this was in 2006).

As you can see, the Crony Capitalists' Wall Street's system rewards Marketing and Sale (the "story") of the deals ("listing") to the investors, the reality of goes on in Main Street is of secondly importance (if at all) and Fiduciary Duties to the investors is an alien concept. I wondered why doctors, lawyers & accountants (professionals) have fiduciary duties but this concept somehow has eluded the highest paying jobs in America (not counting the Celebrities in Entertainment world and Technology billionaires in "Virtual world"). As to the financial derivatives discussion, the risks might have been so called "diversified" [re-insured], passed the buck down to the lowest man in the totem pole... the inherent risks associated with the actual projects themselves (in this case high risks housing mortgages) were never really addressed and true enough, the housing bubble burst in 2008. When the financial crisis happened in 2008, I was naïve and was expecting the authorities to crack down on Wall Street, make them become more accountable to the small investors. Introduce the fiduciary duties expectations on the bankers so that they can be individually and personally held responsible. Sadly, as history has shown us, it became even worse, the divergence of Wall street from Main street actually accelerated.

When the commodities futures exchange in Shanghai was started in China, over 90% of the trades has no real physical underlying transactions, the prices in the futures traded had NO correlation with the prices of the real hard physical assets, there were also no Industrial representatives in the futures exchange, they were all financial plays. More like Casinos masquerading as financial exchanges. Has Wall Street also turned into Las Vegas too?

Quick Summary

We've now clarified the Socialism, Communism, Big State Government and Democracy are forms of government that's defines the distribution of Political Power while Capitalism and State Planned Economies addresses the Markets mechanism and distribution of Financial Power (wealth). We've seen that the Free Market Capitalism always outperforms the State Planned Economies, that Democracy also outperforms the Big State Governments (be they Socialist or Communists States, with power aggregated in hands of only a few). But we have also seen that Democracy and Capitalism can easily be abused by the people themselves for short term gains, enabling power to start aggregating in the hands of few. Now we start to see a very important trend!

Myths and Misunderstandings about Democracy and Capitalism

Democracy (the Demos – the citizen body) is the opposite of Monopoly of Political Power (eg. Tyranny, Monarchy, Oligarchy. This is what Big State Government; Socialists or Communists will bring about, aggregation of power into hands of few). Democracy does NOT assume all humans are equal, let alone should have equal material rewards or financial status. It is precisely the recognition that humans are NOT equal in their abilities, that the basis of democracy stems from; to fight for equal basic human rights(NOT entitlements) for all, equal opportunities and a level playing field for all. If humans are all equal to begin with, then there would be no need to be constantly vigilant to demand equal rights. The Biggest Lie that the Communists, Socialists and now Liberal Socialists like to propagate and sell to the naïve (or the Low to use Orwell's words) is the Myth that all men shall be equal, see quote from Orwell from 1984 at beginning of the chapter. Consider also "those who are conscious of superior ability desires freedom" – quote from Durant.

The great irony is the misunderstanding that Democracy preaches for all men to be equal is the time-tested rallying cry used repetitively by the socialists and communists for abolishing the current existing establishment which if successful, will eventually lead to Socialist and Communist Big Government States, essentially translating into aggregation of power into hands of a few.

Could this be a simple misunderstanding? How's the Democracy's ideals of equal human rights, gets so easily twisted into Myth that all men shall be equal in rewards and status? Any reasonable person will understand it is not possible nor fair to have all humans be equal in rewards and status as humans are not equal in abilities to begin with.

Just like the Welfare Abusers, the prime motivators for the buyers of the message are sloth and greed, as they believe that being equal with others who are more capable or hardworking than themselves, they will gain something for nothing (without understanding that under the new rules of all receiving same rewards, the motivation for hard-work, innovation and initiative all disappears and the only logic now is to do as little as possible. Since the output is now constant, one minimizes one's input to achieve maximum returns on input, it becomes a race to the bottom. All will have equal rewards of 0).

As to the seller of the warped message, there's 2 types, the Social Justice warriors; real romantics that truly believe in the simplicity, romantics of undifferentiated goodness that totally ignores reality but lives in their own idealistic worlds or the second type are problem profiteers that hopes to benefit personally from destroying current Democratic establishment of America. We've already seen in Introduction that Democracy is unstable and fragile, why is that so?

In De l'esprit des lois; The Spirit of the Laws by Baron de Montesquieu in 1748, argued that Republican Governments along the lines of Democratic Ideals, could function only in small geographic areas like Greek city states and Swiss cantons, where the representatives remain aligned with the interest of citizenry who elected them, pointing out the Roman Empire as it grew too large, eventually gave up its Democratic roots too. We'll see in later chapters, how James Madison utilized David Hume's arguments to counter his 'Montesquieu-quoting' opponents, during the Constitutional Convention in Philadelphia, summer of 1787.

Throughout the book, we'll see the various factions that's challenging Democracy in America. We'll discuss these challenges in great details and the necessary steps to overcome them. Here's a quote from Samuel Sidney McClure of McClure's Magazine fame, the True Progressives that were shaping American politics and business at the beginning of the 20th century, helping to breakup Monopolies by taking on the All-Powerful Trusts. [as differentiated from present day neo-Progressives; the Incumbent Monopolies in Mass Media & Social Media networks, also making their impact on politics by indoctrinating the Politically Correct ONE VIEW of the World and chanting political Slogans of the Activists Corporations backed by Wall Street Funds].

Here McClure was describing the corrupting influence of the Monopolies on the American Society in late 19th and early 20th century:

> *"the three stories [as introduction to stories by Tarbell, Baker and Steffens] constitute an arraignment of American character, particularly the American contempt of law… Capitalists, working men, politicians, citizens – all breaking the law, or letting it be broken. Who is left to uphold it? …. there is no one left: none but all of us… the public is the people. We forget that we all are the people; that while each of us in his group can shove off on the rest the bill of today, the debt is only postponed. The rest of us are passing it on back to us. We have to pay in the end, every one of us. And in the end the sum total of the debt will be our liberty."*

> Samuel S McClure, 1903

From McClure's words, we can sense the fragility and susceptibility of Democracy & Capitalism's mechanism to the corruption and manipulations of the powerful. We now have one piece of the answer, Democracy can be abused and exploited by the Rich, Powerful, even the People themselves; for short term gains (we saw that earlier in Madison's arguments too). These forms of greedy Abuse of Welfare & Charity, Abuse of the goodwill and trust of fellow Americans, are similar to exploitation of Public Goods or Tragedy of the commons, if these abuses are not restrained in a timely fashion, they will lead to eventual collapse of Democracy and subsequent transformation into a Big State Socialists form of Government (Consolidation of Power in the hands of few, opening the door to a Tyrannical Regime)

Democracy needs a conjuncture of number of factors for it work, a society with a strong and large Middle-class that's well educated and enlightened (as differentiated from indoctrinated), able to exercise independent reason and apply logic with the confidence to follow ensuing inferences to their conclusions, inculcated with Values of Valour, Self-Sacrifice, Honour, Awful Virtues described by Adam Smith, and Ethos as explained by Aristotle.

Only a large Middle working class with a sizable aggregation of Intellect, Financial Wealth, right Values and the ability to reason and leverage their common sense, only the Middle Class can check the power of the High, for the Low that they are too much crushed by drudgery to be more than intermittently conscious of anything outside their daily lives [1984, Orwell]

> *"Happy families are all alike; every unhappy family is unhappy in its own way."*
>
> Anna Karenina by Tolstoy

With All the necessary factors present, as in Leo Tolstoy famous quote about happy families in Anna Karenina, Democracy [like perfect Competition, Free Market Capitalism] needs to stay in Dynamic Equilibrium, in a state of balance or Homeostasis. If the balance is disrupted and not allowed to re-adjust itself, then the Democratic [as well as Capitalistic] system's self-sustaining mechanism starts to fail and the entire system starts to atrophy and breakdown towards a lower energy system like a Tyranny, Monarchy, Aristocracy, Oligarchy form of government [or a socialists', communists' planned economy].

Therefore, we can also argue that Democracy [like perfect Competition, Free Market Capitalism] to be a Higher Energy System (higher in dynamic collective nous), is more difficult to sustain for any prolonged periods, any disruption, deterioration or reduction in this Energy system and it will tend towards the other forms of government [or Corruption, Monopolies, eventually Planned Economies] of lower Energy content.

Lastly, how Democracy promotes personal Freedom might be an easy concept to explain to an individual, but the Entirety of Democracy, how it works from the society's perspective and the Synergistic Value it derives is difficult to explain conceptually. In fact, it is rather counter-intuitive how allowing individuals' freedom can lead to a vibrant, growing and stable society, wouldn't it lead to abuse and anarchy instead? Answer lies in achieving balance, but how to define where the balance is?

Three Intangible but Critical Key concepts and their interface, makes democracy work [in America]

Ethos (Values like Valour, Self-Sacrifice, Honour), Alignment (Assabiyyah) and National Identity are integral to proper functioning of Democracy. Values, Ethos and Awful virtues like Discipline, self-restraint, moral rectitude, righteous anger at wrongdoers are instrumental in proper functioning of Democracy as they allow the society to achieve balance and prevent the unrestrained Abuse that leads to Anarchy. The Restraint comes from the internalized Values of the individuals themselves; with their clear understanding of the consequence, that constant Abuse will destroy the foundations of Democracy. Next is the concept of Alignment (Assabiyyah - strong sense of group solidarity) of Americans and the third is the National Identity of United States of America (the Belief in and acknowledgement of the existence of the USA Entity, which the globalists undermine).

All these three concepts are abstract and extremely fragile, can they survive under the onslaughts from Social Media, Mainstream Media and Academia that propagates subterfuges [globalism, neo-socialism, welfare is a right, etc.] and brainwashes the naïve and young into mindless P.C. rhetoric repeating drones with No Real Values and deletes their nous (thinking and reasoning abilities)? Now that we understand the fragility of Democracy and the powerful motivators of its Abusers, let's review Capitalism and its short comings.

> *"The real puzzle about economic decision making was figuring out why "the spontaneous interaction of a number of people, each possessing only bits of knowledge, brings about the state of affairs ... Which could [only] be brought about by deliberate direction by someone who possessed the combined knowledge of all these individuals" - something that was clearly impossible. And yet, this is exactly what happens in the economic marketplace."*
>
> - Friedrich August Von Hayek

Laissez-faire Free Market Capitalism

Hayek's answer: Markets are clearinghouses of information, where individuals discover what is useful or valuable to them and then make their preferences known to others by buying or alternatively selling those things that are of lesser value to them but hopefully not to others.

Free Market Capitalism of perfect competition is the opposite of Monopoly of Financial Power (wealth) in hands of a few. The generally-held view [propagated by the Media] that Free Market Capitalism means Monopoly of wealth is again another myth and misunderstanding. Perfect Competition in Market is Capitalism at its most efficient form with millions and millions of independent individual decision makers with perfect information that makes up the market and forms the 'Adam Smith's invisible hand' that will guide and allocate Financial capital to best projects that generate highest returns for their respective investors (the Ideal market situation).

Monopoly and aggregation of wealth creates inefficiency in capital allocation from a Market's perspective as the number of independent decision makers decreases exponentially, lack of competitive projects and investors destroys the efficiency of the Market too. Thus, when we start to see large Monopolies of Banks that are Too Big to Fail, we know there's No longer Free Market Laissez faire Capitalism, these are Red Flags that the Financial Markets are No longer operating efficiently; Crony Capitalism now reigns. Here we also see the immense danger of the Abuse of Capitalism by the Supra-Rich Too Big to Fail Banks aided by the recent Fed's QEs (as well as decision by Nixon to unilaterally remove the Gold Standard in 1971). We'll discuss the solutions of how to align Wall Street with Main Street in Chapter 5 & 8.

If music be the food of Love

> *"If music be the food of love, play on; Give me excess of it, that, surfeiting, The appetite may sicken, and so die."*
>
> - Act I, Scene I Twelve Night by Shakespeare

Are the Globalists and neo-Socialists romantics? All in love with the idea of love itself? With their own Infatuations and self-indulgence? We now know these "façade of ideologies" marketed and sold by the progressives are nothing even remotely close to the reality (which is always flawed and never perfect). Why then do so many misinformed people buy these misleading slogans and mantras? We need to understand that for some, Facing Reality can be difficult and scary, instead they prefer to live in ignorance, giving in to luxury of self-indulgence just like the Duke of Illyria. Ignorance is Strength

Key question we have to ask ourselves, are we dealing with the sheep chanting "Four legs good, Two legs Bad"? or the pigs teaching them? Find out the answers and the various roles of the Civil War Participants in the next chapter.

Chapter 3

Key combatants of the Civil War

"Both parties deprecated war, but one of them would make war rather than let the nation survive, and the other would accept war rather than let it perish, and the war came."

- President Abraham Lincoln, Second Inaugural Address, 1865

It is snowing in America

Singapore is a small country (city-state), at its longest 30 miles from East to West. Some of its less informed habitants uses their own city as a benchmark when talking about other countries like USA or China. After listening to international news; they would make comments like it is snowing in America or it is flooding in China. Comments like that would obviously sound strange or even amusing to the Americans or Chinese, yet you will also often hear comments like; the Democrats want more social welfare or the Republicans want their second amendment rights.

To better understand the current Civil War, we need to clearly identify the combatants; know their agenda and understand their mindset. As any consumer product company that wishes to increase their market share over its competition, they would start with a market segmentation exercise to understand the market better, then develop different strategies for each segment.

Let's try to do the same with various parties of this Civil War, starting with the government and politicians (elected & non-elected), the Executive and the administrative bureaucracy (K Street apparatchiks), the Judiciary, the Legislative (Senate, House of Representatives).

Next, the **Opinion shapers**: Media, Celebrities, Academia, Activists 501c3 special interest groups, Internet Social Media, News

Sponsors: Wall Street Financiers, Technology Monopolies Moguls, Traditional low margin businesses

Federal In-State Government Officials, Unions Leaders, quasi government agencies and related-contractors

Students, Social Welfare Beneficiaries, Demographic Alteration immigrants

Last but not least, the largest group, the American People, consisting mostly of Professionals, Workers, Laborers, Voters

Wow, that's quite a few categories, let's discuss them one at a time and decide which side of the Civil War they are on, and also put them all on one page diagram for easy reference. Also, in the later parts of this chapter, let's explore their agenda and mindset too.

Let's start at the top of power structure and influencers. It's not the Executive nor Legislative branch, it's the sponsors "bank rolling" the campaigns for all politicians, they're the real puppet masters pulling the strings behind the scene, you'll also see that the puppet masters strongly influence a multiple of other opinion shapers too. So, let's put them right at the top of the food-chain, the top 1%. Below the puppet masters, let's put the next layer of puppets; first level puppets, Executive, Legislative and Judiciary branches.

Below the "tip of the iceberg" of the small Executive lies the much larger Administrative branch to support the Executive. This 4th branch of the government has grown organically into a gargantuan bureaucracy that regulates over 90% of all Federal Government rules. You probably heard some of their names like HUD, EPA, DOE, DOL, EEOC, BATFE, BLM, FTC, FAA, IRS, SEC, FHA, HHS, the list goes on…

In 2007 these large bureaucratic organizations issued 2926 rules and regulations while Congress issued only 138, and in 2014, 3554 were issued by them against 224 by congress. Do the simple math, the Admin Branch is now responsible for over 95% of Federal rules and regulations, and that's only part of the problem. Because the Administrative branch is so large and well resourced, they've acquired multiple roles, which in effect has essentially overridden the check and balances of the 3 separate branches of government (Executive, Judiciary and Legislative). The Admin Branch now also adjudicates over 10X the cases by the Federal Courts, they have assumed responsibilities of the three branches, all rolled into one, they have access to much resources and NOT answerable to the voters (they are neither elected nor have term limits). The Administrative branch, aka K Street (Deep State Faceless Bureaucrats) are more powerful than any of the three branches of the government.

As a start, for ease of identification, let's discuss the leanings of each group in this Civil War (using the 2016 Elections as a reference). Understanding their leanings is important, but leanings can change, what's even more critical is to understand their mindset and agenda, for their leanings are shaped by both.

The elected Executive is obviously GOP, the legislative leans GOP too but not overwhelming as Senate right on the edge. The Judiciary is obviously Democrat, of the recent appointments, Obama 331, Bush 330 and Clinton 379 that already totals more than the existing number of Federal Judges. Thus, if you use length of time to retirement (an average) and work backwards, you can deduce most in the Judiciary Branch are Democrat leaning Judges.

Next is the Administrative Apparatchiks, are they GOP or Democrats? We can safely reason that at this point in time (after 8 years of Democrat in the WH), the Admin Apparatchik is overwhelming Democrat, it is purely about self-preservation for these Bureaucrats, staying within their "comfort zones", their cushy life-time guaranteed jobs and enjoying the Power that comes with the positions. This is a really sweet spot, great Powers but with NO associated responsibility to the American Voters. They are accountable to NO one, except perhaps their own bosses within the organizations.

Their 'Elected bosses' come and go every 8 years, maybe even 4 years if luck smiles on the Apparatchiks. What's more, as in all Bureaucratic organizations with NO competition, the managers have no clue what their subordinates, peers or even bosses are doing (sloth & ignorance seldom get into the details). By extension of the Federal Apparatchik in DC, there's another layer below them, government officials, State officials, Union Leaders, Government Unions, Contractors for government projects, etc. this group also can vary but as an extension of the Federal Apparatchiks, they would naturally lean towards the Democrats side, under the last WH administration. Indeed, we actually do have strong evidence, of how the DC's Administrative Apparatchiks votes [via their political contributions].

> *"...95% of all the donations of Federal Employees' went to Hillary Clinton, 97% of all the donations of the Justice department went to HRC, 99% of all the donations of the State Department went to HRC."*
> - Former House Speaker Newt Gingrich, on the 2016 General Election

Next up, the Opinion shapers. We can identify 5 Key categories: a) Traditional news Media (Newspapers, TV, Cable News, Magazines, etc.), b) Activist groups; setup as "charitable organizations", c) Internet News, Searches, Social Media, d) Entertainment Celebrities (actors, singers other glamor stars) and lastly e) Academia which clearly influences the students.

But wait, it is not over, with the success with the Immigration policies or rather lack of enforcement of existing policies, there has been a large influx of new "undocumented" Illegal people in this country. Also with majority of our government spending on social benefits and welfare, there must be a large group of beneficiaries from these welfare and benefits programs. Where do you think these 2 groups would lean? Being the direct beneficiaries, they would likely vote to continue if not increase their benefits and protect their stay in this country (all 'safely' registered as Democrat Voters; courtesy of the DNC).

Finally, we get to the American Voters that has NO vested interests other than for their families, their values and future of their country. Here I would place it as relatively evenly split. Looking at the chart below, the boxes are not to scale, by number of people. The American public is much larger if drawn to scale. But by their influence and visibility of 'Opinion-Shapers', the chart makes its point.

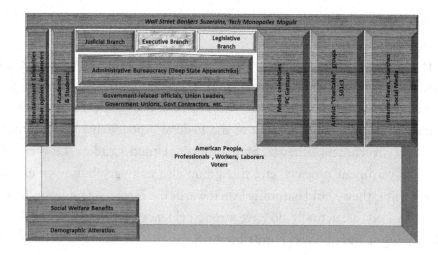

From Chart above, you have got to admire the Democrats for how well planned and brilliantly executed their Strategy for Control of Public Opinions and manipulation of perceptions of the Masses. No wonder Hillary and co. ordered the fireworks for her celebrations.

With such a complete Dominance of the Mainstream Media, Social Media, Academia, all set in perfectly coordinated motion, by the Activist Corporations and sponsored by the Ultra Rich Top 1% Wall Street Suzerains and Tech Street Monopolies Giants, some Democrats might ask how did the Election 2016 happened the way it did? The real question for GOP and America is how did absolute control of Mainstream Media News and Social Media Information streaming become so lopsided? Let's try to answer both questions.

> *"The terrorists were at war with us, but we were not yet at war with them. For more than 20 years the terrorist threat gathered, and America's response across several administrations of both parties was insufficient…."*
>
> - Dr Condoleezza Rice on 8th April 2004 during the 9th public hearing of the National Commission on terrorist attacks upon the United States

Asymmetric Warfare, Appeasement by President Bush 43rd & Blitzkrieg Victory in Election 2008

Asymmetric Warfare: "… is war between 2 sides, whose relative military power differs significantly, thereby causing their strategy or tactics to significantly differ too". The Americans used it against the British in the Revolutionary War, the Vietnamese used it against the Americans, the Afghan Mujahideen against the Soviets and the Al-Qaeda against America in the 9/11 attacks.

Why did the GOP's complacent Deep State politicians (the ones painted as 'white old men' by the neo-Dems) not see it coming? How did they get so 'off message' and completely blindsided? So detached and isolated Media-wise? The results of the 2008 and 2012 Election showed the power of the Opinion Shapers at work, the two landslide victories validate our chart above that shows the complete dominance of the neo-Democrats in Legislative, Judiciary, Administrative, All Opinion shapers, etc. In 2008, 365 Electoral Votes to Democrats' candidate Obama vs 173 GOP's McCain and again in year 2012, 332 votes to Democrats' President Obama vs 206 GOP's Romney.

Strangely, the 2008 Elections has much parallel to the runup of Nazi's victories in beginning of WWII. President Bush 43rd continuous appeasement policies to the neo-Dems allowing the setting up of Sanctuary Cities, rapid build-up of well-funded Activists Corporations, plus the 'new weapons' of Internet Social Media [Mass Indoctrination], all came together to produce the Blitzkrieg Victories in 2008 and 2012 for neo-Democrats

To understand the birth of this neo-Democrats 'Ideology' and history of its growth over last 5 decades, we need to trace its roots to the Vietnam War era. In the '60s as Mao's Cultural Revolution started raging in China, America was also having its own troubles back home; period of identity crisis for young Americans, self-doubt and juvenile rebellion. Lots of Anti-War protests around the country, anti-Vietnam War, anti-American, anti-colonial powers, anti-authority, anti-establishment emotions were all around. President JKF was assassinated in 1963, Reverend MLK was assassinated in 1968. Remember, most of these protests were then against President Lyndon B. Johnson (Democrat President) and later President Richard Nixon (GOP President). Thus, we can see that they (the protestors) were neither leaning towards Democrats nor GOP, they were simply anti-establishment protests.

Born 1909 in Chicago and also gone to school there, Saul Alinsky died 1972 in Carmel by the sea, California. During the '60s movement, Alinsky made a huge impact on number of Liberal Progressives who are key players in today's political stage; Hillary Clinton, George Soros being two of them. Alinsky's works: Rules for Radicals (1971) and Reveille for Radicals (1946) had inspired the birth of the new Democrat 'Ideology'. We'll explore the detailed Ideologies of the neo-Dems later. We shall also see how the neo-Democrats ideologies, their strategies, tactics morphed and transformed from the 60s, incubating, growing and adapting on multiple platforms and finally all re-emerging together, into the American political stage again in 2008, the Perfect Storm. But we're getting ahead of ourselves.

As the '60s turned into the 70s, the Vietnam War ended, the protests subsided. In 1980, Ronald Reagan beat President Jimmy Carter to become the 40th USA President, Reagan ushered in a new wave of America self-confidence and belief in USA's future again. By 1991, the Soviet-bloc dissolved, USSR is no more and Cold War is over. Throughout the '90s the economy was generally good, President Bill Clinton was head of the country. From the mid-90s to early 2000s, first the .coms, then the Internet and Technology Revolution started and Wall Street have their new darlings in Silicon Valley.

Up till 43rd President George Bush's term in office, any historical observer might have thought that the radical views of anti-establishment, anti-American Ideologies had become a thing of the past. They couldn't have been more wrong. Just like virus which can remain dormant for a long time once introduced into the body of its new host (festering, away from sight, refusing to be purged), just waiting for the right conditions to resurface and multiply. Similarly, ideologies can also remain dormant and then re-surface again at the right moment. Like Al-Qaeda and ISIL ideologies remain hidden in the minds of their believers, the anti-establishment, anti-American ideologies also grew stronger, away from public view, in the minds of their believers too.

All these time, they have been patient and very Strategic. Since the 60s, the *pro-left Academia, Liberal Mass Media, Progressive Entertainment celebrities had diligently continued their un-yielding march to absolute domination over the unsuspecting public's opinion. In the beginning of the millennial, they received a huge reinforcement from the virulent spread of *Activist groups (more accurately Activists Corporations as they now have hundreds of Billions of Assets under management) have been diligently setup by George Soros [is coming back to the rescue, he has not forgotten his mentor Alinsky], other similar-minded Wall Street Suzerains, Tech Street Monopolies Moghuls [also started to join in the fray as they began their meteoric rise boosted by Wall Street's confidence and the QE monies]. Ford Foundation alone has over $ 12 Billion, Soro's Open Society has min of $20B; with him recently pledging $ 18B.

Per list attached, the likes of ACLU, NARAL, NAACP, MALDEF, Planned Parenthood, etc. are all Activists Corporations. There are thousands of these 501c3 Activists Corporations with hundreds of Billions under their management. The value of their assets is bigger than the Valuation of entire Airline Industry's Market Capitalization in US Stock Market or that of the Automotive Industry's Market Cap, which would easily translate into tens of Billions of Cashflow per year, purely from the returns on investments without drawing down on the Capital itself. This means that in perpetuity, the Activist Corporations will have tens of billions of cash every year to spend on anti-Establishment, anti-Law & Order, anti-American or any other Activities they deem fit. The virus has truly spread out of control, is the demise of the host now inevitable?

Just so that you can feel the deep spread and penetration in our society by these Activists Corporations. As of 13 years ago, these were the Member Organizations of the America Votes coalition in 2004 Election cycle. They would definitely be much richer, numerous and more powerful now.

	Names of Activists Corporations
1	ACORN (Association of Community Organizations for Reform Now)
2	ACT (America Coming Together)
3	AFL-CIO (America Federation of Labor – Congress of Industrial Organizations)
4	AFSCME (American Federation of State, County and Municipal Employees)
5	**AFT (American Federation of Teachers)**
6	**ATLA (Association of Trial Lawyers of America)**
7	Brady Campaign to Prevent Gun Violence
8	Clean Water Action
9	Defenders of Wildlife Action Fund
10	Democracy for America
11	EMILY's List

12	Environment 2004
13	The Human Rights Campaign
14	League of Conservation Voters
15	**The Media Fund**
16	The Million Mom March
17	MoveOn.org Voter Fund
18	Moving America Forward
19	Music for America
20	NAACP – National Voter Fund
21	***NARAL Pro-Choice America***
22	**National Education Association**
23	National Jewish Democratic Council
24	National Treasury Employees Union
25	Partnership for America's Families
26	People for the American Way (PFAW)
27	***Planned Parenthood Action Fund***
28	Service Employees International Union (SEIU)
29	Sierra Club
30	USAction
31	Voices for Working Families
32	Young Voter Alliance
33	21st Century Democrats
34	America Votes
35	ACLU (American Civil Liberties Union)
36	NAACP (National Association for Advancement of Colored People)
37	MALDEF (Mexican American Legal Defense and Educational Fund

Yet, Powerful as they are, the Activist Corporations is only one piece of the entire puzzle. The *Federal Courts are now held sway over by the Activist judges with the Supreme Court being the last bastion of reason split even at time of writing. The Administrative branch (*K Street apparatchiks) after decades of being on 'auto-pilot' all seemed to have found religion under the last WH's encouragement (religion of Sloth and Avarice), just watch how they are all religiously resisting the new WH Executive team now (who's re-introducing Accountability and personal responsibilities after over 3 decades of rudderless meandering of the Federal Bureaucrats). The *social welfare and benefits programs continue to get rolled out. The *Demographic Alteration Immigration policies continue to be pursued.

Last but not least, with the new Technology monopolies forming in Silicon Valley since last decade, the Wall Street Suzerains have found new powerful Ultra-Rich cronies / allies (with similar interests and agenda) to help *Bank-roll their vision of diversion strategies (to maintain status quo of their monopolies of power and wealth), to help *disseminate and indoctrinate their Politically Correct ONE View to the feeble minded, self-righteous followers and users. Technology Monopolies Moguls like Jeff Bezos, google, Facebook founders; Mark Zuckerberg) and even better yet, the Internet News, Searches algorithms, Social Media now totally dominates and controls the Millennials' News, Media's Rhetoric!! Reinforced by the Traditional Media of Newspapers, TV, Cable News, etc.

The neo-Democrats now have Total dominance [from all the *Forces discussed] of the World News and Opinions, yet *Non sufficit orbis*, The World is not enough – motto of Philip II of Spain. For even as they controlled all channels to broadcast their messages, just to be certain, better have the Media and Politically Correct Gestapo do their policing more diligently; bringing legal action against [rounding up] all the non P.C. people with diverse ideas in both the Academia and Media worlds too! As the Sheep (Mass & Social Media) were bleating the political slogans in Animal Farm, the Dogs (Activists Corporations and their lawyers, ATLA) were intimidating the opposition into submissiveness.

In the meantime, what were the Deep State GOP politicians doing? They have been using the same old political tactics over and over again, they have become complacent and egoistic. It has become obvious; even to their own voters, that they are not committed nor passionate in their causes, inconsistent in their messages, often becoming distracted and lazy, allowing all voters to see that they are purely in the campaign for selfish and personal reasons. They were still living in their vain and self-absorbed world and had no clue that they'll be up against an inspired, passionate and ideologically convinced candidate from the Democrat side. Or perhaps the old school (deep state) GOP camp had resigned themselves to fate that they have no way to beat the slick upstart neo-Democrats, so they resigned themselves to merely be the cronies of the powerful Interests groups, collect their fat paychecks, shamelessly flaunting their [self-perceived] 'well-deserved and hard-earned' entitlements and influence.

If you look back at the neo-Democrats' history, you cannot help but admire the tenacity, great patience, sheer persistence, vision of Strategic planning and will to meticulously Execute the countless individual appointments over decades (in the Judiciary, Administrative, etc.), the setup of the 501c3 Activist groups, etc. All cumulating into the perfect election, of all the pieces coming together, emerging victorious in 2008 and repeating the feat again in 2012 (despite a lackluster first term, strength of Media Power!). Their Glorious success story, crushing the complacent GOP, the arrogant deep state white old man, who surely didn't see it coming.

That's the beauty of Asymmetric Warfare, when one side adopts new tactics and strategies and the other remains complacent and sticks to same old outdated tactics, you get shocking outcomes. The political leanings of the "opinion shapers" definitely help explains the results of 2008 and 2012 Elections. Final Score 365 to 173, that truly sums it all up.

Not only did the GOP get thrashed twice, the sheer number of Activists Corporations,

Sanctuary Cities and Activists Judges has continued to proliferate out of control till the inmates are practically running the asylum for last decade.

You might ask the question, is there really a Civil War? Isn't that a little over-stating things? If you had watched C-span and seen how the senators attacked everyone of cabinet nominees and subsequently the Supreme Court nominee, you'll understand that the neo-Democrat Senators definitely believe there's a Civil War, the Media Celebrities and PC Gestapo on TV and Cable News definitely believe they are in a Civil War as they reject the choice of the American people as ONLY they know better.

Even as the 2016 Election Campaign unfolded, it was a most divisive campaign which we can understand as both sides are vying for the coveted price of WH. After the Election night, and results have been tallied and re-tallied, the powerful professional politicians via their crony Jill Stein then requested for a recount, after which the entertainment celebrities asked the Electorates to "vote their conscience", then the boycott of the President Inauguration, next the relentless assaults on the cabinet nominees, followed by the leaking of transcripts of tele-conversations, contents of phone calls with foreign head of States, never-ending discussions about Russian Hacking, subsequently verbally assaulted on the Supreme Court nominee, Special Investigation, the list goes on and on.

But Why? Are the professional politicians afraid someone might move their cheese? After all, the neo-Dems have built a humongous infrastructure and that needs to be fed via the Federal Coffers (your tax money) or have the American people committed the unthinkable *Thoughtcrime* by not voting as they were told by the Media?

Regardless, the Headlines are out: There will be NO Power Sharing! The P.C. ONE View is right! It is always Right! The pure Hatred and viciousness exposed thus far from the neo-Democrats demonstrates one thing, this Civil War isn't going away anytime soon. Just as when the American Civil War started in 1861, this Current Civil War is not ending anytime soon as the neo-Democrats still retain their Total Dominance of the Mainstream Media and Social Media, with it these neo-Democrats Progressives will omit any negative news against themselves [sexual offenses, conviction of corruption and fraud], fabricate lies and subterfuges out of nothing [Russian Hacking], push forth the simplest, easiest to sell and most popular messages to gain ratings [leadership via popularity polls, or aka Leading from Behind]. This is the Power of Mass Media Dominance

> "*Who controls the past controls the future; who controls the present controls the past,*" 1984, George Orwell, "*.. You believe reality is something objective, external existing in its own right. You also believe that the nature of reality is self evident... But I tell you... That reality is not external.. Whatever the party holds to be truth is truth. It is impossible to see reality except by looking through the eyes of the party.*"
> [think CNN, MSNBC, NYT, CBS, ABC, PBS, NBC, USA Today, Washington Post, Internet Social Media]

> *"One of the most pervasive political visions of our time is the vision of liberals as compassionate and conservatives as less caring."*
>
> – Thomas Sowell

The Glory of the neo-Democrats; behold we give you The Perfect President

Why neo-democrats? To understand the ideologies of the neo-Dems better, we need to trace it to their origins. There were two clear and distinct separate movements in the '60s. Firstly, there was the Civil Rights movement led by Reverend Martin L. King Jr., the racial segregation and discrimination laws were indeed disgraceful, ugly and yet a regrettable part of American history. Reverend Martin L. King Jr.'s peaceful approach to protests was honorable, its cause was grounded in substance of Injustice, its aim to have equal rights and call for triumph of social justice is most respectable. He was so convinced in the righteousness and morality of his cause that he already knew the outcome to be a certainty. Reverend Martin L King Jr. advocates the peaceful approach as he was already thinking of the social integration and reconciliation process (after the eventual triumph of the African American Cause), as President Lincoln had been planning for the reconciliation of the North and Southern States before the surrender of General Robert E. Lee. That's the hallmark of Visionary. This reconciliatory and power sharing approach is valued by those leaders who care about the end results for the society and community impacted by their actions.

By contrast, the other anti-war, anti-establishment movement wasn't anything like the Civil Rights movement. It was anti-Vietnam War, Anti-colonial, Anti-American, Anti-establishment, the premises must be that the Communist Vietnamese must be honorable, the British, French colonial powers must be exploiting the colored people in Asia. Yet, the reality is that these protestors in USA has never been in South East, let alone speak their language nor lived in SE Asia countries. You can now see that just like the neo-socialists in chapter 2, these '60s protestors merely conjectured up their image of the downtrodden Asians exploited by the Evil Colonial Masters. They are like the Duke of Illyria .. in love with the idea of love itself.

From the seeds of the 60s Anti-establishment movement, the neo-democrat ideology started to get its first big boost in early 90s when International Financial Looting (currency speculation) made George Soros extremely wealthy. After 9/11 Soros started to deploy his Strategy of Extreme Activism Corporations with ready access to the Wall Street's & Global Financial Resources. His vision and actions nearly 2 decades ago gave birth to a movement that has more Financial clout than either the Gaming Industry, Aerospace Industry or Automotive Industry. As we'd witnessed, this neo-Democrat party [with Deep Anti-Establishment roots from the '60s] stepped into the spotlight and spread its wings in full glory in 2008.

As we can safely infer that Saul Alinsky and his counterpart radicals in the 60s wasn't impressed with democrat President LBJ then nor any other earlier Democrat Presidents. In fact, this is the precise difference between the neo-democrat party now and the old democrat party prior to 2008's spectacular Victory, the ideology of neo-democrats grew from the '60s anti-establishment movement. These anti-establishment roots of the neo-Democrats is the key to understanding their current mindset and gives us a better ability to interpret their actions. As the French Revolutionists in 1789, the Russian Bolsheviks Revolutionaries in 1917, Islamists during the Arab Spring in 2011, the unspoken intent of the neo-Democrats is to topple the existing establishment. As after all these revolutionaries succeeded in overthrowing the incumbent powers, they all proved unable to rule any better, all eventually devolving into either anarchies or tyrannical regimes. Perhaps now, we can understand President Obama's open embrace of and compliments to BLM, Antifa and other Activists groups, constantly riling up Hate, Wrath against Law and Order, pricking open old wounds about racism, sexism, LGBTQ, etc. sowing discord, spreading division amongst Americans, when he has been the President of the country for 8 years (those 'anti-establishment rhetoric' are the only skills he knows, being too arrogant to learn any new useful ones to properly govern and make the country's economy better. He did wisely learn the tricks of the poverty pimps to push the Free HealthCare agenda to the greedy and slothful as their 'Rights')

The Earlier Democrat Presidents from FDR, Truman, JFK all the way to President Bill Clinton (Yes, Bill Clinton. Remember they were "dead-broke" when they left the Whitehouse?), they might have different ideologies and priorities from the GOP Presidents but the end goal is similar, to make America a better, stronger, richer and more equitable country. They merely see different means and priorities to achieve the same ends. Essentially, they were the loyal opposition, perhaps USSR and the Cold War helped reinforced the "common enemy syndrome" and recognition that ".. we are two sides of the same coin.." The Democrats of pre-2008, knew how to embrace diversity of ideas and compromise in ideologies so as to work together for a better America. They cared enough about America to compromise.

The current neo-democrats come from a very different thread, without the threat of the Cold War, schooled in the anti-Establishment ideologies, they are self-proclaimed Globalists (unlike the old school nationalists). The neo-Dems do NOT see a better, richer, stronger, a more equitable, more harmonious America as the end goal. No, they see a borderless Globalist World, end of Nation States. Unlike Reverend MLK nor President Lincoln, they do Not see a need to plan for any form of harmony or reconciliation of this country in the future, because they know that they are Right! In the beautiful world of Duke Illyria where Music be the food of Love, why bother about painful reconciliation with others? Why bother to empathize with them? It is much easier to self-indulge and live in the world of being in Love with the idea of Love itself. Are neo-Democrats similar to the avant-garde of the *Romanticism movement in support of the French Revolution? Or are they more like the Tyrannical Regimes that later transformed the idealism of French Revolution into Reign of Terror? Russian Revolution into Russian Dictatorship?

As they are showing to all Americans, the neo-Democrats will NOT accept diversity of ideas from others, they do NOT want to accept the New Elected Administration as leaders of this country nor other Americans' views besides theirs. What about Freedom of speech? Is it possible to have freedom of ideas without the need to tolerate, compromise with diversity of ideas from others? How can that be logically possible? Wait, yes, that can only be possible if everyone says the same thing right? So neo-democracy is the freedom to force everyone say the same thing! Now, that's starting to sound like the sheep in Animal Farm chanting Four Legs good, two legs Bad

Quick Summary

Up till this point, we've seen the various parties involved in the Civil War and which way they lean in their political beliefs. We started to notice how lopsided the public opinion shapers (influencers) are with the Internet Social Media, Mainstream Media, Academia and Entertainment Celebrities all neo-Democrats progressive leaning, bolstered by the well-funded Activists corporations with their hundreds of Billions of Assets under management sponsored by Wall Street Financial Looters and Tech Street Monopolies Giants. We've also seen the self-serving K Street apparatchiks [administrative bureaucrats], the Judiciary and Legislative branches all corrupted to furthering their self-interests instead of serving the American People. Next, we've seen the combination of all these various interest groups working together in unison [all working in symbiotic relationships with each other, all working together in parasitic fashion towards the ailing America host] to effect the amazing Blitzkrieg Victories for neo-Democrats in 2008 and 2012 Elections.

We saw the proliferation of the Activists corporations and amazing wealth of funds they now possess. Their reach and influence is beyond anything that ever existed in the history of this country. We've also witnessed the Deep State Politicians on both sides, also chanting meaningless slogans and enjoying their great perks and living in luxuries without doing anything out of principles nor for the American people. The power of the Mainstream Media and Social Media is self-evident in the hordes of non sequiturs and snowflakes they've indoctrinated. And lastly, we saw the rise of the neo-Democrats that does NOT compromise with their fellow Americans and wishes war rather than let the nation survive. The neo-Democrats that has no links to the Democrat parties led by President Franklin D Roosevelt, President John F Kennedy nor even President Bill Clinton, but essentially was born from the '60s Anti-Establishment roots of likes of Saul Alinsky passed on to George Soros, Hillary Clinton and finally to President Obama. For all their Socialism demagogue, racism sophistries and Globalism subterfuges, if you strip away all these facades of lies, in their core lies only the Uncompromising ideology of Anti-Establishment, Anti-America and Self-Enrichment.

Which still leaves us the question of why the results of Election 2016 happened the way it did, we'll discuss that in chapter 8: Closing of the Western Mind. For now, we have identified the combatants, let's understand their Agenda and Mindset too.

To do that, we need to first understand societies' decision-making process; and to distinguish between rational and irrational [cultural] behaviors. We need to remember the difference between the individual's versus the society's perspectives when it comes to decision making, for depending on which perspective, the decision can be very different.

> *"Both parties deprecated war, but one of them would make war rather than let the nation survive, and the other would accept war rather than let it perish, and the war came."*
>
> - President Abraham Lincoln, Second Inaugural Address, 1865

Collapse - Why do some societies make Disastrous Decisions?

In his book; Collapse, how societies choose to fail or succeed, Jared Diamond gave great explanations in his answers to the question above, he also pointed out the weaknesses of a society's decision-making process. He identifies 4 separate stages: Failure to anticipate, Failure to perceive it once it has risen, Failure to attempt to solve it after it has been perceived and lastly Failure to succeed in attempt to solve it. For our discussion here, let's focus on the *Failure to attempt to solve* the issue after it has been perceived. We know from experience that companies, institutions and geographical regions have their own culture, to facilitate ease of discussion here, let's call that organizational culture.

This organizational culture helps guide the organization's decision-making process which works differently from (but linked to) an individual's decision-making process. Let's use a simple example to point out the difference between the organization's (country's) vs the individual's perspective. Driving on the interstate highway, when driving on the interstate, some drivers go slower while others go faster right? That's simple enough, just like diversity or different preferences of the drivers. The generally accepted convention is that the slower traffic keeps to the right lanes while allowing for the faster traffic to pass them on the outer left lanes. That's logical too, it is a way to reconcile between the different preferences of the drivers. So far so good. Now what happens when you have drivers road hogging the lanes at slow speed? Imagine on a 3 lane highway, all 3 drivers driving at the same speed of 30 miles per hour in all 3 lanes for over 50 miles? What happens then? Assuming no accidents, there will be a huge traffic jam behind the 3 drivers on that highway, now most people will immediately say that's stupid, the drivers on the left lanes should keep right and let other drivers pass, right? We so instinctively use the "organizational perspective" (country's perspective) that we don't even notice it, of course the slow drivers should keep right and let others pass, the highway system is meant for ALL drivers not just for the 3 clowns hogging up the 3 lanes. How about the 3 clown drivers going at 30 miles per hour? What about their individual perspectives?

If you are a selfish driver who doesn't care about the other drivers, having no traffic in front of you is a nice drive (in fact, you can even point out to those criticizing you for not understanding that you can only go at 30 miles an hour because that's your personal preference, they are sexists, racists, islamophobic, xenophobic, etc..) from an individual's perspective, there's nothing irrational at all, they are merely protecting their personal interests. This is an extreme example I just gave, the drivers would move off the left lanes and let other traffic pass as it is SO OBVIOUS to all, what they are doing is selfish and inconsiderate (you can drive at 30 miles, no one cares as long as you keep to the right lane). But in the real world, issues are a little more complex and less transparent. More often than not, that we cannot see the selfish behaviors of those around us nor understand their personal agendas.

Let's use the example of the Kleptocrats in congress, imagine the Congress People enjoying their powerful influence and good paychecks, the nice panache or even "aura" that comes with being a senator. What if they are incompetent for the job, don't understand the details or just can't be bothered to get into the details of the bills that they are passing? Or not aligned for the interests of their voters? Would the voters know? Probably not in a timely fashion for most voters, others might figure that out after sometime. For other voters that would not get into too much details or new concepts, they'll probably never recognize the incompetence of their senators ever! Now imagine from the senators' perspective, would they willingly move to the right lanes and let other faster traffic pass them? Would they voluntarily resign from the Senate and let more capable and well-intention new Senators replace them? Of course NOT, because now the drivers causing the traffic jam isn't so obvious, is it? But if you don't call the GDP growing at 1-2% a traffic jam? What do you call that? Ah Yes, that's due to globalism.

Now that we've clarified the individual versus the society's perspective. Back to Jared's analysis of Organizational Behavior (or shortfalls in societies' decision-making process). He separates the weaknesses into Rational vs Irrational Behavior. Under Rational behavior, there's Conflict of Interests, Tragedy of Commons and fact that Decision makers can be Insulated from others in the society. Under Irrational Behavior, there's Clash of Values, "sunk costs" effect, Religious or Personal Values, previous false alarms, dislike Messenger, ISEP – "It is Someone Else's Problem", Crowd psychology, "group think" mentality and finally Psychological Denial. I will briefly summarize what he means by each category emphasizing on those traits more relevant to our situations. For detailed explanations, you might like to read chapter 14 of Jared's book.

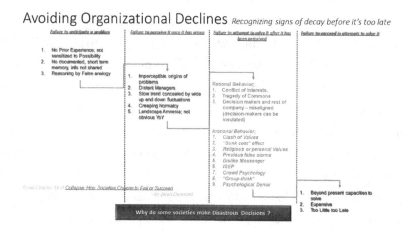

Ideally, the decision-makers should be representing the entire society who would be affected and making the best decision for everyone's interests, when they merely act to further their personal interests that is Conflict of Interests. Simple. These Conflict of Interests' behavior is termed Rational as the actions of the decision-makers are logical although immoral or even illegal (if the laws had been quick enough to catchup) and causes harm to the society as a whole.

The Tragedy of Commons happens when a resource is communally owned but can be exploited or harvested by many (eg. Over-fishing in the oceans, logging in Amazon and Indonesian forests, pollution by the China factories, poaching animals in Africa, unrestrained greed of the Welfare Abusers, Free Healthcare, Free Education, etc.), since the Resources are communal, what the poachers, polluting factories, loggers, fishermen do is also rational and logical.

Another condition that allows the selfish decision-making powerful elite who prioritize personal interests over those of the rest of society, is their ability to Insulate themselves from the consequences of their actions. (eg. In cases of High Crimes, drug-related turf wars, etc.) The politicians, Celebrities, Bankers are all protected in their rich neighborhoods, gated compounds and armies of security guards, it is the average American voters that suffers from High Crimes, proliferation of Drugs on the streets, illegals abusing welfare, etc.

As to the category of Irrational (Emotional) behavior, the distinction isn't so much between the decision-makers and the rest of the society. Here, both the decision-makers and the general society share the same values or psychological mindset. Here most of the terminologies of Irrational Behavior are pretty self-explanatory, the "sunk costs" effect refers to situation when we've invested too much (either emotionally or financially) into something to abandon it or move on. Crowd psychology (going with the masses) and "group think" are same phenomenon except "group think" refers to a smaller and clearly identifiable group.

Two Useful Tools to gauge and understand hidden Agendas

"We were dead broke when we left the Whitehouse" Hillary Clinton herself made this comment to Diane Sawyer in an ABC interview in 2014. Remember when we explored the neo-Democrats vs the old-Democrats? Here, we categorized President Bill Clinton's term from 1992 – 2000 as old-Democrat. Why? The Clintons were dead-broke when they left the Whitehouse, how's that relevant?

Recall when we were using the 3 lane Interstate highway example and how the decision makers' Conflict of Interests with the American Voters' might NOT be as Obvious to the average voter? That's because the personal agendas, Power networks, relationships and influences are not transparent to the outsiders. The politicians are NOT wearing their personal agendas, power relationships on their sleeves for all to see. Just like the icebergs that sank the Titanic, you can only see the tip of the iceberg not what's below the waterline, but Wait if you have sonar, you can see what's below the waterline.

The **Financial Gains Sonar** that detects Conflicts of Interests. Financial rewards can be a Powerful tool to help detect existence of Conflict of Interests, that's why most private financial records of Top 1% are safely guarded away from the public's prying eyes.

In a fair transaction, there's exchange of value, example when you buy a pair of shoes, the goods come to you and the money goes towards the seller, Fair Trade. The Top 1% power brokers are no dummies, when they reward their puppet politicians with $$$ cash (or in other forms.. which would make it even harder to track), obviously they get something back in return. The logic is simple, if whatever the Top 1% needs from the politicians is already per their official duties and NOT a conflict of Interests for the politician, then there would be no need to pay the politician for merely doing their job.

Thus, Hillary's comments are very interesting as she later tried to clarify that they subsequently did very well for themselves. If you read between the lines and use their Financial wealth as a gauge, up till 2000 President Bill Clinton and Hillary Clinton gained recognition and power but didn't make extra-ordinary profits (didn't get super rich). Yet subsequently, they did very well for themselves financially. Using Financial Sonar, that would simply translate into President Clinton had still been working for the American Voters till 2000 when he stepped down as President. That's why I categorized him as old-Democrat for his 1992 – 2000 service to this country.

Would all payments be in financial form? Obviously not, it can be in goodwill, favors owed, access to privileges, technologies, valuable information and news) that's why Conflict of Interests are not always so obvious.

One more useful Tool to help assess Leadership before we start mapping out and understanding the agendas and Mindset of the Civil War combatants, that's **Personal Sacrifice**. The leaders' behavior and demonstrated Values like Edge, Belief and Value System and Personal Sacrifice as against "Jump on the Bandwagon", Mainstream Media Glamor, 'leading from behind' mindset. These 2 different forms of Political Leadership can be summarized down to a) degree of difficulty and b) Risks.

Being on the "cutting edge", pioneering spirit is Difficult, trying and Risky! The second form is much more safe and personally rewarding! To better illustrate this point, let's look at some examples: President George Washington, President Abraham Lincoln, Reverend Martin Luther King Jr, 孙中山 Sun Yatsen, Vladimir Lenin. Although leaders in different countries of different ideologies they share common traits, they endured great hardships for their beliefs and made tremendous personal sacrifices for their countries and cause. At the time of their deaths, none of these leaders made personal gains, enjoyed personal privileges for themselves nor their families. All the Power and Influence they had was in service of their countries and their causes.

Contrasted with the likes of Chairman Mao Zedong, Joseph Stalin, Fidel Castro, you'll see the stark differences. These second group of Leaders might have started off with the right intents but later became Dictators and enjoyed lives of great personal power, privileges and influence.

"… Power corrupts and absolute power corrupts absolutely"

- Lord Acton.

Thanks to the 2 terms limits on the Presidents, we don't get Dictators here. We cannot see the beliefs in their minds (anyone can talk about Change), but we can see the Personal Sacrifices made and Financial Rewards accumulated by the Elected Politicians. If we look at these Professional Politicians enjoying their lives of influence and privileges, all growing fat, dumb and happy in last 3 decades, we can see that they are really doing it for the American People, right!

This second form of **"Hardship, personal Sacrifice" Radar** needs the readers to go deeper in understanding the finer details of specific issues and personalities, when used together with the **Financial Sonar** these two weapons are useful to figure the agendas of the politicians, media celebrities, Wall Street suzerains and the Tech monopolies' Moguls. Think Clintons, Obamas collecting millions for making speeches to Wall Street, tens of millions of guaranteed book deals with Activists and special interests corporations. As public servants, these Politicians that have made no visible sacrifice for this country but instead reaped great (obvious) financial rewards for themselves, that's only the tip of the iceberg of how much wealth had been extracted from the American people (middle working class) and put into the hands of their sponsors (Top 1% puppet masters) bringing income inequality to its highest level in America's modern history.

Another way to sum up **Hardship, self-sacrifice Radar** on the leadership is to assess if they are confronting Uphill struggles, facing great challenges [against the relentless attacks from the Mainstream Media, rhetoric of Hate from the Deep State Politicians] as versus the going down paths of least resistance with much personal rewards, enjoying self-enrichment, the comforts and accolades of leading from behind [similar to the rich and famous lifestyles of Hollywood Celebrities].

Quick Summary

We now understand the difference between the individual and society (organization) decision making process due to difference in perspectives. Also, we've learned the Rational vs Irrational (Cultural) behaviors that influences the decision-making process. We've introduced the leadership assessment heuristics like **Financial Gains Sonar, Hardship and Self-sacrifice Radar**. Through the book, we'll continuously introduce more assessment tools.

We might initially be surprised how the Political Opinions Shapers (Influencers) are so lopsided, but as one understand more about the societies' decision-making process and how individuals are personally motivated by selfish reasons, always heading down paths of least resistance, with so few to look after the interests of the society [America's interest], you add weak non-existent Leadership in the last Administration and atrophying Traditional American Values of Self-Sacrifice, Honor, Hard-work, personal Accountability, Valor, lack of Ethos and Awful Virtues, all under the relentless onslaught of the progressive Media and Academia, and now it doesn't seemed so amazing anymore.

As we know, each civilization goes through its growth phase and finally the Decadence phase (when there's lack of growth). Now we'll explore the real and unstated agendas and motivations of each parties in this Civil War starting with the Rational Behaviors.

> *"political language… is designed to make its lies sound truthful and murder respectable, and to give an appearance of solidity to pure wind." Per George Orwell "Defenseless villages are bombarded from the air. The inhabitants driven out into the countryside, the cattle machine-gunned, the huts set on fire with incendiary bullets: this is called pacification. Millions of peasants are robbed of their farms and sent trudging along the roads with no more than they can carry: this is called transfer of population or rectification of frontiers. People are imprisoned for years without trial, or shot in the back*

*of the neck or sent to die of scurvy in Arctic lumber camps: this is called
elimination of unreliable elements.*

Unmasking Washington DC, Facebook and Hollywood

We'll discuss the rational behavior of each category of players in this segment, let's also brain-
storm the various possible reasons, we'll then triangulate with information and knowledge publicly available plus observation of historical trends and evidence.

Let's start with the Wall Street Suzerains, what motivates them to get involved in the political
game? Does it give them pleasure to exert influence on the puppet politicians? Probably Yes, ability to influence the world affairs and culture does feed one's ego. There's another more practical
reason which started it off, self-interests. As we'd discussed some of the Wall Street challenges in
last chapter, there's a lot to be fixed to realign Wall Street back with Main Street economy. The
Wall Street Suzerains' biggest concerns is that their playground of limitless wealth gets properly
regulated and the "monopolies Banks too Big to fail" (the Assets concentration in top 5 Banks
today has reached over 50% of the entire market, this has increased from less than 10% in 1990)
gets broken up into smaller Banks and the Industry trends towards a perfect competition market
that's efficient and better serves the country. Then there would be no extra-ordinary profits for
the Wall Street Suzerains and their vast wealth and empires would get curtailed. Their source
of immense power would be contained, they would become like other Industries that have to
compete fairly and deliver Value to the customers or go out of business. They would now be held
responsible for their mistakes and be accountable to their fiduciary duties to their investors (big
and small). That scenario must never ever happen, God forbid!

Only by ensuring that the Federal Banks [the Feds] do NOT intervene in our Free Market
Economy, plus the restructuring of the Bank monopolies can the Wall Street be realigned back
to help support Main street growth. The unproductive wealth trapped in the Wall street system
might be driving Stock prices and other financial assets up in last decade but it isn't translating
into increased productivity in our economy or any new Significant technological breakthroughs.
Just like in early twentieth century when Theodore Roosevelt broke up the Industry Monopolies
to create better Free Market competition, this Wall Street Major overhaul is long overdue by at
least half a century. We now see why the Top 1% Wall Street Suzerains needs to protect their
Monopoly playground against Free Market Capitalism competition and mechanism. Remember,
no one controls the free market, it is moved by Adam Smith's "invisible hand".

Besides 'strongly influencing' the politicians, the Wall Street Suzerains also directly and
indirectly control numerous "charitable organizations" aka 501c3 Activists organizations. These
neo-Democrat Liberal Activists 501c3 organizations are much more pervasive than you can imagine. (they include George Soros' Open Society, Ford Foundation, Black Lives Matter, Planned
Parenthood, America Votes, MoveOn.org, America Coming Together, The Media Fund,
American Federation of Teachers, National Treasury Employees Union, National Education
Association, Music for America, etc.) As you can see now, many of the pro-Liberal neo-Democrat

Activists on all the TV, Cable News programs make their successful careers in these huge and powerful organizations. The Net Assets of just the progressive Environmental groups alone are over $ 9.5B, the Ford Foundation (no longer linked to their founders) has over $12B, the left-wing funding organizations together has over $100B in Assets (that's bigger than the combined Market Cap of GM and Ford Motors together). They also don't pay any taxes, being defined by IRS as "charitable organizations". With some much funds and resources, activists organizations are no longer some amateur "hippie" protestors like back in the 60s, they are now huge corporations and better funded, more professionally organized than many industrial companies.

The next biggie are the Ultra-rich Tech Monopolies Moguls. As George Soros, the Tech monopolies Moguls like to influence and shape Public Opinions too; Jeff Bezos (founder of Amazon, personal worth now over $ 75B) buys The Washington Post to help propagate the Politically Correct ONE View. Just like the extra-ordinary profits made by the Wall Street Bankers, the Technology Industry is now dominated by large behemoths like Amazon, Google, Facebook, etc. enjoying their monopolies, buffered from new competition by their size (they enjoy economies of scale) and financial strength, remember that they get most of their funds via the Wall Street Investors. Likewise, they would like to preserve status-quo for themselves. Logically, the Technology companies that generates real Cash flows and are competitive Globally would be more independent of the Wall Street and neo-Democrats' influence at Rationale level but still susceptible at emotional, non-rationale level (crowd psychology).

The Vain Entertainment Celebrities, the Parvenus Mainstream Media Celebrities both have done very well, raked in huge fortunes for themselves under the neo-Democrats rise so they would like to keep the gravy-train going and continue to widen the power-distance between themselves and the average American voter.

The Academia has become a Super-Size commercial Industry, so highly profitable with accumulated wealth that puts most traditional Industries to shame. Universities & Colleges has become a Major Category of Institutional Investors. The Endowment Funds of the top ten Universities total $ 169.3B as of end of FY 2015 Harvard's endowment fund alone amounts to $ 38B. Remember, this is just the Top Ten Universities' endowment funds. As a comparison, the Market Cap of the entire Casino and Gaming Industry stands at $ 107B, entire Airline Industry at $ 150B, Automobile Industry at $ 152B and Hotels, Resorts & Cruise lines at only $163.5B. The Academia staff has always been pro-left and obviously the students would be too. This high margin business also gives you a glimpse why the "snowflakes" culture is becoming so prevalent. In the past, the Students were "the products" of the Universities to supply the growing Economy (companies, organizations, etc.) with talent and professional workers. The better trained and educated the graduates are, the better the credibility of the Universities and kudos to their Alumni. Now the students have become the customers, providing the high Revenue and High Profits for the Universities (with such crazy exorbitant Tuition Fees). What do you say to your high-rollers in the Casinos? Are you getting the service you expect? What can we do to make your experience better? Therefore you have birth of safe-spaces, micro-aggression, etc. whatever the high-rollers expects, the Casinos provides.. that's good service.

The Agenda of the Administrative Apparatchiks and their extension at the Regional and Local levels are mainly self-preservation of their Jobs, power, security and the undue influence linked to their positions. Culture of lack of accountability in the large Bureaucracy can also appeal to some apparatchiks after decades of reveling in such "comfort zones". In some cases, these K Street apparatchiks have devolved further into self-serving *Eunuch Organizations that have NO Real nor Valuable Intelligence on our enemies like North Korea, instead only capable of eavesdropping on the White House's conversations with Australia, Mexico and leaking to the Mainstream News Media. Not able to open an iPhone in domestic terrorists acts nor find any details in Vegas shootings but fully vested in Russian hacking bamboozle; the FBI has become a sad and sick joke on the American people.

The Government Unions also belong to this extension of Apparatchiks, they are now also intertwined with the pervasive, wealthy and professional Activists 501c3 Corporations, just as the FBI & NSA Eunuch Organizations, the Activists Led Teachers Unions are vested to protect their Fat budgets, Federal subsidies for Public Monopoly Schooling (if you call that **schooling) instead of allowing competition from private sectors; who have proven track records to deliver many times the performance for only a tiny fraction of the costs. Here, we need to clarify that there's nothing wrong with the teachers themselves at operational level, however, we know that monopolies organizations always get bloated with Overheads, Inefficiency, corrupted practices at the top and middle management with lack of competition over time.

*Eunuch Culture describes one who's afraid of the external enemy but Hates the internal fellow citizens (you can see much Eunuch Culture being broadcasted to the snowflakes, praising North Korea, Iran, Islamists Regimes and Hating the current American Leadership), it has much in common with the Anomic man. Quoting Robert MacIver from 1950

> "... anomie signifies the state of mind of one who has been pulled up by his moral roots, who has no longer any standards but only disconnected urges, who has no longer any sense of continuity, of folk, of obligation."

> "The anomic man has become spiritually sterile, responsive only to himself, responsible to no one. He derides the values of other men. His only faith is the philosophy of denial. He lives on the thin line of sensation between no future and no past."

> ** "Schools are no longer institutions of learning. They are laboratories of progressive indoctrination. Encouraging critical thought has been replaced by demanding regurgitating of the leftists ideology to get a passing grade. These days, students know how to address the transgendered with the proper pronouns, but they aren't able to do basic maths."

> – Sheriff David Clarke Jr.

Thanks to the 2016 Elections, we now see the political cronies in last Administration for who they really are. Many of them (as in State Departments, DNCs, CNNs, Personal Campaign managers, liaisons to Muslim brotherhoods, etc.) are being paid multiple times by 2 or even 3 organizations for doing the same job of kissing up and kicking down (buttering up to their bosses and pushing all the work and responsibilities downwards in the organization).

Now you can see the Civil War combatants all having strong reasons and personal vested agendas to continue Status Quo for themselves. You might ask the question, how is that a Conflict of Interests? To answer that question, we need to understand what American voters wants, how do America, as a Nation achieve the aims of the American people? Are the professional politicians still aligned to the interests of the country and its people? In chapter 4: we'll explore in detail what are American Ideals? In chapter 7: How to untie the Gordian knot? We'll look at many of the specific issues and you'll see more clearly the conflict of interests. Here's a short concise answer to the conflict of interests. Firstly, the Patriotic Americans don't despise the wealthy, they are not jealous of other American's Wealth. The election of Billionaire Donald J. Trump as President Trump is clear evidence of that.

Being practical people, Americans wants the Economy to grow, they want jobs, they want a better life for their families and themselves, a better future for their kids. Ideally, they would like a more level playing field for themselves, the opportunity to compete for good jobs, for more Meritocracy in the system, a sense of Fair play. They do not demand equality in outcome for all, but they would like Equal opportunity to compete freely. Meritocracy and Culture of Excellence will determine the outcome of the competition. As we'd seen earlier, Equal Outcome means the death of Competition, end of Freedom to compete. The Practical and Ideal Goals of the American Voters are aimed along the same path. They rest on 2 fundamental beliefs. Free Market Capitalism leads to Wealth Creation, Competition leads to Excellence. They also have the Confidence in themselves that, in a Free Market Competition with a level-playing field, their abilities and self-confidence will bear them the desired results. The Practical goals are the desired outcomes, the Ideal goals are the means to get there!

At this stage, some readers might already be able to sense the conflict of interests with these Wall Street Suzerains, Tech monopolies' Moguls. This is a "clash of values" feeling. It is at an intuitive level, "our values systems" exist in our psyche at such a subconscious level, we notice something uncomfortable without consciously being able to put our fingers on the exact concern when a "Clash of personal Values" happens.

The current state of economy is America is lackluster to say the least, China has overtaken USA as the World's largest economy (GDP by PPP, Purchasing Power Parity) in 2015. Wall Street and Main Street are no longer aligned. The middle-Class (the backbone, the heart and Soul of this country, the families that will produce the next Steve Jobs, the next Bill Gates, the next Warren Buffett) is declining rapidly even as the good paying manufacturing jobs goes overseas. Meaningful Technological breakthroughs have slowed down. Even as the free market economy shrank under the last administration, the Big State Government Controlled Bureaucracies grew their endless Regulations and Policies that further crushes the free market economy. To reverse this downward trend and bring growth back to America, a number of initiatives needs to be put in place:

a. Wall Street needs to be better aligned to support Main Street's Economic growth, Bank Monopolies need to be ended or descaled for many smaller banks to compete. Fed intervention needs to be stopped for the Free Market Capitalism to work again and allow Adam Smith's "invisible hands" to reshape this country as it had for last 200 plus years

b. Govt Regulations and policies to be reduced to a minimal as the Administrative Apparatchiks organizations needs to be cut down to a mere sliver of its current form. Allow for Industries to self-regulate

c. The Universities and Colleges classes can be audited by volunteers, introduce international competition via internet. Numeracy must be a compulsory class in College. Foreign languages, Mathematics and Accounts be strongly encouraged so that the Students actually learn something, and not be treated like "high rollers" in the casinos. The college tuition fees need to be lowered substantially, and any involvement by Activists Corporations needs to be fully disclosed to the students, parents and public

d. The Internet Monopolies needs to be also broken up to enable smaller entrepreneur start-ups to compete freely, instead of being bought up and acquired by the larger Monopolies currently; lessening the passion and drive for real technological breakthroughs, killing off potential meaningful innovations that might have added Value to this country and the world Economy.

e. Encourage Competition from Alternative voices, Diverse views, remove the barriers to entry for new entrants and descale the Media Conglomerates. The Mainstream Media Celebrities specializing in only Entertainment needs to move aside for real Journalists (likes of Ida Tarbell's intellectual prowess) to research the severe challenges currently faced by this nation and its citizens. Topics like: Our decline in technology compared to the Chinese. The extent of influence of the Wall Street suzerains, the Tech monopolies' Moguls over the Internet Social Media and the huge wealth and Assets of the Activists Corporations. But wait, aren't these the real bosses and "puppet-masters" of the current Media Conglomerates? There's your conflict of interests.

We also note that the Wall Street suzerains, Tech Moguls, Politician, Celebrities, Apparatchiks, Academia, Activities corporations are all INSULATED from the Economic decline of the main street Industries unlike the average Americans, at least for now. How is this the case? Remember the limitless Financial money created in Wall Street? It only enriches certain groups and stays within those groups. This is similar to Monopolistic Industries with High Barriers to entries. For our current discussion, suffice to say that the Great Wealth of the Hollywood Celebrities, Media Celebrities, the Wall Street suzerains, the Tech Moguls insulates them from the economic decline. Same with the Job security enjoyed by the Administrative Apparatchiks, while the Activists

Corporations provide not only job stability but also great life-long career opportunities, both groups are also insulated from the main street Americans.

Now we've seen the obvious Conflict of Interests and the fact they (the neo-democrats) can be Insulated from the rest of the American Voters, we can see the traffic jams in our earlier interstate example. We now understand the personal reasons why the 3 drivers are road hogging the 3 lanes. What can we do to relieve the traffic jam?

The Take-away here is very simple, if someone already has a personal vested agenda, it is waste of time trying to reason with or have a real discussion with them. You are barking up the wrong tree. Why are you talking to the puppet? Are you talking to the Sheep or the Dogs? You need to figure what who is the real puppet master, what are his/her motives and what you can personally do to further your own cause. Not voting for the Professional Politicians is a good start!

Organizational Cultures and Values – shaping Irrational behaviors

We've addressed the Rational behavior aspects identified in Collapse – How societies choose to fail or succeed, let's review the Irrational or perhaps more Emotional behaviors. Clash of Values is the main focus in this segment. What are Values and where do they come from? Values are linked with Cultures. They help define what is judged as good or bad within a Culture. There are different Cultures; National Cultures, Geographic Regional Cultures, Organizational Cultures. Being a part of each such Cultures would help shape the Values we hold dear. The overlap and interplay of larger Cultures would produce sub-cultures (eg. Within the Japanese Culture, perhaps a strong Disney Company culture? thus it would be a unique sub-culture within Japan, a bland of American and Japanese). How about personal Values? Sure, individuals have different experiences and thus might also have different Values from other individuals within a larger and similar Culture. Values from our parents? Sure, our parents being the greatest influence in our early stages of life would have significant impact on our personal Values system. Whether Cultural or Personal, Values are shaped by past experiences; past experiences of ourselves and past history of the Culture that we are part of. Real Values are internalized within our psyche, they work at the sub-conscious levels which makes us want to resist new conflicting values as and when we come across them as we grow up and come into contact with other cultures or even work in different companies with different organizational cultures. What happens when these different cultures come together for one individual?

There's a number of ways to deal with the situation, a) stay within similar cultures, that's easy enough right? Since all the folks share the same culture and same values, you don't have to adjust your personal values. b) just ignore the new cultures & values, my culture is superior and heck with the others, c) don't resist, just adopt the new values wholesale and d) the most demanding is to try to reconcile between the existing Values and the new Culture and new Values. The last case needs constant assessment and again re-assessment of your old values systems and comparing with the new Values, absorb and integrate what's useful and superior, reject what's in conflict with existing values. But it also needs one to re-configure old and existing values too, what if some are outdated or even outright wrong? It puts one in a state of mental dissonance and stress. When one challenges one's own existing Values and those passed down to us from our parents, grandparents, does that make us unfilial? It makes us feel small and insecure. But the alternative to just ignore new values and different cultures makes us weak and unable to adapt. The constant reconciliation is the right answer but most difficult one. The constant never-ending configuration, re-configuration, de-configuration and then re-configuration can drive one insane. It helps to understand that Values and Cultures are shaped by prior experiences. So if you can understand your own experiences, history of your culture and then the history of the new culture you are in contact with and the prior experiences of the people you deal with, it helps put things into context and gives you a better perspective of things and lessens some of the stress from ceaseless reconciliation.

Obviously, most sane folks would do less of d) and more of a) to c) categories. If you have been attentive, you might point to c) as a weird approach If Values are internalized and work at a sub-conscious level for a person, how can one just adopt new values wholesale and ignore their existing old values? Case a) and b) are simple enough, but c)? I would say Yes, that approach in itself is also a kind of Values too. In chapter 5, we'll discuss more about this Phenomenon, for now, let's just call it "Cut and Paste" Values.

Imagine, for one individual the internal "clash of Values" is already shown to be so stressful and complex. Let alone we're now talking about Clash of Values between over 135M people. So what Values are we discussing about in the specific case of the Civil War now? For that we need to take a step back to understand Organizational Cultures and Values and how environment and history shape their Culture and Values. Then we come back into the present groups of combatants to understand their mindsets.

Here's is a Risk vs Rewards chart. It explains the High Risks, High Rewards concept in Financial Investments. Simple idea, when you hold higher Risks Assets, in an efficient market, you would be rewarded with higher returns. Similarly, if your risk preference is lower, the financial returns would be correspondingly lower too. This concept is pretty intuitive and logical, you should remember that the assumption is that the market is efficient. If there's any extra-ordinary profits, it gets arbitrated out quickly.

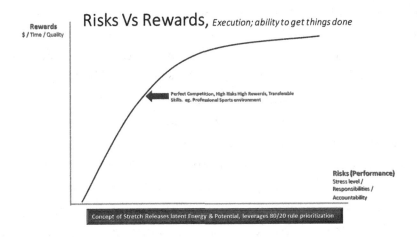

Using the same idea, I had re-produced a similar chart but instead of Financial Investment, it is of Risks and Rewards for Professional Talent in an efficient Labor Market.

The assumption of an efficient Labor Market when the Talent is mobile and the Market is transparent. It works generally well for Professional Sports environment when the rewards for the talent increases as their performance goes up to higher levels. The better sportsman gets paid better, logical? Similarly in the efficient Management Talent market, the logic holds that top management talent performing at each higher level of responsibilities (with promotion) gets paid better too.

Along the curve is the efficient and Free Market, thus when talent transfers, they'll be compensated at the free market rate, they get rewarded for their Performance (as in the efficient Financial Markets, where risks translates into rewards). What happens above or below the curve? Above the curve is interesting as the someone gets compensated above Free Market rate, how can that be possible? Well we had been assuming an efficient and Free Market similar to a Perfection Competition Free Market Economy where there's no "extra-ordinary profits" to be made. In instance of an inefficient Market, as in the case of Monopolies Industries, they can and do make "extra-ordinary profits", usually there's barriers to entries for new competition too. So in an inefficient Market or Industries, the individuals or companies relying on their ability to block new entrants (barrier to entry) into their Markets, corner off their markets and make "extra-ordinary profits" for themselves. This is no longer free market competition. Can you think of such instances with regards to the various Combatants of the Civil War?

Let's review the organizational Cultures of the "perfect competition free Market" companies as against those of "monopolistic nature" companies. Just like in humans, where their experiences shape their culture and values, it is the same for organizations too. The environment in which the company exists, shapes its Culture and values too. There are many Management books written about company's and organizational cultures, will do a quick summary. Companies need to compete and thrive to survive, prosper and grow. Depending the Industry and environment that they are in, *the critical success factors* for the companies are different. Over time, these *critical success factors* will help shape and determine the company's culture and Values.

In the Technology companies in growth phase, ability to Innovate, "thinking out of the box" mindset, willingness to take risk and try new ideas, new approaches in the R&D would be Critical for them and be a competitive advantage for these Technology companies. For consumer products (b2c) companies, Branding and Marketing strengths would provide them with the competitive edge. Large Manufacturing companies would reply on costs efficiencies, economies of scale and superior quality of their products to provide the competitive advantage. You'll notice that it is never only one particular critical success factor but a combination of several factors that leads to the success of the company to outcompete and outperform. Amongst the critical success factors that contributed, one or two would be higher in priority and these few key driving critical success factors will shape the eventual culture and values of the companies (organizations). Other critical success factors would be to create Barriers to Entries, sometimes with government support like Government licenses, regulations, support via policies, subsidies, etc. For start-up companies in their early stages, ability to get Investors' Funding can be a critical success factor too.

Now for companies or organizations in highly competitive environments with less barriers to entry, ever-changing landscapes, competitors with constantly evolving strategies and tactics, merely replying on their identified critical success factors is Not sufficient to remain competitive. They all need a more powerful critical success factor, People. Talented, passionate, committed people to lead as Management in all departments of the organization. Talented, passionate, committed people to excel in R&D, Finance, Marketing, Sales, etc. you get the picture. Besides paying them well, what else would motivate and attract such talent and energize their passions and commitment to the organization?

A **Winning Culture of Meritocracy**, Excellence, Accountability, Hope. Talent wants to be differentiated, recognized and valued for their contributions. That can only happen when there's personal Accountability. They plan ahead and need to see limitless potential and opportunities in the future of the organization, they need to see Hope in their own future with the company. Good people wants to be part of a winning team, they want to compete and win. They also understand Excellence and thus appreciate Meritocracy; may the best person win! Talent wants to be held responsible, they wish to Control their own Destiny, Freedom to pursue their dreams, freedom to share their ideas and listen to and debate other diverse ideas. They love this learning process and approach. They love to try and tinker with new ideas, not afraid of setbacks nor to put in tremendous amounts of hard work to achieve their dreams. Where do you see such Organization Cultures?

One good example is in Sports. You'll witness such Culture of Excellence prevalent in great sports teams; Olympics, Football, Basketball, you name it. The other place is the US Military. Some very well run companies also exhibit this kind of Culture. I call them Living Companies (you can read about such companies in Built to Last, Good to Great both by James C. Collins and The Living Company by Arie de Geus). To have the great joy to be part of such a Culture is the most beautiful experience and makes you able to recognize such Cultures anywhere. One other result of such a Culture of Excellence and Meritocracy is Diversity. Diversity in Ideas and Diversity in Talent. The logic is simple, because nature is unbiased, raw talent is everywhere around the world. To preclude any population from competing is bad strategy, you want to avail yourself to the biggest pool of talent. Through free competition based on Merit (Performance based Culture), you will have a diverse Talent at the end of the process. Note that Diversity is a result of the Culture of Excellence and Meritocracy, not some quota to be made. Any talented individual clearly understands that fact of nature. Just like Distillation process (where the distillate is separated from the residue), the Culture of Excellence & Meritocracy allows the talented and Best rise to the top. This process is elegant, dynamic and beautiful (as a contrast, quotas are ugly, clumsy, man-made and egoistic). This Culture of Excellence (performance based Culture) allows the organization to adapt to the competitive and ever-changing environment, the Living Organization (just as a living organism) can keep adjusting and adapting to the constant changes and challenges of its environment.

Next, companies and organizations that are Monopolies in their Industries and enjoy Barriers to entry against competitors. What kind of Culture would they exhibit? Culture takes time to form, in the early stages of the company or organization's life, the reinforcement of the barriers to entry and consolidation of its position as monopoly is fundamental to its survival. The company Increases its market share and size to start enjoying Economies of Scale (grow in wealth and establishes networks). To ensure continued Government support in policies, regulations and subsidies, it integrates into the government itself. What better way to ensure the barriers to entry are unbreakable and be able to continuously enjoy the government protection? Become part of the government and control the opinion shapers and influencers.

Once they have successfully consolidated their position of power as "monopolies" what culture will they adopt? This is where it gets really interesting, since the Organization Culture is NOT a Critical Success Factor to the company (the successful assurance of Barrier to Entry against external Competition is the critical success factor here), it can adopt any Culture it wants right? Yes, they can and do adopt different forms of cultures but eventually over time they start to gravitate towards a similar type of Culture. Think of the Banking agencies, Casinos, government agencies, bureaucracies, etc. what Cultures do they share? Culture of Compliance and Obedience, not just compliance to laws, compliance to authorities, compliance to those in power within the organization. Why? In absence of the external environment and competition shaping the organization's Culture, over time the shaping force is people. But unlike in Competitive environments where Talented People are required to adapt to the competition, here in these Stable environment, it is Human Nature that begins to shape the culture of these companies. In absence of competition and challenges, the Human Nature that manifest is Ego, remember Lord Acton's words (power corrupts)? Let's call this Culture of Compliance & Ego.

Culture of Compliance and Ego. What behavioral patterns come to one's mind? Complacency, Comfort Zone, Risk Adverse, fear of change, fear of free market competition, lacks clear personal responsibilities (when something goes wrong, I was just following the procedures), "In-groups" vs the rest (seniority based), Large Power Distance (Power distance describes how easily an individual gets promoted to or even above those currently above them in the organization, small Power Distance would indicate high possibility, large Power distance would mean low chance).

In a Bureaucratic Culture, since it is NOT performance based, it would be Large Power Distance because unless you are in the "in-group", for the rest, it would likely be seniority based so the possibility of getting promoted above your superiors would be minimal. Contrast that with a performance-based Culture, if you are capable and worked hard, there's little reason why you don't get promoted. One other behavioral pattern would be the inability to empathize or tolerate diverse ideas.

Now, if we look back at the Culture of Excellence and Meritocracy, the traits are exact opposite. Is this by design? Obviously not so, but why are they the opposites in so many areas. The answer is this kind of Monopoly Culture forms due to Lack of Design. As a person needs to exercise constantly to stay fit and strong, skills when not regularly practiced, will atrophy into weaknesses. With lack of constant competition and challenges, Culture of Compliance and Ego will grow in this Stable, Comfort Zone. Due to the stable conditions, the Culture doesn't need to adapt to changing environment or reacts to competition. Therefore, through neglect and abandonment, the traits of the Culture of Compliance and Ego, are the absence of the very same Values and traits (or opposite to) that we see in Culture of Excellence and Performance. It forms via the path of Least Resistance, like brown stuff flowing downhill (mud).

This Culture of Compliance and Ego exists all around the world, but it America, it takes makes an interesting mutation. Before, I get into the details of this form of mutation, I want to share an incident that happened a few years back. Some of you who might have had the opportunity to visit or live in Asia, you might know of a tradition that the Chinese (in SE Asia) burn paper offerings to their deceased ancestors, mostly in form of paper money, could be paper house, cars, etc. Couple of years ago, after a number of lengthy meetings with the largest Steel company in China, we just saw some folks burning these paper offerings. One of my American friends asked me why they were doing this? As a jest, I replied that they were burning the paper money for their ancestors to bribe the "officials" in the underworld. Later, upon thinking further, it isn't very far from the truth. It is to facilitate the ancestors in the underworld to better their conditions and since bribery in China's 5000 plus years of history is so pervasively practiced, it isn't a shock to any Asians that the paper money would help make their ancestors "lives" better and facilitate attaining additional privileges with the officials in the underworld. Many of the older overseas Chinese wouldn't find that proposal shocking. Noticed that I said Overseas Chinese. In China, after a full decade of Cultural Revolution, many of these "traditions" have been deleted (doesn't mean the practice of Bribery has ceased in China).

I share this joke to illustrate a major Cultural difference, in other parts of the world, the Culture of Compliance and Ego wouldn't need any disguise, in fact in some parts of China before 2012, Values of Decadence and Excesses are celebrated as sign of great Success and symbol that you've made it! We are Rich and proud to flaunt it, bribery is as natural as sun rising in the east, in fact if someone accepts a bribe from you, they honor and trust you (in case, you don't understand. Bribery is a serious crime, if you don't know or trusts someone well, you will refuse the bribe. For you might end up in jail if that person reports you. If you are reading this part, you must be American). Which help explain why the Culture of Compliance and Ego needs a disguise in

America. Because the traditional American Values and Culture was so steeped in Self Reliance and Freedom to pursue one's dreams (with Freedom comes personal responsibilities), etc.

The neo-Democrats' real Cultures of Compliance and Ego translates into Values of Decadence which for most Americans would be unacceptable, so this is where it gets really interesting. Everyone knows the traditional American Values; Diversity, Freedom of Speech, Tolerance, etc. so the wolf in sheep's clothing creates the P.C. (politically correct) Culture and Values.. it is a set of "Cut and Paste" Values that tries to mimic the Culture of Excellence except it de-emphasize the Competition and Excellence part and plays up the Diversity and Tolerance part. Makes it much easier to Market and Sell! Selling Values of Self-Reliance, personal Accountability, Resilience, Free Market Competition, etc. might frighten the less courageous. So, what is easier to sell?

To make the P.C. Culture easy to sell, they "cut and paste" ideas that appeal easily to those seeking paths of least resistance. Make it simple and easy to remember, drop the personal Accountability, Competition, Self-Reliance concepts.. too "uphill" to sell (even many parents fail to impart such Values to their children… they are hard to practice). Instead sell them easy "downhill" ideas that appeal to selfish human nature: Freedom of Speech means that others have to accept whatever you have to say, Tolerance means that others have to tolerate your failures, or incompetence, Diversity means one can play the race card in any situations, etc. As Hillary Clinton had pointed out, there's a Public side and a Private side. So the neo-democrats also have 2 sets of Values, the private side is the real Culture of Compliance and Ego. The Public side is the P.C. "cut and paste" set of Values which they constant chant but NEVER practice. Now we understand their true 'values'; shaped via their Culture of Monopoly of Power. The P.C. Culture is rooted in hypocrisy and pretense.

Remember we'd discussed earlier that Values operate at a sub-conscious level? The neo-democrats real values are Complacency, Egoistic, Large Power Distance, Fear of real competition, Fear of change, etc. that's internalized. The P.C. "cut and paste" Values are just a set of Mantras and Slogans that they chant. It is never internalized nor practiced. If one values of Diversity, Empathy, Tolerance and freedom of speech, etc. How can one be so self-righteous? If everyone has freedom to speak their minds and express their real opinions, how can there be NO difference in opinions? If you practice tolerance and understand diversity, you will understand diversity in ideas and be able to empathize with different ideas. Then where does all the self-righteousness come from? Since there's such a huge variance between their real values which constantly shows through in their actions and behavior and what they chant as their P.C. "cut and paste" Values, some might call them hypocrites! But you don't understand, this is much more than just being hypocritical, it is literally a matter of life and death for the neo-democrats. This is really NO joking matter. Just as after the last Civil War when all the Democrats were the slave owners and the GOP fought to free the slaves then? Yet how did they (the neo-Dems) pull off the stunt and re-invent themselves as the champions of the African Americans? That's a real class act and now again the neo-democrats have pulled off another bait and switch, with their real Culture of Ego and Decadence, they now sell themselves as champions of P.C. Values!

You cannot help but appreciate the marketing skills in pulling both these 2 acts off. Can you now imagine if they are Unmasked for their true Values? And have you wondered why they are so good at lying?

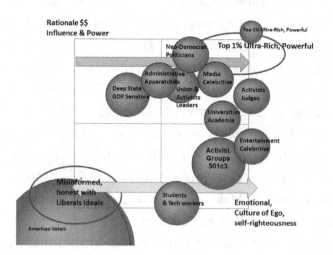

I plotted the chart for the Current Civil War Combatants' Agenda and Motives, on the y-axis the Rational incentives driving their agenda, and on the x-axis the Emotional, Culture & Values driving their agenda. Someone high on the y-axis has strong Rational reasons, high on the x-axis would be Emotional, Cultural Reasons. The top right-hand corner would be both Rational and Emotional reasons. As I started plotting the neo-Democrats groups; the Top 1% Ultra Rich, the Activist Corporation leaders, Activist judges, Media Celebrities, Academia, neo-Democrats Politicians, etc. One thing I noticed was that there is a strong overlap between the Rational reasons and Cultural Mindset (I couldn't find enough space to put all the groups into the top right-hand quadrant!). No wonder the neo-Democrats are so passionate and determined to win this Civil War! Their livelihoods, their self-righteous view of the world and massive Egos (for some) all in unison screams for Victory or Death!

Remember 9th November 2016? The Media Celebrities, the Elites breaking down on TV? Some even crying? Believe me, this isn't just their livelihood anymore, it is all in, their Psyche, their Self-Righteous 'Values', their Prideful Egos, wait what happened to tolerance? What happened to accepting Diversity (other fellow Americans with different opinions)? Now you see their true Values; Hate thy neighbors, Hate thy fellow Americans, Hate the poor, Hate the deplorables! Despise them, despise the non-college voters! How dare they vote otherwise? We are the Top 1%, we are the Super-rich, we are always Right! We'll show you, it is not over yet!

> *"… First they came for the Socialists, and I did not speak out. Because I was not a Socialist. Then they came for the Trade Unionists, and I did not speak out. Because I was not a Trade Unionist. Then they came for the Jews, and I did not speak out. Because I was not a Jew. Then they came for me, and there was no one left to speak for me…"*
>
> - Martin Niemöller (1892-1984)

P.C. Gestapo, be afraid, be very afraid

President Trump did his homework when picking his nominees for his Cabinet positions and the Supreme Court too. Names like Rex Tillerson, James Mattis, John Kelly, Wilbur Ross, Andy Puzder, Steve Mnuchin, Ryan Zinke, Ben Carson, etc. All of them extremely successful in their respective professional fields, competing freely in the commercial, Military, professional free markets world. Rising to the top in their fields and proven themselves repeatedly over decades and lifetime of accomplishments. If you had watched the confirmation hearings of the Cabinet and Supreme Court positions, you would have witnessed for yourself how well qualified these individuals are when they answered the questions put to them. Their lifetime accomplishments speak for themselves too.

You will also observe the extreme behavior of the neo-democrats politicians as they put forth their questions. No, not questions, more like accusations and insults. Yes, they were hurling baseless accusations at the nominees, making self-righteous opinions and bias conclusions right at the start of the hearings even before bothering to start asking any questions! Any independent thinking individuals would be appalled and shocked at such a Spanish Inquisition style hearings conducted by the neo-democrats politicians. This is pure Extremism, the pure Hate and Bias directed at people that they do NOT personally know at all? These are supposed to be US senators? Forget about extending professional courtesy, the sheer disdain and utter contempt that these neo-democrat Senators are demonstrating to the nominees lacks even the basic courtesy one would show to another fellow human being. The formation of extreme opinions about another human being without knowing them personally is the root of Racism! This is the power of the P.C. Gestapo, self-righteous Hate directed at their opponents and fellow Americans, now you see their real Values! The viciousness of the attacks were truly shocking! Whatever happened to Empathy and tolerance?

The P.C. Gestapo aka wolf in sheep's clothing is so vindictive and intrusive that even Navy-SEALs are afraid of them. Yes, our toughest US Navy-Seals (feared by our enemies) would want nothing to do with these P.C. Gestapo, if you had witnessed the Spanish Inquisition process on C-Span, you will understand too. Being personally shot at by the enemies is one thing, having your families and love ones raked over coals of public ridicule and humiliation in a never-ending witch-hunt is quite another. Vice Admiral Robert Harward (ex-Navy SEAL) turned down the position of National Security Advisor to President Trump, Vincent Viola turned down the Army secretary position, Philip Bilden turned down the Navy secretary position, all citing personal reasons. Andy Puzder (CEO of Carl's Jr and Hardees) had to withdraw from Secretary of Labor position after the extreme witch-hunt too. The outcome of the last Election has allowed us to see Extremist neo-Democrats shedding their sheep's clothing. Can you see them now? The vicious Dogs of the Activists Corporations, ATLA? Even the Media Celebrities unmasked themselves and were fully revealed to us, donning their Media P.C. Gestapo uniforms, when they so viciously attacked the widow of a fallen hero of the US Military. Even for the radical Media's neo-democrat extremists, that was a new low.

If we think ISEP (it's someone else problem) and continue to do nothing about the Media and P.C. Gestapo, there will be no one left to speak for you when they come after you.

> *"America has the proud satisfaction of having furnished the world with the greatest, wisest and meanest monopoly known to history."*
> – The History of a Great Monopoly, Henry Demarest Lloyd, 1881

> *".. In Spain, for the first time, I saw newspaper reports which did not bear any relation to the facts,"* George Orwell about the Spanish Civil War 1937.
> *"I saw great battles reported where there had been no fighting, and complete silence where hundreds of men had been killed. I saw troops who had fought bravely denounced as cowards and traitors, and others who had never seen a shot fired hailed as the heroes of imaginary victories; and I saw newspapers in London retailing those lies and eager intellectuals building superstructures over events that has never happened. I saw, in fact, history being written not in terms of what happened but of what ought to have happened according to various "party lines"*
> - Orwell about being skeptical of everything one reads, especially when it comes from or comforted those wielding power

Liberals and Progressives of Elections Past

Over a century ago, there were Professional Investigative Journalists in America. Henry Lloyd was writing about the American Trusts' Monopolies over their respective Industries in 1881 (more specifically referencing Standard Oil), he might as well be referring to the current Mainstream Media & Internet Social Media's strangle hold Monopoly over the unsuspecting American Public. Around the end of 19th century, Ida Minerva Tarbell pioneered investigative journalism, took on Standard Oil (most powerful corporation of its time) and succeeded in helping to trigger its breakup. Her dogged research, following "paper trails" helped provide a foundation for anti-trust law. Tarbell was part of *McClure's Magazine's* team including Lincoln Steffens, Ray Stannard Baker were all of the Progressive Age that understood their responsibility to explain an increasingly complex, often unfair and corrupt system to the public, that in-depth muckraking is needed to uncover the Monopolies' unethical practices. Theirs was a time when there was sincere Hope to alter the national ethos to minimize inequalities among individuals, when real Investigative Journalists were actually ferreting out waste, fraud and abuse to afflict the comfortable and comfort the afflicted.

The young Bob Woodward and Carl Bernstein of The Washington Post, aided by an informant, took on then President Nixon's administration in 1972, Nixon resigned in1974 after the Watergate scandal consumed the nation.

The Boston Globe reporters Michael Rezendes, Matt Carroll and Sacha Pfeiffer under the leadership of editor Walter "Robby" Robinson and Marty Baron took on the Roman Catholic Church in 2001. They exposed the Church for cover-up of sexual abuse after John Geoghan, an unfrock priest had molested more than 80 boys. They did intense investigative journalism, interview victims of sexual abuse, try to unseal sensitive documents to provide proof of the Catholic Church's a cover-up.

Notice the common tread among these professional journalists? When they took on the larger establishments, the eventual outcome was uncertain, they had to invest large part of their lives into the tedious and laborious investigative work. This sacrifice of personal time [years and decades], effort and chapters of their lives in these long and arduous "uphill fights" with uncertain future rewards requires tremendous dedication and belief in their cause. You might also see the similar personal sacrifices made by Great Leaders like Washington, Lincoln, Martin L. King Jr, Lenin, Sun Yat-sen 孫中山, etc. They all had a Greater Cause with no Financial rewards!

Now we contrast the muckrakers of yesteryears with the present day Media Entertainment Celebrities that aids the Rich and Powerful, cronies and lackeys to the Top 1%, making their millions indulging in their rich and famous lifestyles. Accomplices to the Activists Corporations; sponsored by the Wall Street Suzerains and Tech Street Monopoly Giants, joining in the abuse and affliction of the American people, the working class middle class tax payers. Spreading ignorance, Globalists and Socialists Propaganda, riling up racial hatred and anger.

The stark difference is for all too see. The present Media Celebrities and their P.C. Gestapo have become The Establishment! These Media monopolies, ABC, NBC, CBS, MSNBC, CNN, NYT, Washington Post, etc. (6 companies own the hundreds of TV channels you watch) have a near complete strangle-hold on the Main-Stream Media's "news". The combined Corporations' Resources, viewership, market-share easily dwarf that of an ailing FOX News, since Roger Ailes' passing. The personal wealth and riches of these Media celebrities, accumulated over years of protection from Free Market competition, has afforded them luxurious lifestyles of the Rich and Famous that would put many of our ex-Presidents to shame. The Media Celebrities begins to look more like the Hollywood Entertainment Celebrities (just like the Pigs looking more and more like Humans at the last chapter of Animal Farm). They have become the Monopoly themselves!

Ida Tarbell wouldn't be able to recognize the "works" of "self-proclaimed" journalists these days, where is the work and effort put into these publications? They are just opinions on others' opinions, there's no independent attesting to the so call "facts" presented, no long periods of painful and laborious research. In quest for quick turnaround and fast payback, many of these present day writers thinks up a story which they figured would sell well to their readers, then they do their "research online"*, ie. googled one, two existing article (probably someone's opinion), "cut and paste" and voilà you have a NYT or Wash Post report. Then the CNN, ABC or MSBNC would pick that up and start talking about the NYT article and entire mainstream media would be buzzing the same unsubstantiated "news". This kind of "circular reference news" would go on for a few days till the next "news" cycle the following week. The neo-democrat senators and Activist Judges would also reference the comments made on CNN, ABC, etc. and start using them as Facts! This is amazing! What the neo-democrat senators and Activist Judges are using (relying on) for their decision making are groundless "Facts", Opinion Reports that had less work put into them than a Peanut or Garfield comic strip you read on Sunday morning. This is pure Laziness, egoistic and self-righteous on part of the NYT reporters, but the CNN News celebrities are worse in their total lack of professionalism and finally the Worst of them all, the neo-democrat Senators, politicians and Activists Judges! Where's their duties to the American Voters to at least get the basic facts right? Is it so difficult? Even the Pixar production crews put more effort into an Animated movie! This is what happened when you have monopolies of Power!

In absence of free market competition, the "News Media" has become Monopolistic Institutions that has been left unchallenged for decades. Their Final Intellectual collapse happened after they sidle up to and allied themselves with the last Presidency and Executive branch, for the entire 8 years President Obama could do NO Wrong. The Monopoly Media have become laid back, "resting on your laurels" mindset has taken over, there's no longer insights nor research but one can still clearly hear the sheep bleating the familiar political slogans, a rather reassuring tone to some.

As the News Media officially got appointed as the neo-Democrat' Propaganda Arm and knighted as P.C. Gestapo in 2008, the Great payouts continued, the easy money poured in for them, champagne flowed, glamour in the spotlights, the journalists of old have all transformed into crass Entertainment Celebrities, the Great Dying of Intellect Professionalism and Responsibility to American People was completed!

All these huge payouts for doing simple and repetitive work that they've mastered long ago at the start of their careers. When one keeps doing the same work over decades, their minds become Closed. When they get paid easy and Great sums of money for doing it, their egos grow exponentially and now they will do anything to defend and protect their lavish lifestyles (paychecks). Power and wealth has corrupted the pioneering spirit of the investigative journalists. That spirit lives no more. As Tarbell would probably infer the Politically Correct One View of the World to be Antithetical to democracy, "were they not potentially a more subtle form of [mental] slavery, more dangerous because less obvious?"

For the Media Celebrities, their Rational Behavior and Culture of Ego both support a common Agenda. If you watch a thousand news stories from the neo-democrat propaganda arm, a thousand of them would be negative about the current President of the USA. If you roll a set of dices a thousand time and they show the same results, wouldn't you think the dices are loaded? Bashing President Trump is not an "uphill" fight, everyone is doing it. It is just crowd mentality, it is a "downhill" easy and safe bet! The viewers are guaranteed and the viewers' satisfaction is guaranteed too. This is a symbiotic relationship, both the News celebrities and their viewers stay in their respective "comfort zones", the Mainstream Media celebrities stay in their "golden rut" making easy money repeating the same "news" (President Trump sucks), while their viewers gets reassured continuously that their views are right (President Trump sucks), snowflakes mentality, like 2 year old kids watching the same cartoon over and over and they are so proud that they can anticipate what's going to happen next.

Remember we had discussed about the Media Celebrities that vowed that they will leave

America if Donald J. Trump get elected? Now, over a year after President Trump had been inaugurated into the Oval office, where are they? Now we understand why the Celebrities will never leave America not even to Canada, it is not just giving up their million-dollar jobs, their fabulous lifestyles, it's also about the Fear of Change, Inability to adapt, fear to step outside their comfort zone, their Egos, sense of Self-righteousness, their Complacency will be challenged in a new country, they'll need to deal with new set of Cultural Values, etc. This is the Best proof that all the rhetoric about globalist world, borderless world, building bridges not walls are meaningless blather to them. Their real Values show again, just talk the talk, never walk the walk!

> *"we can no longer doubt that the crisis is arrived at which the good people of America are to decide the solemn question, whether they will reap the fruits of that Independence … and of that Union which they have cemented with so much of their common blood, or whether by giving way to unmanly jealousies and prejudices, or to partial and transitory interests, they will renounce the auspicious blessings prepared for them by the Revolution, and furnish its enemies an eventual triumph."*
>
> - James Madison to George Washington on 8th Nov 1786

Parasitic Behavior and the Eunuch Mindset

I had mentioned earlier that Media Celebrities and their Viewers are in a symbiotic relationship. That is true for the short run, but for the long run it is parasitic as the viewers are mis-informed continuously and becomes ignorant and gets blind-sided (results of the 2016 Elections would come as a big surprise to many of the CNN, ABC, CBS, NBC viewers). The Media celebrities continue their ride down the "golden rut" while the Viewers becomes ignorant and closed minded (staying inside your comfort zones for decades tends to do that to you), who do you think is the parasite and who's the host? Just like the drug lords selling the drugs to the junkie, in the short term, the junkie is also happy too. In the long term, the drug lords get super rich and the old junkies gets replaced with new junkies as the parasite would move to new hosts too. The timeframe is key difference here. To the junkie, their timeframe is only the moment of enjoyment (just a snapshot in time), the drug lord obviously has a longer timeframe in mind. Similarly, for the Media Celebrities and Hollywood Celebrities, what timeframe are they looking at? Obviously longer than their viewers.

A side-bar on different views on timeframe, remember at the beginning of this chapter, we discussed the Wealth of Top 1% Insulating them from the shrinking economy, increasing crimes, etc. There's also another factor insulating them from the deterioration of this country. That is their selfish view of timeframe too.

In contrast, the American patriot not only wants to do well personally, he wants his family to do well and the Country to do well. The Top1% are selfish, they have done very well for this lifetime and most likely for the remainder of their lives. That's where it ends for them. Whatever happens to America when they are gone,, who cares? But the country cares.. America's timeframe is longer than the top1%, the Patriots also care, they want their kids to do well in a rich country, a growing country, they want their beloved country to do well even after they are gone. They want their Values to live on. We revisit these Values in next chapter.

When President Obama invited the neo-Democrat Media Celebrities to join him in the White House, they too formed a Symbiotic relationship too. The Media would lavish praise and endless adoration on the President. In return, they would be elevated to status of providing the President with "advise and consul" on the country's policies and receiving Presidential Awards for their contributions. They would not just be reporting events after they happen, they would be consulted for their "insights and expertise" on various policies, obviously only in appearance. But as in showbiz, appearance is all that matters! Both sides are happy with the arrangement. This might be symbiotic for both parties, but this sad arrangement is Parasitic for the American Voters, parasitic for the Country. For 8 years, there was no independent nor transparent media coverage on the Executive branch, for personal gains, the Media Celebrities forgot about their duties to the American public as quickly as the Wall Street Bankers forgot about their responsibilities to the little investors.

The very people supposedly standing in the vanguard of those documenting the societal shifts have abandoned their sentry posts and taken up well-paying jobs either as cheap entertainers of the Mainstream Media, completely missing out on the declining economic affairs of this great State over last 2 decades (attributing all woes to Globalism Cult of President Obama), missing coverage on the rapid descent into poverty of the American Families (whites & blacks alike), failing to foresee the negative impacts of Internet Social Media on this Society's [country's] Institutional Learning abilities, not a single article about the accumulation of $10T of debt under last Administration, etc.

Or worse still, some had actually started working for the Top 1% and aiding them in looting from the middle-working class Americans by pushing agendas like Global Warming, Free Healthcare, Free Education, etc. growing the already gargantuan Federal Welfare Expenses that's funded by your taxes.

> *"If the watchman sees the sword coming and does not blow the trumpet, and the people are not warned, and a sword comes and takes a person from them, he is taken away in his iniquity; but his blood I will require from the watchman's hand."*

> Ezekiel 33:6 (KJV)

".. So much of the left-wing thought is a kind of playing with fire by people who don't even know that fire is hot." George Orwell ".. Intellectual Liberty .. Without a doubt has been one of the distinguishing marks of western civilization, … if this war is about anything at all, it is a war in favor of freedom of thought."

Under President Obama's Midas Rule, everything turned into Gold (at least for the Mainstream Media Celebrities and neo-democrats Politicians). Not even a tiny whimper about the Highest Income Inequality after spending $ 3 Trillion on Welfare every year, nothing about the 8 years of stagnant economy after doubling of the national debt from $10 T to $20 T, nothing about the rise of ISIS in Iraq & Syria, about the poor decisions made in Benghazi and subsequent cover-ups and lies, about the un-constitutional affordable-care Act; forcing millions of Americans to buy this "healthcare Insurance" which is just an additional tax, and how it has been "phased in"; staggered out such that its full disastrous impact will only explode in 2017 [designed by intent for the s*** to hit the fan only after he leaves office].

Nothing about the clear conflict of interests of politicians running their own private foundations while still in office, nothing about the Secretary of State having their private email servers and using private email addresses for State Departments' work? Anyone with any common sense knows that they are not supposed to use private emails for work related matters, let alone work that relates to the country's National Security? And who in their right minds would setup a private email server at home for work emails? Unless they have much to hide from their employers who happens to be the State Department of USA. The Intent to conceal is self-evident by the very Existence of the private server. Yet endless excuses are fed to the American viewers, cartoon video on youtube caused the Benghazi attacks, the explosion of the National Debt is due to the 2008 Financial crisis and saving the auto-industry.

The Sad Reality is that the viewers have short attention spans and minimal understanding of any complex issues. They were relying on the Honesty and Integrity of the Media to tell them the truth? What Naïve viewers, worshipping their Ministry of Truth; Ignorance is Strength, Socialism is Freedom, the Parasites are indeed doing much damage to this country and its future generations.

Remember we had asked two questions earlier about were the neo-Democrats Romantics like the Lord Byron, Percy Shelley of the early 19th century believing themselves to be the Avant Garde of the human spirit?

> *"Whether a society knows it or not, its artists are the advance guard of the human spirit, they are able to see further, grasp with deeper insight, reconcile the conflicts in the human soul more fully, and then chart a course forward that the rest of humanity later only dimly and imperfectly follows."*
> – The Cave and the Light, Arthur Herman

We now know them to be parasitic, so they cannot be Romantics, what's the difference? The Romantics are intellectuals who actually believe in what they write, they live their lives per their values espoused. Romantic poet Percy was inspired by Plato's dialogue Ion, where Socrates praises the art of poetry "for a poet is a light and winged thing," Socrates says, "and holy, and never able to compose until he has become inspired, and is beside himself, and the reason is no longer in him." His works "are not of man or human workmanship, but are divine and from the gods... it is God himself who speaks, and through [the poet] is conversing with us." Shelley believes the poet's ability to dream the impossible dream yet make it reality through his work applies not only to the arts, but also to every form of human creation, stating in his *Defense of Poetry*, poets as 'the unacknowledged legislators of the world.'

Percy had been expelled from Oxford for advocating atheism, he later quarreled with his Dad and ran away with a sixteen-year-old waitress, which didn't work out. He later met and fell in love with Mary Wollstonecraft's 15 year old daughter also named Mary in 1812, when he was a married man and father of two children. Facing opposition from Mary's father (her mother had died shortly after childbirth), they eloped to Europe in 1814. Marrying in 1818 after the suicide of his first wife, Percy himself died in 1822 in a boating accident, leaving Mary Shelley a widow at age of 25. If the name Mary Shelley sounds familiar, that's because she conceived of and wrote *Frankenstein* in 1816 at age 19 in a summer get-together with Percy Bysshe Shelley (her lover at that time), Lord Byron and his physician John Polidori, at Villa Diodati near Lake Geneva. Due to the eruption of Mt Tambora volcano in 1815, the summer of 1816 at Lake Geneva was completely rained out and constantly in torrential cloudbursts.

Confined in the house by the rain, to pass time, they spent hours discussing about current scientific theories and experiments especially those of Luigi Galvani who showed that the legs of dead frogs can be stimulated to movements by electric currents (the word Galvanize comes from), questions about can the dead be brought back to life by electricity? Lord Byron then suggested each member of the group write a horror story. From the intellectual exercise, the Novel Frankenstein was born. Interestingly, from the same exercise, Dr Polidori wrote his own scary story which he later published in 1819 as The Vampyre (a likely precursor to Bram Stoker's Dracula in 1897). Lord Byron besides fame as leading figure of the Romantic movement, a poet who penned Don Juan, She Walks in Beauty, etc., Byron also joined the Greek War of Independence fighting the Ottoman Empire, for which Greeks revere him as a national hero. Lord Byron set sail for port town of Missolonghi in December 1823 in a small ship packed with livestock, four horses, medicine for an army of one thousand men, and chests full of gold coins and forty thousand British Pounds in bills of exchange. In April 1824, Lord Byron (father of Ada Lovelace whom we'll discuss in chapter 5) died from fever and dysentery in Missolonghi, he was thirty six years old. Romantics so believed in their idealism that suicide was an occupational hazard in 19th century for young romantics. Romantics take their own lives in pursuit of their idealism, while the only life that the parasitic is taking, is that of their host, the American Society.

So, we know that the neo-democrats are No Romantics, neither are they intellects, but one question still remains, Why are they so good at lying, at Marketing and Projecting their desired self-image? Well we saw that President Obama employed the help and support of the Mainstream Media to help build his 'Brand Image', so the Mainstream Media is a critical ally to the neo-Democrats, managing all their **Public Relations** matters. Next, we saw that Soros had invested huge Financial Capital Outlays in the Billions to facilitate the Activists Corporations take-over of K Street and Tech Street.

Yet all these are not the most critical reasons what they are so good at lying. We know that with their Culture of Monopoly, they lust for Power, have great Avarice, Envy others' good fortune.

Sheltered from Competition they become lazy, ignorant and slothful, also extremely Prideful and full of hubris, from all these lies the answer [no pun intended] to why they lie so well.

As they possess all these negative traits, they can instantly recognize similar negative traits in others that they then quickly exploit to their advantage and further their own agenda and interests. For example, they recognize the insecurity and vanity of the Entertainment and Mainstream Media parvenus, so they appeal to their pride and ego to come to the White House and receive special Presidential Recognition for contributions, knowing full well Greed will take care of the rest. While in the case of an honest man might ask the uncomfortable question, what contributions did he make? Matthew 25:37-39

The neo-democrats tap into and exploit the weaknesses of parvenus Media Celebrities [Egoistic insecurities of intellectual potemkins in this case] to help propagate their lies. Their sophistries are also easy to sell to the slothful that wants Free Welfare, Free College, Free Healthcare, to those that wishes all man to be equal; all ready audiences already with a rational agendas, to be on board. They also have an innate ability to appeal to the mutually shared *negative traits like sloth, Avarice, ego, Pride, Lust, hubris, Guilt and envy in their target audience such that they can mutually attract each other and spread their lies and deceit like wild fires. People who cannot make anything happen [deliver results] tends to be very good at talking [or lying] for that's the only thing they know.

Interestingly, the opposite also happens for capable, hardworking and intelligent folks too, their values also attract each other to come together in organizations with Culture of Growth and Excellence. This is the Power of Culture! Observing the characteristics of the Culture of Monopoly goes long ways towards explaining the behaviors of individuals.

*these are all traits of the Shame Culture, which we'll discuss in chapter 8

"[in a Culture, organization without deep intellectual roots], minor success brings about overconfidence and the belief that good times last forever; minor setbacks send people into a state of nervousness. in this situation, the rootless Parvenus lends his ears to rumors of all kinds. Nothing is too absurd for him to listen to and pass on to others." The quote from Dr GKS could also be describing the Dance of the Mediocre Intellects between three parties, a) the Vain Greedy Mainstream Media Celebrities, b) the Sloth & Hubris behind the Social Media's rhetoric of Tech Giants and lastly c) their hordes of mindless self-righteous mob of an audience.

Ratings, Sensationalism and the Roman Colosseum

There's another function the current Media Celebrities play, Distraction. As Civilizations weaken and decline, the alignment for the good of the country weakens as selfish individuals makes Rational decisions to put their personal gains above that of the country. We can see such behavior repeatedly in human history as decline of Roman Empire, Chinese 明Ming Dynasty, Ottoman Empire. The Roman gladiator games serves as a distraction to the Roman citizens and populace from the political and economic problems of the day, similarly to our Media now Sensationalize "news" to gain ratings. Ratings is the name of the game, truth is an inconvenience, insights and reason are a bore in the Daily Entertainment 'news'.

Orwell's views on corruption of Power and Role of Journalism;

> *The abuse of Power in all its forms, but especially by the totalitarian State, whether left or right should be exposed. The hypocrisy of some in the left in believing that it was not only permissible but mandatory to suppress the facts if doing so helped [their cause]*

From Orwell's quote, we can also understand some of the Media parvenu celebrities' shallow mindset,

> *Orwell's confident conclusion, after mixing with the rich at Eton and then with the poor in the subbasement of a Paris hotel and on the streets of London, was that "the average millionaire is only the average dishwasher dressed in a new suit."*
>
> – Thomas E. Ricks in Churchill & Orwell

An Appeal to Professionalism

If there are any real Journalists left out there, Liberals or Conservatives, I would like to share this four words 饮水思源, it translates literally into; when you're drinking water, do remember it's source. The larger context is to remember your roots, where you've come from, how you had got to your current state. Remember all the events and processes that contributed to your accomplishments, including the Culture then that allowed you to grow, the hard-work, the sacrifices, the passion you had felt about your cause? Be honest with yourselves, has wealth changed your perspectives? Is your ego directing your behavior and actions these days? Any honest human know this fact: Power does corrupt, unless you make a great conscious effort to rein in your ego constantly (we'll discuss how the Great Leaders manages to keep their egos in check in Chapter 7: How to untie the Gordian knot)

There's an Allegory about a Monkey with a sword crossing the river in a boat. Half-way across the river, the monkey accidentally dropped the sword into the river, since the monkey couldn't swim, it couldn't retrieve its sword immediately, so it marked an X by side of the boat where it has dropped the sword. When the boat the other shore, the monkey started to fish for its sword at spot where he had marked X. any observer would note the foolishness of the monkey, but in real life many people also forget about the past cultures and environment that had helped made them where they are now. As they become more senior and successful, they enjoy the status, wealth and Large Power Distance! They easily forget that they could never have reached their current positions if the Culture of small Power distance (that allowed their rise in the past) had not existed then. Their selfish egos take over, they now reinforce the Large Power distance Culture to protect their current status and block new competition from rising. The Culture of Monopoly, Decadence replaced that of Meritocracy in the Mainstream Media thus excellence gets replaced by compliance and mediocrity. The monkey cannot find his sword of excellence anymore, and once again, we have a traffic Jam when the 3 lanes' drivers are all driving at same speed.

> *"Politics is perhaps the only profession for which no preparation is thought necessary."*
>
> – Robert Louis Stevenson

> *"… It has been said that politics is the second oldest profession. I have learned that it bears a striking resemblance to the first..."*
>
> - President Ronald Reagan

World's second oldest Profession and the Deep State Professional Politician

In the Rational vs Emotional, Values chart, you might have noticed that I had separated out the Deep State GOP politicians with the neo-Democrat politicians. Many of the neo-democrat politicians share the common Culture of Ego and self-righteousness with the Top 1% elites, Media Celebrities, Entertainment Celebrities, etc. while the Deep State GOP politicians are Rational in pursuing their personal selfish reasons, they tend to be less Emotional about the issues and much more Machiavellian, thinking about their self-preservation. Don't get me wrong, all politicians are out for themselves, but the neo-democrat politicians share the similar culture to their supporters while the Deep State GOP politicians are just doing it for the money.

In March of 2002, the McCain-Feingold Act was passed with Funding and support from George Soros' Open Society Institute. This Act regulates political speech by banning private organizations from advertising on TV or radio for or against any candidates, 60 days before the General Election. The Media Networks are exempted from this law. This law blocks private citizens from pooling resources together to express their political views yet it allows the Media Networks to do so! You already know what the Media P.C. Gestapo going to do. The Civil Libertarians were stunned when the Supreme Court approved the McCain-Feingold Act in December 2003 (effectively allowing the Media P.C. Gestapo full monopoly on political speech during the Election season).

This is what Judge Antonin Scalia wrote in his dissenting opinion: "… who could have imagined that the same Court which, within the past four years, has sternly disapproved of restrictions upon such inconsequential forms of expression as virtual child pornography, tobacco advertising, dissemination of illegally intercepted communications and sexually explicit cable programming would smile with favor upon a law that cuts to the heart of what the First Amendment is meant to protect: the right to criticize the government?"

Feingold is a Democrat, so he has similar agenda with George Soros, fact that he wants to regulate Political speech in favor of the Democrat propaganda-arm Media having a total monopoly is understandable. But the other senator? That's Rational behavior but definitely not Emotional driven. Guess the World's Oldest Professionals don't get too emotional with their clients.

> *"Politicians are the same all over. They promise to build a bridge even where there is no river."*
>
> – Nikita Khrushchev

Other Emotional Behaviors that contributes to Societies making disastrous decisions

We've discussed Clash of Culture in great detail. Now we cover the rest quickly, Sunk Costs behavior is an emotional behavior. If you've made financial investments based on certain information available to you and the financial assets decreased in value. Then you received new information that tells you that the financial assets you hold will fall further in value. The logical response would be to take the loss and sell those assets, but since you have already incurred some loss, there is an emotional hope that the assets will rise in value and you wait for it to rise before selling it. If you lean towards the second reasoning, that's sunk costs effect at work. It can be dangerous if it triggers another response to average down the costs in the hope of the eventual rise, that's putting in good money after bad money. It all sounds academic and simple enough here, but when it concerns emotional and large Financial Investments, it will become very real!

Crowd Psychology, Dislike Messenger and Psychological Denial are self-explanatory enough. Let's round up the various groups on the chart of Rational vs Values. You can see for yourself that Students and Technology workers have the least Rational Reason for their behavior. The crowd psychology or Dislike messenger works on their emotional psyche when they are in the Universities that gives them great enjoyable experiences while fleecing them of their tuition fees. But when they leave the Colleges and Universities, they will be stuck with a huge debt (there's no free lunch) and if the economy continues to performs as it has for last 15 years, the light at the end of the tunnel would be that of an on-coming train! The students and Tech workers are still young, if the country and the economy continues its decline, they will be able to personally experience third world living conditions without having to travel overseas. It is already the case in many rust belt towns and cities and it will continue if many tough decisions are Not made soon.

The workers in the Activists groups are more incentivized Rationally as they do get paid. The Entertainment Celebrities are extremely emotionally vested as their culture of Egos and self-righteousness fits them to a Tee. But Financially, they had enjoyed the monopoly of Hollywood for a long time and been rich for a long time. They didn't need to kiss the god father's ring rationally, but then again no one would mistake the Entertainment celebrities for their Thinking prowess. To the Academia and Entertainment Celebrities, John 3:3 (KJV) "… I will tell you the truth, unless you are born again, you cannot see the Kingdom of God.."

Show me the Money!

As we come to the end of this chapter, a quick recap, we had started looking at the Rational Behavior and followed the money! That has led to our understanding of different perspectives and knowing different Agendas and Mindset of different Combatants in this Civil War. We have also seen how Power and unrestrained Egos can corrupt the human spirit, also produce extreme views that have no room for empathy for others, that the world revolves around themselves.

Last category on the chart of Rational and Cultural motivations for the Combatants in this Civil War are the American Voters. They are at the lower left-hand corner of the chart. They have NO personal selfish Rational or Emotional gains from this Civil War. They just want the Country to be strong, the economy to be strong for their Families, friends and themselves. They love their families, hope American Values to be strong and the country to be there after they themselves move on. Only Great Values and Love can transcend time, the selfish cannot take their wealth with them.

Which brings us to a few questions, what are American Values? We'll address that in next chapter 4. Also, we had shared with you the parasitic behavior of some groups that were complicit in furthering their personal interests as they exploited and harmed this Great Nation. We know that the parasites were Killing the host, the other question is this: is the Host dead? Is it like termites devouring the deadwood, gorging themselves fat. Is America deadwood? Will the host be able to resist the parasites with its white blood cells, anti-bodies? We'll address that in Chapter 8: Closing of the Western Mind and discuss how the Civil War will unfold.

Chapter 4
Ideals of America

"Youth is the seed-time of good habits, as well in nations as in individuals. It might be difficult, if not impossible, to form the Continent into one government half a century hence. The vast variety of interests, occasioned by an increase of trade and population, would create confusion. Colony would be against Colony.... The intimacy which is contracted in infancy, and the friendship which is formed in misfortune, are, of all others, the most lasting and unalterable. Our present Union is marked with both these characters: we are young, and we have been distressed; but our concord hath withstood our troubles, and fixes a memorable area for posterity to glory in."

- Common Sense, 10th Jan 1776 Thomas Paine

As we started the discussion about the Clash of Values in the last chapter, let's explore further what are the American Values that this Great Nation holds dear? This is both an easy and challenging question, let's try a couple of approaches, we can start with brainstorming a list of Values that we deem important by looking at key milestone historical documents like Declaration of Independence, Gettysburg addresses, landmark speeches, etc.

Next, we understand that the external Environment shapes the Culture and Values, so let's understand and empathize with conditions during the Pioneering Days, Declaration of Independence, Civil War period, Manifest Destiny, Western Expansion, the Gilded Age, both World Wars and the Great Depression, Cold War, Space Race, etc. we'll see if these Culture and Values are manifestations of their external environment?

We'll compare these American Values identified with those of Cultures of Excellence and Competition. We'll look at three precious resource; Financial Capital, Human Talent and Ideas (birth of new Ideas, how dreams become reality). How competition and interplay between the three helps shaped this country and how the American Values lineup with these processes. Lastly, we'll explore and understand the P.C. snowflakes culture and if Politically Correct is the new American Values?

Control your own Destiny or someone else Will! – Jack F. Welch Jr.

I first read this book about motivational and management practice in the General Electric Company and its related Culture in the '90s by Noel Tichy and Stratford Sherman in 1995. Since then, I've had the fortune to be part of such a company's culture for the next decade, to live and help share these Values and Culture, to experience personal growth myself and help energize growth in others. Since this was my first experience of American Values, I jotted down the first values that came to mind when reading Jack Welch's quote above: Self-Reliance, Personal Accountability, Leadership

You might ask why start with these Values? Why not start with Personal Liberty, Freedom of Speech, Freedom and Diversity of Ideas? Yes, Liberty and Freedom is fundamental to American Values. To be Free also means one has to be ready to take personal responsibility for the Risks that comes with Freedom! The young and impressionable wants to have freedom but none of the risks associated with it, an interesting juvenile perspective. Thus, my first experience of American Values: Self-Reliance, Personal Accountability, Leadership.

Self-Reliance and Personal Accountability, NO excuses, take personal responsibility, grow up and learn to overcome challenges that you come across. Learn to persevere and push-on in difficult times, learn new skills to accomplish your objectives, build new relationships and support networks as necessary, strengthen and develop personal traits. Understand, Integrate and Excel in new Cultures! No excuses ever! Ok, we understand these Values, where does Leadership come in here?

True Leadership is earned, not bestowed nor conferred upon, it is derived from self-confidence which in turn, comes from overcoming personal challenges. Once, you have learnt to fully embrace the Values of Self-Reliance and Personal Accountability, Leadership comes naturally when you have conviction in your cause. You see similar themes and Values in The unanimous Declaration of the thirteen United States of America. The Colonies decided to be self-reliant and take responsibility to control their own destiny by breaking from the British Crown. They know that there's no turning back after this declaration, as the founding fathers, they were then leading the country in a new direction based on stated founding values of Freedom and Liberty (a Radical Idea in its days, a new form of government never tested). If the 'rebellion' (in the British's eyes) were to be put down, many would be hanged, including obviously all the signers of the Declaration.

For someone living within their own Culture, it might be more difficult to see their own Culture through the eyes of an outsider. For many outside Cultures, they would see the American Culture as Aggressive, Competitive, Passionate. I added Competitive and Passionate because they contribute to the "perceived aggressiveness", Others probably see Americans as Aggressive, Rude and Ignorant. Being passionate in your beliefs is important, passion provides the Energy and Motivation to Compete and Succeed! Competition is even more critical, Free Market Competition is the process of how Financial Capital, Human Talent and Ideas are a) differentiated, b) most effectively and efficiently allocated in the market and c) continuously refined and re-refined. We'll elaborate more in later part of this chapter.

Individual Liberty and Freedom of speech, Diversity in Ideas. Free Speech and Diversity of Ideas are interlinked, Free speech allows Ideas to become "fleshed-out", more concrete as they are being described, explained and elaborated. Free speech allows Diverse Ideas to grow and spread as more people understand and subscribe to them. Free Speech allows for Debate and discussions of ideas that leads to refinement and increased sophistication of ideas. Debate and Discussion is a form of competition of ideas, the MOST critical factor is Toleration and mutual respect for Diverse Ideas from each other. P.C. (political correctness) is the New Fascist! Remember that when you see the P.C. Gestapo, discriminating against new and diverse ideas, that in essence marks the decline of a culture and its people.

Traditionally, the American Culture has embraced Diversity, not passing judgement on others' opinions and doesn't discriminate against new ideas (this was before the rise of the P.C. Gestapo and their Social Engineering brainwashing), it used to encourage risk-seeking individuals to try new endeavors. That coupled with a toleration of Failures has allowed the growth of revolutionary new markets and industries; Hollywood, Las Vegas, Silicon Valley, Jazz music, Rock and Roll, etc. all these would Never have been possible in a socially engineered state! The P.C. Gestapo would have weeded out the likes of Steve Jobs, Bill Gates, Elvis, Beatles, Michael Jackson, Walt Disney, Hitchcock, so on with their ceaseless brainwashing. Innovation and creativity is only possible in Cultures Tolerant of Failures, Tolerant of Diverse new Ideas, without which we would never have companies like Apple, Microsoft, Disney, google, Amazon, Facebook, etc.

A Proud National Identity, Visit to the DMZ – Panmunjom (JSA)

In May 2007, I had the opportunity to visit the DMZ – Demilitarized Zone in Korea. Before we started the tour, we were briefed at the visitors' center. During the briefing, the tour leader talked about the axe murder incident in 1976, when two United States Army officers, Arthur Bonifas and Mark Barrett, were killed by North Korean soldiers on August 18, 1976, in the Joint Security Area (JSA). He didn't get into whole lot of details. After he finished, I noted that on 3 separate occasions, 3 different Americans, an elderly lady, a middle-age man and a younger teenage girl all went up to the tour leader (who was doing the briefing earlier) and asked what happened to the North Korean murderers?

Were the murderers brought to justice for killing the 2 American officers? You could sense their sense of injustice about the murders in 1976, and this was in 2007; over 30 years later. That is National Identity, Americans take Great Pride and have much Confidence in their Country! This is alignment, when a Country and its Culture is strong, its people are proud, have great sense of identity and all aligned to the cause of the country. I wonder what will happen today, 10 years later, will the flag-burning, "I am ashamed to be American", "Trump is not my President" snowflakes care? Will they care about the murder of their fellow Americans? Probably not, they are too busy being ashamed.

There's something about America

I have always been a big fan of the summer Olympics games, I remembered the 1984 LA Olympics; USA had boycotted the prior summer games in Moscow, Carl Lewis was the super-star in '84 Olympics, matching Jesse Owens' record with 4 Olympic Golds medals from 1936.

The Rio summer Olympics was a welcomed break from the 2016 Election, esp. from the politicians' inciting violence against cops. The ceaseless and meaningless charges of "Racism" against Law and Order, the violence incited by the "poverty Pimps" are just downright disgusting!

Against this backdrop, we watch the competition of various events unfold in Rio. As I was watching the different events, swimming, gymnastics, athletics, etc. I couldn't help but notice the stark difference in diversity of the USA teams as compared with the other countries (their teams are mostly racially homogenous). USA is practically the one country with largest Diversity of Talent represented and Winning! All the "racists" accusations are politically motivated to score votes. Just look at the teams from Germany, Finland, Sweden, China, Japan, Russia, Turkey, Kenya, etc. since they all appear to be so racially homogenous, are all these countries racists? Why are all other races in their countries not represented in the games? where's their minorities?

Strong, Meritocracy-based, Growth Cultures have always tapped into their available Talent and Resources to Win! This is what you see happening here, it is perfectly logical, it is survival instincts to use all your available resources to beat the competition! Since America is an immigration country with diverse populations, to deprive yourself of over 30-40% of your human talent isn't just stupid (white non-Hispanic Americans make up only 62.6% of population), it is suicidal behavior if winning is your objective. The minorities are not only represented, resources are made available to all, the best athletes of all races are integrated into winning teams! This is triumph of the human spirit, of Esprit de Corps, of e pluribus unum!

From day 1, America has relied on its Racial Diversity to overcome the most difficult and challenging times, African Americans troops had been instrumental in winning the American Revolutionary War! In Bill O'Reilly's Legends & Lies: The Patriots, written by David Fisher, in chapter 8: Forgotten Heros, you can read it for yourselves how the 9000 plus African American troops helped America win the Revolutionary War. The likes of Jack Sisson, James Armistead (later Lafayette); who spied for General Marquis de Lafayette and provided intelligence that led to the British surrender at Yorktown, William (Billy) Lee (aide to Washington), Jordan Freeman, Lambert Latham, the formation of 1st Rhode Island Regiment, etc.. the list goes on. I had wanted to do a short summary, but their contributions had been so pervasive throughout and such an integral part of the war, it would not be right to do a summary of a summarized version.

Another interesting bit of American History; the Lone Ranger cowboy legend was inspired by a real US Marshal named Bass Reeves (an African American man). He was offered the position of US deputy marshal in 1875 by Judge Isaac Parker to help bring law and order to Western District of Arkansas (74,000 square miles of western Arkansas and the Indian Territory). Bass was incredibly courageous and capable, he spoke 5 native American Indian languages, was a crack-shot, skilled tracker and a man of Great Integrity! In the case of Bass Reeves, facts were truly stranger than fiction. In the 1870s, after the Civil war when the westward expansion was underway, life in the Indian Territory was harsh and extremely challenging, here personal abilities and skills triumphed ignorant stereotyping follies (racisms is a form of stereotyping). Interestingly, the Indian Territories was the most racially integrated regions in America then, we observe in the toughest conditions, Meritocracy rules and racial diversity naturally becomes inevitable!

African American soldiers contributed enormously in both the World Wars, Jesse Owens single handedly put Hitler and the entire Third Reich to shame in the 1936 Olympics. Michael Jackson was the first World's Super Star, he was the face of America to the Billions of people outside of America! General Colin Powell, Secretary Condoleezza Rice, Presidential Candidate Herman Cain, Presidential Candidate Dr Ben Carson, (just to name a few) achieved great success. When Barrack H. Obama was elected as President Obama (the 44th President of the USA) in 2008, it came as no great surprise to rest of the World. Racial Inequality concerns is an extremely sensitive topic, let's address that in more depth in Chapter 7: How to untie the Gordian knot? For now, my proposal is just this: America has Diverse Talents and it's not afraid to embrace and leverage these talents!

Quick clarification, the Value of embracing Diversity is having the equal opportunity for Diverse Talents to compete freely in a Culture based on Meritocracy. With a transparent set of rules and a level playing field, may the Best person win! Allow the natural abilities of various racial background to develop and excel. Free Market competition is the Key, it is not a quota system that demands a pre-determined outcome.

A Healthy Respect for Career Choices, another Great American Value is the Freedom to pursue one's passion and dreams as their careers. This laissez-faire attitude ('relative' lack of judgement culture) towards career choices might be taken for granted or seem "natural" to Americans. A society that refrains from judging nor discriminating against individual's career choices, that respects their rights and freedom, provides the passion and self confidence in all professions, as all are viewed equally.

In other societies, due to traditional Cultural values or Social Engineering designs by the Dirigiste State (due to preconceived ideas or lack of resources), certain fields of studies, businesses or industries might be deemed "unproductive", "unrespectable" even "decadent". Per traditional Confucian ethical values, professions like Entertainment or even Military isn't favorably viewed upon; 秀才遇到兵 有理说不清, 好男不当兵好铁不打钉.

Even as late as in 1976, Under Mao's leadership Communists China still viewed the merchants class and the Capitalists Intellects (national bourgeoisie) as inferior to the Workers and Farmers Class, this is in line with the Socialists idealism, as we had discussed earlier, it is only with Deng's practical introduction of "capitalism approach" 黑猫白猫to boast China's economy it began to take off and modern day China exist as we know it. During the Cultural Revolution, many of these "national bourgeoisie" [deemed Capitalists] were forced to manually labor in the villages and farms 下乡.

In other Culturally Biased societies (Career-oriented, Status conscious), careers in Sports, Entertainment, music, arts would be considered unproductive and inferior to professions like doctors, lawyers, engineers, accountants. The social stigma of being considered a "failure" would be too much to bear and most kids would never plan to pursue such frivolous, pathetic careers, becoming an embarrassment to their families. Here, all top students would be shepherded into the professional careers (either Socially engineered or through self-selection due to strong cultural bias), whether they like it or not (no such luxury of pursuing one's dreams or interests). Those that cannot make the grade for the top professions would be then "left-over" to be allocated into the other careers (3rd or 4th choice, by default either whatever we allocate to you or nothing), so those individuals would naturally be less passionate and less self-confident in their new "left-over" careers; knowing they couldn't make the first cut. This form of artificial social stratification would determine one's station in life within that society.

In America, besides the ability to tap into diversity of Human Talent, this relative lack of discrimination or judgement in career choices has enabled a) individuals to pursue their dreams, and as a result allow for new industries and businesses to sprout up and b) best allocation of talent in their various fields of passion and expertise. This is something that the Big State Social Engineering, Central planning cannot emulate. Big Government State planning cannot allocate such diverse talent into Hollywood, Rock & Roll, Jazz, Classical orchestras, Broadway shows, Operas, Architects, Sculptors, artists, Archaeologist, Professional Sports, Information Technology, Military Navy SEALs, Airforce Fight Pilots, Academia, etc.. you get the picture, their personal passion and talents guide them there with the help of Free Market Competition! It is the Adam Smith's "invisible hands" guiding the human talent and potential just like it guides Financial Capital in the free market. This luxury of pursuing one's passion and dreams isn't available to many around the world. The self-confidence that comes from success in these diverse (otherwise non-existent) career fields, generates energy and passion that would be absent in the socially engineered societies or culturally bias ones.

Now we've seen the most efficient allocation of human talent, let's move on to the Values of Free Market Competition laissez-faire in three most precious resources, Financial Capital, Human Talent and Ideas.

Competition, Competition, Competition

We had discussed Capitalism in chapter 2, so we'll focus more on Free Market Competition of Human Talent and Ideas here. Just like Financial Capital, Human Talent and Ideas are also mobile and flows freely under the proper competitive conditions.

In the chart below, you'll see the 3 categories of Financial Capital, Human Talent and Ideas, they are all inter-related as ideas and human talent are closely linked. The Passion, Motivation and energy drives Competition, the continuously competitive process a) differentiates the best ideas, talent and projects with financial returns on Capital, b) refinement and adds to sophistication of Ideas, people & projects, c) allocates talent, capital & ideas in most effective, efficient manner in the market and d) eliminates uncompetitive projects which would have their remaining capital, talent and ideas reincorporated into new competing projects again.

Diversity ensure all the human talent and potential are tapped into (the best from any race, sex, ethnic, etc.) Merit immigration provides much additional Energy and Talent. Global Capital also flows into the system as well (USA in this case). Tolerance of Diverse Ideas and Talent allows for a level playing field free market Meritocracy Competition. Freedom of speech allows for Debates, brain-storming and discussion of Ideas to grow in sophistication and spread in its reach to more people.

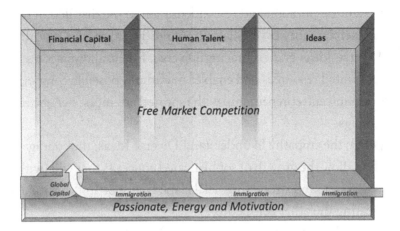

In the following chart, I added a) the continuous competitive process within each of the resource categories and b) the interface between the 3 resources.

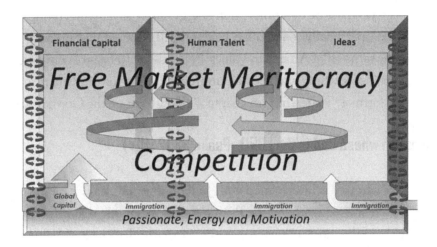

The best ideas will attract the best talent and capital to support its growth. Similarly, the best talent can develop the best ideas and also find the financial capital for its winning strategies too. The various combination goes on... Various projects, organizations, companies, industries will search for the winning combination of the 3 in the continuous competitive process. Unless otherwise disrupted, this Competitive process will continue in its virtuous cycle, growing from strength to strength. At some stage, certain feedback cycles might get disrupted (eg. Crony capitalism, Federal Big State Government steps in) or certain parts start to fail [lack of competition and growth, or degenerating of ethos] and then decay will set in (ending the Capitalist Free Market and the Democratic government).

Notice that the Values hold the entire Competitive Process in place. Self-reliance and Personal Accountability gives the Self-Confidence for individual to compete. Passion, Energy (aggressiveness), armed with Financial Capital provides the driving force to Free Market competition. It fuels the competition and the "Adam Smith's invisible hand" to find the best allocation of Capital, Talent and Ideas just as Heat is the energy for expansion of gas to fill the space. The constant competing and refining of Ideas and Talent [over numerous iterations] is similar to the analogy of continuous and constant evaporation and re-condensation in the distillation process (distillation column), separating each category of distillates from residue, all useful for different purposes.

Tolerance of Diverse Ideas and embracing Diverse Talent allows access to biggest pool of these two extremely limited resources and enables maximum possible competition. Tolerance of Failures allow risk-seeking entrepreneurship with repeated attempts; benefitting from their prior experience and learnings.

Freedom of Speech, the empathy to understand Diverse Ideas, the courage to debate, discuss and brain-storm ideas allow the growth of sophisticated concepts that will (with great human talent to execute, deliver results and strong Financial Capital supporting) eventually become Reality after successfully beating the other competitors.

You can see many of the American Values as necessary precursors for the conditions to be right for the Free Market Competition to work for Capitalism and also Democracy to triumph (Talent and Ideas can rise to their maximum potential in a Democracy!)

One other quick comment on Leadership Style to facilitate and allow American Values to continue growing. This style must be dynamic, High energy, aggressive, with courage to understand and debate diverse ideas, personally competitive, holds oneself Accountable, in short, the Leadership must share most of the same set of American Values! A Leader with Fear of competition, arrogance and ego impeding his/her learning and spell an untimely decline for the American Values. We'll explore this Parasitic form of "leadership" in chapter 7: How to untie the Gordian knot?

Blessed is the nation whose God is the LORD.. Psalm 33:12 (NIV)

The founding of this country is intertwined with Judeo-Christian Values, with the Pilgrims arriving in 1620 followed subsequently by the Puritans. It is inevitable that after nearly 400 years, Christianity would have the most influence over the American Psyche and Values.

Interestingly enough, although Christianity has had a huge influence over the Founding Fathers and many of the Presidents since, the Government (State) and the Church has pretty much remained separate. If you look through all the documents that forged the Nation; Declaration of Independence, Constitution, Bill of Rights, etc. you will see many references to God, rights to religious freedom and civil liberties but not a single quote from the Bible.

> *Bill of Rights, December 15, 1791 - Amendment I*
> *Congress shall make no law respecting an establishment of religion, or prohibiting the free exercise thereof; or abridging the freedom of speech, or of the press; or the right of the people peaceably to assemble, and to petition the government for a redress of grievances.*

This separation of Religion and the State is key to Religious freedom for all religions (we'll visit this important aspect again in Chapter 6 : Religious Empathy). This separation doesn't run counter to Christian beliefs as noted in Gospel of Mark:

Then Jesus said to them, "Give back to Caesar what is Caesar's and to God what is God's." And they were amazed at him.

Mark 12:17 (NIV)

The Christian beliefs in the ten commandments helped maintain some basic semblance of civility, law and order during the pioneer days and later in the westward expansion when the Law enforcement couldn't keep up quickly enough. Not to mistake old west as paragon of virtues but it would be much worse without the fear of God in many of the folks.

The Judeo-Christian Values of humility, forgiveness and empathy is so deeply ingrained into the American Values that it not only helped our forebears endured the hardships and triumphed against adversities they faced, it is also those same Christian Values that the P.C. Gestapo and Activists Corporations try to exploit when pushing for open borders, "undocumented immigrants" and enlarging social welfare! Build bridges, not walls. Help the Poor. Forgive those that trespass against us. These Christian Values are so deep in the American sub-conscious that they feel bad even when having justice served to these illegal criminals. Then how do we reconcile the Christian Values of Forgiveness to ensuring Justice is enforced? Jesus wasn't wrong in preaching Forgiveness. He was teaching the people to deal with their personal hatred, anger and loss. He wasn't preaching to Caesar how to administer the Roman Empire! The role and responsibility of the Government is above that of the individual. It is the government's role to ensure safety for its people, law and order in the country, secure its borders and justice is upheld in America. For the individual to move on from their loss suffered, forgiveness is the first step. And for the P.C. Propaganda arm of neo-democrats, to exploit the good Christian Values, confusing them with the government's responsibilities to its people, is just downright despicable!

Exodus, John and Ephesians

As we'd just witnessed the P.C. Gestapo and Fascist Propaganda Media exploit the cherished Christians Values by confusing the perspectives of the government with that of the individual, we ask ourselves what perspective should we adopt with regards to the P.C. Gestapo, Propaganda Media? There's a couple of different perspectives in the Bible. One of the more commonly known is in Gospel of John:

".....So when they continued asking him, he lifted up himself, and said unto them, He that is without sin among you, let him first cast a stone at her..."

John 8:7 (KJV)

Here Jesus teaches us not to be judgmental of others and exercise Empathy. Would the evangelicals refrain from judging the P.C. Gestapo? There's 2 other interesting perspectives in the Bible, one in Exodus 32 when Moses descended from Mount Sinai with the ten commandments and saw the Israelites worshipping the Golden Calf, the other in Ephesians 6 when Paul (assumed) gives advice to his readers on maintaining healthy relationships within their communities. You can read parts of Exodus 32 and Ephesians 6 by googling or picking up any Bible and decide which perspectives works best for yourselves. I personally like The Armor of God part

> *"..11 Put on the full armor of God, so that you can take your stand against the devil's schemes. 12 For our struggle is not against flesh and blood, but against the rulers, against the authorities, against the powers of this dark world and against the spiritual forces of evil in the heavenly realms. 13 Therefore put on the full armor of God, so that when the day of evil comes, you may be able to stand your ground, and after you have done everything, to stand. 14 Stand firm then, with the belt of truth buckled around your waist, with the breastplate of righteousness in place..."*
>
> Ephesians 6:11-14 (KJV)

> *"...Darkness cannot drive out darkness; only light can do that. Hate cannot drive out hate; only love can do that..."*
>
> Reverend Martin Luther King Jr.

Gandhi, Martin Luther King Jr. to "Guns and Religion"

As Advocates for nonviolent civil disobedience, Gandhi and Martin Luther King Jr. are visionary in planning for the reconciliation process after they have triumph in their cause, their selfless personal sacrifice allows them to transcend their enemies, bring hope and self-respect to millions in their generations and future generations thereafter. In psychology terms, we can understand that they were elevating their supporters from the Dependent stage (being oppressed) to Independent and onwards to Inter-dependent stage!

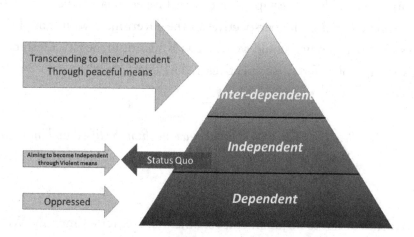

In the chart above, you can see two different approaches for the oppressed to become Independent and ultimately Inter-dependent. If one can see some possibility to reason with the oppressors and appeal to the greater cause (as Gandhi and Martin Luther King Jr did, with the British parliament and the American political systems respectively), the non-violent approach would be superior as it allows for future reconciliation with the oppressors. In such environment of preferred peaceful co-existence, resorting to violence would be counter-productive and ends up in quagmire of endless violence for both sides. Proponents of using violence in such cases either a) cannot understand (too emotional wrapped up), b) don't care about the suffering of their supporters or c) have a different agenda altogether!

> *".... You go into these small towns in Pennsylvania and, like a lot of small towns in the Midwest, the jobs have been gone now for 25 years and nothing's replaced them. And they fell through the Clinton administration, and the Bush administration, and each successive administration has said that somehow these communities are gonna regenerate and they have not. And it's not surprising then they get bitter, they cling to guns or religion or antipathy toward people who aren't like them or anti-immigrant sentiment or anti-trade sentiment as a way to explain their frustrations...."*
>
> - President Barrack Obama in Apr 2008 and Dec 2015

Act I, Scene I Enter: The Poverty Pimps - We Love you back

Why would the President of a country with 400 years of Judeo-Christian Values and Culture say something like that? The very country that elected him President. He didn't say it once but twice, the second time in Dec 2015 in interview with NPR. This shows you the utter contempt and disdain he has for people that he doesn't know personally; this is the hallmark of Racism (pre-judging others by their skin-color without bothering to know them personally). He loves to play the race-card for himself but it is comments like these, that shows you how much he really loves the American People! Here you can see the Ego, Arrogance of a Closed Mind who already knows it all and knows himself to be always right. We'll explore more of this Parasitic Leadership behavior in Chapter 7.

Coming back to the present day, Activists approaches of BLM (Black Lives Matter), Antifa corporations encouraging Cops Killings and Anarchy in America. As leaders of this country, President Obama and Secretary Hillary Clinton both kept pandering to these BLM Activists corporations? doesn't take a genius to figure out who the Poverty Pimps and Race Baiters are. Unlike the Civil Rights activists in '60s, there's no higher cause here! Hopefully time and history will be the judge of their "accomplishments".

> *"I look to a day when people will not be judged by the color of their skin, but by the content of their character"*
>
> - Reverend Martin Luther King Jr.

We should be careful and not confuse the current Liberal Professional Activists with the Civil Rights Leaders in the 60s. The current Activists are no social workers, they do NO productive work but instead are professional Problem Profiteers (aka poverty pimps), together with the Professional Politicians, these Problem Profiteers are the scourge of the American Society, they actively attacks and destroys the American Middle working class by leeching & exploiting the Welfare and other Federal Benefits Expenses paid for by the middle working-class Americans.

These current Activists Corporations are Full Time Professionals Career Activists have NO real job other than to lobby special interests for Federal Welfare, Benefits, Grants, Loans, etc. that amounts to over $ 2.8 Trillion annually (funded by your tax money). Contrasts these professional activists trial lawyers, opinion shapers, influencers for the Social Media, Main Stream Media, etc. to the likes of Rosa Parks and Rev Martin Luther King Jr. who had real productive full-time jobs as seamstress and Baptist minister (contributing towards the American Society) before circumstances made them take on their Activists Causes.

The accelerated Rise of these numerous modern Activists Corporations after the turn of millennia, strongly correlates to the sharp rise in Federal Welfare & Benefits, Grants, Loans, etc. all together bringing about the sharpest rise in Income Inequality in America, reaching its highest since late 20s (the highest in last hundred plus years).

We'll explore in more detail in chapter 7, for now the logic is simple, the middle working class are wage earners or small business owners; their wealth (via taxes) has been transferred by the Deep State Politicians to their sponsors; those behind the Activists Corporations (in forms of Federal projects loans, grants, welfare & benefits payments, etc.)

The Growth Culture, Values to overcome Adversity and Challenges in the New Frontier

By now, we've understood that the traditional American Values and Culture is very close to the Culture of Excellence, Meritocracy and Performance based on Free Market competition. We also know that the environment shapes the Culture and history of America (since the declaration in 1776, till recent years) has been of Growth, overcoming adversity, triumphing over the dynamic environment challenges (eg. Pioneering Days, Declaration of Independence, Civil War period, Manifest Destiny, Western Expansion, the Gilded Age (Industrial Age), both World Wars and the Great Depression - adversity, Cold War – external threat, Space Race – noble challenge).

Just like the best sports teams that faces constant changing competition, America needed a Culture that unleashes its Best Ideas, Greatest Human potential and Talent to help adapt and overcome its environment and competition. It is essentially a Growth Culture!

Velocity = Distance / Time
Acceleration = Velocity / Time
Force = Mass * Acceleration

December 25th 1991, the USSR Soviet Union is dissolved, the largest external threat to USA is no more, so begins the gradual and imperceptible "slowing down of the World's Super-Power" (one might comment that the USA's GDP has continued to increase since 1991). Yes, the GDP has continued to increase and it rightly should. Just as if you stop accelerating the car, it will continue to move, the speed will start slowing down but the car will continue forward until the speed eventually becomes zero and there's no additional distance travelled.

To elaborate on this analogy, if the size of GDP is the distance covered, then the velocity of the car would be the GDP growth % yoy (year over year). If the GDP growth % keeps increasing every year, then the car is accelerating and moving at faster speed. One might ask, how can the GDP growth % yoy be increasing? When the number of new Industries created far exceeds the slow decline of old industries (it is like a growing company with many successful New Products Introduction in addition to their existing Mature Products, this overlap would accelerate the company's growth), the net increasing number of vibrant industries will accelerate the GDP growth % (as experienced by USA after WWII and China in more recent years). The Growth Culture is what enables the formation of new companies in fields of new endeavors and resulting new Industries!

Just as a comparison, since 1990 till 2015, the average GDP growth rate for China has been 9.7% per year, India at 6.5% and USA lagging at a 2.4% (China was catching up, going at a much faster velocity for 25 years and overtook America in 2015 in size of their GDP by PPP). With zero to miserly low GDP growth % in last 15 years (GDP Growth Rate above 4% would be a sign of relieve for any Administrative team, above 5% respectable), the growth Culture in USA had to be spluttering to a halt and true enough, the last significant New Industry was the Internet-related Technology Industry (likes of Cisco Systems in late 90s) growing in the late nineties continuing into the middle of last decade.

The beginning of Google, Facebook (social Media), Tesla, all the countless Unicorns start the age of the negative operating Cashflow, all with minimal profits, instead thriving on the speculative investments from the Wall Street Suzerains funded by the Federal QEs monies and not on real profits from main street paying customers. Which leads us to the question, what does the Culture of the Monopolies look like? They are the Politicians, Wall Street Bankers, Casinos and lately IT Monopolies' Moghul Culture; "rest on your laurels" mindset, Large Power Distance, Risk Adverse, Fear of Change, Fear of free Market competition, Egoistic, Arrogant, etc. (sounds familiar per the Politicians? Media Celebrities?)

Rise of these Decadent Cultures seems to coincide with the decline in the Traditional American Culture and decline in the middle Class of this country, decline in Main Street. This is NO mere coincidence. Crony Capitalism Cannot create real wealth for the working middle class of society! Wall Street monies from QEs Cannot create real vibrant Industries! Financial Capital alone without the Culture of Excellence, Performance, without the Free Market Competition, cannot bring out the real Human Talent nor the creative Genius' Ideas. It can only feed a bunch of cronies and make them fat and happy.

The Unicorns, Green Renewable Energy companies, Teslas of the world, without Free Market Competition to refine their ideas and human talent, without the Culture of Excellence and Performance to embrace Diverse Ideas, to promote debates, to motivate the passionate aggressiveness of their employees, they would all just be "pushing on a rope". The Wall Street monies would keep coming in, the Federal subsidies would keep coming in, their "startup stage" is their Status Quo! They are essentially SUF (Start-Ups Forever). That's how the situation will remain until we revive the American Culture of Free Market Competition. Descaling and breaking up the Monopolies of the Wall Street Suzerains Bankers and IT Moghuls would help accelerate the process.

Remember we had discussed the Conjuncture and factors leading to the Age of Discovery (which eventually catapulted Europe to World's centerstage) in 15th century. They were a) beginning of the age of discovery, b) invention of printing press and c) schism in the Church. How can these three factors revive the Traditional American Growth Culture? A Growth Culture needs Growth to fuel it, because USA economy has been stagnant for last 2 decades, the Decadent Culture has grown more prevalent!

We already have b) the Internet and Social Media, it is like the printing Press, it can disseminate information and knowledge quickly to all. The challenge is the content that is circulating in the internet now is GIGO (Garbage in Garbage Out), no Diverse nor innovative ideas! Because we lack c) and a). The schism in the Church with rise of Protestants challenged the Monopoly of the Medieval Catholic Church and brought in new radical ideas and views. We need to break the P.C. Propaganda Media and Monopoly of google search and social Media's shallow and idle talk. The professional journalists still left in Mainstream Media (if any) needs to help by reporting on the Crony Capitalism of the Wall Street Bankers and Suzerains and stop being their stooges (we'll elaborate more on this P.C. Gestapo cancerous infection in next chapter 5 and chapter 8: Closing of the Western Mind).

Lastly, we need a new Frontier! We need a) Age of Exploration again, the new challenges presented and knowledge acquired from Deep Space Exploration, from Moon Colonization, from Mars Colonization to other planets' tera-forming will inspire all Americans, Democrats or GOP towards a common objective again. It will fill the internet with meaningful new knowledge for debate and constructive discussions again instead of the meaningless blather about others' babble (circular references of meaningless garbage you hear in the Mainstream Media is just sad). We need new Stretch Goals to re-energize the American Values of Growth and Excellence (more on this stretch goals in chapter 9: American Order and Better World for All)

> *"Democracy cannot succeed unless those who express their choice are prepared to choose wisely. The real safeguard of democracy, therefore, is education."*
> - President Franklin D. Roosevelt

Per FDR's quote, the importance of education and teaching values to the younger generation of Americans cannot be overstated. So, what are the values of the new American Generation?

A Whole New World

Is the Snowflake Culture the new American Culture? Let's explore and understand what these new Values are, in next chapter, we'll discuss in detail the formation of this Culture and various forces that shape it. We'd also briefly touched on the fact that the students are now the "high-end" customers in the colleges that charges exorbitant tuition fees, which in turn panders to the whims and fancies of these "snowflakes".

Snowflakes are sheltered individuals that share common traits like Fear of Competition, Risk Adverse, Fear of Change, Intolerant of diversity of Ideas, self-righteous, egoistic, lacks empathy towards diverse opinions different from theirs and embraces the P.C. mindset, Progressives' Culture. Their sense of insecurity prefers Blurred accountability, their lack of competitive nature always chooses the Path of Least Resistance. Snowflakes are the perfect targets for the infectious P.C. virus that attacks those weak in will power, with a severe case of enlarged ego.

The P.C. Culture (offers paths of least resistance and appeals to human weaknesses) is designed to provide a sense of security for those inherently insecure. Chanting the simplistic and meaningless P.C. slogans and mantras appeals to their "we are always right, we know it all" arrogant selves. NOTE, it has to be simplistic! Ideally a Binary view of the world. Make it too complicated (God forbid), and they'll get lost after the first sentence! Snowflake Culture is a symptom of a Decadent Culture and Declining Society, if it keeps growing (which the neo-democrat P.C. activist corporations will do their utmost to stimulate its growth), it means the P.C. One View cancer is spreading out of control and the Host (America) is dying.

One wonders, if the Snowflakes know so little, have so much insecurity, why are they so arrogant and Intolerant to those with different Opinions and Ideas from them? It's precisely because they are so insecure that they cannot empathize with diverse ideas from their own. They need to have Certainty in their lives, there cannot be ambiguity, for uncertainty makes life too stressful for their insecure egos. They need a "Model Answers to life" and voila the P.C. Activists corporations appear with it; Borderless World, Build Bridges not Walls, Socialist Good Capitalist Bad, Global Warming Earth is Dying, etc.

> *The function of education is to teach one to think intensively and to think critically. Intelligence plus character - that is the goal of true education.*
>
> Martin Luther King, Jr.

Snowflakes drive by looking at their rearview mirrors never through the windshield

We all have a little snowflake in us, our values and decisions we make in life either encourages snowflake mentality to grow or we grow up and overcome that Insecurity. Snowflakes prefer a Static view of life, a Dynamic view makes it too complex, too challenging, life is always changing, too much stress! Like the 2 year-old watching the same cartoon show over and over again so that he/she can anticipate the next scene, the snowflakes loves their P.C. Model answers to life, Model answers to living their lives.

I guess they share the same mindset as the college professor's Leading from behind Strategy, wait for things to happen in the world, then take my time to figure out how to explain the events to my class (weeks, months after the fact). Notice that the Academia and P.C. Media Celebrities share the same traits? They all Lead from behind, see life in their rearview mirrors (comment on events after they happen)? A similar virulent strain, entered the Whitehouse in 2008, where do you think the Leading from behind Strategy came from?

My parting advice for the Snowflakes, avoid herd-mentality, overcome the P.C. mantras and slogans, overcome and transcend the P.C. Gestapo, the social engineering fascists. You will be proud of yourselves. 自强不息 it means tireless, never ending self-improvement

> *"Only Thing We Have to Fear Is Fear Itself": FDR's First Inaugural Address.*
> President Franklin D. Roosevelt

Chapter 5

Alan Greenspan, 'Snowflakes' & photocopiers

"The natural effort of every individual to better his own condition.... is so powerful a principle, that it is alone, and without any assistance, not only capable of carrying on the society to wealth and prosperity, but of surmounting a hundred impertinent obstructions with which the folly of human laws too often incumbers its operations."

- Adam Smith in Wealth of Nations

"It is not from the benevolence of the butcher, the brewer, or the baker, that we expect our dinner," Adam Smith in Wealth of Nations, "but from their regard to their own interests."

Discipline, self-restraint, moral rectitude, righteous anger at wrongdoers, what Adam Smith call the "awful Virtues", "the virtues of the ancient Stoics and of the Calvinist Kirk were just as necessary to life in society as were civility and compassion, because they policed the sometimes volatile frontiers of our dealings with others."

- Arthur Herman in How Scots invented the Modern World

We have witnessed the beauty of the Free Market Competition (Meritocracy), including Capitalism workings in Chapter 4. Yet we know the US economy hasn't been too great in the last 15 years despite the accumulation of over $20 T of debt till date, in large part due to QE measures designed to stimulate it. Why is that so? Is Capitalism no longer working properly in USA? Let's meet the man that started it all.

The man who broke the American Free Market Capitalism

We can look at many sets of numbers, the combined Balance sheets of World's Central Banks, sum of business debt and non-financial market equity, money market rates, yield of the 10 year U.S. Treasury note, etc. For simplicity, let's work with a number most people are familiar with, the

National Debt of $20 Trillion (as of 2016). It is the largest contributor of the "artificial liquidity" that has been flooding the U.S. financial system (leading the rest of the world to do likewise) in last three decades. Who started this crazy money printing activities that the rest of the world copied?

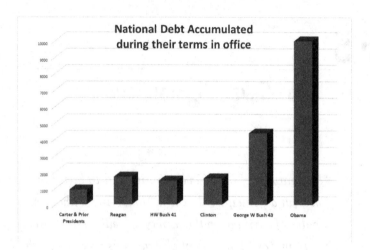

From the chart above, it would look like President Obama incurred the most National Debt under his watch as President, that is correct but President Obama didn't break the American Free Market Capitalism. He did do many other things but this is not his doing. How about the Fed Chairperson? Did Ben Bernanke do it? Look at the chart below, Ben Bernanke added over $9.3 Trillion of debt from 2006 to 2014 when he was the Fed Chairman. Ben definitely made the entire world notice the United States of America's lack of Financial Rectitude, that $9.3 Trillion of reckless money printing, to bail out the Wall Street Suzerains, while the rest of the World were all watching intently, all with clear understanding of the Feds' intentions with the QEs! Surely the series of QEs on the heels of 2008 Financial Crisis made America lose its moral authority as a world leader. So, Ben Bernanke must be the culprit, he did all the QEs (Quantitative Easing) from Nov 2008 – Oct 2014. Bernanke surely did, but he is just the Apprentice, the real master is his predecessor, Alan Greenspan. See the next chart.

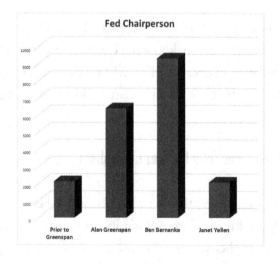

Expressed as a % of the existing National Debt that each of the Fed Chairperson "inherited" when they took office, Ben Bernanke's $9.3 Trillion pales in comparison to his teacher, Mr. Greenspan. Alan Greenspan added $6.4 trillion in National Debt against the $2.1 Trillion of debt that he "inherited" in 1987 when he started. That's over 300% increase compared to Ben's 110% increase over the $8.5 trillion of existing debt when he started as Fed Chairman in 2006.

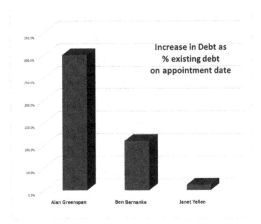

In addition to the crazy money printing, Alan Greenspan also slashed interest rates from 6.25% to 1% between Dec 2000 till mid 2003. He also created the "too big to Fail" institutions by requesting others to support them, when they have clearly become insolvent. His disciple Ben, merely continued his simplistic, 'band-aid' approach (aka immoral ways) and forced many of the Banks to "buy up" the non-performing assets and acquire, merge with these insolvent "too big to fail" entities in the aftermath of the 2008 Financial Crisis. Ben also kept the fed funds at 0% for 8 years which Yellen continued till the recent increase. With the 3-prong attack on Capitalism, "artificial liquidity", 0% interest and mergers of mega-Banks, Alan & Ben destroyed the Scarcity of Resource principle and hobbled the Free Market mechanism.

It's no wonder Main Street is declining while Crony Capitalists, Wall Street Suzerains, IT Monopolies Moghuls are laughing all the way to the banks (to be exact, $20 Trillion of Debt that the American Tax payers now has to pay!). The Wall Street Wealth is no longer allocated by Free Market, it is now monopolized and allocated by the Gargantuan Banking Monopolies (aka Too Big to Fail Banks), instead of the hundreds of millions of independent decision makers that make up the Free Market, just a few key decision makers in the Too Big to Fail Banks can now strongly influence the market!

For more details on Wall Streets' nefarious activities, you would like to read Trumped! By David A. Stockman

How much is $20 Trillion of Debt?

When a number gets too large, sometimes it becomes meaningless as the average person doesn't deal with such large numbers on daily basis. Also, how does the $ 20 Trillion debt matter to the average Joe on the street anyhow? The P.C. Propaganda likes to sell the idea that the rich should pay for it! Yes Sir, the solution to all problems is to tax the Super-Rich; the faceless and nameless Ultra-rich of top 1%, that sounds like a really great idea by Comrade Bernie (aka Col Sanders). Except (wait a minute), the Soros Open Society, the Wall Street Suzerains are the masters of likes of Hillary Clinton, President Obama, etc. all the Politicians, Activists take their cues from the Top1%, all the United Nations, EU, World Bank, IMF are heavily influenced by the Wall Street Suzerains, they are the number one beneficiaries of the $20T "artificial wealth" created but mostly kept within the Wall Street Crony Capitalists circle. Income Inequality goes through the roof, above even the pre-WW II days, yet the Economy has remained stagnant in last decade despite all the QE measures. Yet Comrade Bernie says: Get the Top 1% to pay more tax.

Yeah right, the Ultra-rich top1% is going to help pay down the $20T debt, if Comrade Bernie or Pocahontas Warren even comes within a mile of George Soros' and Wall Street Suzerains' Cheese, President Obama, Secretary Hillary Clinton (the lackeys and underlings of the Top 1%) followed by ANTIFA & BLM are all going to come rushing in so fast, they'll make Usain Bolt look like a crawling tortoise. Comrade Bernie or Pocahontas Warren will be slapped so hard by President Obama & Hillary Clinton that they'll end up back in the Pilgrim days, Pocahontas should be familiar with that environment; oops sorry, she ain't no Native American (just a lying phoney). Since Comrade Bernie or Pocahontas Warren are just acting and pandering for votes, then who is the faceless and nameless person who is paying for the $ 20 Trillion debt? Go look in the mirror, you. Yes, the average Joe, the American people will be paying for the $ 20 trillion debt, with 321 million Americans, that will work out to approx. $62,300 per person. If you have a family of 4, your family owes a debt of about $ 250,000 with $800 left over for your change. That's the Change that President Obama was talking about.

How about the IT Monopolies Moghuls? The likes of Jeff Bezos, Amazon, Google, Apple, surely those should be rich enough to pay if you can get them to. Surely, they belong to the Top 1%? Assuming that they and all their shareholders are willing to help out, besides making empty, meaningless rhetoric about how the government should give "free money" to the poor.

Let's look at the Market Capitalization of their entire companies (not merely their personal wealth), with the latest Stock prices (mid-April 2017, updated again in Apr 2018)

Top Ten most Valuable American Companies Market Cap as of 19th Apr 2017		Top 10 Most Valuable American Companies (Market Cap) dated 11 Apr 2018	
Names	$$ 'Billions		$ ' B
Apple	741	Apple	879
Alphabet (Google)	585	Alphabet Google	714
Microsoft	505	Microsoft	711
Berkshire Hathaway	404	Amazon	696
Amazon	432	Facebook	488
Facebook	407	Berkshire Hathaway	483
Exxon Mobil	344	JP Morgan Chase	380
Johnson & Johnson	330	Johnson & Johnson	349
JP Morgan	304	Exxon Mobil	329
General Electric	259	Bank of America	307
	4,310		5,336

Therefore, if we sell the top ten most Valuable American companies, we cannot even pay down half the debt that President Obama added during his term in office. We will still be left with $15.7 Trillion of debt (Now Updated for Apr 2018, we've gained $ 1B of Value in Market Cap of top ten most valuable companies. Thanks to Market confidence over last one and half year, or since the 2016 Elections)

What if we throw in the entire Market Cap of the Swiss Exchange (SIX)? Even though Swiss wouldn't be helping America pay off our debt. Sorry, the entire Swiss Exchange is only $1.5 T, it will take 13.3X Market Cap of Swiss Exchange to pay down the $20 T debt. Or 27X Apple Companies, Or 40X the entire Aerospace and Defense Industry's Market Cap. The most successful movie franchise Star Wars was valued at $42B by Fortune in Dec 2015, at that valuation, it will take 476X Star Wars Franchise to pay down the National Debt. The entire NYSE (New York Stock Exchange) Market Cap is about $ 20T on a good day, perhaps we can just give away the entire NYSE in exchange for the debt obligations?

Sadly, we cannot do that as large part of the NYSE isn't owned by Americans, there's tremendous foreign wealth invested in both NYSE and Nasdaq (how much is anyone's guess, perhaps we can ask the Media "Journalists" to do their job for a change instead of babbling about Russian hacking all day long, how much of the S&P 500 companies are held by Foreign entities and persons through the Goldman Sachs, Private Equities, various Funds, etc.? the answer might be an eye-opening one). Alas we still have no solution.

How about "globalizing certain regions" of America? Perhaps sell Hawaii to the Japanese and sell California to the Chinese? That might work, that is exactly what had happened to China during the decline of the Qing 清 dynasty; Hong Kong "leased to" British, Macau to the Portuguese, QingDao to the Germans, Taiwan to the Japanese, Heilongjiang region to the Russians, Dalian to the British, Russians, Japanese & back to Russians, Shanghai as concessions to British, French, Germany and Americans. The Japanese and Chinese just happen to be the 2 biggest holders of the U.S. Treasury Bonds, so that just might work! Eureka!

You might say that "leasing out America's lands" wouldn't happen because of our strong Military Force, that is correct for now, yet the fact remains that we have a $ 20 Trillion debt. As it happens, we don't have just one Major Debt problem, we also have the Highest Income Inequality since pre-WW II days, a fast disappearing middle class, a largely stagnant economy and a broken Capitalist market. Only Good news here, is that all the issues are inter-related.

You might remember in last chapter, we saw the beauty of how the Free Market Capitalism (perfect competition) works so well with free flow of wealth, Ideas and human talent competing with and reinforcing each other. This process is held together by traditional American values of respect for hardwork, personal responsibilities, the right to compete freely, thrift, Discipline, self-restraint and moral rectitude. Culture of growth, passion for Excellence, reverence for Meritocracy, freedom of speech, diversity of ideas and rights to debate are all crucial.

We will see how without these Values, what Adam Smith calls Awful Virtues and Aristotle terms Ethos, to hold the Capitalism (ideal of perfect competition) Process in place, it starts to break apart, losing its efficiency and effectiveness resulting in all the problems we'd just mentioned.

Discipline, self-restraint, moral rectitude, righteous anger at wrongdoers,
what Adam Smith call the "awful Virtues", "the virtues of the ancient Stoics

and of the Calvinist Kirk were just as necessary to life in society as were civility and compassion, because they policed the sometimes volatile frontiers of our dealings with others."

- Arthur Herman in How Scots invented the Modern World

Awful Virtues, Nicomachean Ethics and Crony Capitalism

In August 5th 1971, Nixon announced his New Economic Policy and ended the convertibility of the US dollar into gold by foreign central banks, thereby closing the gold window. Since 1971, the US dollar is no longer backed up by Gold reserves, since US had been such a dominant economic force in the world since the end of WW II, the dollar has also become the de facto currency of commerce in world trade. Therefore, whenever the Feds do QE s, the supply of dollar in the world increases.

You might remember in economics 101 classes, when some third world countries' government print tons of money, their economy will see huge inflation and eventually collapses. Why has that not happened here in America so far? Well for one, the entire world trading system uses US dollar (why do you think China, Russia, Iran, etc. had been trying, with limited success thus far, to conduct trade without the US$ or perhaps even to replace the US$ with a portfolio of weighted International currencies).

Since most other world currencies float freely (to some degree watched closely by their governments) against the US$, USA (with Greenspan's, Bernanke's leadership) doing such QEs unilaterally impacts the other countries of the world without their consent. If they do nothing, their currencies would appreciate against the US$, if they follow suit in printing more of their own currencies to maintain the exchange rates, they will face inflation pressures within their countries and economies too. With such irresponsible actions by the US Treasury & Fed Banks, America lost its moral leadership amongst the leading world nations. One might say, who cares about morals, the Economy is the Most important!

Most True, the economy is the key, the rising tide raises all boats, strong economic growth is crucial, but we should not forget that the awful Virtues (Discipline, self-restraint, moral rectitude, righteous anger at wrongdoers) that Adam Smith referred to, helps safeguard, regulates and reinforces the Free Market Capitalism working in smooth fashion with minimal intervention from the government.

The series of QE actions under Greenspan (beginning in '87) and Bernanke (the most obvious being the series after the 2008 crash) is the biggest contributor to Income Inequality in USA, it has created Crony Capitalism and tampered with the proper functioning of capitalism mechanism in free market, reason why the Economy has pretty much remained stagnant in the last 15 years. We will cover the issues of Income Inequality, Crony Capitalism and the stagnant economy in more details in chapter 7 and 8.

When the Big State Government steps into the Free Market Economy, it always pollutes the springs of perfect competition, replacing it with putrid elitism, cronyism, mediocrity worshipping mediocrity. The ultimate proof would be the stagnant economy, high unemployment and decimated middle class (if the crony capitalism trend does not reverse itself, you will start to see a shrinking economy, one more like the communists or socialist States). Greenspan, Bernanke and their cronies at the Fed Banks believe they can 'cheat the system' by complex financial engineering and printing 'free money', forgetting that one always pays the Piper.

As of 2012, the Debt had exceeded America's GDP in the entire history of the nation. Alan Greenspan, Ben Bernanke with approval from President George W Bush and President Barrack Obama sure didn't do the American people any favors, but wait that's not all Folks, Mr. Greenspan still has more to contribute!

Quick Summary

We've now seen Greenspan and Bernanke, by pushing the QEs and mergers of the Banks (forcing them to acquire ill-liquid assets of failed Banks) has fostered Monopoly in America's Banking system, this has crippled the Free Market Capitalism mechanism. The artificially created QE wealth effect has not spread into the Main Street. Tech Street and Unicorns did receive some QE monies; but not allocated via the Adam Smith's 'invisible hand' but by the Wall Street and K Street Cronies' hands into the Tech Street & Renewable Energy's cronies hands (their critical success factor not being great technology but the ability to repeatedly gain access to funds).

Setting the interests rates at 0%, plus the fact that the Fed's QE money are printed out of thin air and not from hard-earned profits from Main Street business destroys the Scarcity of Capital principle needed to properly allocate capital for best and highest return of investments. We now understand why the Mainstreet and Wall street has diverged and secondly, why the Free Market Capitalism Mechanism is NOT working effectively.

JP Morgan, beginning of Fed and Industries' Accountants

There's one other minor point, the Federal Reserve System was setup in 1913, after John Pierpont Morgan led a series of earlier Buy-outs of healthy companies to stabilize them (after prior stock markets crashes). JP Morgan had persuaded other leading financiers to group together and secure additional credit to buy stocks of assets rich and healthy operating companies. As powerful as JP Morgan and these Financiers were, they were still subjected to the rules of Risks and Rewards of the Free Market, thus they had 'rolled up their sleeves' and worked directly with the Accountants within the Industries, thereby knowing exactly which are the healthy corporations with strong assets-backed balance sheets and the best potential for future growth (ie. they definitely did their Due Diligence homework).

Now we have Feds Bureaucratic Apparatchiks with no personal skin in the game, doling out free QE – Taxpayers monies to Mega Monopoly Banks which in turn bases their Buy opinions recommended by bank analysts with the most sophisticated modeling skills working on questionable basic assumptions; as they've never actually worked in any Industries. Some of these structural fixes would be addressed in chapter 8

"To educate a person in mind and not in morals is to educate a menace to society."

- Theodore Roosevelt

The Fathers of 'Snowflakes'

On Oct 29th 1929, Wall Street crashed after a decade of excesses, the roaring twenties. For next 12 years, America struggled through the Great Depression. After WWII, the post war American economy grew at a phenomenon rate growing from $200B GNP to over $500B between 1940 – 1960. That's 2.5X in 2 decades, that was the rise of the American Middle-Class.

When we observe nature, light waves, sound waves; the sine or cosine waves, they oscillate around a balance point or plane. That happens due to presence of feedback cycle. In last chapter, we had also established that Culture and its external environment are also interlinked, the challenging and adverse environment will shape a Culture that can handle adversity and adapt to the challenges! This is also a feedback cycle. This form of feedback cycles in nature can be viewed as a form of adaptation, if the natural feedback loops are broken (small adjustments), then the subsequent forced disruption would be much more traumatic for the entire society (major adjustments)

In the last 3 decades with Greenspan's and Bernanke's "artificial liquidity", they broke not only the Financial Capitalism's feedback Loop. They also broke the Cultural feedback loop and that led to the growth of the 'snowflake' Culture! You don't see any 'snowflakes' during or after the Great Depression, most folks would be grateful to have a job and more than willingly to work hard for an honest paycheck. We know the CCC was formed and helped contributed towards projects like the Hoover Dam (completed under budget and ahead of schedule, when was the last public project that didn't exceed budget?). With hardship, it forges resilience in the population, this mental toughness and self-discipline helps the society overcome hardship and become more adaptable.

Sadly, because of the lack of feedback cycle in the last 3 decades, the snowflakes grew up in their "wealth bubble" cushioned from the conditions of the Great Depression that they logically should be experiencing now. Instead they are sipping their Starbucks coffee, living their borderless world in the apple shops. I mentioned "wealth" as they are not truly rich, just like the $ 20T of debt all Americans jointly owe, the Tuition Fees Loans are also waiting to be repaid too. The snowflakes each owe (not counting their debts on credit cards), an average of over $ 100k of student loan, on top of the $62k (QE debt) that they got stuck with courtesy Mr. Greenspan, Mr. Bernanke, President Bush 43rd and President Obama, that's how wealthy they are. The snowflakes' future has already been mortgaged by the Four Wise men, they just don't know it yet.

After a decade of excesses in the 20s, the Crash of 1929 and the Great Depression lasted for about 12 years. Now after 3 decades of lack of Real market feedback and adjustment, why do you think the economy is Not growing? Any genius can see that Mr. Greenspan, by sticking that $ 20T of debt on the balance sheet, for future generations of Americans to deal with, has mortgaged Americas future which truly qualifies him as one of the fathers of the snowflake generation!

Who is the other father of the snowflakes? The one behind the shadow government of Activist

Corporations pushing all the buttons behind the President Bush 43rd and President Obama's administration, George Soros is the other father of the snowflakes. Talk about the ideological disaster for America, the radical, fallacious self-proclaimed disciple of Karl Popper. He who, failed to understand the substance behind *The Open Society and Its Enemies* (1945), but mimicked the form into his Open Society Institute [activists corporation], while Popper was writing against the totalitarian Communists Regimes in Soviet Unions, the Fascists Regimes of Nazis and Mussolini and his 'self-proclaimed' disciple turned the attacks against Democracy and Capitalism, taking aim at America and utilizing Open Society Institute as instrument of anti-Establishment, anti-America, spreading internal decay since the turn of the millennia.

On top of this "pseudo wealth" bubble, you add the toxic and shallow Rhetoric of the Mainstream Media and their partners in crime, the "Power Establishment with complete Monopoly of Internet" [all under the Top 1%'s control], that has completely brainwashed all the millennials to become imbued with a sense of welfare entitlement, expecting free money from the government, free healthcare, free college education, etc. This has become the Land of Entitlements from the Big Government.

History has taught mankind that there's no such thing as a 'free lunch', yet the mainstream liberal media, ivy league academia and neo-Democrats' demagogues insist to the millennials that Free Healthcare, Education, etc. are their rights and Big Government (controlled by Top 1%) is going to pay for them by taxing the Top 1%? I guess they all suffer from "Undifferentiated Goodness". William F. Buckley Jr. coined this term when he described Eleanor Roosevelt (the grandmother of Political Correctness).

"To Buckley, she (Eleanor Roosevelt) embodied the worst of what in subsequent decades would be called political correctness: the mindless application to every issue of a platitudinous egalitarianism whose practical effect invariably is to expand the reach of totalitarianism."

- A Torch Kept Lit by James Rosen

Hers is the age of undifferentiated goodness, of permissive egalitarianist. Mrs Roosevelt's approach to human problems, so charming in its Franciscan naïveté, was simply; do away with them - by the most obvious means. The way to cope with Russia is to negotiate.... The way for everyone to be free in the world is to tell the U.N. To free everyone..... The way to solve the housing shortage is for the government to build more houses... All this is more than Mrs Roosevelt writing a column. It is a way of life. Based, essentially, on unreason; on the leaving out of the concrete, complex factor, which is why they call it "undifferentiated" goodness. Mrs Roosevelt's principled bequest, her most enduring bequest, was the capacity so to oversimplify problems as to give encouragement to those who wish to pitch the nation and the world onto humanitarian crusades which, because they fail to take reality into account, end up plunging people into misery...... "*with all my heart and soul,*" *her epitaph should read,* "*I fought the syllogism.*" *And with that energy and force, she wounded it, almost irretrievably...*"

A Torch Kept Lit, William F. Buckley Jr.

Profession by Isaac Asimov

This is a nice novella published in 1957 by Isaac Asimov whose family emigrated to USA from Russia in 1923 when he was three. It is a science fiction version of Social Engineering, if only Social Engineering is as simplistic and benign as people getting taped for their professions. Don't get me wrong, I love the story and twist at the end. Isaac Asimov is a great writer. Sadly, in the real world, human's attempts at Social Engineering, building their Utopian societies are ugly, cruel, twisted and stupid. They always end up disastrous for the human subjects experimented on, generations of sufferings, millions of lives lost, the communists have been trying social engineering, big state planning for a century now. The Nazis are big into Social Engineering too, many of the Asian countries practice mild forms of State Planning and Social Engineering in the name of achieving economic progress. The progressives are also selling their brand of Social engineering in the form of P.C. [politically correct] Propaganda along with their Socialist Big State Plans for Welfare.

But unlike the Lenins of the world who actually believe in their ideology (right or wrong ideology is a separate discussion), these neo-Democrats are just pushing for personal gains and power grab. It is obvious to see their true agenda, how can millions of American patriots put their future, the future of their families into the hands of a bunch of faceless and nameless bureaucrats? Yet, the neo-democrats are ceaselessly pushing for Big State, Big Government Control, why? Big Bureaucracy means NO accountability with large budgets and resources for them to enjoy. By the time the implosion happens, the parasites are long gone and have had their free lunch (life-time of lunches that is).

There's always a time lag, by the time USSR dissolved in 1991, Stalin already had his "glorious reign", killed millions in the gulag and died in 1953. By the time Deng put China back on the right track with Capitalist reforms for their economy, Chairman Mao had also killed millions with his Great Leap forward and deleted China's traditional Culture of 5000 years with his decade of Cultural Revolution and passed away peacefully in 1976. If cumulative naivety of America allows the Progressives neo-democrats to push their Social Engineering and Big Government Control agenda through, generations of Americans will suffer too. The neo-democrats politicians (we know them) will also get away with their life-time of free lunches, just like Mao and Stalin had already passed away when their regimes collapses. Here's the funny part, just like the average Russian in '90s and average Chinese in '70s left holding the bag after their esteemed leaders pass on. So will the snowflakes be holding the bag too. Most of them are young enough to be still around in 20-30 years time.

Before we get too ahead of ourselves, let's understand the snowflake Culture in more detail. Let's understand the backdrop of how this Culture grew up. Then let's analyze the P.C. Cultural and Values brainwashing and indoctrination by the Media Gestapo and neo-fascist Activist Corporations with a little help from the Academia Con-men. Lastly, we'll also look at the power of technology's subtle but powerful influence on the mindset of the snowflakes. With this lethal and potent combination, the snowflakes don't stand a chance! Probably the same chance as a real snowflake in the Arizona desert in summer.

Google
Climate Change, Globalism
Understanding the Millennial's perspective;
A long time ago (in a Galaxy far, far away), there were no Apple Stores

Actually, it wasn't not that long ago, the first Apple store was opened on 19th May 2001. The other day I was in an apple store trying to get my mac book air repaired, I've had it since 2010, looking around inside the store the customers are all in jovial mood, they are mix of different races and background in harmonious interactions with each other. Apple retail store is a good concept well executed; they are wide, spacious and well designed. An apple store in Shanghai is as well designed as the one in Hong Kong or any other apple store in USA. Interestingly, the city in USA with most Apple Stores is NYC with 7 (as of April 2017), followed by Las Vegas with 4. Shanghai also has 7, Hong Kong has 6 and Beijing has 5 Apple stores. If you view the world through the eyes of an Apple Store or Apple TV Commercials, there's your Globalization, Ethic and Cultural Diversity with people of different races mingling together happily in a borderless world. So what's wrong with that picture? If you cannot see the beauty of the world and beauty of diversity in such commercials, you must be racists, sexists, xenophobic, islamphobic, etc. By the way, these are not just commercials nor advertisements, they are reality because whenever I'm online, that's what I see. I see them at least 10 - 20 times a day from google, yahoo, FaceBook, whatsapp, wechat, Instagram, twitter, snapchat, msn, anywhere and everywhere online, etc.

It is the same when you are in Disneyland too, there's diversity by Culture, by races, by ethnicity, families all together and enjoying themselves. There's Disneyland in Shanghai, Hong Kong, Japan, Europe, Orlando, FL and Anaheim, CA, that's pretty Global too. Why can't you see the beauty of the borderless global one Earth vision? Why do you still cling to your antiquated "guns and bibles"?

Toy Story was first released in 1995, Pixar became a household name instantly overnight! It was not just a box-office hit, it was a real break-through for animated films, a milestone in cinematography. Toy Story must have made the entire Pixar team Real Proud, it must have vindicated Steve Jobs, forced out of Apple since 1985. Steve eventually returned to Apple in 1997 and began the revival of a company on verge of bankruptcy and the rest is history. If one grows up in a world where Animated movies are already the norm, watching Idealized Disney, Hollywood, Pixar (later bought by Disney) movies, spending most of their time online (virtually) and hanging out (physically) in Starbucks and Apple Stores (or equivalents), you might be able to empathize with the experience of the snowflakes better.

The emergence of the Internet and related-Technology (Social Media, etc.) Culture also produced interesting experiences and behavioral patterns too, much more "Texting" type of interactions, more online reading, via smartphones, iPads, Kindle, etc. Here we present the stage and backdrop that the snowflakes entered. For those who knew a world before the Internet, a world that saw Personal Computers concepts launched by Apple in late 70s and early 80s, those folks that prefer reading hardcopy books to iPad, Kindle reading, sometimes it might be difficult to understand the mindset of those that grew up in a world when the Internet and social-Media related Culture reigns supreme and molds the mindsets of its users. A lot of the behavioral patterns are subconsciously shaped by this Internet and social-Media related Culture.

Here we will separate the unintentional versus the intentional impacts on the Snowflake Culture a) Culturally and b) Internet, technology-related. In this segment, we'd started off with the Unintentional impacts, thus far, the apple stores, the Disneyland perspectives, the movies takeaways (moral messages), they are Unintentional Cultural Impacts on the snowflakes. They are intentional design by Apple, Disney, Pixar, Hollywood to please their customers but not their intention to create snowflakes.

Monte Carlo, Monaco, Las Vegas, Macau, Singapore, Atlantic City. They all have beautiful Casinos, when you first step into these beautifully designed Casinos, you are overwhelmed by the glamour, so much buzzling activities, their sheer scale and grandeur are so impressive, the water fountains of Bellagio, pyramid lighting of Luxor, views of the Mediterranean sea from the Monte Carlo Casino. When you are inside the Casino on the gaming floor, looking for the exit, you will find it much challenging then when you were entering earlier. Don't worry, it is by design, you didn't lose your way. Most of the casino patrons are happy with their experience and the casinos put up the facade and show for their guests just as Apple, Disney, Hollywood do the same for their customers too.

But while most casino customers wouldn't confuse the casino with the real outside world, some of the young and impressionable Apple, Disney customers could actually mix up the two. Since the Disneyland in Orlando and Shanghai look the same and the Apple Store in Hong Kong and San Diego look alike, why isn't this the Globalized World? Sounds logical right?

There are many consequences of the snowflakes not being able to differentiate between the "subset & idealized world" (façade) created for them and the larger "whole set world" complete with imperfections of reality. They try to stay in that sub-set world instead of facing the reality of the larger real world, here they can avoid confrontations, they assume there's unlimited resources in the world, choose path of least resistance and yield the chance to deal with the larger whole-set world's imperfections, they abdicate the chance to learn to overcome hardships and challenges, to control their own destinies. They forfeit all the great learning opportunities in the school of hard-knocks, gave up contributing towards making the imperfect world a better place! Instead, they choose the semblance of control by hiding in their idealized sub-set world created for them. Next, we'll explore some of the Unintentional Technology related impacts on the snowflakes.

Texting while Driving

Why do people text? Why is there a texting Culture? Along the spectrum of people interactions; ranging from personal face to face, video conference, phone conversations, texting has to be slowest in speed with least amount of information exchanged. Face to Face meetings would be maximum in both speed and feedback obtained (including non-verbal cues), followed by video conference, phone conversations would also be faster and also more feedback in hearing the tone of voice, pauses between, etc. Of the whole lot, texting is the slowest with minimal hints of the other sides' emotions and inner thoughts. Since it is the most inefficient, Why text then?

Perhaps due to Availability? sometimes the other party might be busy, then texting would be more polite; for it allows them to respond at a more suitable time for themselves. it also allows more time to screen the message for errors before sending. But seriously, how can you say something wrong over the phone? Well, we've just touched on another snowflake Culture, it is precisely the lack of feedback that the snowflakes prefer.

Texting allows snowflakes their safe space as they have time to screen and re-screen their messages, to google for answers which they cannot do in face to face or live phone conversation. It allows them to appear to know as much as they can google quickly. In real live conversations, their slowness in response, their lack of confidence in their voice or lack of passion in their "strong beliefs" through non-verbal cues would be obvious to others. That's why snowflakes prefer texting or perhaps texting culture create more snowflakes (catch 22). Would Face to face conversations mean micro-aggressions? I guess it would be if you call out their hypocrisy, pretense or dim wittedness (essentially to call out Reality), or perhaps it is sexists, racists, xenophobia, etc.

Reading Digitally

When the iPad was launched in Apr 2010, they were really amazing, very soon after, I was able to read National Geographic off the iPads, it was an amazing experience with the video-clips embedded and the moving images that would have been impossible to reproduce in the hardcopy magazine. I tried e-books off the kindle (amazon) or nook (Barnes & Nobles), interesting but not quite as spectacular as the iPad. There's a proposition that hardcopy books are on decline because everyone is switching to e-books or just reading articles off the internet, which I respectfully disagree with. Hardcopy books are on decline, this is a undisputed Fact! But only a small portion has been replaced by e-books; personally I love reading magazines or novels off iPads, Kindle, nooks or whatever digital format works great! A large portion of the 'sober reading' has disappeared due to cultural change, it has evolved (or devolved depending on your perspective) into speeding scanning of Headlines or watching short video clips. Here Speed is of the essence not self-attained insights nor substance, you can forget about any complex concepts!

I would like to make a comparison between hardcopy reading Vs e-Reading, for there are still critical advantages to reading off hardcopy books too. They come in very handy when you are reading about complex issues which you might like to resolve and internalize. When you read something, a few processes are happening a) you are absorbing the new information presented to you (so the information goes from medium to you), b) you are also reconciling the new information with what you already know or your prior experiences or personal Values and c) the agenda and experience of the author. Because of the 3 processes happening simultaneously, a hardcopy book makes for better reading when dealing with complex ideas and concepts. Why? First a) it allows you much longer time at the subject matter, staring at the screen for hours can make your eyes really tired, b) more time also allows you to reflect on what you had just read, reconciling between what you had just read versus your personal experiences will create new insights, c) hardcopy allows easier random access as against sequential access in the digital format (random access also possible now in digital, just not as quickly as on hardcopy), random access gives the reader a better overview of the topic very quickly, d) hardcopy allows for multiple access and alternating between chapters to crosslink related ideas and concepts, e) hardcopy also lets the user draw, jot down, write, markup the pages to speedily capture his/hers personal thoughts and insights as they cross his/her mind and lastly f) because of all the above, the user can choose to have a much more Active experience as versus a digital copy which is relatively more passive.

We understand that many of the functions are also becoming available in the digital copies, I also read from Kindle too but at this time they are still too slow and antiquated. By the time you typed in 1 idea, the other 2 related ones might have fleeted away g) doodle and scribbling also allows ideas to form, somehow typing doesn't feel the same as graphs and charts in capturing complex ideas and simplifying them for the readers quickly [we are after all still visual creatures, much more powerful to express concepts visually].

My point about the snowflake Culture is this, reading digitally might also encourage more passive behavior and more accepting of whatever one reads as you either accept all or reject everything you read. Hardcopies allows you to cross out sections you think is BS and yet circle and markup sections which you find more insightful. If you have already developed the reading behavior I am describing, one can go back and do the same in the digital format, but if you have never developed those reading habits, the digital format will "unintentionally" [subconsciously] encourage you to be more passive in your reading and thinking style.

Watching short clips of news "summarized version of summaries"

In these fast pace world, who has time to be reading long articles, let alone books? Or even hardcopy books (that's really old school). This is very true, that's the real reason the hardcopy book industry is dying. The snowflakes are watching summaries of summaries of comments and opinions. The shorter the better! Get right to the point, tell me what to know, tell me what to say, tell me what to believe! I just want to be in the know! With attitudes like these, it makes snowflakes perfect targets for brain-washing! We'll visit that interesting process soon.

The Principles of Newspeak

> *"Newspeak was the official language of Oceania and had been devised to meet the ideological needs of Ingsoc, or English Socialism. In the year 1984 there was not as yet anyone who used Newspeak as his sole means of communication, ... it was expected that Newspeak would have finally superseded Oldspeak (or Standard English, as we should call it) by year 2050."*
>
> - 1984 by George Orwell

Googling for answers to everything (Headline: *"Newspeak"* roll-out is ahead of schedule!)

I am King of the World! This is funny, when one of my friends discovered google search, this was around late 2011, yet the late adopter kept going around telling anyone who would care to listen, advertising about "his discovery". google search is a great tool, and some might even find it indispensable. It does have a huge impact to the snowflakes' mindset. We'll address the unintentional effects here and more Intentional Impacts in last part of this chapter. The concept behind the results of google searches, Wikipedia, google maps locations, etc. is that the most common answer is the right answer! For most part, this would hold true. But any thinking person with some experience in life should be able to explain why most common doesn't always mean it's right or most sophisticated. In fact, the most average cannot be the cutting edge. The leading minds and most innovative talent should be the most rare, if that's the case, then their voices would be easily drowned out by the masses of the average person right? So how can the google, with the most common answers be of any value to the cutting edge or leading minds?

We also need to differentiate between the different subject matters of what we are googling about (which is what the snowflakes and Media Gestapo doesn't do, in their minds all facts are facts). Let's start with the easiest, physical locations on earth, with the exact longitudes and latitudes coordinates and GPS, the locations on google maps cannot be wrong. Yes and no, the coordinates will not be wrong, but the identifications of certain rare locations could be pinned incorrectly. Remember individuals pin them. The more common locations would be corrected, the extremely rare might not always be correct. This is especially true on foreign language spellings. For example, the local Portuguese or Greek names would be correct, but many tourists will try pin the locations in English and possibly pinned the wrong café in Rio or pub in Rhodes.

How about spellings, words meanings on google search? They are mostly good since English language is common. Past neutral Events that are *apolitical* are usually good. How about getting your News on internet? The so called "News on internet" is free, since no one is paying for it, the most readily available "News" would appear to the Internet User (it would be driven by google's search algorithms and cookies too). Just like commercials and advertisement that keeps popping out to entice the dollars from your wallet, the most readily available "News" are also paid for by someone; by those that have an agenda, that is to shape your thinking and get your votes!

On more complex issues that require Analysis of multiple variables, with many implied assumptions that aren't common knowledge, then the internet would be a difficult place to get useful information quickly and easily (it is possible to piece the final answers together after much hard work and effort into investigations). Just as one would NOT become a rocket scientist or neuro surgeon by googling, yet we can find answers for complex data analysis, financial or legal analysis by googling. Are the Actuarial scientists, CPAs, Lawyers, CFAs out of jobs now? In cases where you need deep accumulated knowledge base, trying to google answers to such questions is like trying to short-cut professions that took decades of personal investment of time and dedicated hard work to build (not to mention accumulated knowledge, experience and insights) and implicitly relying on conclusions put together by others whom you know nothing about; not their technical expertise, their relevant professional experience, nor their agenda? Many would put more effort into deciding what they'll have for lunch, yet they'll believe whatever they read on the internet without question?

Quick re-cap, the snowflakes Culture might be shaped by the google mindset ("unintentional" impact to society) believing that they can google the answers to everything and do not distinguish between the subject matters of what they google.

Just as a con-man cannot pull off the con unless the victim gets greedy, the Intentional P.C. Brainwasher cannot feed you false news and fake analysis unless you are lazy and try to use google as short-cut for understanding complex issues. The slothful are more susceptible to be brainwashed. More to follow on the Intentional Impact on Snowflakes

> *"Freedom is never more than one generation away from extinction. We didn't pass it to our children in the bloodstream. It must be fought for, protected, and handed on for them to do the same."*
>
> - President Ronald Reagan

> *"Each new generation born is in effect an invasion of civilization by little barbarians, who must be civilized before it is too late."*
>
> - Thomas Sowell

Indoctrination in the Ivy League Academia

From President Reagan and Thomas Sowell's quotes, we can sense how critical it is to protect our education system and younger generation. It is the Achilles Heel of America, if so, how did we allow the neo-Fascists Social Engineers, the P.C. Gestapo, the Activists Corporations to brainwash our young into snowflakes? In chapter 3, we had mentioned about the students becoming the "high rollers" in the Colleges as they are the biggest Revenue Generators for the schools' explosive endowment Funds! So that's one reason that contributed to the rise of snowflakes.

We can think of another reason for the P.C. Cultural and Values brainwashing, the indoctrination by the Media Gestapo and neo-fascist Activist Corporations of the snowflakes, they want their Votes!

But here's another 3 important reasons for the Intentional Cultural brainwashing of the snowflakes. With help from the Academia Con-men, the Academia Colleges with the snowflakes is a) the perfect testing ground for the neo-fascists Progressives' message and Social Engineering experiments (equivalent to Product Testing in the commercial world). b) training ground for the Activists Corporations (staff training), and c) Recruiting for the neo-fascists Propaganda Media (talent pipeline)

That's all well and good Strategy, but how to execute on this Strategy? Be it the Progressives, Propaganda or Activists Corporations, they need a way in to get to the snowflakes. Just as the Wall Street Suzerains, control the Politicians, Media, IT Moguls (Wolf control the shepherd and sheepdogs), the Activists, Progressives, Social Engineers also learn from their Bosses [aka sponsors]. They reach out to the shepherd and sheepdogs in the Academia too. Provide Incentives of making huge contributions to endowment funds? Or are the Activists witch-hunts? Perhaps mere threats of witch-hunts is enough? Appeals to the Liberals mindset of the Academia? Always works best with both a pull and a push (appeal plus potential threat) and also both Rational and Emotional reasons as we had witnessed with the neo-democrats politicians, Media Celebrities, etc.

Just appeal to the Liberal Academia's romanticized version of Globalism and Socialism and they show be eating out of your hands; they do already have their life-time of free lunches as Professors.

Speaking of Romantics, I really like this quote from Stephen R. Platt,

> *"... and when we congratulate ourselves on seeing through the darkened window that separates us from another civilization, heartened to discover the familiar forms that lie hidden among the shadows on the other side, sometimes we do so without ever realizing that we are only gazing at our own reflection.."*
>
> - Stephen R. Platt in Autumn in the Heavenly Kingdom....
> the Epic Story of the Taiping Civil War (1851 -1864, few
> outside China know of this Civil War that claimed over
> 20 million lives by conservative estimates)

Or perhaps, the Academia bunch are just like Eleanor Roosevelt, full of Undifferentiated Goodness?

Back to executing the indoctrination strategy, Ok, now we have the Academia on our side, what next? Simple, we know that human nature always chooses the Paths of least resistance. They like to stay in their Comfort zone, any self-respecting snowflake would find it Difficult to face reality... stay in their bubble! Safe space, be Risk Adverse. Human weaknesses like Sloth and greed so we need a Simple message, simple is always easiest to market and sell.

Now comes the real test, would they be dumb enough to buy a "Cut and paste" message? One that doesn't link to any semblance of reality. A romanticized version of Globalism and Socialism that doesn't stand up to any deep analysis. One that will breakup into gibberish when the students learn to think intensively and to think critically for themselves. Luckily for us the Academia Professors already bought into the romanticized version long ago. So we're good there too, this is good, we are nearly out of the woods now.

Lastly, we need to convince them that they can have the comfort of knowing all the Model answers to life, we can teach them all they ever need to know about dealing with the challenges of the future.

Good Business leaders, Commercial Executives with real-world experience or Military Leaders who have fought real wars, will tell the kids that there is NO such thing as a model answer to life! They have to learn and figure out for themselves as life and the challenges it presents are Dynamic and never Static! Shucks.. we are stuck, how do we sell to the snowflakes that life is Static and they can drive their cars by looking in their Rear view mirrors (looking into the past instead of looking into the future)?

"Sanctuary in which exploded systems and obsolete prejudices find shelter and protection, after they have been hunted out of every other corner of the world."

Adam Smith after studying at Oxford for 7 years describes an average university

"The most fundamental fact about the ideas of the political left is that they do not work. Therefore, we should not be surprised to find the left concentrated in institutions where ideas do not have to work in order to survive."

– Thomas Sowell

Beware the Academia Con-men

Thank God for the Academia Romantics, they are truly a god sent! Romantics that make their living by studying the past and living in the safe, secure world of absolute certainty (the past)! We wait for events to unfold around us and then we analyze them and re-analyze them, once we have consensus and everyone is on board (god forbid anyone rocks the boat), we reveal our insightful and infinitely wise analysis to the eagerly awaiting snowflakes and then bathe in the full glory of their sincerest adoration!

So we just leave it to the academics to sell the snowflakes how to navigate (drive) the static world with a static picture. The snowflakes have to (follow closely now, you don't want to miss any details) take a picture through their windshield before they start their cars, then print the pic to the highest resolution and biggest possible size, ideally cover the entire windshield. It is very important to get to the highest resolution as you cannot miss any tiniest detail. After that stick the pic on your windshield, next step is going to be very easy now, as you already have the picture printed to the highest resolution! You cannot miss any details now. So next step is just to start up your car and drive around looking at the picture on your windshield. You should be all set and reach your destination in 15 mins. All the details have been captured and analyzed in the picture on your windshield. There, you are all set for life

> *"Too much of what is called 'education' is little more than an expensive isolation from reality."*
>
> – Thomas Sowell

Ada Lovelace, the photocopier and the Turing Test

What is the advantage of a photocopying machine versus scanning a document into softcopy on a PC (Personal Computer), then printing a hardcopy? Although a photocopying machine can only reproduce from hardcopies to hardcopies (some can also scan these days), the main advantage is speed over the Personal Computer! If all you need is from one hardcopy to many hardcopies, then the photo-copying machine is way faster!

There many advantages of scanning into softcopy is a) ability to retain a copy on the Personal Computer, b) ability to disseminate via emails or posting to the cloud, etc., c) ability to convert into word doc and make changes and d) print into different versions or amended drafts at later stage. Now if we do this, we scan into softcopy, pdf, convert pdf into word, print the word doc exactly as the scanned copy. Or just merely photocopy 1 copy also. Yet the end result is the same if you are ONLY looking at the end product of the one hardcopy, in fact the scanning process requires much more processing power and ends up slower (it has much more future potential of the softcopy retained that we'd discussed, it is NOT apparent at this stage). I am using this as an analogy.

When I was back in college, I noticed a strange phenomenon, when the lecturers gives an overloaded syllabus in a very short time frame, the students couldn't help but memorize the materials to score well in the immediate standardized tests or exams. A few weeks or months later, they have nearly zero recollection of what they had memorized even though they might have done very well during the tests and reproduced exactly what they had memorized for the test. They were essentially behaving like photocopies .. very strange observation.

If the academia doesn't wish to encourage too much intensive and critical thinking, just load up big time on the syllabus and conduct standardized tests that rewards memorization and regurgitation behavior. The snowflakes will learn very quickly not to ask questions nor to think too much as it wastes their precious time to memorize. True learning becomes extremely inefficient as compared to memorizing and regurgitating! You can change their learning behavior in a heartbeat!

As I was reading The Innovators by Walter Isaacson, about Ada Lovelace's (Lord Byron's daughter) Notes by the Translator published in 1843 and Alan Turing's later work and question : Can machines think? It suddenly occurred to me that Processing Power is the answer to the phenomenon about learning I just described earlier.

In a real learning process, a) the learner receives and understands the information presented to him/her, b) he/she then assess if information is useful to oneself, c) learner then uses personal logic to vet the information received is logically sound and reasonable, d) next the learner also reconciles the new information received with his/her personal experiences in life, or pre-existing knowledge or expertise on the matter, e) the more astute learner might also review the personal agenda as well as Competence (level of expertise) of the Information provider. All the steps/toll-gates a) to e) are done instinctively and subconsciously (almost instantaneously), if the learner doesn't agree with any above 'tollgates', either from logic standpoint or personal past experience or personal knowledge, he/she will reject the new information, f) only if the information passed all the prior 'checks' does the learner start "practicing" the new information, to internalize the new facts or analysis. After much repeated practice does new information truly gets assimilated and internalized. This way of learning will require much more processing power than just memorizing and regurgitating, which is a definite proof that college or higher education doesn't always translate into learning.

Memorizing and regurgitating is only at the Knowledge (lowest level of learning), the ability to Recognize or Recall depends the processing power of the individual. While the earlier way of learning requires the individual to achieve a minimal Application level of learning (after Knowledge and Comprehension), the better ones will start to move into Analysis and finally into Synthesis after reconciling their ability to apply with years of personal work experience.

In the "pseudo learning" process, the lower processing units only need to clear one hurdle, understand enough to repeat the information provided; to recognize and hopefully able to recall. The real challenge would be that they cannot even repeat information that's too complex or detailed, so the neo-Dems simplifies the message till it becomes binary; four legs good, two legs bad, Socialism good, Capitalism Bad, all neo-Dems are kind and all GOP are evil. All the other steps are skipped, no reconciliation needed.

Despite all the help, the low processing units might still forget the information after some time due to lack of processing power (aka memory space), thus the genius of binary view of life devised by the manipulators. One cannot help but also see the irony in Ada Lovelace's insights realizing that 'punched cards' can be coded to program any machines back in 1842; fast forward to 2017, all programming are based on series of 1 & 0 (a binary form of instructions). Just as binary coding is used to program machines, so is a "binary view of the world" leveraged to manipulate and program the lower processing units amongst us.

Once these units are programmed with this 'binary view of life', it is extremely difficult to debate or discuss any diverse or new perspectives as their need for certainty, fear of change makes it impossible to invoke any reason in them. One needs to empathize with the low for it took them years, even decades master the few political slogans, can you imagine their stress to memorize new slogans?

> *"Schools are no longer institutions of learning. They are laboratories of progressive indoctrination. Encouraging critical thought has been replaced by demanding regurgitating of the leftists ideology to get a passing grade.*

These days, students know how to address the transgendered with the proper pronouns, but they aren't able to do basic maths"

– Sheriff David Clarke Jr.

Instead of teaching the young to learn and reason for themselves, to understand the logic behind the concepts so as to be able to work from first principles. The youth of America has only been trained to memorize sound-bites, indoctrinated to repeat slogans of subterfuges and mantras of sophistries. In short, the Liberal Ivy League Academia has substituted adaptable learning skills through logical reasoning, with standard hardcoded conditioned reflexes.

Alan Turing summed it up elegantly in his response to Sir Geoffrey Jefferson in 1949 (a famous brain surgeon) "Not until a machine can write a sonnet or compose a concerto because of thoughts and emotions felt, and not by the chance fall of symbols, could we agree that machines equals brain," to which Turing's reply "the comparison is perhaps a little bit unfair because a sonnet written by a machine will be better appreciated by another machine." For most 'machines', sonnets are unnecessary when political slogans would more than suffice.

Snowflake Culture is the greatest attestation to the success of the brainwashing efforts of the Progressive Social Engineering P.C. Gestapo, together with the Academia con-men and help of Social Media, they have successful taught the snowflakes how to think! Interestingly, we'll observe later in this chapter that the anomic Culture is not unique to just the snowflakes.

".. The party fights any tendency to delve into the depths of a human being, especially in literature and art," .. "What is not expressed does not exist. Therefore if one forbids men to explore the depths of human nature, one destroys in them the urge to make such explorations; and the depths in themselves slowly become unreal." .. The result, he warned was that ".. In the East, there is no boundary between man and society."

- Czelaw Milosz Polish poet and diplomat,
The Captive Mind written in 1953

Social Engineering

In Marxism, bourgeois nationalism is the alleged practice by the ruling classes of deliberately dividing people by nationality, race, ethnicity, or religion, so as to distract them from initiating class warfare. It is seen as a divide and conquer strategy used by the ruling classes to prevent the working class from uniting against them (hence the Marxist slogan, Workers of all countries, unite!).

A more astute reader might notice that the neo-Dems divisive rhetoric constantly dredging up racism, sexism, religious differences, rich vs poor, LGBTQ, etc. instead of emphasizing e pluribus unum (assimilating from many into one : Americanism). By deliberately and constantly focusing on the divisions and differences, the neo-Dems social engineers the masses into believing they have no hope of unity amongst themselves and only hope lays in the Big State Government to control everything for them.

For if the people are already united as one, then the neo-Democrats would have no role to play, the problem profiteers needs The Problem to exist to justify their very own existence, or better still for the problem to get worse, so that they can grow bigger and stronger!

> *"It is the mark of an educated mind to be able to entertain a thought without accepting it."*
>
> – Aristotle

Other attributes of LPUs (Low Processing Units), or what Orwell simply called *Low

Following up from the section on Ada Lovelace and Turing test, we shall explore other attributes of the Low that makes them easily susceptible to manipulations of the Social Engineers, aka Mainstream Media P.C. Gestapo. The Low prefer a static instead of dynamic view of the world, once they have figured some issue out (usually a binary view of the world as discussed earlier), the conclusion will always be cast in stone. They do not comprehend contingency, that outcomes can be contingent on many different variables and varying from situation to situation. Their fear of change leads to a strong preference for risk adversity, dislike for fluidity and dynamism that comes with growth.

The *Low usually fails to understand history in the context of the values and cultures as of the particular point of time and place (eg. All slave owners are evil, all Confederates are evil). They cannot imagine nor fathom that the cultures and conditions faced by the ancient Greece, Romans, the early pioneers in America, American Revolutionary War, Civil War, etc. yet they are quick to judge and criticize others based purely on the Next article they happen to come across in the social or mass media (due to their conditioned reflexes).

They also frequently exhibit the "This Is Where I Came In" syndrome, believing events and 'news' exactly as presented to them and when they first became aware of them without ever bothering to research back into history to the cause and effects leading up to this point. They also fail to follow up on such situations over time (no continuity) after the initial exposure (eg. Middle East Syrian Civil War, Israel Palestine conflict, China's Trade imbalance with America, NAFTA trade deficits that America suffers from, etc.), such that each 'New' incident are always viewed as isolated events and perceived exactly as the next 'News article' present the situation to them [they are true photo copying machines with minimal memory retention capability].

They have tough time understanding multiple different perspectives on any particular issue, let alone the agenda of the individuals championing each different perspective. Inability to see and understand other's perspective also handicaps their ability to emphasize with diverse ideologies different from their views (doesn't mean they have no emotions). They tend to have difficulty with complex issues involving much details, have limited concentration timeframe (very short spans), usually some challenges with details & memories even of their own past (we are not talking patients suffering from illness). *Per George Orwell in 1984 as quoted in beginning of chapter 2

All these attributes make it difficult for the Low to forecast (various different scenarios) into the future based on existing variables and assumptions. Their only view of future is the same as present, failing to understand syllogism and that different variables will drive different outcomes of the future. If the rich and powerful top 1% controls the government, wouldn't a Big State Government (needed to give more entitlements) enable the Top 1% to have more control over the rest of us in the future? Wouldn't giving up rights to arms help enable this Big State Government dominate over the people? If we truly have freedom of speech, why do we have to be Politically Correct? If we truly value diversity, why do we hate differing views so much?

Once you add sloth, selfishness, fear of change and ego to the toxic mix, then one can see why the Low happily abdicates their free will, freedom to reason, to think logically in lieu of Political Correctness.

> *"Knowledge has always been the enemy of Extremism, and for the most radical elements among Alexandria's Christians (in late 4th century AD), the books in the Serapeum (Great Library, College in addition to Temple) were a threat. So they simply destroyed them"*
>
> - Rise and Fall of Alexandria, Justin Pollard & Howard Reid

Convergent Evolution through search Technology and Social Media

In the late 90s and early millennial, when the internet first became popular, it was envisioned that many diverse views and perspectives will thrive! Democracy will triumph and Big Government Socialists Communist States will fall. Of course, the USSR had already dissolved in 1991, so the conventional wisdom was that China the next largest Communist country, North Korea, Cuba, Vietnam, Laos & Myanmar all will become democratic societies very soon by end of the millennia. Well the millennia came and went, the Y2K problem came and went, so did the prediction that communist parties will fall also came and went. In fact, most of the Big State Govt have learnt to use the Internet to weed out diverse ideas and voices. It is also the same in USA too. Look at the power of the Activists corporations and Politically Correct movement in shaping the Snowflakes Generation! We had discussed some of the unintentional impacts of the search technology. Let's touch on the extreme bias and intentional impacts on the snowflakes and other unsuspecting internet users.

If you wish to understand more deeply about any current political issues and try searching for any remotely Politically-related words or terms, you will get a humongous diarrhea-like dump of "news", Prescriptive reports of Skewed data, Skewed and bias analysis, misleading representations that the Politically Correct Gestapo, neo-fascists Propaganda arm of Progressive Social Engineers put into the internet! You know the *reports are prescriptive as they already start off with the

Conclusion on what you should be thinking and 'supported loosely' by a couple of anecdotal data points (ideally emotional examples, tearjerkers are good).

*Any college kid should know that any half decent report would start with an observation and description of the situation being investigated, after which a draft hypothesis is put forth, prelim data gathering followed by testing to see if we have the right sample size, renewed data gathering and re-testing. Only if we're satisfied that we have the right representative population sample do we even begin the analysis of data collected. Only with proper analysis do we build correlation and start exploring causation, after months if not years of testing those factors with highest correlations and verified some to be actual causations rather than symptoms do we propose a tentative conclusion. The entire process can be sped up when possible with experience, high processing power and luck but the discipline and rigor never short-cut!

But wait a minute, doesn't the cookie and search algorithm supposed to be customized to the individual user? If I have never search for any political reports before or gave any indication whether I am pro-Democrat or pro-GOP, how is the google search dumping all these neo-democrat, P.C. Gestapo reports and analysis to me?

If you are looking for neutral articles that deals with concepts of Mercantilism, Socialism, etc. in an un-bias way, you can find them eventually, that is after going through 30 minutes of scanning through loads and loads of propaganda glorifying Socialism and slamming protectionism practices. You also have to keep refining your search too. Long story short, you must already know what you are looking for to find it! If you are a new to these concepts and ideas, you have NO chance to get a neutral or balanced education via the google search (which is supposed to be neutral?)

The biasness isn't just that it is difficult to find the articles, when I finally did managed to locate a free version of the article online via google, the Amended article had missing pages (exactly the 2 pages explaining tariffs and mercantilism worked in the country's favor). I finally had to buy a version of the book off kindle to get the missing pages. The only reason I knew where to look was because I had read the book in print before, remembered the concept and made a mental note to retrieve the details at a later stage.

> *"…Nothing in all the world is more dangerous than sincere ignorance and conscientious stupidity…"*
>
> - Rev Martin Luther King, Jr.

Are the IT Monopolies Moguls in with the P.C. Gestapo and neo-fascists Activists?

Is Jeff Bezos, Mark Zuckerberg, etc. supporting the Politically Correct Agenda? We know for a fact all their investors' monies are from Wall Street. We know that they have all publicly acknowledged to be extreme Pro-Left Progressives. So we know they have both the incentive to do so and history of supporting the neo-democrats' cause. But we cannot tell if they gave the edict for their search algorithms to be "modified".

I would lean more towards incompetence. Incompetence of their Middle management, to avoid the neo-fascists Activists and P.C. Gestapo legal harassments and public witch hunts. And also the incompetence of their Junior Un-professionals Tech workers who cannot separate their professional duties from their emotional snowflake Values. What is fiduciary duties? what is professionalism? What is dedication to Excellence? These vocabulary are not in the snowflake Culture nor in that of their Masters' Culture of Ego and Self-Righteousness. Difference between masters and their underlings is that the Masters are insulated from stagnant economy with their personal huge wealth, even as America declines, the Tech workers are not insulated, they still have their loans and debts to pay off.

Contrast the current sloppy Culture of Sloth with: The Spirit of analysis and a rigorous discipline of testing all premise, the endeavor to explore and systematization of all knowledge behind *Encyclopedie* by d'Alembert and Diderot between 1751 – 1772, where Reason would confront falsehoods with "solid principles to serve as the foundation for diametrically opposed truths," whereby "we shall be able to throw down the whole edifice of mud and scatter the idle heap of dust" and instead "put men on the right path." – Denis Diderot

Instead of The spirit of intensive debates, exchange of ideas and intellectual discussions behind Republic of Letters, Select Society, Lunar Society, Mirror Club, Poker Club, Oyster Club, so on during the Age of Enlightenment, all the Internet Revolution (at this stage) has brought about a Culture of the MOB (Millennials Oriented Broadcast) where the Mass Ignorance floods the web, Fake News if repeated enough times by Mainstream Media becomes REAL and Mass Emotional Hysteria is guided by paths of Least Resistance.

Just like the French Revolution in 1789 or the more recent Arab Spring, the IT Revolution has been hijacked by Radicals and extremists of the neo-Democrats, who just like Maximilien Robespierre, Louis-Antoine Saint-Just and co, refuses to compromise, instead looking for an Idealistic solution that ended in Failure (as it wasn't rooted in reality). One needs to ask if Bezos and Zuckerbergs of the world are Romantics whose view of the world ignores reality (following in the vein of Eleanor Roosevelt's Undifferentiated Goodness), are they wicked, or merely stupid is one of the most difficult questions of our time, and at certain moments a very important question.

At first glance, one might lean towards Romantics with huge egoistic ignorance towards human nature, free market capitalism and workings of societies. On deeper analysis, the agenda of their Wall Street investors (Crony Capitalists) probably dictates their agenda. For all their wealth, it appears that these one trick ponies are nothing more than buffoons and whores to the Wall Street Capitalists that can make or break their stock prices and thus ultimately their companies. Unlike the more traditional industries with strong operating cashflows, most of these Unicorns Technology monopolies have astronomical PE multiples (Price over Earning) and even lower Price over CashFlow. Many have negative operating Cashflows, so it is all a confidence game to the Wall Street Investors which leaves many of them easily vulnerable to loss in confidence (easily shaken by negative press, by savage assaults by the Dogs of the Activists Corporations) in their future potential.

> *"Who controls the past controls the future; who controls the present controls the past", 1984 by George Orwell, ".. You believe reality is something objective, external, existing in its own right. You also believe that the nature of reality is self-evident, But I tell you... That reality is not external... Whatever the party (the internet) holds to be truth is truth. It is impossible to see reality except by looking through the eyes of the party (results of Google)."*

News, Fake News, Opinions of the uninformed and misinformed Egoistic Media Celebrities

Some days in the future, those watching the CNN, MSNBC, etc. 'News footages' might wonder to themselves, is this the Entertainment section, National Enquirer: Martians with "Model Answers to Life" have landed news?

Whenever you log into MSN, Yahoo, the crazed Hatred, anti-Trump, anti-GOP news? It's like 99.9% of the internet is policed 24/7 by the Politically Correct Gestapo and the neo-fascists Propaganda arm of Progressives. Same Blind-Hate when you switch on cable-TV channels CNN, MSNBC, CBS, NBC, etc. There's no detailed research, no thoughtful analysis, no useful insights, just a bunch of self-important ranting, Entertainment Celebrities telling you their precious opinions and what and how you should think.

We have already seen how the professionalism and cutting-edge Culture of Ida Tarbell's investigative journalism has long been replaced by shallow, Idle Pomp of Self Glorifying Media Celebrities (all unworthy successors), gaggle of sycophants in CNN, NBC, literary pretenders in NYT, grammarians buffoons in Washington Post should at best qualify only as Entertainment SNL or Big State neo-Dems' propaganda arm instead of masquerading as Independent News agencies.

So the Real question is, Are you getting your 2 Hours of Hate from the Ministry of Truth every day?

> *"There is no education like adversity"*
>
> – Benjamin Disraeli

> *"Associate yourself with people of good quality, for it is better to be alone than in bad company."*
>
> – Booker T. Washington

Rise of the Anomie Culture in America

Due to combination of sheltered lifestyles of the snowflakes, Thanks to the $20T of new money creation by Greenspan and Bernanke. This dual lack of adversity and lack of growth had weaken the traditional American Values of Endurance, Courage and Fortitude as these can only be brought forth by hardship and adversity. As we'll see though out the various chapters, this anomie state is shared by many segments; K-Street administrative apparatchiks, Deep-State politicians, snowflakes in schools, the Academia, social and Mass Media (aka Fake News, slothful and egoist 'journalist', opinion grammarians, etc.), Technology Monopolies and Entertainment Celebrities. They all share common traits like being spiritually sterile, responsive only to themselves, responsible to no one. They deride the values of other men. Their philosophy is of denial, they live on the thin line of sensation between no future and no past.

See the Mass Media ridicule traditional American Values like Valor (exhibited by police officers during shootings), they (the anomie Media Celebrities) mock and laugh at virtues like discipline, self-restraint and moral rectitude, makes fun of Vice President Pence's religious beliefs, calling him names? They praise the cowardice of the wrong-doers, police officers that run away from danger and the deep State politicians supports illegal criminals in sanctuary cities against law enforcement officers.

All these K-Street administrative apparatchiks, Deep-State politicians, snowflakes in schools, the Academia pseudo-intellects, social and Mass Media Celebrities, Technology Monopolies Moghuls and Entertainment Narcissistic ego-junkies all share a common state of mind of one who has been pulled up by his/her moral roots, who has no longer any standards but only disconnected urges, who has no longer any sense of continuity, of folk, of obligation. This is so simply because they all live in Cultures of Monopolies and Decadence without free market competition. Sheltered from adversity and competition, their ego grows out of check and becomes disconnected with realities of life. Their chosen paths are always the paths of least resistance, short term comfort and *happiness [*per Mary Wollstonecraft's quote in chapter 8]

The Anomie bunch, while they themselves are risk adverse to change (god forbid anything should challenge their Monopolies, or put an end to their luxurious and decadent lifestyles), yet they are quick to judge others, the Media Celebrities criticize and focuses on any perceived negatives of current administration without learning more about the facts and history nor allowing time for the policies to gain traction and deliver results, the Mainstream is negative on every issue to the point that it is actually becoming rather comical.

As we sum up our observation of this culture and behavior that has infected this generation propagated and sped up via the IT Revolution (merging of P.C. Internet News and Celebrities Main Stream Media Cult), the Living in the Now, Feeling is All, Instant Gratification, Lack of personal Accountability, it is Culture of Anomie. With the pervasive use of 'memory holes' by both PC. Gestapo Mainstream Media and neo-Fascists Activists on the Internet, the Anomie Values is now challenging the traditional Culture of Excellence and Judeo-Christian American Values.

Déjà vu: This is not a New Story

Interestingly from a different perspective, this kind of Spiritual Malaise, exemplified by the Liberal Progressives values (or rather the lack of) demanding free welfare, free healthcare, free education, etc. is not a new story.

Through human history, with unprecedented periods of peace (demise of USSR in early 90s) and pseudo-wealth (though QEs) benefiting only those in Monopolies and Activists Corporations; sloth, decadence and malaise inevitably starts to set in. For sadly, Desirable Virtues like fortitude, endurance and courage can only be brought forth through intense competition, hardship or war.

"Daring ideas are like chessmen moved forward; they may be beaten, but they may start a winning game."

- Goethe

"It has ever been my experience that folks who have no vices have very few virtues."

– President Abraham Lincoln

"A pessimist is one who makes difficulties of his opportunities and optimist is one who makes opportunities of his difficulties."

– President Harry S. Truman

Admiration of the Can-Do Spirit and Respect for the Daring

It used to be Great Daring to attempt and try new endeavors, Courage to attempt the Impossible was respected and looked up to, now it has become the ugly "leading from behind values" of the neo-democrat progressives in Mass Media, where Globalization and Big Government is a given and any attempts to try reverse the Huge Trade deficits for America is being ridiculed and mocked as 'leading to Trade Wars' and how terrible thy consequences.

We must Remember they (anomie) deride the Values of others, they frown on the Can-Do and Daring Spirit of others, for Fear of Change from their precious status quo, fear that Main Street America might succeed and start to Grow and the decadent monopolies exposed for what they truly are, that real free market competition would be re-introduced once again to invigorate the renaissance of this country once more.

The prior status-quo of a weak America, an America without growth, without free market competition, one with the largest wealth inequality suited the neo-democrat progressives just fine as they then would have more arguments for a Welfare State which would increase more Federal Funds and a bigger Cheese for them, true Problem Profiteers at heart they are.

Makes one wonder, the Traditional American Values of Growth, would we see no more?

Ode: Intimations of Immortality from Recollections of Early Childhood – By William Wordsworth

There was a time when meadow, grove, and stream,
The earth, and every common sight,
To me did seem

Apparelled in celestial light,
The glory and the freshness of a dream.
It is not now as it hath been of yore;—
Turn wheresoe'er I may,
By night or day.
The things which I have seen I now can see no more…

Many Dangers of Avarice

If something is too good to be true, it is! Remember at beginning of his chapter how Greenspan tried to financial engineer economic growth through "printing free money"? it worked for a while in 80s and 90s as the American families leveraged up and spent more thus expanding the economy then. When the Main Street's growth slowed after the initial surge of the IT Revolution in early 2000s, printing more money didn't translate into Economic growth, it created a Crony Capitalism Culture where the Wall Street is no longer correlated to Main Street growth (real economy), instead (as we shall see in chapter 7), we have the largest Income Inequality since the Great Depression, a dying middle class in America, a $ 20 Trillion debt, a broken Free Market Capitalism system, a generation of 'snowflakes' and a stagnant economy for over a decade. Worst of all, the specter of the Big State Government looming over the horizon (Obama Care, $ 3 Trillion on welfare each year, behemoth K Street staff size, etc.) Remember, one always pays the Piper! How the academia conmen and Social Media sold the snowflakes a bag of $20T debt and a bill of goods for the Book of Model Answers to Life? You cannot be conned unless you are greedy or egoistic

Con of the century, how a Nation sold its future generations for $20 trillion of Debt in return? Snowflakes have left the building with Alan the Piper

…But there's a Tree, of many, one,
A single field which I have looked upon,
Both of them speak of something that is gone;
The Pansy at my feet
Doth the same tale repeat:
Whither is fled the visionary gleam?
Where is it now, the glory and the [American] dream?

End of Book I

Chapter 6
Religious Empathy

أبو عبد الله محمد بن علي بن محمد بن عربي الحاتمي الطائي *Abū ʿAbd Allāh Muḥammad ibn ʿAlī ibn Muḥammad ibnʿArabī al-Ḥātimī aṭ-Ṭāʾī, Ibn Arabi (1165 – 1240) was greatest sufi master (Shaykh Al-Akbar) from Murcia Spain preaches that: Every single human being was a unique and unrepeatable revelation of one of God's hidden attributes, and the only God we will ever know was the Divine Name inscribed in our inmost self. This vision of a personal Lord was conditioned by the faith tradition into which a person was born. Thus, the mystic must see all faiths as equally valid, and is at home in a synagogue, mosque, temple or church, for, as God says in the Quran: "Wheresoever ye turn, there is the face of Allah."*

– Islam, Short history by Karen Armstrong

Religious Freedom, Religious Tolerance and Religious Empathy

In Chapter 4, we'd seen the separation of State and Religion ensured religious freedom in USA. Religious freedom for the individual means each person can practise his / hers own religion, there would naturally be others practising their religions; different from yours, that in turn would imply religious tolerance if we were to be in peaceful co-existence. Seems pretty simple thus far. If we try to understand the religions practised by others, that would be religious Empathy.

How is it we never hear the neo-Democrats, Politically Correct Gestapo chanting religious empathy? Always screaming religious freedom? They have only 1 perspective, their Politically Correct one; the one and only view, which is always Right! So the neo-Democrats, neo-fascists Propaganda Activists never need to empathize with anyone. No need to even chant Empathy, let alone learn nor practice empathy.

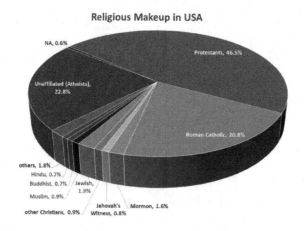

Looking at the chart above, 2 things jumped out at me, first was how small the population of Muslims in America is, only about 1% and secondly, the large unaffiliated which I would guest to be Atheists is about 22.8%. where would the atheists come from? They cannot be from Muslims or the Jews. They cannot be Communists who were not allowed to practise (at least officially) religions. Their families (parents and grandparents) must have had practiced certain religions, right? The immigrants from Latin Americas should be Catholics. Unless the new immigrants into USA stopped practising their previously held religious beliefs, I would guess that a large part of the Atheists are from families previously practising certain Judeo-Christian religious beliefs. Maybe because of lack of time (too busy) or strong influence of modern science and technology, they have over the years or generations placed less priorities in going to Church (under Sharia Law, Apostates are punishable by death).

Coming from a Multi-racial, Multi-religious, Cultural and Language society, one clearly understands the critical yet implicit responsibility of the Mainstream Media, never to rile up Religious rhetoric & emotions. Yet in recent years, in spite of the religious mix in the USA, there is such a disproportionate Media coverage on Islamophobia, outraged rhetoric about infringing on Muslim's rights, so on and forth, one might expect the Muslim population to be closer to a 15-20% (in Singapore it is about 14.3%). Judaism is double the Muslims, the Hindus and Buddhists are close behind the Muslims are 0.7% each, yet you never hear any news about infringement on Buddhists or Hindus rights?

Unlike the Judeo-Christian religion that was at the heart of the founding of this Nation, Buddhism, Hinduism, Islam, Taoism had little to do with the beginnings of America. Till the moment Cassius Marcellus Clay Jr. [Muhammad Ali] converted to Islam in 1964, one wonders how many in America had heard of nor known much about Islam. In fact, just as Taoism, Buddhism, Hinduism, most Americans probably won't know much about the history of Islam.

Understanding the Glory of Islam & its Contributions to Human Civilization

To better appreciate any civilization, we need to learn about its history, know more about both its strengths and weaknesses. Let's do a quick view of the Muslim Civilization, see their glory during the Ottoman and Mughal Empires and major contributions to the human civilization.

The Hindu–Arabic numeral system of 0 – 9, the combination and relative position of the digits to denote its value, that plus the symbol 0 was developed in Hindu subcontinent and adopted by the Arabic mathematicians in Baghdad before being spread westwards and eventually into Europe. Later on, Muslims mathematicians extended the decimal numeral system to include fractions, the decimal point notation was also introduced in the middle east region. Much of the knowledge of the ancient Greek and Romans were also adopted by, further developed in the Muslim world and protected in their libraries, which later helped sparked the Renaissance in Europe. Much of the studies in modern day science, mathematics disciplines were also developed by the Muslim world. Any words beginning with Al (The), Algebra (integral part of Mathematics), Algorithms, Alchemy (chemistry) were all pioneered by the Muslim scholars. Islamic Astronomy was already a well-developed science by 10th century, centuries ahead of anything remotely close in Europe.

The splendor of the Ottoman and Mughal Empires at their height of power and the resulting architectures remains unparalleled till this present day. A visit to the Taj Mahal in Agra, India or Sultan Ahmed Mosque (Blue Mosque) in Istanbul, Turkey would attest to that. The enlightened approach of Sultan Mehmed II in 1453 of protecting the aya sofya (Hagia Sophia) Church and converting it into a Mosque when Constantinople fell to the Ottoman Turks speaks volumes of the advanced stage of the Muslim civilization by that time. Contrast that with the sack of Jerusalem by the first Crusade in 1099, the needless killings and bloodshed of Jews, Muslims and believers of other religions by the "Christian" Knights. We see this contrast in civility again in 1189 – 1192, the third Crusade, Saladin (Ṣalāḥ ad-Dīn Yūsuf ibn Ayyūb) was much more strategic in his planning, exercised restraint and portrayed himself to be more merciful to the victims of war as compared to his European counterparts who again allowed their soldiers to indulged in looting and bloodthirsty killings of the civilian populations.

The Ottoman Empire and civilization stretched from 1282 – 1923 and had the entire middle east under its control including Turkey, Egypt, Greece, Bulgaria, Romania, Macedonia, Hungary, Palestine, Iraq, Jordan, Lebanon, Syria, Parts of Arabia, Much of the coastal strip of North Africa. It was the second longest Empire in recorded human history (over 640 years) after the Byzantine (Eastern Roman) Empire from 330 – 1453 AD

History of the Early Islamic World

In year 610 AD, Prophet Muhammad went to Mount Hira (near Mecca in modern day Saudi Arabia) to meditate, the archangel Jibrail (Gabriel) appeared to Muhammad, asked him to recite the words of Allah (God) revealed to him, which Muhammad did (114 سورة Surahs). Those recitations became the Quran (the Muslims' holy book, 86 surahs were revealed between 610-622 AD when Mohammad was in Mecca). Muhammad started sharing Allah's messages with his families and friends, his public speaking attracted large audience and the believers in Allah's message grew. The Authorities in Power in Mecca felt threatened and started to persecute Muhammad and his followers so they moved to Medina in 622 (here, the remaining 28 surahs were revealed to Muhammad)

In Medina, Prophet Muhammad followers' grew quickly in size and capability, perhaps their appeal to egalitarian principles touched a chord in life under the harsh desert conditions. 2 years later, they defeated a large Mecca army at Badr in Arabia and by 630 AD, Muhammad's forces have captured Mecca. Prophet Mohammad died in 632 AD. Unlike Jesus who lived (the man) during a time when the Roman Empire was getting consolidated under Augustus Caesar, growing in Military strength and expanding Roman presence throughout the known human world (with another 450 years before the fall of the Western Roman empire), Muhammad (the man) lived during time when the Eastern Roman Empire and the Sassanid Persian Empire were exhausting each other's waning strength through many battles and long drawn-out wars with each other. As Jesus preached love for all and early Christianity expanded without military conflict within the Roman Empire, Prophet Muhammad also preached love and equality but early Islam expanded at a Phenomenon Rate after Muhammad's death for next hundred years, largely through Military expansion (by the sword).

The process to document Allah's message (they were previously memorized and shared orally) after Muhammad's death began under Caliph Umar (ruled from 634-44) so the Quran [recitation] came about shortly after the Prophet's death. For Christianity, the attempts to select the gospels [canonical gospels] for compilation of New testament only began over 300 years after Jesus's crucifixion and subsequent resurrection. 4 canonical Gospels made it into the New Testament; Matthew, Mark, Luke and John, the rest, including the Gnostic Gospels were not sanctioned by the Roman authorities and left to the desert sands till they were discovered in 1945 in Upper Egyptian town of Nag Hammadi.

Islam, Christianity and Judaism are all monotheism, they believe in one god. Prophet Mohammad called the Christians and Jews People of the Book as he believed that God previously revealed himself to humans through other prophets like Musa (Moses) and Isa (Jesus). Muslims believe themselves to be descendants of Abraham also, through the line of Ishmael (first son of Abraham).

In Islam, there should be no image of God, the symbol; Arabic calligraphy al-ilah means The God. The Arabic calligraphy you see in the mosques are truly beautiful! There is also the traditional Muslim belief that the Temple Mount in Jerusalem (where the Al-Aqsa Mosque now stands) was Qiblah for over 13 years, from 610 CE until 623 CE (the direction that Muslims face when praying). In 624 – the Qiblah became oriented towards the Kaaba in Mecca. When Muhammad was preaching Allah's words, he was spreading Allah's message to the polytheism and idol worshippers, the people of the book were not his target audience.

Whatever Mohammad's plans were for future of Islam, on how it should be further developed and spread we'll never know. But when he died in 632AD, Muhammad had already created an extremely powerful force, a combination of religious ideals with egalitarian appeal and a strong militaristic culture. This potent mix would push aside the 2 declining Eastern Roman Empire and Sassanid Persian Empire, if you look at the map of middle east, the expansion of Islam is truly amazing, in 10 years after Muhammad left Mecca, they have conquered the entire Arabia peninsular, in 30 years of the Rashidun Caliphate (first 4 'rightly-guided' Caliphs), Islam has conquered the entire Persian empire and most of the territories Eastern Roman empire (save Anatolia). The speed was astonishing, phenomenon growth, perhaps a little too Fast!

The leadership of Islam, Muslim ummah transferred to Abu Bakr (أبو بكر عبد الله بن أبي قحافة الصديق) Mohammad's father-in-law, who continued to be both the political and religious leader. Here we take a quick recap before looking at the history of the Rashidun Caliphate, a) the political is also the religious leader; little separation of power, b) use of Military Force has allowed the growth of Islam and will continue to drive its growth over the next century, c) growth of Islam over the century will be extremely fast and d) the Quran was composed soon after Muhammad's death, all 114 Surahs were revealed to Muhammad during his lifetime.

Rashidun Caliphate الخلافة الراشدة

Starting with Abu Bakr; from 632-634 CE, Umar; from 634-644 CE, Uthman; 644-656 CE, Ali; 656-661 CE & ending with Al-Hasan ibn 'Ali in 661 CE.

Because Muhammad did not appoint his successor before he died in 632, there were a number of factions with their respective contenders. Ali was Muhammad's cousin and raised by Muhammad and his first wife Khadija, Ali married Muhammad's daughter Fatima and thus was also Muhammad's son-in-law. His supporters believe someone related to the Prophet should succeed him, they are known as Shia Muslims (party or Shia of Ali). Others contend that the Caliph should be the person most able to maintain the Sunna (teachings) of the prophet, so they are known as the Sunni Muslims. The Medinan Ansar ('helpers' to Muhammad in Medina) also debated which of them should succeed him in running, the hosts and loyal companions of Muhammad, nominated Sa'd ibn Ubadah ibn Dulaym (سعد بن عبادة بن دليم) as their candidate for the Caliphate.

A shura (consultative) council met and chose Abū Bakr 'Abdallāh bin Abī Quḥāfah aṣ-Ṣiddīq (أبو بكر عبد الله بن أبي قحافة الصديق) (Abu Bakr was Muhammad's father-in-law, father of his wife Aisha) as the 1st Caliph. He kept the entire Muslim Ummah together. 2 years later Abu Bakr died, probably from natural illness (or rumored to be poisoned). If he died from natural causes, Abu Bakr would be the only Caliph of the Rashidun Caliphate to do so. The other 3 Caliphs were all murdered. The next to succeed Abu Bakr was Umar ibn Al-Khattāb (عمر بن الخطاب), 'Umar was also Muhammad's father-in-law (father of Mohammad's wife Hafsah). Umar ruled for 10 years and led the rapid Islam territorial expansion over the Byzantine and Sassanid Persian Empires, conquering the entire Persian Empire by 643 AD. In a morning prayer session in 644, 'Umar was assassinated by a Persian slave (Piruz Nahavandi).

Uthman ibn Affan(عثمان بن عفان) also a son-in-law of Prophet Muhammad succeeded as the 3rd Caliph, under 'Uthman, the Rashidun Caliphate reached its largest territorial expansion and the Quran compilation project (initiated under 'Umar) was completed. 'Uthman was killed by protestors in 656, they broke into his house and killed him as he was reading the Quran.

The last Caliph of Rashidun Caliphate was 'Ali ibn Abi Talib(علي ابن أبي طالب), as discussed earlier, 'Ali was Muhammad's cousin and raised by him and his first wife Khadija. He is the rallying call for the Shiat Ali (Shiites) Muslims. 'Ali ruled for 5 years (Civil War broke out within the Muslim Ummah during Ali's reign) from 656 – 661 when he too was attacked and assassinated by a Kharijite while praying in the Great Mosque of Kufa, dying two days later.

الحسن ابن علي ابن أبي طالب Al-Ḥasan ibn ʿAlī ibn Abī Ṭālib (Hasan), succeed ʿAli as the second Shiʿite Imam. He abdicated after six months.

With end of the Rashidun Caliphate, the Umayyad Caliphate started under Muawiya. At this stage, we can do a quick summary of the 30 years of Rashidun Caliphate after Muhammad's death, seems like there's lots of violence, power struggles, great military success? With so much power and resources at stake, it is not difficult to imagine the power struggles, cloak and dagger intrigue. Yet even by history's standards for murders of head of states; 3 assassinations within 17 years? ¾ of the Caliphs? Why? All the factors that existed in 632AD we had summarized contributed to it. The Empire expanded too quickly, too many large and diverse groups, populations with different interests came under the Caliphs influence in a very short span of time. The early years of Islamic Empire was experiencing growing pains of its government from tribal rule into that for an Empire in a span of 30 years! Since the growth was on steroids, the growing pains followed suit. All the conflicting interests and needs of multitudes of diverse factions cannot find ways to be represented, as all the power converge into 1 person; the Caliphs (only their inner circles can reach them). If there are different leaders as Religious head, Executive branch, Legislative and Judiciary Branches [as an example], the various interest groups have a better chance of finding voices to represent them.

Since all the Caliphs believe themselves to represent Allah too, then they must be administering Allah's will on earth, what else can explain the rapid success and expansion of Islam? So, where's the justification to compromise with the diverse groups when Allah is clearly on your side. Which leaves only one avenue left for these unrepresented groups, Violence! We should also not forget the culture of Military force to further Allah's will, the jihad, the expansion of dar al-Islam (House of Islam) against the dar al-harb (House of War). If we using force to further Allah's cause is perfectly natural, why should we not use force against our enemies to further Allah's cause too?

After Prophet's Muhammad's death, the religious fervor, Ideologies that Prophet used to unite the tribes around Mecca and Medina, started to give way to the traditional tribal feuds, beginning since his death, declining rapidly and by the time of 'Ali's murder (nearly 30 years later), escalating into an all-out Power Grab on steroids as the Power and Resources at stake has increased exponentially from tiny tribes within Arabia into the largest Empire in the world since the Roman times! By the end of the Rashidun Caliphate, Religious compassion is clearly taking a backseat to the Intoxicating Effects of Power! It became increasingly obvious that Religion was just a rallying cry to expand the Umayyad Caliphate territories for additional resources and rewards for the "power hungry" Caliphs. One needn't talk about assassinating one opponent, they will kill entire families and slaughter entire tribes if needed be to stay in Power! And that's exactly what happened, with events leading up to and cumulating in Karbala, Iraq in 680 AD.

The Day of Ashura

الحسن ابن علي ابن أبي طالب Al-Ḥasan ibn 'Alī ibn Abī Ṭālib (Hasan), the elder son of 'Ali and Muhammad's daughter, Fatimah, the grandson of the Islamic Nabi (نَبِي, Prophet) Muhammad, and the 5th rightly guided Khalifah, abdicated to Muawiya of Umayyad Caliphate in 661. He lived in seclusion after that and died in 670 AD (suspected of being poisoned). Hasan was a compassionate man and he abdicated to Muawiya to end Civil war within the Muslim ummah, in the Hasan-Muawiya treaty, Hasan ibn Ali handed over power to Muawiya on the condition that; he be just to the people and keep them safe and secure, and after his death, that he does not establish a dynasty.

In 680 AD, Muawiya died and his son Yazid I took over as Caliph of the Umayyad dynasty. A number of Muslim leaders voiced their opposition, among them was Husayn ibn Ali, grandson of Muhammad and younger son of Ali. الحسين ابن علي ابن أبي طالب Al-Husayn became the Third Imam of Shi'ites after the death of his older brother, Al-Hasan, in 670 AD.

Yazid I asked for arrest of Husayn (Hussein) in order to force Husayn to pledge public allegiance to Yazid as the sole leader of the Muslim ummah. Husayn and his family escaped from Medina to Mecca. In Mecca, Husayn received word from Al-Kufah, Iraq that there are many (army of tens of thousands) awaiting him to lead a rebellion against Yazid and take his place as the rightful heir (Prophet Muhammad's grandson) to the Prophet's successor. After much deliberation, Husayn made the fateful decision, he and his family with 70 warriors left the safety of Mecca towards Al-Kufah, Iraq.

They never made it, they were intercepted by Yazid's 4000 strong army and slaughtered after being besieged for 7 days without water. Husayn's party was mostly women and children, with 70 warriors; who all rode out to meet their deaths, against an army of 4000 on the Day of Ashura. As his infant 3 month-old son was dying of dehydration, he begged his enemies to show mercy to the children, the baby was pierced with an arrow as Husayn held him aloft. Husayn himself was beheaded and head impaled on a pike and brought back to Yazid. Uncountable atrocities were committed, Husayn's remaining family (those still alive) were sold into slavery. All the corpses were left to rot until nearby villagers came out to bury them in a mass grave named Karbala ('place of trial and tribulation').

Karbala becomes the symbol for Shiites anguish at injustice till this day! The powerful graphic imagery of the legendary martyrdom of الحسين ابن علي ابن أبي طالب Husayn ibn Ali, grandson of the Prophet. With such a powerful rallying symbol even against their own Caliphs, what will they do against the Un-Islamic, Apostate Muslims? Against the جاهلية Jahiliyyah? Against the دار الحرب Dar al-Harb?

Less than 50 years after the death of Prophet Muhammad, his great grand children, entire families of his grandson was all slaughtered in cold blood, in the Caliphs' quest for Power! Those seeds of radicalism are planted less than 60 years after the beginning of Islam. Reading about the fate of Husayn ibn Ali and his family, one can feel the deep sense of injustice, even some 1300 years later. That's why the Day of Ashura as a day of remembrance can also be tapped into for much more powerful emotions against any authorities, against any enemies.

Before we continue further, let's clarify an Important fact, Extremism, Radicalism are Human Traits, they can be associated with any Religion, with any Culture. We are discussing Islamic Radicalism due to the events that has transpired in last few decades. If this had been in early 5th Century, we'll be discussing about the barbaric acts of Christian Radicals, Cyril's Parabolans in Alexandria, murdering peaceful pagans, flaying Hypatia alive with broken pieces of roof tiles.

We'll briefly highlight a few of the Islamic Faylasufs' Achievements in Falsafah, and discuss the conditions through History of Islam that led to the flourishing of great Muslim philosophies and sophisticated religious ideologies which might come in useful to help redress the current Radical religious extremism.

أبو عبد الله محمد بن علي بن محمد بن عربي الحاتمي الطائي Abū ʿAbd Allāh Muḥammad ibn ʿAlī ibn Muḥammad ibnʿArabī al-Ḥātimī aṭ-Ṭāʾī, Ibn Arabi (1165 – 1240) was greatest sufi master (Shaykh Al-Akbar) from Murcia Spain preaches that

> *Every single human being was a unique and unrepeatable revelation of one of God's hidden attributes, and the only God we will ever know was the Divine Name inscribed in our inmost self. This vision of a personal Lord was conditioned by the faith tradition into which a person was born. Thus the mystic must see all faiths as equally valid, and is at home in a synagogue, mosque, temple or church, for, as God says in the Quran: "Wheresoever ye turn, there is the face of Allah."*
>
> – Islam, A Short history by Karen Armstrong

Islam - Age of Reason

When the Culture and Traditions of Greek and Roman pagans was under attack, when the Culture of Diverse Ideologies, Skepticism & questioning was under onslaught by Blind Radical Christian Faith in early 5th century, when the libraries and museums of Alexandria were being destroyed and the knowledge, wisdom of Ancient Greece was gradually being forgotten, when Europe entered into the Dark Ages, it was the Rising Islamic Civilization that came to the rescue. In Europe, Islam carried the Torch of Human Reason for a thousand years; a period starting from the Closing of the Western Mind in 5th Century AD till the Renaissance in 15th century AD Europe.

Many scholars attribute to Muslims scholars, the preservation of the Ancient Greek works of Aristotle, Plato, Ptolemy, Euclid, etc. But it was really much more than just copying and translating books, Muslim Scholars in Cairo, Aleppo, Damascus, Isfahan, Bagdad, Cordoba, Toledo, Tunis, etc. not only kept the knowledge alive, they were practicing and further developing on those knowledge and philosophies. It was the likes of Al Farabi (872 – 950 AD), Alpharabius, Ibn Sina (980 – 1037 AD), Avicenna, Ibn Rushd (1126 – 1198 AD), Averroes that inspired European scholars and philosophers, the likes of Albertus Magnus (1200-1280 AD), Thomas Aquinas (1225 – 1274 AD), William of Ockham (1285 – 1347 AD), etc.

Ibn Khaldun's (1332 – 1406 AD) work Al-*Muqaddimah* (Introduction to History) was way ahead of its time in the understanding of societies' behavioral sciences. He emigrated to Tunisia from Spain during the Reconquista of Muslim territory in Spain (Cordoba in 1236, Seville in 1248), the last Muslim city-State of Granada was defeated in 1492, same year as Columbus' Voyage to the New World.

We'd discussed Islamic achievements in Sciences, Mathematics and Astronomy at the beginning of this chapter, in the field of Architecture, the Pointed Arch was also a gift from Islamic world to the Western architectures, you see the pointed Arch in all the Tracery with the beautiful stained glass windows of the European Cathedrals.

In fact, the birth of the beautiful Gothic Architectures; ever so representative of western civilization, really came from the Crusades' learning from the Islamic Culture & Civilizations, which was way ahead of the Europeans. Christopher Wren (architect of St Paul's cathedral in London), in his history of Westminster Abbey (1713) noted: "This we now call the Gothick manner of architecture .. tho' the Goths were rather destroyers than builders I think it should with more reason be called Saracen style.. " (Saracen, Muslims or Arabs). The Dome of the Rock completed in Jerusalem by 692 AD would go on to serve as inspiration to the Domes of St Peter's 1591 (Renaissance Style), Les Invalides 1706 (Baroque) and St Paul's 1710 (English Baroque) a thousand years later!

The *muqarnas* style Vaulting that we can see in the Seljuk's caravanserai in early 13th century (lodgings for traders with storage for their goods and stables for their animals) could later be seen integrated into the Architectural styles of the Ottomans across their Huge Empire, Safavids in Persia and Mughals in India.

Great Islamic Philosophies and Religious Insights

Through the long history of Islamic Civilizations, we can find many instances of flourishing of diverse ideologies resulting in advancements in various fields. In fact the entire period starting from the wane of the central power of the Abbasids in early 10th century till the 16th century after the establishment of the three Islamic Empires, Ottomans, Safavids and Mughals, for about 700 years, Great Cultural Cities of Learnings can be found all across the Islamic world, from Cordoba, Toledo in Spain, Tunis, Cairo, Aleppo, Damascus, Bagdad, Isfahan to Mughal India under Akbar the Great. Sufism and Falsafah (positive sciences, logic and metaphysics) would be practiced and Faylasufs (philosophers) held in the highest esteem.

It is during this time in mid-10th century that the Ismaili Fatimids established themselves in Cairo (al-Qahira, the victorious) ruling over North Africa, Syria, most of Arabia and Palestine. While in Iraq, Iran and Central Asia the Amirs (Turkish army officers) seized power and setup their independent states, still acknowledging the Abbasid Caliph as supreme leader of the ummah. Remember the Optimal-fragmentation Model that Jared Diamond described? Similar conditions existed for the Islamic civilization then, for even as the Seljuk Turks came to power from mid-11th century till early 13th century before the Mongols appeared on the scene, the religious power of the caliphate had remained balanced by the separate powers of the political rulers.

The Mongols introduced the Military Style efficient bureaucracy government to the Muslims but no religious doctrines of their own, in fact, the Mongols were tolerant to diverse religions and most of them converted to Islam. Later as the Mongol power started to weaken in the 15th century, the 3 successor Empires of the Ottomans, Safavids in Persia and Mughal in India all adopted the Military Style Efficient Bureaucracy government. We'll trace chronologically a number of the great Faylasufs and their philosophies.

As in the subsequent, European Age of Enlightenment later, there was No contradiction between the Islam religion and Falsafah (Philosophy and Intellectual Reasoning), they seek Enlightenment in Sufism that they practice and Intellectual Reason in Falsafah. Faylasuf Abu Ali Ibn Sina of Persia (Avicenna to the West) and Faylasuf Abu al-Walid Ahmad ibn Rushd of Spain (Averroes to the West) helped inspire the renaissance of skepticism towards blind religious faith in Medieval Europe.

In Aleppo, Yahya Suhrawardi of Persia (1154 – 1191) founded the school of illumination Al-ishraq, saw true philosophy as a marriage between disciplined training of the intellect through Falsafah and internal transformation of the heart by practice of Sufism, reason and mysticism go hand in hand and both are essential in the seeking of the Truth.

Spanish theosopher Muid ad-Di Ibn Al-Arabi (1165 – 1240) urged Muslims to discover *alam al-mithal* (active imagination) within themselves, everyone should look for the symbolic and hidden meaning of the scripture. Muslims should train their imagination to see below the surface (beyond the material world) to the sacred presence residing all around them. Since every single human being was a unique and unrepeatable revelation of one of God's hidden attributes, and the only God we will ever know was the Divine Name inscribed in our inmost self. This vision of a personal Lord was conditioned by the faith tradition into which a person was born. Thus, the mystic must see all faiths as equally valid, and is at home in a synagogue, mosque, temple or church, for, as God says in the Quran: "Wheresoever ye turn, there is the face of Allah." This view aligns with the Quranic belief that one God could reveal himself in any rightly guided religion.

> *"Rivers, ponds, lakes and streams - they all have different names, but they all contain water. Just as religions do - they all contain truths."*
>
> - Muhammad Ali

عصبيّة

From Tunis, Abd al-Rahman ibn Khaldun (1332 - 1406), Ibn-Khaldun wanted to discover the underlying causes of this change. He was probably the last great *Spanish Faylasuf*, his great innovation was to apply the principles of philosophic rationalism to the study of history, hitherto considered to be beneath the notice of a philosopher, because it dealt only with transient, fleeting events instead of eternal truths. But Ibn-Khaldun believed that beneath the flux of historical incidents, universal laws governed the fortunes of society. He believed that it was a strong sense of group solidarity عصبية *(asibiyyah)* that enabled a people to survive and, if conditions were right, to subjugate others....

His masterpiece *Al-Maqaddimah*; an introduction to History, was widely read by later Muslim Empire builders and also 19th century Western historians Ibn-Khaldun as a pioneer of their scientific study of history. Ibn Khaldun uses the term Asabiyyah to describe the bond of cohesion among humans in a group forming community. The bond, Asabiyyah, exists at any level of civilization, from nomadic society to states and empires. Asabiyyah is most strong in the nomadic phase, and decreases as civilization advances. As this Asabiyyah declines, another more compelling Asabiyyah may take its place; thus, civilizations rise and fall, and history describes these cycles of Asabiyyah as they play out.

Ibn Khaldun argues that each dynasty (or civilization) has within itself the seeds of its own downfall. He explains that ruling houses tend to emerge on the peripheries of great empires and use the much stronger `asabiyya present in those areas to their advantage, in order to bring about a change in leadership. This implies that the new rulers are at first considered "barbarians" by comparison to the old ones. As they establish themselves at the center of their empire, they become increasingly lax, less coordinated, disciplined and watchful, and more concerned with maintaining their new power and lifestyle at the centre of the empire—i.e, their internal cohesion and ties to the original peripheral group, the `asabiyya, dissolves into factionalism and individualism, diminishing their capacity as a political unit. Thus, conditions are created wherein a new dynasty can emerge at the periphery of their control, grow strong, and effect a change in leadership, beginning the cycle anew.

Ibn Khaldun also further states in the Muqaddimah that "dynasties have a natural life span like individuals", and that no dynasty generally lasts beyond three generations of about 40 years each. In the first generation, the people who established the civilization are used to "privation and to sharing their glory (with each other); they are brave and rapacious. Therefore, the strength of group feeling continues to be preserved among them". In the second generation, when the dynasty moves from "privation to luxury and plenty", the people "become used to lowliness and obedience ... But many of the old virtues remain" and they "live in hope that the conditions that existed in the first generation may come back, or they live under the illusion that those conditions still exist." By the third generation, the people have forgotten the period of toughness "as if it had never existed ... Luxury reaches its peak among them, because they are so much given to a life of prosperity and ease. They become dependent on the dynasty ... Group feeling disappears completely. People forget to protect and defend themselves and to press their claims ... When someone comes and demands something from them, they cannot repel him."

Ibn Khaldun's work on social dynamics, organizational alignment and Institutional Learning is truly incredible as it was nearly eight centuries ahead of its time, his family emigrated from Spain and settled in Tunis. "when there is an entire alteration of conditions, it is as if the whole creation had changed and all the world had been transformed, as if there were a new creation, a rebirth, a world brought into existence anew." Ibn Khaldun reflected on his experience.

صدرالمتألهين Mulla Sadra (1571 – 1640) founded school of philosophy and spirituality in Isfahan linking both disciplines, teaching that a philosopher should be rational, scientific yet be able to cultivate imaginative and intuitive approach to seek the truth. Arguing religious intolerance as a perversion of Islam, Truth shouldn't be imposed by force and intellectual conformism was incompatible with true faith. *Al-Afsan al-Arbaah* (the fourfold journey), Mulla Sadra described how a Leader should divest himself of Ego, receive divine illumination before he starts to transform the mundane world linking political reform to spirituality. Ayatollah Khomeini was deeply influenced by Mulla Sadra's teachings.

In India, Akbar (1542 – 1605) brought the Moghul Empire to its peak in India in an environment of diverse religions (Hindus, Buddhists, Jains, Jews, Christians, Zoroastrians, Sunni Muslims, Ismailis, etc.). the Faylasuf King (who's own bent towards Sufism and Falsafah) created his own Sufi-order stressing Divine monotheism (Tawhid-e ilahi), expressing the Sufi Ideal of sulh-e kull (Universal peace) and mahabbat-e kull (Universal love)

Through these Faylasufs of great intellect spanning vast stretches of time and geography, we can glean two time-tested concepts [powerful insights] that was handed down from the Greeks Philosophers to the Islamic Faylasufs and later to the Scientific Philosophers of the Enlightened Age of Europe. If we were to also observe the Chinese Philosophers between the Spring Summer and later Warring States, you'll also see similar trends too.

First, there is no contradiction between Religion, Philosophy and Science reasoning or logic (perceived contradictions are due to our own lack of understanding which would be subsequently resolved by i) advancement of human knowledge, ii) deeper insights into our religious interpretations, either would be opportunities to better ourselves). Second, Allah (God) reveals himself to all rightly guided Religions, only humans might call him by different names.

Times and Conditions that allow for blooming of Philosophical, Religious Diversity and Sophistication

The societies fostering growth of Ideologies are stable, successful and exudes self confidence in their accomplishments, when there isn't an overwhelming Consolidation of Power. Such conditions exists when there's a separation of Religious and Political Powers, when there's many separate independent political units as during the weakened political power of the Abbasid Caliph, Decentralized Seljuks under Vizier Nizamulmulk, or various ghazi warrior leaders running their respective amirates under the Mongols. Or as in Spain from weakening of Umayyad till end of Reconquista 1492, or as Mughal India under Akbar when the diversity of multiple religions also brought forth the Tolerance of Diversity of Ideologies.

Next, we explore the individual Faylasufs' personal traits (as compared to the Religious Zealots seeding the Radical Ideologies), they are optimistic, positive in personal attitudes like Ibn-Khaldun. Most of them are cross-discipline trained with great knowledge in Sciences, Mathematics, Philosophies and Religious texts (as opposed to being confined to only Religious study). Their ideologies enjoy interactive feedback in two ways. First, positive and constructive discussions to refine and challenge their ideas with others (like Select Society, Republic of Letters, etc. of the later Age of Enlightenment). Second and even more importantly, they have avenues to contribute certain degree of positive influence on their societies with their writings; with Progress, they can see Hope (which starts forming a virtuous cycle).

Later in the chapter, as we continue to trace the growth of the Radical Ideology, we will see a stark contrast between these two branches in Ideologies. The radical religious theologians are every bit as intellectually powerful, their grasp of religious concepts as strong as the Faylasufs we'd just observed. But the times they lived under were much bleaker for the Muslim society, during rise of British dominance in India with the Mughals decline or later the same can be said in the Middle East, Egypt, Jordan, Syria, Palestine, etc. with rise of Western Influence there after end of the Ottoman Empire.

> *"Terrorists are not following Islam. Killing people and blowing up people and dropping bombs in places and all this is not the way to spread the word of Islam. So people realize now that all Muslims are not terrorists."*
>
> - Muhammad Ali

Modern History of Middle East; Seeds of Radicalism

Not all seeds grow into trees, as a matter of fact, most never do. They just have the potential to do so, they need the necessary conditions. Temperature, moisture, air, and light conditions must be correct for seeds to germinate, you'll also need a common Enemy, a strong Motivational Force that resonates, able leadership to a) weaponized ideologies and b) provide training, means.

When most Americans think of Radical Islamic Terrorism, they might think of Islamic terrorists' attacks against Western societies. Yet for most of Islamic long history till date, there was no motivation to attack westerners, let alone civilians. There was no reason for any Muslims to do so.

When did the roots of anti-Western sentiments start to take roots and how did the religious ideologies become weaponized against the western societies and later civilians? Some pseudo-scholar politician gave the Medieval Crusades as the reason why the Muslims hated the Europeans. That's a load of baloney, the first Crusade was from 1096-1099, that's over 900 years ago. Many events that came after had demonstrated this statement to be nothing but widely publicized Ignorance. When Saladin (Ṣalāḥ ad-Dīn Yūsuf ibn Ayyūb) صلاح الدين يوسف بن أيوب retook Jerusalem from the Crusader knights in 1187 after 88 years of Christian control, there was no crazy massacre of the Christians in Jerusalem. When Sultan Mehmed II محمد ثانى conquered Constantinople in 1453, he didn't go on an extermination of the Christians or destruction of Christian architecture. The reality is that in both those instances, the civilization, organizational skills, the strategic thinking of the Muslims were ahead of their opponents and their ability to overcome them was a matter of time, patience and careful Strategic planning. There was no need for radical and blood thirsty behavior.

To get a quick understanding of the Modern History of Middle East, let's start with T.E.

Lawrence and the Arab Revolt. Not the Arab Spring that started in Dec 2010 in Tunisia. The Arab Revolt (1916-1918) in WWI that eventually toppled the Ottoman Empire in 1923 (which had survived for nearly 650 years). The irony was that the British and French were on the same side as the Arabs Muslims and supported them in their fight against the Ottoman Turkish Muslims. (so where's the "deep hatred of Christians since the Crusades"). Sadly, after the initial "success" of toppling the Ottoman Empire (the British had achieved their aim, together with their allies; including the French, they had emerged as victors of the WW I conflict), the British never lifted up to their end of the bargain to the Arabs.

The British needed to reconcile between taking care of the Russian's, French's interests (both their allies), the Arabs' interests, British's own interests and also learn, understand the complexity and Diversity of Middle East that the Rashidun Caliphate was faced with nearly 1280 years ago. The Religious diversity; Sunni Muslims, Shiite Muslims, Christianity, Judaism, Greek Orthodox, etc. You layer the racial and Ethnicity dimensions on top of that, the British Foreign Office and diplomats didn't have much of a chance. They also missed the opportunity to have a Jewish State setup in Middle East with a supportive Arab Leadership in form of Emir Feisal, son of Sharif Hussein of Mecca, both key Leaders in the Arab Revolt. Or did they? Did the British Foreign Office make "mistakes" in handling the designation of territories from the old Ottoman empire?

Unlike their American counterpart, the State Department, which took over the world center-stage only after second World War, the British Foreign Office had already been at its game for nearly 300 years leading up to WW I. In 1916, while bank rolling and supplying the Arab forces under Emir Feisal (T. E. Lawrence actually participated and commanded Arab troops together with Feisal in the Aqaba campaign), with limited use of British troops, the British also met up secretly with Russian and French diplomats to divide up the Arab lands amongst themselves. This document became known as the Sykes-Picot Agreement. Sharif Hussein (Feisal's father) had agreed to help the British overthrow the Ottomans based on British's promise to support establishment of local Arab governments afterwards. The British even had a signed agreement [Hussain-McMahon's correspondence] with Sharif Hussein and Emir Feisal of which they would not keep to the Arabs, for their need to keep their WW I allies happy and their National Interests of ensuring Oil supply for its Industries and modernization meant their promises to the Arabs will have to take a back seat.

In Nov 1917, the Arabs learnt of the Sykes-Picot agreement from the Turks. The Bolsheviks had just overthrown the Russian Czar and publicly released the agreement. The Turks wanted to reveal the underhanded conduct of the British to their Arab allies in hope breaking that alliance, yet the Arabs remained loyal to their agreement and fought out the last year of the war against the Ottomans, continued allied with the British.

Aftermath of the Arab Revolt, from Ottoman vilayets to League of Nations' Mandates

As the Qing 清Dynasty (1644-1911) was dying in China, China was the sick man of Asia to the Western powers, the dying Ottoman Empire (1256-1923) was the sick man of Europe. With the loss of territories due to Arab revolt, being on the losing side of WW I, it was just a matter of time before the end of the Ottoman Empire, the signing the Treaty of Sevres in 1920 by Sultan Mehmed VI certainly didn't help. (notice the last Byzantine Emperor was Constantine XI when Constantinople fell to Sultan Mehmed II? Guess naming after your Great ancestors doesn't confer their Values, Experience and Insights to oneself, nor able to help halt the eventual decline and ending to in their empire's histories; we see this common theme of subsequent ruling generations grasping at the form (mere procedures) and missing out on the substance in a vain attempt to emulate their ancestors of past glorious eras.

The Sultan, by agreeing to the severe terms of the treaties, (renouncing claims to all non-Turkish territories, demobilize their armies, create an Independent Armenia, an "autonomous" Kurdistan under British control, Greece would exercise control over Aegean islands in Dardanelles, the straits between Mediterranean Sea and Black Sea would become open to public shipping), lost all semblance of respect left for the Sultanate and created huge opposition within his "remaining Empire".

Mustafa Kemal Ataturk, already a highly respected Military leader [from his victories in Gallipoli], refused to de-mobilize the troops, setup the Turkish National Assembly that refused to ratify the treaty of Sevres, launched the Turkish National Movement that led to the Turkish War of Independence. After 2 years, all the foreign armies were defeated; including the Armenians, Greeks and the French. The Brits and their allies signed a new Treaty of Lausanne in 1923 with Ataturk's Ankara government, and the Sultanate was no more. The new treaty was much more favorable to Turkey, ending all capitulations to Europe started since 1500s, no European sphere of influence in Turkey, no independent Armenia nor autonomous Kurdistan but the British and French get to keep their control in Iraq and Syria and Turkey gets recognition as Independent Nation!

League of Nations (newly formed after WW I, for promoting peace through international cooperation) was responsible for deciding what happens to all the territories renounced by Turkey (no more Ottoman). Article 22 of the Covenant, put forward by the League of Nations in 1919, essentially proposed a Mandate System for transferring control of these areas previously under Ottoman Rule, the idea behind this Mandate is that these previously Ottoman territories are not yet capable of independent statehood and therefore should be entrusted to the supervision of "advanced nations" to responsibly administer the territories on behalf of the league until the people of these territories had developed sufficiently to govern themselves. Whatever kernel of truth in the Arab's lack of experience in self-government, it is also an extremely politicized Mandate against the Arabs.

Luckily for Americans, there was no League of Nations to settle the dispute between the 13 colonies and the British Crown in 1776, otherwise the colonies would be put under supervision of "Advanced Nations", as they were not yet capable of independent statehood. There will be no declaration of independence, no constitution, no USA. The League of Nations is also a sham, it is just a political crony to the larger Powers behind the screen, just as the United Nations, IMF, World Bank, etc. are now all cronies to the real Powers, where the money is, the Wall Street

Suzerains. The League did such a stupendous job promoting world peace that WW II followed right on the heels of WW I, just 20 years later.

The Ottoman Empire was divided up in early 1920s, the Mandates were agreed by the Allied Powers at San Remo, Italy in 1920 and then confirmed later by League of Nations. Syria and Lebanon went to France, Palestine to the British, Mesopotamia (Iraq) to British, with a responsibility to create a Jewish national home in Palestine. As for Sharif Hussein and Emir Feisal, they had the short end of the stick, their army raised in attempt to become King of Syria was crushed by the French at the battle Maysalun in 1920. By 1925, the Saud family had defeated the other 2 major Arab powers in Arabian peninsula, the Rashid family and Hashemites (Sharif Hussein of Hejaz province; comprising both Medina & Mecca), entered Mecca and expelled Sharif Hussein. The British agree to offer Trans-Jordan and Iraq to two sons of Sharif Hussein as partial fulfillment of the spirit of the Hussein-McMahon correspondence, the Hashemites rule Jordan till this day.

Emir Feisal ascend to throne of Iraq in 1921 with British support, hoping to rule through him. Iraq is a new political entity that comprises of 3 former Ottoman vilayets; Basra, Mosul & Baghdad. The Religious, ethnic, social, sectarian divisions that the British would have had leveraged (pitting one against the other) to control the much larger local population as they had so effectively pulled off in India for about 350 years, became a challenge for King Feisal trying to build Iraq into a single independent Nation. The fact that Feisal wasn't a native of Iraq didn't help, coupled all these problems with the British wish to exert its influence in Iraq made the 12 year rule a constant struggle for Feisal. He died in 1933 from ill health and exhaustion at age of 50.

This is where the Western influence starts to take on the Face of the Enemy. In the past, the Sultan of the Ottoman Empire is the Caliph, now no more Sultan, the French control Lebanon, Syria, the British control Iraq, Palestine, Trans-Jordan and Egypt.

Prior to the arrival of the Western Powers, Mecca and Medina were under the protection of the Ottoman Caliph, this was an interesting political, religious arrangement between the Sharif of Hejaz (province covering Medina and Mecca) and the Sultan of the Ottoman Empire since 1517, as long as the Sharif acknowledged the Ottoman Sultan as Caliph, the Sultan has claim over all the Muslim lands, in return, provides "protection" over ولاية الحجاز Hejaz vilayet and leaves it relatively autonomous.

Now this equation has also changed. The British and French are not even Muslims, they belong to the دار الحرب Dar al-Harb (House of War), the British and French are out for their own interests and subordinates the Arab's interests, so there's a common enemy and a strong Motivation now too. The Weaponization of the Religious Ideologies into Religious Radicalism is an interesting study of the works of Islamic scholars and activists.

جاهلية Jahiliyyah, تكفيري Takfirism, دار الحرب Dar al-Harb; Rise of Radical Ideologies

History is a continuous flow, experiences of individuals under certain conditions, in particular physical locations and junctures of history produces new ideologies which in turn will shape future history. Since they are all inter-twined, the chronological time clock can be transcended by ideas. Scholars can reach back into the past to learn past ideologies that's faded into obscurity, revise and re-vitalize them for new consumption. With the new "colonial" administration of the Muslim lands of Egypt, Syria, Palestine, Iraq, Jordan, Lebanon, etc. there would be much frustrations, anger and even hatred against these western powers, ideologies of Jihads, Dar al-Harb, Takfirism, Jahiliyyah, etc. any of which can be easily revived to serve current needs. Let's spend some time to understand more.

		Mughal Empire	1526-1857		
		Babur	1526-1530		
		Humayun	1530-1540		
			1555-1556		
British India	1612-1947	Akbar	1556-1605		
		Shan Jahan	1627-1658		
East India Company (EIC)	1612-1757	Aurangzeb	1658-1707	**Maratha Empire**	1674-1818
Company Rule in India	1757-1858				
British Raj	1858-1947			Chhatrapati	
British Rule in Burma	1824-1948			Shivaji	1674-1680
Princely States	1721-1949			Raja Pratap Singh	1808-1818
Partition of India	1947			Raja of Satara	
				Peshwa	
				Moropant Pingle	1674-1689
				Baji Rao II	1803-1818

The Mughal Empire ruled over the Indian sub-continent from 1526-1748 (finally dissolved 1857), they were Muslims while the main religion in India has traditionally be Hinduism. As early as 1600s the British started to take a strong interest in India with setup of East India Company (EIC).

The last strong Mughal Aurangzeb (his father Shah Jahan built the Taj Mahal) died in 1707, the empire started its long decline. قطب الدين أحمد ولي الله بن عبد الرحيم العمري الدهلوي Shah Waliullah Dehlawi (1703-1762) witnessed the decline of Islam amidst environment of growing British influence, the main religion in Indian; Hinduism was starting to regain popularity as the ruling Mughals' power weakens. New ideas as Capitalism and Free Trade are introduced. Dehlawi sees a similarity to جاهلية Jahiliyyah, the time before Islam was revealed by Muhammad and there was multi religions and ideologies. He proposed that moving away from Islam core religious beliefs has caused the declined in Islamic Culture and Civilization so Dehlawi calls for bringing the core tenets of Islam back to forefront of dawa (Proselytizing and religious education), goal is to purify Islam and bring it back to "basics" (ignorance of Allah leads to the ills suffered by Muslims all around the world). Islam needs to be purged of جاهلية Jahiliyyah; pagan ignorance just as Muhammad had previously purged Mecca by Force.

These "purifying" themes would merge with earlier concepts by Ibn Taymiyya of تكفيري **Takfirism**, "ex-communicating" another Muslim unilaterally, just by declaring him/her to be un-Islamic, an Apostate! Two Powerful pieces of Ideologies coming together.

You might also notice that Indian Islamic scholars Activists have been working on their ideologies earlier than their Egyptian, Jordanian, Saudi counterparts. The Islamic scholars' encounters with the British occurred much earlier in Indian in 17th Century versus the 20th Century for Middle East scholars.

ابو الاعلى مودودى Syed Abul A'la Mawdudi (1903-1979) is also another Indian Islamist scholar, founder of Jamaat e Islami (largest Islamic organization in Asia), his work led to establishment of Pakistan in 1947, as separate from India, when the British Raj was dissolved. This is what Mawdudi taught ".. everything in the universe is 'Muslim' for it obeys Allah by submission to His laws..".

In the eyes of Mawdudi and the faith of Jamaat e Islami; Islam is not a 'religion' in the sense this term is commonly understood. It is a system encompassing all fields of living. Islam means politics, economics, legislative, science, humanism, health, psychology and sociology. The believer must be a 'slave of Allah', with 'absolute obedience to Allah' representing a 'fundamental right' of the creator, since the believer does 'not have the right to choose a way of life for himself'.

Muslim Brotherhood, Rise of the Islamists

حسن أحمد عبد الرحمن محمد البنا Hasan Al-Banna (1906-1949) was an Egyptian watch-maker, school teacher, widely read and self-taught religious activist. He was also the founder of Muslim Brotherhood, killed by Egyptian secret police in 1949. سيد قطب Sayyid Qutb (1906-1966) also an Egyptian writer and the Muslim Brotherhood strategist. Sayyid Qutb internalized the teachings of Mawdudi and Dehlawi's Jahiliyyah جاهلية, he then built on these and added the idea of not just going after the un-Islamic, Apostate Arab Leaders to be the targets of his Muslim Brotherhood, but also going after their puppet masters in America as well. He was able to form these ideas as he was invited to United States after the second world war, after living in USA for 2 years, he wrote Milestones (an influential work on Global jihadism and essential text for Al-Qaeda and other jihadists groups) in 1964 when he was imprisoned on charges for plotting assassination of Egyptian President Nasser.

To Qutb, Islam was a universal system offering the only true form of freedom: freedom from governance by other men, man-made doctrines, or "low associations based on race an color, language and country, regional and national interests". Islam's modern mission, in Qutb's view, was to overthrow them all and replace them with what he took to be a literal, eventually global implementation of the Quran. The culmination of this process would be "the achievement of the freedom of man on earth, all of mankind throughout the earth." This would complete the process begun by the initial wave of Islamic Expansion between 7th – 8th century, the first 100 years that we had witnessed earlier in this chapter.

مجاهدين The Mujahideen, Islamic Patriots that defeated the Evil Empire

عبد الله يوسف عزام Abdullah Yusuf Azzam (1941-1989) was a Jordanian cleric, theologian and father of Modern Jihad. Azzam achieved a number of feats that his scholar predecessors didn't and couldn't accomplished. Azzam wasn't just intelligent, knowledgeable and articulate as all the other scholars, he was also a great leader of men, organizer, motivator and most important, practical man of action. All the great literature is good reading material, but how to make it into reality? Azzam made all the pieces come together and added a couple more of the missing pieces to transform modern jihad into a reality!

Soviet Union invaded Afghanistan in Dec 1979, مجاهدين The Mujahideen became a powerful symbol worldwide for resistance against the Russians. Also, Jihad would no longer only be self-strive for personal betterment, against cultural or political influence but it now means full scale military war. The local Afghan Guerrilla tribal Mujahideen warriors would bear the blunt of the resistance over the next 10 years till eventual Soviet withdrawal in 1989, international support was also forthcoming, especially from USA as this was still in the heights of the cold war. Stinger Missiles, financial support, you name it. USA was on the side of the Mujahideen, they were patriots defending their homeland, for most part all true.

Azzam introduced 2 new concepts that connected all the previous ideas together into a working model (like pieces of a puzzle). First a) jihad went from local to Global. Prior to Azzam, jihad movements tend to be local Muslims protecting their own territories. Azzam made the call to jihadists all around the world to join the afghan Muslim brothers fight the Soviets. He was persuasive enough to make it happen and delivered on Global Branding of Jihad in support of Afghan's resistance against the Soviet Union's invasion. Secondly b) he also by-passed the traditional requirement that a holy war has to be declared by the legitimate authority of a caliph by redefining Military resistance as an individual's duty!

Azzam issued a Fatwa: Defense of the Muslim Lands,

> *If a piece of Muslim land the size of a hand-span is infringed upon, then jihad becomes a personal obligation on every Muslim male and female, where the child shall march forward without the permission of its parents and the wife without the permission of the husband.*

He also quoted the Koran, chapter 9, verse 39

> *If you march not forth, he will punish you with a painful torment and will replace you with another people, and you cannot harm Him at all, since Allah is able to do all things.*

Azzam was so successful in his redefinition of Jihad in the political and geostrategic environment of the cold war that Jihad was widely accepted, and even viewed very positively by the Western Media. I can clearly remember the mujahideen branded as patriots fighting for their homeland message in mid-eighties, lionized all around the world on Newsweek and Time covers.

Azzam was also the teacher and mentor of Osama bin Laden and persuaded bin Laden to come to Afghanistan and help the jihad, he knew of Osama's ability to help secure funding for the jihad movement and also skills to move those funds around the world with his Saudi background and global contacts. Azzam was killed in 1989 in Pakistan and the leadership of the Al-Qaeda plus 55,000 warriors resources from the Arab Mujahideen Services Bureau passed on to Osama bin Laden.

Osama made one addition to the Jihad movement, he started using it against civilian targets, women and children. There were a number of attacks against WTC, NY in 1993, USS Cole, etc. But it was on Sept 11 2001, the entire World took notice. Now we ask ourselves, the Religious Radicals are against the Western world, especially the British and French for intrusion into Muslim homelands after 1920s, ok we can understand, but why USA?

Beginning of American Entanglements (I)

Let's list the more recent major events that USA has engaged with the middle east region, with benefit of hindsight 20/20, add some comments to those engagements.

1979 Iranian Hostage Crisis, this toppling of the American backed Shah and capture of American hostages was a definite blow to American's standing in the Middle East. 1983 Bombing of USA & French Peacekeeping forces in Beirut, Lebanon led by Hezbollah, Iran, and Syria is part of accelerating trend of terrorist acts against western forces in Muslim homeland.

1991 Gulf War after Iraq's invasion of Kuwait, this must be the last war led by USA with strong World support including large Coalition force comprising of several major Muslim countries against Iraq; the likes of Saudi Arabia, Egypt, Syria, Morocco, Kuwait, Oman, Pakistan, UAE, Qatar, Bangladesh, etc. Besides the wisdom of building the large coalition force with major Muslim Powers co-leading the expulsion of Iraq from Kuwait (another Muslim country), President H.W. Bush also made the wise decision to leave Saddam Hussein in power as a counter-balance force to Iran in the Middle-East! This decision was viewed by many back home as 'not finishing' the job and leading to the 2003 Invasion of Iraq by 43rd President George W. Bush (his son). Again, with hindsight 20/20, the Invasion of Iraq in 2003 had subsequent World-Wide consequences!

There was one other minor detail that resulted from the 1991 Gulf War, when the Saudi Royalty decided to go with the USA led coalition instead of relying on Osama bin Laden's offer of help with his Al-Qaeda fighters, it focused Osama on USA as the Great Satan as Al-Qaeda's biggest enemy. To Osama, the invasion of Muslim holy land (in this case Iraq) by so many American troops was unconscionable (to Osama's personal ego) and must be punished for their acts against Allah! That brand of thinking led to the 9/11 attacks in 2001 against America destroying the World Trade Centers in New York and damaging the Pentagon in DC. The heroic acts of passengers on board United Flight 93 prevented further deaths and destruction.

2001 Invasion of Afghanistan in retaliation of 9/11. The US Intelligence had correctly traced the attacks to Al-Qaeda and Osama bin Laden who was in Afghanistan and backed by the Taliban regime there. We need to remember that while the majority of the World sympathized with America over the 9/11 attacks, there's a part of the Muslims population all around the world including in America, who rejoiced at the results of the attacks, they probably saw it as retribution for years of intervening in the Middle East affairs, this is also true in South East Asian Muslim countries too. In less than one month after the attack on America, Operation Enduring Freedom was launched on 7 October 2001 together with the United Kingdom, this time there was no large Coalition force, let alone Muslim countries forces but wait, there is support from Northern Alliance forces. The Afghan Northern Alliance was setup in 1996 against the Taliban with allies like Iran, Turkey, Tajikistan, Russia, India (as Taliban was backed by Pakistan), Uzbekistan, United States (after September 11, 2001) & Turkmenistan). Iran (Shiites) furthering their self-interests, supported the Afghan Northern Alliance against Taliban and Al-Qaeda (Sunnis).

The countries with USA in Operation Enduring Freedom are UK, Australia, Germany, Canada, and the Northern Alliance. The result, the Taliban government (supported by Pakistan and Saudi Arabia) was toppled and Al-Qaeda moved from their bases in Afghanistan. USA achieved their objectives but this wasn't as well received by the rest of world nor as successful as the Gulf War '91. Till this day, America is still engaged in Afghanistan which is bad optics and one more pathetic excuse for the Radical Islamic Terrorists to target civilians all around the world. The British practice of working with Arabs Muslims leveraging their self-interests against the Turks Muslims in WWI seems a superior strategy.

Upsetting the Balance of Power in Middle East, 2003

President George W. Bush 43rd received intelligence that Saddam Hussein had weapons of mass destruction that threatened world peace and needed to be dealt with. This led to the 2003 Invasion of Iraq in search of weapons of Mass destruction.

Looking back, this is a big lose lose for America and the World and the Iraqi People too. USA ended with a huge debt from financing the war with nothing to show for it, except causing military power imbalance in Middle East leaving Iran now as the most powerful Nation there. Iraq entered into chaos with the collapse of Saddam's government and USA subsequently entered into an ill-conceived Nation-building strategy in Iraq? Iraq is an example of poor strategic decision making about Foreign Affairs, as a knee-jerk reaction to domestic public opinion drummed up by the Progressive Media and Press. Yet, the all 'too-real' resulting civil wars, slaughter and instability in Middle East surely does the world no favors. The 2007 troop surge in Iraq was a good move towards stabilizing the situation there but an expensive one for America.

Arab Spring started in Tunisia in Dec 2010, subsequently we saw sporadic and haphazard USA's involvements (always reactive); in Egypt, Libya, Iraq, Iran and Syria [look at Chart A]. Let's briefly discuss some of the more Strategic countries with impacts to USA and rest of the world. America didn't start the Uprisings, some might make the (weak) argument that spread of democratic values via the internet, could be traced to America. We'll visit the Arab spring in more details later. For now, let's look at the impact [from USA's perspective] on some of the Major Middle East countries and what USA did or didn't do in the most critical junctures and the results of "leading from behind" or 'reactive to polls' Strategies

A)

	US Ally?	Strategic to USA?	US Action in respond to Arab Spring Uprising	Grade	The Result
Egypt	Pro-US	YES	Supported the Islamists Muslim brotherhood, and requested President Mubarak to step down	1	The Islamists lost control to Radicals, before the Egyptian Military stepped in and resume Law and Order
Libya	Neutral	NO	Actively Destabilize	2	Lapsed into ISIS and Al-Qaeda control
Syria	Anti-US	YES	Nothing, subsequently delayed response	1	Civil War till date
Iran	Anti-US	YES	Nothing in support of Pro-Democracy Demonstrations	1	Anti-American Regime remained in Power

Scale of 1 - 5, 1 Worst, 5 Best

B)

	USA	Target	ROW
1991 Gulf War	5	3	5
2001 Invasion of Afghanistan	5	3	4
2003 Invasion of Iraq	1	1	2
2010-present Arab Spring	1	1	1
2011 Withdrawal from Iraq	3	1	2

Scale of 1 - 5, 1 Bad and 5 Good

2011 Iraq withdrawal, while relatively neutral for USA, was a complete disaster for the Iraqi people, for the entire middle east region. Its effect was relatively neutral to America. USA left behind tons of military equipment (M1 Abrams Tanks, Humvees, machineguns, etc.) for our Iraqi ally government which all went into ISIS / ISIL's (Iraq's Al-Qaeda became ISIL) hands once the US troops pulled out. It also coincided with the Arab Spring with many huge Muslim countries spinning out of control into chaos. Till this day, the Syria Civil war still continues and millions of refugees are fleeing into countries all over the world as we speak. Needless to say, the scorecard for USA's performance in the Arab Spring looks terrible, but most reasonable folks would agree that America didn't start the Arab Spring.

2012 Benghazi, Libya. Compared to Egypt, Iran and Syria, Libya isn't as Strategic to the US Interests yet, USA led a NATO coalition in March 2011 to topple Muammar Gaddafi's government. As you can expect, a peace loving democratic party magically appeared and rule over Libya and the people of Libya lived happily ever after! Obviously, that didn't happen, although the snowflakes might buy it. Al-Qaeda and ISIL filled the power-vacuum when Gaddafi's regime fell, together they shared power in Libya.

On 9/11 in 2012 (11th Anniversary of terror attack on America), the Al-Qaeda led coordinated attacks on a) the US ambassador compound which they successfully breached and killed the ambassador J. Christopher Stevens and another ambassador staff. The Al-Qaeda fighters also attacked b) the CIA office and managed to kill more Americans but they never breached the CIA compound before help finally arrived. Many of the Whitehouse officials lied about the attacks and whitewashed the entire event because the US General Election was in November; instead blaming the well-planned, well-coordinated attacks by Al-Qaeda, to be a result of some anti-Islam cartoon on youtube. Great example of an Incompetent administration using the Media to cover-up it's mistakes.

This wasn't a Strategic Event but it did showcase to the world at large the corrupting influence of Power and how American's Media has become the Liberal Left's accomplice and enablers! And the sad ignorance of the snowflakes who buy into it whatever the Media has to feed them, no matter how ridiculous or absurd; An anti-Islamic cartoon on youtube leads to surgical strike by Islamic Special Forces that successful took out America's ambassador in Libya on the Anniversary of Sept 11th. Our Glorious Leadership by leading from behind, missed out on the Democratic Revolutions in Iran and Syria, enabling the rebels to be crushed by the totalitarian forces… oops, never mind the last sentence

Let's review table B, is a quick summary of The Major Wars & Events in Middle East with USA involvement, from the Multiple perspective of USA, of the Target country (people of country, not regime in Power) & the Rest of the World. Scale of 1 – 5, 1 is Bad and 5 is Good,

The '91 Gulf war was relatively neutral to the entire population of Iraq, it wasn't great for Saddam's regime but they recovered to rule for another 12 years till 2003 when USA invaded again. Overall the 41ˢᵗ President did well. The 2001 invasion of Afghanistan in retaliation to the 9/11 attacks could be sympathized with by most non-Muslims countries. The Afghan people also relatively neutral as it was the Taliban regime that was targeted by the Americans. The invasion of Iraq was bad judgement (remember we have hindsight 20/20), lose lose for all. The "Polling reactive" Strategy was bad for all when the events for Arab spring unfolded. As discussed earlier, withdrawal from Iraq was neutral for USA but bad for the Iraqis and rest of middle east and subsequently rest of the world too.

The report card over last 4 decades of the American Leadership's Foreign Policies doesn't look stellar for sure, but does it warrant the killing of civilians, women and children? The radicals in Al-Qaeda, ISIL/ISIS certainly thinks it does, yet there has to be more reasons for USA to become their targets.

America's Inheritance of the Israel-Palestinian conflict, its Policy in Support of Israel (II)

The Mandate system per Article 22 of the Covenant of the League of Nations, had British oversee Palestine with the responsibility to create a "Jewish national home" there. So in 1921, the British split the territorial into Palestine (west of Jordan river) and TransJordan (78% of the land). Jews were forbidden to settle in TransJordan and thus the Jewish settlement was limited to the smaller western section, while Transjordan later became the Jordan as we know today. When the British announced its intention to withdrew from the region in 1947, UN proposed partitioning Palestine into 3 parts, Jewish, Arab and the Jerusalem portion under UN control to protect the holy site of Judaism, Christianity and Islam. The Arabs rejected the proposal (as they had rejected all previous proposals by the British for power-sharing between the Arabs and Jews in the past).

After the British withdrew, the Jewish Palestinians proclaimed the creation of a Jewish Palestinian State: State of Israel on May 14, 1948. A day later the neighboring Arab states invaded Israel with the help of Arab Palestinians already fighting the Jewish Palestinians. The Arab-Israeli War lasted 10 months, Israel on one side and the Arab league (comprising Egypt, Jordan, Iraq, Syria, Lebanon and Saudi Arabia, volunteers from Muslim lands like Yemen, Pakistan, etc.) on the other. By March 1949, Israel had defeated the Arab league and has control of most of the land of the Mandate except for Gaza strip (occupied by Egyptian Military) and West Bank (occupied by Jordanian military). This remained the case till 1967 when the 6-Day war (Egypt, Jordan, Iraq, Syria, Lebanon against Israel) broke out, at the end of which the West Bank, Gaza strip, Golan Heights of Syria and Sinai Peninsula of Egypt all came under Israel control

Last Major confrontation was between Israel and a Egypt-Syria alliance in the 1973 Yom Kippur War concluding in a UN brokered cease fire 22ⁿᵈ Oct and 25ᵗʰ Oct 1973. This battle raised tensions between US (backing Israel) and Soviets (backing Syria and Egypt), the end of which led to 1978 Camp David Accords and return of the Sinai Peninsula to Egypt. Egypt became the first Arab country to recognize the Israel State and establish peaceful and normalized relations with it. Egypt continued its drift away from the Soviet Union, left the Soviet influence and became Pro-West (pro-America) till President Obama in the 2011 Arab Spring, decided to support the Muslim Brotherhood back revolution against then Egyptian President Mubarak.

Up till 2009, America Leadership had pretty much been supportive of Israel in the Middle East conflicts against the Arabs States, after the British withdrawal. It is understandable how these actions contributed to the hate from the Arabs against USA.

This is Where I came in ... how the Liberal Media hates Israel and made the world see 'reality' through their eyes. The Media's Perception of Reality is Reality! (III)

Partly to insert their relevance (more like irrelevance), partly due to ignorance of historical context & perspective but mostly due to Greed, the self-proclaimed 'altruistic' Liberal Mainstream Media felt it is their sacred duties to protect the "weak and downtrodden" Muslims from the Evil small Satan Israel and Big Satan America, stirring up and magnifying the hatred of those in conflict in Middle East into one of Global Scale. The groundwork to painting America as the big Enemy Target for the Islamic Radical Terrorists has been laid! Fanning the Flames of Ignorance, Hatred and Ira (wrath), the Liberal Left Mainstream Media; indirectly helps and supports the Islamists rhetoric by painting Israel and America as the aggressors in Middle East.

The situation in the Middle East is already complex as it is without the additional ignorance generated by the dim-witted in Liberal Media; deleting whichever portions of history they didn't fancy into memory-holes, ensuring becomes impossible for the millennials to see reality except through the eyes of the Politically Correct Gestapo. We'll explore the details in next section, how George Soros and his henchman Jeff Sachs lobbied for Global War on Poverty after 9/11 events and pushed for support and funding to the Islamists States like Palestine Authority and Hamas in 2006.

The Global War on Poverty (IV), Great Avarice and the Biggest Ruse Ever Pulled Off, for we suffer fools all too gladly

In chapter 2, we introduced George Soros and saw how he made Billions from exploiting the International Financial Markets and its numerous loopholes and flaws in the 90s. Soros is also very good at exploiting crisis like 9/11 to push forth his personal agenda under guise of non-sequitur demagogue, to spread his radical neo-democrat ideologies through his 501c3 Activists Corporations, creates funding for his personal agendas and set the stage for future on-going exploitation of the broken and corrupted international organizations. George Soros is an intelligent and strategic man, if President Obama is the poster child (aka mouth piece) of the neo-Democrat Party, George Soros is the brains and wealth behind the foundation of neo-democrat Party (Father of the neo-Democrats)!

After betting against the British Pounds in early 90s and the Asian Developing Economies in the late 90s where Soros succeeded in causing both to collapse and making Billions for himself in the process, this is what George Soros had to say in his book, The Crisis of Global Capitalism in 1998. He "confessed" that financiers like himself were largely to be blamed, for they had allowed greed to overwhelm their humanity. ".. The (Global capitalist) system is deeply flawed,.. As long as capitalism remains triumphant, the pursuit of money overrides all other social considerations." George Soros wrote. He saw that the International Financial System had loopholes, got super rich exploiting it and then pointed out that the system needs to be fixed? Why? He lobbied for himself to head up the international bureaucratic organizations to address these issues. He was hoping that USA would also get impacted by the Asian Financial crisis as it spills over globally, that way Soros would get to change the USA Financial sphere too. But the Asian Crisis didn't impact USA as Soros expected, so he didn't get his chance then. The capital investors that were losing confidence in Asia needed to find a safe harbor, so instead of a domino effect of collapsing economies as Soros expected. The capital flight found safe harbor in the USA market and strengthened the market at home. But Soros is tenacious and will eventually get his way, and he didn't have to wait too long.

In Sept 11th, 2001 the Al-Qaeda terrorists struck America and Soros saw his new opportunity! In the midst of the chaos and sadness, George Soros pushed his narrative with United Nations, IMF (International Monetary Fund) and President Bush in the USA. He also got Laura D'Andrea Tyson (former Clinton advisor) and Jeff Sachs (formerly from Harvard University whom Soros hired) to help him further his message and "solution" to address Global Terrorism which is: Terrorism arise because of Poverty, Global corruption and weak governance arise because of Poverty! The solution is War-on-Poverty, create anti-poverty programs, setup world funds to sponsor and help the poor countries (funds to be managed and distributed by Soros and his cronies).[2] Per Soros, Tyson and Sachs, it is perfectly alright if these poor countries have corrupt governments or sponsor terrorism. If we keep giving them more money, the government will become less corrupt and the terrorist activities will stop because we have providing them so much funds! Let's take a step back and analyze their message and proposed solutions.

Terrorism doesn't arise because of poverty, there are hundreds of poor countries all around the world in Africa, Asia, Latin America, etc. you don't see all of them as terrorist countries. Radical Ideological fed by Religious extremism combined with a deep sense of Insecurity (personal inadequacies) creates vengeful streak, a lack of Empathy, lack of tolerance, yet these conditions still need a trigger event. Any events that creates a perceived sense of injustice to the "victims"; stirring up strong emotions of wrath (which the Mainstream Media constantly provides without end, ceaselessly fanning the flames of Hatred), and terrorists becomes committed once they can find the means of doing it. We can see so many cases of self-induced (home grown) terrorists in recent years.

Next, poverty doesn't cause corruption, quite the contrary, corruption causes poverty as the

---

[2] Per The Shadow Party by David Horowitz and Richard Poe, Unholy Alliance: Radical Islam and the American Left by David Horowitz, The Big Lie: Exposing the Nazi Roots of the American Left by Dinesh D'Souza

wealth gets aggregated in the hands of a few which doesn't help stimulate the economy nor grow it. If the money flows into the hands of the middle-class through the free Market mechanism, the economy and wealth in less developed countries will grow and lift them out of poverty through the money multiplier-effect (increasing velocity of money).

Lastly, the proposed solution is downright stupid! Fund the under-developed countries? Any kid would have heard of the saying, "..give the person a fish and you feed him/her for a day. Teach him/her to fish and you fed the person for life!" if the intent is really to help the third world countries, then the corruption of their government, the economic development plans for the next 2 decades for those countries, their industries, infrastructure developments, the markets that they will need to export into, the growth of their internal domestic Markets, the overseas investors that they need to attract, the education systems and schools that needs to produce the skilled labor to build and operate the factories, to manage the growing companies and Industries, etc. the To-Dos list, Strategic plans, resources and skills needed would be way beyond America's current capabilities. How can you solve Poverty by funding it? This is purely a Distraction and personal self-enrichment Strategy and as we can see with the UN voting against America's support of Israel, they're just a bunch of corrupt, self-serving entities, out to increase their personal wealth and singing whatever tunes that gets the funds.

Stupid and illogical as it was, many people loved this 'Soros developed' narrative and bought into it lock, stock and barrel. UN Secretary General Kofi Annan hired Jeff Sachs to implement the Millennium Project to lead the War-on-Poverty. Jeff Sachs even wrote a book The End of Poverty. The Canada Free Press calls the Project: "the largest global wealth redistribution program ever conceived" IMF will be issuing SDRs (Special Drawing Rights) to fund this "End of Poverty" projects.

These End of Poverty shenanigans were in early 2000, now nearly 2 decades later and tens of Trillions spent. Has the world become a much richer place? Has world hunger disappeared? Where did all the money go? There's been many more terrorist acts, that's for sure! Iran has gotten much stronger and richer, ISIL, Al-Qaeda, etc. has gotten richer and well-funded as of end of Obama's term. The neo-democrat Activists Corporations has also gotten extremely rich and powerful and declaring all Out War on the American middle-class and traditional American Values, on the traditional Christian Values! The SDRs and Free International Money is definitely flowing, not into the hands of the poor but into the hands of those with vested interests, International problem profiteers, [aka Globalists Pimps].

Before we proceed to more evidence of Soros and Sachs, urging the support of "impoverished" Middle East states, that's headed by radical Islamists, let's take a step back and review "conceptual framework" of their proposed solution and why it is logically flawed. This is important, as the same concept applies to Environmental Protection, Global Warming, Social Security, Racial Income Inequality, other Domestic Welfare Subsidies programs which we'll discuss in Chapter 7, Untying the Gordian Knot.

Aids and subsidies, A) you never fix a problem by subsidizing it. By subsidizing, you will just get more and more of it because you are encouraging it! Aids should be a one-time, short term solution to tide over certain critical times, per when disasters strike Hurricane Katerina, earthquakes, floods, etc. to fix a problem, you have to find the root causes and remove those causes not just put a band-aid over them! If you reward someone for not working, wouldn't you get more people not working?

Next, B) the funds to aid those under-developed countries are too puny, only a "drop in the bucket" to truly address the reality of poverty problems faced there. You need to take the sum of money allocated and then multiply by a thousand and tens of thousand times, how? What's is needed to truly address the Poverty Issues which we'd briefly discussed earlier are: the corruption of their government (as this determines how the wealth gets distributed), we need a free market Capitalistic economy that promotes competition that will properly allocate the wealth distribution per the fairest means of hard work, abilities and ingenuities of the population, only then the Middle Working class will grow! Thus, we'll need the Strategic economic development plans for the next 2 decades for those countries, their industries to grow, their infrastructure developments, the identification of foreign markets that they will sell their exports to, the growth of their internal Markets, the overseas investors that they need to attract, their education systems and schools that needs to produce the skilled labor to build and operate the factories, the talent to manage the growing companies and Industries, etc.

Only by creating a real robust economy and free market that can sustain itself for future to come can we truly help the under-developed countries! (only then you have taught them how to fish and it takes minimal of 2-3 decades). We also saw a similar challenge summarized in chapter 2 with George Rosen's Patron and Client relationship of corruption.

Finally, C) Creating more Global Bureaucracy and setting up more International Committees are definitely not the way to go in fixing any problems! These bureaucracies; with their unjustified pay-scales and underserved influence, have absolutely NO accountability, no one takes responsibility for any actions or results. When all are jointly accountable, it means NO one is accountable! You will need dedicated, passionate individuals to lead and be held accountable, individuals who are NOT in it for the money. If certain people need the social, charity jobs purely for the paychecks, power and influence, then somethings' really fishy and their priority is to keep their 'jobs' (aka perks and benefits) as long as possible, NOT to get the Job done!

Anyone who has had any substantial work experience would be able to see these 3 fundamental flaws in the proposed "solution" and Soros is no fool, why is he proposing such "solutions"? He is setting the stage for his never-ending and torrents of Cash-flow so as to preserve his 'legacy', impose his ideologies and world views on the American middle class! We'll see how each of the 3 flaws in addressing the real problem actually supports his hidden agenda perfectly! A) First, aids and subsidies will never fix the real issue, they make it bigger and never-ending as selling drugs to junkies and more junkies, you will get a never-ending cash-flow stream. Similarly, with the aids to the under-developed countries, the UN and IMF will be funding such projects till eternity when the cow comes home [Soros and his cronies will get their unlimited and endless funding].

Secondly, B) although the amounts are too small to properly address the real poverty issues in those countries, they are not puny to support Soros' and Sachs' real agenda; setting up various activist corporations. Remember, Sachs was the director of these Projects and able to direct where the aids go towards. These "puny sums" to aid the entire country populations will NOT be "puny" in the hands of the recipient organizations for purpose of their intended goals. They will become well-funded and very powerful to perform their required tasks! Lastly, C) Bureaucracy is the worst organization structure to get real work done or tasks accomplished, but they are best for NO accountability! So when the funds become "mismanaged" or no visible results after decades, Everyone in UN, Millennium Project and IMF are jointly accountable!

What a perfect cover, also the excess staff that can be on double or triple paychecks working for the State, Charity-foundations, World-Aid organizations can be easily utilized to perform many personal tasks or agenda for Soros or Clinton as we had seen with many on her campaign also working for the State and Clinton foundation at the same time! So employing such "elegant, beautiful solutions" provides ever-lasting resources (Financial as well as people resources) to Soros and his neo-fascists Activists Corporations! You might have noticed similar concepts employed elsewhere by the likes of Al-Gore in the situation of Renewable Energy with much subsidies set aside to support new Unicorns of renewable energy whose critical success factor is to obtain subsidies from the US Government!

If we use the example of building up Economies over 2-3 decades of dedication and hard-work of their Leadership teams and citizens of the country together (exactly what the 4 Asia Tigers economies were doing till Soros crashed the Asian Economies in 97-98) equates Earning their paychecks, then making the Billions from just crashing their economies (betting against them .. shorting the market) would be much easier (equating to legal Stealing). The Moral of the story here is that Stealing [financial looting] is much easier than Earning your paycheck! But Soros is smarter still!

Stealing from Individuals brings little money and you get a bigger reaction from that individual because when you steal $1 from him/her, he/she loses $1, there's also 100% accountability here as it is his/her personal money! Stealing from the Government or Wall Street is much easier and faster! First, you can steal a lot of money quickly! Secondly, the responsible bureaucrats protecting the money couldn't care less when the money gets stolen, why? It is NOT their money (OPM, other people's money) and they never get blamed, being well hidden and shrouded in the bureaucracy, it is the Wall Street's fault, it is SEC fault, it is the Fed's fault. Who the hell is Wall Street? You get the picture, there's no Accountability! And thirdly, the victims feel minimal pain from the loss, even delayed feedback as in the $ 20T debt as the pain hasn't even began to spread back to the Americans yet. Why minimal pain? It is spread out over a large number of victims. As an example, if you steal $320M from the US Government, each of the American loses $1, the thief gets $320M, who has more incentive? The thief to perpetuate the crime or the 320 million Americans losing $1 each? Ohh yes, the conscientious Bureaucrat in DC will stop the crime, right

So after stealing from the country, what comes next? Stealing from International Organizations is even better! now you can steal $7 Billion, and each person on earth only loses $1 each, if you think the bureaucrats in DC have no responsibilities, the clowns in UN & IMF will put them to shame in the competition of Who wants to have NO accountability? That's why the EU (hard to imagine idiots even worse than DC bureaucrats) clowns have run Europe so much faster to the ground then USA (in the race to Poverty, Corruption & Chaos, the EU and UN do seem to be way ahead)

Now let's return to the Great Successful War on Poverty. If you find it difficult to believe that IMF or UN could be funding some of these Radical organizations, let's review some of the comments made by Soros and Sachs, that will provide some insights into their ideologies.

> *".. After 11 September, the American public has become more aware than before that what happens in the rest of the world can affect them directly and there are important foreign policy decisions to be made. This awareness may not last long, and I am determined not to let the moment pass."*
>
> In his book: George Soros on Globalization as he was getting the IMF's support for his Global War on Poverty in March 2002

> *"whether terrorists are rich or poor or middle-class, their staging areas – their bases of operations – are unstable societies beset by poverty, unemployment, rapid population growth, hunger, and lack of hope. Without addressing the root causes of that instability, little will be accomplished in stanching terror."*
>
> Jeff Sachs in his 2005 book The End of Poverty

In Jan 2006, when Hamas (an Iran-backed terrorist group) became the majority in the Palestinian Parliament, Sachs argues for West continuation in funding the Palestinian Authority and Hamas by writing "Almost daily the United States and Europe brandish threats to impose economic sanctions… The most recent threats are towards the new Hamas-led government in Palestine… such tactics are misguided… cutting aid is likely to increase turmoil… a newly elected Palestinian government should be treated, at least initially with legitimacy."

"we needed to address the deeper roots of terrorism in societies…. that are misused and abused by the rich world, as have been the oil states of the Middle East." Sachs also wrote in his book The End of Poverty blaming the USA as occupier in Iraq in 2005

Laura D'Andrea Tyson also promotes the Millennium Project as best antidote to terrorism stating that "It's time to step up the global war on poverty.." in her Business Week article in Dec 2001 clearly also of the view the Poverty is the root cause of Terrorism. This tricky sleight of hands might even sound 'logical' to some as they employ trickery, leveraging the misconception of correlation to equate causation (States sponsoring Terrorism might appear 'poor' relative to Western States; that's correlation, but to draw the conclusion that 'poverty' caused terrorism is the magic trick that the razzle and dazzled the uninformed). On closer look, although Afghanistan and Pakistan might be poor we now understand that corruption causes income inequality thus poverty for the masses, just as in many of the Arab countries that supports and trains the terrorists are oil rich but also suffers from Income Inequality too.

Just as in Global Warming, we cannot prove a 1:1 relationship that burning fossil fuels caused Global Warming, similarly from public information, we have no direct evidence that the funds controlled by Jeff Sachs and George Soros went towards the Terrorist activities (we'll need professionals to ascertain that fact, perhaps some Real Journalists has the courage to embark on that journey?), but as in Global Warming, there sure is a very strong correlation, not to mention the obvious alignment these two ideologies share against a common enemy.[3]

If some good coordinated effort is focused on uncovering the money trail from the Millennium Projects or other George Soros related 501c3 entities [which he'd openly declared to be for Global War on Poverty] to the Terror or terror-related groups, it would probably help solve many problems at home too. Which would be the secret of untying the Gordian Knot, solving multiple issues with one solution!

If you think that the Radical groups like Palestinian Authority, Hamas, Hezbollah, ISIL, Al-Qaeda, Muslim Brotherhood are far away in the deserts of Middle East, you might like to think again.

Up close and personal; Radicals @ Home (V)

How close? Hillary Clinton's right hand aide, Huma Abedin (remarked by Hillary to be the daughter she wished she had) was working for a company related to Muslim World League (creator of Al-Qaeda) before Hillary offered her a job. Her boss was Abdullah Omar Nasseef (wanted by authorities for connections to 9/11 attacks). Huma's mother and brother are leaders of the Muslim Brotherhood as was her father (deceased). Huma is the board member of the Muslim Students Association also related to the Muslim Brotherhood. When Hillary was Secretary of State, President Obama sided with the Muslim Brotherhood in Egypt and asked then Egyptian President Mubarak (longtime ally of America) to resign and step aside for the Muslim Brotherhood to come into power. When the Egyptian military later toppled the brotherhood and assumed power, President Obama cut off all military aid to Egypt forcing the Egyptians to seek support from the Russians after decades of Pro-USA stance (since 1970s)

How about John Kerry's daughter? She is married into the Iranian Ruling hierarchy and John Kerry was Secretary of State while the negotiations for the Iran deal was on-going? Isn't that a huge potential Conflict of Interests? What kind of ethical standards? And where's the Media Coverage?

President Obama's closest White House adviser, Valerie Jarrett (who's been dubbed Obama's "work wife") who was born in and spent her early childhood in Iran has great affinity and sympathies for Shiite Muslims and Iran. Jarrett in an interview with David Samuels of Times magazine about their early upbringing overseas influenced both hers and the President's policies towards all things Muslim ".. what it was like for both of us to live in countries that were predominantly

---

[3] Per The Shadow Party by David Horowitz and Richard Poe, Unholy Alliance: Radical Islam and the American Left by David Horowitz

Muslim countries as formative parts of our childhood… I remember (Obama) asking me questions that I felt like no one else has ever asked me before…. Oh, finally someone who gets it."

As you can see, from Valerie Jarrett own words about both hers and President Obama's views on Muslims and Islam because both of them had spent their formative years in "predominantly Muslim countries as formative parts of our childhood". What does that tell you? Quite a lot actually, does it mean that they would be bias in their decisions towards Muslim countries? Most likely they would be sympathetic, Yes probably.

Even more importantly, it demonstrated the arrogance and dishonesty of this line of thinking. Truth 1: Americans mostly have minimal International Exposure with Zero overseas Cultural Experience and folks like President Obama and Valerie Jarrett know that so they prey on this lack of experience by claiming they have lived overseas as kids and thus they feel that they know more about Globalism than the average Americans. Here's the reality, Yes, most Americans know Zero about overseas Cultures, so does President Obama and Valerie Jarrett. By publicly indicating that because they lived overseas as kids and thus they know what Overseas Cultures and only they "get it"? that's like putting your childhood holidays experience on your professional work CV; passing it off as Global Exposure. Having great childhood memories is great! We all have nice and beautiful childhood memories but to allow those memories to influence our professional decisions is a Crime, claiming to know Islam and understand Muslims because of your childhood memories is pretentious at a personal level and downright irresponsible (at professional level), creating unnecessary danger for Americans in the International Arena! Both of them do NOT speak Persian or Kurdish nor Indonesian, Obama lived in Indonesia between age 8-10 before he returned to Hawaii. We'll cover more of this lack of Culture Experience later in this chapter.

Sleeping with the Enemy

How the Radical Liberal Left's 'Ideology' is aiding and abetting the Radical Islamic Terrorists in Targeting and Killing Innocent Americans. This segment discusses how the Radical Liberal Ideology [just like the AIDS virus] has handicapped the USA's counter-intelligence efforts [body's immune system to battle] against the Islamic Radicals for the last 8 years, and also contributes to the failure of our law enforcement in stopping the Radicals (Islamic in this case) from killing Americans back home. Many counter-intelligence officials have noted our USA counter-intelligence narrative on the Islamist enemy, is being controlled by (and under the control of) Muslim Brotherhood Islamist front groups and supported by Liberal left's narratives that regards Islamism as Progressive. No wonder we have NO counter-intelligence! In fact, with the new administration in the Whitehouse, we can now see clearly how the NSA, FBI, etc. hasn't only been subverted, they have been totally re-wired (reprogramed) to do the easiest tasks of least resistance and lowest risks, instead of their intended functions.

The Muslim Brotherhood has been labeled a Terrorist organization by Saudi Arabia, Egypt, United Arab Emirates but not in USA, UAE government labeled two American groups as affiliates of Muslim Brotherhood, the Council on American-Islamic Relations (CAIR) and the

Muslim American Society as terrorist groups. President Obama ignored all these Intelligence and Insights shared by Saudi Arabia, Egypt and UAE, instead he (in his personal great wisdom) outlined a Key Element of his Strategy against Al-Qaeda (disclosed by inside sources) called PSD-11 (Presidential Study Directive 11) in 2011 based on advice by his trusted Muslim Brotherhood advisors and his childhood insights into the Muslim world when he was 8 and living in Indonesia, 2 years before he returned to Hawaii to live with his grandparents.

Another feedback from a concerned American counter-intelligence analyst, The Center for Security Policy has documented successful Muslim Brotherhood subversion efforts in USA and overseas; including several Brotherhood supporters identified as key advisors to Obama! Surprising? Hardly, President Obama already revealed his support for the Muslim Brotherhood in Egypt's situation in 2011. These subversion efforts helped contributed towards the successful formation of Islamic State in 2014 in Syria and Iraq.

We know that FBI has been under subversion for over 8 years, the current FBI lexicon (language which agents can use) does NOT include Jihad, Muslim, Islam, Sharia, Al-Qaeda, Hezbollah, Hamas, instead using the generic term: violent extremism. Seems like the FBI has been made impotent by the Politically Correct Gestapo, it's a wonder there hasn't been more "work-place" violence. Even the National Intelligence Strategy in 2009 makes no mention of Jihad, Muslim nor Islam.

The slothful lackeys in FBI, NSA, etc. have now been enervated to a point of producing No intelligence on North Korea, none on the Middle East countries, cannot open an iPhone, yet they know how to spy on their fellow American Citizens, leak phone conversations of President Trump, like dogs forever barking up the Russian Hacking Tree. Why? Easy, Paths of Least resistance, high risks to get caught by North Koreans, Iranians, Syrian, etc. possibly death. Leak info on fellow Americans or the current Administration? Just as Comey, making millions from his book deals with the Liberal Progressives Activists Corporations, became a celebrity (at least to the snowflakes)! The P.C. Gestapo, Radical Liberal Extremists reigns supreme in the age of President Obama and continues the Civil War against the American People. We shall return later to how President Obama's anti-American perspectives and also the Liberal left infatuation with Islamist both stems from Cultural Ignorance and Egoistic Arrogance!

To know more and get more details about George Soros and Jeff Sachs, you might like to read:

The Shadow Party, by David Horowitz and Richard Poe. Possibly also Big Agenda, by David Horowitz

As we'll see in a while, there's a lot of money to be made in Terror Business

Follow the $$ trail; Organized Crime and Organized Terror, the rise in Age of Anti Establishment, Anti Law & Order

All sorts of criminal activities in Drugs, Weapons, Money Launderers, Human & Narcotics Trafficking, extortion, oil smuggling, kidnapping, etc. operated by terrorists, States-sponsoring terror activities, drug cartels. All working closely together as they share synergies and common agendas, the cycles investments and funds generating activities reinforces each other and produces tons of cash which goes back into supporting their respective activities so the cycles continues.

Merging of these various groups is happening because these are "high-return on investment" activities, profitable "high margin" business, estimated $1 trillion of illegal funds just from corrupt officials around the world each year. We need professionals to trace the network of funds that's supporting the terrorists' activities and also all the parties involved in it. Sadly, the Terror Business is becoming very lucrative business. You might remember that when Azzam brought Osama bin Laden on board to help the jihad, it was because of his skills to raise funds and move them around too.

Just like the 501c3 Activists Corporations that have Billions of Assets under management, the Terror Organizations can also setup entities with assets under management, the returns from their Assets becomes an on-going cashflow stream to fund their daily terror operations and activities. If financially astute, they can quickly become financially independent of their donors, investors.

All they need a one-time startup capital like (same concept as) getting investments from Venture Capitalists. Some funds get invested into the activities described above, some funds can also be invested into equities for capital gains right? Whichever can generate higher returns on investments for the investor, if the money launderers are doing their jobs right, who knows where the funds come from and what they get used for.

One would believe with the amount of money we are talking about, the professionals hired by the criminals, terrorists, terror States should be able to give FBI, CIA, US Treasury Department, DEA a good run for their money (assuming the K Street apparatchiks would even attempt to do their jobs).

Between 1942 – 1943, Churchill saw part of his task with the Americans as "bringing them into touch with political issues on which they had strong opinions and little experience."

The Ambivalent Superpower since WW II (VI Foreign Policies)

The sixth reason why America has become the Enemy of the Religious Radicals is Overreach and Naivete in America's Foreign Policies.

Before 1923, the Arabs were under the rule of Ottoman Turks, the West had relatively less interactions with the Arab Muslims. Since the Turks were also Muslims, they are joined in دار الإسلامDar al-Islam, also the Ottoman Sultan was their Caliph so there really no justification for any kind of religious wars. All that changed after WWI as we saw, but most of the attacks then were against British and French as they were occupying Syria, Lebanon, Iraq and Palestine, it is only after WW II, as America assumed World Stage Leadership, that the anger and hatred starts getting directed towards USA? Could that be a contributing reason too?

Well, increased interactions would definitely lead to increased opportunities for conflict, question really should be, need these increased interactions lead to conflicts? Not necessarily, in fact when TE Lawrence first came into contacts with the Arabs, the experience was extremely positive to the point that the British were able to ally with the Arabs against the Turks (both of whom are Muslims, TE Lawrence and the British were able to turn the concept of Dar al-Harb دار الحرب and Dar al-Islam دار الإسلام completely on its head. The traditional concept prior to the Arab revolt was that the House of Islam is united and needs to expand against the house of War (any territory which is not within the Muslim control).

For hundreds of years before the collapse of the Ottoman Empire, most of the affairs would have been handled locally within the various geographical levels of Vilayets, sanjak, kaza, nahiye (they were similar to the Federal, State, County, City, Municipal levels). Even at the highest level of the vilayet, they are much smaller regionally than what the British, French drew up for Syria, Iraq, etc. (ignoring the traditional ethnic and sectarian boundaries). You can refer to the chart on page 12 of the various Ottoman vilayets. These Vilayets, sanjak, kaza, nahiye would have been able to reflect the ethnic and sectarian differences more accurately, able to address and accommodate the Armenian, Kurds, Shiites, Sunnis differences more easily. The same organization of the administration in case of China 省, 市, 县, 镇, 乡, 村, 户 where the geographical Cultural, Regional and historical allegiance makes a huge difference where 关系 relationships matters, Not ideology.

Here, although USA also is administered at various difference levels State, County, City, Municipal, but for countries like China, India and Ottoman Empire, their local geographical regions carry with them thousands of years of ethnic, sectarian, religious and Cultural differences that might be challenging to understand, let alone bridge in short time periods. Americans might only understand these differences at conceptual level but not Internalized enough to leverage and exploit them, British did but they had other agendas (not to a peaceful and well-integrated country but to exploit the locals' differences to further British interests).

Another example of the British's Awareness of other countries' Cultures and their experience in exploiting them: British's control (started with influence) in India for close to 350 years with minimal military expenditures, page 13 chart. You can see how the British has presence in EIC there since 1600, but as the Mughal empire weakens and later the Maratha empire also weakens, the British quickly took the opportunity to increase their control and influence!

We can continue to analyze each of the British colonies and see similar patterns, but that's not necessary, the case in point is that UK has much longer exposure as a World Power and America still has much to learn about how to use minimal military force (none would be best) to achieve their Strategic Objectives.

America's Debate between Strategic Objectives versus Morals and Ideals in Foreign Policies

Yet, the Unsolved debate between security interests and the importance of promoting humane and legitimate governance. Henry Kissinger deliberates between maintaining Order and furthering the Ideals of Morals, Democratic rule in America's Foreign Policies.

> *"… Both elements are important. Neglecting a democratic future; assuming we know how to shape its direction, involves long term risk. Neglecting the present by ignoring the security element risks immediate catastrophe. The*

difference between traditionalists and activists hinges on that distinction.
The statesman has to balance it each time the issue arises…."

- World Order by Henry Kissinger

I plotted the 2 following charts for discussion purposes, the first is between Order (on y axis) and Morals (on x axis). The Best case would be at the top right hand corner, fulling both the Morals Obligations and achieving World Order. The worst would be bottom left hand corner, achieving neither purpose. Let's discuss each of America's recent Middle East involvement, plus other Military examples for comparison purpose. Beside Strategic Vs Morals tradeoffs, we'll also look at Short Term Vs Long Term Objectives, Intent of the Strategy Vs the Level of Competence in its Execution (ability to deliver from high-level Strategy to final actual results).

America's participation in WW II achieved both purposes, doing what is morally correct against the dictatorial regimes and also help to restore World Order. As we'd discussed earlier, the 1991 Gulf War also helped achieved World Order by evicting Saddam from Kuwait and Morally right by most counts (the large Arab coalition with USA was great feat of accomplishment, Kudos to the 41st President), but I put the effort in RED instead of BLUE because, one ask the question, was such large scale invasion really necessary? Could we have achieved similar objective by a smaller force or through economic pressures? Also, America didn't gain anything of value from the 1991 Gulf War, instead we planted the seeds of Hatred in Al-Qaeda (Osama) that eventually led to 9/11 attacks.

Similarly, with the 2007 Surge and National Building Ideals of 43rd President Bush, they helped maintained Order in Iraq and protected the Iraq citizens but both at huge expenses to America so they are RED too. We're not bias against nor complimenting President Bush 43rd, the 2003 Invasion of Iraq was a terrible decision (with hindsight 20/20), but given the fact that it already happened and America was already involved in Iraq, the 2007 surge and Nation building strategy was the last resort available and made sense then (the most logical one of a bad situation; one that Bush 43rd had gotten USA into).

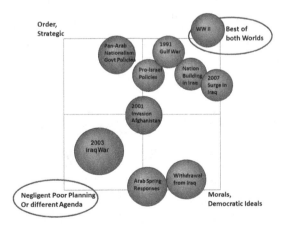

The politically motivated withdrawal from Iraq and the haphazard Arab Spring responses were terrible from World Order standpoint, however the Withdrawal made Moral sense to rest of the World as USA had no business being in Iraq.

Here's the interesting but pointed Policy, support of the Pan-Arab Nationalist (strong man) governments produces better World Order but not Morally correct as many of the strong-man are dictators, here's the dilemma that Henry Kissinger was deliberating about. But the alternative of supporting rebellion against these strong-man regimes are even worst! Look at the case of Syria? Because of the delayed America's support for the rebels, we have the Syria Civil War from 2011-present. Millions are now homeless and displaced all over the world! Thousands have lost their lives, families broken up, they are homeless and without a country. All these suffering in the pretext of democracy? What utter hogwash and hypocrisy! Because of American failure in Leadership, first the failure to act decisively (strong Military action right from the start of revolution) would have toppled Assad's regime then! If we had missed that window of opportunity, then let nature takes it course, if Assad's regime could have stem out the rebellion, there would at least be peace for the Syrians. But the American Leadership under Obama then decided to intervene subsequently and support the rebellion (due to public opinion in USA??) thus prolonging and dragging out the Civil War! This is the result of Leading from Behind! Millions and Millions have suffered due to what? Due to the USA Internal politics of appealing to the popularity in the Polls? If I were a Syrian refugee, lost my family, suffering as a result of the American Leadership via Polls, I would indeed be a bitter soul.

Invasion of Afghanistan satisfy the American agenda to topple Taliban, deny Al-Qaeda operating bases in Afghanistan and chase after Osama bin-Laden but it didn't contribute much towards World Order nor rank high in Moral justification. Still as a response to 9/11, the Afghan invasion is more "understandable" than the Invasion of Iraq which would probably rank as the worst war since Vietnam, of not accomplishing much in Strategic value yet accumulating a huge war debt for the American people.

Knowing the background of the Israel-Arab conflict tracing back to WW I and the League of Nations Mandate, Americas support of Israel helped maintained Order in the Middle East especially with the success of Camp David's Accord in 1978. Morally, it didn't make USA many friends with the Arab Nations plus the crazy Liberal Media went nuts over this policy (of course the Liberal anti-establishment Media would still have gone crazy, even if America leadership had supported the Arabs' cause instead of Israel, they would probably then be accusing their leadership of antisemitism).

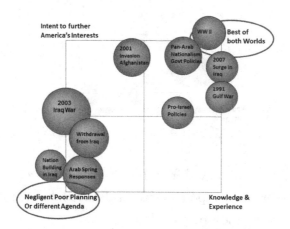

President George W. Bush made a terrible decision going into the Iraq war in 2003 (hindsight 20/20), but with the memories from the 9/11 attacks still fresh, perhaps we give him the benefit of doubt that he had the right intent for the American people and was trying to further American interests. Here's chart of Observed Intent of American Leadership Vs the knowledge and experience (competence) each administration had.

In this second chart, the 2007 Surge of force is made after learning about the situation and better understanding with over 4 years being embroiled in Iraq, so both Intent and Knowledge are good. In contrast, Nation Building in Iraq was a disaster as it doesn't serve American interests at all and still demonstrates a lack of understanding of the complexity of administering Iraq (even Emir Feisal, himself a Muslim had failed after 12 years of trying). The re-building of Japan after the WW II was more successful, but Japan was much more homogenous and it still took decades to accomplish.

The pan-Arab Nationalism Policies is a Strategic approach for benefits American interests with minimal commitment of USA troops. The strong-man regimes, from the local people's perspective, some innocent would be unfairly treated, imprisoned and even tortured, yet compared to the Civil War in Syria and state of anarchy in Iraq after US Troops withdrawn in 2007, most would still prefer political & economic stability with some semblance of civilization over complete chaos, senseless slaughter & anarchy (all in the name and pursuit of a worthless "dream of democracy").

The biggest haters of the Strong-man regimes are the Liberal Radical left Media. In hopes of pleasing their own egos, armed with Popularity Polls results, Hillary charged in as Queen of the Liberal Progressives and led the efforts to topple Gaddafi in Libya, President Obama after initial delay also started to support the rebels against Assad's regimes. Look at the plight of the Syrian, Libyan refugees. All in placation of the Liberal Radical's Left's Egos, Poll results! And they are still not done yet, that'll be more to come.

George Soros had this to say in the aftershocks of 9/11 attacks "…. September 11 has shocked the people of the United States into realizing that others may regard them very differently from the way they see themselves.." and he went on to argue for his War on Poverty agenda. In this particular instance, he did get one thing right, the general naïve and innocence of Americans when it comes to Foreign Policies.[4]

中国 China, translated it means Middle Kingdom, Heaven is above, Earth is below and in between is the Middle Kingdom where all civilization revolves around. This was the view expressed by Qing Emperor Qianlong to Macartney's delegation in 1793. Subconsciously, many Americans think of the World to be alike America, not through arrogance but innocence and naivety. This also includes the Radical Left Media with their humungous egos and likes of President Obama too. Even the wise Henry Kissinger isn't immune to this perspective (pretty natural since he is an American). But their responses are all very different, let's review each of them.

---

[4] Per Unholy Alliance: Radical Islam and the American Left by David Horowitz, The Shadow Party by David Horowitz and Richard Poe, George Soros on Globalization in 2002

> *"We have no eternal allies, and we have no perpetual enemies. Our interests*
> *are eternal and perpetual, and those interests it is our duty to follow."*
>
> - Lord Palmerston on British Foreign Policy

This is the view expressed by Lord Palmerston about British Foreign Policies, compare this to Henry Kissinger's comments earlier on the debate between Order and Morals & Democratic Values. Notice how Palmerston's comments to be more succinct, practical and Machiavelli.

Let's compare some of the **UK and USA Foreign Policy strengths** and areas for improvement, these charts are subjective and the specifics are open for discussions, certain differences between the British and American Foreign Policies are highlighted for comparative purpose.

	United States of America	United Kingdom	Comments
Timeline	70 years	350 years	USA from 1945 - 2015 (approx), UK from 1600 - 1947 (approx)
Strategy	5	5	capacity to learn, Institutional Learning (similar enough) Culture
Knowledge	5	5	capacity to learn, Institutional Learning (similar enough) Culture
Strategy Vs Morals	3	5	UK Strategic in approach, USA debates Democracy Issues
Insights into Foreign Cultures	1	5	UK has longer periods of Global Exposure, USA's approach "..Do to others as you would have them do to you..." Luke 6:31
Strong: 5			
Neutral: 3			
Weak: 1			

First, you'll notice that UK had (after the defeat of the Spanish Armada in 1588) over 350 years on the World's center stage vs US over the last 70 years, that's about 5X longer. On Strategy and Knowledge, both can learn about their opponents equally well, thus I ranked both as the same. On Morals, USA deliberates about the Strategic Objectives vs the Morals, Democratic Values and tries to find a balance. The UK's approach was much more Machiavelli and Strategic. Lastly, on Cultural Experience of the countries, regions engaged with, Britain (in their 350 years as key player on World Stage) has also demonstrated itself to be a keen student and observer of the cultural, religious, ethnicity of their opponents and then being able to exploit them well to Britain's advantage.

Why is this so? Besides having 5X longer exposure, Britain has always been a small country, compared to Indian and China, its population is tiny. UK is also a maritime Nation, when it's representatives are overseas in India, China, Middle East regions, Africa, etc. they are just a small faction of the local population so they have to rely heavily on Strategy, Intelligence and understanding of the local cultures, etc.

Superior Size and Strength makes for Bad Strategy (David v Goliath) and that's what America has, superior technology, Military prowess and relative to UK, America is a large country. As a result, unless a strong conscious effort is made by its leadership to imbue itself with a deep sense of crisis, it would have a lower tendency to learn, to leverage and exploit the Cultural differences of their opponents to their advantage. America has a stronger tendency to adopt a "Middle Kingdom" mentality!

"Much of this has been seen by later scholars less as being based upon a sober calculation of the country's real interests in the world than as reflecting an immaturity of foreign policy style, an ethnocentric naïveté, and a wish to impress audiences both at home and abroad - traits which would complicate a "realistic" American foreign policy in the future; but even if that's true, the United States was hardly alone in this age of imperialist bombast and nationalist pride."

- Paul Kennedy in Rise and Fall of the Great Powers, describing America's involvement in World Politics beginning of 20th century

Lack of Experience with, minimal Insights into Foreign Cultures

I was going to address the Morals Vs Strategic Goals issue before the Lack of Exposure into Foreign Cultures, then I realized that this "lack of exposure" caused the Moral Issue to surface in the USA Foreign Policies discussions. Thus, let's address the Foreign Culture challenge. America is a Big Country; 48 contiguous plus Alaska and Hawaii. It is the world's largest economy in absolute US$, most Americans have minimal interactions with overseas Culture and other religious beliefs (global virtual friends on the internet doesn't quite count, social media, live chats, etc. isn't the same as living in a Culture for years, even decades, learning to speak their language, having serious conflict of interests and then being able to resolve these conflicts in a foreign Culture where you are the minority and cannot speak their language).

Even when most Americans do have the opportunities for interactions with Foreign Cultures, they tend to Project themselves outwards instead of Absorbing inwards due to their more passionate and "aggressive" culture. It takes much effort to consciously rein yourself in, keep silent and listen. Many Cultures tend to avoid confrontations, so they just stay silent, doesn't mean they agree with you!

In absence of developing insights into other Cultures [culturally tone-deaf], there are 3 responses (Strategies) that manifested themselves.

A) First and most common is the Projection of one's own Values and Beliefs onto the other Foreign party. It is almost instinctive, tool of Empathy … a kind version of that would manifest as: "…Do to others as you would have them do to you…" Luke 6:31 (NIV)

Remember the Dilemma on Foreign Policies that Henry Kissinger was deliberating about?

"…Neglecting a democratic future; assuming we know how to shape its direction, involves long term risk.." and yet "… Those committed to democratization have found it difficult to discover leaders who recognize the importance of democracy other than as a means to achieve their own dominance… They were interested in Democracy only if it installed their own

> *group; none favored a system that did not guarantee its own party's control of the political system. A war conducted solely to enforce human rights norms and without concern for the geostrategic or geo-religious outcome was inconceivable to the overwhelming majority of the contestants... The conflict, as they perceived it, was not between a dictator and the forces of democracy but between Syria's contending sects and their regional backers."*
>
> - World Order by Henry Kissinger, referring to the various power groups seeking to displace Assad's regime in Syria

Did you noticed how many times the word democracy, democratic, democratization, human rights kept coming up? Mr. Kissinger wrote "...a war conducted solely to enforce human rights norms...was inconceivable to the overwhelming majority..." How was it inconceivable to Mr. Kissinger that Democracy and Human Rights Ideals are "nice to have", a luxury that rest of the world might not yet be able to afford? Why do Americans [leaders] assume that what they want, is what others want? They project that their own Values is what other Cultures aspire to?

The larger parts of the World have cultural backgrounds and histories that are not rooted in Democracy. Democracy isn't top of the list for the average person in these countries. 安居乐业 Peace and Social Stability in their countries, Jobs, Wealth, Happiness. Democracy is NOT the only way to achieve these goals, a stable government and a strong economy are higher priorities!

To become embroiled in chaos of Civil War in pursuit for Democratic Ideals? How is it inconceivable for Americans to understand such simple needs as Peace and Social Stability in their countries, Jobs, Wealth, Happiness is more important? Treat people as they want to be treated! Not as you would want to be treated!

The More you interfere and invade Muslim lands, the more reasons for Jihads against Americans, seems pretty straightforward to me. If you truly want to help us, please stop supporting Civil Wars in our countries. Let us have peace and stability as a start for now! 揠苗助长 (aiding the sapling's growth by tugging on it). The different historical, religious and cultural background influence the likelihood of success as well as speed of acceptance of Democracy into each society. Even for America, with a populace that had a relatively common historical, religious and cultural European background, yet from the time of Mayflower to the American Revolution, it was approx. 150 years, each society needs to reach a certain stage before Democracy can be properly leveraged and harnessed as form of government.

Projection of American Values and Culture onto a Foreign Culture might be an honest mistake, but still a terrible Mistake with far reaching consequences around the world!

B) The second version of dealing with Lack of understanding of Foreign Culture is even more surreal: they Fantasize and have their own infatuations. This group comprises largely of the neo-democrats Radical Extremists and neo-Fascist ONE VIEW of the world Activists. When you see them on cable-TV, Social-Media, in Hillary's Campaigns, in the Whitehouse sidling up to President Obama. You can tell they are ignorant Americans, born and raised here in America.

They do NOT speak with an accent, their rude, obnoxious "in your face" behavior is a dead give-away.

Immigrants coming into this country in search of a better life for themselves and their families do NOT go protesting on the streets for free speech rights, religious freedom rights, women rights, gay rights, LGBTQ rights, racial inequality, Global Warming, Environmental Protection, etc. Immigrants are rational people and the have higher priorities and better things to do, like looking after their families. Get a good job! Ensure their kids go to good schools, their families get to live in a good and safe neighborhood! Just like the folks in Middle East, a better life, peace and stability, jobs, better future for their families, prosperity are their priorities! As for any rational human.

Only someone born and raised in this country and most likely Paid and Incentivized [by activist corporations] can ever afford to take these "basics needs" [just a simple hope for a peaceful life with jobs] for Granted and idle away their time chanting political slogans, mindlessly protesting about abstract ideals not linked to any semblance of reality. (abstract ideals which they have little understanding about)

Only someone who has enjoyed the Protection of the 1st Amendment and all the Luxury of Human Rights afforded and protected by this country their entire Lives, sheltered and coddled by the American human rights, NOT understand the fear of REAL physical harm, imprisonment and possibility of physical torture by the Authorities in Power (as in Iran, Pakistan, Turkey, Russia, China, North Korea, Libya, Saudi Arabia, Iraq, Syria, Egypt, Cuba and the lists goes on in Middle East, South American, Mexico, Africa, Asian countries)! Question, if these hypocrites neo-Democrats and Radical Fascists Activists are so Pro-Islam, why are they NOT living in the Middle East countries under the strictest Sharia Law Discipline? Under Sharia Law, punishment for Theft is amputation, punishment for Apostasy is death, wonder what is the punishment for Protesting, Rioting and Looting in Iran? If we use the same logic per Sharia Law, Apostasy is punished by Death, what would happen to the 22.8% of Atheists in USA that were previously from Christian background? Wouldn't that be Apostasy too? That would translate into about 73M Apostates in America (22.8% of 320M = 72.96M).

C) Exploit the Naïvete. The Third version of manifestation of this Lack of insights into Foreign Culture is Exploitation! As the Poverty Pimps do, someone always figures out a way to exploit the plight of the unfortunate and uninformed.

We shall cover the second and third form of responses in more detail later.

孙子兵法 and the New Marshall Plan

Now back to the dilemma between Strategy Vs Morals? Or phrased differently, the issue of furthering Morals and Democratic Values as an objective of Foreign policies per Henry Kissinger's comment earlier. The British doesn't seem to have that problem, were the British Leaders all immoral people? Or are the American Leaders Overly Idealistic? If we start off the Invasion of

Iraq with the publicly Stated objective as to further Democratic Values, yet subsequently start to lean towards a more Strategic objective (such as arrest growth of radicalism, or political stability in Middle East which might mean working with strong-man regimes), the world will then see America as hypocritical right? That's the challenge American Leadership needs to balance and negotiate.

For 350 years, the British had no such problem addressing Moral and Democratic Values as an Objective of their Foreign Policies because they didn't confuse their Foreign Policies (aimed at external parties and countries) with their Internal Politics back home in Britain, they also do NOT project their image of themselves onto their opponents or colonies overseas (in fact, Americans didn't have their confused foreign policies back in WWII either).

Earlier, we had touched on America's Lack of Insights into Foreign Cultures and as a result projecting their own Values and Aspirations onto the Citizens of Foreign Countries. Perhaps we are confusing the Foreign Policies (External) Objectives with America's Internal Demands by the Liberal Left Activists for a more "Humane and Democratic" Islamists Governments in the Middle East, to be propped up by the USA government as President Obama supported the Muslim Brotherhood [an Islamist group] in Egypt against President Mubarak. Support of the Islamists by neo-Democrats and seeing Islamists as Progressives helped plant of the seeds of Radicalism back home against fellow Americans. Strategy via Polls (aka leading from behind) is in essence a circular reference in logic (non sequitur)

孙子兵法

Developed between the Spring, Summer periods and Waring States periods in China, the works of 孙子兵法Sun Tze provides another perspective. In his first chapter Estimates 计划, 始计, Sun Tze indicated the 5 fundamentals to consider before engaging in Military conflict. This is before the design of Military Strategy by the Generals and Military Leadership. The 5 fundamentals are Moral Influence (道, 法), Heaven (weather), Earth (terrain), Command (Leadership) and Doctrine (Military Discipline, organization efficiency, Culture of Excellence, etc.)

Moral Influence, 道 in Taoism would mean The Way, as in 道义as in righteousness 道義, this isn't a Military Strategy but the Moral Influence of the Emperor over his citizens, the alignment of the citizens to the country and its head. 法 means law, how the country is governed by the Emperor. If the country is well governed and the Emperor has the interests of his people at heart. Then with the strong Moral Influence backing the Military, the chances of success would be greatly increased. This Moral Influence is built-up over time between the demonstrated actions of the Emperor for his subjects, way before any Military conflict is even conceived. Other cultures might use Solidarity, Esprit de Corps (French) or Asabiyyah (Muslim) this form of Alignment in the Society (organization, team, etc.)

In America's case, this Moral Influence perhaps can be equated with the Moral Justification to the American public for engaging in War. War is an expensive and High Risk, the people should be fully behind its leader before Military engagement starts. The President must have the

Moral Mandate of the American People before the war starts! Obtaining the Moral Mandate is the Job of the President! The Secretary of State is an External Function designing the Foreign Policies. The President has all the rest of the Secretaries of Interior, Commerce, Education, Labor, Treasury, etc. to work on and improve what's Internal (Domestic) to America. The Secretary of State is clearly a more Strategic view of the World than just the Military but clearly aligned with the Military (Externally focused) as far as Sun Tze's view of the world. The British named their Foreign Office more appropriately (it sums up the perspective more succinctly). Before the war starts, the Military Leadership (Secretary of State and Secretary of Defense) also has to decide the Strategic Objective (Foreign Policies) of the War is.

To spread Democratic Ideals and Morals by war as an objective? To topple existing regimes and setup democratic governments as our Military Objectives?

If you don't see by now how ridiculous these two Objectives sounds? Especially as Objectives of a country's Foreign Policies? You are probably still Confusing America with the World. Firstly a) if you are trying to impose your view of the world onto others, you are the same as the Radical neo-Democrats, trying to spread the Ideology of Democracy by Military Force? We know what's best for you and we are going to stir up your country into chaos of Civil War in order to achieve what we believe is best for you.

Secondly b) if indeed, the wish is to setup Democratic and Humane Governments, then the Military intervention should be only <1% of the effort, for the rest of 99%? where's the Ideological War element? Where's the Funds for Rebuilding after the war? Even more importantly as we'd discussed, USA needs to show up with ready-made democratic Governments that will live in Iraq, Syria for next 2-3 decades. Build up their Economies, Industries, Education, Infrastructures, etc. where's the Marshall Plans for Iraq, Syria? If we had spent $6 Trillion on War in Iraq, then where's the $ 60 Trillion (just a ball park number of ten times) in Cash just to help re-build Iraq, let alone Syria, Libya, Afghanistan, etc. Just these 4 countries will cost and add additional $240 Trillion to our current debt of $20Trillion. We'll need to send maybe 500,000 professionals into each country to help build up their Economies, Healthcare, Education, design their Industries growth, etc. These professionals need to live in Iraq for next 2 decades at minimal, all 2 million of them in Syria, Libya, Iraq, Afghanistan. Hope we're getting the picture here, if USA's own Education and Healthcare is already struggling, we cannot even fix our own economy and we wish to build up other countries' economies? Let alone those with totally different Cultural and religious histories from us? We should stop day-dreaming! Objectives like Nation Building might sound like a good idea to the Idealistic Liberal Left Progressives and the Mindless Press or even a Morally correct thing to do, Strategically and Realistically it is pure Idiotic Madness!

Only the Hollywood dreamers, incompetent imbeciles politicians that uses the public opinion polls to build their 'strategies of leading from behind' would ever state such mindless nincompoop objectives. Leaders are supposed to lead their people because of their superior wisdom and insights from relevant experience, if they lead from behind, using public opinion polls (Obama, Hillary) as their compass, the entire nation would be in circular reference, going in circles like a dog chasing its own tail.

"The task of the leader is to get his people from where they are to where they have not been."

– Henry Kissinger

Just as George Soros and Jeff Sachs' dream about flooding the corrupted countries with Cash to solve the terrorist problem is Stupid, building Democratic Governments in parts of the World that's not ready or not appropriate is also pure stupidity, and there seems to be an intense competition going on here. If we truly want to help the people of these countries, we have to start by working with existing government (strong-man or no strong-man), only on stable grounds (Political stability) can the seeds of economic growth be planted. When the economies are such that basic necessities are addressed, their Rule of Law ingrained over decades, to protect their lives and assets, Education systems that have produced generations of middle-class workers that can understand and willingly to defend Democracy, when Free Market Economies and Free Market Capital Markets are linked and integrated with rest of the world (when they can see the future for their families), then Democracy will find the suitable environment to flourish and grow.

From the Dilemma that Mr. Kissinger expressed on USA Foreign Policies, besides the Projection of American Values unto others, there's also a number of other interesting observations I wish to share:

a) seems like there's a Mix-up in the sequence of Events, the Moral Justification for War has to be given by the people before the War starts (if you refer to Sun Tze), in America's case for Vietnam War and the Iraq War, it seems like the President didn't get the Moral Mandate to go to war from the people? At least not from the Liberal Left Media's perspective, who seems to be working to undermine the War efforts in Vietnam and also Iraq and Afghanistan? If there was NO Mandate from the people, the President shouldn't start the war, however if the Mandate had been given, then the Liberals efforts to continuously undermine the war by spreading subversive messages would be treasonous, they would in fact be aiding the enemies' ideologies by undermining American's values and beliefs. In fact, President Franklin D. Roosevelt foresaw and warned about such activities by the fascists sympathizers in America during WWII, the same with the Communists sympathizers throughout the Cold War. Perhaps the speed was too fast, American troops were already in Afghanistan less than a month after 9/11, to get the full mandate of the people?

b) Confusion in the direction of messaging, it seems like in order to pacify and persuade the Liberal Left Media not to continuously undermine the Mandate from the people (if that had been given), the Foreign Policies was an attempt to satisfy the internal American Activists' demands / wish-list and NOT truly addressing the Strategic Interests of the country.

This is a case of the tail wagging the dog, instead of coming up with the Strategy before we enter into the war, and then communicating to the Americans the Strategy (goals and objectives to be accomplished), we're coming up with a 'Strategy' to appease the Liberal Media who's against wars in Vietnam and Iraq. See the proof in the pudding from the various quotes below, from Henry Kissinger and George Shultz both ex Secretary of States.

"… Those committed to democratization have found it difficult to discover leaders who recognize the importance of democracy other than as a means to achieve their own dominance. At the same time, the advocates of strategic necessity have not been able to show how the established regimes will ever evolve in a democratic or even reformist manner. The democratization approach could not remedy the vacuum looming in pursuit of its objectives; the strategic approach was handicapped by the rigidity of available institutions…"

- World Order by Henry Kissinger, published in 2014

".. They were interested in Democracy only if it installed their own group; none favored a system that did not guarantee its own party's control of the political system. A war conducted solely to enforce human rights norms and without concern for the geostrategic or geo-religious outcome was inconceivable to the overwhelming majority of the contestants… The conflict, as they perceived it, was not between a dictator and the forces of democracy but between Syria's contending sects and their regional backers."

- World Order by Henry Kissinger, referring to the various power groups seeking to displace Assad's regime in Syria

"Americans, being a moral people, want their foreign policy to reflect the values we espouse as a nation. But Americans, being practical people, also want their foreign policy to be effective."

- George Shultz, Secretary of State under President Ronald Reagan

What George Shultz was saying sounds similar to the dilemma that Henry Kissinger was deliberating, but it has a much easier answer. Effective Foreign Policy equals getting the job Done! Period. If Americans are a moral people and had internalized their Moral Values as such, then we have nothing to worry about Immoral Foreign Policies or Immoral means used to have Effective Foreign Policies, right?

In conclusion, this Dilemma only arises as we try to solve Multiple Objectives, addressing too many diverse parties, mixing up sequence of events, putting Impossible, Impractical goals as Objectives for "beneficiaries" that don't want them to begin with. It arises because we Confuse America's Internal Political challenges with the External Challenges that our Foreign Policies should be addressing.

Fatal Attraction, the most dangerous enemies are here in America, up close and personal

In addition to the external challenges America faced in dealing with the Radical Islamic Terrorism (some created due to World Events beyond America's control, some created due to our own ignorance in Foreign Policies), there's a number of internal factors actively encouraged by the Radical Liberal neo-Democrats that's really unnecessary self-inflicted damage. We've seen how the Liberal Media helps paints Americans as the Big Satan, supporting Israel (small Satan) that 'kills and bullies the poor innocent Palestinians women and children' story line so wide spread and pervasively indoctrinated, they've become the Liberal Mass Media's Tales of Modern Arabia for the Snowflakes after they had outgrown their Disney Fairy Tales.

Besides the Liberal Progressive Media creating sympathies for the terrorists, George Soros and Jeff Sachs' argument to fund the fundamentalists' associated States in their Global War on poverty. We shall now see how these 2 groups are conducting Ideological warfare on the behalf of the Radical Islamic terrorists and doing such a successful, respectable job thus far! They also worked with the third group, the incompetent Liberal Progressives Politicians that based their perception of the Islamic Fundamentalists on Infatuation and make belief. Infatuation that Kills. We have seen how the US Counter-Intelligence, FBI, NSA etc. had all become Incapacitated by the Muslim Brotherhood and their own sloth from lack of active service. With the lack of Counter Ideological Warfare against the Radical Terrorists, they became stronger ideologically and have been winning in the 8 years under Obama, that's an undeniable fact.

Let's briefly explore this Culture of the Liberal Left neo-democrat's infatuation with Radical Islam to being perceived as Progressive? [Of true spirit of Islam, the shallow juveniles would obviously have no idea about]. Let's also see how the 'Global War on Poverty Pimps' profiteering from others' suffering, before concluding this chapter with the Solutions of how to pacify and eliminate the Hydra of Lerna.

Infatuation with Radicals burning, skinning both Muslims and Christians alive? Infatuation with Radical Islam, stems from the Ideologies of the Islamists schooled in Western education, lives in Western Societies, enjoys the freedom of free speech offered to them in these western societies but feels a deep yearning for their Middle Eastern Roots. Yet, they cannot fit in the Middle East as their western upbringing in now part of their culture which they refuse to admit to themselves. These hopeless 'idealists Islamists' looks down on their cousins in Middle East as unpolished, uncivilized, unschooled in the finer understand of Islam, blind-faith zealots or barbarians. They see the strong-man dictators are barbaric tyrants from the dark ages. In their minds, their new brand of Islam is the future, Ideal and pure, separated from the ugliness and selfishness of man.

Just like the avant garde Romantics supporting the French Revolution, these western-trained Progressive Islamists wishes the love of Allah to spread across a Stateless Muslim land where all Muslims are united in their love for Allah, where they as the avant garde legislators will lead the next stage of Islamic Glory to its new heights! That is the vision of these new prophets of Islamic Faith. Except for a small problem, they are not in touch with reality, they are Not accepted by the real Middle East Muslims with very different Culture and Traditions, they forget all the 'Barbaric Strong-men' currently in power, as the borderless internet culture of will miraculously replace the strong-men with peace loving romantics. These global-style Islamists refuse to associate themselves with the western societies (their adoptive countries), think that they are above the blind-faith uncivilized goats back in their ancestral lands and cannot reconcile between their dreams with the realities in the Middle East except blaming Israel, blaming America, blaming western societies. Israel, America, western societies need to apologize for their sins and then help build up Middle East for the Islamists per their vision so that they can rule in the most enlightened fashion for the entire world to admire, marvel at the glory of Allah. The truth is that these are just wannabes, mediocre intellects using whatever little they googled about Islam to escape from realities of the real world but you can see similarities with the snowflakes living in their star-bucks and apple shops world. Juvenile mindset of refusing to reconcile with realities of life, instead hiding in their pretentious make-belief world.

The reality is that these Radical Infatuated Progressives through their shallow association with the Islamists, pretend to know Islam or the Muslim culture, when in reality, their rhetoric is nothing more than made-up loads of hogwash, conjured up by pompous, egoistic imbeciles, with too much idle time on their hands. The pure Hypocrisy, if you hate the Americans way of life so much and embrace the traditional Sharia Law, what are you doing in America? Why are you not practicing real Sharia law in Middle East? What? You cannot fit in with your fellow Muslims? Or you were born in the land of the Great Satan? Does Sharia Law encourage Free speech, protesting and rioting in Middle East? Why are you not in Iran, Saudi, Iraq, Syria helping the refugees? Furthering Human Rights in these countries? Sharia law states amputating limbs for stealing, what's the punishment for rioting and looting? What's sharia law say about abortion? Women rights? We understand that Sharia law clearly states that women are not the equivalent of man and needs to be beaten when deemed appropriate by the husband. In view of Diversity, we fully respect your rights.

These Idle Talkers, Self-gratifying Egoistic Hypocrites, instigating the Civil Wars in Syria, in Libya through Polls, sponsoring and perpetuating terrorism and violence in Middle East. Just as the Hollywood Celebrities all threatening to leave America but none ever did so, the same with these Radical Islamists Activists all hiding in America with none living in Middle East speaks volumes, all the rhetoric are just made-up lies for consumption by the feeble-minded and enrich the Terrorism Profiteers!

Below are few Activist corporations that works closely with the Muslim Brotherhood on Ideological Subversion; coining terms like Islamophobia, Islamophobe. They are American Civil Liberties Union (Sanctuary cities), Center for Constitutional Rights and Center for American Progress 501c3 – headed by John Podesta (before becoming Hillary Clinton's campaign manager)

Quick Summary

We now understand the history of Islamic Civilization better and the beginnings of Radical Ideologies against the British and French in Middle East after fall of Ottoman Empire, later against the Soviets in Afghanistan and the beginning of entanglement with America as it replaces Britain as the World Power after WWII. America's support of Israel in the Middle East conflicts didn't win it many Arab friends either. The Entanglement with the Religious Radicals only got worse after 91 Gulf War and 2003 Invasion of Iraq, which with hindsight 20/20 America could have avoided. Nonetheless, the support of Israel and Middle East Entanglements could be viewed as comprehensible Foreign Policies.

The other 4 factors are completely self-inflicted and arose due to combination of personal Avarice, ignorance, incompetence, selfish egoistic reasons. The Global War on Poverty led by Activists corporations that funds the Islamists States sympathetic to and harboring Radical organizations, the imbeciles politicians and liberal leftist celebrities infatuated with their 'self-love' about progressive Islamists together with their Disney's Arabic Fantasies. Next, the slothful and ignorant nincompoop of Mainstream media selling their mindless hogwash against the Jewish people in Israel and last but not least, the Mono-Culture, 'Middle Kingdom' cultural tone-deaf foreign policies makers pretending to be foreign affairs experts, while seeing everything around the world through their American Democracy human rights' lenses.

> *"we do not think you can do it by national defense, We think you can do it by moving forward to a new world - a world of law, the abolition of national armaments with a world force and a world economic system."*
>
> - Clement Attlee, Leader of the British Labor Party speaking for the mainstream opinion in 1935 on pursuing peace in Europe

2009 Apology Tour, New Lawrence of Arabia II; The Incompetent fool yet honorable man

Lawrence of Arabian; TE Lawrence (who helped convinced the Arabs to revolt against the Ottoman Turks), who learned the Arabic language, first arrived in Syria in 1909 as a 21 year old (not 8 year) doing research for his Oxford thesis on Influence of Crusades on European military architecture. He trekked across Syria completing his thesis and later joined an excavation expedition to ancient city of Carchemish. Lawrence learned about the Arab culture, worked along the men as one of them and visit the workmen in their homes. Lawrence earned their respect, became close friends with the Arab and loved the Arab Culture. Throughout his time in the Middle East, Lawrence became an apologist for the Arabs and often criticized the British Government siding with the Arabs instead.

If the above Quote from Clement Attlee in 1935 sounds familiar, that's probably because we'd been listening to 8 years of Never Ending Appeasement in Foreign Policies (2008 – 2016), Appeasement to Tyrannical Regimes, Terrorists sponsoring Regimes, Appeasement to Iran, to North Korea, Hubris Ignorance to ISIS (calling them the JV team), Indecisive paralysis to Syrian Civil War (leading to millions of refugees displaced from Middle East). America's revised doctrine in Foreign Policies; Appeasing our Enemies and Abandoning our Allies, all started in 2009.

Before we get into President Obama's Foreign Policies, let's see if we can learn from past history on Policies of Appeasements. In the early 1930s till beginning of WWII most of the British leaders adopted policies of Appeasement to the rise of Hitler's Nazi Germany (fatigue from the last Great War, British foreign policy of maintaining 'global status quo' to facilitate British Trade, Rising Economic and Military Strength of Germany was indeed formidable and at 'peer status' of the British Empire). The poster child for this appeasement policy towards Hitler and Nazi Germany was Neville chamberlain but many British leaders were also supportive of it then. History of WWII showed us that appeasement only allowed the Enemy to grow Bolder and become Stronger, some also saw President Roosevelt's appeasement to Joseph Stalin emboldening the Dictatorship Regime in USSR too.

What History has proven, which our common sense logic can support; a) Appeasement is only a temporary solution as delaying tactic, there has to be a middle and longer term Strategy, b) the Enemy will become Stronger and Bolder over time, making the future engagement tougher, c) a power would only appease another power that it perceives to be of 'peer status' to itself, strategically or tactically for this is just pure common sense, a much stronger force wouldn't use appeasement as policy against a much weaker opponent? Let's fast forward to 2009 and see what happens

When President Obama came into office in early 2009, he started his "around the world apology tour", making several speeches between March 2009 – June 2009 apologizing for America's Foreign Policies for last several decades and how America had exploited and abused the interests of other countries, people of Color, etc. especially in Middle East to the Muslim countries. President Obama is no TE Lawrence, he doesn't know anything about the Middle East nor Islam nor the Muslim Culture or does he? He knows that he lived 2 years as a kid in Indonesia and Indonesia is a Muslim country, but most importantly, he was very close to Edward Said in Columbia, Edward was a Radical Palestinian, therefore those views and perspective were deeply ingrained into his psyche, that would also qualify for his shinning CV as an expert on Muslim Lands, this is especially so, since most Americans have 0 experience on Foreign Culture, 2 years might not be a lot but 2/0 is infinitely more. Not to forget, President Obama is such a great orator, with such great gifts of speech he had become the 44th President of the United States and even won a Nobel price already in his 1st act in White House! Now armed with his tutelage from various mentors since young, including Frank Marshall Davis (in Hawaii), Edward Said (in Columbia), Robert Mangabeira Uger (in Harvard), Jeremiah Wright (in Chicago) and Bill Ayers (also in Chicago), President Obama already has all the answers to the challenges facing the World (all USA's fault).

Now with his "practiced to perfection" presentation skills honed in the University of Chicago, President began his apology Tour for USA. Since President Obama is all about Theatrics and Optics, he is a huge celebrity and the neo-Democrat Media Adored and Idolized him and he could do NO wrong, for the next 8 years President Obama walks on water every day and puts Jesus Christ, Mohammad, Abraham, Buddha all to shame! Only the racists, xenophobic, islamophobic FOX News dares asks him 'rude and fact-based' questions, how boorish and uncivil, For President Obama is an Honorable Man.

After his Apology tours in 2009, in Dec 2010 the Arab Spring starts and spreads across the Middle East countries, we had already discussed President Obama's responses and the results of Civil War in Syria, Libya, Iraq with the refugees fleeing to all parts of the World, speaks volumes for his great accomplishments. For President Obama is an Honorable Man.

In 2011, President Obama orders the Complete withdrawal of all Troops from Iraq without leaving a smaller contingent to safe-guard a 'Green Zone' for our Iraq allies and supporters leaving all of them to the brutality of the invading Enemy forces, allowing the Rise of the Islamic State, yet this is also a great accomplishment For President Obama is an Honorable Man. Many babbling nitwits from Hollywood acted in Movies about War in Iraq, Afghanistan, etc. with names like Green Zone, yet they (like photocopying machines) didn't understand diddly-squat about the Green Zone concept and loudly applauded President Obama's decision to withdraw completely from Iraq and allowing the power vacuum for ISIL to expand into, For President Obama is an Honorable Man.

As we had witnessed, against the Intelligence provided by UAE, Saudi Arabia and Egypt, President Obama consults with the Muslim Brotherhood and issues his Presidential Study Directive, PSD-11 to curb and subvert the US counter-Intelligence against the Radical Islamic Fundamentalists, essentially rendering the FBI impotent against the Radical Islamic Terrorists and clearing the way for ISIL's growth. Yet this is also a great accomplishment For President Obama is an Honorable Man.

As History had shown us, Appeasement by President Obama made the Terrorists & Tyrannical Regimes Bolder and Stronger. The Syrian Civil drags till this day with the refugee crisis spilling into many countries in Europe, causing immense suffering to those losing their families, loved ones and homes.

Ironically, just like the British who watched and learned the Cultural Insights about their Foreign opponents carefully, President Obama also watched and learned the Cultural Insights about Americans carefully when he returned to USA at age 10. And as the British exploited their knowledge and insights of the Foreign Cultures to further British Interests, President also exploited his knowledge and insights of American Culture to further his personal agenda and beliefs. Exploiting their Naïvete to coverup for his Incompetence in Foreign Policies (which can be forgiven at the beginning of his Presidency for he had no experience then, but his Arrogant refusal to learn through the 8 years makes it unforgivable).

Yet President Obama is an Honorable Man. Why is President Obama such an honorable man, you might ask? Simply because the Mainstream Media are racists and judges a man by his skin color. Since it would not be Politically Correct to call him out on the truth due to his skin color, the Mainstream Media calls him an Honorable man.

To know more about the Honorable Man's accomplishments, you might like to refer: iWar: War and Peace in the Information Age by Bill Gertz, Unholy Alliance: The Agenda Iran, Russia, and Jihadists Share for Conquering the World by Jay Sekulow, Defeating Jihad: The Winnable War by Sebastian Gorka and The Field of Fight: How We Can Win the Global War Against Radical Islam and Its Allies, by Lieutenant General (Ret.) Michael T. Flynn and Michael Ledeen.

Censorship Rules set by President - First, it must be True

The New York Times - 1941
Washington, Dec 9th - President Roosevelt laid down two primary rules of censorship of war news today, reserving to himself and high-ranking officials the right of decision over material released.

News to be released, he said, first must be true, and then it must pass a test whether it conforms with a rule that it must "not give aid and comfort to the enemy."

Λερναῖα Ὕδρα To Slay the Hydra of Lerna (of Greek Mythology), Exploring Solutions to Radical Religious Terrorists

We've now seen clearly all the challenges and understood various perspectives of the Radical Religious Islamic Fundamentalists challenges. We've also better understood the subterfuges and subversion activities by the Liberal Left Mainstream Media, fanning the flames of ignorance, Hatred and Ira (wrath), undermining the American Patriotism with Globalism sophistries, later we will see the dangers of such 'globalism' mindset perpetrated via the French inept education system in 1940. See President Roosevelt's solution against the mindless Mob of a Press aka Mainstream Media.

Let's understand mindsets of Capable Leaders throughout History, those that do NOT lead from Behind via Popularity Polls: Here's a summary of Richelieu's career by Henry Kissinger in World Order

a. Indispensable element of a successful foreign policy is a long term strategic concept based on careful analysis of all relevant factors.

b. The statesman must distill that vision by analyzing and shaping an array of ambiguous, often conflicting pressures into a coherent and purposeful direction. He or she must know where this strategy is leading and why.

c. He must act at the outer edge of the possible, bridging the gap between his society's experiences and its aspirations. Because repetition of the familiar leads to stagnation, no little daring is required.

> *"We have no eternal allies, and we have no perpetual enemies. Our interests are eternal and perpetual, and those interests it is our duty to follow."*
> - Lord Palmerston on British Foreign Policy
> *Forti nihil difficile* - Benjamin Disraeli

From the Richelieu, Disraeli and Palmerston, we glean the correct approach [The able leadership mindset] to solving this new Challenge has to have a New solution, we need to be brave to leave the "shores of safety" and stretch our minds for unconventional solutions and from Palmerston, we should partner with any possible friends however "unlikely ones" for the solution. The necessary Bravery, not merely against the Radicals Jihadists Militants in the fighting Units of ISIL, Al-Qaeda, Hamas, etc. but also Bravery against the even more Real and Acute fear coming from the Radicals Jihadists in Americas' Mainstream Media and neo-Fascists 501c3 Activists Corporations back home because that's where they can get you and your families' credibility with smears and alleged "whatever accusations" their Trillions of Funds and hundreds, thousands of Lawyers can cook up.

> *"In France between the two world wars, the teachers' union decided that schools should replace patriotism with internationalism and pacifism. Books that told the story of the heroic defense of French soldiers against the German invaders at Verdun in 1916 despite suffering massive casualties were replaced by books that spoke impartially about the suffering of all soldiers - both French and German - at Verdun. Germany invaded France again in 1940, and this time the world was shocked when the French surrender after just six weeks of fighting - especially since military experts expected France to win. But two decades of undermining French patriotism and morale had done their work."*
>
> - Thomas Sowell

As Thomas Sowell had pointed out, the power of Academia, Mainstream Media. Social Media in shaping the public's perception which in the case of the French soldiers in WWII translated into lack of will power, rapid capitulation and surrender. This highlights an important epiphany in our 'war on terror', as complicated as the Islamic Radical Terrorists threat is, even more complex is the Radical Virus threat we face back home.

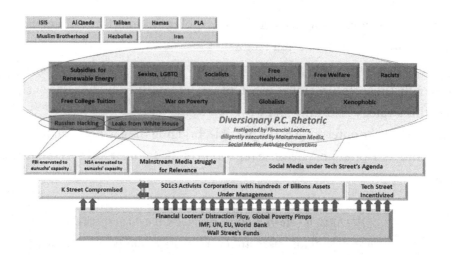

The larger Threat is the Diversionary P.C. Rhetoric put out by the Financial Looters. Although these Financial Looters didn't create ISIS, Al-Qaeda, etc. (some of the Failed American Foreign Policies did contribute), but the diversion has been so successful that despite spending trillions of tax payers' money, the situation at the end of the honorable man's reign is much worse in Middle East than prior 9/11. The Diversionary tactics of the Financial Looters combined with the sheer ineptness and Greed of Political Leadership in America over last 2 decades has transformed the Middle East into a living hell for many of its residents, it has also incapacitated the K Street's Federal Agencies into self-serving Palaces' Eunuchs; afflicted by Sloth, Avarice and Hubris, that knows only to appease our enemies, abandon our allies and attack its new Leaders (elected by the American People).

Just as the AIDS virus breaks down the victims' body immune system, this Virus spread by the Financial Looters & previous Greedy Political Puppets (aka Wall Street's Cronies) has caused K Street to be compromised and now attacks the American People instead of the enemy (NSA White House Leaks, FBI Russian Hacking). If Not for ISIS (the common flu), we would never have known about the Radicals neo-Democrats' corrupting our K Street Apparatchiks FBI, NSA, etc. (the terrible AIDS virus breaking down America's immune system). We definitely need a peaceful and intelligent plan to address the Radical Liberal Progressive Jihadists back home in addition to the ones in Middle East.

On the engagement with the Radical Religious Islamic Fundamentalist issue, let's start with the Facts, there's 1.6 Billion Muslims in the World and growing, purely on Religious Ideological perspective, we can group them into Radicals, Moderates, Reformers. The Islamic Radicals are only a small group but sadly the Reformers are an even smaller group. The Moderates might not be directly doing the killing but a substantial portion of them sympathize with the Radicals. To address the Radicals Ideology, we need help and Leadership from the Islamic Reformers.

It is true that the Islamic Fundamentalist threat is Not like the Imperial Japan and Nazi Germany crisis back in 1941, nonetheless, it is an existential and complex one. For the first time since WWII, we are up against a well-funded, tenacious, ideologically sophisticated enemy on a Global Scale. Like the Vietnam war, it is asymmetric and we cannot see the enemy but unlike Vietnam War, many of the enemies now lives amongst us in NYC, Paris, London, Barcelona, Brussels, etc. President Trump made the comment during his election campaign that in WW II the enemies wear uniforms, now they can strike us at home anytime and we have no way of knowing who they are.

Under the last administration, the Islamic Radicals seemed to be winning the Ideological War, Many Americans, led by the Radical neo-Democrats Politicians and Radical neo-Fascists Activists corporations are not only rooting for the Radical Jihadists, but also supporting their affiliated organizations financially, ceaselessly broadcasting pro-Islamists' propagandas and rhetoric. That is what happens when you lose the Ideological High-ground, when there's no counter-Intelligence (all blocked and rendered impotent by PSD-11). Under the last administration's 8 years of appeasement and avoidance strategies, it really looked as if the complex and tedious solutions to this Radical challenge seemed too large to undertake and perhaps not worth the effort to engage the Enemy and USA should just leave it be.

Luckily, we now have a new leadership and administration that is willing to engage and start to resolve this complicated crisis. We ask ourselves is it worth it? So much effort to counter just a small bunch of Radical Terrorists? True, if you only see ISIL, Al-Qaeda, Hamas, Hezbollah, etc. (ie. Only the fighting arm of the Militant groups), they are not quite like the Russian military in their size, but if you expand to a) Entities and b) States Funding them, c) the available Funds, d) Funds Generating Organizations and e) Ideologies spread by the f) Activists corporations, g) Islamic Radicals h) Radical Liberal neo-Democrat Media, i) Social Media controlled by the Tech Monopolies Giants all strongly incentivized to support the Diversionary P.C. rhetoric of the Financial Looters from Wall Street, then it would take detailed planning and deep understanding to untangle this mess.

危机, 机会 in Chinese, the same character appears in Crisis and Opportunity because with Great Difficulty comes Great Opportunities (or with High Risks comes High Returns)! If we can solve the Radical Islamic Terrorist Challenge for the World as in WW II, we will also help solve 60-70% of the *problems we currently face in America too (the same thing happened in WWII, America was still struggling the Great Depression since 1929, by helping out the World, America also helped Grow its Own Economy into the World's Super Power! Showing that Unselfish acts can lead to the Greatest Returns)

*Radical Islamists is merely a flu, it is the pervasive spread of Activist Corporations inside K Street, Tech Street masterminded by the Financial Looters in Wall Street that has caused the immune system of America to become severely impaired

1991 Shock and Awe, 2017 Intelligence about the entire Hydra

In 1991 Gulf War, under Military leadership of Gen Colin Powell and Gen Norman Schwarzkopf Jr. USA demonstrated overwhelming Force to overcome Saddam Hussein Forces. This time round, the enemy is much more evasive and tenacious. It is like the Hydra of Lerna in the second Labor of Heracles, every time you cut off one of its heads, two more will grow in its place and it has been going on for last 8 years. This Hydra is well nourished and flooded with Funds and highly revered by America's Radical Liberal Media and neo-Democrats, sympathized with by many Moderate Muslims. That's the reason it is difficult to eliminate once and for all.

To defeat a worthy opponent, we need to learn and understand it before devising the strategy to take it on. Let's start with the Ideology, you have seen some of their writings and ideas. Concepts well explained and reasoned out, the Islamic scholars and theologians are not some mindless people blowing themselves up! They are well read and knowledgeable, intensely passionate in their beliefs, dedicated and can be extremely persuasive. Their ideologies are well formulated as they were articulated in their writings and teachings. It would not be easy to take on and challenge such sensitive religious beliefs, we need to understand each component of the doctrines and respect the immense danger they pose before attempting to find allies in the Muslim religious ummah to disavow certain components of such ideologies, just to break the linkage in logic that links the various concepts together. Just like during the Gulf War, having a Large International Coalition fronted by countries like Saudi Arabia, Egypt, Jordan and UAE is crucial to get the Muslim community buy-in and support.

Let's look at the following 2 charts on the complete Make-up of our esteemed adversary the Hydra of Radicals [the Islamists, the Terrorists, the Ignorant & Greedy Mainstream Media, infatuated Progressive Radicals back home, Activist Corporations with limitless Funding]

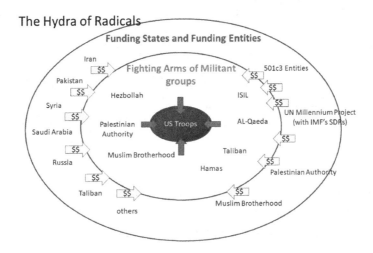

There's 3 categories of opponents here, the ones we see (a) opposing our troops, the ISIL, Al-Qaeda, Hamas, Hezbollah, and the ones we don't easily see (b) the States Funding the Militant groups (Iran, Syria, Pakistan, Russia, etc.) and (c) the Entities Funding them (we discussed the Millennium Projects, etc. earlier). With the never-ending funds coming in, little wonder, the Hydra's heads keep growing back so quickly!

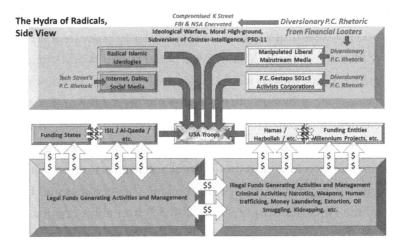

But that's just one piece of the puzzle, let's look at the side view of the Hydra. Like the enemy troops caught between the Pincer maneuver of Coalition Troops in '91, now the US troops are also trapped in an everlasting war between:

1) the success of the Radical Islamic Ideological aided by the (a) Subversion of US Counter-Intelligence, (b) manipulative 'sympathetic' coverage by the Radical Liberal Mainstream Media, & (c) Social Media's pro-radicals' coverage, 'enemy friendly air-cover', all jointly provides the Hydra complete dominance (Moral High ground) of the Ideological Front and the

2) the Funds being multiplied exponentially through re-investment into High Returns and low Risks a) Criminal Activities and b) other Legal Funds Generating Activities in Wall Street.

As you can see, our coalition-led assaults on the Physical locations occupied by ISIS/ISIL, important as they are, is only a small piece (2% of Strategy) of the entire puzzle. What we really need to step up (98% of Strategy) are the twin efforts of:

a. learning, understanding the Ideology warfare. Forming a Middle East Led Coalition in this New Age of Falsafah to be championed by Islamic Faylasufs all around the world and

b. tracing the Funds Flow of the Terrorists and their sponsors. And then cutting off their nourishment

Both are vital to winning the War against the Hydra of Radicals, both will contribute to World Peace on a much larger scale than what meets the eye.

As we've learnt, it is the Diversionary P.C. Rhetoric that's sowing so much distraction, discord and exacerbating the already complicated situation. Thus, the first step to simplify the solution, would be to take the Diversionary Rhetoric out of the equation.

In Name: International Coalition of Peace; Finance & Economic Council

In Substance: Incisive focus on Funds Flow & Audit

Military Campaigns had been sustained via Financial backing throughout History. Since the current combatants do not wear uniforms, it makes it harder to know their identities, yet we still have the Financial & Ideological Trails. Money-Men better Get to Work! Once the funds are cut, the enemy's capacity to continue the war would be severely reduced. We know that the entities for funding and the processes for re-investments have already been setup and put into motion since last decade. These entities [interrelated to IMF, UN's Millennium Project, Muslim Brotherhood, Palestine Authorities, etc.] have also gotten very rich and powerful, growing richer each day from the returns of their investments in crimes (both illegal and legal crimes in Wall Street).

Here's the good news for America, success in tracking these entities and their possible affiliations with many of the Activists Corporations, 501c3 "charitable" organizations should help resolve 60-70% of all of America's Domestic problems. The domestic 'mindless rhetoric' will all start to disappear, leaving only the important real Domestic challenges, some of will start healing by themselves without the neo-Fascists Activists Corporations constantly pricking at the old wounds. The current administration can start focusing on fixing the real problems with our Poverty, Education, Social Security, etc. as the Activists groups 501c3 entities' funds, are interlinked. (for example; Black Lives Matter, Planned Parenthood, Teachers Union, etc..) We can eliminate many birds with one stone here too.

If our Money-Men are no longer at the cutting edge of current technology (let's face it, our Intelligence have been left impotent for last 8 years and Technology moves way too fast. Case in point, remember how FBI needed apple to open an i-Phone?), we'll seek help from the Russians, Chinese and Israel to teach our Intelligence personnel, they have incentives to stop the Terrorists too. Think Lord Palmerston, we have no eternal allies, and we have no perpetual enemies. The

Russians, Chinese and Israel will be more than willing to cooperate with us to eliminate the mutual Islamic terrorist threat, you'll just hear the Radical Islamic Activists in America with their political witch-hunt once more.

Capital Punishment needs to be strictly enforced for Treasonous Crimes

We need to focus Effort to Audit all the Terrorists related Funds 501c3 Activists Corporations' books, and all those of their affiliates too, for last 2 decades and uncover any irregularities, linked with K Street's contributions as well as existence of audit trails linking Wall Street Financial Looters with the UN [Millennium project], IMF, World Bank's funds as well as any suspicious Foreign Regimes.

Any IMF issued SDRs are Red Flags, any Bank accounts linked with Muslim Brotherhood, Palestine Authorities, Iranian or Iranian-related Funds thoroughly investigated. Through audits, strongly encourage those responsible for bank signatories to be brought in for cooperative interviews. 1800-Hotlines setup for potential whistle blowers, civic minded and Patriotic employees to support our efforts to protect Americans against terrorism.

Any Leaks by NSA, FBI, Social Media and Mainstream would need to be pursued as vigorously as the WWII's Nazi's spies and Cold War Communists' covert Operations. Go Direct Model needs to be employed to target the crypto Radicals and fellow travelers back home in America. Those that lead the subversion and sabotage activities against this country. There are many sympathizers for the Radicals too. We will also need to amputate away the gangrene portions of FBIs, NSA, CIA and various K Street Apparatchiks. Failure to do so will only result in a Dead certain future for this country's fight against external threats.

The Radical Jihadists back home will resist to their last dollar, yet we shall Fear NOT them, Remember Benjamin Disraeli's motto "Forti Nihil Difficile" [To the Brave Nothing is Difficult]

> *"In violent conflict with each other [between Sunni, Shia], they're united in their commitment to dismantle the existing regional order and rebuild it as a divinely inspired system."*
>
> - Henry Kissinger in World Order

Pan-Arab 'strong man' Rule Vs Islamists' Vision in Middle East

To avoid an overly idealistic approach of how to solve the Radicalization issues, let's first view the Middle East as it has been shaped since the end of the Ottoman's Empire. As Henry Kissinger explained in World Order, the Pan-Arab leaders respect the balance of power via State lines defined geographically via UN. The Islamists, the more radical groups that promised to replace all the existing systems with a new Religious based Middle East Order, that'll exist across all States.

The Islamists vision to rebuild the entire Middle East sounds like the Idealistic (Romanticism) that set forth the French Revolution and Russian Revolution which ultimately led back to tyranny which is where the Pan-Arabs had been for last 60 years. Tearing away all establishments would be too traumatic for the civilizations to survive and too much would be lost before any meaningful recovery can restart. The Pan Arab regimes respect the balance of power & geographical State Lines, they are (like it or not) the current power establishment in Middle East and you actually have someone we can negotiate with, thus the most logical and sensible approach would be to work with the existing Pan-Arab regimes in hopes of gradually working towards a more democratic society over time. There's a major caveat, where are the *selfless reformers willing to sacrifice themselves in pursue such Risky and Thankless endeavors? Would the global-styled Islamists volunteer? Would they be willing to move to the Middle-East and live under Real Sharia Law for next 2-3 decades to help spread democracy in Middle-East? Would these westernized 'romantics' be accepted by their Muslims in Middle East? I think we already know the answer.

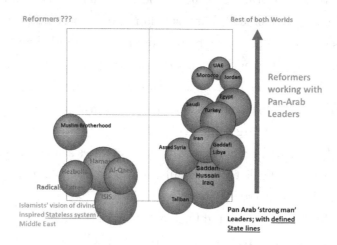

Muslims Allies to help lead and champion the cause of reforms (Go Direct Models)

UAE, Jordon, Morocco, Egypt could be leading contenders to facilitate and advise on the directions and Strategies, we can see that with the stability afforded from the Pan Arab government, some of those pro-west regimes have slowly adopted a more liberal stance with extended interface with the West. That's the key, as in the part, trading brings wealth to both cultures, increased exposure to the Global Trade, Foreign Investments into these countries and Tourism helps the Pan-Arab move towards more democratic regimes (relatively) as wealth in the middle class increases.

We'll have to use the Ockham Razor to cut out the corrupted Middle-man in UN. A convincing case to help spearhead the Middle East's coalition would be the End the Civil War in Syria to allow rebuilding of the country and return of its citizens back home? Ending the Civil War would be a sure sign of Good Faith [as corner stone] to start the Reform Process, it would also elevate the pressure of refugees on Europe as well as countries like Turkey, Jordan, etc.

Engagement on Ideology grounds Globally, Please step forth, The Great Reformer!

As critical as the Radical Ideology crisis is, there's an equally important issue to be addressed. As we'd noted earlier, there's 1.6B Muslims and growing, we have to find some kind of common understanding between rule of law and the religiously laws. One major challenge that the Israelis have found out in their negotiations with Palestinians is that there's NO de facto head of the Muslim or Arab communities, no Caliph of the Muslim Ummah to speak for all Arabs or Muslims.

Yet the threat of Islamic religious Radicals has become more pronounced in recent years as unlike in the past when Muslims were living within the boundaries of their Nation States, many are now within the European Union and more coming to USA, this is fine if Muslims are the minorities as the current Western societies are well tolerant towards all religions. But this will NOT be the case when Islam becomes the dominant religion (even as the majority of Muslims are NOT Radicals). One cannot deny the fact of (as the Radicals are highlighting to the World now), the Incompatibility of the Religious views, how is it going to work then? There are many questions that needs to be asked and answered jointly with Islamic scholars and religious leaders to prevent wars and unnecessary bloodshed in the future!

Let's address the Radical Islamic Religious issues and also try to solve both challenges at the same time. We need to look for Common Ground, form an International Coalition of Peace headed by Islamic Countries (supported by USA and other Allies), seeking help and co-leadership from Russia, China, Saudis, UAE, Egypt, Jordan, Israel, etc. all with skin in the game for themselves. China and Russia have major challenges with their Muslim populations and it is in their Best interests for the reconciliation of the Islamic Radical Ideologies with the Acceptance of Global Peaceful co-Existence with other "misguided" religions in eyes of Islam. Addressing and Hopefully Disavowing the Radical Jihadist Theologies is critical, various leading Mujtahid (a jurist, one who has earned the right to exercise independent Reasoning when formulating Islamic legislation) should issue Fatwahs against the Radicals, the Sharif of Hejaz, شريف الحجاز Protector of Mecca and Medina needs to help make a stand against them too.

Let's start by addressing the Religious Islamic Radical's Ideology, which is rooted in history and religious quotes, unlike the 'mindless rhetoric of neo-Fascists Dems', these Radical theosophers have an intellectual bent, they saw the injustice to their fellow countrymen at a time when Western Powers were on the rise around the World, driven in large part by the Industrial Revolution. As intellectually capable as they were, there was nothing they could do to reverse the decline of the Ottoman, Mughal empires, etc. They were confused between what's 'controllable' and what's 'not controllable' by themselves thus creating a deep sense of Insecurity, that coupled with their great intellectual prowess on the religious texts, translated into religious zealotry. Contrasts that with the Faylasufs that were lucky enough to influence Progress in societies through their works, thereby seeing Hope for the future.

"when there is an entire alteration of conditions, it is as if the whole creation had changed and all the world had been transformed, as if there were a new creation, a rebirth, a world brought into existence anew."

- Ibn Khaldun reflected on his experience, his family emigrated from Seville (due to Reconquista) to Tunis, at 17, he lost both his parents to the Black Death, produced *Al-Maqaddimah*; an introduction to History in 1377

This new Coalition would be one of Peace, but backed by Military from various countries. As only under the protection of the Coalition Forces, would the Islamic Scholars and Reformers (protected by their Government and Coalition forces) step forth to discuss the real challenges and incompatibility with other world religions. To then be able to search for Peaceful Religious Doctrines for all.

This **International Coalition of Peace, Council of Religious Studies**, needs to highlight and address questions to whomever can constitute the Muslim Ummah (like the Council of Nicaea back in 325AD) questions like:

a. application of Sharia Law, should non-Muslims follow Sharia Law?
b. The 4 Madrassa Teachings
    a. Kufr (disbelief, denial of Islam), Shirk (saying anything against the oneness of Allah), or irtidad (apostasy) are all to be punished by death
    b. Non-Muslims are to be subjugated, only Muslims should rule the world
    c. World must have only one Caliphate and no governments needed)
    d. Modern Nation-states is Kufr
c. The House of Islam vs House of War Ideologies
d. What is the definition of Muslim Land? If NO Muslim has been invaded, why are there Islamic killings against innocent civilians?
e. Can Individual Muslims declare Jihad without the Caliphate's approval?
f. Is Allah God to all? Where do non-Muslims stand in the House of Islam?
g. Religious vs Secular/Political Leadership?

While many of these answers might seem straightforward to some, let's hope we can get the same answers from the 'Muslims ummah'. If they are, let it be officially agreed to and declared to all Muslims globally to disavow the Radicals Jihadist and declare the Extremists as UN-Muslim and issue Takfiri against the Radical Muslims.

We might find it not as straight-forward as you think, Most of the good Reformers in Islam (they are the scare minority) already sees the challenges of these Incompatibility and the need to reform and reconcile the Radical Beliefs and certain interpretation of the Religion. The separation of Religion with the State is not as pronounced in Shia Islam. But None of them will ever step forth to identify these contradictions for fear of their lives and families lives. Much work remains to be done, below are some suggestions:

Leading Ideologies to be studied together with Religious Texts

Explore the Akbar the Great's Divine Monotheism (tawhid-e ilahi), sulh-e kull, Universal Peace, mahabbat-e kull, Universal Love.

Study the Literature and Philosophies of Ibn Arabi's Face of Allah in all rightly guided religions

Science, Philosophy and Religious studies

Glorify and promote the Great works of Ibn Rushd, Ibn Sina, Ibn Khaldun, Mulla Sadra, etc.

Promote Practice of Sufism & Falsafah

Open the Gates of ijtihad (ability to see Reason, apply logic with Religion), to spread the teachings of mujtahids (an organized, systematic doctrine with training in application of Reason, Logic in various Fields beyond mere Legal judgements)

As the Muslims Leaders lead the coalition, western nations acting only as facilitators. Always Be sensitive to the Extreme Dangers faced by the reformers, also attuned to the Cultural Sensitivities (not to appear as arrogant, dismissive, always be honest and sincere). Clearing away these Radical Ideologies will also open the way for more transparent integration and assimilation of religions and cultures all around the world. If they are left un-resolved, and left to fester, then sad to say, the current Violence will only the beginning, not even tip of the iceberg of what we'll be witnessing in the Future!

عصبيّة

e pluribus unum

Hopefully we can eliminate the Diversionary P.C. Rhetoric from the equation asap, George Soros, the Great self-admitted Global Financial Profiteer [per his book *The Crisis of Global Capitalism* in 1998] together with his cronies in Wall Street, Tech Street and K Street have done the world a great disservice. Distorting the perception of the problem and impeding the solution of the challenge for nearly 2 decades now. Aiding and abetting the Fake 'TE Lawrence' in mishandling the entire Middle East debacle in last 8 years, also confusing Bush 43rd The Wise, into Nation Building blunders in Iraq, thereby causing untold sufferings, loss of lives in Middle East over last 2 decades. This entire package is clearly America's and we owe it to the world to unburden the world of it.

At some stage, when we have mutual understanding and able to reconcile the Ideology differences, there is light at the end of the tunnel and chance for mutual respect and cooperation. we should also start planning to teach our kids, the young and impressionable, the Importance of Religious Freedom, the Fragility of religious peace and sacredness of Religious Empathy. We must teach it in schools through the re-vitalized Education Systems and also broadcasted through America's National Message Media. Always promote Learning and Mutual Understanding.

Bearing in mind to ourselves that Military action always be avoided and if absolutely necessary, be kept to a minimal, just enough to help bring about ends to Civil Wars and promote sustainable balance of Power in the Regions.

Freedom of Speech is Important, but always be respectful, for Religious Freedom is Fragile. Never ever let the Radical Activists stir up Racial Hatred and Religious Ignorance ever, a Global Solidarity against Terrorism. It's NOT about *Political Correctness, it is just stupid Common Sense!

Chapter 7

How to untie the 'Gordian knot'?
Different perspectives on various challenges

Take a look at the back of your dollar note, the Great Seal of United States, the pyramid has four sides each aligned with the 4 points of the compass. At the lower level of the pyramid, one will be either on one side or on the other (thus can only see from one side but not the other sides), only when one gets up to the top (the points come together), the eye of Reason opens up to be able to understand all sides' perspectives. This is a State created in the name of Reason, not in the name of Power.

When one descends from the eye of Reason (due to Pride, Greed, Envy, Lust of Power, of Wealth), they will naturally be able to see only one side again (Ignorance and drudgery once again dominates).

Seeing Multitude of Perspectives

Another analogy in photography, when I got my first SLR camera with a 28-300mm zoom lens, I was ecstatic with the zoom function, it was as if you could have unlimited new perspectives in your repertoire of photographic images. This is really a neat and powerful tool! Many folks when they discovered google search might have felt the same 'empowerment' of been able to know so much more and always knowing the right answer might make one feel smarter?

Much Later, I realized the zoom function doesn't give me different perspectives, it allows me to focus on certain subjects with more emphasis but my perspective does Not change, unless I move myself, walk around. It requires much more effort to get different perspectives.

Similarly, with google and internet search, it doesn't give you different perspectives (unless you already know what you are look for), it merely gives you the most popular perspective. Google doesn't always give you the right answer, it gives you the most easily available and popular answer (as we'd discussed in chapter 4, on very basic data, google works fine but for more complex and sophisticated analysis, it merely provides you with the most easily available report). The Moral of the story here, to get multiple perspectives is possible, but it will take much effort and discipline, lots of both. 'Shortcuts' attempting to be 'in the know' without expending any effort on your part, merely gets you hoodwinked into blathering [paid for] political slogans, just as you would be repeating advertising slogans of [paid for] informercials.

知不知上；不知知病。夫唯病病，是以不病。聖人不病，以其病病，是以不病。

- Lao Tze 老子

Knowing what you do not know is a strength, thinking that you know is a weakness

Only by recognizing you are sick, then you will seek a cure

The Sage is well, as she sees her illness and treats them, and thus remain well

By design, there can be many interpretations of just this short verse from Tao Te Ching (Dao De Jing), so let's just focus on a few concepts. You have to be honest with yourself to learn, pretending to know when you do not will never allow you to learn new knowledge.

知不知上 another concept: knowing a couple of perspectives on a topic doesn't mean you announce you know the topic, by listening to another explain their understanding to you, might teach you a new perspective.

不知知病 not knowing what you don't know could be due to innocent ignorance or egoistic behavior, if it is the former, it might be possible to shed light to ignorance with patient education, if it is the later, you can never add more water to a cup already full.

夫唯病病, 是以不病 you need courage to face reality, only then can you address the problems in an unemotional way and devise an objective solution to the problem.

聖人不病, 以其病病, 是以不病 the sage doesn't always know all, by understanding her own shortcomings and constantly learning new perspectives, knowledge and insights does the Sage tirelessly work towards incremental wisdom.

Having the discipline to control your ego and humility to know your areas of weakness will allow you to learn from various subject matter experts, being able to learn from everyone in their areas of expertise is like Active Transport concept (able to move molecules against concentration gradient). Always having an open mind is like always having an empty cup, ego keeps your cup always full no new perspectives or knowledge can enter, humility drains the cup empty.

Let's brainstorm a number of ways to gain new perspectives (all would require much effort and discipline); 1) moving to and living in a different Culture will show you a new perspective. 2) Learning and immersing yourself in a new language might help you see a one too. 3) Having friends (real friends) from many different levels in a society would help you see through their eyes and gain different perspectives. 4) Study, Immerse and internalize new Religious concepts or other new subject matters can also help provide new perspectives too.

True commitment to any of these endeavors would require significant dedication of time, energy and resources. It would be equivalent to taking everything that you've learnt and accomplished till date, then add an additional 50-70% on top of that, in order to accomplish each of these new endeavors. Who has time and energy to pursue such activities? You are right, most don't.

The real question then, if you have your own perspective, can you imagine others might also have their perspectives and if they are different from yours, can you tolerate the difference? I imagine we already know the answer to that question for the snow-flakes, neo-democrat celebrities and neo-fascists Activists.

> 莊子 *Zhuangzi (370 – 311 BC) puts it in another way, "we should not be dismayed to find that there was no such thing as certainty, because this "confusion" could lead us to the Way. Egotism was the greatest obstacle to enlightenment. It was an inflated sense of self that made us identify with one opinion rather than another; ego made us quarrelsome and officious, because we wanted to change other people to suit ourselves. Once people stopped arguing about doctrines and theories, they could acquire the "Great Knowledge". Instead of claiming that this could not mean that, they began to see that all apparent contradictions formed a mysterious, numinous entity. This coincidentia oppositorum brought them to the hub of the wheel, the axis of the Way."*
>
> – The Great Transformation by Karen Armstrong

"the pivot at the center of the circle, for it can react equally
to that which is and to that which is not"

Why the need for new and different perspectives?

To untie the Gordian knot, to see the solution, it would help to see all the various perspectives (angles) at the issue. As in the Photography analogy earlier, if you do Not move yourself, you cannot get a new perspective, you can zoom into any subject matter and get real closeup shots but the relative positions of your subjects are fixed; what's on the left, middle and right. You are still viewing the world in a relatively "static 2D view". Only if you walk around, the relative positions of the subjects start to change and switch around, arguing about an issue with only 1 perspective is like arguing about the relatively positions of subject matters, what's on left and right, but if you view the same subject matters from different perspectives (or angles), their relative positions to each other start to change. Only now you are seeing the 3-D world. By having a multitude of perspectives, you can see the "approximate reality" as best as possible. $\sum$ of all perspectives $\simeq$ Solution to Gordian Knot, We need more effort to Think deeper!

Instilling discipline into our Decision-Making process

We also need more effort to Think Clearer! Stereotyping is a "short cut" [heuristics] decision making process that everyone employs. It relies on past experience or the "most widely held conventional wisdom" instead of re-assessing every new situation from scratch each time (which will be too time consuming). A perfectly innocent example would be when you see a bear or a lion, you assume it is dangerous and can harm you, although you probably have never encounter a bear or lion in the wild, this is a perfectly logical assumption based on common knowledge that bears and lions are powerful predators.

For majority of decisions we make on daily basis, this "short cut" [rule of thumb] method works fine, the challenge comes when some people gets lazy and starts applying this "short cut" method to other humans too. When we meet a person new to us, instead of assessing him/her with an open mind, giving them time and opportunity before forming a perception of them, we pre-judge them based on unfounded "short cuts". If you pre-judge humans based on race, sex, religions, etc. the P.C. Gestapo has already coined and painted them into the most heinous crimes. Yet, interestingly, Pre-judging people without making the effort to know them personally is the basis of Racism! And the ones most guilty of these types of pre-judging acts are the previous-slave owners democrats and also the current Radical P.C. Gestapo neo-democrats (who cannot tolerate views diverse and different from themselves? Who calls other Americans 'a basket of deplorables' or was it "a bucket of losers'?)

So how do we become more Consciously aware of our own decision-making flaws? Can we improve, Internalize New discipline into our decision-making process? 知不知上, becoming conscious of potential flaws is a Huge step to strengthening one's weaknesses. Let's review couple of decision making tools used in Management discussions and analysis, before discussing proposals for solutions. As this is not a management book, I will only cover the key concepts behind them.

Pareto Analysis or Pareto Charts identifies the top contributors or causes of any concern we are trying to solve. It quantifies the contributing reasons instead of anecdotal stories. Obviously, the sample size must be as large as possible, and as representative of the entire population size without any bias during sampling.

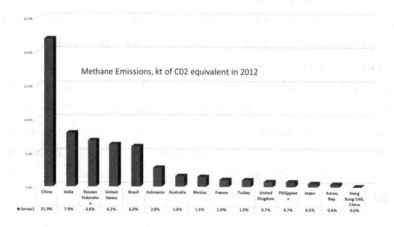

Methane Emissions, kt of CO2 equivalent in 2012

	China	India	Russian Federation	United States	Brazil	Indonesia	Australia	Mexico	France	Turkey	United Kingdom	Philippines	Japan	Korea, Rep.	Hong Kong SAR, China
Series1	21.9%	7.9%	6.8%	6.2%	6.0%	2.8%	1.6%	1.5%	1.0%	1.0%	0.7%	0.7%	0.5%	0.4%	0.0%

Looking at the example above on Methane Emissions, you'll notice that China which has slightly more people than India has 3 times the Pollution of India. Russia which has less than half the people in USA has more pollution than USA. Brazil which has less 2/3 of USA population has as much Pollution. Japan has 130 m people 6X Australia's yet Australia has 3X more Methane Emissions. You wonder why Al Gore is not getting China to be at India's level, Russia and Brazil to be at level comparable to USA per capital (per person) and Australia, Mexico, etc. to be at Japan's level? We'll discuss more on Global Warming later & introduce you to Climate-change Pimps.

The Fish-Bone

Couple of examples of Fishbone, you write up all the various categories of Causes that have effect on the problem (defect) and list the more detailed sub-cause within each category. Used together with Pareto analysis, this two tools form a powerful combination to solving the problems.

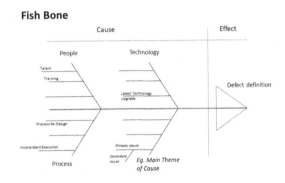

FMEA 6 Sigma (Failure Modes and Effects Analysis)

In the FMEA, you notice that they analyze each defect by severity of impact, frequency of occurrence and chance of detection. High Severity, Frequent Occurrence and low chance of Detection would be very bad. Self-radicalized Islamic Terrorists might fall into this category? We can use all the above tools to objectively resolve the Radical Jihadist Terrorists, High Crimes, High Abortion rates, High Welfare expenses challenges easily.

The Radical Liberal Activists and P.C. Gestapo Media always using anecdotal emotional stories to confuse the uninformed and misinformed Naïve audience isn't doing anyone Favors. Therefore, as we solve the Funding challenges for the Terrorists (in chapter 6), we can eradicate all the 501c3 Activists Corporations and finally we can start working and (Truly) Solving the problems this country faces!

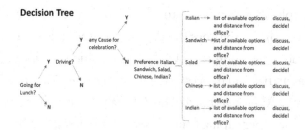

Decision Tree shows the thought process, logic behind decision making. It allows an objective and un-bias look into the logic of each decision, the considerations that went into each decision and if all options have been considered or all required information made available to the decision maker. For those not familiar with this tool, starting with a more common and repetitive task would be good way to learn (perhaps like where to go for lunch? See chart above)

Process Maps (Flow Charts) helps identifies the critical paths and "bottle necks", it can also be leveraged to determine probability of success. Process Maps can be used for high level processes and drill-down each process into sub-processes and so on into individual tasks. We can start combining individual's tasks and decision making into their decision trees and map out the logic. This combination of Process Mapping and Decision-Making Logic forms the basis of process Improvement, streamlining and IT process automation.

If there are many sub-processes, the **probability of defects** increases. If you have 5 steps to completing the final product (or solution) and each step has a 10% probability of defect, the final product doesn't have 10% chance of defect, it has a 41% chance of defect. This is just probability. The logic behind it is that it just needs to be defective in 1 step (or sub-process) out of 5. If you only have 2 steps, then the probability of defect is 19%. With the vast complexity of Nation Building in Iraq, the number of tasks would be infinitely more complex and that's why is was simply silly to assume we have any shot at making it work in the Middle East.

One last comment on process-maps, they are also very useful for identifying the "bottle necks" or critical paths in the entire larger operations. That is what you need to address to improve the larger process by opening by the "bottle necks", addressing that particular constraint.

Strategic Alignment Tool

Below is a Strategic Alignment planning chart, it shows how each department (even down to individuals) are aligned and linked to the Strategic Goals of the Organization. Should be rather useful to vet the rouge bureaucratic Apparatchiks.

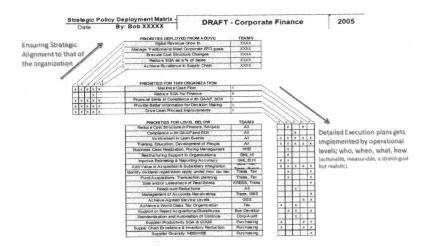

Scarcity of Resources Assumption / Approach

Nature Never Waste, Resources are limited, this is Life. People who tell you that we can solve War on Poverty by giving the developing countries money, people who tell you that illegals can come into this country and be on welfare because the world has unlimited resources, Top 1% is paying for everything, are thinking you are stupid! Let's shine more light, in hope of illuminating the darkness of ignorance; we'll quickly discuss a few more concepts before starting to untie the Gordian Knot.

Concept of **Satisfy v Optimize Solutions**, depending on Priorities and Resources available. When we are designing the solutions we need to bear in mind if the issue is high or low in priority and the resources available to solve it. Under the constraints (could be due to resource, time, technology, moral & ethics, etc.) we can either have a solution merely satisfies, but not necessarily the optimal solution. It is ok if the concern is not a high priority or critical one. That way we can conserve the resources expended.

Concept of **Efficiency and Effectiveness of Solutions**, an efficient solution addresses the problem in faster and expends least resources but it might not be the most effective solution. The most effective solution ensures the problem is solved most effectively and expending as much resources and time as necessary. When certain issues are not the most critical, efficiency can be a huge plus especially if you have resource constraints. It might not be the Best, but it sure is Value for money and time. An example, if you arrive at the rental car office to pick your car, if they don't have your preferred car, would you take the next best one available and be on your way? Or would you wait, stay in the Hotel for a few days till your most preferred rental comes in? You will get the exact car you want but waiting 2 days for it? Or paying for the Best Dinner in Bay Area for $1000 bucks v getting one that's comparable (not the best) for $180 bucks?

Cancer of Bureaucracy and Mother of Rules. Bureaucracy to an organization, is like cancer to the Human body, it will grow and spread and soon the organization becomes dysfunctional. It no longer performs its intended function but exist for its existence sake (paying the payroll of the employees, all of them making and following meaningless rules). No room for bureaucracy. You need good rules not many rules. Notice the bible states the Ten commandments, not 25,000 commandments! Bureaucrats create Rules and Rules justify more Bureaucrats to administer them, it goes into a vicious NEVER-ENDING cycle. Nothing ever gets solved and as the opportunities to resolve issues pass us by, they then unnecessarily become more and more complicated due to delay in addressing them. Plus the idiots are blocking the way of anyone trying to address the problems. Collecting their paychecks to spout nonsensical rules and misleading the Naïve and Innocent.

Subsidies is an addictive drug, this is simply rewarding bad behavior, if you keep subsidizing something, you will get more and more of it. It naturally becomes an incentive for the activists interest groups to ask for more; the intended end-user gets miniscule while bulk of Federal Funding enriches the sponsors of the activists corporations, as we've already seen that in the Clinton Foundation, less than 10% gets applied to the projects. Per their own accounts, they are only 10% efficient.

Any help should be a short term, temporary Crutch. Subsidizing Renewal or Green Energy is just a ruse to distract from the subpar performance of a subpar leadership and also making good money at the same time! There are many ways to encourage renewal Energy, subsidies is definitely NOT one of them.

Paralysis from Analysis

We need good and disciplined planning and preparation but also need action and implementation, no amount of planning can substitute for adaption and adjustments along the way, establishing a great feedback mechanism is instrumental to the eventual success. Analysis without action is like going around in circles, pure doing without thinking is like going in a straight line. Doing without thinking or thinking without doing would lead to disaster. Their combination is like a spiral, doing and thinking at same time, continuously adjusting and finetuning even as we progress in implementation of solutions. The entire process of continuous feedback to adjust strategies into effective solutions is Execution.

A parallel train of thought, Aristotle categorizes all forms of knowledge into theoretical, technical or practical. Pure theory (*espisteme*) is about knowing and understanding, practical knowledge (*praxis*) is about doing, technical (*techne*) has to do with making and Productive Knowledge.

This 'mindful hand' interaction between mental and manual labor is an essential component of the Industrial Revolution contributing to scientific innovation.

Always Leverage Free Market Competition

As we have already seen in Chapter 4, Free Market competition is essential to America's success. We not only need free market competition in the Financial Capital Markets but also in Human Talents and also Ideas too. Lastly Leadership is just as Important! We shall cover Leadership in much details later in this chapter.

Smaller P&L has better Accountability

小國寡民。使有什伯之器而不用；使民重死而不遠徙。雖有舟輿，無所乘之，雖有甲兵，無所陳之。使民復結繩而用之，甘其食，美其服，安其居，樂其俗。鄰國相望，雞犬之聲相聞，民至老死，不相往來。

- 老子

Lao Tze wasn't making comments about running Profit and Loss (P&L) business segments, he was talking about the same concept of having accountability at the lowest regional level. Small countries with few citizens are best run such that they can have the Best Quality of life, much personal wealth, understand the priorities and finer things in life. Small countries with Leaders having clear accountability can provide efficient and effective administrations for the people and make their lives so Great such that they have no desire to leave for other countries.

The same concept is leveraged by Global Businesses where responsibilities and resources can be allocated to the most operational level to solve the issues with fastest turnaround time and tackled by folks with the best knowledge as they are closest to the problems! It is also the same in the Military too, within the platoon, each section of 6-8 soldiers is led by a section leader. You want it to be small so they can react with great Speed, the section leader has great Self-confidence to make decisions and take responsibilities. Keep the Strategy and Doctrine Simple so that every soldier knows what they are!

Ideally, in USA, first the County, followed by City and only then Municipal should have the empowerment and resources to deal with issues. As much of the laws should be handled at the State level. Federal is furthest away, knows the least [the distant manager] and should intervene as little as possible. We'll discuss more of this in concept of Descaling of Complexity Theory.

Per last chapter, the Ottoman Empire was at its height under Suleiman the Magnificent (سلطان سليمان اول) the detailed daily administrations were executed at various Ottoman vilayets and below. These Vilayets, sanjak, kaza, nahiye would have been able to reflect the ethnic and sectarian differences more accurately, able to address and accommodate the Armenian, Kurds, Shiites, Sunnis differences more easily.

We also see the same organization of the administration in case of China 省, 市, 县, 镇, 乡, 村, 户 where the geographical Culture and history makes a huge difference where 关系 local relationships makes for ease of government.

This same concept also came up in the 1787 Constitution Convention in Philadelphia. The conventional wisdom then was summed up by Montesquieu's Spirit of the Laws published in 1748, postulating that only a small community, composed of persons who all knew one other or nearly so, could perpetuate true liberty. A large continental republic was doomed to tyranny; as only the rule of the strong could maintain order in face of conflicting interests over large differing geographic distance, which would breed civil conflict. This view would be in favor of the States to remain Independent and merely revising the Articles of Association.

Madison (with Washington, Hamilton, Jay) wanted a much stronger Federal government with clear Constitutional powers and mandate. Thus Madison quoted David Hume's work under Essays, Moral, Political, and Literary, titled *The Idea of a Perfect Commonwealth* 1754, in which David Hume disagreed with Montesquieu "although the people as a body are unfit for government," he wrote, "yet when dispersed in small bodies" – such as individual colonies or states – "they are more susceptible both to reason and order; the force of popular currents and tides is, in great measure, broken…. The parts are so distant and remote, that it is very difficult, either by intrigue, prejudice, or passion, to hurry them into any measures against the public interest." We know the outcome of the Philadelphia Convention and also the subsequent Bill of Rights.

There's 2 points worthy of note here. One, there's no conflict of idea between David Hume and Montesquieu, just as the smaller bodies have better accountability and faster feedback cycles, thus the elected leader would have to prove his/her competence in ensuring the regions or bodies (be they counties, colonies, states) are well governed and efficiently run to win re-elections. The people when within small groups also focus on clearer accountability as the impact of a poorly run community would impact them personally (and their families) negatively within a short time. In a Governing body over huge geographical region, it would be harder to hold the elected leader accountable, also the people might be roused by popular currents, demagogue, emotions, etc. (as Hume pointed out, gridlock at the public level guarantees liberty at the private level), Hume's model of how the democracy would is ordinary voters would elect local representatives, who would elect the next tier of representatives, and so on up the political alder in a process of refinement that would leave the leaders at the top connected only distantly with the original electorate, thus enabling them to make tough decisions that's good for the country in long run by might be unpopular in the short run. Hume has made his democracy model more sophisticated and added more layers to Montesquieu.

We will re-visit the validity of some these assumptions by Hume which Madison adopted in the Virginia Plan. Madison called this layering effect (of elected representative): Filtration, essentially the answer to concerns about How could a republic bottomed on the principle of popular sovereignty be structured in such a way to manage the inevitable excesses of democracy and best serve the long term public interests?

Major components of the Gordian Knot

By sharing all the earlier management concepts with yourself (the readers), hopefully it can help open your eyes as to how they (apparatchiks) should really be thinking if they are indeed trying to solve the problems instead of the Politically Correct Baloney they are feeding you. Let you see that the apparatchiks are not interested in fixing any issues but politicizing together with the politicians, so no one is driving the damn bus!

Anyone who has ever picked up a self-help book, would know that the 101 in Self-Help is to focus on Positives! Never highlight the negatives because you will subconsciously start focusing on the negatives and it will become a self-fulfilling prophesy! Understanding this approach, why are the neo-democrats always complaining about the system, the unfairness, the racists, sexists baloney when they were the ruling party with President Obama in the White House for the last 8 years? Pandering to the violent Activists Corporations?

Just as all the Deep State Politicians (both GOP and neo-Democrats alike) they are NOT interested in fixing anything, they are just selling you the Paths of Least Resistance, nonsensical Ideologies that's easiest to sell and easiest to chant. The Poverty Pimps as well as the Deep State, just wish to have Power for the sake of Power, enhancing their personal agenda and wealth. Their behavior speaks for themselves, Don't listen to what they say, watch what they do! We've grouped the domestic challenges into **6 Major categories**:

1) National Sovereignty (Borders, Refugees, Law & Order)

In Chapter 1, we've discussed why National Sovereignties (political entities) are still the most logical and practical governance bodies to safeguard the safety and well-being of its citizens. How the 'globalism' ideology is merely sophistry born in the 1960s in America; concocted by a bunch of self-obsessed 'juveniles' indulging in their delusional views of the world, who've never lived overseas, understand other Cultures nor speak other languages.

These neo-democrats Hypocrites are always chanting slogans and building bridges, yet you never see them in Syria, helping the refugees? We've already witnessed the hypocrisy of the Hollywood and Media Celebrities claiming to want to leave America and all the parasites are still here. Similarly, all the Idiotic self-proclaimed "Pro-Sharia" Apostates; Ignorant of Islam, Ignorant of Allah, all enjoying their wanton lives in the Land of the Big Satan when they should be serving Allah and helping their fellow Muslims in the war-torn land of Levant, Syria & Iraq?

As the American people have indicated clearly: The National Sovereignty Reigns. Wall, Fence or natural barriers, the Borders should be and are being enforced. All other countries; China, Russia, Mexico, etc. all enforced their National Boundaries, Borders. Thomas Hobbes' social contract still stands, the last time I checked humans are still physical beings, we have Not virtual forms living within the internet. Why do you think the Hollywood Celebrities have bodyguards, Facebook, google & IT Monopolies Moghuls have high walls, fences and security systems around their private estates?

We love the energy, talent and ideas that new immigrants bring into America, which is why merit-based immigration is and always has been the way to go for the last 200 plus years. When something is working well, don't have to fix it dummy!

The refugee problems in the Middle East due to the sad accomplishments of the last administration throughout the Arab Spring and then interfering in Libya, withdrawing from Iraq and supporting the Civil War in Syria caused Millions to lose their families and lose their homes. If we truly want to help the refugees, the civil war has to stop (it is within our powers to stop the civil war, just stop interfering), let some peace accord be reached and rebuilding begin, that way, the refugees can return home and rebuild their lives again. This is the correct solution but as usual, the neo-democrats would be chanting some paths of least resistance, easiest to sell mantra. Yet they have no wish to personally step up to volunteer adopting the refugees under their personal care, NO walls just let the refugees come and the Federal government to take care of them. As usual, some faceless and nameless entities will solve the 'world hunger' problems, this unsophisticated nonsense, glorifying Ignorance and Egoistic tendencies is really disgusting.

Domestic Law and Order must be maintained, political stability is the foundation for the Economy to growth and wealth to be created. Advocates of violence, rioting, looting are poverty pimps and it should be enacted into law for the victims of these violence to sue the neo-democrats politicians, neo-fascists activities corporations for inciting the violence and causing harm and injury to others. We need to build a feedback mechanism to hold the Poverty Pimps accountable! More needs to be done than the usual police work. The source of these violence has to be addressed. Currently, there is no accountability nor responsibilities by these neo-democrats Parasites from harming our communities, spreading ignorant ideologies and inciting violence that kills our citizens. Instead, these parasites are getting super rich from these immoral and nefarious activities, no wonder the poverty pimps are growing gangbusters into Celebrities, going on TVs, going to the White House, appearing on Talk-shows, hosting their own TV shows, morning show, late night shows, you name it! When they get rewarded so handsomely for their selfish and deceitful behavior, you know that you'll be seeing a whole lot more of these nonsensical ideologies coming your way! We need a counter-intelligence against these Radical neo-fascists corporations (BLM, other 501c3 entities) that's promoting violence, rioting and looting.

We have also see in chapter 4, how to reconcile between the role of the individual (in forgiveness of "those who trespass against us") and that of the government in administering, enforcing Law and Order (we can analyze the causes of the crimes using Pareto analysis and Fishbone chart, then devising the solutions leveraging FMEA to address the severity and frequency of occurrence. Raising the severity of punishments can dramatically lower the frequency of occurrence without having to employ large amount of additional resources into policing, these resources thus saved can then be used towards Education which will further lower crimes. That is a positive self-reinforcing cycle

2) National Debt, Tax the top 1% Super Rich, in the end you always pay the Piper

In Chapter 5, you've seen Mr. Alan Greenspan's hubris; cooking up the $ 20T debt and avoiding the Great Depression? Well, guess what, Americans lost their entire snowflakes generation to the Piper of Debt. We had also realized that President Obama and Hillary Clinton's Masters are NOT going to pay for the $ 20T of debt, that in reality the weakest and least able to defend themselves will pay the price (as in case of Pro-choice that we'll discuss later). Thus, with the affliction of the snowflake Generation, the next American generation will still be paying for the $ 20T debt, that's not going anywhere. That's a Lose, Lose 赔了夫人又折兵. In the end, you always pay the Piper!

3) Global Warming the Inconvenient Truth

Here's the Inconvenient Truth about Climate Change, the Only thing powering the Renewal Energy sectors are the Winds of Subsidies and Solar Rays of Tax rebates! I am not disputing that there's a strong correlation in the amount of Carbon that humans are releasing into the atmosphere and global warming (climate change). But going from high probability of Global Warming to Federal Subsidies is the skill of the Media's con artists pulling another fast one on the innocent 'snowflakes'

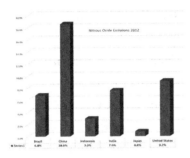 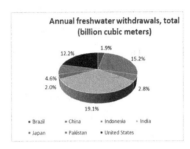

If we do indeed wish to address Global Warming, besides attempts at slowing it down [CO_2 carbon dioxide emissions has been increasing 1.6% per annum from 2005-2015], there should also be many other Major Global Initiatives (achieving Gaia Equilibrium; alternative sustainable sources of energy, Exponential Increase in Space Exploration, Mars Colonization, etc.). Slowing the current rate of pollution should be only one of multiple initiatives to protect the human civilization as we know it.

There's many challenges on slowing down the current pollution that's not properly addressed after over a decade and a half of high visibility talks, conferences, huge investments of tax payers' money and empty promises of new technologies to come. Earth is a common resource and every nation pushes for its own agendas; from 2005-2015, CO_2 emissions has increased annually by 4.2% for China, 6% for India, 7.3% for Bangladesh, 3.7% for Indonesia, 2.9% for Argentina, 4% for Brazil, 3.5% for Iran, 5.2% for Saudi Arabia, 5.2% for UAE, while decreasing by -1.1% for USA. China now contributes 27.3% of CO_2 while USA is at 16%. In the last decade, the biggest contributor to increasing global pollution is China, India would probably be the next in line. There's no way to mandate the slow down, any mutual agreement could only be loosely enforced at best.

China and India also uses Coal as a large part of their energy source which is cheapest but most harmful to the environment, China uses over 50% of the whole world's coal consumption with India at 11%, both increased at 3.7% and 6.5% per annum for last decade. Both China and India are also inefficient for producing more carbon emissions measured against fuel consumed, China consumes 23% of all primary fuels, produces 27.3% of CO_2 pollution, India consumes 5.5% of all primary fuels, produces 6.8% of CO_2 pollution. After over a decade of the high visibility talks, as of end 2015, Renewables make up 3% of total fuel consumption. As you can see from the facts above, they are public information from any major Energy Research organizations, since there's no way to mandate to the countries, focusing on technology breakthrough is a better approach as it would provide competitive advantage to the successful party.

At this stage, Japan and India as the Model countries for all to emulate, they have the lowest pollution for their population size. They lead in Renewable Energy implementation in their respective countries. The top Pollution contributors have to come together led by China, USA, India, Russia, Brazil, Indonesia, etc. The aim should be decrease of CO_2 pollution by 2020. USA could also lead its own efforts in reducing its carbon footprint and also supporting India, China and other countries in the research for new Technologies.

We will brainstorm many ways [to achieve Gaia Equilibrium in chapter 9], but Federal Government's subsidies and Tax rebates are definitely NOT the solutions. The Politicians and Apparatchiks are the last people to know anything about new technologies and their commercialization efforts! Politicians talking about free-market failures are just a bunch of lying con-men, the only thing that Subsidies and Tax rebates ever do is to enrich the fat cats cronies and friends of the politicians, the very ones that tirelessly lobbies for those subsidies and tax rebates to start with.

Subsidies doesn't drive "grid parity", subsidies never drive technology breakthrough, in fact, subsidies have the exact opposite on the company's behaviors; it takes the company's focus off technology and onto lobbying for more subsidies! Lobbying efforts becomes the main focus, while technology takes a back seat, becomes stagnant, while the marketing to investors (razzle and dazzle) becomes the key priority. We now have many renewable energy companies all started off on welfare of Federal subsidies and growing rich on the speculative greed of Wall Street gamblers. Marketing their 'so call technologies' takes precedent over real research and development work, personal accountability and passion, have no place in these companies, Tesla is the poster child for such companies. All its cars Sales were propped up by tax rebates for its customers, its cashflow comes from its Wall Street investors, the customers are just a small sideshow for the investors to feel good about the 'future prospects' of the company.

Solyndra is sad example of US tax payers' money gone down the toilet, $850 million to be exact. It was a Solar panel manufacturing company that the Department of Energy loan $535 million under the leadership of Prof Steven Chu. Long story short, the company made a series of strategic mistakes, including building a huge factory in Germany based on unproven speculative technology not yet commercialized. Building up its supply chain before receiving any orders for shipments and failure to reduce it's costs of manufacturing for commercial viability. Thus the company went under when the Chinese companies flooded the market in 2011 with much cheaper solar panels with older technology (the new breakthrough even if it had succeeded wouldn't have been able to command the price premium anyway). Prof Chu might have good technical background, but he doesn't know much about driving manufacturing costs down, the various stages of commercialization, Market competition, streamlining process improvements, supply-chain management, cashflow and financial discipline. The Federal government should not be anywhere near investing tax payers money with leadership from technical scientists. But wait, the show is not over on Solyndra, Prof Chu in his infinite wisdom decided to make the DOE (Dept of Energy's) $535m loan subordinate to Investments from affiliates of George Kaiser (Obama fund raiser) of $75m of rescue money. Kaiser knew what he was doing, Solyndra from all its losses was sitting on $350 of NOL (Net Operating Losses that can be deducted off taxes of profitable companies). With the appropriate tax structure, Solyndra's tax losses would be worth 4.6X more to Kaiser, the only rescue was the tax NOLs. Again you see the lack of commercial experience play out. That's why Federal and Government Apparatchiks should not handle US Tax Payer's hard earned money.

If you think the Solyndra smells fishy with President Obama's Fund Raiser friend doing so well financially when the US Tax Payers' paying the bill for the failed investment. And It wasn't a one off, the Obama administration also provided loans of $ 530m to Fisker Automotive (EV) and $ 270m stimulus money to A123 which makes electric vehicle batteries. Long story short, both these companies were again badly managed, producing poor quality batteries that burst into flames, buying a failed GM plant in VP Joe Biden's home state of Delaware (arranged by another Obama's fund raiser John Doerr), very poor gas millage from "well to wheels" poorer than a Ford Explorer. Fisker got another $ 170m installment from Dept of Energy for design work. VP Al Gore and actor Leonardo DiCaprio were also investors in Fisker Auto too. A123 filed for bankruptcy in Nov 2012 and Fisker Auto in Nov 2013. Most of Fisker's assets, the designs, rights to a plug-hybrid powertrain and a manufacturing facility in Delaware to the Chinese company Wanxiang. That's another great use of the US Tax payers money to provide Chinese companies with EV (Electric Vehicle) designs, plug-hybrid powertrain rights. Do we need to keep paying for the Washington's Bureaucrats to repeatedly prove to us their incompetence and lack of business judgement? And in the meantime, as the US Tax payers are getting poorer by the day, the crony Fat Cats are getting richer, fatter and China Companies are buying up (2 cents to a dollar) whatever technologies falling by the wayside as these failing companies implode.

We can keep going on for more cases. In fact, I was in Western Tennessee number of months back, some renewable energy company wanted to build Wind Turbines there outside of Fairfield Glade, TN. Again it was a sham, TVA had no need for the power, the local residents had no need for the Wind Turbines nor the Inefficient power it would generate but the company wanted to do it anyway purely to secure Government Subsidies, everyone is playing the Subsidies Game! This is stupid waste of Tax-payers money achieve nothing in return.

In chapter 3, we'd discussed about the Tragedy of commons (Jared Diamond's book Collapse), Global Warming is the textbook case of Tragedy of Commons, the best prerequisites for overcoming such a challenge was clearly stated which we hope to emulate (and find if not currently available) the conditions for success. A) Homogeneous group of individuals that has learnt to trust and communicate with each other. B) They see a common future for themselves and their heirs. C) They must learn to police themselves with clearly defined boundaries and consumers of such resources.

It is a real challenge for the entire World to step up to address this issue together as there's no accountability and no ownership. There's no real urgency nor desire to fix the challenge. What you are currently seeing is just Politics and semantics are work. Having the Federal Apparatchiks address such challenges; by pushing for subsidies as the solution is a prime example of 'Distant managers' at work (Distant Managers, are those with least experience, least relevant expertise and furthest from the problem, being put in charge to attempt solving them).

And you'll start to notice a parallel case, of how George Soros and Jeff Sachs pushes for UN and IMF (again Distant Managers), after 9/11 attacks, to address War on Poverty? Only the Innocent and Naïve confuse Politics with real solutions and only the Egoistic can be conned by the "Global Warming" pimps. 不知知病, not knowing what you do not know is a weakness, not knowing what you don't know and pretending to know, stems from the combination of Ignorance and Ego.

4) Healthcare, Welfare and Social Benefits

America's Healthcare was already way over priced to begin with, then along came President Obama with his genius neo-democrat pseudo-intellects to the rescue. The same ones that added $ 10Trillion of debt in last 8 years, the Perfect President with the Perfect solution; one rigged and perfectly timed to blow up when he leaves office and blames everyone else. Here we again have 'distant managers' at work, yet they managed to name the solution right, quite appropriately called the Affordable Healthcare. Great! That's the only thing they got right. The idea to make Healthcare affordable is the right Idea! How they went about it was a total Disaster, an extremely disgusting failure due to complete lack of market dynamics and a deep seated desired for Big Government Control over (aka 'be responsible' for) the American People's Lives! Obviously all the freebies sounds great when marketed by the Angels of Welfare, as Rights to Healthcare! Hell, any freebies would sound great as a Right! forget about the marketing.

Let's look at what is currently wrong and the steps forward. The Obama's admin wanted more Welfare, so they added Welfare into Healthcare, calls it Obama-care, and intentionally mixed up the whole discussion. They essentially forced other Healthcare users to subsidize the ones "unable to afford Healthcare", the Supreme Court had called it what it is. It is a TAX on the other Healthcare Users and that's how they justified it 5-4. Americans cannot be forced to buy products they do NOT want to, but as a form of TAX, you have to pay TAX that the government imposes on you (selectively, note that not all pay this tax).

There's also no differentiation between the different Needs (intentional and by design) of the Healthcare users and thus no opportunity, for competition amongst the Insurance providers via market segmentation strategies. That's the Admin's wholesale plan, designed to force the other users to help pick-up the tab! If they had allowed differentiation, then there will be competition from service providers to address the different needs of different segments of patients, then the Welfare Costs (of those that cannot afford Healthcare) cannot be loaded on the Normal Paying Users of Healthcare.

To solve the challenge, we have to remember the goal is to make Healthcare affordable for all. NOT to load HealthCare costs onto other users! The welfare element must be removed from the Healthcare issue and addressed separately! If other government costs need to address that, it would become a separate additional item in the Benefits Category. Healthcare costs to be addressed separately, in fact if we can make Healthcare affordable, then we do NOT need more Federal welfare expenses, right?

How to make HealthCare affordable? Back to the Basics

To start with, we already had too many players (parties) involved in the USA Healthcare system (pre-Obama's admin intervention); we have the Insurance providers, Employers, Employees, Healthcare Service Providers, Doctors, Patients, pharmaceutical companies

Here again, there's a mix-up of concept of Healthcare and Insurance. They are NOT the same thing, these are two separate and distinct concepts. In America, it has become a given as Healthcare Insurance. This is NOT the case in many other countries. Concept of Insurance is to cover an event of minimal probability happening, not when you need to use it regularly! That's the only way for Insurance Industries to exists, users pay minimal amount but gets covered for Catastrophic accidents, because there are many users and the probability of Catastrophic accidents happening is low. The Model works. If the incidents happen frequently like once a month, then it is NOT Insurance but routine doctor visits. What has that to do with Insurance? Healthcare is something you use on regular basis. Catastrophic Insurance is something you hope never happens to you; as in Event of a severe Accident or a Major Illness that needs major operation or treatment. 1st step is to separate this 2 distinct segments.

Next, we note that the Law of Demand and Supply is NOT working in Healthcare Industry in USA. Too many parties being intertwined minimizes the opportunity for Free Market competition. For the price of Healthcare to come down, the Law of Demand and Supply has to work again, we have un-tangle the mess of multiple parties' involvement. Per the 2 charts below: 1st chart addresses the Healthcare and Insurance issue (before the Obama-administration making a bigger Mess out of an existing mess). There's no feedback loop between the employees, healthcare providers, Insurance agents nor the employers that's buying the Insurance.

NO Demand and Supply relationship between Service Provider and Patients

Wastage everywhere between Insurance Companies, Healthcare Providers, Pharmaceutical Companies, Patients bear unnecessary burdens => High Costs of Healthcare for Patients

The employers just make the payments to their employees directly and let the patients be the decision maker. That will re-establish the Law of Demand and Supply in the Healthcare System. Insurance companies should just address catastrophic Insurance as they are meant to do. Stay the hack out of Healthcare! Let the service providers (doctors) deal directly with the patients (employees).

**Need To re-establish Demand and Supply
between Service Provider and Patients**

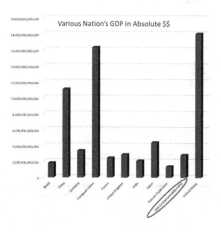

The Patient has to be in the center, they choose their Healthcare Service Providers, their Catastrophic Insurance coverage as needed and the medication recommended by the Doctors

Minimal Wastage in the systems => Patients pays low costs of Healthcare

NO Government involvement, NO Need for any Welfare Costs, NO additional Taxes for the Tax-payers!

Once we resolve issue and lower the Healthcare Costs with an efficient system, there is NO need for the government to get involve. We already have affordable Healthcare! Dear Federal Government (aka Distant Managers) please stay out of our Lives!

Just as in Chapter 6, the USA Foreign Policies trying to address World Order & Stability and setting up Democratic Governments in Middle East at same time? Trying to address too many issues at same time ends up Solving none of them and creating more Gordian Knots!

> *"My fellow Americans, ask not what your country can do for you, ask what you can do for your country."*
>
> President John F. Kennedy

Social Welfare, Benefits

The USA spending on Welfare and Benefits at approx. $2.8T will make it about the same size as the entire UK's economy! The 6th Largest "Economy" (this is NOT a plus, it is a minus) in the world behind, USA, China, Japan, Germany and UK. In fact, it might overtake UK depending on the budget each year. Amazing, isn't it? The level of decadence, the handouts to those not working in America is more than all the wealth created by the entire working population of United Kingdom? You wonder what happened to those values espoused by President JFK? In place of President Kennedy, we now have Comrade Bernie, appealing to one's Greed and Sloth, repackaging them as Rights!

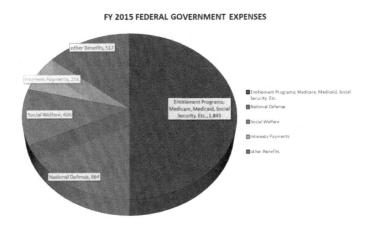

FY 2015 FEDERAL GOVERNMENT EXPENSES

Just the same logic as Subsidies, the more Welfare and Benefits payments you put out, the more recipients will come forth, what do you expect? Subsidies is an addictive drug, rewarding certain behavior, the more you give subsidies, the more of that certain behavior [welfare abusers] you will get. Remember the Durants' quote in chapter 2 "…Utopias of equality are biologically doomed, and the best that the amiable philosopher can hope for is an approximate equality of legal justice and educational opportunity. A society in which all potential abilities are allowed to develop and function will have a survival advantage in competition of groups."

Just to clarify, FICA that funds Social Security and Medicare is Not a Welfare BUT, America's Social Security and Medicare has loopholes, each larger than the hole in our ozone layer, it needs a long overdue overhaul. The International Best Practice in Social Security has closely monitored Individualized Accounts, tracked to accuracy higher than personal Bank or Shares Investment Accounts. Even with the technologies in the 60s and 70s, most advance Asia Countries had already been tracking and closely monitoring individualized Social Security contributions, from both Employee and Employer, which pays dividends modeled after the 401K, ROTH accounts, fraudulent and fictitious accounts audited on monthly basis.

Welfare should only be reserved exclusively for a very small group of infirmed elderly, veterans or children born with severe disabilities. Any portion of society on Welfare represents the Sad Loss of human potential and productivity for America. A large portion on welfare represents a dying host from parasitic invasion.

"Sedan-Chair Mindset" and the wisdom of President Obama's step father

Lolo was Obama's stepfather when he was 8 years old living in Indonesia. Lolo found Ann's (Obama's mother) leftist and anti-American Ideologies impractical and naïve, while he was trying to survive and prosper in Indonesia, where the hard realities of a developing nation doesn't shelter the growth of romantic leftists' dreams very well.

Lolo's thinking much more pragmatic than idealistic. "Guilt", Lolo told Ann "is a luxury only foreigners can afford." Wise words indeed, only the 'greenhouses of academia' (or virtual worlds of Social Media) in developed countries can breed such non-functional mindsets. Many Americans might feel this "guilt" that they are doing well because they were born in America, if they had been born in Africa or Middle East, they might not be so lucky! Many white Liberals also feel this "white guilt" that they are privileged and doing well for themselves or even perhaps the Hollywood Celebrities feeling that they have gotten lucky in this life, while others might not have been so lucky as themselves.

This so called "guilt" is their personal emotions to handle and I have no comments but here is where I have a concern.

Their response is what I would coin as "sedan-chair mindset", they feel "guilty" as they are sitting in a sedan chair while being carried by others but instead of having the courage to get off the sedan-chair to walk, they actually encourage more people to get onto the sedan-chair! Unlimited resources, Rich Top 1% is going for pay for everything, Debt spending, mortgaging the future, out of sight out of mind mentality, or in case, don't understand don't matter or can't understand can't impact me mindsets.

This stupid mindset is killing this country! The snowflake Liberal mindset supporting more Entitlements, more Benefits for the "less fortunate" is simply downright Idiotic! If you want to help the less fortunate, roll up your sleeves and head down to the "inner cities" to teach in the schools, to donate your personal wealth to the poor. Stop being such a hypocrite when you are obviously NOT paying for these entitlements nor benefits. Get off the damn sedan-chair and walk, help carry (personally) the real disabled or handicapped people if you can, but stop asking more people to get into the sedan-chair when you are NOT the one carrying it!

With certain **exceptions** like Veterans (VA) who'd served, sacrificed, bled for and protected this country with their lives, disabled children and the infirmed elderly.

Ethically, Entitlements and Benefits are Immoral and Revolting, as it encourages Sloth and Greed. Philosophically, it represents Great and Tragic Loss of Human Potential, It is Ideologically subscribed to by the naïve and non sequiturs as their selfish, short-term thinking and simple-mindedness believes that it is just Free Money, Others People Money. Strategically, they cripple the Economy and Capital Free Market (it encourages minimal participation in workforce and growing the economy). Financially, they are inefficient and wasteful, with huge "overheads" to administer (for example, in Clinton foundation >90% overheads with less than 10% of each dollar contributed turning into real benefits for the intended beneficiaries). The standard for overheads vary between Industries or Businesses, but an efficiently run business should have <15% overheads (in fact, for many high Margin IT / software companies, the overheads can easily run in the single digits). Free money, other people's money? We should remember McClure's words, "… [in the end] there is no one left: none but all of us… the public is the people. We forget that we all are the people; that while each of us in his group can shove off on the rest the bill of today, the debt is only postponed. The rest of us are passing it on back to us. We have to pay in the end, every one of us. And in the end the sum total of the debt will be our liberty."

Happiness lies in the joy of achievement and the thrill of creative effort
- President Franklin D. Roosevelt

We should measure welfare's success by how many people leave welfare, not by how many are added.
- President Ronald Reagan

"We want every American to know the dignity of work, the pride of a paycheck, and the satisfaction of a JOB WELL DONE."
- President Donald Trump

FDR during the Great Depression, with his great wisdom started the CCC, now we need the Civilian Conservation Corps to be revived and Energized all around America, Allow the Growth of Human Potential, treasure it, don't kill it by feeding it greed and sloth!

5) Sexists, LGBTQ, Pro-choice topics

"I was taught that the way of progress was neither swift nor easy"
- Marie Curie

Newsflash: the women's rights & suffrage movements started in 1848 in America

I had first became more aware of the history of Women's suffrage movement when we visited Geneva and Seneca Falls in 1999. Elizabeth Cady Stanton (1815-1902), Seneca Falls Convention held in 1848 in Seneca Falls, New York, Susan Brownell Anthony (1820-1906) these women were pioneers on the cutting edge of the Women's rights and suffrage movement, inspired by earlier works such as *A Vindication of The Rights of Woman* by Mary Wollstonecraft in 1792. All these women going against the grain and sacrificing much in return for upholding their ideals and rights. They don't make major money nor reap financial profits from their life works.

"Children will never be properly educated 'til friendship subsists between parents. Virtue flies from a house divided against itself and a whole legion of devils take up their residence there.'
- Mary Wollstonecraft

A country that makes itself unavailable to the talent, intellect, ideas and resources of women is only at best, at half of its true Potential. How can such a society be competitive with the rest of the world at large? Intellect transcends Race, it transcends Sexes, anyone who doesn't understand this simple fact wouldn't seem to have much of it.

To the innocent and Naïve, the cutting-edge might sound like a really cool, while in reality, to be at the forefront cutting edge of any ideology is extremely painful, lonely, never-ending sacrifices, against insurmountable odds with no assurance of success. If one eventually does prevail, the Ideals and rights won are usually the only rewards to show for. When at the cutting edge, one will inevitably get cut too and its painful (try moving your finger along the razors edge, same concept as staying on the Risks and Rewards curve that we saw in chapter 3 and will explore further in appendix X). Please do not tarnish the memories, dedication and sacrifices of such Pioneering Intellects by associating them with the current "poverty" pimps, "healthcare" pimps, "global warming" pimps.

Now we even have Suffrage profiteers? These neo-Democrats Activists are rewarded handsomely and paid Huge dollars by the Activists corporations, giving speeches to Wall Street, Publications of Best Sellers, the professional politicians that trade in 'deals' and favors, excel in graft and pull. They are obviously in it for the money, making re-makes of re-makes of previous blockbusters. We are so glad for you and your successes in reaping in the Big Bucks, but please pardon us for not watching your movie Madam, we've seen this movie before, too many times.

As for their impressionable supporters, since your idols politicians of graft are acting rationally getting handsomely rewarded, if you're not getting paid, you either belong to the non-rational category or better to ask for your money back.

LGBTQ

There's some recent research in genetics that purports the idea that there are many sexes, sex isn't binary as either female or male and attributes it to human chromosomes, the National Geographic in Jan 2017 has several articles concerning sex identities, biological sex and sex expressions.

There might be another explanation for sex identities misaligned to the biological sex. In Hinduism, Jainism and Buddhism, the concept of re-birth or Reincarnation is common to all three religions. If we could entertain the idea of reincarnation, then the logically, there would be a 50-50 chance we share the same sex as in previous life-times right? assuming we were in human form in previous lifetimes. This idea might be too much of stretch for Americans but many Asians; Indians, Japanese, Chinese, etc. [over 50% of world's population] are comfortable with the concept of re-birth.

Regardless of the explanations for the LGBTQ's behavior, we all might be missing the point in trying to justify or defend it. Perhaps we just forgotten what it means to be human. Remember we had discussed about stereotying and pre-judging people without knowing them personally? The people that attack LGBTQ are fearful of others different from themselves. If others do not harm you, there's no need to attack them. If others attack you, you must be stupid if you don't defend yourself. Let's just use our common sense, and cut out the parasitic lawyers from the equation, more left for all to share.

Here again, the neo-fascist activists and neo-democrat LGBTQ Pimps steps in and exploits the situation and politicize anything that furthers their agendas of sowing discord and generating chaos such that those trying to run the country has NO time to address the Wall Street Super-corruption nor be able to focus on apprehending the nefarious Heads of Radical Activists Corporation inciting violence, flag-burning, looting, rioting all around America as they are busy addressing transgender bathroom issues.

> *"...human weeds,' 'reckless breeders,' 'spawning... human beings who never should have been born."*
>
> Margaret Sanger [founder of Planned Parenthood]
> in *Pivot of Civilization*, referring to immigrants,
> African Americans and poor people.

Pro-Life vs Pro-Choice

Superficially, the issue here seems to be about women's rights to have an abortion which elicit the simple answer that she has the right to decide for herself, it's her life and her baby right? This logic seems straight forward enough. Of course, the neo-fascist Activists motto "Sell the Easiest Ideas, Market to the Simple, Exploit their Ego and show them the Path of Least Resistance". Works like a charm all the Time!

There's also another line of reasoning that can sound pretty logical too; posing the question: who's going to take care of the baby? The State? From birth till 16-18 years, age that they can work and contribute back to the society, the kid would be a burden, a liability to the society (who's going to feed them, house them, educate them?), and very large one if that number is substantial.

> *"... that average negroes possess too little intellect, self-reliance, and self-control to make it possible for them to sustain the burden of any respectable form of civilization without a large measure of external guidance and support."*
>
> - Francis Galton, letter to the Editor of The Times, June 5 1873

Origins of the Ideology behind Planned Parenthood, Racist Liberal Progressives

Modern Eugenics come from Greek εὐγενής (meaning noble, well born) is an Ideology developed by white elitist progressives in UK around the later part of 19th century, it is the same ideology behind Planned Parenthood and Nazi Eugenics programs. Not only were the Liberal Progressives in America big subscribers to this ideology, the Nazis started the racial doctrine by learning from their American counterparts about racial ideologies of Eugenics who a head-start on the Germans.

Sir Francis Galton (knighted in 1909) was Charles Darwin's half-cousin, was an English Victorian statistician, progressive, polymath, sociologist, psychologist, anthropologist, eugenicist, tropical explorer, geographer, inventor, meteorologist, proto-geneticist, and psychometrician. Francis Galton was a pioneer in modern eugenics, coining the term itself, and the phrase "nature versus nurture", he had read the works of his half-cousin Charles Darwin, Origin of Species, his theory of Evolution and Natural Selection. Francis then applied those concepts to humans, seeing "desirable human qualities" as hereditary traits and how the genetic quality of the human population can be improved by human intervention and practices. This ideology became extremely popular and spread to most of Europe, USA, Canada in early 20th century. American progressives embraced eugenics, it became an academic discipline and received funding from various sources. The American Eugenics Society was formed in 1921, the same year that Margaret Sanger founded the American Birth Control League, which later became the Planned Parenthood Federation of America.

The Facts and Numbers behind Planned Parenthood, the Trail of Blood

In 2011 alone, approx. 3000 babies are aborted each day (that number has decreased 8.6% since then per AP report), but here's the strange stats, of all the abortions by Planned Parenthood, African Americans make up 37% when they only makeup 13% of America's population. That's a skewed ratio of nearly 3 times what it should logically be.

Per documentary film: Maafa 21 released by Life Dynamics in 2009, they exposed the Planned Parenthood's use of words like 'population control', 'family planning' are really code words for a genocidal effort aimed at minorities, mainly African Americans. In 2011, Mark Crutcher followed up by releasing a detailed research and study; Racial Targeting and Population Control, to support this claim. This report established a couple of facts, most of the Planned Parenthood Clinics are established in a) zip codes with high proportions of African Americans and Hispanics, b) very often in zip codes that's a number of times the States' average, c) and in zip codes that are disproportionally high in minorities compared with the States average, there are Multiple Planned Parenthood facilities! if you might like to read Crutcher's report, here's the url link

http://www.operationrescue.org/wp-content/uploads/2016/09/LifeDynamicsRacialReport.pdf

The blueprint for the Planned Parenthood Strategy was clearly outlined by Gunnar Myrdal in his 1944 book, *An American Dilemma: The Negro Problem and Modern Democracy.* Today Planned Parenthood operate the Nation's largest chain of abortion clinics and 80% are in minority neighborhoods.

In 2007, they aborted over 300,000 babies while only making 5000 referrals for adoption (if you were an unborn in 2007, you are 60X more likely to be aborted then be referred for adoption by Planned Parenthood). The reality is that they have Quotas to be met, Social Engineering out the "undesirables", 'feeble minded' by race (this is negative eugenics). They received over $350m in taxpayers' money in 2009 alone in support of their operations. Their founder, Margaret Sanger who was active with both the Klu Klux Klan and the Eugenics movement in early 20th century would be proud of her creation. Here's more abortion facts and numbers that you never hear from the Lackeys of Activist Corporations, aka the Mainstream Media;

- *75% of the abortions are from poor, Low Income families*
- *African Americans are 3.8 times more likely to have abortions than White Americans*
- *Those on Medicaid are 3 time more likely to have abortions than those not*
- *More African American Babies are aborted per week than All other causes of African Americans deaths put together!*

Fyi, when you see any abortion reports by Alan Guttmacher Institute (AGI), understand this fact: AGI is NOT an independent agency, it is the research arm of Planned Parenthood. Alan Guttmacher was once the President of Planned Parenthood and Vice President of the American Eugenics Society.

With such brutal and glaring facts, you would think the African American Leaders would be going after Planned Parenthood Big-Time right? Well, yes and no.

In 1970, Rev Jesse Jackson was speaking out against birth control and abortion. Jackson saw these things as "warfare" against the poor, the disabled, and minorities. In 1973, he stated in no uncertain terms that abortion was "genocide." These were his exact words

> *"Abortion is genocide. Anything growing is living… If you got the thrill to set the baby in motion and you don't have the will to protect it, you're dishonest… You try to avoid reproducing sickness. You try to avoid reproducing deformities. But you don't try to stop reproducing and procreating human life at its best. For who knows the cure for cancer won't come out of some mind of some Black child?"*
>
> Reverend Jackson, JET MAGAZINE MAR 22, 1973; P. 15

In Jan 2017, President Obama also vetoed a legislation that would have defunded Planned Parenthood. Rev Jesse Jackson has also since reversed his pro-life stance and has been completely silent in face of all the Pro-Choice and Planned Parenthood gain in momentum and strength for last 3 decades. Why? The Activists Corporations Coalition that funds the neo-Democrats, funds America Votes (headed by Nancy Pelosi) includes Planned Parenthood Action Fund, NARAL Pro-Choice America, AFT (American Federation of Teachers), amongst many other 501c3 Activists groups and corporations that George Soros supports and helped setup.

Greed, Lust for Power and wealth corrupts young idealistic activists from the 60s & 70s, transforming them into the Poverty Pimps of today, we see Lord Acton's words in action.

Protecting Lives and Teaching Responsibilities

The combination of Pro-Choice Planned Parenthood has been successfully implementing their genocide activities and atrocities against human lives for nearly a century now, as its 100th birthday approaches, it looks to continue its great success. We've seen the powerful ideologies, the birth of modern eugenics, sponsored by Carnegie and Rockefeller groups earlier on and now the George

Soros' Activists Corporations, the 501c3s Planned Parenthood Action Fund, NARAL Pro-choice America, the PP Politicians who reversed their earlier Pro-Life stances, selling out their cause, now gratefully "kow-tow"-ing to the neo-fascist Activists stooges.

There's another Key factor that allows all of these atrocities against the unborn babies to happen, it is rooted in ignorance. The lack of knowledge, lack of forward planning and resulting reactive behavior of continuously choosing the path of least resistance. Let's use the decision tree concept to illustrate how one comes to make the decision to abort the baby, with each "decision point", the green colored answer would lead away from final abortion action.

From this simple Decision tree, you can see how many "wrong turns" due to lack of planning, 'knee-jerk' reactions down paths of least resistance, were taken before getting into the "dead-end" decision of aborting their babies? Any small amount of planning and thinking ahead would most likely have avoided the ultimate dreadful decision to be made.

Below are the responses from women as reasons for their abortion;

- *22% Inadequate finances,*
- *22% Not ready for responsibility,*
- *16% Woman's life would be changed too much,*
- *13% Problems with relationships, unmarried,*
- *12% Too young and/or immature,*
- *8% Children are grown; she has all she wants,*
- *3% Baby has possible health problems,*

- <u>*≤1% Pregnancy caused by rape/incest,*</u>
- *3% Others*

From here, you can see that rape, incest and baby has possible health issues, the Key reasons you hear from the Pro-Choice camp's argument makes up *less than 4%* of total abortions. The majority, in fact close to 90% is due to lack of planning, lack of knowledge or ignorance in short.

Education would be the best means to combat such ignorance, not just Education in School, Education via media, via commercials, social media, etc. The simple knowledge to use contraceptives and practice Safe Sex with protection should be taken up as crusade by the Pro-Choice and Planned Parenthood right? Yet, if they had been successful in their education, why are 3000 babies murdered via abortions each day? The teenagers have obviously not been taught to planned for anything, but the Racists Activists Liberals killing thousands per day have Planned very well to secure their Federal Funding paid for by your Tax dollars.

Guess teaching our young generation personal Responsibilities, skills of Planning ahead, value of Human Lives, the courage to protect the unborn and weak takes much effort, time and heart! It is a "uphill" and tiring climb yet protecting these lives are important, they are all human potential, these lives born in America has the potential to become the next Bill Gates, President Obama, Rev Jesse Jackson, George Soros, Steve Jobs, Thomas Edison, Michael Jackson, Rev Martin Luther King Jr., etc. Killing human potential has the larger impact of killing the next Einstein, Stephen Hawking, etc. that could help spark the next transformation of human civilization.

Yet, the ugly neo-democrats Activists are always beaconing, always Selling paths of least resistance, teaching the shirking of responsibilities and sticking it to the weakest and those not able to defend themselves. NO personal responsibility NO personal Accountability ever.

Quick Summary and Clarifications - Darwinism

Myth and Misunderstanding about Darwin's Theory of Evolution, we often hear phrases like Survival of the Fittest, Adaptability linked with Darwinism. Some might incorrectly believe that Evolution means the Fittest Animals adapt best and thus survive and reproduce more offspring similar to themselves, this incorrect interpretation then gets borrowed by the Social Darwinism believers, the Progressive Racists who then added more myths and sophistries to justify their racists views. Here we sought to clarify these myths. In Darwin's Theory of Evolution, it is not the individual organism, animal, insect, reptile, etc. that adapts, it is the species that adapt.

The species adapt over many generations (shorter life spans of insects translates to faster evolution), through probability of life; certain genetic traits enable them to compete better than others, over many generations these genetic traits gets enhanced in the species as those individuals possessing such genetic qualities tend to out-compete those without so they reproduce and pass on such genetic traits to their young. These are all through probability, it does Not mean that individual birds, animals with that trait will outcompete another without in its lifetime, there's just too many other variables in play in one lifespan but over hundreds of millions of insects, animals, etc. over thousands of generations, the probability will work itself out to produce the most competitive traits that allow each species to adapt and survive. Thus, Survival of the Fittest species.

Each individual animal, bird, insect cannot adapt its genetic traits in its own lifetime, the species as a whole adapt because the less competitive traits tend not survive over time, to be reproduced into the future generations. Mass Competition over generations produces Adaptation.

It is even more important that we understand, most of what we see to be desirable human qualities or traits are mostly Values taught and practiced by (Ethos) our parents, elders, they are not genetically passed down from our ancestors (as in case of skin, hair, eyes color, etc. skin-deep attributes). This is the biggest distinguishing factor between humans and other creatures, humans can learn and adapt their mindset within their own life times, animals and other creatures cannot.

Social Darwinists just like Progressive Racists are being overly simplistic in attributing [what they called] 'human traits' to genetics and shirking off individual responsibilities, denying one's ability to control one's own destiny. They stereotype people, then cook up myths and subterfuges to justify their racists behavior.

"Nature is written in mathematical language."

– Galileo Galilei

Casino, Statistics and Probability

Statistics and study of Probability is Mathematics, Probability is not Racists, Sexists, homophobic. A higher probability does not mean something will happen. As when one visits a Casino, the odds are always in the Casino's favor, but it doesn't mean you will lose money each time you game in the Casinos. It is also Important to note that Correlation does Not mean Causation.

Clarifying these concepts is critical as we too often hear progressives chanting police brutality and President Obama citing disproportionate high or low racial statistics means racisms. Whenever we observe a high correlation of variables in statistics, it prompts us to investigate further into the details behind the variables measured, listing a number of possible causes. Once we've identified the key causes, we objectively address the solutions to remove the causes creating the negative effects. If we had addressed the correct causes, then in due time, the negative effects will be observed to fall to a ratio similar to other races. That's how issues get resolved in objective and unemotional fashion. Understanding Mathematics allows human invention, discoveries, innovation and progress, lack of its understanding allows the spawning of sophistries like racism, sexism, LGBTQ, etc. by the problem profiteers.

"There is another class of coloured people who make a business of keeping the troubles, the wrongs and the hardships of the Negro race before the public. Having learned that they are able to make a living out of their troubles, they have grown into the settled habit of advertising their wrongs – partly because they want sympathy and partly because it pays. Some of these people

do not want the Negro to lose his grievances, because they do not want to lose their jobs."

- *My Larger Education* by Booker T. Washington
in 1911 describing the 'problem profiteers'

6) Poverty Traps set by Poverty Pimps, the long and arduous Path to personal success has to be Illuminated by Light of Education and self-confidence to avoid Emotional baggage

In chapter 4, we had touched on America's history of leveraging and using its Diverse Human talents. This view I expressed earlier was a Global International view of Americans and African Americans, from outside in, unemotional and disinterested in any local politics. Of all the various challenges to untie the Gordian knot, this one is the most emotionally charged and complex to understand. It is complex as there is a self-fulfilling prophesy element that is constantly affecting the outcome, thus sort of a 'circular reference' syndrome. We'll elaborate more in due time.

First, I started with the outsiders' perspective on this topic, then I listen to the Mainstream Media and Social Media's perspective of the 'exploitation of the negros' by the whites, etc. This is very easily accessible, it is plastered all over the internet, cable TV, airwaves, anywhere you look or listen. Then, I figured perhaps I should understand the perspective of the Black, Minority Leaders which I watched and listened to their views followed by listening to the views of the White Academia with their white guilt rhetoric. The Mainstream Media, Black Minority Leaders and White Academia all share the same view about the terrible exploitation of the Negro population in America.

Still it puzzled me with many inconsistencies of so many successful Entertainment, Sport Celebrities and President Obama being so popular in 2008 Elections winning such a landslide victory? From an outsiders' perspective coming into this country in 1998, the African and White Americans appear to be Culturally relativelly closer, compared to the Asians or Chinese, in fact they share a common history over last century, watch the same sports, similar entertainment tastes as compared to the Europeans or Latin Americans.

This 'white guilt' complex was also a puzzling one to me, it defies all reason and logic. There are obviously people exploiting the African American communities, but the people doing the exploiting obviously do NOT feel any guilt otherwise they would NOT be doing the exploiting, on the other hand, the ones NOT doing the exploiting, why do you need to feel any guilt since you didn't exploit anyone? Finally, after much searching and reconciling, I found the key in the writing and literatures of the Independently Successful, capable African Americans (Independent because they are NOT lined up with the Mainstream Media nor made their Wealth from being a Problem Profiteer, to use the words of Booker T Washington). From their perspectives, I was able to understand and reconcile the 'inconsistencies' of the wealthy, successful Sports and Entertainment Celebrities mentioned earlier, learn that the 'white guilt' complex is a condition that the feeble-minded suffer from, manufactured by the Mainstream Media and Academia aka Problem Profiteers.

The reality is that many African Americans are still caught in Poverty Traps, and the very

REAL and Heavy Emotional Baggage constantly stirred up by the Media, neo-Democrats (aka poverty Pimps) for self-enrichment. As I read the passage below from Mason Weaver, [a successful author and motivational speaker], I asked myself, is it merely coincidental? Or is he blaming Democrats for the ills upon the African American community? I also realized there is a common thread linking all the events together.

> *"The problem is the constant beat down of poor people under the Democratic Party. The party of slavery, black codes, slave hunters, lynching, the KKK, White Citizens Council and plantations is still creating and managing slavery in America. Dr. Carson gave a tremendous presentation to those employees at HUD. It was full of hope, framed by his own personal successful life. It should have been greeted as a new era in poverty reduction. But the old party that stood in the Little Rock High School door denying black children an education, the same party that turned dogs on the civil rights demonstrators and the same party that had to be taken to court to allow black folks to vote is attacking the idea of prosperity. Democrats, who didn't want black folks to use the same bathroom with them, are eager to allow the gender-confused to use any bathroom they choose."*
>
> - Mason Weaver, former member of Black
> Panther, author & motivational speaker

Let's look at the chart below, the African American Community has suffered 3 Great Injustices, the 1st Great Injustice is Slavery which ended in 1865 by President Lincoln, the 2nd Great Injustice was the Exploitation by ex-Slave Owners who continued to exploit them after the End of last Civil War as President Lincoln having successfully held the Union together, had also made the ultimate sacrifice. President Andrew Johnson was a southern sympathizer, he didn't share Lincoln's vision for the reconstruction, therefore the chance for African Americans to turn their new-found Freedom into better Equality was lost in 1865.

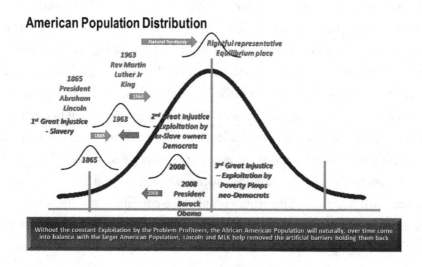

Since the 50s, Rev Martin Luther King Jr had been leading and working tirelessly for racial equality in America, in 1963, made the I Have a Dream speech and led the successful Civil rights movement against the Democratic government headed by President Lyndon B. Johnson. More barriers were removed for the African Americans to advance themselves and again as President Lincoln earlier, Rev Martin Luther King Jr also made the ultimate sacrifice in 1968. Rev Martin Luther King Jr's success for the African American's cause can be seen in the rising affluence of their families from 60s into the 80s, the increased in wealth of their communities is also matched by the successful careers of the talented in music, entertainment, sports, various other fields, also came financial wealth, social recognition and status. Finally, in 2008 Barack Obama was elected as 44th President of America.

The 3rd Great Injustice is the current exploitation by the Poverty Pimps incessantly riling up their Emotional Baggage, this disgusting form of exploitative rhetoric moves the communities backwards and keeps them tethered in poverty traps. In 2008 President Obama became the first African American president, and Hopes were high for African American Communities to be able to finally stop the Poverty Pimps ceaseless exploitation and start addressing the REAL causation of Poverty Traps like to have better education, address drugs abuse and drugs-related crimes, teenage pregnancy, family structure issues, Reliance on Welfare, etc.

Sadly, President Obama never addressed nor even attempted to solve any of these difficult challenges, he merely put the Poverty Pimps' rhetoric on Steroids and made the Ultimate Self-Enriching act of pandering to the Activists Corporations funded by Wall Street's Financial Looters, increasing his personal Net Worth from nothing in 2008, to tenths - hundreds of millions by 2017. If you look at the chart, if the entire America's population is represented by the larger normal distribution curve, and the African American community being a subset of it, represented by a series of smaller normal distribution curves. Since human capabilities are equally endowed in all races, then without barriers to entry (with free market competition) the average of the African American communities should be same as the average of the American Nation. We've seen that barriers to competition (like slavery, exploitation by the Liberals ex-slave owners, Liberals progressive poverty pimps/problem profiteers' exploitation), these barriers are represented by Red arrow pointing from right to left. They are the Great Injustices. The Green Arrows pointing from left to right represent successful attempts in breaking these barriers. When barriers are removed, the natural tendencies to compete will move the African American's average towards that of the national average.

You'll notice very interestingly that when great leaders made great personal sacrifices (by removing barriers to competition) the society benefits and moves forward, when Ugly Politicians enrich themselves, the society suffers and moves backwards. As we know all races are gifted similarly by nature, intellect, talents, etc. without 'artificial barriers' / exploitation by others, the African American Community should naturally move towards an equilibrium with the larger American Society over time. It is the constant exploitation by the Poverty Pimps that creates unnecessary barriers, otherwise the African American Community would have put down their emotional baggage long ago and move out of the poverty traps. The very fact that they (majority) haven't done that is the strongest proof of the self-fulfilling prophesies of Racisms rhetoric, self-evidenced in the Poverty Pimps ill-gotten wealth. The very success of African Americans in Entertainment, Sports, other fields and the Election of President Obama in 2008 is the strongest Proof that the racial barriers had been removed and paid for by Rev Martin L King Jr.'s blood 1968.

And NO, per Mason Weaver's passage, it is NOT a coincidence that Slave Owners were Democrats, President Johnson's government that set dogs on peaceful protesters, deny black children education were Democrats and the current Poverty Pimps; Al Sharpton, Jesse Jackson, Maxine Waters, etc. led by President Obama are Democrats. It is NOT a coincidence as history has shown us it is always easier to steal from the Poor than from the Rich, Bernie and gang lies a good rhetoric about taxing the Top 1% when in reality the Top 1% in Wealth hardly pays any *Income Taxes. When in reality, President Obama, Bernie and most Elected, non-Elected Officials in K Street are mere lackeys and cronies to the Activists Corporations with their real Puppet-Masters in Wall Street and Tech Street.

In the following sections, we'll elaborate in more details what we'd just covered, they were in the order of 1) the Success of 1960s Civil Rights Movement, 2) the second Great Injustice in 1865 after the Civil War and efforts of Frederick Douglass against the historical amnesia about the Blacks Cause then, 3) 2008 and the 3rd Great Injustice Chief Problem Profiteer cranking up the Racism Rhetoric! And 4) the Hopes and Aspirations for a Bright and Better Future for American Families.

The Success and aftermath of '60s Civil Rights movement

We had witness the courage and transcending wisdom of Reverend Martin Luther King Jr. and other civil rights leaders in 1960s to use non-Violence protests against the segregation laws, for black's rights to vote, labor rights, and other basic civil rights. Most of these rights were successfully enacted into US Laws with passage of Civil Rights Act of 1964 and 1965 Voting Rights Act. Rev Martin Luther King Jr. and the Civil Rights Leaders won big time against the Democrats, a long overdue victory too. They had the Higher Cause on their side and they didn't resorted to violence, they had both Moral grounds and the "logic of all men created equal" on their side, thus Justice prevailed and the average African American families enjoyed rising wealth, social status and opportunites into the 80s.

Less than 20 years after the 1963 speech, MJ's album Thriller was released and was a World-Wide Phenomenon, a year later Carl Lewis won 4 Gold Medals in 1984 LA Olympics equaling Jesse Owens record set in 1936 Berlin Olympics. The success of MLK's civil rights movement is self-evident to the entire world, from the 1970s till beginning of the Millennia, African Americans have excelled in American Sports, Entertainment, Military, Government and various other Industries. The outside world doesn't see American just as white or black or Hispanic, in fact, the Music, Sports, Comedies, Hollywood Movies' Super Stars are all disproportionally African Americans! Names like Michael Jackson, Prince, Lionel Richie, Billy Ocean, Stevie Wonder, Diana Ross, Janet Jackson, Paula Abdul, Gloria Estefan in the 1980s, who remembers any white music artists? Madonna? For 13% of the population, that's pretty impressive. In Comedies, Bill Crosby, Eddie Murphy dominated comedies in 80s, Will Smith, Chris Rock then followed in Comedies. The affluence and wealth of the African American families started to become evident in the mid-80s due to cumulative effects over 2 decades of good progress.

In Professional Sports, NBA, NFL Football, Athletics, Boxing, Olympics, etc. (yet you don't hear of racial inequality in NBA? In NFL? Of course not, it is just common sense as that's talent and ability translating into a larger representation). The lists of Celebrities and Super Stars goes on, there are also examples in many other fields too, for example in the Military and Government, we had mentioned Gen Colin Powell earlier, Sec Condoleezza Rice, Presidential Candidates Herman Cain, Ben Carson both succeeded in Business and Neuro-surgery fields. In fact, in Entertainment and Sports the representation is disproportionately skewed, in favor of African Americans, this is Not because it is racists but simply because they are more talented. Many in the Mainstream Media love to use the word Disproportionate when addressing the statistics of crime, education, wealth or even incarceration to mean racism, this incorrect and illogical reasoning only goes to show the lack of comprehension of the user or their disdain for their audience's lack of knowledge in basic mathematics and statistics (correlation does not necessarily indicate causation).

Since the 60s, the racial barrier has been successfully removed by Rev Martin Luther King Jr and other leaders, otherwise, there is no way to explain the success of all the talented individuals since then (the reverence of Rev MLK speaks to his success). But sadly, the terrible poverty pimp politicians makes it extremely challenging (an uphill fight) for most African Americans to succeed in leaving the poverty trap. Whites, Hispanics, Asians, etc. all can be in Poverty traps, it has nothing to with racism. In a more racially homogeneous society like India or China, there are millions and millions of extremely poor Indians or Chinese, but it wouldn't be any racial issues because they are from same race and look similar. For the poor that are still in the Poverty traps and we have to solve this challenge and unleash their talent and energies for the advancement of America.

Just as in naming the Radical Islamic Terrorist problem, we need to address the right issues, naming the issue correctly as a Poverty Trap is a start, otherwise, we'll always be barking up the wrong tree. We also need to be sensitive to the strong emotional element involved too.

The Second Great Injustice, aftermath of the American Civil War

In 1865, at the end of last Civil War, the former slaves owned nothing because they had received only freedom. Now 152 years after the end of last Civil War, the African Americans are still disproportionally stuck in the Poverty Traps. As we've seen, it becomes an opportunity for the unscrupulous to exploit which they do so on a daily basis and making fortunes for themselves. There is also another less obvious but equally powerful emotion that completes the equation [emotional trap], resulting in today's Poverty Trap challenge (aka Racial Inequality challenge to the exploitative neo-democrats).

In 1865 as the XIII amendment was passed by the Senate on April 8, 1864, and by the House on January 31, 1865, the end of the Civil War draws towards its close, President Abraham Lincoln was already planning for the integration of the South back into the Union. In Lincoln's mind, it wasn't just about winning the war over the south, the slaves have also been freed and their rights to freedom are also now enshrined in the US Constitution.

The Next step will be to address their future in the United States of America. Unfortunately for America, President Abraham Lincoln never got to oversee the Integration of the South back into the Union, neither was the Freed Slaves' Future addressed. Otherwise the freed Slaves might have been able to play a major role contributing to the Reconstruction in the South or even the Westward Expansion. Secretary of State William H. Seward did proclaim the XIII amendment's adoption in Dec 1865, Seward also went on to acquire Alaska from the Russians (a stroke of genius that was ridiculed in its time).

After the end of the Civil war, the slaves were freed and their future might have looked promising for a short while, it wasn't long before the Democrats (ex-slave owners), were back and re-asserted themselves again over their previous 'properties' and dominance over the African American communities in the south. Although President Abraham Lincoln freed the slaves (both via the war and via the US Constitution) in form, and gave his life doing so, he didn't get to address their plight after the war ended, so in substance, the African American ended back under the dominance of the Democrats (their ex-owners). Freedom and True Equality are two different things. This is the **second Great Injustice** to the African American community in USA.

As historical amnesia befell the African American race towards the end of 19th century, after the end of the Civil War, Frederick Douglass (name he chose in 1838 at age 20 after escaping from slavery, was inspired by a character in Sir Walter Scott's poem *Lady of the Lake*), had described himself as "one isolated in the land of his birth – debarred by his color from congenial association with whites … equally cast out by the ignorance of the blacks." Douglass was an influential Pioneer abolitionist when President Lincoln issued the Emancipation Proclamation in 1863, he was later called to the White House to discuss strategies for emancipation the next year.

He attended the White House reception in 1865 following Lincoln's second inauguration and also supported the Republican Reconstruction plans in 1866 and part of a delegation that met with President Andrew Johnson to push for black suffrage. Douglass campaigned for Ulysses S. Grant who won and became president in 1868. By March 30th in 1870, Congress passed the 15th amendment giving the African Americans the right to vote. Douglass was appointed to a number of positions by President Grant, President Rutherford Hayes, President James Garfield and finally President Benjamin Harris in 1889 (6 years before Douglass' death in 1895). For all his tireless efforts, the fugitive Slave that rose from bondage to become the foremost orator-editor-activist for the abolition movement couldn't do much more for the freed slaves.

This is where I came in – by Bee Gees;

Act IV, Scene IV Enter: The Poverty Pimps, the Third Great Injustice 2008

The best attestation to Rev ML King's success is the election into office of the 44th President of USA in 2008 (for 2 terms). This was a great victory, a landslide victory over Sen McCain. It was also a victory for America, it now has its first African American President! All those suffering from white guilt should be vindicated, right? many might even have voted for President Obama just because he was African American to prove that they are NOT racists and collect their Certificates of Absolution. Sadly no one checked his qualifications, experience nor background, it would have been racist to even dream of doing something like that! Thanks to this type of "white guilt" complex in Liberal Mainstream Media, who's been totally negligent in their duties to the American people, allowing President Obama to walk on water for 8 years, creating additional $ 10T in debts, Syrian Civil War to proliferate; which led to millions of refugees around the world, the rise of ISIS, the breakup of the African American Families, further deterioration of the Income Inequality in America and the worsening economic status of the African Americans. All on his 8 years watch as leader of this country.

In the last section of this chapter, we'll analyze the strengths and weaknesses of President Obama and also some of the previous Presidents too. For this part of the discussion, I wish to just highlight 2 untruths that President Obama Marketed and Projected as his "experience and knowledge".

First as we'd witnessed in chapter 6, he projected the image that he has Global Experience or Exposure as he had lived overseas. The reality was that he was a kid of 8 years old, this is the logic of the non sequiturs. Perhaps it's the white guilt talking? This is utter nonsense and has caused millions of Syrians, Libyans, Iraqis their homes, families and for some their lives due to his arrogance and unwillingness to learn about the reality in Middle East, instead relying on his "personal expertise and insights" about Islam gleaned from his childhood memories about Indonesia, plus advice from his designing Muslim brotherhood advisors.

Secondly, he also portrayed this image that he knows the plight of the African Americans because he is born in USA and he is also racially African which would make him African American. The reality is that his father was Kenyan and Obama grew up in Hawaii (which in form, is part of America, but in substance, is culturally the most distinct from any other American States). There is no personal experience of his which would let him relate nor understand the challenges faced by the African American community in mainland America of 48 States. So, what's President Obama going to do for the African American community? Does he really care?

We know he was being untruthful in his projection of himself having experiences and skills which he doesn't have. Perhaps he just likes to brag to get into office, nothing wrong with that [let's not judge him too early]. Let's watch his behavior after he comes to into power in 2009. With hindsight 20/20, there were some things which he didn't do which should raise some red flags about his real intentions about helping the African American communities. First, having owed his success of becoming the first African American President to selfless endeavors and sacrifice of Rev MLK, you don't hear him say much about ".. standing on the shoulders of giants.." in acknowledgement of Rev MLK's sacrifice and contribution to the African American people.

Next observation, as in any relay races, when it's your turn and you get handed the baton, you will run as quickly as you can to finish the race or pass on the baton to the next runner, right? Instead, do you see President Obama start to address the real Poverty Issues with the African

American communities? Does he address the Planned Parenthood concerns with the African Americans? Does he address their social and family structural challenges or their "room for improvement" in education and much needed attention to place education as their highest priority? No, he didn't do any of these. Instead he Rewind and amplify the rhetoric about Racism, about Racial Inequality, Racial Grievances, anything that is Racially dividing, an America that elected an African American President is telling that entire world that America is a racists country, and they heard him loud and clear as most African Americans back home, [this is power of self-fulling prophesies, as one becomes more self-conscious of the differences, it actually magnifies them].

We already know the 101 in Self-Help is to focus on Positives, focus on the Solutions! Never constantly indulge in the negative problems without solutions, because you will then subconsciously start focusing on the negatives and it will become a self-fulfilling prophesy! Does President Obama not understand such a simple concept? Obama is not stupid, that is a fact, so why is he stirring up old wounds and fanning the flames of Hatred and Anger with the African American communities?

> *"The problem isn't that Johnny can't read. The problem isn't even that Johnny can't think. The problem is that Johnny doesn't know what thinking is; he confuses it with feeling."*
>
> – Thomas Sowell

In 2009, besides doing his Apology Tours around the world, President Obama also received a Nobel Peace Prize, less than 10 months after he gets into the White House (for talking about need for world peace)? The same Norwegians that was going to give the 1939 Nobel Peace Prize to Adolf Hitler. Ever since then, Obama besides also giving out Presidential awards to media, entertainment celebrities or anyone he has any use for, has also been incessantly fanning the Flames of Anger and Hatred, pandering to Black Lives Matter, Antifa (most recently even personally setting up OFA, another Activists Corporation) activists that incites Violence, rioting and looting.

Leveraging the Hollywood and American Media's influence around the world, as President Obama cranks up his rhetoric on Racism, Racial Inequality in America, the world also starts to see America as Racists and backward in Racial Equality; all this nonsensical back-sliding after decades of good progress since '60s in removing Racial (but NOT Poverty) barriers, cumulating in his own election to become the 44th USA's President, yet the world now sees Americans as racists since American Media is reporting it so it must be true, right?

> *"Grief is the agony of an instant; the indulgence of grief the blunder of a life."*
> - Benjamin Disraeli

There's injustice all around the world through human history, Asian Colonies, the Latin American Colonies in Central and South Americas (the great dying; estimated 85-90% of indigenous population died, under the Spanish), slavery practiced in Caribbean, Africa, etc. (in fact, word slave comes from Slavs). The Arab Muslims were the largest Slaves traders in Africa when Dr Livingston was getting public attention towards the sad plight of the African people in 19th century. In spite of these, of all the countries under colonial rule, all with history of slavery, not one single country openly advertises about its historical grievances on a daily basis [unlike the 2 hours of hate we see from Mass Media, Social Media]

> *"Racism does not have a good track record. It's been tried out for a long time and you'd think by now we'd want to put an end to it instead of putting it under new management."*
>
> – Thomas Sowell

Many of these Asian colonies only became independent after second world war some as late as the '60s, in the case of the apartheid system in South Africa, it only ended as late as 1993, when Nelson Mandela was elected as first President of South Africa in May 1994. Yet despite receiving their 'redress' only recently, you don't see the Portuguese, Spanish, Dutch, Belgian, German, English ex-colonists protesting about their old grievances on daily basis. The reality is this when left alone, Humans move on with their lives, leaving history behind, remembering and learning from it but never wallowing fruitlessly in the past.

> *"In various countries and times, leaders of groups that lagged behind, economically and educationally, have taught their followers to blame all their problems on other people - and to hate those other people."*
>
> - Thomas Sowell

Now we see the Poverty Pimps for what they really are. The PPs [problem profiteers] like Al Sharpton, Maxine Waters, Al Green, Elijah Cummings, Jesse Jackson and Suzerain of PPs, President Obama. If one were to learn more about lives of Rev MLK and President Nelson Mandela, you'll note their tireless work over decades, driven by virtues, ethics and self-sacrifice made by these giants of men, this stands in stark contrast to the Czar of Problem Profiteers who only talks a good game with shallow understanding of the real challenges and no follow through actions, except making more grandiose speeches and making idealistic empty promises; totally disconnected from realities.

> *"If you have always believed that everyone should play by the same rules and be judged by the same standards, that would have gotten you labeled a radical 60 years ago, a liberal 30 years ago and a racist today."*
>
> – Thomas Sowell

The Mainstream Media are Racists, and the major contributor to the African Americans' current plight

They see Obama as a Black person and treats him differently from other previous leaders. This is exactly the basis of racism. If measured by the same yard stick [a short & shallow one], President Obama's performance at a superficial level, might be equivalent to that of President Bush 43rd, who's no intellectual giant. These Media sycophants will allow President Obama's foot to rest on their necks, neglecting their duties over last decade [Ezekiel 33:6], never highlighting any mistakes of and not providing checks and balances to the power in the Oval office during Obama's terms.

But their worst crime in last decades is against the African American communities by constantly propagating the Racism Hate rhetoric and being the biggest Accomplice of President Obama and the other Poverty Pimps in not allowing their victims to move on with their lives and achieving their fullest potential. Their Daily Dosage TV Broadcasts and Internet Social Media Postings consist of 2 hours of Hate and 1 hour of self-Pity without Fail.

Together with the Ivy League Academia, the Mainstream Media has also conjured up and continues to manufacture the 'White Guilt' complex, sold to any dim-witted snowflake subscribers indoctrinated in Art of No Logic. Periodically, it also afflicts the Super-Rich whites; the media and entertainment celebrities who wishes to appear as sympathetic to the Black cause without bothering to learn the details, so they just hit the FB LIKE Button for "White Guilt' and nobly assumes the mantle of welfare and social justice warriors (taking on arduous tasks of saying the Federal Government should donate more of other Tax Payers money to 'Welfare'). This is the same logic behind the 'sedan chair mindset' that we discussed under the Welfare Discussion.

Now we know who's been creating more problems instead of fixing them. We need to deal with the solutions and try to minimize the damage done by these Poverty Pimps. When you are in a hole and wish to get out, the first is to stop digging, we have to remove the influence of the 'problem profiteers' as it is way too easy for them to constantly riled up emotional grievances, Anger, Hate, Self-pity, distracting the American populace from focusing on their strengths and excelling in their areas of talents.

> *"Groups that rose from poverty to prosperity seldom did so by having their own racial or ethnic leaders to follow."*
>
> – Thomas Sowell

A Brighter and Better future for All American Families

We've seen that President Obama had utilized his 8 years in office to stir up Resentment and Hatred (pandering and endorsing BLM, Antifa activist groups; his anti-Establishment actions were visible for all to see in addition to saying all the idealistic superfluous 'save the world', 'love all mankind' comments and cashing out big time personally with his popularity), thanks to the PP Czar, the racial divide is now more challenging to bridge, the Poverty situation of the African

American family has deteriorated. The true worthy successor to continue Rev MLK's legacy has now passed on to Dr. Benjamin S. Carson, Sr., M.D. the Secretary of HUD (Housing and Urban Development)

As the late Great MLK had once demonstrated, transcending the opposition by non-violent approach, lifting the oppressed from the "dependent" stage to Independent and onwards to the Interdependent Stage on moral high grounds. It would be wise for us to follow in his footsteps by out-flanking the throngs of PPs to reach the American Families directly, transcending the white-guilt Media and Academia Cronies to achieve the Higher Cause of Unlocking the untapped Human Talent available and acknowledging the past Great contributions of the African Americans to this Great Nation!

The Funds to the dirty PP Politicians needs to be diverted directly into the hands of the American Families in forms of Books, Food, Computers, warm clothing for winter, education for kids, etc. To fight crimes and poverty isn't merely more policing, the real solution is economic growth! By cutting out the ugly Problem Profiteers Activists Corporations, taxing their 501c3 entities and diverting away their funds, the economy will grow, Jobs and Education opportunities provide the path to a brighter future, this is the wisdom of the Indirect Approach!

善為士者, 不武; 善戰者, 不怒; 善勝敵者, 不與; 善用人者, 為之下。是謂不爭之德, 是謂用人之力, 是謂配天古之極。

Lao Tze

The Indirect Approach. The Best warriors need not battle, The Best Generals does no needless Destruction, the Best Strategists does not rejoice confrontation. The Best Leaders serve their people and country. The transcendent Leader does not impose but guides and leads his people by maximizing their potential, thus furthering the limitless boundaries of Nature.

"The black family survived centuries of slavery and generations of Jim Crow, but it has disintegrated in the wake of the liberals' expansion of the welfare state."

– Thomas Sowell

Kern G. Lim

To protect the American Families from the Evils of Drugs, Crimes, PPs and Genocides, we need to provide a host of constructive activities, like Education, Sports, Local religious groups, outdoor activities, summer jobs, numerous positive Role Models of Sportsmen, Military Leaders and heroes that'll impart positive attitudes and Values to American families such that we might unleash and draw from their fullest talents and potential. Muhammad Ali's vision: the need to instill American Pride and teach Black Pride in the communities.

> *"The Nation of Islam's main focus was teaching black pride and self-awareness. Why should we keep trying to force ourselves into white restaurants and schools when white people didn't want us? Why not clean up our own neighborhoods and schools instead of trying to move out of them and into white people's neighborhoods?"*
>
> – Muhammad Ali

> *"I've been everywhere in the world, seen everything, had everything a man can have …. America is the greatest country in the world."*
>
> - Muhammad Ali

> *"The people made worse off by slavery were those who were enslaved. Their descendants would have been worse off today if born in Africa instead of America. Put differently, the terrible fate of their ancestors benefitted them."*
>
> – Thomas Sowell

> *"Thank God my granddaddy got on that boat."*
>
> - 1974 Mohammad Ali's response when asked for his impression of Africa, after he returned to the United States from Zaire, where he fought George Foreman.

American Pride, Black Pride & Right Values, Positive Attitudes all jointly Building Harmonious and Happy Communities with Great Future

HUD is not merely about building houses, it is about building homes, communities and a bright future for Americans. The plan should start with the end desired goal, which is a bright future with Great Jobs, Great Economy.

It should be demand-pull, there should be a pitcher and a catcher. We start with the Jobs (the 'Pull'), the various Industries, Businesses that can provide jobs and career opportunities. Sports, Music, Entertainment, Military, Industrial, Services, Food and Beverage services, Technology, Academia, Tourism, etc. We also focus on the Education (in support of the process), teachers, schools, Sports, Outdoor activities, Music, Arts, Religious Studies, etc. any opportunity to educate, impart knowledge and teach values.

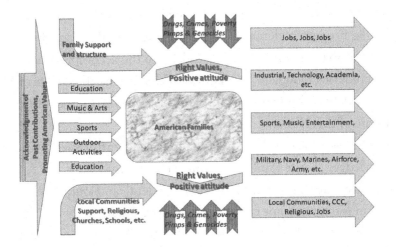

Now that we have a pull and push, we also need to have the structure, process to keep it going in right direction, we need to ensure local communities support (hopefully from the Church and school leadership), the family's support and structure needs to be addressed, currently certain Federal Welfare policies encourage single parent families, perhaps better welfare for dual parent families? We'd discussed healthy activities as a defense mechanism against the corruption of drugs, crimes, poverty pimps and genocide activities.

> *"And as we let our own light shine, we unconsciously give other people permission to do the same"*
>
> - Nelson Mandela

> *"It's the repetition of affirmations that leads to belief. And once that belief becomes a deep conviction, things begin to happen."*

> *"I am an ordinary man who worked hard to develop the talent I was given. I believed in myself, and I believe in the goodness of others."*
>
> - Muhammad Ali

Role Models [likes of successful sportsmen] are Key as they can teach and share the right American Values, Values that support a Culture of Excellence, Culture of Meritocracy and free market competition, Religious Values be they Judeo-Christian, Islamic, Buddhist, Hindu Values, Values of positivity, overcoming challenges and difficulties, we would also need to acknowledge the numerous past contributions of African Americans to this countries' history and success.

Need to discuss Positive Values in the education syllabus, have open discussions about the positives and over-coming hardships and great difficulties! This positive approach must triumph over and conquer the current negative resentment about racial inequality; wallowing in self-pity (destructive and poisonous).

Have more Memorials (have competitions for their best design) to celebrate the Bravery and selfless Courage of the Forgotten Heroes from our Revolution War (Jack Sisson, William 'Billy' Lee, James Armistead, Prince Whipple, etc.). Celebrate the accomplishments of Jesse Owens, Gen Colin Powell, Frederick Douglass, Muhammad Ali, etc. and the talents of Michael Jackson, Prince, etc. celebrate accomplishments not only of the past but also for the future, as reinforcement for the growth culture of this Nation.

Teach the young how to avoid the Poverty traps and identify the Poverty pimps through education and knowledge. White Americans and African Americans are Americans, working together to make a better future for both is "inter-dependent" and logical behavior, (as we all aim to co-exist peaceful in the same home call America), there are no "sell-outs", no "Uncle Toms".

To escape the Emotional Traps (Hatred, Wrath, Self-Pity, etc.) which distort reason, we need to focus on the strengths and innate talents of the individuals, celebrate their successes! Brainstorm in small close trusted groups, the possible sources of emotional insecurity and then address their solutions.

Violence is never the solution, Gandhi and MLK are both shining examples of understanding non-Violence, yet many PP Politicians in previous administration were pandering to the BLM activist corporations, why? Not just for their votes but more importantly, the politicians and neo-Democrats activists are all funded by the same Wall Street Suzerains, they serve the same master and drink the same Kool-Aid. We must resolve to help Americans escape the Poverty traps & leave their emotional baggage behind once and for all. Thus, allowing them to realize their fullest Potentials and harness their Talents, for 13% of America's population is too much wasted human potential and talents.

> "Hating people because of their color is wrong. And it doesn't matter which color does the hating. It's just plain wrong."
>
> – Muhammad Ali

> "For to be free is not merely to cast off one's chains, but to live in a way that respects and enhances the freedom of others."
>
> - Nelson Mandela

> "Peace Eternal in a Nation United"
> - as inscribed on the Eternal Light Peace Memorial dedicated in 1938

The Dogs that didn't bark at Charlottesville

In August 2017, Violence erupted in Charlottesville, VA when groups of protesters confronted each other, one of contributing reasons for protest was the removal of Confederate Memorials and Statues in remembrance of the last Civil War. We know what the journalist pretenders Mainstream Media and Social Media presented; attacking President Trump for not criticizing the supposed KKK-affiliated protestors 'quickly enough' and couple of corporate CEOs quickly withdrew their participation in the President's Manufacturing Jobs' Council citing similar lame excuse as the Mainstream Media. All that shallow rhetoric, we know as it is simple and plastered all over the Media.

Instead of frantically gouging on the garbage fed by the Mainstream Media, if one watches the videos of the fighting between the 2 groups of protestors, any independent thinking person would observe both factions to be equally violent, both ANTIFA and KKK are equally guilty of Violence and President Trump is right to criticize the use of Violence by either side. Any person with common sense understands it takes two hands to clap. ANTIFA is a violent Fascists Radical Activists organization that uses Violence against Diversity of Ideas, against any group that they disagree with and deem justified to be attacked with force (that is the very spirit of Fascism). The Mainstream Media Dogs didn't bark at three critical events impacting the American Public in Charlottesville.

First, the Mainstream & Social Media didn't bark at their fellow Dog ANTIFA owned by the same masters, strongly influenced by the activist corporations and ultimately financed by the Financial Looters from Wall Street. Set up of such violent Activists groups sponsored by whomever should be seriously investigated and diligently reported to the American Public. Clearly, we can see where their priorities lie, and duties are not to the American People but to their paymasters behind the scenes.

Next the CEOs, why some of them leave the Manufacturing Jobs Council? We know that President Trump wants to move manufacturing jobs back to America, that might not be the wish of the CEOs as they work for their shareholders with mission to increase stock price with income and earnings, and moving jobs back to America might not help the short-term earnings of the company, we discussed this issue in chapter 1, Henry Kissinger's point about economic and political entities. Highlighting this conflict of interests can help educate the American Public about the challenges in bringing jobs back to America; we'll discuss solutions to these challenges in next chapter.

Finally, on the removal of Civil War Memorials, 152 years after end of the last Civil War, is the highest epitome of stupidity, the crowning achievement of the progressive Mainstream Media and Academia. It's level of ignorance that cannot even be rivaled by the ISIS radicals destroying the archaeological treasures in Syria and Iraq (ISIS had a rationale reason, they looted the treasures for sale and destroys whatever's left to cover their tracks). This level of mindless frenzy just might be the milestone in marking the beginning of the dark ages of western civilization.

> *"In great deeds, something abides. On great fields, something stays. Forms change and pass; bodies disappear, but spirits linger to consecrate ground for the vision-place of souls. And reverent man and women from afar, and generations that know us not and that we know not of, heart-drawn to see where and by whom great things suffered and done for them, shall come to this deathless field, to ponder and dream, and lo! the shadow of a mighty*

presence shall wrap them in its bosom, and the power of the vision [shall] pass into their souls."

- General Lawrence Chamberlain expressing the underlying purposes of such memorials at a monument dedication at Gettysburg in 1888

Historical Amnesia of the American Civil War

In the aftermath of the American Civil War in 1865, one cannot even to scarcely imagine the anguish felt by the returning veterans to their homes and lands in the South, all totally devastated after four years of war, previously bountiful fields now abandoned and overgrown with weeds. Cities like Atlanta, Mobile, Charleston, Columbia, New Orleans, Richmond all burnt down to ash heaps of desolateness, feelings of despair and emptiness made even more heavy for many ex-Confederates with amputated limbs and sense of hopelessness all around. Even then, these are considered the lucky survivors as over 750,000 Americans lost their lives to the Civil War. All the infrastructure in the South was destroyed completely, homes, buildings, farms, bridges, factories, roads, ports, rail lines all needed to be rebuilt. Law and Order was nowhere to be found while hunger and shattered lives was pervasive everywhere in the South.

Despite all the bitterness and humiliation, they found the courage to persevere and Reconstruction began, it was a long and painful trudge back to respectability but by 1870s, the South has acquired the self-respect to face reality and openly referred to their struggle in the Civil War as the "Lost Cause." As the Union veterans were hailed as 'saviors of the Union' in the North, the ex-Confederates soldiers were respected in the South as 'keepers of the Faith'. As the Union Veterans formed the Grand Army of Republic, the United Confederate Veterans was formed in the South. By the late 19th century, the healing process had begun to gain traction and the nation had emerged stronger through the conflict, the bitterness subsided to acceptance of history passed, pride in keeping to one's Faith, self-respect from having had the conviction to defend those Beliefs and also pride in the growth and strength of their country as America achieves its Manifest Destiny and the approach of the 20th century lauded as the American Century.

Reading Ida Tarbell's letters to the veterans and their responses back as she researched her work on Lincoln we can also sense this sense of 'moving on' on both sides and bonding as a new Nation emerges. This post war camaraderie can be clearly seen in battlefield reunions especially in 1913, the 50th anniversary of the battle of Gettysburg and again in 1938, the 75th anniversary when President Franklin Roosevelt addressed an audience of estimated 400,000 people on 3rd July, looking down at the front section, where old men sat wearing hats, stiff collars, and holding canes. Roosevelt said, "All of them we honor, not asking under which flag they fought then – thankful that they stand together under one flag now."

"As the Civil War passed into history, former enemies found themselves linked in what The Red Badge of Courage author Stephen Crane called "a mysterious fraternity." They were bound by shared sympathies for the

younger mean they once were and for the sacrifices they made. Of all the thoughts of that war, those remembrances offered the least controversial ground upon which they could relate. Many began to realize that they had not been enemies at all but brothers in suffering. This mutual respect was the gateway to a lasting peace in the United States. The soldiers would never forget, but they could forgive. They were all living reminders of the greatest test of American statehood. The war was bigger than individual animosity; human commonality drew them together.... We say they are all gone now. They are not. The past is forever speaking to us. And it speaks with many voices. Those Civil War generations went through an indescribable hell to carve a pathway to the future. We are that future. The America we know was born in 1865."

- After the Civil War by James Robertson

When the bough breaks, the cradle will fall, has the American Civilization has fallen from its heights of enlightened souls that had come together in mutual respect after the last Civil War, to the depths of present day ignorance of radicals destroying the Confederates Memorials? The very souls that went through indescribable hell (forging a United States of America), to allow the current generation of Americans the luxury to forget and abuse their own history is an ironical Tragedy for the country. The fact that the Mainstream Media and Social Media chose not to address it or carelessly dismiss these inexcusable acts as 'statues of ex-slave owners' is the REAL SHAME in Charlottesville!

"Education is the most powerful weapon which you can use to change the world."

– Nelson Mandela

"Human history becomes more and more a race between education and catastrophe."

– H.G. Wells

6b) Beware the hollowgast; the invisible Pimps in Public Education

Speaking of cradle, the cradle of civilizations lies in their Education System. Even here, the American Education system (Public Education) is seriously infected by the parasitic virus. The American Federation of Teachers (AFT), National Education Association, AFSCME (American Federation of State, County and Municipal Employees) are Activists 501c3 "charitable organization".

Let's cover the 'conflict of interests' of government Unions, for the power relationships in government unions are unlike labor unions in the private sectors. In the Private sectors, where the management reports to the shareholders, and pushes on labor to extract more profits, the labor in private sectors thus Unionize in order to increase their bargaining power against management.

In the case of Government Unions, the elected officials are essentially elected into their offices by the local residents; many of whom would naturally hold jobs in local communities (eg. Teachers), by Unionizing, they can become powerful enough to influence the results of the local elections. Which is a huge 'conflict of interest' as they can now hold the elected officials (aka their bosses) hostage and can place their own agenda above all the other residents. For example, the Teachers Union can be very powerful and pushes their elected officials for more benefits for themselves. The top officials get rich and becomes the local 'elite' in their communities (thanks to their advantageous Union positions), send their own kids into private schools and NOT focusing on addressing the challenges in the Public-school systems as they have now become "insulated" from the impact of poor public education.

Why do you think the Teachers Union opposed their new Sec of Education like there's no tomorrow? She just might direct funds away from their 'personal kitty', towards the kids in real need of getting a good education. To clarify, we are not referring to the teachers (operational level) themselves but the officials behind the scenes, the administrative overheads, you'll just need to review the complete set of budgets and financials to pick out these groups. They might be fewer in numbers but their share of the Total payroll and benefits are substantial, in the commercial world, we might know them as middle and upper management, the executives, they probably go by same titles in government, non-profit, non-government organizations.

Because they are not at the front line or operational level, to the lay-man they are invisible. But they are NOT invisible in the accounts and payrolls. To flush out all these pests and parasites, the Accounts and Financials is always the Best Place to start, that goes for the K Street anomic Administrative Apparatchiks too. Even as we Must encourage diversity in ideas, in ideologies, so we must eradicate the parasites and purge poverty pimp virus from the systems, protect America against Virus threats and infections.

Fortes Fortuna Juvat, We will untie the Gordian Knot

Just as when we first look at the Challenge of Radicals In last chapter, it looked rather formidable to take on, so does solving the challenge of untying the Gordian knot for domestic issues too. Many of issues of the Gordian Knot are 'interlinked', Solving one challenge will also help 'untangle' other challenges too (they are 'synergistic' in that sense).

And as in Heracles against the Hydra of Lerna, if you chop off one of the heads, it will grow back into two heads. Therefore, we need to address all the challenges simultaneously (in parallel), only then can we see the entire problem (get a feel of how large it is), figure out where they are inter-related and understand the key nexus groups; the flow of funds that feed them.

How to Kill many birds with one stone? Can the camel to go through the eye of the needle?

We know that we don't have the luxury nor resources to address the challenges individually and sequentially (too slow plus they will 'grow back'), we have to knock a number of them 'out of the park' with one swing!

Many of the challenges are inter-related, so as we start to address some of them, the others become simpler to tackle. The next realization is that most of the challenges are created by a few common sources, by removing the cause of the issues, many of the seemingly un-related issues will disappear.

Lastly and Best News of All, by removing the causes of the issues, we'll also be looking at areas of Growth Opportunities for the American Economy; eg. by targeting the cause of Income Inequality, we'll also be boosting the Economy and Job growth!

We have a big fat Administrative Bureaucracy of Federal apparatchiks in Washington DC, issuing meaningless Rules that's killing this country's economy, innovativeness, free-market competition, etc. Their Culture of Entitlement is decadent and egoistic. These Deep State Bureaucrats feels threatened as the American people had put into office an outsider, with his outsider cabinet leadership team too. It has been a long while since DC had seen volunteer public servants and the decadent professional politicians are fiercely resisting the change demanded by the American people.

The Federal budget had been deficit for over 17 years, last time it was breakeven was under Bill Clinton. So we have the perfect opportunity to kill 4 birds with 1 stone and yet the new administration might have missed the first swing. We could have a surplus budget since the 1990s, remove all the ugly Federal Apparatchiks and remove the Federal Rules; barriers to this countries' economy, drive Cultural change and introduce the traditional American Leadership Values into Washington DC's organization just by cutting the budgets of all the Bureaucratic organizations by over 80%. That will drive the sense of crisis into these fat cats!

That will also clear out all the decades of clogged up sewers in Washington DC organizations, cutting the layers of idle "middle management" and paper / emails pushers. Let the ground staff do their jobs, the organizations should be flat. Entire organizations should be at most 3 layers; from operational level staff up to the Secretary of Departments (including the Secretary as 1 layer), operating at 20% of budget will weed out all the noise and allow the secretary of each department to learn "first hand" which are the most crucial and remove all the filters and red-tape!

Tracking the Terrorist Funding might possibly help clear out some of the Activists Corporations of "charitable nature" 501c3 locally and relieve pressure on many of the Gordian Knot issues. These two Hydra of Radicals are interlinked in more than one way, for they similar Cultures of Radicals, Strong Passions rooted in Ignorance. As noted in last chapter, the counter-intelligence is crucial, we need to address the Lies and Ugly Deceit of the neo-democrat Radicals as well and show them to be the shameful Poverty Pimps that they really are! Once we've remove the dirty, malicious neo-fascist Activists propaganda and activities back home, 60-70% of all domestic problems will disappear overnight! The descaling (re-structuring) of the Big State Governments' apparatchiks in DC will solve the remaining 30% as strong Economic Growth, good paying Jobs return to America and Income Inequality will start decreasing Big Time. You think this is too good to believe? We'll show you the opportunities and potential in this and following chapters!

We'll discuss more of the "synergistic" solutions in next 2 chapters. For now, we can safely conclude that the Federal government is NEVER the solution for individual's problems. The more it gets involve and creates more rules to regulate, the more mess it creates till a point of complete chaos and the individuals will stop following the meaningless rules!

A Huge Hammer cannot be used to stich a piece of clothing together, only a needle can. Different tools solve different problems. As a start, one needs to understand all the minutiae, all the intricate interdependent variables and start quantifying, prioritizing the key drivers, definitely NOT broad-brushing the issues and stirring up sentiments, playing on emotional baggage.

We now know from experience and observations, whichever the challenges, the Poverty Pimps will always recommend Federal Government as The Solution; using subsidies, grants, loans to address them. Simply because that's how the pimps get their money! We'll show you exactly how that happens, but first, let's introduce the father of the Czar of Poverty Pimps and how it all started.

> *"..the experience of history brings ample evidence that the downfall of civilized states tends to come not from the direct assaults of foes but **from internal decay**, combined with the consequences of exhaustion in war.."*
>
> - B.H. Liddell Hart in Strategy

Rebels without a Cause, Birth of the Anti-American Virus

We'd witnessed the birth of the Ideological Virus that sprouted internal decay in 60s America; the virus then festered but stayed relatively dormant for decades, until the Leadership and Values of this country became weak, that's when the ideological virus started to multiplied so rapidly that decadence has spread over 50% of this country's population in less than 2 decades since the turn of the Millennium.

As the Civil Rights leaders led by the late Rev Martin Luther King Jr. marched for their Rights, a bunch of neo-democrats tried to copy and emulate their actions but had no real substantial cause to fight for (the reality is that their lives are too good after the post-war Economic boom in America and they have too much idle time on their hands; these juveniles were lashing out against authority, sick and tired of the disciplined fashion that they've been brought up), so they needed to invent their reasons for protest [against the Democratic party in power].

Act II Scene VII

Enter the Witch-doctors, Anti-establishment Shamans Saul Alinsky and his adoring young fans (George Soros and Hillary Diane Rodham, Hillary who? She's such a big women's Lib but leaches onto her husband's last name like no tomorrow .. Branding is of utmost importance especially for Parvenus who cannot make a name for themselves!)

Per the Witch doctors and shamans of the old days before emergence of modern sciences and its later dominance, Earthquakes were caused by the Gods being angry, perhaps with need for human sacrifice. It was not possible for the witch doctors and shamans to know about Plate-tectonics (which was only validated in late 1950s), fault-lines, subduction or continental collisions so they invented their own explanations.

So, in similar fashion, the neo-witch doctors and Shamans Saul Alinsky and his romantics proposed that Racisms, Colonial exploitation activities, etc. made America and Western Nations rich, and the other people of color around the world poor, to justify their 'righteous anger' against authority, establishment and even America. The Vietnam War was being fought so that blended in pretty well with their "new proposed Anti-America, Anti-Establishment Ideologies".

As we learnt from History, the conjuncture of Age of Discovery, invention of the Printing press and schisms in the Church allowed Europe to breakout into a new Age. On the heels of the Reformation followed the beginnings of Age of Enlightenment, multitude of key Events like the numerous European wars, the combination of British mercantilism, State protectionism and subsequent Free trade that allowed Britain the conjunctures of having the Textiles industries, discovery of coal and early use of steam power that led to the Industrial Revolution in Britain which then quickly spread into Europe. All of these events also interlaced with the colonization of the New World, the Great Dying, Slave Trade, colonization of Africa, American Revolution, colonization of Asia, French Revolution, Reign of Terror, Rise of Napoleon Bonaparte, Louisiana Purchase, The Alamo, Mexican War, American Civil War, and on and on, you get the picture, History is dynamic and courses through multiple rivers of time, the intersections of events in time, all have causation effects.

Philosophy of Causation that Aristotle categorized into material, efficient, formal and Telos (purpose). Racism didn't cause the colonization by the European powers, quite the other way, Racism came about after decades and centuries of colonization experience. Avarice of the Asia's wealth, Fall of Constantinople to the Ottomans helped trigger the Age of Exploration in 15th century by Portugal and Spain, followed by the other European Powers. Ming China's withdrawal from their Naval expeditions in early 15th century, voluntary abdication of their early lead in Naval exploration had allowed the European Powers (Portugal and Spain, followed later by Holland, Britain, even France) to catchup and then overtake its sea prowess. Europe's 'optimal fragmentation' model [Jared Diamond] where no one major power dominates, allows competition and numerous conjunctures of events to happen, Age of Exploration, Reformation of Church, Age of Enlightenment and then Industrial Revolution that eventually allowed the European Powers to dominate over the old agrarian Empires and set up their colonies, which they then proceeded to exploit. The simple Take Away here; Competition drives Progress!

Understanding about the Causation and all of us living through the rivers of time is like learning about the plate-tectonics that provides a better appreciation of the present, an ability to forecast the future, rather than to blame the ghosts of past racism and be praying to the shamans of neo-Dems.

From *chapter 4, we also learnt that a) Free Market competition for financial Capital (capitalism), b) free market competition for Human Talents and c) free market competition for Ideas, in combination helped to drive the huge economic growth in USA after the WW II into 1960s (the near total destruction of the developed world manufacturing facilities after WW II leaving only America's intact also presented the opportunity for the miraculous Economic Growth). To understand all of these would require not only knowledge of history but also of World Powers' Foreign Policies, knowledge of Economics, Financial Markets, etc. which the neo-witch doctors (Saul Alinsky) and their lackeys obviously lacks nor wishes to learn.

But here's the irony, the witch doctors [of old days] might have been ignorant in real knowledge (about the plate tectonics) but they were not ignorant in understanding human nature and how to exploit the shallowness and egoistic human nature (Ignorance and Want). Similarly, the neo-democrats witch doctors are also wise to sell their proposed anti-American, anti-Establishment ideologies to a bunch of their lackeys, obviously George Soros and Hillary Clinton subscribe to this ideology, Obama's mother Ann also a firm believer in the Anti-American rhetoric. Saul Alinsky understands human nature's ugly side and his book: Rules for Radicals, 1971 taught Soros, Hillary and subsequently Obama very well! Anti-American rhetoric can make one a multi-millionaire [billionaire in the case of Soros].

One might also notice the 1960s Anti-colonial, Anti-American Ideologies in America were led by white Americans who have never been in Asia, Middle East nor speak any Arabic nor Asian languages. These are People with no understanding of Foreign Cultures nor lived in Foreign Cultures (except President Obama, he lived in Indonesia when he was 8 years old for 2 long years).

Just as the Eugenicists attributing White Superiority in the 19th Century to superior genetics or hereditary traits are shallow, so are the Leftist Ideologies of Anti-Colonial, Anti-American (Racists causing people of color immense suffering), just as shallow. Both their Ideologies and explanations are similar in that they are both only 'skin-deep' in their logic. The Liberal Media's anti-establishments' lies and sophistries if not properly clarified becomes dangerous slogans that gets repeated through Social Media [as dangerous as the Nazis misunderstanding of racial superiority led to The Holocaust]. Thus, we need to put these crazy anti-colonial and anti-slavery arguments to rest once and for all.

It is important to understand the anti-Establishment Roots of the current neo-Democrat party, once we become aware if it, we start to understand all the endless protests, rioting by activists corporations BLM, Antifa, anti-cops, anti-Law & Order groups started by George Soros during President Bush 43rd and all spreading like Wild Fires being fanned by President Obama. They also conveniently provide a very nice distraction from the lackluster economy, highest income inequality in recent history of America, high unemployment rates and huge job losses for last 2 decades.

* In addition to Financial Capital, Human Talent and Ideas, to ensure success, there is one other Key ingredient: Leadership which we will discuss in detail shortly.

> *".. how a government came into being – whether by democratic or representative means, or by hereditary rule or even by conquest – mattered less than what the government did when it got there. As long as it promoted progress and protected the rights of the individual ad property; as long as it kept pace with social and economic change and expanded opportunities for everyone, then it was a good government, no matter who was in charge. If it did not, then it was a failure, no matter how many people voted for it."*
>
> - Dugald Stewart (1753 – 1828), How Scots Invented the Modern World, by Arthur Herman

A good measure of a Government's performance? Science of Legislature, Efficient Bureaucracy

What makes a good government? Per Dugald Stewart, putting forth the argument for Efficient Bureaucracy, a government that deliver Results serves its people better in long term, than one that tries to win short term popularity by pandering to ignorance and greed of the people.

Growing the economy is important, creating jobs and wealth for the hardworking folks, building roads, rails, infrastructures, power, clean water and utilities in the colonies. Expanding trade for the colonies benefits everyone and spreads wealth into the middle working class, building schools and bringing mass quality education lifts the poor colonies into a better platform than their previous rulers had ever done for them.

> *".. on the one hand, self-government was the fruit of civilized advancement and a goal for any people. On the other, the general welfare of a modern, complex society profited most from applying "the science of legislation," in Dugald Stewart's phrase, which increasingly meant rule by experts and bureaucrats."*

Liberal Imperialism, Dominions and British Commonwealth

Dugald Stewart replace Adam Ferguson as Chair of moral philosophy in 1785, his lectures put Adam Smith on the intellectual map, Dugald served as the intellectual bridge between Scottish Enlightenment and Victoria Age; his students included two future prime ministers of Britain, Lord Palmerston and Lord John Russell, also a James Mill who wrote the History of British India that gave birth to the Idea of Liberal Imperialism, also coined 'The white man's burden' by Rudyard Kipling.

The History of British India by James Mill in 1817 (father of John Stuart Mill), clearly reflected Stewart's question between a self-government by the locals in "colonies" as against a government applying 'the science of legislature', if the society as a whole benefited more from the later, why shouldn't the British replace the corrupted local rulers that have been abusing their subjects for centuries and instead replace them with efficient bureaucrats [public servants with no entitlement mindset] well trained in the 'science of legislature'? This mindset started a new Imperialism, the Liberal Imperialism.

> *"How feeble is a system of Iniquity!" he wrote as he watched the local rulers at work. "How weak is injustice!" Charles James Napier 1841. The remark reminds us of the sober truth that many of the traditional regimes the British toppled, both in India and elsewhere, had spent centuries making their subjects wretchedly unhappy. When their fate hung in the balance, most of their populations would refuse to lift a finger to save them. For native peoples, the British might not be their first choice. But, in many cases, thanks to Scots like Napier, they were better than what they had.*
>
> How Scots Invented the Modern World, Arthur Herman

British Commonwealth's principle: that if a former colony was given the choice, it would prefer to remain associated with Great Britain than try to go it alone. This insight was enunciated by Lord Elgin when he communicated to his Superiors in Whitehall in mid-19th century, "if London were to give Canadians their Independence, that they might actually strengthen their ties to Britain". Lord Elgin realized this insight when he was the governor-general of British North America (later Canada) in mid-19th century, as the colonies became Dominions and later Independent nations. Yet they are still associated as the Commonwealth Nations, nearly 180 years later, the XXI Commonwealth Games, held every four years, just concluded in April, Gold Coast Australia this year

> *"...On the positive side, "the seeds of progress and modernization" were planted in most places by imperialist powers, in the form of "official agencies and business enterprises. ..... In many of the third world countries this process [had] been subverted by unethical business practices and corrupt administration, and unless the situation [was] changed, less developed countries [would] not be able to emerge from poverty, no matter how much aid they [received] from rich nations".*
>
> - By *Dr GKS in 1979 at Barbara Weinstock lecture in Berkeley

*[we'd introduced Dr Goh Keng Swee in chapter 2, to know more of his accomplishments, you could refer to - In Lieu of Ideology; An Intellectual Biography of Goh Keng Swee by Ooi Kee Beng].

Most well-intentioned Intellects and Leaders in Asia; who wishes their country progress and prosperity would never dwell on the meaningless pessimistic rhetoric about past colonial misgivings. In fact, they generally acknowledge the administrative and infrastructural legacies they had inherited from the British; respect for rule of law, a democratic system of government, high esteem for public education, western scientific mindset of factual proof & discovery, the Ideal model of an efficient public civil service that's free from corruption, etc. They would take all of these strengths and build on top of them to make their countries better and stronger (this is the most logical way).

Only the most incompetent and corrupt government would rile up their masses into hysteria, or whipped mobs into frenzies with blind hate, that accomplishes nothing except hurt the future of the country and its people. They do so, to cover-up their incompetence in running the government, fear of the people seeing through their kleptocracy and inability to add any value to the country other than purely benefiting and enriching themselves [rent seeking behavior].

The anti-establishment anarchists employ racists demagogue to gain power from incumbents, the incompetent incumbents in power also uses similar tactics to distract the people's attention away from their kleptocracy regimes based on cronyism, mediocracy and corruption.

Below is a record of events during the second opium war in China (over lapping with the Taiping Civil War) which eventually led to the burning of the Summer Palace, which was just outside Beijing.

> *"The hours passed patiently, and the men on the ships saw neither imperial soldiers nor any kind of overt hostility from the crowds of peasants that traced their progression from shore, walking along beside them as the ships puffed their white smoke and pushed upstream against the current. These were not the howling masses of Chinese made famous by the missionaries under attack. Nor did they appear as the incensed citizens of a nation invaded. The men on board the ships could find nothing to indicate whether they cared one way or the other about the fate of their emperor. (Indeed, for the mass of Chinese peasants the existence of the emperor was a distant abstraction, a choice made by Heaven in which they had no parts.)"*

Autumn in the Heavenly Kingdom - Stephen Platt

From this passage, we can note 2 glaring facts, the people when left alone are NOT howling masses, people as individuals do not lead their lives in crazed frenzy, mass hysteria, nor do they seek to wallow in self-pity, indulge in pessimism from the past. Left to their own devices, individuals tend to leave their past emotional baggage behind and move on towards a better and happier lives for themselves and their families.

The second observation: when the local rulers, (be they the Chinese Emperors or the Indian Maharajas), have become corrupt and inept, abusing their subjects for centuries which raises Dugald Stewart's question; if 'science of legislature' can do a better job for the people, isn't that a better government for them? If their lives have improved significantly, the reasonable individual would know their ruler has done a good job, be he/she an Indian, Chinese, Scot, English, etc.

All Asia territories were under European influence (in some shape or form), many were colonies to the British, French, Spain, Dutch, Portuguese, Germany, even some to Japanese and America. Yet, now China, India, Japan (never a colony but under American influence after WW II), Korea, Taiwan, Singapore, Thailand, Malaysia, etc. have progressed and advanced (to different degrees) from their colonial days. Many Asian cities have done spectacularly well for themselves; Beijing, Hong Kong, Taipei, Singapore, Seoul, Shanghai, Tokyo, etc. have all advanced and surpassed most American and European cities. How did they do it? They didn't dig up meaningless anti-European, anti-Colonial rhetoric, they didn't waste any time living in the past or being angry, they were too busy building their future!

Most of Central and South America nations were Spanish and Portuguese colonies with widespread Slavery. Same with Most of the Caribbean countries with Slavery practiced by the British, French and Spanish in a much more ruthless and brutal manner, Slaves had a significantly shorter lifespan in the Caribbean compared with in America (most aren't allow to have families). Yet despite all of the above, you will also NOT any crazed rhetoric about anti-Spanish, anti-colonial, anti-French, Racisms, white privilege, etc. in these countries either, why? Again the same reason as in the Asian Countries. People move on to build a better life and brighter future for themselves and their families.

Only here in America, the meaningless and disgraceful rhetoric about Racism and Slavery, Racism against African Americans, Racism against colored people, Sexism, etc. overwhelms the Mainstream News Media, Internet, Social Media, etc. Someone is working very hard to produce that Frenzied state of mind, someone wants to prevent the individuals from progressing and achieving better lives for themselves. In the post-revolution days, the founding fathers described them as smoldering, ever-shifting gatherings of factions or interest groups with partisan agenda. Now, we call them Activists groups, or more accurately Activists corporations (501c3) like BLM, ANTIFA, etc. organizing Protests, rioting, looting, removing Historical Statues from this countries' historical heritage, exactly like the ISIS radicals destroying the archeological treasures of the Levant, or the 5th century, Christians Radicals in Alexandrian burning the books of the Great Library.

The problem profiteers exploit the misfortunates of others and constantly aggravate the wounds, never allowing healing to happen. I am not denying the unfortunate realities of the past, but we need to focus on the future, allow our ability to reason to transcend our basic passions and escape the emotional trap.

The Radical mindless neo-democrats of Liberal Media have sold their souls for fame and wealth, becoming the pathetic mouthpiece of the neo-fascists Activists Corporations. These treasonous traitors have failed the American Public, never reporting any of the mistakes of the Obama's administration for last 8 years (as he could do NO wrong). Worse still, they had been spreading ignorance and untruths to the naïve, innocent and ignorant American public; producing the current *Anomic* Snowflake Generation handicapped with no ability for Reason (nous); the most precious gift within our Psyche, relegated to Romantics where feeling is All. Peddling the evil mischief of the Poverty Pimps and trapping the individuals in an endless cycle of pessimism and negativity, permanently trapped in Emotional Purgatory of Wrath, Hate and bitterness and never unleashing their true potential in their lifetimes.

Now after over 2 decades of misrule by incompetent and unqualified leaders, under the combined relentless onslaught of the Fascists One View Media, driven by the K Street cronies' greed, supported by the Activists corporations' wealth; sponsored by the Wall Street & Tech Street suzerains, (all jointly promoting lies and sophistries that Healthcare and Welfare are rights, constant rhetoric about racism, sexism, anti-cops, etc. just as the third world developing countries' inept rulers do), America has devolved back into a Developing Nation and once again, facing the same set of challenges that our fore fathers had envisioned and feared would threaten this country over 240 years ago.

The Idea of a *Perfect Commonwealth* described by David Hume and Madison is No More, the checks and balances built into the system of government by the founding fathers is No More, corroded and corrupted by the insatiable avarice of politicians, egoistic greed of the Mainstream Media, sloth and hubris of K Street cronies, the deceitful activists lackeys and their greedy, immoral Wall Street, Tech street sponsors, and finally aided and abetted by the ignorant snowflakes clamoring for their free welfare. All working in perfect unison with different agendas, finally breaking down the concepts of "dispersed in small bodies,… more susceptible both to reason and order; …. Parts are so distant and remote, that it is very difficult, either by intrigue, prejudice, or passion, to hurry them into any measures against the public interests.".

After decades of Incompetence and Decadence under the Deep State Politicians, the grand elegant design of democratic government by our Founding Fathers has been broken and atrophied into a third world government structure of corrupted kleptocrats; predicated in essence on the fundamental relationship of the Patron – Client Culture described in *Rosen's Peasant Society in a Changing Economy*. The Healthy Free Market has been replaced by Crony Capitalism in Wall Street and numerous Monopolies in various Industries (incl. Tech Street, Mass & Social Media).

> *Most of the founding fathers clearly understand the threat to long term public interests comes from the people themselves who are easily swayed by demagogues with partisan agenda, popular currents, "when the government is the mere instrument of the major number of the constituents, … when the greatest threat to the rights of the people could be public opinion."*
>
> – The Quartet, Joseph J. Ellis

Quick Summary

By now, we hope you can see clearly the anti-establishment, anti-America roots and why they are constantly spreading lies and subterfuges about various topics we've covered in last 7 chapters. As problem profiteers (aka poverty pimps), they personally benefit, handsomely rewarded by the Ultra-rich activists' corporations, their sponsors the Wall Street & International Financial Looters while at the same time, the public's attention is diverted from the Incompetence of the previous Administration and also the Corruption of International Financial & Wall Street Crony Capitalism's failures to grow Main Street's and America's Economy. In next section, we'll show you how the QEs and Federal funds flow to their beneficiaries and how Inequitable the Tax policies truly are.

སྒྲོལ་མ

Eye of the White Tara's all-seeing Nature. Within Tibetan Buddhism Tārā is regarded as a Bodhisattva of compassion and action, 多羅菩薩 in Chinese Buddhism and Japan too. Tārā is also known as a savior of Sentient beings, as a heavenly deity who hears the cries of beings experiencing misery in saṃsāra (cycle of rebirth).

White Tara has seven eyes. She has three eyes on her face, the third eye in her forehead symbolizing her ability to see the unity of ultimate reality, while her two other eyes simultaneously see the relative and dualistic worlds. She has one eye on each palm of her hands and feet, showing that all her actions are governed by her ultimate wisdom and compassion. It is said that White Tara's seven eyes enable her to clearly "see" all beings in all the realms of existence. Her expression is one of the utmost compassion.

With the all-seeing eye of suffering, seeing eye of Sloth and Pride, that leads to decadence and incompetence which eventually causes suffering to all. All seeing eye of Ignorance and Want. We now need to Show the Ugly Poverty Pimps for who they really are. Let's show the American People where and how the PPs (Professional Politicians) get their money; in chapter 5, we had discussed Greenspan's $ 20 T debt, the High unemployment rate, the Income Inequality, stagnant USA Economy, broken Capitalism mechanism and disappearing middle-class Bourgeoisie. And in the earlier section, we'd also discussed the observation why the neo-Dems Fascists PPs always come back to using Federal Funds as the Ultimate and ONLY solution to all the issues and challenges, that they had raised 'awareness' through the Mainstream P.C. Gestapo Media. Now we'll show you how all the pieces fit together and why Federal Funding is always the ONLY solution.

See the Income Inequality chart below, updated till 2010. Couple of observations, you'll notice that the last high point in the Income Inequality was in late 1920s (before the 1929 Wall Street Crash), throughout the WW II it stayed low, through the economic Boom of USA from '45 – '60s (fueled the rise of middle class in USA), and remained that way till the late 1980 when it started to creep upwards. A strong Middle Class equals lower Income Inequality.

You'll also notice that every time the stock market clashes, the income inequality dips, in 1929, in 2001, 2008 and then picks back up again. The Rich has their wealth in the Stock Market. As at the time of writing, the Income Inequality would be above the high of 1929 level (the highest in last 100 years of American history).

There are 3 key contributing factors to the Huge rise in Income Inequality. Tax Policies, QEs and Federal Funding to various Welfare and Activists Groups. You will probably be able to find lots of literature about how USA government isn't taxing the rich enough and should tax them more heavily to subsidize the poor and exploited working class. Tax policies do have certain impact on Income Inequality, but the QEs since the 80s by Feds and the Annual Federal Funding of $3 Trillion of Tax payers money into Welfare, Entitlements, Grants, Loans would have substantially bigger impact to Income Inequality. Also, the Tax policies impact is Not what most Americans know them to be either.

Top 1% Taxpayers are NOT the Top 1% Wealthiest in this country

A couple of short notes on Taxation, trying to tax the rich to help the poor would never benefit the poor. It will only cause the entire economy to shrink and everyone to become poorer (it is literally killing the goose that lay the golden egg). It will benefit certain deceitful individuals in the short term, but eventually the entire economy will shrink simply because heading down this path of 'taxing the rich' actually ends-up targeting the middle working class (the Bourgeoisie); that invest to increase their own productivity, as a result growing the larger economy, the middle working class also works with creativity and ingenuity, adding value and efficiency into the entire system. The strong Middle Class and a strong economy in any country has an extremely strong correlation historically (from empirical evidence) and also very logically intuitively as the middle class (they have the conjuncture of enough wealth, brains and education, large enough in numbers to make a difference) being the backbone of any society through human history. The Middle Working Class constantly re-invest back into the economy as they need to stay efficient and competitive, as they do Not enjoy the barriers to entry as the Monopolies.

As we had already shown you in chapter 5, all the top 10 most Valuable American companies' market capitalization is only $ 4 plus trillion, only enough to take care of 1 year of America's Welfare and Entitlement Expenses. So, this approach (going after 'the rich') definitely wouldn't work.

Next fact, The Middle, working class American works and collects a paycheck, this wage is taxed by IRS as employment income. It is the most straight forward income and easiest for the Taxman to get their hands on as the employers also report what they pay (wages) to their employees too. As we've already noticed earlier, the Rich are holding much of their wealth in the stock market, setting up companies and selling them off through IPOs, google, Facebook, Amazon, twitter or selling them to (through M&As) to the likes of MS, Intel, google, Apple, etc. The capital appreciation of the shares and also their valuation methodology as reported to the IRS, with deferred Income accounting. Also, contributions to charity organizations are NOT taxable, all makes the 'income' not as clear-cut as the wages. The Top 1% super rich do NOT collect wage income, when the bulk of their income doesn't come from wages, it is more challenging to understand what their true wealth is, let alone be able to tax it.

Next, the wealthy benefitting from the annual $ 3 Trillion of Federal Expenses also gets murky too, as much of the influence and benefits accrued here are also not wages, the goodies would be in form of project funding, probably loans and donations to charity organizations; just like the Clinton Foundation (all 501c3 companies deemed as charity organizations that are tax exempt) all the activist corporations are also tax exempt too. So now you see the Wall Street funds which are already difficult to monitor as income by the IRS flowing into the hands of the Activists corporations (which are tax exempt) as assets under management, the income generated from the funds belonging to such activist corporations would never come under the taxman's jurisdiction ever.

Thus, we come back to the middle class wage earners and small business owners that ends up shouldering practically All, if not Bulk of the Tax Burden. To avoid confusion, I will call this group the middle-class, working bourgeoisie. The Clintons, Obamas and Activists Corporations call these middle working class people the "Top 1%" intentionally to distract the REAL problem in the US Economy, when in fact the Real Top 1% in wealth are the George Soros, Bezos, Zuckerburg, the Wall Street Bankers, Global Funds owners, etc. (whose wealth range between hundreds of billions into the trillions) who are their Donors and effectively their Bosses. Notice that Obama and Clintons get paid millions by Wall Street (Goldman Sachs, etc.) to make speeches?

We cannot Tax the truly wealthy Top 1% rich to give to the poor (realistically not possible due to their lackey politicians, and also conceptually wrong). What we do need to pay close attention to is leakage from the Economic system into non-productive sector; which is the REAL top 1% does. Why do we call that leakage? Because they will never re-invest those ill-gotten funds into real Main-street businesses, real factories that will hire real workers. They will park their money as assets under management with the activist charity organizations that generate returns from Wall Street (hopefully if they are risk adverse, those looking for higher returns might even invest those funds in other avenues overseas projects that give even higher returns; and standards that FCPA might question, etc.)

These 'leakages' will still hold up the stock market (Wall Street) but will NOT grow the real economy (Main Street) as no real substantiate additional workers have been hired. Just as wealth in the hands of the middle-class, working bourgeoisie, have multiplier effects for the entire economy thus benefitting all, which when they leak into the hands of the non-Productive sector like the Top 1%, the Real Mainstreet economy stay stagnant even as the Wall Street's 'virtual wealth' appears to be growing but benefitting only a few (in the top 1%). If more wealth leaks from the Main Street economy (via taxes paid by Middle Class into welfare payments into hands of the Activist Corporations) out into the non-productive sector, the Real Economy will start to shrink (you will see contraction in Real economy). We need to a) stop the Federal Expenses leakage and also b) encourage the 'virtual wealth' in Wall Street to flow back into Mainstreet through Investments into factories, infrastructure and other productive areas of Mainstreet economy!

There are two charts below, one ones the Current YTD (Year to Date) $ 20T debt or QE effects by the Fed Banks increasing since the 80s. The net impact is $ 20T of wealth extracted from the US Taxpayers (it has not been passed down to you yet) and transferred to the Fed Banks to the Wall Street Investment Banks, Equity Funds, etc. who then 'invest into' the various sectors like Technology (Google, Amazon, Facebook, etc.), Unicorns companies, Renewable Energy sectors (like Tesla, Wind farm companies, etc.). The Industrial and Service sector also have equity appreciation but only a relatively small piece of the pie.

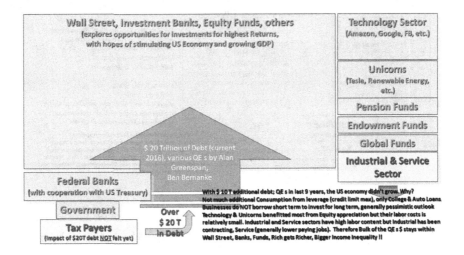

Now we understand why with the additional $ 10T in debt (since 2008) to stimulate the economy in 2008 (QE s to save auto-industry, to help stabilize the Financial banks and Institution, etc.), the main-street economy has hardly grown. Only a trickling has gone back out into the hands of workers in the Main Street. Most of the QEs' 'virtual wealth' has stayed in Wall Street and benefitting the Technology sectors, Unicorns, Renewable Energy companies in wealth (remember only in wealth on paper in Equity Value, not necessarily into Operations Improvement, Technology Innovations, etc. as those real improvements need great leaders to execute into effect, real Value Creation cannot be simply conjured up from the thin air by the Fin wizards from Fed Banks, nor the Great Used-Car Sales men who work in league with Wall Street Investors, to attract their bloated funds)

You can also read from the chart that individuals cannot borrow those QE funds even at the low interest rates as they had max out their credit limit in last round of Housing crisis. Only the auto-loans and student loans got loaded up again to credit limit.

The Industrial and Service Businesses also cannot borrow short term loans for long term investment payout, especially when the future doesn't look at all optimistic from 2008 – 2016 under weak leadership when the Inmates were running the asylum.

Now that you really see the beneficiaries of the last $ 10T QEs, does it surprise you that the Bezos, Zuckerburgs, Elon Musk, Al Gore (renewable energy) are so outspoken to protect their 'extraordinary Gains'. Their ulterior motive is to protect status quo, even as main street economy is Not growing as they personally had benefitted from the Crony Capitalism system.

Since the students have been loaded up to the credit limit to memorize their *Model Answer to Life in the Academia and now snowflakes are stuck with the loan, why do you think Comrade Bernie is lobby for their Votes and by promising Free College Loans? Events always happen for a deeper reason if you are willing to search and understand. *Bernie is right as Logically Propaganda should be Free

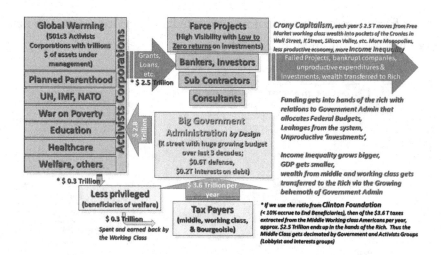

Next, let us review the Annual benefits that accrue to the Activists, Lobbyists corporations that work for the Real Top 1% (the Soros, Bezos, Zuckerburgs, Musk, etc.), the amount is about $ 2.8T that leaves the middle-class working Americans to gets transferred to the Cronies related to the K street Administration.

You can see that approx $ 3.6 T gets taxed from the US Tax Payers, of that about $ 0.6 T goes to the Military expenses, $0.2T paying Interests for the debt. About $ 2.8 Trillion goes into welfare, entitlement payments, subsidies and other Activists groups in terms of grants, loans and subsidies. We know there's much leakages into non-Productive sector again as in the earlier case for multiple observations. The Renewable Energy sector has made no significant breakthrough in technology in last 2 decades despite huge influx of Tax-payers money. We can see that there's lots of money spent on Marketing Renewable Energy as an Industry and Global Warming Killing the Earth rhetoric by Al Gore, etc. the Real significant break-through accomplished is how efficiently and quickly the 'Renewable Energy companies' are now able to apply for and receive their yearly grants, subsidies and loans from the government K Street bureaucrats in DC.

Next, we also know that the Clintons and Al Gore were pretty much dead-broke when they left office in 2000 (by their own admission), yet, each of them are sitting on easily over $ 300 million in wealth (this is public information), so the Global Warming Pimps must be getting their money somewhere right?

In spite of the annual $2.8T of welfare spending, we still observe that all the various issues and problems (that the interests and activist groups represent) have not improved, be it the country's welfare problem, healthcare, education, Poverty issues have not shown any improvement.

As for Global Warming only the Activists groups getting paid have become very efficient at applying for the subsidies and funding and also experts in marketing their cause as well, but never into actually in fixing the real technology challenges, otherwise they will have no reason to apply for the funding next year, right? so if we use the same ratio from *Clinton foundation, a 90% SG&A or only 10% actually accruing to the intended recipient of the funds, that would imply over $ 2.5 Trillion leaves the productive Economy and gets into the hands of the Activists, Interests corporations and K Street Cronies. Why do you think the K street Administrative (aka Deep State) are resisting the new Executive Team so vehemently? They have been without Accountability, with the absolute Power to allocate over $ 2.8 Trillion per year to whom they see fit, what do you think the benefits and influence that accrue back to them be right? Moving someone's cheese of $ 2.5T per year, can become a matter of live and death, that's why only leaders willing to make those ultimate sacrifice themselves successfully moved the society forward (like we saw in case of President Lincoln and Rev Martin Luther King Jr for the African American's cause)

Perhaps now, we can understand the NSA leaks, the negative language from the deep State, the pure Hate and disdain for the New Sheriff and his team in town? This a clear case of Who Moved my Cheese ($2.5T of Cheese annually, to be exact) and it refers to the Idiotic main stream News Media too.

*instead of the Clinton foundation ratio of 90%, if we assume only 35% inefficiency, it still amounts to a hefty $1 Trillion dollars of untraceable goodies to K Street and Activist Corporations annually.

We've all heard of the saying, "Give a man a fish, you feed him for a day. Teach a man to fish and you feed him for Life!" Everyone's heard of this saying just as the other saying about NOT to focus on the Negative aspects of Life (they get self-reinforcing)

Yet, we have observed that every issue and problem that the Activists Corporations brought can be solved by different methods, but all starting with deeper understanding of the issues and then addressing the issues directly, quantifying the causes and then prioritizing them, eventually teaching those closest to the issues to resolve the issues themselves (in other words teaching them to fish for themselves). Yet, we have discovered that in all the issues, the Activists, Interests Corporations always push for Federal Involvement and always Federal Funding as the solution? Now we finally see the faces of the Poverty Pimps, they are enriched from the process. If we truly wish to help solve the issues, we have to engage with the people directly and spent time to understand the causes of the issues and then give them the resources directly to solve the problems themselves, time, knowledge, changing existing habits, dismantling old and forming new organizations, training, money and finding good people are all elements needed to solve the problems.

The Pimps always ask for money as solution because they can siphon off the money. They ask for Welfare payments @ the Federal level as it is too high level and no accountability once the funds get disbursed out. The victims of the crime also do not feel the impact as close to them as the theft gets spread out over tens of millions of tax payers, same issues as highlighted by Jared Diamond in Collapse of Societies. ISEP mentality as everyone thinks it might be a 'victimless' crime. The Pimps benefiting gets handsomely rewarded (Al Gore) while the victims (US Tax payers) loses only an additional $ 10 - $ 30 each to the 'Global Warming subsidies for Gore and Co.', and they probably are not even aware of the crime as it went in a round-about way too.

You will never see the celebrities (aka Poverty Pimps) Roll up their sleeves and personally go direct to source of the problems, to help the situation (like living in Indonesia or Brazil to stop the destruction of forest canopy, in Syria to help peace talks between ISIS, Bashar al-Assad, Kurds, so that the refugees can return home, or perhaps negotiating with the Drug cartel in Mexico to tackle the drug problem in America, working in the American Ghettos and Inner Cities to setup schools and provide Education for the kids there,

Instead it is always to have the government come up with funds (extracted from Tax Payers) to sponsor whatever the so-call "needy" issues. That's how they siphon off their cut of "the funds", the money "contraction effect" is 90% Leakage from the Productive and Healthy Economy.

Raise awareness, Marketing to the Naïve so as to shape public opinion, generate support for Federal involvement, and then milk the Federal Subsidies for personal enrichment, push negative rhetoric and pessimistic hopelessness to the deluded who become despaired, trapping themselves in Emotional purgatory of Hate and Bitterness.

In Summary: A Big State Government (similar to the Communists countries) is what the Activists Corporations; Poverty Pimps, push for as they make their money from the Federal Subsidies (about $ 2.5 trillion per year). Combined with the Crony Capitalism ($ 20 Trillion to date, thanks to Greenspan, Bernanke and their Fed Cronies), more and more wealth is extracted from the Middle Bourgeoisie, working class (productive sector) and into the hands of the Super Wealth (Bezos, Soros, Zuckerburgs, Musk, etc.) and K Street Cronies (with their sub-contractors, consultants working on farce projects); both unproductive sectors of economy, thus Income Inequality Increases, Middle Class shrinks and Economy stays stagnant. We now have all the pieces of the puzzle;

The Victim:	American People (Middle, Working Class)
The Suspect:	Real Top 1% (Soros, Bezos, Zuckerburgs, Musk, etc.) Poverty Pimps, Activists Corporations (Obama, Al Gore, Clintons, Sanders, etc.) K Street Admin (deep State, McCain, Comey, Mueller, etc.)
The Crime:	Kleptocracy from American People for Self-Enrichment
The Motive:	Wealth, Power, Ego
The Evidence: & Self Admissions Of Guilt All the Above =	Un-Accountable Wealth, Self-Evident Behaviors, association with Wall Street Incessant calling for Federal Funding on ALL Issues by the Activists groups, High profile Intervention by IT Moghuls, Wall Street Suzerains, Celebrities Unemployment in Main Street, Stagnant Economy, Crony Capitalism, Activist Groups still pushing for more Welfare budgets, Global Warming Grants, Loans, Income Inequality despite Trillions spent, etc.

"Government's first duty is to protect the people, not run their lives."

- President Ronald Reagan

As President Reagan's quote about the role of the government for protection. It is not to involve itself in Social Welfare, managing the economy, Global Warming, Free healthcare, etc. Minimal

Federal Government Intervention is best for the country (exception being the breaking up of Business Monopolies), yet the liberals and socialists wishes Big Government Expenses such that they can siphon off the taxes paid by the middle working-class Americans. This is a wake-up Call! We cannot ever have the Inmates running the Asylum again, the sad state of K Street, Activists Groups, Crony Capitalism needs to be addressed to revived the Stagnant Economic situation of America.

We see an exact parallel in chapter 6 when various individuals such as Soros, Sachs etc. after Sept 11, argued for Global War on Poverty in replication of the Domestic War on Poverty in USA. In the same way, the funds from UN, IMF, etc. gets managed by various fund managers to be used to help the poor in 3rd world countries. Many have gotten extremely rich while the poor in both America and Globally have fared far worse due to increasing income inequality.

> *"Foreign aid might be defined as a transfer of money from poor people in rich countries to rich people in poor countries."*
> - Douglas Casey, Classmate of Bill Clinton at Georgetown University

Ethos and the Peasant Society

When I first read the writings by George Soros and his crony Jeff Sachs about third world countries' poverty and how the solution is War on Poverty, regardless of the corruption in the Third World Countries, I was so amazed, then infuriated at its absurdity and blatant disregard for human intelligence. We know the reason and motivation for their self-enrichment, but to say and write something so illogical is bizarre beyond comprehension, the fact they managed to pull off the stunts of getting the IMF support and setting up UN Funding from Kofi Annan attest to the severe corruption of these Organizations.

Interestingly, the solution to both the economic problems faced in 3rd World Countries and present-day America would stem from common Values. Virtues as morality and ethos are critical to breaking the incestuous patron-client relationship and ending the vicious downward spiral into poverty.

Recall in chapter 2, George Rosen's Peasant Society in a Changing Economy 1975, as quoted by Dr GKS in 1979 about business morality in less developed countries with regards to the Patron – Client relationship; "…unless the situation [of unethical business practices and corrupt administration] was changed, the less developed countries cannot emerge from poverty, no matter how much aid they receive from rich nations." The working Middle Class in Less Developed countries just as in America constitute the beating heart of their economies. They spend, re-invest in themselves (education, training for themselves, their kids), the small businesses owners re-invest to continuously grow their businesses and thus the middle working class generate the highest money multiplier for the economy.

In the case of the Patron-Client (K-Street, Wall Street/Tech Street Monopolies), the Super-Rich Client Monopolies created via such a corrupted set-up, are too few in numbers compared to the middle-class to generate any substantial impact on the velocity of money (or significant multiplier effects). The monopolies also invest relatively less compared to the numerous small growing businesses as their monopoly creates a barrier to entry and prohibits new competitors while the small businesses need to constantly re-invest to stay ahead of the competition and thus generate a far greater growth of wealth for the larger economy. This same logic holds true in America as in Developing countries.

Dr Goh KS quote about Morality and Business Ethics still apply today in both Less Developed Countries and also in Developed Countries too as we had seen earlier from the Relationship between the K Street Deep State (Patron) and the Wall Street Suzerains, Silicon Valley IT Moghuls (Clients) replicates exactly the incestuous relationship between the Political leaders (Patron) and Industrialists (Clients) in Less Developed Nations. This Patron-Client relationship (symbiotic between K Street & Wall Street, but Parasitic by both on the American People) seems to transcend Nations and also Time too.

The illusion of Equality amongst men as described and explained by Will and Ariel Durant. George Orwell says it slightly differently in 1984 as both are quoted in beginning of chapter 2. Out of kindness comes charity to help the less fortunate, the Problem Profiteers makes huge killings from gouging the Federal Welfare payouts and destroys the Free Market in the process as they [the clients] grow into gigantic Monopolies (of Financial Wealth) and decimating the Middle working class in the process. This push by the socialists (PP themselves) also sets up the stage for the Big Government (Patrons who holds monopoly of political power as the K Street Apparatchiks in DC) into eventual Totalitarianism as described by Friedrich August von Hayek.

Since we've already seen the end Results of the Central Planned Economy, Big State Government leading to eventual Totalitarian Government and Tyranny in chapter 2. Let's move on to another Key Important Element for Economic Success.

An Essay on History of Leadership in the Growth Culture

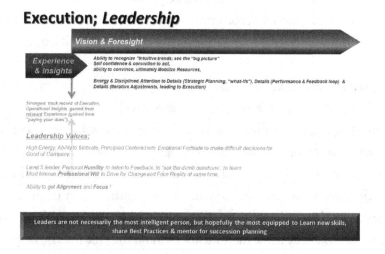

Per Henry Kissinger's summary of Richelieu's career as quoted in last chapter; let's paraphrase what a good leader should be able to accomplish:

a. A good long term Strategic plan on foreign policy which should be consistent over time, based on detailed analysis of bottom up facts with clear ability to distill relevance and priorities

b. He/she must be able to internalize mass of detailed information, conflicting agendas and crystalize the plan of execution in a simple, actionable and reality-based vision. This has to be done under intense time pressure and incomplete information.

c. He/she must understand and face reality and yet be able to stretch the potential strength and confidence of his society to achieve a Stretch Goal (Vision)

While Mr Kissinger was elaborating on the leadership and skills expected of the wise Statesman, while the above Chart, was done in 2006 to explain the expectations of Leadership. In both instances, you can see the distinction between past and future. Let me explain the chart quickly, the red vertical line (left side of page) with arrow pointing downwards to the Leadership Values denotes the Present. The Leader has gathered all his Experiences and Insights from the past up till this point (present), the lighter blue (horizontal) arrow pointing to the right of the page denotes the future (in timeline). At the present, the leader cannot see the future, however he can rely on his prior experience and insights to help him. He also has to rely on his Values (face reality, personal accountability, etc.), Expertise and perhaps most importantly, the ability to learn New skills, adjust and adapt strategies along the way to navigate the future to accomplish Stretch Goals (Visions) for his company / country. Both are similar concepts, from similar perspectives on Leadership, explained differently.

In the 2016 Election Campaign, the GOP leading candidate made many references to his belief in the exceptionalism of America, his wish to make America Great again, and in Free but Fair Trade. His opponent, presidential candidate Hillary Clinton made this remark on a couple of occasions "… we are only 5% of the world." As her justification on why America must have free trade with rest of the world. She was referring to the population size of America in case you were wondering. In Economic Size, America was over 25% of World's in 1960, about 22.5% in 1980 and still the largest and most lucrative single market in the whole.

SHARE OF THE WORLD'S ECONOMIES IN 1960

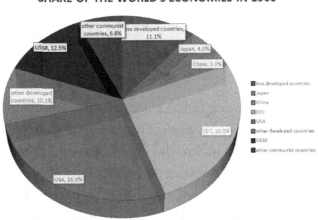

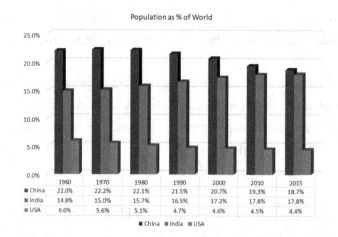

Why would a country with 5% of the world's population have an economy over 5X of its population as % of the world? The witch doctors and Shamans (let's call them Global Socialist Poverty Pimps) have already explained their Ideology, it's because of Racism, colonial powers, exploitation of people of color, so on. We have explored the combination of Free Market Competition in Financial Capital, Human Talent and Ideas to be the driving force in USA post-war economic boom. I promised you that we'll bring Leadership into the discussion.

I also made this chart about exponential growth in 2006, the row row row your boat comment was just added after I heard Hillary's comment on the 5% population. The y-axis is the returns to the organization, the x-axis is the resources invested by the organization. Under different types of Leaders, you will get different returns.

Under the Competent Leaders with right Values to further the organization's interests, the ability to stretch himself/herself to learn new skills, the humility to listen to more competent subject-matter experts and the Belief in Stretch Goals to accomplish the impossible (example: American exceptionalism, the beauty here is that the belief in its future potential yet facing current reality at the same time, makes it become real), you will get the Exponential Growth curve. Great Leaders recognizes and can tap into intangible assets like human potential, self-confidence, hope, imagination and unleashes all these raw potential, into tangible economic growth, innovation, improving quality of life. All of the dynamism can be possible under the Free Market Competition Capitalism Model and Democratic Ideals which we discussed in chapter 4. Great Leaders can also understand the limitations of present constraints, identify the most critical challenges and distill down the priorities within their solutions; quickly isolating the 'bottlenecks' and highlighting the 'critical paths'.

Under incompetent leaders with NO Values [does not believe in self Discipline, nor stretch goals, with no personal accountability to American people], other than to further his/hers personal agenda, interests, NO interests nor ability to learn anything new (I already know all the answers), no humility to listen to anyone besides himself/herself and doesn't want to have any defined goals (or anything even remotely measurable of his/hers performance in office), you will get the curve of diminishing returns. *defined as Rent Seeking behavior per Joseph A. Tainter's *The Collapse of Complex Societies*; "Outputs of civilization and governments decline per unit of input when measured in terms of public goods and services provided."

The linear growth (straight line) is just hypothetical, purely academic as by adding more people, you will get more internal politicizing with NO returns to the organization. Adding more financial resources will also become wastage or overheads (like the >90% overheads in Clinton Foundation).

Row Row Row your boat? Under the incompetent leader is like rowing the boat allegory, their mindset is simple, if you want the boat to go faster, add more people. They always ask for more resources because they cannot stretch themselves to learn and help the team. Under this boat analogy, even if I were to add 25,000 rowers, can we row across the Pacific ocean? How about the logistics of food and water along the journey? Can we have a boat to accommodate 25,000 rowers? Where will they sleep? Can they all row in perfect coordination? Under the competent leaders, is like the Polynesian Voyagers; the Wayfinders, they don't need 25,000 rowers, they learnt to read the stars to navigate, read the ocean's currents and the wind, etc. That's the difference in Leadership

Hillary's comments about the 5% in population demonstrates 2 matters, she doesn't believe in America's Exceptionalism. And her logic could be extended to the eventuality that America's economy should also be at 5% of the World's economy (makes her job pretty easy now right? as she can already justify why the economy will keep shrinking till it is 5% as America is also only 5% of world's population, right?) that's how "global Socialist Poverty Pimps" think, always thinking of excuses to cover their incompetence. If you are with her, an economy that shrinks to 5% of the world's (that means it will only be about ¼ of its current size), if you are on her boat then, you are probably one of the many Galley slaves rowing her boat.

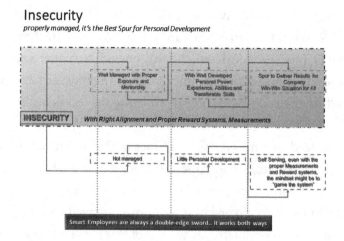

Everyone has Ego, it is rooted in Insecurity. All Great Leaders feel insecurity (esp. when young), but not all insecure people become Great Leaders. The difference is the Values learned and Personal Development when they were young. The two charts explain the dynamics, let's start with chart above.

The 2 separate paths of an Insecure Employee, the top half shows what happens when the Insecure employee is well managed in his/her younger days with the right mentorship and exposure, the end-result is win-win for both the employee and the organization. The bottom half of the same chart shows the same employee, not managed with little exposure to rights Values, and no personal development with minimal transferable skills, the end-result is a mind-set to 'game the system'.

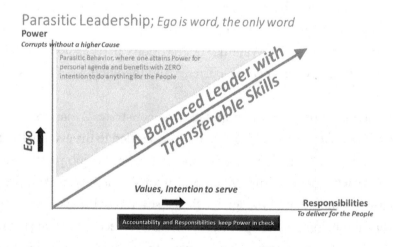

Now let's look at the next chart, the y-axis is the Power a leader manages to acquire, the x-axis are the responsibilities that he/she takes on personally. Only the leader can take on the responsibility himself/herself, the company or country can expect that of him/her but if he/she doesn't believe in his/her heart in those responsibilities, then it is very easy to side-step doing anything for the people, (especially with all the power and resources already acquired). The Power and Resources given to the leader is obviously meant to solve issues and deliver on goals for the country and people, in the event that the leader with poor Values realizes that he/she cannot fulfil solving those issues or deliver on the goals for the country, the next easiest approach is use those same resources to 'side-step' the responsibilities and give *excuses; it is like the analogy of 2 hikers outrunning the Bear, the hiker doesn't need to outrun the bear, he just needs to outrun the other hiker, similarly, the incompetent President doesn't need to be smart enough to fulfil his duties to the American people, he just needs to be smart enough to pull the wool over the American people's eyes (as President Obama has demonstrated for 2 terms with the help of his accomplice, the main-stream Media).

* You might recall that when Obama was asked by NPR why some would blame him for the lack-luster economy in 2015 after 7 years at the helm, his answer was that they were racists

Starting at the bottom left hand corner, the growth in Power (driven by Ego) has to be matched by the increase of responsibilities to deliver more for the people (can only be countered by the right Values internalized within the Leader), this balance will force the Leader to acquire new Skills to help deliver on his new responsibilities. This process is continuous and iterative, additional Responsibilities needs additional Power plus additional Skills to meet those responsibilities to deliver for the people, and it repeats again and again. The 'linear growth' line going from bottom left to top right hand corner denotes the transferable skills acquired by the leader to serve his/her people. The ↑ pressure of the Ego has to be matched by → the Values of the Leader to place on himself/herself more responsibilities, the resultant vector force ↗ can be witnessed in the new skills or insights that the leader demonstrates in solving new challenges that arises (making the prior un-controllable factors become more 'controllable' via learning new skills, insights).

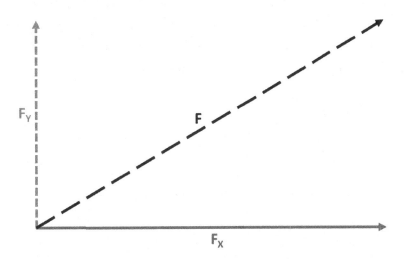

These cycles of learning have to continue on, anytime the cycle breaks, acquiring more power without wishing to add new responsibilities? The seeds of corruption are sowed.

To Most, the definition of corruption is theft of public funds or similar acts. To me, the inability to fulfil one's job's description and giving tons of excuses is also corruption. Between President Bush and President Obama, they incurred about $ 15 Trillion of debt for America, whether it is intentional or unintentional (we can argue about the intent till the cow comes home), the damage is already done. Hypothetically, if between the 2 ex-Presidents they had just taken $ 1 Trillion each, the intent might be clear, but the damage to American would be far smaller, we would only be looking at $7 Trillion of debt instead of $ 20Trillion.

Incompetence is as guilty as Intent, as far as the impact of Damage is concern. To the victim who died from drunk driving, it doesn't matter anymore the intent of the driver, the victim is dead. Or does intent matter?

Since this isn't a management book, I am not going to go deeper into Leadership, one last note on **Dynamic Leadership**. As we have witnessed in chapter 4 on the Free Market Competition of Financial Capital, Human Talent and Ideas all interacting together, it is extremely Dynamic and every changing environment. Therefore, the Leader also have to be extremely Dynamic and constantly learning new skills to cope with his/hers changing environment and competition. The one trick pony cannot make it here!

In the old agrarian societies, the one trick pony can rule the country if properly coached and mentored when young. The leadership styles will vary according to the Cultural settings as well. In many Asian Cultures, there is a lot more respect for Positional Power, due to the large power distance, the Asians generally defer authority to those in Power and seldom challenge those in Power. Asian leaders would rely more on Positional power (relatively) as compared to the American counterpart who needs to rely more on Personal Power (their personal transferable skills; dynamism, insightful, the ability to learn new skills to help and lead the country).

All leaders will use a combination of various types of power, I was referencing the varying emphasis different leaders will utilize in different cultures. President Obama (intuitively) understood this point when he made comments about how it would be easier to implement certain policies in China as compared to USA, he understood the 'tops-down' approach very well, like most that rely heavily on Positional Power do. Those one trick ponies, 'Leading from Behind', most 'tops down leaders' prefer positional power as it is the easiest to wield.

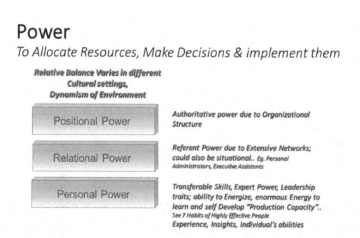

20/20 Assessment of America's Leadership through last 3 decades

In chapter 4, we had remarked how the Growth Culture in America started to wane after the end of the Cold War (in 1991). We compared the Growth Culture to the Engine of America. The size of Economy is like the distance covered, the pace of growth of economy to the speed and increase in number of new Industries (or simply, increasing the % growth in GDP every year) to the acceleration of America's growth. The same applies in positive or negative direction, with Growth Culture going strong, the acceleration of America's economy is increase (as it did from 1940-1960), in the reverse, with engine shutting off (decline of the growth culture), the economy also starts to slow down (becoming more visible in last 2 decades). However, there is always a 'lag effect'. Any driver understands this intuitively, when you step on accelerator, it takes some time for the car to pickup to desired speed. If you merely take your foot off the accelerator, it also takes the car some time to come to a stop. Yet when it comes to the country, they fail to apply this concept, for a country the size of America, it would take decades after the fact to fully comprehend each President's contribution to America. A great example of this 'lag effect' is Sec of State Howard Seward's acquisition of Alaska and how it was ridiculed in its time. Many are now acknowledging the contributions and leadership of President Reagan in the 80s and defeating the USSR. History (if America tides through this current waning phase of decline) should also judge our 41ˢᵗ President George HW Bush positively.

In fact, looking back to President Ronald Reagan, President George HW Bush was probably the last 'technically qualified' President of USA. Of course, we have the benefit of hind-sight 20/20, starting from President Clinton onwards, it seems to become a pure showmanship play. If you are hiring a legal counsel of 20 years work experience to head up your internal legal department, would you hire someone with NO legal experience but a used-car sales man with 20 years of sales experience? But in 1992, with the cold war's threat over, America elected the flamboyant Bill Clinton over George HW Bush as president of United States. How can Bill Clinton have better experience than George HW Bush's track record (from WWII veteran pilot, US Ambassador to UN, RNC Chairman, CIA Director, 8 years Vice President under Ronald Reagan, current President)? Perhaps since Cold War is no more, let's relax a little and pick the less qualified but Mr. Most Likeable? And true enough, it wasn't a disaster, in fact, the 90s economy was pretty good (relatively speaking compared to last 2 decades) and the Internet, Technology Industry grew (last truly new Industry in USA), this is the 'lag effect'. The fully loaded super-tanker can continue for up to 15 miles after cutting their engines. President Bill Clinton didn't contribute big time, but at least he didn't do any damage, he was 'reputed to be a people person' and smart enough (知不知上) to know he didn't know, so he left things alone and tries to listen to his advisors? The same cannot be said for the next 2 Presidents. For both their track records (again we say this 20/20), both their Domestic and Foreign Policies were pretty bad. Alan Greenspan and Ben Bernanke continue to put us trillions into debt with nothing to show for in the US economy and the policies in Middle East were disastrous for the inhabitants there, ask the refugees.

I guess the only topic left for discussion between 43ʳᵈ President Bush and 44ᵗʰ President Obama is their Intent to help America and Americans. Most Americans will agree the President Bush was no Einstein, but his decisions for nation-Building in Iraq and also increase American troops in Iraq although misguided and incorrect moves for America strategically, perhaps demonstrated his wish to do the right thing. As for President Obama's intent? I think it is best summed up in the following speech:

".... You go into these small towns in Pennsylvania and, like a lot of small towns in the Midwest, the jobs have been gone now for 25 years and nothing's replaced them. And they fell through the Clinton administration, and the Bush administration, and each successive administration has said that somehow these communities are gonna regenerate and they have not. And it's not surprising then they get bitter, they cling to guns or religion or antipathy toward people who aren't like them or anti-immigrant sentiment or anti-trade sentiment as a way to explain their frustrations...."

President Barrack Obama in Apr 2008, which he repeated in Dec 2015

In 1876, King Leopold II of Belgium declared his peaceful humanitarian objective of exploring and 'civilizing' Africa as he convened a Geographical Conference in Brussels, all the delegates became convinced of his altruism and hailed him as the leader of Europe's humanitarian mission in Africa. Over 30 years later, the population in Congo had declined by 70% from 30 to 9 million due to abominable exploitation, maltreatment, atrocities and abuse by their Belgian 'humanitarians', thank goodness the US President is no King and terms in office limited to 2 with checks and balances by the Congress and Judiciary branch, yet one wonders how would one's cruel intentions to exploit racial divide and Americans in Poverty Traps (be they black or white Americans) be judged 30 years later?

Act V, Scene IV Exit: The Wall Street Suzerain and the 'Czar' of Poverty Pimps

Now that we've seen the Parasites for who they truly are, how do we get back to Free Market Capitalism, grow the economy, create New well-paying Jobs, buildup the Middle Income class again?

It all Starts with the Right Leadership

A Leadership that Serves the People, A Leader that puts the Interest of the People before himself, one who doesn't seek wealth for himself but dedicated to the cause of building up this great Nation once more. A servant of the American People. One not corruptible by entice of wealth because he/she is already wealthy?

Matthew 20:25-27 New International Version (NIV)

25 Jesus called them together and said, "You know that the rulers of the Gentiles lord it over them, and their high officials exercise authority over them. 26 Not so with you. Instead, whoever wants to become great among you must be your servant, 27 and whoever wants to be first must be your slave—

江海所以能為百谷王者, 以其善下之, 故能為百谷王。
是以聖人欲上民, 必以言下之；欲先民, 必以身後之。
是以聖人處上而民不重, 處前而民不害。
是以天下樂推而不厭。
以其不爭, 故天下莫能與之爭。

Due to their low position, the Rivers and Seas receive their power from the countless streams feeding them.

The Sage Ruler receives all her power from the People, so the people's needs and interests naturally come above hers. She listens attentively as their servants to understand and hear them

The people feel not the burden of the Sage Ruler, she leads them purely to further their cause

All recognizes her wisdom and never tires from the guidance of the Sage Ruler

As she seeks no personal glory, All the Great accomplishments will be in her name

.

Chapter 8

The Closing of the Western Mind; the American Civil War

The American Crisis.

> *"These are the times that try men's souls, The summer soldier and the sunshine patriot will, in this crisis, shrink from the service of their country; but he that stands by it now, deserves the love and thanks of man and woman."*
>
> - Thomas Paine

In Chapter 3, we'd explored and understood how the Radical neo-democrats had monopolized and controlled the 'opinion shapers' of the mainstream Mass Media, Internet News, Academia, with help from the neo-fascist Activists groups, Entertainment celebrities, etc. In fact anything that remotely looks like it has some influence over public opinions has been infiltrated, dominated and manipulated to become the propaganda arms of the neo-democrats, any independent thinking soul can see that fact. Then how did the 2016 General Election results turn out the way it did? Russian hacking? FBI against Clinton? White-lash?

Here's the reason. Imagine the scales of Justice, On one side, you have Presidential candidate Hillary Clinton, in her corner you have ex-President Bill Clinton, ex-VP Al Gore, sitting President Obama, sitting first lady Michelle Obama, sitting VP Joe Biden, all the movie, music, entertainment, Media celebrities, Academia, Top 1%, Wall street Suzerains, IT Monopolies Moguls, etc. and in the other side, you have Donald Trump. Surely, by all conventional wisdom the outcome is fairly (just to be conservative) certain right? and all the political pundits placed their bets, this should be an easy one. No one saw the only person standing with Donald J. Trump, how could they? This person is invisible and has long since been forgotten, this person is the American People. So, the American people made the difference, but why? Why would the American people stand with Donald Trump?

Simple answer, they must be stupid! Yes, Americans must be real imbeciles, Hillary Clinton already called them out, basket of deplorables, bucket of losers, non-college educated [per the words of Mainstream Media's elites]. By the standards of the educated Liberal Academia, the elites of Harvard, Yale, Princeton, Stanford, etc. (with their $38B endowment funds), these 'less educated' Americans have no idea what's going on. Of course, by the same standards of these "educated Academia", the likes of Albert Einstein, Steve Jobs, Bill Gates, Thomas Edison, Nikola Tesla all have no Idea what's going on too, as none of them went through the elite Academia system of America.

The reality is that the so-called 'Less Educated' Americans (per Mainstream Media), just happens to be Independent Thinking folks that don't drink the Kool Aid of the Radical neo-democrat Media Gestapo Propaganda. They that have not been indoctrinated, are still able to exercise their reason and logical thinking. To understand the truth, one doesn't need to be a genius, one just needs to stop clamoring over each other; stop chanting the mindless mantras and slogans of the P.C. Gestapo and neo-fascists propagandas.

The American people suspected collusion for a while, this 2016 GE proved their suspicions right with the FBI acquitting Hillary's obvious 'apparent' breach of national security protocols and all the other wiki-leaks revelations. The desperate Bias of President Obama's entire throng of cronies coming out in support of Hillary, all the Activists Judges throwing away their sheep clothing and vehemently condemning people that they know nothing of, except through the tainted reporting and made up blatant lies of the sycophant grammarians in Mainstream Media repeated religiously by the impressionable snowflakes texting and tweeting in Social Media.

The American people had long suspected the sheepdogs and shepherd to be colluding with the wolves. How did they see the light? As it turns out, not all Americans worship the celebrities of Ignorance and Want, nor vainly repeat the mindless mantras put out by the Mainstream Media and Social Media, in hopes appearing "knowledgeable".

Interesting Eye Opener: Form over Substance

As a side-bar, a quick note on 2 similar concepts in the Accounting, Auditing and Legal professions. Form and Substance. Form refers to Compliance with the Disclosure requirements of Financial Statements, Substance addresses accurately representing the real state of business & nature transactions. Making the minimum standard would be making the form (in blind compliance with the rules) but not truly reflecting the real substance [accurate state of business or transaction] to the users of the financial statements, that is Form over Substance.

There's a Similar concept in Legal profession, Spirit and Letter of the Law. Letter is to follow exactly as the law states (to the letter), Spirit addresses the concept or the Principle that the law is trying to address (the 'intention' during the drafting of the law). The Spirit guides both the General Rule of the Law (stare decisis), as well as the exceptions to the Rule. Here again, the letter is the lower standard to meet. In Mathematics, when solving Calculus Optimization problems with Constraints, merely clearing the constraints is Satisfying, while Optimizing is getting the Best solution under all the given constraints. Satisfying is the lower hurdle to clear. We had touched on Satisfied Vs Optimized Solutions in chapter 7.

You might have noticed by now, that the Pseudo Intellects, the Educated Academia, Celebrity mainstream Media, Social Media & Internet searches are only meeting the lower standard of addressing only the form but not the substance, addressing the letter but not the spirit. There seems to be a correlation between the 'paths of least resistance', sold to the 'snowflake junkies' and lower standards of the 'Academia con-men' drug pushers. Of course, if the Academia is already of low standard, then the students they produce would be of even lower standard. That's Shallow and Shallower.

Form over Substance is the single Best differentiator (setting hidden agendas aside) between the mindless horde of Progressives Liberals plus the Deep State Politicians and their cronies against the patriotic supporters of current new Administration of Law and Order in the White House. Those used to the form of typical Politicians reject a non-Political President dissimilar in the traditional form, it also makes them uncomfortable and mad as they had taken huge efforts and immense investment of their time to remember the shibboleth form without ever understanding the real substance. Those supporting the present Administration understands that the Substance is the Key to unlocking the Potential of America and making this Nation Great again. The intent and heart are pointed in direction of the North Star.

I - Why is the Civil War of 'Ideology' and Information fought here in America?

Most would acknowledge Silicon Valley, USA to be the birthplace of the Modern Internet; where its foundational Technology and early Culture took roots. One might ask the question, why is this 'Ideological', Information War being fought here in USA and not in other parts of the World? India and China are biggest users of the Internet, Asia alone makes up > 50% of all the internet users of the world, Europe makes up about 17%, while the entire North America only makes up 8.6% of the world's internet users. Why is there no Internet War of Ideas in EU? In Russia? In Sweden? or Finland? The 1st and 2nd amendment is part of the answer.

The early promise of diverse ideas, growth of diversity with the internet turned out to be all but a Big lie. As in all new emerging technology, only in the early phases of development did the 'new insurgents' enjoy any initial advantage. Soon enough; as 'break through' slows down, the revolutionary turns into maturity stage, the Incumbents in Power would catchup and learn to leverage the 'new technology' too and turn it around to control ideas and ultimately the people.

In last decade, as the development of internet slowed (relative to its initial explosive growth) and the Net culture started to settle into predictability, most of the governments in power around the world have learnt to control and use the internet to do their bidding of 'managing the thoughts and ideas' of their citizens. In fact, it is proving to be a 'god-sent' weapon for 'brain-washing' as the internet is much more pervasive, (esp. with the explosive growth of smartphones in last decade) into its users lives and operate at an even more 'subconscious level' in manipulating them. Compared to the 'clumsy and awkward' mainstream media where the lying media celebrities needs to be paid top dollars to babble some stupid nonsense for their adoring fans to lap up. The users now actually believe the experience is unique to themselves when they are searching on the Net, they believe that they are 'in control' of the process (without understanding the search algorithms, internet news, availability of reports and articles on the Net can and are being 'managed').

In China, Russia, Socialist countries' the government does the job of the filtering and 'managing' the Net for their citizens, while in America, the neo-democrat P.C. (Politically Correct) Gestapo, IT Monopolies Moguls, their social media tech cronies and neo-fascist Activists Corporations do the same job of selling 'paths of least resistance' via simple political slogans. Many EU countries follows the P.C. liberal progressive media garbage in American; simply because its easiest to sell and always along the paths of least resistance. 'Snowflakes' lapping up the P.C. nonsense from CNN, MSNBC, ABC, CBS, etc. is a Global phenomenon, 'Stupidity is indeed Borderless' too, stupidity transcends Race and Culture. Why are the Germans admitting all the Middle East refugees (when other Muslims countries aren't); without first understanding the implications of Sharia Law, without considering the challenges of their cultural, religious integration, the practical question of immigrants' lack of language skills and prospects of landing jobs in their new homes? The P.C. Virus that overwhelms reason and logic.

We understand that Politically Correct Virus is infecting not only USA but most of the Western Civilized societies too, but it still doesn't completely answer the question, why is America resisting the Monopoly and dominance of the 'Internet and Mainstream Media' dominance of a ONE P.C. ideology? While we don't see the resistance in other countries? We just agreed that they are also infected by the P.C. Virus too. Does America have anti-Virus software that the others don't?

Over hundred years back, America had faced a similar threat of Business Monopolies too; *Progress and Poverty* in 1880 by Henry George who wrote and posed the question "partnership of land and labor which produces wealth, Capital… since labor created capital, how had Capital [through monopolies of trusts] held itself superior to Labor?" To Ida Tarbell, "Labor has been made dependent on Capital by Capital's theft of Land which God gave to all." We see a similar trend a hundred years later, humans invented the Internet, how did the Internet now influence and dominate the human's thinking? Through the monopoly of Mainstream Media & Social Media [as the monopolies of trusts], the internet has replaced the Reason, Nous of humans [for those willing to abdicate it], which God gave to all. Only in America, are there Independent Thinking humans with Common Sense, still fighting on against the tyranny of the P.C. One View Gestapos Media. That's why the last bastion against the P.C. Fascists is being fought in America.

Most other countries in the World are more subservient to authority, many are used to being dominated by their Government, indoctrinated by their Mainstream Media, they have long been conditioned and tamed to 'kow-tow' to Power! They all bow to the Culture of Conformity. That's the reason why the last 'resistance' against the domination of a ONE P.C. Culture is fought in the very land that birth the Internet. Politically Correctness is not a new phenomenon, it was not invented in America, in fact Political Correctness was practiced in Ancient China 指鹿为马 incident (when the entire Imperial Court followed the Chief Eunuch's lead in calling a deer a horse) during end of the Qin Dynasty秦朝, also in Chairman Mao's China, under all Communist Regimes, under the Nazis, the Fascists, Socialists dictators, this is their de-facto tool of choice as the incompetent leader's preferred 'top downs' approach leadership style.

As we'd discussed, in the Introduction, Democratic Rule is an extremely rare phenomenon in human history and it usually does not persist for long periods. Many Americans might be under the impression that Democracy is the predominant form of government around the world, while on the surface it might appear so, but the reality is that this appearance of 'democratic rule' is pretty shallow and can be easily overturned in a heartbeat! The deference to Dominance of the Politically Correct Culture of the Mass Media and Social Media, around the world is the greatest proof of this mirage.

One should not forget that USSR and the Eastern bloc only ended in early 90s [which might not have happened if Capitalism and Democracy had been severely weakened from Internal Decay as now, thereby not providing any viable alternative to Communism]. China is still a communist country and many others are either socialists, under military oversight or thinly veiled 'democratic' with elections nothing more than mere formality.

Long before the spread of the Internet, most of the other societies have already been pre-conditioned to bow to (in deference) those in power and authority. During its early start when the Internet mind-set started in late 90s, it might have given them a sense of 'new-found' freedom, but when it quickly mutated into a P.C. (Politically Correct) Culture of ONE 'correct view' of the world, the folks in EU, China, Russia, Asian countries do NOT reject this approach as they had always been 'conditioned' to think this way for generations (they have all surrendered their freedom of speech long ago).

Only the Disobedient Americans reject this view of the World! Americans still have some Free Spirit left in them, we can still see True Freedom of Ideas & Diversity in action, this Civil War against Conformity is the Best Proof that America is a free country Ideologically. Armed with its 1st and 2nd amendment, the only country in the world that truly allows freedom of ideas to grow and flourish, which gave birth to the internet, is resisting the Monopoly of P.C. Culture, desisting the Mass Indoctrination of the Social Media and Mass Media. Only in the Land of the Free, Home of the Brave, The Creator (of Internet) refuses to 'kow-tow' to its own Creation.

In fact, while the IT Revolution might initially have seemed like a great tool for democracy when in actual reality, its merging with the traditional mainstream media has presented The Best opportunity (yet) for extreme pervasive, intrusive indoctrination with no limits into individuals personal lives (especially with smartphones, tablets, etc. the brainwashing has become 24/7 which leaves nothing to chance anymore). We can already see from the last decade that the Internet with the Main-Stream Media has become intensely Uniform in 'P.C. Ideology' and totally dominated by the Neo-Fascist Democrats. This powerful combination [of Technology and Media] has brought about the Great Dying of Diverse Ideas in last Decade. A similar societal crisis with its own set of cultural challenges was being experienced at the start of Industrial Revolution in later part of 18th century in Britain.

During the Scottish Age of Enlightenment, the intellects foresaw the changes happening to their traditional lifestyles, as we had seen in chapter 2, they discussed about it in their Select Societies, Poker Club, Oyster Club, Tuesday Club, etc. Adam Ferguson wrote about the cultural impact in his *Essay on the History of Civil Society published in 1768*, in it he praises the old way of life with courage, honor, integrity which was being destroyed by the commercial society's (new Industrialized World) over specialization and mental mutilation. Ferguson is on same page as all his fellow literati (likes of Dave Hume, Adam Smith, Lord Kames, Andrew Fletcher and Jean Jacques Rousseau) about the societal changes happening due to 'division of labor', 'partition of employment'. Unlike Hume and Smith who saw that the benefits outweigh the price, Ferguson was more pessimistic and saw commercial society (Industrialization and capitalism) leading to tyranny instead of Liberty.

The *History of Civil Society* was well received in Europe, well read by the leaders of the German Romanticism movement and also Wilhelm Fredrich Hegel who absorbed many of Ferguson's ideas and phrases into his own philosophy later strongly influencing Karl Marx who (together with Friedrich Engels) started the Marxism Philosophy which in 1917 Russian Revolution did turn into Communism and thus tyranny (becoming self-fulfilling prophecy for Ferguson). The later Romanticism movement in Europe (later 18th and early 19th century) had many supporters for the French Revolution which turned into the Reign of Terror, a total failure as system of government and a Great Disappointment for the Romantics (including likes of Lord Byron, Percy Shelley, J.M.W. Turner, etc.) Ironically, it was Britain; birthplace of the Industrial Revolution, the country that compromised, adapted and adjusted to the effects of Industrialization and Capitalism that successfully avoided Revolution and Tyranny of the Big State, which subsequently passed on the torch of Democracy to America.

Another two major inheritance that America acquired from the Intellects from the Age of Enlightenment, for the solutions had been proposed by Smith and Ferguson, to counteract the "bad effects of commerce" they'd identified. Education is one, they advocate public support for a large system of schools that teach the benefits of Civilized culture (values of courage, self-sacrifice, discipline, loyalty, integrity and honor) to reach as large portion of the youth as possible. Schools that teach youth the ability to think for oneself and value of the freedom to be able do so. The other solution was the creation of a citizen militia with ownership of weapons, because when liberty is threatened, to defend all the Values mentioned above, militia training and weapons would be needed. The American Revolution proved them right!

Till this day, America has enshrined the Right to Freedom of Ideas, Speech as well as Right to bear arms in their 1st and 2nd amendment. Again, why is the Fight against Tyranny of the Big State Government being fought here in America?

II - What is the 'Ideology' being fought over in this Civil War?

When I first started writing the book, I had truly believed that the 'civil war' was about difference in ideologies and was hoping to be able to find a common ground or Compromise for the Best Interest of the Country and all its citizens. As I progressed in the research, reading up on the Literature of the Liberals in 19th – first half of 20th century, I realized the current neo-Fascist Democrats has nothing in common with the Liberals' ideologies of yesteryears. In fact, they bear a much stronger resemblance to the Big State Government of the Communist, Socialist regimes, exploiting the masses by appealing to their emotions. Their Dominance over the Internet and Main Stream Media is extremely effective for brainwashing the naïve, the intellectually slothful, yet insecure and egoistic people; who hold strong opinions about events and subject matters which they have very little knowledge and experience on.

Quite unlike the Islamic Radicals Ideology (Chapter 6), there is really NO ideology (Chapter 1,2,7) behind the neo-democrat fascist slogans and mantras. They are all just 'easiest to sell', 'one phrase deep' slogans, make it too complicated, the 'snowflakes' will get lost or confused, remember never overload their puny processors (that's why they love their smartphones so much, besides taking selfies, their smartphone really has more processing power than them). What then is the Civil War for?

This Civil War is really about Freedom, freedom of Individuals against Big State Control, Freedom of Ideas against Conformity & Compliance, War of Freewill against Imposing ONE (Politically Correct) view on all (Everyone). A War between traditional American Values, Culture of Growth, Culture of Excellence against a Culture of Compliance, Culture of Decadence, Culture that glorifies Ignorance, Sloth and Pride (Ego). It is a War between True Freedom of personal responsibility against the Illusion of Equality; this desire of the ignorant and naive for 'idea of equality' will allow the 'socialist poverty pimps' to rise to Power (bait to snare the Low into position of servitude). We know that Power corrupts and ultimately the ones left 'holding the bag' will be the same ignorant ones that sold away their freedom (for a song on equality).

History has shown us this truth countless times (most recently, we have the short story of Communism in last 100 years across various cultures, regions, countries, races, etc. all with one same result) yet the ignorant persists in their ways. Word of caution about the ignorant Radicals, they are dangerous, they aren't innocent little lambs. Wild animals might be considered less intelligent than humans, but they are very dangerous, we must always remember that Clueless doesn't mean Harmless!

From last chapter, we saw how the Activists make their money from the Federal Big State Government, the incestuous relationship between the Patron (Government, K Street apparatchiks, Clintons, Obama, Al Gore) and their Client (Top 1 % Wall Street Suzerains, IT Monopolies, Soros, Bezos, Zuckerburgs), and also how the Wealth gets extracted from the Middle-Income Working Class (productive economy) to the Top 1% and their cronies (non-productive section of economy, idle wealth). Now, let's discuss the Culture of Compliance, Culture of Decadence where the Mediocrity worships the Mediocracy, where Cronyism reigns. This is the Culture of Monopolies of Societies in decline, for if you are not growing, you must be declining in the real and dynamic world.

> *"Happy families are all alike; every unhappy family is unhappy in its own way."*
>
> - Leo Tolstoy in Anna Karenina

To be successful in Life (as in Marriages), many challenges have to be overcome. To be Unsuccessful, one only needs to fail in any of the challenges, thus the unhappy families can be due to multitude of different reasons. Similarly, for Culture of Growth to happen, all the factors have to be aligned for Conjunctures to happen. On-going efforts also have to invested to ensure the Culture of Growth flourishes and continues.

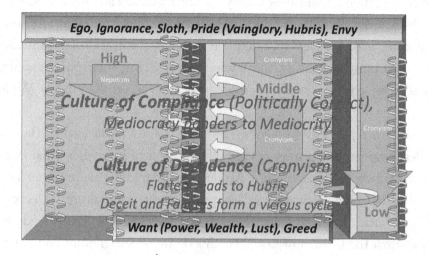

The opposite is true for *Culture of Decline or Decadence, any one of the negative traits can [is sufficient to] trigger the start of the downward spiral of the Culture of Decadence, compounded and accelerated by any additional negatives. Negative Traits are also mutually attractive, people with such negative traits can sense similar traits in others (just as people with positive values also attract those of similar values).

When there's no Growth and Lack of Competition, internal decay sets in, the Rigid Compliant Culture (organization) can no longer adapt to external change, that's why what starts off as Culture of Compliance will eventually morph into Culture of Decadence. The negative human traits are present in all of us and are easily triggered when the Organizational Culture rewards such behavior.

In absence of true benchmark of Excellence (no external competition), sloth quickly sets in. Yet personal Want and Greed will never be satisfied, thus to differentiate oneself, flattery and cronyism becomes a competitive advantage. This would have a new impact (entanglement) on the leadership of the organization, flattery would lead to pride and hubris in leaders which would retard their learning capability as humility is required for True Learning (not memorizing, but internalizing the skills and re-applying the concepts in different situations). You see these interactions between different levels in the organizations resulting in downward spirals resulting in loss of organization's capability and adaptability. Mediocracy starts to be glorified and Incompetence tolerated, eventually becoming the norm. The High is smallest by numbers but has largest Influence in the Organization, the Low has largest numbers but has minimal influence due to, their inability to differentiate between what's 'controllable' and 'uncontrollable', their unwillingness to hold themselves personally accountable and as a result to hold others accountable either. The entire organization forever moves down the paths of least resistance.

Due to the pursue of Want (Wealth, Power, Lust, etc.) and Avarice for more, the downward vicious continuous cycle spirals on without Awful Virtues to counter them (one might note this vicious cycle as compared to the virtuous cycles between ideas, talent & capital under the Free Market Perfect Competition Model). At some stage, the organization will no longer be able to perform its intended function. Interestingly, combinations of different negative traits can generate additional negative ones. For example, we know Ego retards learning ability (a full cup cannot receive more poured water), sloth produces ignorance, you add Ego to the equation and one becomes Ignorant of his ignorance, producing Hubris.

Hubris leads to Failures, to coverup for Failures, Deceit starts sets in too. Deceit becomes the organizational Culture both directions, upwards reporting; [distorting, framing, omitting information] and downwards official communique to the masses. At a personal level, deceiving oneself is being delusional, as in Hillary's Book for her deluded fans; What Happened?

This Culture of Decadence is eerily similar to Viral Infection of an otherwise healthy Host. See the passage below from my college biology textbook A E Vines & N Rees;

> *"we recognize that a system is 'alive' when it shows ability to carry out certain processes, for example when it is able to nourish itself, to respire, to grow and develop, to excrete, to detect and respond to changes in conditions, to reproduce and sometimes to move. But none of these abilities, separately or together, constitutes being "alive", they are merely manifestations of the quality. We can use them to distinguish between living and non-living things, but by so doing we get no nearer to an understanding of the meaning of being "alive". We can approach an understanding by thinking more fundamentally and considering the energy and material relationships which known systems of particles have with their environments. In these terms, systems of particles fall into two main groups. On the one hand there are those which, under the physical and chemical forces of the universe, are tending always to disintegrate passively and be forced towards a lower individual energy content. On the other hand there are systems of particles which, although subject to the same forces, are actively increasing their energy content and material substance by extracting and converting (not creating) energy and materials from their surroundings. Such systems are found only in protoplasm, the "living" substance, Thus a distinction between living and non-living things could be made in these more fundamental terms, that is according to their possession or otherwise of the property of being able to actively obtain and make use of energy and materials from their surroundings, so to increase or at least maintain their own bulk and energy content. The quality of being "alive" with all its manifestations, could then be regarded as the expression of this property."*
>
> N Rees, A E Vines

"The question is often asked, "is a virus particle alive?" In composition, it is protein enclosing nucleic acid, and if these substances are taken separately then each is no more alive than any other individual organic substance. Together, as the whole virus particle, but held in a purely inorganic environment, they are still inanimate, for no virus can replicate under such conditions. The same virus particle inside a suitable living protoplasmic system, however, soon becomes a multitude of identical particles. Has the virus itself actively utilized energy and materials to bring about its own replication or has its presence merely caused an already living protoplasmic system, equipped with the necessary synthesizing machinery, to do the replicating work? If the second of these is correct, then the virus particle cannot be considered to be alive in the sense described above."

From the definitions provided and concepts explained above, we can infer a) life reinforces itself, gaining in energy content, b) the virus does not increase its own energy content by itself but it can infect a host and divert the resources, energy of the host to do its bidding by replicating more viruses; ready to infect new hosts, c) the 'previous host' will die as all of its energy and resources had been re-directed to create new viruses and none to sustain its own continuity. If we now look at it from an organization's perspective, if the organization had contracted the culture of Decadence, it becomes sick and will eventually lose the ability to perform its *intended function (Telos). We can see parallels in the Decadence Culture of Monopolies, the virus infection taking over healthy hosts, Jared Diamond's Collapse of Societies, Ibn-Khaldun's work *Al-Maqaddimah* and also Decline of societies through the *Complexity Theory (works of Chaisson & Tainter).

Complexity Theory

Complex Systems, designed themselves through evolution or the interaction of myriad autonomous parts, they Have Emergent Properties, run on exponentially greater amount of energy and Are prone to catastrophic collapse. In Currency Wars, James Rickards uses Complexity Theory to help explain the currencies and capital market, we'll focus more on the human civilization as a Complex System. Complex Systems have Diverse Autonomous Agents, Connectedness, Interdependence & Adaptation (learning). They also Have Emergent Properties and Possible Phase Transition [when system is in a Critical Stage], at the critical threshold, the system passes from subcritical into supercritical.

Eric J Chaisson; Ratio of Free Energy Flow to Density in a System, More Complex a system, more Energy it needs to maintain its size and space

Joseph A Tainter; Inputs increase exponentially with the scale of civilization, *Outputs of civilization and governments decline per unit of input when measured in terms of public goods and services provided. [at which stage the Kleptocrats are] Rent Seeking, accumulation of wealth through non-productive means. [this is] Similar to Law of Diminishing Returns. When society offers its masses negative returns on inputs, those masses [would logically] opt out of society [thereby destabilizing it].

Black Swan refers to Extreme Catastrophic Events, the Catastrophe cannot be bigger than the system in which it occurs [logical], and Relationship between Catastrophic Risks and Scale is Exponential. In summary Per Rickards; Chaisson shows how highly complex systems such as civilization require exponentially greater energy inputs to grow, while Tainter shows how those civilizations come to produce negative outputs in exchange for the inputs and eventually collapse.

> *"When the system reaches a certain scale, the energy inputs dry up because the exponential relationship between scale and inputs exhausts the available resources... Complex systems arise spontaneously, behave unpredictably, exhaust resources and collapse catastrophically"*
>
> – Currency Wars by James Rickards

عصبيّة *Asabiyyah,* in his masterpiece *Al-Maqaddimah*; an Introduction to History, Ibn-Khaldun (1332-1406), a *Spanish Faylasuf,* argues that it is this sense of solidarity within the group, clan that makes it strong and grow bigger, wealthier and more sophisticated. Under lax and comfortable conditions, the group loses its Asabiyyah, dissolves into factionalism and individualism, diminishing and weakening their capacity as a political unit. Other new units with strong Asabiyyah will replace it and the cycle will start all over again.

Now in America, the Radical neo-Democrat and Fascist Activists groups have thrown the two party system out of balance and out of Alignment. There is NO tolerance for Diversity in Ideas in mainstream media, NO more Culture of Excellence via Free Market Competition. There is the growing Culture of Monopoly, the P.C. Culture (Politically Correct) Uniform ONE VIEW of the World in Blind Compliance to Authority of their Masters (aka. Various factions of Golden Calves); the Wall Street Suzerains, IT Monopolies Moghuls, followed by the Activists Corporations (aka Problem Profiteers), Poverty Pimps, Climate-change Pimps, Renewable-energy Pimps, Globalist and Socialist Pimps, then comes the narcissistic Entertainment Monopoly Celebrities and Main Stream Media Monopoly Celebrities, not to forget the Monopolies of Academia conmen, "aka pseudo intellects", last but not least, the Federal Administrative Apparatchiks Bureaucrats Monopolies (Politicians, Kleptocrats; elected or otherwise), etc. Various Factions all for their selfish agendas all profiting at the expenses of American Public (Tragedy of Commons), all with similar Cultures of Monopoly, Blind Compliance & Decadence!

Most Important Question here is, Can American's reverse this cycle of decay and repel the parasitic Viral infection with their Culture of Mediocracy? As we shall see, many cornerstones laid by the founders have been stolen, discredited and actively destroyed, their dearly cherished Values have now been lost, ridiculed, forgotten and even mocked at.

Prior Assumptions, Cornerstones of America's Constitution being eroded away

In David Hume's The Idea of a Perfect Commonwealth, he pointed out that a Large or extended republic, for all its geographic and social economic diversity, might turn out to be most stable of all. "the parts are so distant and remote, that it is very difficult, either by intrigue, prejudice, or passion, to hurry them into any measures against the public interest." I would propose that this 'largeness' has been shrunk by the proliferation of smart phones, internet and mainstream media all Uniform in ONE P.C. View of the neo-Fascists Dem's demagogue. The threat to the Freedom of Diverse Ideas is most real, if we do nothing to change the Monopoly of Internet and Mainstream Media's Message (Demagogue and Indoctrination), eventually they will bring the entire Republic of Democracy and its Constitution crumbling down in this lifetime.

In Hume's model adopted by Madison, the assumption was also that the elected officials (first level of elections) by the people would have to do a good job for their local community in order to get re-elected (sounds logical right?) Again, there's been couple of updates a) the incompetent politicians [monkey see, monkey do] can now run up huge deficit spending (ISEP to deal with later on), b) rely on the 'helpful' Distortion of perception by the Internet and Mainstream Media [easily bought], c) distraction via the mind-numbing Racial indoctrination and management of expectations of the confused, and lastly d) Big Federal Government expected to step in to help; thereby taking away their need to personally Account to their voters for doing a pathetic job (broken feedback loop).

The elected officials then to help elect the next higher level up and so on, what Madison termed Filtration also assumes that the Elected Officials are able to exercise Reason and has more Common Sense than the Masses (the common man). Again, this assumption has also been 'updated'. Due to the ceaseless rhetoric on racism, sexism, etc. Now the criteria for Elected Officials is based on *quota for race, sex, etc. to be Politically Correct. In other words, 'human photocopiers' that will repeat P.C. Messages without any need to invoke their cerebral function. No Intellect needed, so it is now quite the opposite, due to the change of selection criteria, the Inmates are now running the asylum. Update to Madison and Hume, Political Correctness and Partisan Loyalty have replaced Common Sense as requirement for elected officials.

* this P.C. quota started to gain momentum about 2-3 decades back.

James Wilson's view of the United States Supreme Court providing 'the Power of Reflection', helping to decide whether a particular law fit within the frame of the Constitution, becoming the 'jury of the country.' This assumption also no longer holds true, it has also been "updated" by the P.C. Movement in last 2 decade. Similar to the Elected Officials, Political Correctness, Partisan Loyalty, Racial and Sexist orientation are the main driving force for the appointment of the Judges. All the Activists Judges openly vouch for Political Correctness as their Guiding Mandate, Law is whatever the P.C. One View wants it to be (as the Dirigiste Big State Govt).

> *"Whatever the party holds to be truth is truth. It is impossible to see reality except by looking through the eyes of the party."*
>
> – 1984 George Orwell

The very existence, let alone proliferation of Activists Judges validates this version of PC Update. Two other independent attestation to the blatant disregard for the Law, the Constitution and complete abandonment of Common Sense? The constant encroachment of the Activist Judges in their wish to change the Constitution Unilaterally by themselves is one.

The other needs close observation of the Low. Remember we started this chapter about the

Substance Vs Form discussion? Or Spirit Vs Letter? The Best cases would be meeting both the Spirit and Letter of the Law or meeting both the Form and Substance of Accounting Disclosure. Meeting only the letter but missing the spirit of the Law is just Blind Compliance (same in case of form over substance). If you observe the Low closely, be they the Judges or the Elected Officials, the Low tend to be always harping about the form and the letter but they seldom address the Substance or the Spirit, why? Simply because the Substance and Spirit is more abstract, difficult to grasp; there's the element of contingency, where the same concept can applied in various different situations, while the form and letter can be memorized (we discussed this point in chapter 5). If your judge or elected official under observation doesn't constantly harp about the letter or form, then he/she isn't a Low, he is just wicked and thinks you are stupid.

Lastly, Wilson also quoted Thomas Reid's concept about the 'Common Sense Man'; the fundamental building block of democracy, man as a knower, a judger, who trusts his own senses, his grasp of the facts, and his grasp of right and wrong. In the Federal System that Hume and Madison designed for the American Constitution, the 'Common Sense Man' (envisioned by Reid and Wilson) will be able to see and agree on fundamental 'self-evident truths' and provide the final solution in event of Gridlock arising within the System.

Obviously, this Common-Sense man has been missing in the last 2 decades of American History, let's hope the new elected administration can inspire some Common Sense and untangle the partisan Gridlock that has been haunting America.

What's the take-away here? People makes the difference! No matter how well a system or process is designed, good people also need to understand, then adapt it to the changing external environment. If you have people who are not overburdened with intellect in strategic key positions, you can be pretty certain of the eventual outcome regardless of how well designed a system you have. The current Caliber of the professional politicians, K street administrative 'Public servants' (both elected or otherwise) has probably never been matched in the entire history of this country.

III - How is the Civil War being Waged?

Essay on the History of the Original Thought; Division of thought, Abdication of Reason, Deletion of *Nous*

In the last Transformation, the coming of the Industrial Revolution happened together with proliferation of Capitalism and Age of Enlightenment. The intellects of the Enlightened Age saw the impacts of Industrialization on the society in the early stage of the Revolution, much was written and being discussed, debated (both the positives and negatives) all across Europe even before the Industrialization got into full steam, thus by and large, the ill effects of the 'commercial world' (Industrialization and Capitalism) was being addressed as the events unfolded (not ideal but being addressed nonetheless).

Just as the coming of the 'commercial world', the IT Revolution (by which we include the Cultural impacts of Politically Correct Movement) also have both positive and negative impacts, sadly the gaggle of sycophants in the Internet News and Mainstream Media had overhyped the strengths and potential (much of which never materialize yet) but completely ignored the dangers and harmful effects. Sadly, we are now behind the curve in addressing such destructive effects on the human psyche, the behavioral patterns of both individual and group, the larger group dynamics (interactions) and the contagious fall-out to the larger Society as a whole.

In the early stages of the IT Revolution, there was much hope that it would enable more free speech and expression of ideas, promoting freedom of speech around the world, so on. What a huge disappointment that turned out to be, just like the French Revolution (for the Romantics), which degenerated into the Reign of Terror, just like the Arab Spring in various countries, all the initial euphoria of freedom also quickly turned into consolidation of power into hands of the ruthless radicals with scheming personal agenda, so the same has happened in America and around the world too. In absence of further accelerated new technology revolution, the Top 1% (Incumbents in Power) quickly caught up with the IT Revolution and its possibilities in the early – mid of last decade. It is now merely a mouth-piece for the Proponents of the Big State Government to run everyone's lives as deemed fit by the Politically Correct ONE View Gestapo. Instead of being an avenue of free diverse ideas, it has become the most intrusive and pervasive indoctrination tool ever invented. The cognitive prowess of the human mind has become so enfeebled and dependent on the internet and smart devices that it no longer realizes the differences between facts in the real world versus propaganda in the internet media. The human spirit so enervated, it no longer understands the basic principles of how we had designed, program and created the softwares that makeup the internet and its entire hosts of application we use, instead it has become submissive to the internet and its applications (many people are afraid to challenge, let alone dismiss what they read on the web for fear of being ridiculed by their peers). In this section, let's try to explore how all these sets of behavior started to manifest into their current form.

Before we dive into the details of the Impact of IT Revolution on both the Individual's cognitive as well as the Society's Learning processes, let's first address certain fundamentals of the Thinking Process. Following up from chapter 5, both Alan Turing's (thinks it's possible) and Ada Lovelace's (Not possible) views on the question: Can Machines Think? Both of them are correct, perhaps the question should be put in this form: Are All humans capable of Original Thoughts? The trend of thought goes this way, the answer to Can Machines Think? has a few assumptions, depending on the assumptions, you will get different answers. Can Machines Think like Humans? We immediately assume all Humans think alike or have same cognitive capability which is Untrue, Turing clearly understood this when he made this comment during lunch in the Bell Labs dining room, "No, I'm not interested in developing a powerful brain. All I'm after is just a mediocre brain, something like the President of the American Telephone and Telegraph Company." Lady Lovelace made her "Objections" (as coined by Turing), nearly a hundred years before Turing gave his views in late 1940s. She was a Key pioneer in the logic behind programming but it would have been a stretch for her to imagine the advance for computing powers of our present day back in 1842. She would probably, be assuming 'Humans' to be someone comparable to herself, which most intelligent people assume all others are like themselves as they cannot imagine anything otherwise [case of self-projection]. However, if they (the High Processing Units) have had to work closely in handling complex mental exertions together with others of normal processing capacity, they will very quickly understand what Alan Turing had just expressed is a self-evident fact of life. Everyone is different and have different strengths and weaknesses, this is what makes this world a beautiful and interesting place.

So we come back to the new question: Are All Humans capable of Original Thoughts? Some humans are obviously capable of originality, otherwise human society would never had advanced, our question is framed as: Are ALL Humans? Then, we address what's definition of Original Thought? This is my proposal for consideration: Most People merely repeat whatever they've heard or seen, but because they couldn't remember exactly when or where they were initially exposed to the idea, they think it's their personal view and 'original' thought (that's the trick behind brain-washing, it gets in at the subconscious level). At a higher level, many others also re-configure (mix and match) parts of different ideas to come up with new combination of Ideas, are these Original Ideas? It's always a spectrum (like a bell-shape curve), where is the cut-off for definition of Original Thought? To me, it's the level of detailed breakdown of learned Ideas and re-synthesis of new combinations to form 1) a new advancement from prior logic, 2) finer sub-ideas (descriptions or explanations), or 3) different direction, trend of logic. Whatever your definition of Original Thought (Idea), perhaps we could answer that in Ideal setting most Humans are capable of forming Original Ideas or Thoughts, but in reality, due to the Eternal Sloth, most Humans find no need nor see the Value of Original Thought. Thus answer would be NO.

Let's put forth another question, Can an Extremely powerful computer be programmed to think like an average human being? Turing seems to think so, I would agree with him. In fact, for our routine average day lives, a number of very well design algorithms can suffice for many folks. It is when the unexpected happens that humans can adapt while programmed computers cannot, they need to be reprogrammed. Let's take this one level deeper, to what degree of 'unexpectedness', if the degree is so huge, many humans might also have trouble responding or 'adapting' immediately too. To what degree of sophistication of the programming logic? An extremely complex and well-designed program, with elegant logic loops can address hundreds, thousands or even millions of possible scenarios, allowing computers to respond even faster to 'unexpected'' situations than a mediocre human mind can. The limitation for the computer is that it cannot *program itself (for now), then again, many humans are also one-trick ponies too, they don't constantly upgrade themselves either but rely on old skills learnt in their youth, most humans cannot write a sonnet or compose a concerto because of thoughts and emotions felt either (Sir Geoffrey Jefferson assertion).

Are people being 'educated' ('taped' as in *Profession*) as Machines are programmed? *Should they? If you think no, just go to your social Media pages, internet 'news', or switch on your TV.

Mental Sloth, *The Trojan Horse that no one saw*

Most think of sloth as physical laziness because that's what we can see, but as in all actions it always starts with an idea. Most of us have experienced mental fatigue, after concentrating very hard for a few hours, your mind might just 'go blank' or a few seconds, some described it as 'splitting headache', etc. to avoid such situations, we've devised short-cuts like stereotyping, deferring to others' expertise and experience, etc. Mental sloth aids us in the search for such 'short-cuts', so it can be useful to us adapting 'best practices' from others, perhaps even protect us as a 'release valve' against extreme pressures from mental exhaustion. But More often than not, it is a negative trait, excessive use of stereotyping will lead to wrong assumptions and false conclusions (manifested in racism, sexism, etc.) Mental Sloth also prevents us from learning new skills, from constantly reviewing our perspectives and reconciling them to new feedback, from diving deeper into the facts, context of events, it also blocks individuals from achieving their potential as each human can keep pushing and stretching their learning abilities with NO limits, Mental Sloth retards that process from starting. Lastly, it works in close tandem with Ego to produce Ignorance or it can also join forces with Ignorance to produce Hubris.

Two particular variations of Mental Sloth are extremely dangerous to Individuals; Grandfathered Mental Sloth and Sub-conscious Mental Sloth, because we are not consciously aware of them. The first case is Unintentional due to innovations; eg. Calculators, driving auto-gear, smartphones. Before we had such 'luxuries', we had to do mathematics mentally, drive the stick-shift, remember most of our close friends phone numbers by hard. From personal experiences, we knew that it was possible we 'internalize those abilities to a subconscious level' and they just became daily routine skills. Yet with the new inventions, we 'rest on these laurels' and stop exercising our mental skills in those particular areas.

Next is the sub-conscious Mental Sloth, this second case is subconscious due to personal ego. At sub-conscious level, most people like the feeling of 'being in control' and dislike feeling of insecurity (sense of crisis, fear of the unknown), when we engage in any form of learning, there is always a 'sense of being lost', kind of confusion which we need to overcome. The dislike of such sense of being confused or 'feeling stupid' reinforces the subconscious Mental sloth by always choosing paths of least resistance and substituting real Learning (what we described in chpt 5) by merely repeating what comes easiest.

> *"I do not feel obliged to believe that the same God who has endowed us with sense, reason and intellect has intended us to forego their use."*
>
> – Galileo Galilei

∑ effects of IT Revolution, Dominance of the Politically Correct Culture over the Internet, Social Media, Mainstream Media & Academia = MOB [M.O.B. is short for Millennial Oriented Broadcast]

Impact on Individual's cognitive processes (both Thinking and Learning as they're interrelated)

Everyone's different, thus the impact of the IT Revolution would vary according, however the most significant impact would be on the millennials as they never knew the world before the extensive spread of internet technology through Smart devices, they didn't see nor helped shaped the creation of this IT Revolution. The employees in Disney World knows what makes the Happiest Place on Earth run like clockwork, how they perceive Disney World would be very different from the Visitors who sees a beautiful fairy tale. Similar to the visitors, the millennials would only see and use the end-product of google, Internet, Social Media without knowing the intricate workings behind the scenes and how much of the content could be 'fabricated' out of the thin air without any effort in research nor analysis. The Millennials might even believe much of what they read from the internet as they naturally assume the content providers have some level of integrity, professionalism with NO bias Agenda, which is obviously untrue.

This is where the millennials differ from the visitors to Disney World, even as the visitors enjoy their visit to the Happiest Place on earth, even the kids can tell the difference between the Real and the 'magical' world. The little kids don't expect to see Mickey Mouse in their homes but the Millennials believe 'facts are facts', if I find it on google, it must be true & correct! Here I must clarify, not only millennials hold this later belief, many people who lived through the IT revolution do too. Sadly, they have now forgotten what it was like before that time too, so they too behave the same manner. With this understanding, the definition of Millennials in this section does NOT refer to those born after year 2000, it has a much broader population than that, all those with little experience in life, those that easily forget their experiences, those that always choose paths of least resistance, essentially those with low processing power. For ease of reference in this section, in short we'll call the summation $\sum$ of all the effects of IT Revolution, Politically Correct Movement, neo-fascists Dems' messages intruding into our lives via Smart devices, etc. into one simple acronym M.O.B. (Millennial Oriented Broadcast).

Now with the proliferation of Smart Devices (esp. Smartphones) into many people's bed, the MOB has literally wormed itself into many folks' heads. With a click of a mouse, the 'Big Brother' can now penetrate into millions of brains where Mental Sloth is waiting with open gates to receive the MOB army. In the old days, face to face brain-washing besides being slower; one has to be physically present, TV and Radio did speed up the process, but even then, from visual or verbal cues, people can spot lies or lack of conviction. This non-verbal signs' barrier has also been cleared through MOB technology.

Lastly, the lack of discussion or debate on the MOB Materials completely eliminates the competition of Ideas. The MOB comes across in Unilateral fashion and the recipients gladly imbibe it wholesale without any filtering, 'facts are fact' to the Low. Just in case any remaining Lows might not believe MOB, we still have the Academia Gestapo to reinforce and drill home the indoctrination of Racism, Sexism and Globalism. The inventor of Newspeak would be impressed.

Under the ruthless and relentless onslaught of the MOB, the Anomie Man from '50s has been turned into a New Super-Anomic Creed on steroids. This new creed has short-cut the *Learning process from mere Knowledge recognition; a lower form of knowledge recall, to become directly linked to formation of Judgement. Going from lowest level of Knowledge [ability to recall information], by-passing Comprehension, Application [ability to apply concept to new situation, as in understanding the Substance], Analysis [logical examination of concepts or parts of problem to better under the whole] and finally Synthesis [creation of a whole concept from individual parts and patterns, as the Original Idea].

The Mental Sloth has always been present in us, now with extended reach of MOB; made possible through the IT Revolution, to many of those that allow it to happen, much of Thinking duties has been relieved by the Smart devices, just google for the answers. Googling has replaced Thinking and Reasoning for some people. While Emojis has substituted and become the highest standardized form of Emotional expression for others.

*Normal Human's mental development ranged over 5 incremental levels of complexity from a) Knowledge (recall of data), b) Comprehension, c) Application (ability to apply concept to new situation), d) Analysis to e) Synthesis (creation of whole concept from individual parts and patterns), MOB has corrupted this learning process of certain individuals, linking the recognition of data (lower form of recall) directly to formation of political judgement, essentially conditioned reflexes (eg. Socialism is Good, Globalism is progressive). Conditioned responses doesn't require exercise of reason nor logical thinking, they are also often used in the training of animals too.

Division of Thoughts, Abdication of Reason and Deletion of Nous

Even small amounts of Thinking are exercised, they now 'cut up' or divided into short sections interspersed between Messaging, Instagraming, FaceBooking, googling activities. So the thoughts are NOT connected, they no longer form a coherent string of Ideas or have any logic in their flow, there is no such need for coherence as everything is instantaneous, Only the Present matters, the Past is over and quickly forgotten. Present is All, googling is All. There is no need for reason or logic as google will provide the answer, MOB has the answer to everything, MOB is always there and always has the answers, so why waste any time to remember anything or waste any energy to reason or follow any logic, as long as I say the PC speak, I am in line with MOB so I will be respected and never be in dispute with others. If I follow my personal logic and it ends up with different conclusions from MOB, I will be ridiculed by my friends and peers. Worse, I might even be ostracized and made a 'laughing stock' of. MOB has no Agenda, MOB has always existed, MOB is the Past and my future is safe with MOB, I live in the Present and Present is All – Snowflake in 2017

With the quick Rise and invasive spread of MOB, individuals' richness in personal experience, their interactions, discussions with other people and their personal reasoning has atrophied. As googling, messaging, etc. starts to intrude into personal thinking, it starts to displace larger and larger tracts of thoughts such that thoughts become fragmented into smaller and smaller 'divisions', no longer as a single logical unit. Without real debates and constructive discussions of concepts and diverse ideas, one's learning capability becomes weaken without competition, personal learning and powers of analysis gets substituted with powers of 'searching & googling' (*googling is learning*).

As one abdicates personal reason, his Self Confidence, Conviction and Passion wanes in submission to the MOB. Personal Submissiveness Rules, I am with MOB (I am nothing without the MOB, MOB is everything). As P.C. behavior dominates, the ability to distinguish between reality and virtual gets blurred as the pigs and men start to look alike too [as in Animal Farm by Orwell].

Impact on Societies' (Institutional) Learning Ability

Start of a vicious cycle, even as MOB has weakened the Learning capability and power of Reason of the individual, its impact on society's Learning is exponentially more harmful. As the intent of MOB is to seek control over and compliance of its targets, the success of MOB implies the society's learning (institutional learning) is severely weaken, no surprise as Knowledge has always been the enemy of Extremism. We've seen how MOB achieves its goals on individuals, let's see how the effect spills over into the society at large, distorting some of the properties of Human Civilization as a *Complex System. Under MOB, the agents in our Complex System have become less Diverse and less Autonomous. Their Adaptability [learning through competing] has also decreased significantly.

As many snowflakes and millennials submit themselves to MOB, their *nous* becomes extinguished. Per Plato, each human psyche has three parts, senses, emotions (passions) and nous (reason, thinking). Will power and Focus would describe nous too. As more and more defer to MOB, the diversity and dynamism of the society will decrease as Uniformity rules. With less passionate debates and constructive discussions, it means less competition of Ideas, no New Ideas, the Complexity and sophistication of Ideas declines rapidly, the interactive refinement of ideas disappears together with the breakup of the feedback loop of Institutional learning. As MOB grows stronger, the flames of Independence and Free Will in individuals decreases and the society becomes Predictable. As a whole, the society loses its diversity, dynamism, sophistication and ability to respond to adversity. It becomes Uniform, Static, Predictable and compliant.

Uniformity, Computer Programming, Human Societies' Learning

Let's briefly discuss the strengths of Computer Programming and that of the Institutional Learnings of Human Societies.

Programming the Computers have Accuracy as major advantage, they are also uniform, if you program one, you can program all to exactly similar with latest update and Best Optimal software. The rules and logic behind the program can also be verifiable and made transparent to all. Currently, Computers cannot self-upgrade nor compete amongst themselves to establish better and new programs or software.

From Human Societies' perspective, the individuals are diverse and autonomous, Independent Thinking, but each human has to learn from scratch. At first look, this is a weakness, as it's extremely inefficient compared with programming, and chaotic as different individuals learn at different speeds and all individuals will learn different perspectives per their exposure to varying cultures, experiences, etc. Yet at closer inspection, it can be a strength for the society as it allows for a) adaption for one doesn't learn outmoded skills that's irrelevant in new environment, b) competition from different perspectives [sadly even to the extent of wars and genocides] and c) new learning from 'unexpected new perspectives [that's the power of diversity]. With a Culture of sharing information, the society's institutional learning can be enhanced, competition of ideas through discussions will also increase their diversity and sophistication.

Interestingly, the Brain-washing of snowflakes [Uniformity per Politically Correct ONE View] gives us all the weakness of both Humans Societies and Computer Programming. All brain-washed drones have a uniform Politically Correct One View with minimal Diversity in Ideas, yet does not have the accuracy of the machines. The P.C. One View Culture has the most commonly held view as it needs to be easiest paths of least resistance [equivalent to all traffic go at the speed of the slowest vehicle]. It cannot have the Best nor Optimal cutting-edge update as most of the low processing units will hang ["…it was also found that the stupider animals, such as the sheep, hens, and ducks, were unable to learn the Seven Commandments by heart.' - Animal Farm].

The sophistries of P.C. One View cannot be verified nor made transparent to all as they are non sequitur. The Fascists snowflakes cannot self-upgrade nor learn anything different from the P.C. One View, they are neither autonomous nor independent thinking [for they cannot say any different from the Ministry of Truth], let alone be able to compete amongst themselves, thus no sophisticated nor diverse ideas from snowflakes just as the programmed computers [yet without all the machines' efficiencies].

> *"Tolerance of New Ideas. The long-lived companies in our study tolerated activities in the margin: experiments and eccentricities that stretched their understanding. They recognized that new businesses may be entirely unrelated to existing businesses and that the act of starting a business need not be centrally controlled. W.R. Grace, from its very beginning, encouraged autonomous experimentation. The company was founded in 1854 by an Irish immigrant in Peru and traded in guano, a natural fertilizer, before it moved into sugar and tin. Eventually, the company established Pan American Airways. Today it is primarily a chemical company, although it is also the leading provider of kidney dialysis services in the United States."*
>
> - The Living Company by Arie de Geus, 1997

> *In Decentralization and Tolerance, and the Parable of the Chilean Potato. "Without diversity, the 'uniform' group becomes much more prone to extinction when the environment changes."*
>
> - The Living Company by Arie de Geus, 1997

We can clearly see the Dangers of Uniformity in a Society, it's Predictable, all dependent on a few to think for them, power and resources are aggregated in the hands of a few who will become corrupt and inept. Once the external environment changes or new competition emerges, doesn't take a genius to predict the impending disasters.

Now that we understand the Power of MOB, we can start to see why the Main Stream Media Celebrities and also the IT Monopolies Czars collect such obscene paychecks, it is NOT through the Capitalism mechanism, not the free market perfect competition mechanism that determined their pay-outs, in fact it is exactly the Opposite. These Main Stream Media and IT Social Media

Tech Giants are ALL Monopolies, yet they are most Powerful in that they can sway the public opinions.

The neo-Fascists Dems as well as the Deep State GOP Cronies, all the Politicians, Activists Corporations, Wall Street Suzerains, etc. are more than willing to deploy vast resources towards furthering their agenda (just like Businesses pay to advertise their products, all the Political and Power factions also pay big time to get their agenda out there too), thus the Main Stream Media, IT Tech Giants are all rolling in Cash while peddling ignorance to the American Public and Poisoning the American Society. Just as advertisements are Free to get you to buy their products, so are all the Social Media and Mainstream Media's propaganda, demagogue Freely available to you on the internet. If you are still paying to receive propaganda, you should apply for your refunds.

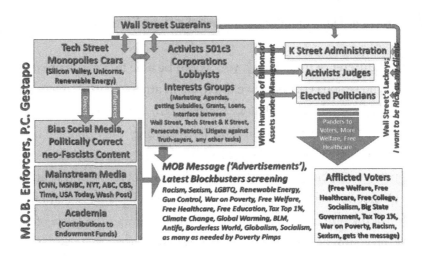

The Mainstream Media, Power of Monopoly

Unlike the Romantics that supported the French Revolution who believed themselves to be Avant-Garde of Human Spirit in early 19th century or the Undifferentiated Goodness of Democrats in 50s that battles syllogism, the current Mainstream Media and IT Monopolies Tech, Social Media Giants CEOs are Ugly and Evil. The earlier two groups might be misguided but they actually believed in their own ideology and willing to personally walk their talk.

Here, the MOB designers are pure Evil and outright Dirty Wicked, there's no ideology in their rhetoric (we've already explored that repeatedly throughout the book), they are vain and shallow hypocrites (very wealthy ones). A bunch of Egoistic Parvenus blissed to be not overburdened with intellect but so insecure in themselves, they are more than happy to be selling lies, peddling demagogue to our youth and the impressionable. Looking at the chart above, you'll see that the M.O.B. messages that's fed to the afflicted voters, is pushed forth from a combination of Social Media, Mainstream Media, Academia and the Activists Corporations [with periodic guest appearances by The Perfect President] whom themselves are sponsored by the Wall Street Suzerains, Tech Street Monopolies Czars. Lastly, you see the Professional Politicians pandering to the afflicted voters while they themselves dance to the tunes played by the Activists Corporations (special interests groups), composed in turn by their sponsors; Wall Street and Tech Street Monopolies' aristocrats. The Activists Corporations are the Nexus of the entire ecosystem.

As President Theodore Roosevelt had pointed out, the irresponsible Press, instead of letting in light and fresh air into the room, lets in poisonous sewer gas, they riled up racial tensions, sow discord and abuse emotional insecurities and turn them into racial Hate and Violence, leaving the victims forever trapped in their endless cycles of Poverty and Racial Divide, all these Evil they do so that they can satisfy their lust for wealth, their greed for power and continue to enjoy their decadent lifestyles. Meanwhile, the poor stays in their ghettos amid never-ending cycles of poverty, Hate, Ignorance and Violence, over five decades after Rev Martin L King Jr. Civil rights march, over 150 years after the Emancipation proclamation. These Poverty Pimps are indeed Evil.

We've seen their Tools of Mass Indoctrination, what's their Strategy?

If it was truly about difference in Ideology, you would be able to see a desire for debate and discussions, yet we see no serious collaborative attempts in any insightful, meaningful debates nor discussions about ideologies. Instead what we see are a bunch of slogan throwing terrorists, mantra hurling activists and P.C. Gestapo 'character assassinating' their political opponents through baseless accusations of "verbal sexual misconduct", wild allegations of 'racists behavior', etc. yet these behavioral patterns are clearly consistent with the conflict resolution strategies employed by the Radical neo-Democrats and neo-fascist Activists. The ATLA [Association of Trial Lawyers of America] is one of the numerous Activists Corporations under the guise of 501c3 'charitable' companies whose job is similar to the fierce Dogs in Animal Farms that tear any dissenting voices to shreds and intimidate Americans into subservient serfs.

The Liberal Progressives have been meticulously planning and setting up 'tax-exempt charitable' corporations dedicated to threatening, intimidating and ripping apart any diverse views from their own and we are still hoping to see Compromise behavior from them?

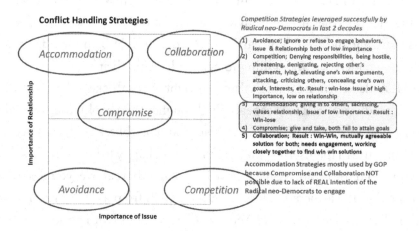

Under the (Blake and Mouton) 5 basic Conflict styles of Avoidance, Competition, Accommodation, Compromise and Collaboration. You will only see 2 Strategies employed by the neo-democrat Radicals and neo-fascist Activists. Avoidance and Competition. The simple reason is that they place the Value of the relationship as Low, they view their opponents as Enemies and not fellow Americans, they have no wish to work together for a better future. The Activists' aims is to have a Big State Government providing Bigger Subsidies, so the parasites can siphon off the wealth from the Middle-Class working Americans. Whenever they are caught 'unprepared' (when they are NOT the majority or when they actually need to debate real facts and detailed issues instead of chanting mindless slogans), they will use Avoidance strategies.

Most of the time, they use Competition strategies. (per the 5 Basic Conflict Model, Competition here doesn't mean Free Market Competition), Competition here entails: Lying, concealing one's own goals, attacking the other party verbally, denying responsibilities, Being Hostile, threatening, elevating one's own arguments, denigrating or rejecting the others arguments, bluffing, etc. The opposing side has been using the Accommodation Strategy; which works for the Radical neo-Democrats and neo-fascist Activists as they get what they want. But compromise and collaboration yielded ZERO results for the American people, as the parasites refuse to yield their ill-gotten spoils.

The current administration is the first to also leverage Competition strategy during the 2016 campaign. All the previous GOP administrations had cowered in fear of avoidance when facing the neo-Fascists Dem's Competition strategies, often resorting to Accommodation which explains why the MOB and P.C. Gestapo had gotten their Radical Agenda so well entrenched into the Deep State Administration. The new GOP Administration had used similar strategy of competition, also elevating one's own arguments, denigrating or rejecting the others arguments, this Strategy has made the Radical neo-Democrats and neo-fascist Activists Mad as Hell (as this was their 'invention') and now they are coming for their Revenge.

Why does the Radical neo-Democrats and neo-fascist Activists see their Opponents as Enemies and only employed Avoidance and Competition as Strategies while the moderate right has tried to use Accommodation, Compromise and Collaboration as their Strategies in the Past?

Getting together to debate and discuss some kind of compromise assumes that these neo-Democrat Activists have some ideological beliefs and well thought out strategies on how to best run the country (or various States for that matter). When the reality is that they have no ideology other than to have a Big State Government with unaccountable faceless bureaucrats that prints free money for everyone and run unlimited budget deficits into the infinity (NO Accountability, NO views of the Future, just grab their personal payouts from the interest groups and enjoy the power and influence in meantime). Any "so call discussions" are no more than mantra-chanting of meaningless PC slogans and empty 'war on Poverty' rhetoric. We have also seen how they (parasites from both political parties) are merely enriching themselves while causing the Income Inequality gap to be the widest in American history in last chapter. This bunch of Parasites are Harming this Country and the American Society.

The future of America (or just the future in general), doesn't exist in the Radicals' plans, they have only a 1 step plan that is to spread their pretentious non sequitur rhetoric of Socialism sophistry, Globalism subterfuge, Equality for all mirage, etc. meanwhile the Socialist Pimps,

Globalism Pimps are all laughing all the way to their banks (owned by Soros). We tend to underestimate the ignorant, believing that we can teach or help them, maybe even guide and counsel them. This approach is equally as Ignorant as the Ignorant ones themselves [ignorant might not be as ignorant as you think, turns out that their self-enrichment schemes are all Pre-Meditated, diligently planned and painstakingly executed to perfection over last 2 decades]. In chapter 3, as we had segmented the various groups, we need different Strategies aimed towards the Poverty Pimps, the Academia-conmen, the Radical neo-Democrat Gestapo Media and neo-fascist Activists corporations, etc. which we address in more details later.

If the GOP supporters and Fair-minded Americans continue to use Accommodation or Compromise as their Only Strategies, this country (and the larger World, we'll explore shortly) will see darker days to come. A combination of Competition, Collaboration and Compromise Strategies has to be adopted swiftly!

There's no easy path ahead, no more delay, no more Appeasement! We have to do the right thing and stop the spread of the Parasites, expose their Shame Culture of P.C. ONE View as it truly is, one that is rooted in insecurity, pretense and hypocrisy!

> *"When Moses approached the camp and saw the calf and the dancing, his anger burned and he threw the tablets out of his hands, breaking them to pieces at the foot of the mountain. And he took the calf the people had made and burned it in the fire; then he ground it to powder, scattered it on the water and made the Israelites drink it. He said to Aaron, "What did these people do to you, that you led them into such great sin?" "Do not be angry, my lord," Aaron answered. "You know how prone these people are to evil. They said to me, 'Make us gods who will go before us. As for this fellow Moses who brought us up out of Egypt, we don't know what has happened to him.' So I told them, 'Whoever has any gold jewelry, take it off.' Then they gave me the gold, and I threw it into the fire, and out came this calf!" Moses saw that the people were running wild and that Aaron had let them get out of control and so become a laughingstock to their enemies. So he stood at the entrance to the camp and said, "Whoever is for the Lord, come to me." And all the Levites rallied to him."*
>
> Exodus 32:19-26 (NIV)

We've witnessed the Powerful Tools (MOB, P.C. Gestapo, etc.) employed by those in Power to drive the Big State Socialist Agenda and decimate the Middle Income of America. We also know that losing diversity in Ideas and Compliance to Uniformity is dangerous for the Society when external changes happen as the society has lost its ability to adapt to changes. In next section, we'll see how the World at large would also be at risk from these Parasites, and ironically How Global Warming would indeed be a cause for concern in near future.

"Moreover, regrettable as it may seem to the idealist, the experience of history provides little warrant for the belief that real progress, and the freedom that makes progress possible, lies in unification. For where unification has been able to establish unity of ideas it has usually ended in uniformity, paralyzing the growth of new ideas. And where the unification has merely brought about an artificial or imposed unity, its irksomeness has led through discord to disruption."

- B.H. Liddell Hart Strategy 1954, 1967

"It was a bright cold day in April, and the clocks were striking thirteen."

1984, George Orwell

Golden Calves of Social Media, 'google funnel'; You must know to google, you cannot google to know

In chapter 5, we had discussed Use of the Internet as Powerful Brain-washing Tool to control the Ignorant. With the google Search Funnel, ALL Ideas are filtered down to / funneled into Uniformity of the P.C. ONE View, as parallel to concept of Convergent Evolution. This filtering out of diverse Ideas is equivalent to burning books in the Fascists, Nazi and Communists reigns. With such emerging Uniformity in views, new and diverse ideas (also championed by CNN, MSNBC, NYT, WP, yahoo, Microsoft, all mainstream Media) and the serendipity or possible Conjunctures of events becomes extremely low for new 'breakthroughs' of human ingenuity to occur. It is serendipity that allows life to happen, it is conjunctures that allow major breakthroughs though human history.

The Google funnel, the new combined tool of Newspeak and "memory Hole" are doing a tremendous job of influencing opinions with the users 'sub-consciously' believing they are in 'in control' of their search and liking the 'personal discovery experience'. So now all the ignorant P.C. ONE View masses have been indoctrinated by the 'google funnel' are all worshiping the Gods of Social Media and praying to the golden calf of Mainstream Media Celebrities. Uniformity has been achieved at expense of Diversity of Ideas and our Society's ability to adapt has been diminished. As MOB strengthens, Scale of the Complex system increases and risks increases exponentially. Society becomes brittle and less pliable.

"... there was a ring of truth to the idea that religious bigotry had after a thousand years of enlightenment finally dragged Alexandria into oblivion. Ironically, however, it was Muslim scholars who were even then preserving and translating the few great works from Alexandria's library shelves that had survived. ... any conqueror might consider the contents of a library as dangerous as the contents of an arsenal. Building that arsenal of ideas had

> *been the driving force behind Ptolemy I's creation of Alexandria, and the insecurity of conquerors and the intolerance of extremists had been its downfall. Alexandria had been a city of ideas where the greatest freedom was the freedom to think, but Roman emperors, Christian patriarchs, and Muslim caliphs had all, in attempting to control those thoughts, whittled away at the library, the city, and the idea that lay behind them."*
>
> - Rise and Fall of Alexandria, Justin Pollard & Howard Reid

The shipwreck of time, Inflection Point for Western Civilization and the Closing of the Western Mind

Remember at end of Chapter 3, we had asked the question if America is deadwood for the termites? We know the parasites are well and getting fat, the question: Is the host dead? No, luckily the host (America as a country) isn't dead, the results of the 2016 General Election clearly demonstrated that. (so the termites was a bad example, but you get the picture)

The fact we are discussing the Civil War is a sign of the body's immune system fighting back, the anti-bodies, white-blood cells and other defense mechanisms are all resisting the viral infection (the 'ideological virus' wreaked on to us by the parasitic poverty pimps). That's the good news, and the bad news?

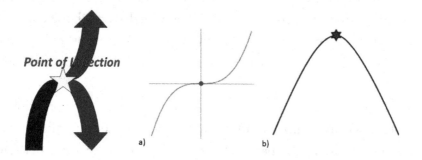

Like it or not, we are at the Cross-roads, the point of Inflection, depending on the outcome of this Civil War, if Individual Freedom wins, we will see the red curve a) where the World's advancement in technologies, science, healthcare advances as it had done so for last 75 years after WW II. If the Culture of Conformity, Politically Correct ONE view wins, America will continue its decline, the pace of World advancement will also slow significantly, it will also be led by Asians, namely China and India.

The logic is simple, America without the Culture of Growth's Engine, the combination of Free Market Competition of Capitalism, Human Talent & Ideas and the virtuous cycles of reinforcement between them (as discussed in chapter 4 per chart on page 89), will definitely fall behind China and India, as population size will then become the 'key driver', determinant of Economic strength (even Hillary knows this one). We might now be able to see why such conjunctures; of multiple conditions to align themselves, are so rare exceptions in human history.

The Western civilization (America and Europe) will continue their downwards slide, degenerate into Uncompetitive, Unproductive Social Welfare States and then eventually into opportunities for the stronger Asian economies to exploit as the western powers did to China, India and Ottoman Empire in 18th and 19th Centuries. The western civilizations will move along the blue curve b).

We have seen this scenario played out repeatedly as civilizations decline for numerous reasons; losing their Asabiyyah (could be roughly translated as sense of National Pride, Patriotism) being one of them. The last time the Closing of Western Mind happened was around between 3rd – 5th century AD coinciding with move of Capital to Constantinople and eventual Fall of Western Rome. Europe then entered the Dark Ages for a thousand years as ONE view dominated, that of the Medieval Church and diversity of ideas was frowned on. Interestingly, it was the Rise of Islam and the Muslim Scholars that helped preserved the ancient Greek knowledge and carried on the Torch of human enlightenment. With ascent of Chinese Technology Giants like Huawei superseding Apple, it does look like a possible and probable future. If the P.C. One View continues to dominate in America, then the Asian Global Power China and India would take over the torch of human civilization from America.

How about the Climate change equation? As the western civilizations slides into impotent welfare states, there will be a transfer of Power in the World Leadership into the hands of the Chinese and Indians, this transfer will probably NOT be a peaceful nor easy one as India and China are Culturally diverse and distinct from each other. Russia, Japan would also be juggling to best position themselves during this re-sorting of World order and leadership.

During these next 4-5 decades of power shift and re-sorting of World Order, you can bet one thing, Climate Change will be of low priority as the rising Nations tussle each other and shove aside the "sick man of the West" (America).

As we're already seeing, China and India are the largest users of Coal as Fuel for their Energy Needs and produces over 35% of the entire world's CO_2 pollution as Coal is the cheapest and quickest for them to satisfy their Energy needs. Renewable Energy is only at 3-4% of the entire world's till date as it simply has not reached grid parity and requires Tax payers money to prop up. In all the current forecasts by Major Energy Producers; BP, Exxon Mobile, Shell, etc. China Petroleum gives renewable energy the lowest growth potential compared to the others who had to appease to their Activist groups back home. What does that tell you? In our scenario of waning American and Western powers, Global Warming will definitely Not be on anyone's radar as it is a simple case of Tragedy of the Commons (everyone abuses it but no one owns it), Global Warming will likely accelerate as China and Indian races to raise the standard of living for their citizens whom still mostly live in poverty now. Fossil Fuel is the cheapest and most economical way for them to raise half of the World's population to Developed Nation's standard of living. And it will increase the carbon emissions exponentially, as there's No real incentive for breakthrough in renewable energy technology (too slow, expensive and doubtful success). As the western powers wane, their government would have no need to pander to their ignorant voters any longer, they would be focusing on learning to dance to Chinese and Indian tunes.

> *"This generation of Americans has a rendezvous with destiny."*
>
> - President Franklin D Roosevelt

The League of Nations, 狐假虎威, United Nations and United States of America's Military Force and why the Accord de Paris (Paris Agreement) is a worthless sham

狐假虎威The fox walks in front of a Tiger, all the animals in the forest scurries away from the fox as he approaches, the fox believes himself to be King of the Jungle after such a display. After WWI, the League of Nations was formed to maintain world peace, 2 decades later, WWII exploded around the world with even larger casualties and bigger number of countries embroiled. How is the UN successful while the League of Nations failed?

There's a number of reasons, President Woodrow Wilson's overly idealistic goal for League of Nations as 'to make the world safe for democracy', his inability to get congress to accept his terms caused his brain-child, The League, to started its life without its most powerful godparent. The Treaty of Versailles was a huge humiliation to the Germans; as the Allies were then seeking to extract revenge instead of seeking just equilibrium of power in Europe [as in the Congress of Vienna after the Napoleonic Wars]. More importantly after WWI, the combination of Industrial, economic & subsequently military powers were evenly matched amongst a number of Nations, Britain, France, USA, Japan, Russia, Germany, all with conflicting agenda and interests.

The League of Nations also has no Military Force at its disposal, it also proved itself unable to represent all the interests of the major world powers then nor navigate their differences to find common ground.

United Nations was form towards end of WWII (Charter was signed 26th June 1945, born on 24th Oct 1945) when all the Military might was shared between 2 superpowers, USA and USSR. Most of the World's economic powers was shared between USA and Western European countries with USSR only 13% of world's economy. Combining these 2 measures (military and economic), USA leading the Western European countries is clearly ahead of the Soviet eastern bloc. Now you see the fox (UN) and the Tiger? Whoever has the strongest Economic and Military Dominance will dictate the Rules. The UN, IMF, EU, etc. are all facades for the Global corrupted Poverty Pimps to make their money, nothing more.

So as America and Europe's influence wanes, a similar multiple world powers scenario will re-emerge as after WWI. UN probably will be relegated to the impotence of the League of Nations, the façade of UN might and probably be dispensed with all together, leaving the few with Nuclear capabilities to decide for the world. Climate change will then take a back seat, as the new world powers race for dominance and exploit fossil fuels (it being the most efficient and cheapest means) to boost their energy needs and fuel economic growth in their respective countries.

We know that Climate Change Effects definitely needs to be addressed, Common Sense tells us that Earth (in its delicate balanced 'homeostasis') doesn't have Unlimited Resources for us to keep plundering, but United Nations, EU, IMF are corrupted dens of thieves, the Paris Accord is just a Hollywood Academy ceremony celebrating all the moving and touching speeches made about Climate Change for that year. When everyone is jointly responsible, it means NO one is really responsible to do anything. UN, IMF, EU, etc. in their current form are merely great venues for the Corrupted Globalist Pimps to make good on their SDRs, but not the organizations to solve any real problems, nor get anything of value done for the ordinary folks.

In next chapter, we'll explore in more detail how to solve renewable energy problems in a 'Go Direct Model' approach (as versus the approach of having huge gaggle of faceless bureaucrats, international funding & SDRs, with no accountability taking charge) and leveraging the Free Market Capitalism mechanism to provide the most efficient and effective solutions.

For the entire history of human race up till the Industrial Revolution (beginning of the Anthropocene Age), all civilizations on earth were agrarian societies. As a large agrarian ecosystem, the Earth could sustain itself and human race, as the human population was constrained by the amount of crops they can growth on this planet. Various human civilizations can rise and fall, but Earth was sustainable and the torch of human civilization can be passed between civilizations as some decline and others rise, as when the Western Roman decline, Europe moved into the Dark Ages but the Islamic Civilization stepped up and held the torch of human civilization till the Renaissance when Europe once again emerged from the Medieval age.

Before Industrial Revolution, before we started releasing large amounts of carbon into the atmosphere and unknowingly started this climate change, the Global Human Population had stayed below 1 billion for entire human history on earth until the 19th century. It has now reached over 7 billion and counting (up 7 times in just last century). Not only has the population size increased, the modern-day comforts enjoyed by the developed countries, all the technologies, all powered by electricity generated by burning (to a large degree) fossil fuels.

This is the simple equation that the Global Warming Pimps never tell you: The Industrial Revolution, together with the release of Energy from the Fossil Fuels, plus a whole host of human inventions and discoveries allowed the rise in human population and all the ease and material comforts, technologies that we now enjoy! Yet the Gaia's clock has started ticking and has been accelerating since then. The agrarian societies were in balance with Earth as they could only grow as big as the amount of crops that they can grow (crops are 'fueled via photosynthesis', light from the sun). Gaia is Safe.

Now we enter the Anthropocene Age and we become out of balance with Gaia, why? The growth in human population, their relative ease of life versus those that lived in the agrarian societies, advance in technologies, etc. are all possible only because of the Fossil Fuel we consume. We (human civilization) owe Gaia a pound of Flesh but she's kind enough to give us time before extracting it back. Time for us to find alternative source of energy, time to find alternative homes besides earth, time to terraform these new homes for human habitation.

But No time for problem profiteers to cry wolf, exploit the good intentions of concerned kids and enrich themselves in the process with no intention to deliver any results other than to 'raise awareness' (aka marketing for more funds). 'Global climate change pimps' has been 'raising awareness' for the last 2 decades and asking for huge international funds to be setup to address Global Warming, unaccountable funds managed by unaccountable faceless bureaucrats that have nothing to show for after 2 decades. The renewable energy sectors technology has achieved minimal advancement in technology, only loads of marketing material to keep raise funds for the 'faceless global warming pimps' that have all made themselves filthy rich in the process. Al Gore left public office with minimal wealth (a typical civil servant), he now has net worth of $ 300 million. Climate Change makes very good business for some, it's just the Inconvenient Truth.

With China and India economy rising fast and their population starting to enjoy the comforts and conveniences of developed nations and no new replacement energy sources in sight, to say that we can stop this climate change effect or even to reverse it is Naïve and just a dumb slogan the "climate change pimps" are selling to the snowflakes, as the climate change clock ticks away, the "climate change pimps" propose to stop time or reverse time? We can only outrun time, how? Ideas, only Ideas can outrun time. What do I mean? Innovation and breakthroughs in technologies, etc. not via stupid subsidies, grants, loans, International SDRs (that's just to fill the kitty of the climate-change pimps), the funds have to be directed very specifically to Institutions with the highest probability of break-though in technology, not to line the pockets of corrupted bureaucrats. We need something of Revolutionary Magnitude, with major impact like the last Industrial Revolution and Age of Enlightenment.

Remember in chapter 1, we discussed the a) Age of Discovery, b) Schism in the Church & c) Printing press to break from the shackles of the Old World in 15th Century? We now already have c) the Printing Press => the Internet (born in America), we need two other events to happen a) Age of Discovery and b) Schism in the Church. The serendipity and conjuncture of these 3 events will break us from the constraints of 'Old World' Earth. The schism in Uniform vs Diverse Ideology is already happening in USA. That's the current Civil War we are currently discussing, the War between ONE View of the world and individual free ideas. If the P.C. ONE view of the world wins, it's like the Medieval Church dominating over all ideas in Europe through the Dark Ages[for a thousand years], over the champions of new ideas (the likes of Galileo Galilei), banning the works of intellects and excommunicating them. Just as the neo-Fascists Dem Activists persecute views diverse from theirs, radicals Antifa and extremists Liberals tear down historical statues following in the footsteps of Spanish Inquisition and burning of 'witches' at the stake.

These neo-Dem P.C. Gestapo might not be worthy successors of the muckraking Investigative Journalists but they are definitely worthy successors to the Radical Parabolans under Cyril of Alexandria (around 5th century AD). This dominance of ONE View with little tolerance for diversity of Ideas, only started to recede with emergence of Renaissance, Age of Discovery, Reformation and the Protestant movement spread across Europe in 16th century and (later into America) resulting in the Age of Enlightenment (17th and 18th century), all cumulating into the Industrial Revolution that brought us here.

If the freedom of Ideas does prevail in this Civil war, then we will still need one more event to happen for this conjuncture to happen, that is Deep Space exploration, Human Colonization within Solar System ('Near Space'); in Mars, Moon? And beginning of Terraforming other planets. This is the Age of Discovery that can unlock the shackles of our Old World Earth. Growth of this kind of magnitude will also drive the economy revitalization and ascent of this country, start to provide all the millions of Great-paying jobs. Only by pushing the limits of our knowledge and science can we truly find the technologies for renewable energy, real affordable and working technologies, real as in Not marketing clips, not in Movies, real as in people working on the moon, living on Mars and as human lives depend on it.

Real Robust Economic Growth for next 2 decades will bring back the traditional American Values of Growth Culture, Culture of Excellence! Value Creation Growth and Growth Culture goes hand in hand and reinforce each other as we have seen in the Free Market Competition Model of Capitalism. Not the subsidized malformed imitations of 'renewable energy' companies that lives on Federal subsidies and the greedy speculative monies of Wall Street. Only with the new Age of Space Exploration and Discovery can we have proper use of the Internet and its true potential of leveraging human ideas and creative solution to help solve challenges we will face on Mars, Moon and eventually in deep space! Only then Mankind achieves its potential and Telos. (one cannot imagine the height of human's potential & ingenuity is taking selfies and posting on social media?)

If the P.C. ONE view of world wins, the conjuncture of new Age of Discovery will NOT happen in USA, neither will it happen anytime soon. The Global Heating clock will pick-up and accelerate the race will be on for next conjuncture to happen before Earth becomes un-livable for human race. Between China and India, where will the next conjuncture happen? I'll bet my money on India, some will not agree as China is already way ahead of the economic race, Infrastructure-wise China is also way superior to India. I choose India as the country is democratic and new Ideas are more likely to grow from diversity. China has become Capitalist as we had discussed but it is still very much a Big State-controlled (tops down) socialist country will be very effective and efficient in executing their State Policies. But not necessarily best place for new Ideas to gain traction and gather momentum. But as America continues to decline, the next conjuncture will likely not happen within the next 30 years. But it can still happen within the next 50 years with a hopeful outlook.

Do we have 50 years before the Global Heating clock runs out and destiny catches up with humans? If you are a Climate Change fan (and believe in the fragility of earth's ecosystems), then the planet is also at stake here in this Civil War. If you are not a Climate change fan, then you'll just need to learn Chinese and Hindi in the next few decades, not so bad. If you live in Europe, you also might need to live under Sharia Law too, (many European cities would likely be addressing the integration of Sharia Law into their existing legal systems), man does has more rights under Sharia Law, while the LGBTQ might not be too welcomed. Now we've addressed what's at stake in this Civil War, let's see what we should do or can do?

> *"we can no longer doubt that the crisis is arrived at which the good people of America are to decide the solemn question, whether they will reap the fruits of that Independence … and of that Union which they have cemented with so much of their common blood, or whether by giving way to unmanly jealousies and prejudices, or to partial and transitory interests, they will renounce the auspicious blessings prepared for them by the Revolution, and furnish its enemies an eventual triumph."*
>
> - James Madison to George Washington on 8th Nov 1786

"The terrorists were at war with us, but we were not yet at war with them."
Secretary of State Condoleezza Rice

IX - When is the Civil War being fought?

Open your eyes, it is in many forms all around, everywhere. The parasitic Alinsky virus has been incubating in this country since the 60s. The Cold War kept the virus dormant, but with the thaw in the early 90s after end of Cold War, the virus started to multiply, quickly reaching its exponential growth phase in last decade, that when the host [America] started to manifest multiple serious symptoms of Huge Income Inequality, sluggish economy, Unemployment, Explosion in Welfare handouts, etc. Just like the War on Terror, this is a form of Asymmetric Warfare, we know now that it isn't a war of Ideology, but it is a very real War nonetheless, it is a much tougher War than War on Terror.

This is a War for survival against Parasites within the infected host, that's weakening its Growth ability, (over a decade of stagnant Economy, Massive unemployment). Remember the wise words of B.H. Liddell Hart "The experience of history.... the downfall of civilized states tends to come not from the direct assaults of foes but from internal decay"

Let's review both the actions of these neo-Fascists Dems MOB, aided by their Deep State GOP colleagues and the results of what they've wreaked onto this Nation. We'll group the Impacts in 3 categories per Causation and Intent of those responsible, note their interesting sequence;

A - Incompetence, sloth and Hubris

Many of the elected officials at both State and Federal levels couldn't even run municipals to save their own souls, let alone run the country. The following impacts here are caused by sheer Incompetence, enabled through sloth and hubris.

Stagnant Economy for last 2 decades, yearly Budgets deficits, $ 20 Trillion of Debt, Massive Unemployment, Rise of Crony Capitalism breaking the Free Market Capitalism mechanism (Greenspan & Bernanke understand impact, Bush & Obama are just plain ignorant about the economy). Appeasement to Tyrannical & Terrorists Regimes abroad, allowing proliferation of ISIS (calling them JV team by last admin team is blind egoistic ignorance), Appeasement to Iran and North Korea, repeated Indecisive Delays leading to Syria's Civil War; Displacement of millions of refugees. Abandonment of our Allies; Israel, Egypt, Saudi, UAE, Jordan, Turkey, etc.

We have also witnessed firsthand, the 'globalists pimps' with no prior Foreign Policies experience like Valerie Jarrett and President Obama who knew and still knows nothing about Muslims Culture or History, their claim to fame was to have lived in Muslim countries when they were toddlers and in Obama's case 8 years old. They were also too slothful and egoistic to do their homework and learn on the job, instead they made decisions on Foreign Policies based NOT on Insights or knowledge about the Middle East countries but based on their childhood memories of Muslim lands or even worse based on influence and ill advice from the Muslim Brotherhood.

The incompetence of these 'globalist pimps' are causing millions of Syrians, Libyans and Iraqis to lose their lives, their families and homes (In case of Iraq, President Bush started the mess). Policies of Appeasement to Tyrannical & Terrorist Regimes in Middle East and Asia emboldens them ultimately causing much suffering to the innocent populace under them.

As an interesting point of reference, under Athenian Democracy of the Greek polis (the model on which modern democracy is based), Incompetence of council members in government posts was punished by fines, exile or ultimately execution as their mistakes causes loss of lives just as Incompetence causes lives in war and major destruction of wealth in present day!

> *"He knows nothing; and he thinks he knows everything. That points clearly to a political career."*
>
> – George Bernard Shaw

B - Avarice & Envy

Greed to enrich themselves, giving in and pandering to the Activists Corporations and collecting their personal rewards produces;

Highest Income Inequality since 1920s, Unproductive Welfare State with Uncompetitive Wages, a broken HealthCare system, billions of Tax-Payers monies poured into farce Renewable Energy companies,

In chapter 2 and 6, we've also understood how the 'socialist pimps' like Bernie Sanders and Liz Warren make their political career out of a Big Lie about a façade of Socialists Ideals, without ever addressing the challenges and complexities ALL Communist (socialism in action) countries struggles with for last century and had not been able to overcome till date. The snowflakes still living in their socialist illusions & dreams from which when they do ever awake from, they find themselves forever trapped in the Dark Ages dungeons of the Big State Tyrannical Regimes. For the first step for the Elite kleptocrats to lord over their serfs is to disarm the populace and arm only themselves (the most powerful of weapons being the Monopoly of the Mass Media)

C - Lust for Power, wicked and deceitful

Finally, to hang on to their power and distract from their Incompetence, they create deceitful lies and distractions and also collecting their goodies from the Activists Corporations, Lobbyists, Interests Groups

Racial Tensions and Violence against Law and Order, Mindless Divisive Rhetoric (Racism, Sexism, etc.) divides the nation, killing its Asabiyyah (National Unity and Patriotism), losing a complete generation of snowflakes to ignorance; becoming an immense liability to society and humankind

The rhetoric during the campaigns leading up to the Elections are ugly on both sides but understandable as both are contesting for the coveted price of the Presidency. But the Post-Election behavior of the Radical neo-democrats says it all, the wolf has taken off its sheep's clothing and openly inciting and praising violence, flag burning and rioting. It continues till date over a year after the Inauguration Day, this is just plain anarchy behavior by the neo-fascists activists with the neo-democrat P.C. Media Gestapo encouraging and egging them on.

And the Deep State Politicians; the poverty pimps, climate-change pimps, socialist-pimps and globalists pimps, All the neo-democrat politician pimps 'grand-standing', shouting the same 'one phrase slogans' in the House of Representatives, in the Senate, on C-SPAN. They see their fellow citizens as their personal enemies as they feel their lifestyles of perks and unearned wealth being threatened, this is typical Eunuch Mentality. Hard to imagine all these mindless Violence, Anarchy, the very crescendo of human Ignorance and Mob-like crazed Hysteria, meticulously and intentionally planned, choreographed by their elected officials. These neo-Fascists Dems would sow discord and wreak Anarchy on their country to distract public attention from their own Incompetence, failures and greed. Then again, we'd witnessed such behavior time and again as they surfaced repeatedly throughout human history.

> *"The French Revolution replaced the landowning aristocracy with the money-controlling business class as the ruling power, but a similar result occurred in the nineteenth-century England without bloodshed, and without disturbing the public peace. To break sharply with the past is to court madness that may follow the shock of sudden blows or mutilation. As the sanity of the individual lies in the continuity of his memories, so the sanity of a group lies in the continuity of its traditions, in either case a break in the chain invites a neurotic reaction, as in the Paris massacres of September 1792."*
>
> Will & Ariel Durant, The Lessons of History

In the 1930s, the Decade leading up to the Holocaust, the Allies had adopted Policies of Appeasement to the Fascists, Nazis and Communists Regimes in hopes of maintaining status quo. As many GOP and Independent Americans had also adopted Appeasement Policies towards the neo-Fascists Dem's Activists' groups use of Violence against Law and Order. We know from history appeasement only emboldens the opposition and increasing their never-ending demands.

We should remember the end Results of Appeasement leading up to WWII and the Holocaust. The attacks of Nov 9 and 10th, 1938, **Kristallnacht**, became known as beginning of the Holocaust, marking the first instance of state-organized mass violence against Jews. Similarly, the Policies of Pandering & Appeasement to Violent Activists groups (in last decade); likes of BLM, Antifa, set-up of Sanctuary Cities harboring violent illegal criminals marks the state-sanctioned mass violence against Cops, against Law & Order and the American people. We ask ourselves what are we appeasing to?

> *"Violence takes much deeper root in irregular warfare than it does in regular warfare. In the latter, it is counteracted by obedience to constituted*

authority. Whereas the former makes a virtue of defying authority and violating rules. It becomes very difficult to rebuild a country, and a stable state, on a foundation undermined by such experience."

B.H. Liddell Hart Strategy 1954, 1967

Dangers of Unrestrained Protests, Violence, leading to Anarchy

From chapter 7, we'd learnt and witnessed the Pro-choice, Planned Parenthood's genocide activities (in the African American and minorities communities). These days we also see the on-going rioting, flag-burning, pro-violence against cops activities by neo-fascist activist corporations like ANTIFA, Black Lives Matter. In full realization of dangers of violence and anarchy to our country, the PP Politicians like President Obama and Sec of State Hillary Clinton continues to pander to these neo-fascists activist corporations (BLM, ANTIFA, Pro-choice, Planned Parenthood, etc.)? Their actions clearly signal their Intentions and how much their truly value this country and its people.

The neo-democrat Activists continues their anarchy activities, praised by Radical P.C. Media Celebrities and pandered to by the poverty & socialist pimps. This is a wake-up Call! We must curtail these violence-agitating neo-Democrats PP Politicians and Radicals in Mainstream Media, who's constantly encouraging and sanctioning Violence against our Law and Order officers just like the French Revolution's Reign of Terror, or the start of Holocaust with State sanctioned violence against the Jews.

No more appeasement, we have to put an end to the numerous Open Society's sponsored neo-Fascists Activists corporations (BLM, Antifa, etc.) from continuing to incite violence. Through history, we've witnessed the violence of the Russian Revolution, the French Revolution, Mao's Cultural Revolution in China, the Syrian & Iraq's Civil Wars set these entire societies back decades in wealth and in many cases total loss of history, arts, knowledge that will never be recovered.

Human Civilizations, knowledge and wisdom lost cannot be recovered, we cannot allow such fate to happen to our country. Just open your eyes, have you seen the removal and destruction of Confederate Statues by neo-Dem Radicals? The extremists spitting, stepping over and destroying the country's history and sense of Pride. See the similarity with the ISIS Radicals destroying archeological treasures in Levant? Taliban's Extremism destroying thousand years-old Buddhist Arts and Treasures in Afghanistan? As the Extremists Christian parabolans destroying the libraries in Alexandria in 5th century AD?

Radicalism as Extremism (rooted in ignorance) are global and repeatedly shows themselves in different faces. Once such mindset of embracing violence, disrespect of Law and Order take root in a society, Anarchy looms over it and would take even more Force and Violence to restore and reconstruct Law and Order again.

So who are we Appeasing? We know there's no ideology here. Only sound-bytes of advertisements, trailers of Movies coming soon (Titled Racism, Sexism, Global Warming, reruns too). Are we Appeasing to Incompetence? To Theft? To Looting by the Top 1% from the Middle Working Tax Payers? In fact, Looting is already happening;

> *Orwell's confident conclusion, after mixing with the rich at Eton and then with the poor in the subbasement of a Paris hotel and on the streets of London, was that "the average millionaire is only the average dishwasher dressed in a new suit."... as for those who worried about the mob looting in the streets, he responded that "the mob is in fact loose now - and in the shape of rich men." ie. wealthy already looting from the poor*
> — Churchill & Orwell, Thomas E Ricks

Appeasement will only encourage and embolden the Top 1% Looters, their Activists Corporations sponsoring all the protests and violence, leading to the Rise of the Big State Government spending the Annual Federal Welfare Expenses of $2.5 Trillion of the hardworking American middle-income tax payers. Thereby, increasing Income Inequality! Decimating the Middle Class of America forever. We've already understood the mathematics in chapter 7, at 90% inefficiency the Activists Corporations, related K-street participants and their sponsors will receive $ 2.5 T per year, at 35% inefficiency, they will receive $ 1 Trillion of goodies.

No good will ever come from Appeasement to their Avarice, Lust for Power, to the wicked and deceitful. The K street professional politicians after over 2 decades of unearned and underserved Life of Luxury, Glamor and Power that maintaining Status Quo is critical to them, they actively encourage their Mobs to RESIST, to incite violence, to risk Americans to Cultures of Violence, to risk the American Society to Anarchy just so they can ensure their status quo lives of complacency and decadence.

They can only be contained and checked by the Power of Ethos, Awful Virtues, counteracted by Powers of Discipline, self-restraint, moral rectitude, righteous anger at wrongdoers. We all need to step up, support Law and Order, support the Establishment and put an end to these appeasement to radicals. We need to audit and tax these Activists Corporations and their sponsors, Shame the PP Politicians and Shame the Mainstream Media Entertainment celebrities, and lastly minimize the Federal Expenses that's feeding them [cut the Federal Expenses to below $ 1 Trillion and increase the efficiency of reach to the intended end-recipients to over 90%]. If you are afraid of the neo-democrats Gestapo coming after you, we can understand. Many ex-Navy SEALs are also afraid and we can understand your fears.

> *"if someone drops a bomb on your mother, go drop two bombs on his mother."*
> — George Orwell in Feb 1938

> *"the growth of freedom and law, of the rights of the individual, of the subordination of the State to the fundamental and moral conceptions of an ever-comprehending community." were the principles at stake in the coming*

fight, "of these ideas the English-speaking peoples were the authors, then the trustees, and must now become the armed champions,"

– Winston Churchill

Having understood the threat we face, having witnessed their utter Incompetence and total disregard for human lives, let's now review the Strategies for Conflict resolution. The various Issues are obviously of utmost importance, thus Avoidance and Accommodation strategies cannot be the response to the neo-Democrats any more. Collaboration would be offered as first resort, then Competition strategies would be next and last would be a compromise on less Strategic issues.

"... They exhibit a melancholy proof of what our Trans Atlantic foes have predicted; and of another thing perhaps,... That mankind left to themselves are unfit for their own government. I am mortified beyond expression whenever I view the clouds which have spread over the brightest morn that ever dawned upon my Country.... For it is hardly to be imagined that the great body of the people can be so enveloped in darkness, or short sighted as not to see the rays of distant sun through all this mist of intoxication and folly."

George Washington to Henry Lee 31st Oct 1786 after
receiving exaggerated reports on Shays' Rebellion

V - Who are the opponents?

In the Great Seal of USA, the olive branch of peace would always be extended, but as and whenever needed, the lightning bolts of competition needs to cleanse out the Parasitic neo-fascists Activist Corporations, to reveal the Radical neo-democrat's Farce of Ideologies, hidden agenda of the hypocrites Poverty Pimps, Climate-change Pimps, Socialists and Globalists Pimps, their Immoral activities. The Corrupted Monopolies of Wall Street Suzerains and IT Tech Giants Moghuls should also be illuminated for all to see!

The Who, is most critical, we do need close observation and patience to unveil, as there are various levels of Distractions that many Presidents and Politicians helped created or was baited into their creation.

Let's start with the first layer of Distraction:

In 1992, after end of Cold War, the Global Financial Speculating started, first against the British Pound by George Soros, betting against and dumping the Pound. Eventually the Pound collapsed and Financial turmoil swept across the world from Tokyo, Rome to London. Soros personally made over $ 2 B, the Integrated Global Financial Markets had revealed its weakness to speculations by powerful financial players. Soros with his Quantum Fund repeated this speculation activities through the 90s, (in '93 against Deutschmark, in '97 triggered the Asia Financial crisis, and again in '98 against the Russian ruble), sending Financial crisis and disasters around the world and profiting handsomely personally. The American Financial Watchdogs had been expressing their concerns and momentum started to gather for actions against such irresponsible avarice towards end of 90s. Soros knew that if he didn't take the offensive, the Financial Watchdogs would catchup with him eventually.

In fact, after the ' 97 Asia Crisis, Soros did make a very strong attempt to vie for influence over the Clinton administration as lead advisor on addressing such financial crisis that he had created to begin with and then subsequently labeled as *The Crisis of Global Capitalism* (his book published in 1998). After the Asia Financial Crisis in '97, followed by Russian crisis in '98; both triggered by Soros, it looked like financial crisis was going to overrun America too. Soros stood poised to take over the American Financial helm then.

As it happened, he didn't see the entire picture clearly, with the loss of Investors' confidence all around the world, all the funds pulled their money back into America and causing the US Stock Market to strengthen considerably from 1998 – 2000 (Nasdaq rose very quickly with the .com bubble which burst at end of 2000).

But the event that gave Soros his second chance did come on 9/11 2001. We know about the terrorists' attacks, but we didn't know that Soros again lobbied to exploit the events of 9/11. This time Soros and his lackey from Harvard Jeff Sachs started peddling Global War on Poverty rhetoric; *Soros on Globalization* in 2002, *The End of Poverty* in 2005 by Sachs. They essentially proposed that Terrorist around the world arose due to poverty and the Solution is for America and The World (UN and IMF) to give so much foreign aids to these 'poor nations' regardless how corrupted their government are and the problem of terrorism would go away. At the same time, America and The World are responsible for the poverty of these terrorist breeding countries run by Corrupted and Tyrannical Regimes. Many Activists corporations in America (many started by Soros) also started to proliferate after turn of the millennium, growing special interests Activism exponentially into stratospheric levels.

Soros and his neo-Dem cronies also pressured the Bush Admin to help Fund the Global War on Poverty; ie. the Islamists States harboring the Terrorist & Tyrannical Regimes (obviously such that they can manage these International Funds and enrich themselves). Bush 43 didn't buy Soros proposal, but Kofi Annan of UN did, he allowed Sachs to set up the Millennium Project (with IMF Funds) for War on Poverty in the poor countries run by corrupted regimes (you might notice the similar tricks by the Poverty Pimps at home set up the War on Poverty campaigns to collect Federal Subsidies and Funds from unsuspecting American public).

Bush might not have bought Soros' rhetoric about Global War on Poverty but he did sign up for the Nation Building in Iraq, perhaps Bush 43rd subconsciously bought the reasoning about America being responsible to rid the world of Poverty (without realizing that it is Corruption that breeds Poverty, not vice versa. Indeed, if Crony Capitalism continues to reign in America, it's economy will continue to weaken). So now we see the successful launch of 1st layer of Distraction, the Wall Street Suzerain George Soros and all his cronies, in order to satisfy their greed and cling on to their ill-gotten wealth (tens and hundreds of Billions for Soros) and avoid arms of financial justice catching him, leveraged the devastating and confusing events of 9/11 to cover his tracks.

Paraphrasing Tarbell, "all his [*Soros] vast wealth spent in one supreme effort to evade the judgement of men would be but wasted, for a man can never escape the judgement of the society which has bred him", she was referring to Rockefeller. *my words, the 501c3 'charitable organizations' are Tax exempt and serves well as vehicles for multiple purposes of Tax planning for wealth enhancement purposes, Activists and other activities of interests and finally as The Open Society to write into history for posterity one's personal vision and version of 'humanitarian work'.

By middle of last decade, the 1st layer of Distractions had been successfully planted by Soros and his Wall Street Cronies; we must also remember that Greenspan had also contributed with numerous QEs of Free Money. Greenspan retired in 2006 after 19 years and Bernanke took over. 2008 saw the Lehmann Brothers' Major Financial Crisis hit America, more and Bigger QEs (now on steroids), Obama takes over from Bush 43 and starts his own reign of Incompetence (Foreign debacles in Iraq leading to rise of ISIS, Appeasement to Iran, North Korea, Indecision leading to Syrian Civil War, etc.), further QEs under Bernanke with Obama's approval (started under Bush 43 and continued under Obama) so now we have a stagnant Economy, rampant Crony Capitalism, Unemployment and Highest Income Inequality (one could argue they were accumulated effects under Incompetence of 3 Presidents, Avarice of Soros, Hubris of Greenspan and Bernanke, they would be right).

Here comes the next layer of Distractions, to cover up for his own Incompetence and Hubris (as Soros wanted to cover his tracks of Greed and Financial speculations), Obama started to layer the 2nd layer of Distractions, partially as distractions from the problems we've just mentioned and partially to satisfy his personal Greed (we know that the 'Poverty Pimps' all benefit from million dollars speeches and Book deals supported by Activists corporations and their sponsors in turn, from the Federal subsidies to the Activists Interest groups), so the Divisive Racial, Sexists, LGBTQ, etc. rhetoric starts, Climate Change, more Unlimited Welfare, Free Healthcare all put into play accelerated with the Help of the MOB (Internet and Mainstream Media Monopolies) helping to whip the 'snowflakes' in crazed frenzies.

> *"we must not underrate the gravity of the task which lies before us, … or the severity of the ordeal, to which we shall not be found unequal…… This is not a question of fighting for Danzig or fighting for Poland. We are fighting to save the whole world from the pestilence of Nazi tyranny and in defense of all that is most sacred to man. This is no war for domination or imperial aggrandizement or material gain; no war to shut any country out of its sunlight and means of progress. It is a war, viewed in its inherent quality, to establish, on impregnable rocks, the rights of the individual, and it is a war to establish and revive the stature of man."*
>
> – Churchill

We should not underestimate the magnitude and complexity of tasks at hand, to reverse all the wrongs and mistakes made in last quarter of century of irresponsible politicians and lack of leadership is like turning around a Super oil tanker, it takes time and finesse to know which buttons to press and in which sequence to as to unleash the American Economy by fixing the Capitalism and Democratic Engines.

We know the layers of Distractions and who are the main actors, let's move on to what we need to do:

Four Key Areas of Focus

I - Message,

Clear. Simple and Precise Message, multiple avenues of communications to reach-out, Violence is not an option, Acceptance of Diversity, Strategies of Collaboration, Competition [Perfect Competition Model to remove Monopolies of Power, understand Shame Culture and illuminate] and use the Compromise strategy to achieve a better future for Americans

II - Growth (more in chapter 9),

Trade, Services, IP and Eco-Tourism & Economic Growth to leverage America's Industrial & Innovation strength, Space Exploration & Discovery, Gaia Equilibrium, Technology in support of all above initiatives, De-Scale the Federal government by 90%, Increase States' Power

III - Ethos, Awful Virtues

Go after Crony Capitalism, Trace Funds Flow, Audit for Fraud, Abuse and waste, check for segregation of duties, increase transparency, personal accountability, fiduciary duties, legal consequences on negligence, incompetence, violation of any internal Controls procedures, verify Compliance to all Internal Controls, Corporate Governance, Alignment to Corporate Strategy by all levels? Instill Culture of Financial Discipline, review Financial ROI (Return on Investments) on any projects and on any departments, review all loans and grants; ROI, repayable? Audit sub-contractors, check K Street employees' [ones awarding contracts] personal Banking details, related party transactions, use unrelated Internal Auditors

Teach Values of Accountability, Meritocracy, Culture of Excellence, Honor, Self-Sacrifice, Endurance, Personal Responsibilities, self-restraint, discipline, Valor, will power, etc. in Schools and Academia

IV - Ockham's Razor (Simplify & Descale)

Federal Government's Organization Restructuring, Budgets Cuts, Performance Evaluation, Privatization, Target Monopolies, Trustbusting Industries, Financial Institutions, restructuring K Street, minimize Federal Government's involvement in Economy, Welfare, Healthcare, re-Institute Military Draft, CCC (Civilian Conservation Corps), leverage the Go Direct Model, Simplify and De-Scale

We also need to be more precise and Strategically target different segments (the groups that we've segmented in chapter 3, charts on page 42 & 68) with specifically designed Strategies for each.

Market Segment	Strategy	Tactics
Wall Street Suzerains, Tech Monopolies Moguls	Competition	Transparency, Trust-busting Monopolies, Industrial Insights, Expertise from Accountants, segregation of duties between & within organizations, personal fiduciary responsibilities for bankers, legal consequences for negligence, Governance & Compliance, Audits
Activists Judicial	Competition,	More Conservative Judges
Legislative Politicians, Professional Politicians both Deep State GOP and neo-Democrats	Competition, Collaboration later	Professional Journalism with Insightful coverage on issues, Shame Culture
Administrative Apparatchiks (Bureaucracy)	Competition, Collaboration later	Budgets Cuts, Audits, Organization Re-structuring, Privatization, Performance Review, legal consequences for negligence, Governance & Compliance, Eradicate & Uproot Strategy, minimal Federal Government presence
Media Celebrities, PC Gestapo	Competition, Collaboration later	Shame Culture, Eradicate & Uproot Strategy, Additional Competition, Trusting Busting Monopolies, additional licenses
Activists Corporations (501c3), Professional Politicians; Deep State GOP and neo-Democrats	Competition	IRS, remove their Charity Tax-exempt status, Audit, trace detailed funds flow & closely monitor sources of investment income, legal consequences for negligence, Eradicate & Uproot Strategy, minimal Federal Government involvement eliminates needs for Activists corporations
Academia & Students	Collaboration, Competition	Shame Culture, International Competition, Internet, Virtual Teachings, leverage Industrial, Business Leaders Insights, Eradicate & Uproot Strategy, Teach Real Values not self-justification for Greed and Sloth
Entertainment Celebrities	Collaboration	Gaia Equilibrium, Space Colonization within Solar System, Deep Space Exploration, Shame Culture

Market Segment	Strategy	Tactics
Internet News, Search Algorithms, Social Media Workers	Collaboration, Competition	Trusting-Busting Monopolies, International Competition, Shame Culture, remove snowflake intervention and leverage real independent AI logic and algorithms
Social Welfare Benefits	Collaboration	Work, CCC, Draft
Demographic Alteration	Collaboration	Work, CCC, Draft

Laissez-faire Free Market Capitalism (cont.)

We saw how the Capitalism Mechanism works in Chapter 4, saw its beginnings in our recent history from Medici family, Amsterdam Exchange in chapter 2, better understood Adam Smith's brilliance in describing 'the invisible hand' mechanism behind the Free Market, Perfect Competition Model of Capitalism.

We should remember that Monopoly is Not Capitalism, the Working Free Market Capitalism of Perfect Competition is the exact opposite of Monopoly. Corruption of Power that abuses Capitalism and prevents the Perfect Competition Ideal from being achieved or when achieved, from being sustained for any considerable time. Capitalism does NOT make the Rich Richer and Poor Poorer, Human Greed, the abuse of Power by the High, combined with the Ignorance of the Low, allows Income Inequality to happen. Only the Middle can check the High and the Free Market, Perfect Competition form of Capitalism helps them do exactly that, for Capitalism gives as much power into the hands of informed and reasoning individuals to check the corrupted and abusive High. Let's also review this similar concept from a bottom's up approach.

For an unemotional, un-bias and Independent view, let's use a typical Bell-shaped curve of Normal Distribution to represent the human population. Various Human traits and abilities would logically be spread out accordingly in a Normal Distribution (like the bell shaped curve as in chpt 7, page 220). If it is skewed for certain reasons, we can always investigate the reasons why

Now if we follow the logic that human abilities are spread similar to a normal distribution bell shape curve, then extending from that logic, if all gets rewarded fairly [corresponding to their ability per the Free Market] then the Middle working Class would still have a substantial portion of the society's wealth, purely because they constitute such a large segment of the total population. This is the case in America from 1940s – 1980s (Income Inequality Chart in chapter 7, when top decile (10%) of population holds less than 35% of wealth, It is currently now over 50%. Now you see the Rich (High)accumulating majority of wealth and the Low having the opposite end of the spectrum. This kind of distinctive skew instead of a continuous distribution demonstrates presence of Monopoly and barriers to entry. In a Free Market of perfect Competition, you'll not see such skewed wealth distribution. In fact, we tend to see the Worst Income Inequality in Less

Developed Countries, in Socialists and Communists countries (where Power is aggregated in hands of few and where NO Capitalist Free Markets exists). Thomas A. Bland in his 1881 book *The Reign of Monopoly*, explains the same concept as he argued for unhampered competition and a level playing field.

Free Market Perfect Competition form of Capitalism grows the Middle-class population which in turn keeps High and Powerful in check. The Middle-Class (bourgeoise) are the custodians of Ethos and Awful Virtues as they truly understand their value in checking the Corrupt and those in Power.

When there is Economic Growth, a full employment, artificial barriers removed and people are allowed to compete freely, the income distribution curve will assume a shape much more representative of the natural abilities and potential of people. Strangely, it is the greedy and ignorant "desire for all to be Equal" that allows Big Government bringing forth the rise of Monopoly of Power, Income Inequality.

Sadly, the Low are always playing accomplice to the Corrupt Top 1% Problem Profiteers in transforming Democracy into Big State Government as Power is consolidated, for they are either too ignorant (to comprehend), too slothful (to work for and earn what they desire), too egoistic (to be humble and learn), and too greedy with envy to demand Free Welfare, Free Healthcare, Free Education as their rights (you only need 1 negative trait to fail, they have many). And thus, the eternal struggle between the vicious cycles of Decadence against the virtuous cycles of Competition. It is the Values of Ethos, Awful Virtues that sustains and reinforces the Free Market Capitalism of Perfect competition, it's the missing link in the current crony capitalism system. Therefore to revive the Competitive workings of the Free Market Capitalism, this is the first place for us to start for the Economy to recover.

> *"the citizenry had experienced 'a deep feeling of unrest' over a kind of slavery that had nothing to do with race and plantations.... The slavery that would result from aggregations of capital in the hands of a few individuals and corporations controlling, for their own profit and advantage exclusively, the entire business of the country, including the production and sale of the necessities of life."*
>
> - Justice John Marshall Harlan, 1890

The Long and Arduous Uphill Fight Against Monopolies

Back in 1901, McClure and Tarbell were setting their sights to cover the Monopolies of the Trusts (eventually deciding on Standard Oil) when they felt that "the feeling of the common people had a sort of menace in it; they took a threatening attitude toward the trusts, and without much knowledge", so McClure's Magazine aim to give their readers a "clear and succinct notion of the process by which a particular industry passes from the control of the many to that of the few."

One wonder that if Tarbell had felt so much moral outrage at the Monopolies of the Trusts at turn of the last century, businesses that were delivering real goods and services [Steel, Oil, Meat products, railway services, etc.] to the American People at low prices, what would she think of the current Monopoly of the Mainstream Media & Internet Social Media that delivers virtual propaganda, mindless blather, wicked sophistries and empty P.C. rhetoric to the American Public now? One asks the questions along her same logic, isn't the monopoly of thoughts and ideas [form of mental slavery] much more dangerous as they are more subtle and less obvious?

Now over a century later, we again face Multiple Monopolies in a) Internet Tech Industry, b) Wall Street Financial Industry, c) Mainstream Media and Social Media all linked together by the incestuous relationship between the Activists Corporations and K Street's faceless bureaucrats. Let's start by addressing the Wall Street Monopolies, the Few that have become too Big to Fail, Too Rich and Corrupt to Jail.

Ethos and Awful Virtues – Wall Street and Tech Street Monopolies

In Nicomachean Ethics, Aristotle explained "Moral goodness is the result of habit," in Greek, the words for character and custom are the same, Ethos. Learning to be virtuous is not that hard, it's all a matter of practice and learning the habits that go with it. It does need to be constantly reinforced so that people take pleasure in doing the right thing and experience pain in doing bad things. From Aristotle we move forward to the 18th century Scotland, Francis Hutcheson's original notion of innate moral sense and the virtues of ancient Stoics, are both necessary to police the sometimes volatile frontiers of our dealings with others pointed out by Adam Smith as Awful Virtues.

Thus, Awful Virtues like Discipline, self-restraint, moral rectitude, righteous anger at wrongdoers are absolutely necessary to enable our civil society to function effectively, they are not virtues for virtues' sake but an integral and extremely crucial component of Democracy, as well as for Free Market Capitalism to function effectively and efficiently! If some selfish criminal starts to game the system, not playing by the rules (as Financial looters games the International Financial System and continues to do so), others all start clamoring to join in and the system stops working (as in Tragedy of the Commons, exploitation of Public Goods).

Thinking that he can outsmart the Free Market, Greenspan broke the Financial system by destroying Scarcity of Resources (with QEs), and the Free Market (turning Too Big to Fail Banks into Monopolies), we've inherited the inefficient crony capitalism which contributed largely to the stagnant economy, high unemployment and income inequality for last decade. Crony Capitalism needs to be addressed for the Free Market Capitalism to function properly, as long as the K Street Patrons are in cahoots with the Wall Street and Tech Street Clients, Capitalism cannot function efficiently, it would remained forever hobbled by such corruption; described pointedly as the Incestuous relationship between Patrons (Political leaders) and Clients (Industrialists) in Economies of Less Developed Nations - * George Rosen's Peasant Society in a Changing Economy, 1975.

Income Inequality, Stagnant Economy, Crony Capitalism all a result of Activist Groups pushing for more Welfare budgets, Global Warming Grants, Loans, etc. all these QEs, Pervasive Federal Intervention all cumulates to break the virtuous cycle of Free Market Capitalism, analogous to the life giving 'Distillation effects' of Water Cycle being broken.

The Top 1% Tax payers are NOT the Top 1% in wealth, the Wage earners and small Business owners' income are easy to track and thus they pay the most taxes to the government. The truly wealthy like the George Soros, Investment Banks, Funds Owners' wealth isn't in wages, much of their wealth might not even be in America. So in reality, the American tax system extracts wealth from America's Middle Working class, Main Street workers, this gets handed out as Federal Expenses over $ 3 Trillion per year and Feds' QE funds over $ 10 Trillion in last decade. All the QE monies gets into Wall Street and some into Tech Street, essentially into the hands of the Top 1% in wealth. The Federal Expenses gets handed out by K Street Apparatchiks to their buddies and cronies through Global Warming, Renewable Energy Grants, Loans, War on Poverty, Healthcare, Welfare Planned Parenthood, etc. expenses, so the Politicians both elected and non-elected get to join their sponsors, the Top 1% in wealth and increases their wealth in Wall Street Equities again.

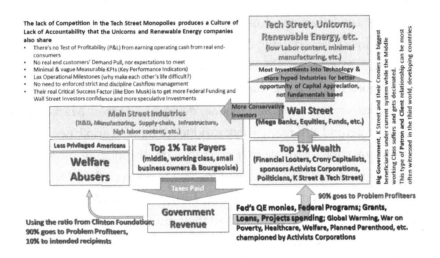

Only a small portion of Welfare actually reaches the less privileged Americans (intended beneficiaries), if we use the ratio in Clinton foundation, only 10% of all donations actually reach the intended recipients, 90% gets siphoned off. To make matters worse, there's now many Welfare Abusers who are literally stealing from the truly poor by competing for their welfare benefits.

The Crony Capitalism in Wall Street doesn't invest their ill-gotten gains back into Main Street Industries and thus the American Middle Class gets even poorer as factories close down and jobs gets lost to overseas, all this while continuing paying taxes to make the Top 1% in Wealth richer. The rampant proliferation of the Activists Corporations, since 2001 all lobbying for the annual $ 3 Trillion of Welfare, Healthcare, Global Warming, Planned Parenthood, Renewable Energy Grants, Loans, etc. is the best attestation of this cycle. Why does Wall Street Crony Capitalists Not invest in Main Street Industries' shares but in Tech street, Unicorns, renewable energy? Besides gaining influence over the Social Media's rhetoric, it's speculative Capital appreciation of hyped up technology shares that matters more than the real 'bricks and mortar' strong operating cash-flows but dull with little opportunity for massive price appreciation, thus momentum Trading easily trumps Fundamentals analysis in the world of Crony Capitalism.

Because the Culture of Monopoly will invariably become Culture of Decadence, expecting the Unicorns and Renewable Energy companies to produce any real breakthrough in real Technology is like pushing on a rope. Per all the factors listed on the top left-hand corner of the chart, one can predict the outcomes which we'll see examples of in the EV industry later. When President Kennedy gave his 'moon speech' in Sept 1962 till the actual moon landing in July 1969, it took less than 7 years for us to put a man on the moon. Vice President Al Gore released his movie about Global Warming in 2006, after over a decade of whining about Global Warming, with DOE invested Billions and Billions of Tax payers money later there's nothing to show in renewable energy technology except tons of worthless marketing reports and materials soliciting for more funds, movies for the snowflakes and impressionable to become Global Warming keyboard warriors [Gore has somehow coincidentally grown his personal wealth from that of a public servant to over quarter of a Billion dollars].

With our present-day state of the art technology and advances in know-how, the track record of the Global Warming and Renewable Energy Technology is truly pathetic! As a comparison in the same period, Steve Jobs released the 1st iPhone in June of 2007 by the time of his death in 2011 (slightly over 4 years), apple has released 5 versions of iPhone and 2 versions of iPad, Steve Jobs has made hundreds of Billions for the apple shareholders, introduced latest touchscreen technologies to the American Masses, created the smart-phone, devices and tablet Markets from nothing in span of 4 years, leaving behind still many more product designs in apple new product pipelines.

To address the crony capitalism, we will need to start introducing more transparency into the Wall Street "too big to fail Banks" and explore how to address the Monopolies, the conflict of interests between various Investment Banking, Insurance, Private Banking, Global Equity Funds, Pension Funds, Private Equity, etc. and all their multiple overlapping functions as a start. Insurance and Investment Banks activities need to be de-coupled. We do Not need more rules to regulate the Banks and Wall Street. We need insightful and meaningful rules that target the heart of the crimes, and also to increase the severity of the consequences with no sacred cows too rich to jail. Perhaps explore self-regulate as in Auditing, Medical profession? De-Scale the Monopoly Banks, minimize Federal Government's involvement, all the Industry to self-regulate for better governance to self the investors, All investors.

We need personal fiduciary duties and personal liabilities of all Bankers [personal accountability] to their clients and All shareholders or investors with serious legal consequences for negligence. We need to immediately start investigating any of Wall Street Suzerains for their possible financial support of the Activists Corporations linked with Global Terror Networks through detailed tracing of the funds flows of the 501c3 entities. The segregation of duties within the Banks' departments, between individuals to be strictly enforced with serious offenses leading to criminal penalties. Regular, frequent ad-Hoc Audits to be conducted by un-related Auditors, the Industries' expertise reside with the Accountants within the Industries not with the Financial Analysts in the Wall

Street Investment Banks or Funds. The Investment Houses cannot rely on their in-house Analysts or Compliance Officers as these are obvious Conflict of Interests stooges. The Bankers themselves will be 100% responsible (personally) for their investments with research from Industrial Accountants reports issued that's public information available to all. The Compliance Officers should also be from unrelated fields, frequently rotated, highly incentivized for uncovering crimes, not compensated for merely checking compliance to rules. Substance of Investigations take precedence over compliance to form. Personal Accountability needs to be introduced as these individuals had been enjoying highest Returns while taking on NO Risks (due to the Banking Monopolies), we need to re-introduce Market Competition and Risks back into the equation.

Trust-busting the 'too Big to Fail Banks' seriously explored and implemented in stages, to be clearly communicated ahead of time to maintain investors' confidence. Once the Wall Street Crony Capitalism is broken and only by addressing and fixing it can we again unleash the potential and energy of the American people and build a strong and vibrant American Economy once more.

Most Importantly, we need to allow the Wall Street [currently virtual] wealth to flow into the Main Street for real investments for the future; producing efficiency in the American labor force, unleashing the innovativeness and creativity of American People once again, thus translating into Real Wealth for all Americans including the Top 1%, a Win-Win Strategy for all. There needs to be a Pull, a Push and a Due Diligence process based on scarcity of financial resources [no more QEs] and returns on investments from Main Street Growth projects with disciplined Cash-Flow tracking.

Quick Summary

A Big Government involved in [trying to orchestrate] the economy and welfare is causing the American Economy to stagnate with languishing high unemployment. The inefficient Crony Capitalism of Capital allocation mechanism [benefitting only K Street apparatchiks and their lackeys, Wall Street Cronies and their creations Activists Corporations] creates the highest Income Inequality in America for over a century. Meanwhile Main Street America atrophies from lack of new investments from Wall Street speculative investors, while the Middle Working class continues to carry the bulk of the tax burden and thus gets crushed under the dual onslaught.

Meanwhile, the Tech street monopolies, Unicorns and Renewable Energy plays get bloated with speculative investments but fails to deliver any real technology breakthrough as their competitive strength (critical success factor) is not R&D, innovation nor manufacturing, but in Marketing and Selling their all-hype visions of the future to the impressionable and speculating fund managers, as well as obtaining Federal Funding (be they loans, grants, etc.) The Welfare Abusers pilfer from the Less privileged Americans and the vicious downward spiral continues year after year.

The only good news is that the virtual wealth is still in Wall Street as Global Investors still have confidence in America (relative to Europe and Asia Stock Markets), therefore we shall now explore how we shall proceed to release that wealth into Main Street, invest in the American worker, increase their efficiency, leverage their innovativeness and Make America Great Again.

Growth Culture, let Wall Street and Tech Street be enablers in support of Main Street

A Growth Culture needs growth to thrive, therefore we need large scale Research and Development, Manufacturing accompanied by Supply-chain and procurement Industries as we strive to grow Global Trade, exponentially increase America's Exports, build, repair and Expand America's Infrastructure. Extensive manufacturing in support of Space Exploration, Colonies on Moon & Mars, Projects of Gaia Equilibrium of sustainable long-term Energy Sources (in chapter 9). All these Projects will re-energize Main Street's factories and provide investments opportunities in companies like Boeing, Bechtel, Caterpillar, NASA and NASA related Technology companies, Northrop, Lockheed, Raytheon, General Dynamics, etc. and all their upstream and downstream companies. Think 10 – 30 times their current manufacturing capacities and another additional 10 – 50 times more for the related suppliers, logistics, R&D, technical services, maintenance, transportation, distribution and installation. This is the Pull.

Just imagine the demands of WWII had birth more than half million new businesses, GM alone had over 18,000 sub-contracting companies and Boeing had over 1400 subcontractors for just the B-29 project itself. If the half million new Industrial businesses merely hires 50 person per business, there would be 25 million more well paying jobs! With a major push into Space Colonization and Exploration, plus Infrastructure projects, America's MainStreet Economy would easily be back in Serious Major business!

The Technology segment will then need to support these real high demand and rigorous testing requirements instead of their current lax standards, new opportunities will open up for new upstarts and innovative competition will sprout up rising to these new challenges and demands. Now Wall Street will have many new Growth Opportunities to invest their funds. Now we'll see real Demand Pull to support our Strategic Visions and Projects. Government needs to be shrunk to a minimal skeletal existence and allow the Free Market to triumph and grow.

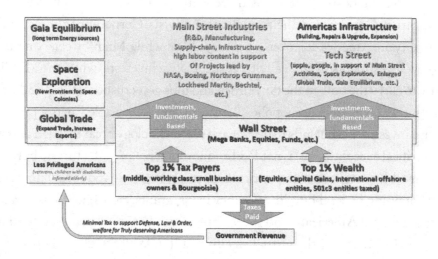

Welfare will only apply to handicapped children, infirmed elderly or Veterans that served this Great Nation, only those truly in need. We will have to eradicate the Welfare Abusers, the K Street bureaucrats, Activists Corporations and their lackeys. Wall Street will naturally become more integrated with Main Street over time as we start streamlining the mega-Banks into smaller and more Industry specialized banks that work directly with the Accountants inside the Industrial Companies such that the Investors now grasp insights into the operational strengths, KPI measurements of management and R&D technology, NPI Commercialization Milestones that decide the successful product launches.

The Tax mechanism has to extend to include the Super-Rich Top 1% in Wealth so that the Middle-Class and Ultra Rich fairly share the burden of Taxation. Income Tax burden should be reduced as we no longer need to feed the K Street Apparatchiks and their cronies, the Activists Corporations and their Lackeys. Main Street Investors together with Wall Street bankers should be making their returns under a healthy Capitalism system, subjected to a proper Risks and Rewards of the Free Market.

> *"Inherited from its Middle Eastern tribal roots, Islamic culture is a "shame culture." Psychiatrist Patricia A. Santy explains that shame cultures are essentially collectivist by nature, and individual behavior in such a culture is shaped by the external opinion of others rather than internal values. Under such a mind-set, whether a person is actually guilty of wrong doing is less important than whether a person appears to be guilty of wrong doing. The individual is focused on honor and shame generated by his reputation in the community rather than on personal feelings of guilt generated by violating internalized values. In a shame culture, if an individual knows he is guilty of wrongdoing but the fact is hidden from his community, his behavior is not affected because the external motivator of shame is not present. This stands in contrasts to the more individualistic mind-set of the West, which has been termed Guilt Culture, placing much greater emphasis on objective values such as truth, justice, and individual rights. In a guilt culture, one who knows he is guilty is expected to feel guilty and behave accordingly, even if he is the only one who knows it, because guilt is an internal motivator. Thus shame culture, by its nature, perpetuates certain behaviors that a guilt culture does not. In a shame culture, individuals are free to engage in wrong-doing as long as no one knows they have done so. They are encouraged to take any course of action necessary to avoid public shame, even if it requires secret wrongdoing, because the extrinsic value of honor is more important than intrinsic values of truth, justice, and whether one is actually guilty."*
>
> – Jay Sekulow, Unholy Alliance

Messaging - Competitive Strategies: Illuminating on the Shame Culture

Islamic Culture isn't the 'Shame Culture', rather it's the Progressives Liberals that is a Shame Culture as Guilt Culture needs the individuals to have internalized Values; of which the Progressives Liberals possess none as we'd witnessed in chapter 4. Thus, the only way that works with the Fascists neo-Democrats Liberals is Shame! We have to expose their lies and hypocrisies, we need to uproot and eradicate their entire sham once and for all, give no quarter as they will show us none. Remember their Shame Culture!

As we address the relationship between Wall Street, K Street, Tech Street and the Activists Corporations, we also have to illuminate and show the American people these incestuous, cancerous relationships. How these radical parasitic neo-Democrats' complete lack of 'Ideologies', hypocrisy of self-enrichment, coupled with the Deep State's hubris, Wall Street's Avarice has produced the toxic Crony Capitalism, Stagnant Economy and Highest Income Inequality!

The Messaging has to be clear concise and simple. What we had thought as self-evident truths in the past was apparently didn't work with many youths and snowflakes. So we must learn from the neo-Dems, they have been the wizards of Marketing. We need to setup mirrors of the neo-Dems' and the Activists Corporations' Marketing arms (sharing of Best Practices) and perhaps hire some of their Top Marketing Talent and learn from the Best! Unlike the past, we have to relentless in our Messaging, Shame Them, expose their lack of understanding of Global issues and Foreign Cultures, show the "globalist pimps" for what they really are.. Same as for their ignorance of Socialist Ideology and history, attack the "socialist pimps" for who they really are. In hope that as we shine light into the darkness, some Common Sense Person might see the light and choose to step out of the darkness and ignorance.

We have to leverage latest technology to increase the avenues of out-reach to all Americans. Stage Proper, intensive Debates and constructive Discussions on un-bias, independent platforms.

Learning from the neo-democrats, we Simplify the Messaging, attack and expose their hypocrisy tirelessly and most importantly, we show how the Financial Funding Networks Operate, follow the money, use the Audit and Financial trail to detect the 'conflict of interests' ill-gotten Payouts. We need to be able to verbalized the concept of ferreting out waste, fraud and abuse to afflict the comfortable and comfort the afflicted, the present American Leadership needs to understand their power and their responsibilities to explain an increasingly complex, often unfair and corrupt system. Even as more in-depth muckraking is needed to uncover the K Street, their cronies and Mainstream Media's Monopolies' unethical practices.

> *"Revolutions erupt when a variety of often different resentments merge to assault an unsuspecting regime. The broader the revolutionary coalition, the greater its ability to destroy existing patterns of authority. But the more sweeping the change, the more violence is needed to reconstruct authority,*

without which society will disintegrate. Reigns of terror are not an accident; they are inherent in the scope of revolution."

World Order in 2014 by Henry Kissinger about
the French Revolution started in 1789

Messaging: Violence is Not an Option, Acceptance & Empathy of Diversity

Per the earlier quotes from Kissinger, the Durants and Liddell, we need to continuously reinforce with all Americans that violence should never be an option. Acceptance of Diversity and Strategies to deal with resistance, more details in next chapter; the path to Compromise and Collaboration with fellow Americans with different ideologies. Not to forget the need Competition Strategies against the parasitic Eunuch Culture, reveal them for their lack of Values and expose their Decadence and Shame Culture

The Nexus - K Street and Activists Corporations

Awful Virtues; *Discipline, self-restraint, moral rectitude, righteous anger at wrongdoers*

Per Chart on M.O.B. Messaging per page 285, we can see that the Activists Corporations are the enablers, go-betweens Wall Street Suzerains, K Street Apparatchiks and Tech Street PC Globalists, you will note that the 501c3 Activists Corporations and the K Street Apparatchiks form the Nexus of the entire neo-Democrats P.C. ONE VIEW Big State Government setup, per the quote from George Rosen's Peasant Society, this is where the *Patron and Client relationships are held together like a tangled web and exactly where we need to Audit and review Internal Controls, Compliance and instill Corporate Governance Discipline. This is the Push.

* "…this incestuous relationship creates an oligarchy of political leaders and industrialists [includes Wall Street and Tech Street monopolies] who jointly control the political and industrial system [incl. Financial, Technology & Media]." As quoted in chapter 2

We'd seen how Billions of tax payers hard-earned money gets poured into "renewable energy" company Solyndra, Electric Vehicles (EV) companies like Fisker and A123 as subsidies, bad loans, etc. all to ending up bankrupt as technologies rights gets sold to China Companies. Yet President Obama's fund-raisers all benefitting big time from such spectacular failures of judgments. These 'climate-change' pimps are as bad as the Poverty Pimps, all needs to be investigated and brought before justice. The DOE projects and investments, loans, Grants and Funds should be intensively Audited by unrelated parties, all recipients of Grants, Federal Funding in any way shape or form would also be Audited with personal responsibilities, criminal liabilities for any individuals' breach, violations of any improper Use of Funds. Losses incurred for 'poor judgement in investments' will be deemed negligence and all liabilities to be shouldered by Federal employees and their associated cronies personally. Loans previously made will be recalled immediately without exceptions. All Personal and Family Wealth would be utilized to help reduce the losses for the DOE or any other Federal Departments. Audits will be retroactive without time limits, any 'poor judgement calls in investments', resulting in losses for the American Tax-Payers will be traced back to all employees remotely associated with these decisions regardless of whether they are still under employment or residence inside or outside of America. With determination, the Ugly Financial Networks of Funding the Dirty politicians by the Activists Corporations will be uncovered as sure as the sunrise tomorrow.

We need to constantly detect and disinfect America of the Globalists and Socialist Pimps Virus and scan for, plus delete the Virus of Climate-change Pimps and Poverty Pimps. We need to be vigilant and always protect America against Virus Threats and Infection.

We need Professionals to start tracing the funds of these Radical neo-fascists corporations. The George Soros Open Society, the Planned Parenthood Action Funds, the Federal Teachers Union, the Millennium Project Funds and connections with each other. They would all owed back-dated taxes to our IRS since their inception if we can prove that they never truly qualified as "charitable organizations" to begin with. These accounting and tax loop-holes needs to be closed and allowed only for their original purposes; eg. the hospitals, VAs. We need to audit and comb through all these 501c3 books for the last 2 - 3 decades and put the crooks behind bars for tax evasion. The financial assets re-possessed from these 501c3 can help the American people pay down the $20 Trillions of debt.

Most critically, Any criminal related, terrorists-related, drugs, narcotics-related activities uncovered in their funding or related investments, should allow the IRS to shut their organizations down immediately and arrest any responsible activist leaders reaping financial returns from such illegal investments. IRS should investigate deeply into these cash-rich 501c3 organizations, remove their tax-free status immediately and explore collecting back-dated taxes to the American People. All findings should be made public to the American people.

For dealings with the Terrorists, narcotics related activities would be construed as Treason, perhaps with possibility of Capital Punishment, only the Fear of Death will make the corrupt see the Virtues of Empathy and Respect for their fellow citizens (instead of calling them deplorables, loser). So Money-men, auditors better get to work for the American people quick, do your job you've been paid to do. Remember the wise words of B.H. Liddell Hart "The experience of history…. the downfall of civilized states tends to come not from the direct assaults of foes but from internal decay,…"

> *"A Ruler, any Ruler, must promote and defend the welfare of all those subject to his rule." William from Ockham inferred from Aristotle's Politics, "to understand this it must first be known that the power of making human laws and rights was first and principally in the people," Ockham wrote in 1328, "and hence the people transferred the power of making the law to the emperor," or whomever they choose to exercise authority over them. All mortals who are born free have the power voluntarily to put a ruler over*

themselves, including the Church and the pope. But the final power remained with the people. So having put the pope in office, the people were now free to end "his raging tyranny over the faithful" and push him out.

The Cave and the Light – Arthur Herman

Ockham's Razor – K Street Apparatchiks & Bureaucrats

The concept behind Ockham's Razor is to remove any redundancy, we can leverage this simple but effective idea in re-structuring as well as the 'Go Direct' Model (made popular by Dell in late 90s). The K Street Administrative Apparatchiks in DC, beset by Monopoly Cultures of Decadence and subpar performance, with incompetence becoming common occurrence needs to be addressed. In addition, the Federal Government needs to be culled back significantly to allow the healthy growth of American Economy and Free Market Capitalism to triumph through massive Privatization initiatives (as Thatcher did for UK in the 80s).

To kill two birds with one stone, we just need to remove the Incompetent and Corrupt, introduce a little Free Market Competition, Performance Review, Peer appraisals, Budget Cuts and organizational Re-structuring to the Administrative Apparatchiks. On the surface, this might seem the simplest and 'controllable' solutions (since they are under the leadership of the new administration), we just need to hire new and better employees and remove the bottom 20% for next 3 years, after which remove the bottom 10% as an on-going practice. With Budget cuts, they would also be Great Costs Savings opportunities as we had already discussed in chapter 7.

There's a big catch, they will be most stubborn group digging in as they have the largest conflict of interests, Who moved my cheese? scenario here. See the Comey case's fall-out? Simple case of Incompetency twisted by the MOB into Special consul Investigation when blatant 'conflict of interests' motivated setup of personal email server which resulted in compromised National Security and loss of Human Lives received absolutely NO Media Coverage by the MOB.

We understand the Need to import a totally new Culture of Growth and Excellence into these Apparatchiks, question is how?

Below is a short extract of speech Dr Goh KS gave to the Officers of Army when setting up the (Israelites assisted) Singapore Armed Forces in 1967;

> *"...Self-deception .. we are given to wishful thinking and believe what is comforting, ... we prefer to be lazy than to work. When such an attitude prevails in an organization. Reports upwards tend to be more positive than situation warrants; so that "everyone can sit back and have a grand time, instead of picking faults, stirring trouble and being nasty to everybody". Finally, incompetence in any organization, encourages self-deception, and the only way to cure this condition is to remove the incumbents. However, when incompetence exists at the top, "removal takes place only as a result of Defeat"*

Values flows Tops down, never bottoms up, to drive change, the Top leader of the organization must change, the new administration has also provided that opportunity of new leaders (many unrelated to the K Street, Great News!). Hopefully, Substantial Budget Cuts will help the new Leaders to drive the much needed Cultural Change as well as create a sense of crisis in the K Street Bureaucracy (that's been decaying and festering in last quarter of century) and also produced a balanced Federal Budget in over 2 decades too. The new Leaders need to zealously drive Cultural Change in the entire Departments, Culture of Competition and Excellence. Frequently Performance Reviews. The Ethical Malaise and Putrefaction in the Federal Government can only be removed by removing All their 'senior leaders', there is no other way as the corruption has been internalized in them over the last 2 decades besides their rational reason to maintain the status quo.

The new Leaders really need to 'roll up their sleeves' (they need to be High Energy and do all the 'heavy lifting' themselves) and learn, know the detailed operations in their departments, only then they understand which activities and projects are of Value to American people, once the new Leader understand all the details and now able to re-prioritize, 80% of all department's (mindless bureaucratic) activities has to end. Keep the operational level staff but redeploy them to new projects, new areas of focus. The 3 immediate layers reporting to the new Leader should be re-structured as that's where all the last 25 years of Decadence Values reside (they were all promoted for exhibiting the undesired corrupted, incompetent and Compliant Values).

It is self-evident that these parasites all need to be re-structured immediately. And if they wish to, they should be allowed to assist in the Audits, to negotiate amnesty for admission of guilt or applauded and rewarded for whistle blowing.

Efficient Bureaucracy, The Gold Standard of Public Service

What is Efficient Bureaucracy, Science of Legislature? What constitutes the Gold Standard of Public Services? The Founding Leaders of America, Lincoln's team through the Civil War, the Scottish Civil Servants under the British Crown in 18th and 19th Centuries, the British Navy from 16th – 19th Century, the Meiji Restoration late 19th century in Japan, the Janissaries that served the Ottomans 14th – 16th centuries, Mamluks leaders of Egypt 13th – 14th Century; only army to defeat the Mongols in 1260 AD at Ayn Jalut, the English Court serving Queen Elizabeth in 16th Century, the British Parliament 18th – 19th centuries, the Legalists serving the Qin Emperors (from 3rd – 2nd century BC) leading to the eventual Unification of China, first generation leaders of Independent Singapore from 60s – mid 80s, Israel's leaders from 40s – 80s, are a few examples, the Mongol administrative in 12 – 13th Century was powerful too later adopted by the three Islamic Empires, Ottomans, Mughals in India and Safavids in Persia.

Let's explore common trends in all these diverse administrations spanning over geography, culture and time. Also we should remind ourselves it is the administrative teams' traits, not the Ruling Class, neither should we get distracted and overly focus on the Individual Leaders' personal traits. All Values of Leadership and Culture of Growth, Excellence still apply, but these conditions are additional requisites for the small admin group that wielded power yet remain uncorrupted custodians, I would propose the following:

Strong Sense of Asabiyyah,

Group, National Identity, you'll see these Alignment of personal interests with that of the group in all instances we shared above. When one is part of such company, its great of honor and pride with sense of purpose. During the Scottish Enlightenment, many Scots referred themselves as North British.

Sense of Crisis

Perception of External Threat to group, American Revolution, Meiji Restoration - Japan, British as Island States, Qin within the warring States, Singapore after Independence, Israel's leaders after its modern day formation after WW II, the Mamluks & Janissaries all started as slave soldiers, etc. all with deep sense of crisis, ever vigilant mindset.

No sense of Entitlement of Power (to hold power for power's sake)

In most cases above, as these leaders are NOT from aristocracy (born into the Ruling Class), here their relationships within the cohort is good enough to achieve greatness for the Nation's interests but not sufficient to replace the ruling class. They understand that they wield power to serve and better the lives they are responsible for; with great powers come great responsibilities.

Leaders of Convictions and Personal Belief in their destiny to shape History

Proven themselves time and again, constantly learning and acquiring new skills, Huge opportunity Costs to serve group; alternatives would be highly lucrative. Understands Integrity, Made personal sacrifices and knows failures, as differentiated from 'talented one trick ponies' using office to get rich and powerful. *Strong Alignment of personal agenda* with the Nation's (Group's) agenda.

This last point is critical as roots of corruption starts when the personal agenda of the custodians of power is NOT aligned with the Group's. They naturally start to put their personal agenda first, abuse of power for personal wealth, influence, quality of life, etc. comes naturally. Self-justifying that they've earned these 'perks of office', feeling sense of entitlement. Ego and mental sloth will extinguish any hopes of them learning new skills and the 'one trick ponies' will apply the only skill they know to all challenges faced by the Group leading to failures and eventual decline of the group (as noted by Ibn Khaldun *in Al-Maqaddimah*)

Such rare Alignment of agendas; between the custodians of Power and that of the group, translating into great successes in human Civilization's history didn't happen through mere coincidence. Conjunctures of so many qualities in leadership didn't happen randomly either. Common

Values and Beliefs shape the Alignment, that alignment coupled with Culture of Growth and Meritocracy distills out the finest qualities in their leadership. When the Leadership exudes these Values, it becomes a virtuous cycle. Take out Values, Virtues and the cycle breaks. Now we've seen the traits of successful Civil Service, let's review our K Street Cronies attributes, do they share any of those we had just discussed?

Sadly, the answer is none, let's understand one trait at a time. Asabiyyah? No, the P.C. Message is Globalists which means no American Patriotism. Sense of Crisis? None, since external threat disappeared at end of Cold War, plus we are Globalists so no external threat, also no threat to their jobs either. Sense of Entitlement? Yes, they've earned these 'perks of office', no threat to their jobs for last 3 decades, they are entitled to hold office and enjoy the 'perks' and doing whatever they deem fit setting their own deliverables and schedules for last quarter of decade as elected officials come and go (Clinton couldn't be bothered with details and enjoying his personal life, Bush too Low Processing to compute anything and distracted by Nation Building in Iraq, Obama too busy with Globalists, Socialists Activists rhetoric and spreading divisive Racists, sexists, anti-American slogans to care).

Lastly, with no competition, no clear deliverables, no sense of crisis in their bureaucratic roles with many 'deserved perks', what would you expect to find in K Street except a complete bunch of incompetent buffoons with huge Egos and Great Sense of Entitlement to Power and their 'deserved perks'? that's why the Razor of Re-structuring is long over-due after 3 decades of Decay. Per the Complexity Theory we'd discussed earlier, this is the most Ideal case for Descaling [simplification] and also case for smaller components too; Deep cut-backs in entire Deep State and every single Department.

Besides the Privatization Strategy, the reduction in Federal Government's powers and responsibilities to be transferred into the State Level and municipal level. Bulk of all Education, Healthcare, Transport, Police and Courts should be at the State Level to drive better accountability and quality of service. The States should have more autonomy and history has shown us that Best Practice is Army, Finances and Foreign Policies stay at Federal Level, all else should be at State level or lower still whenever possible.

> *"The only proper functions of a government are: the police, to protect you from criminals; the army, to protect you from foreign invaders; and the courts, to protect your property and contracts from breach or fraud by others, and to settle disputes by rational rules, according to objective law."*
>
> - Ayn Rand

Joseph A Tainter; Inputs increase exponentially with the scale of civilization, Outputs of civilization and governments decline per unit of input when measured in terms of public goods and services provided.

[kleptocrats become] Rent Seeking, [self enriching] accumulation of wealth through non productive means. [translates to] Law of Diminishing Returns [for the society]. When society offers its masses negative returns on inputs, those masses opt out of society, thereby destabilizing it

Quick Summary

Keeping the Military to protect Americans, and a minimal Welfare for the truly needy as we'd explained. All other K Street should be reduced to skeletal or eliminated altogether. The Economy without K Street's Crony Capitalism will recover and Middle Class will expand and Income Inequality shrink to the great post war days. If we are successful in making real progress, this is What American Economy would look like with Crony Capitalism, K Street and Activist Interests Corporations all systematically addressed.

For the American Dream to be realized once again, the vibrancy in American Economy to thrive and grow, the professional Deep State politicians in K Street and the Activists Corporations need to be descaled big time, their very existence speaks to the dysfunctional and parasitic causes of a society in decline. These Activists are NO Social Workers, they are professional Problem Profiteers diverting wealth from the working middle class Americans into the pockets of the top 1% that sponsors the Activists and influences the Deep State Politicians. As for the shallow ignorant social justice warrior [not personally benefitting in wealth nor benefits except satisfying their egoistic ignorant self-esteem], they need to understand the social consciousness is not activism of mass movements, as civic virtue is a mirage unless anchored in the inner virtue of each individual citizen. Texting and Posting on social media is nothing more than applying emotional liniments for one's personal ego, life experiences teaches us that Virtues and Great Values can only be forged through hardship. Talk is Cheap

> *"When you see that in order to produce, you need to obtain permission from men who produce nothing - when you see money flowing to those who deal, not in goods, but in favors - when you see that men get richer by graft and pull than by work, and your laws don't protect you against them, but protect them against you - when you see corruption being rewarded and honesty becoming a self-sacrifice - you may know that your society is doomed."*
>
> - Ayn Rand, Atlas Shrugged (1957)

"Fondly do we hope, fervently do we pray, that this mighty scourge of war may speedily pass away. Yet, if God wills that it continue until all the wealth piled by the bondsman's two hundred and fifty years of unrequited toil shall be sunk, and until every drop of blood drawn with the lash shall be paid by another drawn with the sword, as was said three thousand years ago, so still it must be said "the judgments of the Lord are true and righteous altogether. With malice toward none, with charity for all, with firmness in the right as God gives us to see the right, let us strive on to finish the work we are in, to bind up the nation's wounds, to care for him who shall have borne the battle and for his widow and his orphan, to do all which may achieve and cherish a just and lasting peace among ourselves and with all nations."

President Abraham Lincoln, Second Inaugural Address, 1865

As the last American Civil draws to a close, President Lincoln made his second inaugural address on a Saturday, 4th March, 1865, just over a month later, he was assassinated. Yet after over 150 years, he still has much to teach us. It is not with Malice that we seek to overcome our opponents in this Civil War, it is "with firmness in the right as God gives us to see the right", it is the Right thing to do.

"One-eighth of the whole population were colored slaves, not distributed generally over the Union, but localized in the southern part of it. These slaves constituted a peculiar and powerful interest. All knew that this interest was somehow the cause of the war. To strengthen, perpetuate, and extend this interest was the object for which the insurgents would rend the Union even by war, while the Government claimed no right to do more than to restrict the territorial enlargement of it"

Just as it was the right thing to do to abolish slavery in the last Civil War, it is also the right thing to do to defend individual freedom, to fight for Freedom of ideas, diverse ideas, our belief in human potential and excellence. It is the right thing to do to overcome the oppression of the "Politically Correct ONE view of the World" Gestapos, to overcome those that seek to injure us, hurt our Ideals and our country. Once again, we have been called to Free the Slaves; slaves of Ignorant and Want.

"We think no disinterested mind can survey the period in question without being inevitably driven to the conclusion that the very genius for commercial development and organization, which it would seem was manifested from the beginning, soon begat an interest and purpose to exclude others. The desire to dominate the industry, was frequently manifested by actions and dealings wholly inconsistent with the theory that they were made with the

single conception of advancing the development of business power by usual methods, but which, on the contrary, necessarily involved the intent to drive others from the field and exclude them from their rights to trade and thus accomplish the mastery which was the end in view"

- Chief Justice Edward White, 1911

"No man chooses evil because it is evil; he only mistakes it for happiness, the good he seeks."

– Mary Wollstonecraft

Freeing the Slaves of Ignorant and Want – Mainstream Media and Internet Social Media

Quoting Walter Lippmann in his book *Drift and Mastery*, "..The law may not have realized this, but the fact is being accomplished, and it's a fact grounded deeper than statutes." Similarly, we now have a situation of Extreme Monopoly in the Social Media and Mainstream Media merged into one.

From Steve Weinberg's book *Taking on the Trust*, as those "…Standing in the vanguard of those documenting the societal shifts. Recognizing the unrest and the yearning of the exploited for clamps on Political and Financial Greed, …" All Americans with Common Sense, have duties to understand the challenges created by the Mainstream Media & Social Media, to help spread explanations and insights to dispel the corrupting ignorance. Monopolies cultures that stifles competition and growth of the American economy that needs to be addressed. We saw the damaging effects of MOB on the Crazed Hysteria of neo-Fascists Liberals and misguided Snowflakes, its incessant fanning the flames of Hate and Divisiveness in this nation.

How to address the Mainstream Mass Media and IT Monopolies Giants stirring up Radical Liberals and the brainwashing by the P.C. Gestapo? The News and Information Technology, Social Medias all started to merge together in Jan 2000 with the Time Warner and AOL deal. This colliding of two giant Industry has killed off most of the smaller outfits and thus losing much of the diversity in ideas, views and opinions. The few large Monopolies that emerged from the collision also prevented the growth of new startups (real ones that makes money from real paying customers, not the 'unicorn startups' raised on the Wall Street crony capitalists' greed and speculation), thus stifling job creation and Industries growth. The result is obvious in the stagnation of both Industries.

We've seen how the Wall Street crony Capitalism has capped the growth of all Industries in America as the Free Market Competition of Capital hasn't been working right for the last 2 decades. Therefore, in addition to Trust-busting (following in the footsteps of President Theodore Roosevelt) of the Wall-Street Mega "too big to fail" Banks, we also have to use Ockham's razor on the Mainstream Media, to slice into shreds the Monopoly that is Temple of the *Anomic Man; present is ALL, with no past and no future.

We will also expose the IT Monopolies Giants to greater competition (eg. Multi-Billion dollar

Social Media Giant FB, since its founding 13 years ago, the experience is essentially the same, other than adding a couple of minor bells and whistles) and transform the decadent Monopolies into young smaller companies with diverse ideas and insights. Most importantly, besides breaking the Monopolies, the free market has to offer financial incentives to new competitors, the new comers need to be able to start sharing the extra-ordinary profits enjoyed at present by the monopolies, the corrupted Media Celebrities need to compete for their obscene multi-million paychecks (as News broadcasters?). Only the profit cycle will ensure the growth of new competition becomes sustainable.

Logically, the current technologies like Social Media should allow self-broadcasts and the proliferation of numerous start-ups, the very fact we don't see new CNNs, MSNBCs, NBCs in recent years is self-evident of the technologies has been hijacked by the powerful Tech Monopolies and turned into M.O.B. aiding the Politically Correct Gestapos.

Not only has the diversity of ideas been whittled out, the quality and standard of output has plummeted into nothing more than crass entertainment. Sophistication and Class declines without passion in their work, just a sense of entitlement for their fat paychecks. This type of degenerated culture of indolence would probably remind Ida Tarbell of the Monopolies or Trusts that she was writing about and helped bring about the anti-trusts laws against.

Tarbell's philosophy of biography "one should start by wiping out of his mind all that he knows about the man, start as if you had never before heard of him,.. everything then is fresh, new. Your mind feeding on this fresh material, sees things in a new way." She understood that every person is complex – not all good, not all bad.

In her letters to the Confederate Soldiers to better understand and incorporate their insights about the Civil War in her work on Lincoln's Biography, "I have been deeply interested in the condition…. Which the disbanding Confederates found themselves[in] at the close of the war, and in their struggles to start in life and to build up the south again… my whole object is to call attention more forcibly than ever been done to the fine heroism of the Southerner in building up the South after the war." From the two instances, one can see the intense professionalism, reality based logic and perspective she adopts. Unlike theses current crazed Radicals Mainstream Media insisting current elected administration is Hitler and destroying Confederates Statues. Less than 30 after the Civil War, America has started to heal with both sides accepting the past reality and facing the future as one country together.

At present, with the never-ending provocation of the Poverty-Pimps Mainstream Media to stir up fanatical riots and Blind Hate, their victims remain trapped in Poverty, still trapped in Purgatory of Hatred, over 50 years after Rev Martin Luther King Jr. Momentous Victory in the Civil Rights Movement, 150 years after the ratification of the thirteenth amendment. Thanks to the relentless race baiting efforts of the ex-slave Owners, their ghosts never going away, forever staying within the Democrat party and still exploiting their ex-Slaves' descendants after all these decades.

Using the Ockham's Razor, we need to have open and Free Market Competition again in the IT Technologies Industries and Cable News Media Networks. Offer Go-Direct Communication

Models to the American public. Break current Monopolies with large number of new entrants into the industry including JVs (Joint Ventures) with any foreign media players (China, India, Commonwealth countries, Dutch, Eastern Europe, Latin America countries).

The slothful pretenders of journalists, unworthy 'successors' to the muckrakers, sycophant grammarians should be revealed as nothing more than the Entertainment Celebrities that they are. These egoistic rootless, parvenus with their hubris should now be subjected to International and Domestic Competition as we all know Monopolies naturally sprout Cultures of Decadence, they kill off new competition and new Ideas which are the very basis of new Growth for America.

> *"If you pursue evil with pleasure, the pleasure passes away and the evil remains; if you pursue good with labor, the labor passes away but the good remains."*
>
> - Marcus Tullius Cicero

> *"A man who views the world the same at fifty as he did at twenty has wasted thirty years of his life."*
>
> - Muhammad Ali

Let the Narcissistic Anomic Entertainers entertain us with their Ignorance

The Job of Hollywood Entertainers is to entertain the American and Global Audience, for their talents they receive a nice and healthy payout. Sadly, that was the vintage Hollywood of yester-years. Over time due to lack of competition, the Culture of Decadence has set in, causing creative passion to die and quality of end product has plunged. The Mediocre starts passing off as talent, the Monopoly Industry with its High barriers to entry, has enabled the same incompetents to reap obscene payouts with no correlation to any value added nor contribution to the society.

This Monopoly Culture also explains why the Hollywood culture is so cliquish, for their 'acting skills' are subjective, the obedient mediocre gets groomed into super stars in this culture of Lowliness. To provide competition in the Entertainment Industry, the current CGI technology could be made available to new 'Self-Directors', such that Americans with good ideas and concepts can make short movies and enter into the market, making profits for themselves and introduce diversity of ideas into the market which hopefully gets picked up by the 'lack of new ideas' followers (aka monopolies)

The current Hollywood's crazy payouts, media attention and 'star power' also has another effect, it corrupts the celebrities and blows their narcissistic egos out of proportion into believing they know enough to make comments about world affairs or the economy, etc. The Media hype also brainwashes their impressionable anomic movie fans into mindless worshipers of the ignorant. We'll explore more of the decline in standards and quality of Hollywood's productions in next chapter.

There's a favorite quote used often by Hillary's campaign as well as the mainstream Media that President Trump's supporters are mostly non-college graduates. This is very interesting behavior is very telling on the mainstream Media's psyche that despises those they deem to be 'inferior' to themselves. We know that the Polling process is defective and depending the person performing the polls, it can be skewed to be as bias as intended so the results obtained about non-college supporters are essentially pretty meaningless. Yet, the comments reveal more insights to us about those clowns quoting it.

First, anyone who's been to college intuitively understands it is merely a conforming routine, rather than any great intellectual exercise requiring special cognitive capabilities. Any intelligent humans can understand the material (those of any real use) in colleges can be easily self-learned, the professors or teachers are merely facilitators (Jobs and Gates as college drop-outs clearly understood that). Only the mediocre that struggled through their studies and 'barely made it' (only they themselves know how much intellectual effort they had to exert) will proudly and loudly self-proclaim to be college grads, because if one found the effort to be easy, they would Not claim it as a batch of honor, right? We'd had already understood from earlier chapters, being indoctrinated is nothing more than being conditioned to repeat standard model answers as many animals, birds can also be trained and conditioned to do.

Secondly, making such quotes about non-college supporters is essentially applying the same logic of stereotyping as racism or sexism, trying to imply that non-college grads are less intelligent than college grads. This kind of shallow and stupid comments are made only by racists and sexists people. Thirdly, unless you are a young graduate with No work experience then the act of graduating college would be your latest achievement right? for Most Graduates, graduating from college would have been a past event superseded since then by numerous acts of accomplishments since then, any honest high achievers would be constantly pushing themselves without ever stopping, thus their last accomplishments (known only to themselves) of overcoming great challenges to learn new skills, to close a complex deal, to cross the finishing line of running a marathon, etc. should be a rather recent event [maybe in last 6 months?], which clown would still be talking about their college graduation unless that was their peak accomplishment in their lives?

To peak in your early 20s? those low achievers definitely share much in common with the Media and Entertainment Celebrities, not that they are College Graduates but that they worship Youth as that was the Best and peak times in their lives, see the likes of irrelevant celebrities like Madonna, Ashley Judd, whole bunch that I don't know how to spell their names. They have not learned any new tricks since their 20s.

If they had kept their mouths shut, some might still have remembered them in their heydays, but just as the Crow opening its mouth and losing its meal to the Fox [Aesop Fables], these old irrelevant Celebrities had to open their ugly big mouths and reveal their pathetic lack of Values, Intellect and Understanding for the Whole World to see. As Mainstream Media Narcissus continues to stare piteously at its own reflection of self-made fabricated 'fake news', only the snowflakes Echo repeats the mindless blather, meanwhile the real world moves on. Google the interesting fate of Echo and Narcissus.

"The whole problem with the world is that fools and fanatics are always so certain of themselves, and wiser people so full of doubts."

- Bertrand Russell

"What is tolerance? It is the consequence of humanity. We are all formed of frailty and error; let us pardon reciprocally each other's folly – that is the first law of nature."

- Voltaire

Monopoly in Academia

The Monopoly Cultures of Decadence and subpar performance in the Academia, incompetence becoming common occurrence, is becoming increasing obvious with the defective end products produced by them. We need to introduce a little Free Market Competition to showcase the standard of Excellence as result of real Diversity (not some 'slogan chanting' feeble-minded progressives' version of diversity). There may be many schools but only a single school of thought. We need more online sharing of real intellectual content, virtual learnings as well as International competitions with India's and China's best brains to demonstrates the atrophied academia as they truly have become. Global Virtual Schooling should be encouraged to share overseas experience and International culture.

First and most important, the costs of college fees has to become more affordable, Competition and Diversity from Virtual Schools' curriculum be supported. International Competition from China, India, Bangladesh, etc. will demonstrate the intellectual abundance other countries and the pathetic state of Uniformity of Ideas in America's Academia. Competition will bring the costs down.

Scoring distinctions in Numeracy subjects should become compulsory for entry into colleges regardless of subsequent courses applied for as Numeracy is fundamental to literacy. Excelling in Foreign languages, mathematics, philosophies encouraged as Best Practices.

The community and Academia to become closer such that the students do not get indoctrinated into mindless serfs which would take them decades to recover, by then we would have lost the opportunities for their creativeness and diverse ideas during their prime years. College professors to do community outreach work and parents to audit university classes were best practices during the Age of Scottish Enlightenment

Business Leaders and Industrial Experts to speak at and lecture in Colleges. Bringing together the Industries and Academia is important as Industries merely doing without thinking is like going in a straight line and Academia thinking without doing is like Paralysis from Analysis going around in a circle. Coming together allows the discussion about the challenges faced in real world of Industries and allow for breakthroughs into new platforms or creation of new Industries giving us the Spiral effect (combination of straight line and circular motions). End users Industries to have input into the process, encourage Industries Leaders to give part-time lectures, more interactions, more dynamism, reduce the 'pure academia' with NO work experience by 50%. More Practicing Professionals; Doctors, Engineers, Accountants, Lawyers, Auditors, etc. from the Industries, less academic babbling.

We have to teach Awful Virtues like Discipline, self-restraint, moral rectitude, righteous anger at wrongdoers. Teach Values of Accountability, Meritocracy, Culture of Excellence, Honor, Self-Sacrifice, Endurance, Personal Responsibilities, self-restraint, discipline, Valor, will power, etc. in Schools and Academia. We need to Teach real Values, not self-justification for Greed and Sloth like Healthcare, welfare as Rights.

Through schools, we have to alter the national ethos of hard-work, demand for a level playing field, unhampered competition to minimize inequalities among individuals. The Academia needs to stop encouraging the Disgusting Greed and Sloth of snowflakes that shamelessly demand to be given Welfare, Healthcare, College Education as rights and justifying free hand-outs. Kids need not pay into the $ 38B Endowment Funds of Harvard just to learn Greed and Sloth, any bozo can learn them without any help and also constantly lie to cover up their true intentions, as President Obama has demonstrated so elegantly.

> *"With malice toward none, with charity for all, with firmness in the right as God gives us to see the right, let us strive on to finish the work we are in, to bind up the nation's wounds, to care for him who shall have borne the battle and for his widow and his orphan, to do all which may achieve and cherish a just and lasting peace among ourselves and with all nations."*
>
> President Abraham Lincoln, Second Inaugural Address, 1865

Make America Great again, Mutual Collaboration for Growth

Growth will be the most Important Element to Making America Great again. The entire next chapter will be discussing Growth for America and the World. Here we'll explore some of the future collaborative efforts to make this country great again. Growth with diligent practice of the right Values of Ethos and Awful Virtues. Driving Growth with the Go-Direct Model, NO parasitic intermediaries' self-enriching Pimps, Please!

Education, Housing and Urban Development

Building Communities with Great Futures for the American families, we touched on this topic in chapter 7. As we increase our acknowledgement of the African American past and present contributions to our country and promoting Traditional American Values at the same time, let us seek help from the influential African American sportsmen and women to help promote the causes. Let's all work together to help promote and build a better future for American families together with the local community leaders, and religious leaders too. Let's go direct and roll-up our sleeves (The divisiveness needs to stop, we promote a great future for all Americans as the common goal). As we gain momentum and get returns, we need to start to show-case the progress in Education and HUD and Share with the American Public. Acknowledge the leadership and help from all sides of the American communities. Show the success of collaboration in Education and HUD.

Social Welfare Collaboration

Civilian Conservation Corps to address the Infrastructural upgrade of America, which should be able to create many job opportunities and relieve the need for social welfare. Also change the welfare policies into a phrase-out mode, all welfare programs have a limited time element from 3 months to max of 6 months (time limit). Any individual welfare recipient that needs welfare after 6 months would need the personal review and approval of the State Governor (who would only have a quota of 50 per year). Get to work, get off welfare! We need to better leverage all this untapped energy and wasted human potential.

We have between a third to 40% of Americans on welfare, this is a huge burden and liability to this country, which is dying from carrying this awful and unnecessary load. Everybody has to add Value to this country, that's the only way the country can grow and become stronger, if anyone subtracts from the country, the terminology is Parasitic. If there are more parasites than the host (America) can bear, the host will die (this is just nature), > 30% is pretty near the limit. Can you imagine a patient with 30% cancer cells in his/her body? The end must be pretty near. If you reward a particular behavior, you'll get more of it. The exceptions for welfare should be made for Veteran Affairs (ex-military), Children born with disabilities, the Disabled charity hospitals. The able should be working and proud of a job well done and earning a honest pay check!

Collaboration in Demographic Alteration

Except for a small portion that is in the Drug and Narcotics trade, we assume (until proven otherwise) that most of the 'undocumented' Illegal Immigrants in America are hardworking folks providing a better life for their families. As long as they are working and paying taxes (and not here on our welfare benefits), we should a) start a process of bringing them from 'undocumented' to 'documented'. Start to understand the number of people we are talking about (we cannot design a solution until we know the extent of the challenge), b) setting up a path to legalization of their status here (obviously, they must add value to this society as in above mentioned). They must serve the country as we all do.

In addition, America has to exponentially bring in brain power to support the Space Exploration and Colonization efforts. Immigrants from India, Eastern Europe with the desired Values of competition, intellectual prowess to bring this country to the next level as the 'damaged snowflakes' recover from their mind damage.

Return of the King, Upgrading the Internet News, Searches, Social Media

Wall Street Too Big to Fail Investor Institution needs to be addressed. Then we start Collaboration with the Technology workers, here we need real leadership for the Technology Industry. Since the last great visionary of technology Steve Jobs passed away in 2011, the information technologies industries have been left in the hands of the Stewards of Silicon Valley.

Remember we'd remarked about Facebook earlier? Since FB was founded in 2004, it was an interesting idea (I started my FB account in early 2006), the experience of the users has stayed more or less similar. Yes, the base of users has increased tremendously so we can interact with many more of our friends. Some additional bells and whistles functions that facilitates sharing of videos, larger cache of pictures, forming collages, emojis, etc. After over 13 years (which in technology time, should be a minimum of 3-4 generations later), where is the Virtual Reality Version of FB? We should access our FB account with VR technology and be able to construct personalized VR homes in FB. Why can't we have VR space/locations recreated from our real life travels pictures such that we can share these VR experiences (from Petra, Angkor Wat, Machu Picchu, Angel Falls, Santorini, etc.) with our friends, and also be able to enter into their VR world (just as we share pics and videos)? Why can't we have VR versions of chat-interactions with our friends as we have chat groups, why can't we have VR groups where we can see each other in VR settings that we choose and have preference for? Let's meet up in Triton, Neptune or perhaps Ancient Rome? Let's have a meeting in VR world of Europa, Jupiter or Titan, Saturn? We'll discuss more of this new chapter in American Order & a Better World for All. Needless to say, there are many more opportunities to dream and create into reality.

Artificial Intelligence also has huge potential if we can link more substantive projects like Space Exploration and Colonization where we can harness the ability A.I. to work over timeframes not possible for humans in space [eg. near light speed space travel, over many centuries in space] or in hazardous environments [surface of Venus, Saturn, etc.] where machines can be sent in place of humans. We'll discuss more about A.I. in next chapter including the current short coming of lack of competition, lack of imagination, inability to self-upgrade or self-program after new experiences.

Only the Visionary Founders of the Technology companies can dream of and transform into reality through hard-work, innovativeness and leadership. Stewards seldom dream, let alone make them into reality. You see, the current stewards were the righthand man/woman of the founders. The founders were the brains and the right-hand man/woman help the founders transform their dreams into reality. The care-takers cannot dream, but they sure can bleat Politically Correct slogans [that's the type of skills that made them janitors to begin with], see the various janitors all clamoring over each other to attack the Administration elected by the American People (not counting illegals brought in to be on welfare paid for by the working Middle Class of this country). Since the hand cannot think nor dream, only the brain can, then how do we allow more visionary founders to step forth?

How do we help bring about the Return of the King? By breaking the monopolies, allowing for smaller and new technology companies to start-up (NO Unicorns here) and their new visionary founders to achieve new dreams!

Tacking a new strategy on Climate Change; Gaia Equilibrium Project

Driving change in Climate Change. At least, there are at Stewards in the Tech sector, in the Renewable Energy sectors, there are NO stewards, they are only crooks and crony capitalists from Wall Streets (oh, I forgot the climate-change pimps). All these shibboleths about Carbon emissions, carbon footprint, carbon credits, we've been hearing these same sound-bytes for over 2 decades with no major breakthrough in field, only Billions of tax payers money distributed to the cronies and friends of those in political power. Disgusting. The Spirit of the Paris Accord was good, but now we need to Leapfrog the Paris Accord with Real Strategies for safe nuclear fusion energy and solar energy harnessed outside of earth's atmosphere.

Execute on tapping the Energy from the Oceanic Winds, Ocean Currents and Geothermal energy from Earth. Once we have dreamt the larger Goals, the technologies will be developed to deliver on the goals. Trying to first develop the technologies is like pushing on a rope. After we've fleshed out the strawman, clearly understood the major stages, milestones and projects to fulfil the larger dream with project schedules and timelines. We can then ask Hollywood's celebrities help to raise public Awareness and support for the new endeavors into Climate Change and Deep Space Exploration. Let them do what they know best, Marketing. We'll also explore more in next chapter too

Let there be Jobs and so there were Jobs?

President Trump's goal to create more Jobs. To achieve this goal, it is obvious that we cannot just wish for more jobs and they will appear. As a shrewd business man he knows that this is not the case. Here again, we have synergistic solutions.

A. A Growth Culture needs a New Frontier to flourish.
B. Jobs also needs to be Demand Pull, other we'll be just be pushing on a rope (as the current lame approach attempted half-heartedly by the 'climate-change pimps' really gorging on our tax payers money as subsidies)
C. We do need to address Climate Change and Deep Space Exploration, planets colonization and terraforming at some point.

Let's kill these 3 birds with one stone (figuratively speaking). By taking on such major projects, jobs will be coming out the wazoo, Growth Culture will again prevail and the entire Human Race again has a champion and world Leader. For funding these projects? How about the $ 3T we spend on welfare annually? Let us Focus on the Goals and Clearly state the Objectives of what we need to accomplish. The rest will follow accordingly.

This time, with NASA, USA Military leading the testing, experimentation, etc. Main Street Factories to get into large scale Manufacturing in support of Lunar and Mars Colonization and other space travel needs. As well as required increase in Exports and Global Trading, Americas Infrastructure Building and expansion. This time we will have concrete operational milestones and strong Execution Culture to deliver results as the renewable energy technologies will have to work perfectly under extreme conditions of space, otherwise our astronauts will be at unforgiving mercy of Space.

Leading into Chapter 9: American Order, Better World for All

Chapter 9

American Order, Global Collaboration, Humanity's Growth

"Vitality springs from diversity-which makes for real progress so long as there is mutual toleration based on the recognition that worse may come from an attempt to suppress differences than from acceptance of them."

- B.H. Liddell Hart, Strategy 1954, 1967

In the Introduction of this book, we'd discussed Symbol of 道 Taoism in the balance of Yin and Yang 阴阳. As the 2 parties alternate in peaceful transition of power (loyal oppositions both working for the good of the country), the country moves forward with stability (in dynamic equilibrium) and all Americans benefit. We've also understood the importance of Diversity for the long term survival for the entity (country in this case) as espoused by Arie de Geus in The Living Company, 1997. Diversity of ideas and beliefs leads to growth, while uniformity of ideas with the P.C. Big State Authority leads to compliance, obedience and ultimately to Decadence and eventually decline of Democracy in America.

The Dynamic dual-party system with different ideologies; mutually compromising and alternating in peaceful transition of Power, as during the days of the founding fathers, Federalists working together with the Democratic Republicans, as President John F Kennedy getting advice from his predecessor President Eisenhower, (where different but Loyal Opposing Ideologies, allowing growth of Diverse Ideologies for good of the country) is beneficial and the right answer for America. However, this successful system rests on 2 Key premises, peaceful transition of power and Loyal Diverse Ideologies for good of the country.

We can clearly see that we've had neither a Peaceful transition of Power as clearly evidence by the ceaseless attacks by the Radical neo-fascists Activist Corporations, the Radical neo-democrat Politicians and the P.C. Media Gestapos, neither do we have Loyal diverse Ideologies; with good of this country at heart. From the careful analysis and observations in prior chapters we've come to clearly understand a) the non-existence of any Ideologies in the neo-democrats slogans and mantras and b) the real nefarious agendas of the Poverty Pimps, Globalist, Socialist Pimps and Climate-change Pimps (how coincidentally, they, their cronies and fund-raisers all reaping off millions of dollars and laughing all the way to the bank too). One never sees the political kleptocrats walk the talk, never see even the tiniest bit of self-sacrifice, only Loads of voracious disgusting self-enrichment, always at the expense of the [faceless] Working Class American Tax payers.

With better understanding of the current Civil War, we can now see the survival of American Democracy is hanging in balance, under the neo-Democrats' Parasitic Invasion; weakening the host to the point where the cherished American Values have been replaced by meaningless Politically Correct Slogans, designed for the deluded by their deceitful leaders. Yet, as we work towards a better future for this country we should clearly bear in mind, whether the neo-Democrat Liberals are Sheep, Dogs or Squealers?

We had already discussed Ethos, Awful Virtues, Ockham's Razor; Go Direct Model & Restructuring, and The Message in last chapter. We'll now elaborate briefly on our definition of Go-Direct Model and Collaboration Strategies to leverage diverse ideologies.

When addressing the solutions for various challenges, Go to the source of the Highest Value creation activities; the people or teams, cut out any in-between redundancy. Be specific and incisive in approach and execution; 3S (Simple, Speed & Self Confidence). Focus on a few Critical 'drivers' (with highest correlation to the desired end result, verify their causation), clearly understand where the 'bottlenecks' and critical paths are in the high priority processes. Know the critical sequence of events that needs to happen and check off all the low-hanging fruits with highest probabilities of success. In short, roll-up your sleeves and go directly to the operational level that makes things happen, cut through all the "mid-levels postmen", hold yourself, hold specific individuals accountable by certain timelines, most important No Committees, Hate Bureaucracy!

Under the Auspices of the Awful Virtues, Ethos of Financial Discipline and Leveraging the Go-Direct Model we will focus predominantly on Growth in this chapter. Before we jump into the specifics of each of the Three Key Areas of growth; a) Growth from Global Trade and Collaboration, b) Growth from Gaia Equilibrium and c) Growth from Space Exploration and Colonization.

"Tolerance and compassion are active, not passive states, born of the capacity to listen, to observe and to respect others."

- Indira Gandhi

"Peace is not unity in similarity but unity in diversity, in the comparison and conciliation of differences."

– Mikhail Gorbachev

Collaboration Strategy in engaging foreign Trading partners as well as our fellow Americans.

Uniformity in ideas signals the start of decline and end of growth. For America to succeed, we all need to accept and embrace diversity in ideologies. Let's discuss the concept of Compromise and Collaboration. Yes, the very conflict resolution strategies that the neo-Dems and P.C. Fascists never entertained nor utilized as they never had any intention to resolve the deadlock. Here, we tack a different strategy [that of cooperation] from last chapter's Competition Strategies as we hope that the incumbents in fields of information technology, NASA, Global Trading partners have the same goals of economy growth for all (win win) and achieving Space Exploration and Gaia Equilibrium to be their mutual objectives too.

With the Awful Virtues, Ethos, Financial Discipline, etc. as 'constraining factors' that we need to meet [satisfy], and Growth as the Key Strategic objective we need to achieve [optimize], we also need to be fully prepared to Compromise and negotiate both Internationally and also Domestically.

In seeking collaboration, we have to remember that this is our aim that together as Americans, we look forward to New Horizons but we must not be naïve to think that there would be NO resistance to our efforts seeking collaboration. The resistance can be classified into 2 categories Rational and Irrational / Cultural (also stated by Jared Diamond).

Let's bear these 2 forms of resistance in mind as we discuss the various Collaboration opportunities highlighted in last chapter.

Rational Resistance (in both Foreign Trade and also Domestic Opposition)

As we move forth to enforce the Antitrust Laws on the IT Monopolies in Silicon Valley [to foster Competition and bring forth Culture of Excellence], those in Power and with Influence would obviously fight the process, this is self-evident. They (the owners) would not be financially any worse off as the smaller companies that are formed from the dissolution of the monopolies would still retain similar share ownership, if anything the aggregate of the share price of the break-up companies would probably be greater than the old monopolies. In short, they would financially be whole (if not better off as in the case of Standard Oil).

As we start to move down the food chain in the organization, it would become less obvious who's power base is being threatened and who would be financially less well off (who's cheese we are moving). When encountering such resistance, it would help to map out the power relationships within the organization, the specifics of these future conflict of interests (financial or otherwise) would not addressed here as we have no visibility, so we'll move on in pursuit of our goals and Excellence in full respect of the law, as we work through the resistance, some will leave the organization. Over time, the pieces will naturally fall into place, however let's be conscious of the resistance and engage with our eyes wide open, if someone is resisting against moving forward, against what seems perfectly logical solutions, the answer could be they have vested interests that's not being addressed as part of the official discussions.

Cultural Resistance (with Domestic Opposition as Foreign Leaders are Rational)

The Clash of Cultures in certain organizations might prove to be more tenacious than Rational Resistance. To be able to convince them into Alignment with our overall Strategic Goals, we need to clearly identify those organizations with high potential of Cultural Resistance before starting the collaborative efforts. For this purpose, we need to clearly understand the existing Culture of these organizations and how close they are to the Culture of Excellence and Meritocracy that we wish to introduce to them. It would obviously vary from organizations to organizations and across different Industries too.

We have discussed the Culture of Compliance and Decadence in chapter 3, we have also looked closely at Culture of Excellence and Growth in chapter 3 & 4, and how it aligns closely to the Traditional American Culture. If the particular organization has strong alignment to the Culture of Excellence and Growth, then there would not be any Cultural Resistance as we start discussing Accountability and personal responsibilities.

Usually for organizations that deliver strong performance [operationally and financially], visible results with 'minimal' investments, Culture of Excellence is usually a given. However, we would not be expecting Culture of Growth and Meritocracy in Unicorns or organizations subsisting on government subsidies or grants (their critical success factor is to raise funds as we'd discussed in chapter 3).

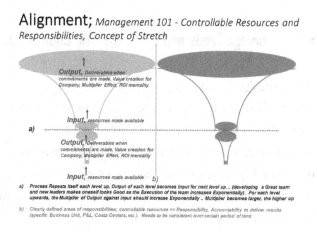

Alignment; *Management 101 - Controllable Resources and Responsibilities, Concept of Stretch*

Output, *Deliverables when commitments are made, Value creation for Company, Multiplier Effect, ROI mentality*

Input, *resources made available*

a)

Output, *Deliverables when commitments are made, Value creation for Company, Multiplier Effect, ROI mentality*

Input, *resources made available* **b)**

a) *Process Repeats itself each level up, Output of each level becomes input for next level up... (developing a Great team and new leaders makes oneself looks Good as the Execution of the team increases Exponentially). For each level upwards, the Multiplier of Output against input should increase Exponentially .. Multiplier becomes larger, the higher up*

b) *Clearly defined areas of responsibilities; controllable resources => Responsibility, Accountability to deliver results (specific Business Unit, P&L, Costs Centers, etc.). Needs to be consistent over certain period of time*

As a sidebar, the concept of 'Minimal' investments implies that the Output should be much larger than the investments, a great 'level 5' leader with a great culture of growth makes that happen (as an example, input of $1 produces output $5 as example), a steward will take input of $1 and produce output of $1 (no value added but protects the wealth to his/her best ability, maybe into 98 cents with 2 cents SG&A 'overheads' expenses). A Parasitic Leader (or a poverty pimp) will take input of $1 and produce output of 5 cents (for shareholders, tax-payers), 2 cents to himself, 10 cents to his cronies, 35 cents to his Fund-raisers, balanced of 48 cents wasted through inefficiency, incompetent decisions and incoherent strategies.

> *"You have to work with your enemy. Then he becomes your partner."*
>
> – Nelson Mandela

Growth by Increasing Global Trade Exponentially, Need to Compromise with Global Partners to achieve win win for all

$GDP = (Ex - Im)\Delta + I + G + C$

G, Government Expenditures is usually inefficient as compared with Free Market, but on certain occasions, it could help stimulate the economy in short term

C, Consumption did increase in the early QEs in 90s as consumers leveraged up to spend (essentially mortgaging their future), but proved ineffective after 2008 as they had all maxed out their credit limit

I, Investments by Businesses for long term growth is a good thing for the economy

$(Ex - Im)\Delta$, a Trade Surplus (more Exports than Imports) means a transfer of wealth into the country, the other way around means a loss of wealth to other countries. The last time America has Trade surplus was in the early 70s, in the early 90s we came close to breakeven, sadly it has been awful for the American Citizens from the late 90s till date. America has been enriching the other countries since 70s (see America's negative trade balance per chart below). We have to turn the situation around, to create Value, so that other countries would desire and willingly exchange for it with their wealth, what can we export that's of Value to other Nations?

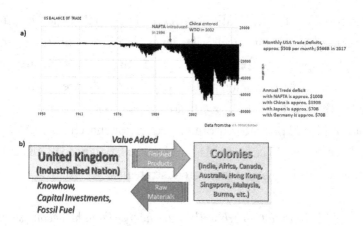

Before we dive into the more complex World Trade Discussion, let's understand the fundamentals, let's look at the UK when it first Industrialized, it gets raw material from its colonies and ships Manufactured Finished Products back to them. Due to its Industrial technology 'knowhow', ability to aggregate wealth (Capitalism) and using Fossil Fuels (burning coal), it adds Value and it able to create wealth for its citizens.

This same concept has persisted till modern times, the Developed Countries sends Finished Products to the Less Developed Nations while importing Raw materials from them. Because the Less Developed Countries only exports raw materials, minimal Value is created and they are poorer (purely from economic sense, obviously there are other factors at play, like Corruption). The big exception had been Oil & Gas, from 70s till early this century, the Middle East was very rich from Oil Sale as the entire world [needs energy] relied predominantly on the Wellheads in Middle East during that period.

Another change was that a number of countries started to transform from Less Developed into Developed countries, starting first with Japan and West Germany becoming powerful exporters by 70s, than followed by the Asia 4 dragon economies between 70s – 90s (South Korea, Taiwan, Singapore and Hong Kong). This process wasn't merely Industrialization but also the adoption of Democracy into their societies' values, this enabled the free-flow of Ideas, Talent and integrating with the World's Capital Markets, thus bringing in Capitalism (essentially similar to the America's Model we saw in chapter 4), all these countries started to run trade surplus with America (trade deficit for America). These countries (mentioned) were able to raise their entire population through widely spread, high quality education into skilled work force of the highest caliber. Many MNCs (Multi-Nationals), likes of HP (Hewlett-Packard), Exxon Mobil, General Electric Company, Phillips Company has had huge investments, factories, etc. in Asia since 70s. All these lined up with the conventional wisdom that since these economies can produce the same quality finished goods for lower costs, they 'out competed' America in efficiency. To stay ahead, America needed to continuously innovate and remain technologically superior with more Value Creation. Now we move forward to the 90s and another major player started to make its impact on World Economy, China.

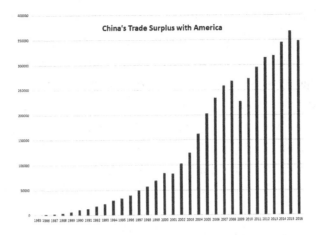

Unlike the other countries, China is not democratic but as we'd seen earlier, under Deng Xiaoping, it has embraced Capitalism thus avoiding a fate similar to the collapse of the USSR. In fact, anyone's been to China knows that it is Capitalism on steroids, as for democracy, it isn't like the Orwell's 1984 version of Big State Government nor the P.C. neo-Fascists Dem's incessant Propaganda. Individuals are pretty much left alone to create wealth through Capitalism mechanism of the free market, the only caveat that they don't rile up public emotions against the Party or get caught for Corruption (much tighter scrutiny now under President Xi). China also has huge pool of talent simply due to its gargantuan population size. With a country of 1.3 billion (official number) integrating into the World Economy you would expect seismic economic impact and true enough China's trade surplus with America is currently about *\$ 350 Billion per year [\$ 500 Billion in some years], it had crossed the \$ 100 B mark in 2002 when China entered WTO.

* \$350 Billion spread among the 320 million Americans is approx. US\$ 1100 paid by each American to China per year.

Using convention wisdom of the 90s Competitive Strategies, an Academia professor might argue that because China has much lower labor costs translating into lower costs of production, they would be able to also 'out compete' America in being more efficient and thus resulting in the Trade deficit for America. This line of argument is overly simplistic and also not updated for numerous events that's transpired since the 90s. In the late 90s, we did much out-sourcing work from America into the less developed countries, in search of lowering our costs of Operations in America. It is obvious that labor costs are much lower in these Less Developed Countries, but the labor costs only makes up 10 – 15% of the entire Finished Product's Cost (depending on the products, the more capital intensive, the lower the labor content). There's also Transportation Costs, Warranty and Product Quality Issues and associated costs. Therefore, the decision to outsource wasn't a slam dunk.

China's labor costs advantage started to erode towards the end of last decade as the Costs of Living (Shanghai, Beijing, Hong Kong's costs of living is above most American cities) started to increase drastically (same effect as Ricardian Bind) coming to a head around 2010 when a number of workers suicides in Foxconn factories in Dongguan, Guangdong forced the Chinese government to step in and demanded benefits to be adjusted upwards, in 2 year period, the effect on payroll nearly doubled. Logically, that effect should wipe out any advantage of manufacturing in China right? Then why has the Trade deficit against China not reduced since 2011?

To clarify, the average worker in China is still very poor by America's standards, made poorer because their real estate prices had sky rocketed due to property speculation by the Top 1% in China. Income Inequality situation is much worse than, or as bad as America's (by China's official reports). The top 1% in China translates to about 15 – 18 million of Super Stellar Rich Chinese [giving Bill Gates a run for his money, that's probably why he's saying that China is over-taking America].

So back to the question, why has the Trade deficit not closed but continues to widen? To move production facilities would incur some setup costs and lead time needed too, but these aren't the reasons. Two categories of reasons, one is economic and the other is political. Economically, China's costs of production isn't burdened by Environmental Costs and Welfare Abuse Costs. The Pollution in China is terrible and thus there's minimal EPA compliance costs loaded into the end Product.

Secondly, the China worker isn't burdened with Welfare Abuse cost of over $ 3 Trillion annually, that the American worker has to carry, that's right, the Giant Welfare State helps make the American worker Uncompetitive (there's no free lunch), all the Welfare Abusers in America that collecting welfare checks, while NOT working is making the other working Americans carry their $ 3 Trillion of freebies (which ultimately comes from taxes collected from wage earners), thus much less competitive in wages vs overseas workers. In China as in many Capitalist countries, the workers' welfare accounts are specific to their personal contributions, if you don't work then you have no welfare account to draw down from. The State has no handouts for people Not working, unless you are in jail.

Next 2 reasons are political, all the Chinese Leaders since Deng are all extremely intelligent (not surprising since China has the largest World Population to choose from) but China had been Blessed that these Leaders chose to put the interests of their countrymen first, in their dealing with any foreign countries. No BS Globalists nor Crazy Welfare rhetoric, they clearly understood that jobs must remain in China and Local Companies must dominate the scene in China and abroad too. We saw this at beginning of the book, due to the filtering effects of absorbing the talent, knowhow in management, foreign investments and capital in the early days, China had built up their Tech and Financial Giants that dwarfs their US counterparts in Market Size by number of users. All these State Protection for their local players restricts the success of American companies in China and the volume of Exports we can sell into China. If America's trade deficit narrows against China, that would mean disaster for the China Economy and they cannot have that happen at any costs. At risk of explaining the self-evident, if the trade deficit (standing at $ 350 B per year) narrows by $ 100 B, and China knows that there aren't any 'Globalists dummies' out there to pick up a $ 100 B deficit tab, that would mean China's GDP would shrink by $ 100 B, a major Disaster for the country.

The second Political reason can be understood in PPP concept, Purchasing Power Parity, we had seen that China's economy has already overtaken the US economy by PPP adjustments but what does that mean? PPP addresses what can be purchased domestically with local currency, it is a more accurate measure as anyone who has travelled extensively understands this concept, it is what you can buy in the local currency that truly reflects the quality of life in that country. Similar concept as price of a Big Mac (the Big Mac Index), it varies around the world to the purchasing power of its consumers. The quality of life, the true costs of living can be much better summed up by adjusting for PPP. The PPP concept (or index) is a more accurate reflection of costs of living differential which FX should logically also reflect, if it is allowed to move according to Free Market Forces. Under a truly Free Global Market, the price of a product in its local current currency when adjusted via exchange rates back to US$ should be close to its US$ Price, in other words the PPP adjustment factors should be small, otherwise arbitrage happens.

Per the Big Mac Index, currently the RmB is undervalued about 41%, while per the World Bank's PPP Adjustment factor, the RmB is undervalued by approx. 36% which would translate to an exchange rate of 3.89 RmB : US$ 1 or 4.26 RmB : US$ 1 respectively.

But while PPP is academic, owned by the statisticians (for now), while the FX rates are owned by the Policy makers and Political Leaders of the World (in Financial Wars, they can be weaponized to be as powerful as Nuclear weapons in Military Wars).

Now, if we observe the revaluation of RmB against the US$ from 1982 – 2016, we'll note the following; RmB went from 2 RmB to 1 US$ in 1984 to 8.7 RmB to 1 US$ in 1994 (more than 4 times, it's been at 7 Rmb to $1 since 2008). The major revisions were in 1984, 1986, 1990, 1994.

Below is the GDP growth of China till 2000, except for the first red arrow when Deng took over as China's Leader and unleashed Capitalism, the other red arrows all show points of RmB devaluation against US$ which is essentially against all other world currency, see the coincidence along the various revisions of RmB against the US$ from 1984 - 1994? Foreign Exchange Rates; undervalued currency provides the second advantage enjoyed by China Manufacturers.

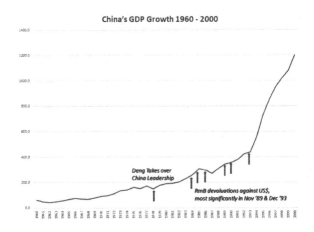

In face of such unfair Trade practices by our Trade Partners, what can America do? The last Admin merely surrenders to all adversaries in area of Trade competition (just as it appeases all our enemies; the Terrorists and Tyrannical Regimes in the area of Foreign Affairs), prefer to tell the Snowflakes the non sequitur story of Globalism as an excuse for the Trade deficits (and calling ISIS the JV team, bribing, paying off Iran & North Korea), thus the first step is the Leadership having the Intent to address and remedy the Trade deficit situation instead of looking for an excuse to lie to the feeble minded mob.

Thank God, we now have a second chance to make this right. Before we jump at the more obvious low hanging fruit (also contentious) of merely addressing the Foreign Exchange concerns, let's explore our strengths and areas for improvements.

Quick Summary:

By almost any measure, America's market is still the single largest and most lucrative in the world, that's why it is so valuable to China, Mexico, Canada, etc. (just search for the largest importers into USA). When you adjust for the GDP per capital, it easily is the most significant world economy with substantial growth potential, observe the confidence level of the Wall Street market rally since 2016 Elections.

$GDP = (Ex - Im)\Delta + I + G + C$

Strong Economic growth rests on the Trade Surplus (Ex – Im) and Business Investments (I) as the wealth created flows directly into the middle working class which generates the highest velocity of money or biggest money multiplier. This is because a) the base of middle class is huge in America and b) they spend and re-invest in themselves to stay competitive, whether through small business investments or education, etc. Over time as the middle-class becomes bigger and richer, the Consumption (C) will naturally grow as well. Generally, Government Spending (G) is inefficient and only occasionally under the gold standard of 'efficient bureaucracy' generates positive short term economic growth.

Remember, the Middle working class is the beating heart of True Democracy and Perfect Competition Free Market Capitalism; key words being Working and Competition, for the decline of the middle working class signals the rise of Monopolies of power (Income Inequality, Culture of Decadence, etc.) all brought about through the Socialists Big Government and crazy Welfare Expenses (G), essentially the transfer of wealth through extracting Taxes from the Middle Working Class and delivering into hands of the Top 1% who influences the Deep State politicians and K Street apparatchiks [think of the QE monies of over $ 20 Trillion YTD, the annual $3 Trillion of Welfare expenses]

> *"American ingenuity is at work day and night finding new methods of production... American industry was raised on a free land, and the spirit of competition that built our machines, which we are now gearing up to a world-record effort, will respond if we all cooperate and keep our thoughts focused on one object – to preserve our American way of life and beat the invaders."*
>
> – William S. Knudsen, Freedom's Forge by Arthur Herman

Current Strengths:

Despite what the Academia conmen tells you, the bottom line is very simple, if the Trade Deficit between America and China is reduced to zero, America's economy will be Net better off (yes, there will be some short term administrative and logistical headaches of shifting production back to America which will benefit all Americans immediately after the initial hump is overcome).. on the other hand, if China's economy reduces by $ 350 B (over 3% of its economy), it has a very real chance of collapsing onto itself(official growth rate has been about 7%), riots and probably revolutions are very real threats when such economic disasters hit China, such threats are so real that their leadership will consider risking Military Wars as an option, offering distraction or excuse to have Military Rule in China to maintain stability.

Understanding China's need for America's Export Market to maintain its own internal political stability is crucial to reversing America's Trade deficit (not necessarily that with China alone), America's Exports to China is less than half of what it exports to Mexico, considering how much bigger the China Market is, we still have great opportunities but need to be cautiously sensitive to China's concerns.

Let's review America's Top Net Exports in 2016, where these Value Creation Industries by Americans still having competitive advantage over other Nations:

1. Aircraft, spacecraft: US$103.6 billion (Up by 60.7% since 2009)
2. Oil seeds: $25.3 billion (Up by 41.5%)
3. Cereals: $16.8 billion (Up by 10.1%)
4. Other chemical goods: $11.5 billion (Up by 9.2%)
5. Plastics, plastic articles: $8.1 billion (Down by -37.4%)
6. Food industry waste, animal fodder: $7.1 billion (Up by 21.5%)
7. Meat: $6.7 billion (Up by 4.6%)
8. Woodpulp: $5.6 billion (Up by 31.1%)
9. Cotton: $4.7 billion (Up by 15.8%)
10. Miscellaneous food preparations: $4.1 billion (Up by 117.4%)

Top American Export Companies in 2016

- Apple (<u>computer hardware</u>)
- Exxon Mobil (oil, gas)
- Johnson & Johnson (medical equipment, supplies)
- Chevron Corporation (oil, gas)
- Procter & Gamble (household, personal care items)
- Pfizer (pharmaceuticals)
- The Coca-Cola Company (beverages)
- Merck & Co (pharmaceuticals)

- Qualcomm (semiconductors)
- Philip Morris International (tobacco)
- Intel (semiconductors)
- Schlumberger (oil, gas)
- PepsiCo (beverages)
- Cisco Systems (communications equipment)
- Boeing (aerospace)
- ConocoPhillips (oil, gas)
- AbbVie (pharmaceuticals)
- Occidental Petroleum (oil, gas)
- Eli Lilly and Company (pharmaceuticals)

From the 2 lists above, we can summarize America currently has three areas of Current Strengths over other countries and we'll also explore other potential strengths.

> *"We are a commercial people. We cannot boast of our arts, our crafts, our civilization; our boast is in the wealth we produce."*
>
> – Ida Tarbell

> *"No one can do what we can do if we all get together," Bill Knudsen liked to boast. Americans' love of freedom, of individuality, of doing things differently from the other guy – these were sources of strength, he believed, not weakness. He believed in the power of the average American worker; as he said "Progress in the world is accomplished by average people," and the power of American business. "American ingenuity has never failed to cope with every specific problem before it… and if we have your support and confidence, we will surely succeed."*
>
> – Arthur Herman in Freedom's Forge

Technological Edge

Aerospace, Healthcare, Information technology, cyber security, Biotechnology sciences, America's lead in all these fields of expertise can be leveraged to help other countries be able to enjoy these advances in science while creating wealth and better education for Americans which will in turn help push advancement in innovations and the frontiers of science further.

In *beatissimum saeculum*; as the Spirit of Golden Age under Emperor Trajan, we need to believe in the future and potential of this country, America has many strengths and advantages, Technology, innovativeness, Industrial Production Potential, etc. has to be all considered together as we'll explore the mindful hand concept shortly. Through making and producing [*Techne*], innovation and creativeness arise, that's why having production in America is important (it is not just about short term profits from low costs manufacturing in China, Mexico, etc.) Innovations and new inventions arise where the Market Needs and Production interfaces, without the production, the innovations will decline and Growth culture atrophy into Culture of Decadence. Besides mere Industrial and Technology advantages, America also has great advantages in Agricultural and Energy resources.

> *"Agricultural work is – as Pope John XXIII described it - a vocation, a God-given mission, a noble task and a contribution to civilization. God has blessed the United States with some of the richest farm land in the world. The productivity of American agriculture is a major success story. Clearly, it is a history of hard and wearying work, of courage and enterprise, and it involves the interaction of many people: growers, workers, processors, distributors and finally consumers."*
>
> – Pope John Paul II, 1987

Ecological Edge

Due to extreme pollution, much of China's ecologies has become severely contaminated which will take decades to recover if ever, thus their critical desire for clean and uncontaminated water, food supplies from overseas might not be fully appreciated. This severe need of China's, could be better leveraged to help America's cause for increasing Food and Water Industry's Exports to China

Energy Edge

Unlike the past when the Oil wells in Middle East reigned supreme, many of those wells have now passed their Peak Production, with the Technology breakthroughs in clean coal, shale fracking, etc. America has become Energy Independent and could easily be a Major Force as Exporter of Energy in near future.

As of 2016, these countries provide America with Trade Surplus (Hong Kong +$27.5B, Netherlands +$24B, UAE +$19B, Belgium +$15B, Australia +$12.7B, Singapore +$9B, Chile & Brazil +$4B each), hopefully we can see a longer list with much larger positive balances (surpluses) soon.

Areas of Improvement:

It is Critical to Decouple the costs of Welfare Abusers from the honest hardworking American's Wages, perhaps leverage Best Practices of having individualized specific Welfare Accounts. Penalize the Welfare Abusers, explore re-Introducing the compulsory Military draft and the CCC (Civilian Conservation Corps) to address the Welfare Challenges. The Welfare Abusers even openly states that they are getting over $ 35K of benefits per year and thus have no incentive to look for work, you know the Welfare Pimps must be extracting their 'pound of flesh' from the $ 3 Trillion of Welfare burden unfairly shouldered by the honest hardworking American Tax payers. Do we continue to suffer these Vicious Parasites Gladly?

Potential Strengths:

Innovation Edge

Since the end of the last American Civil War, with the Westward expansion's risk seeking spirit and combined with its being the natural successor to the Europe Enlightenment, the pace of innovation in America started to accelerate and overtook the UK in the late 19th century. By the beginning of the 20th century, America's Gilded Age backed by the wealth of Capitalism, labors of the populace and the creativity and innovation of the human spirit is clearly starting to surpass its predecessors in the European continent. Americans have managed to hold on to this Innovation leadership till the turn of the millennia as the birthplace of the Internet Technology.

Yet we've listed Innovation Culture only as a Potential not as Current Strength, we've seen there still much work to do to overcome the stupefying effects of the P.C. ONE VIEW Culture, to recover from the decomposing effects of the Decadence Culture of Monopolies of the IT Tech Monopolies Giants. Monopolies always leads to Uniformity, intolerance of diverse ideas, ridiculing American Exceptionalism, mocking efforts and initiatives to reverse the Trade Deficit [chanting their Trade Wars Slogans], belittling attempts to think differently; the cornerstone of innovations and stifling of Culture of Innovation. To reverse such paralyzing effects of Decadence, Conformity to the Politically Correct Culture would require Herculean Efforts by All Americans.

To revive our Innovation Edge, we need to crush the P.C. ONE VIEW's reign of stupidity and embrace diversity regardless of political ideologies, to restructure the IT Tech Suzerains' strangle-hold over resources in Silicon Valley, to allow new growth of ideas and fresh wave of innovations to sweep thorough America again. Probably best to have competing new and larger centers of Technologies in Cleveland, OH, Huntsville, AL, Seattle, WA, Boston, MA, Austin, TX, etc. Nothing helps Innovation like Good-old Competition and Culture of Growth!

Google gone missing!

You might have noticed that Google, FaceBook, Telsa, Amazon are NOT amongst Top American Export companies, in fact only apple is top of the list, Qualcomm, Intel and Cisco Systems are the only tech-related companies on the Export list. Despite being on the highest valued (Market cap-wise), the 'tech monopolies giants' are not exporting any goods nor services [except Apple, most of the other Tech Giants like google, FB, Amazon, etc. have ZERO market share in China; the World's Largest Market by Population size] What does that tell you? We learnt from beginning of the book that many of these 'giants' hardly made any real revenue from their customers, most of their wealth comes from Wall Street Investors that don't value the minuscule 'so call revenue from advertisers' but do like the ability to control the Social Media's rhetoric, with added the perks of Capital appreciation of their shares.

Since the foreign countries wish to receive something of value for their money spent, there isn't anything of value from Facebook, Amazon, Google or Tesla that they would pay for. This is the strongest indicator of the true Value Creation they bring, Amazon does add some productivity domestically for the local consumers, but it has minimal market share overseas. Just a sad cannibalization of all the Retail Industries within America. Any astute reader can see that Amazon shrinks the American Economy rather than growing it, the Retail Industries stimulates Economic Growth as wealth is spread out amongst many more employees along the entire Retail Chain, from Manufacturers to Distributors to franchisers to retailers to Mall and Real Estate owners. The 'productivity gain' that Amazon brings, also has a huge social cost, the lost in employment opportunities of the American Retail Industry is way bigger than a tiny few gained in Amazon's own distribution centers. Under the Old model, when customers visit the Mall, they also spend more, coffee, drinks, movies, etc. (other services) thereby further growing the economy, this 'economic growth' is now lost under the Amazon model.

The reality is many 'tech giants monopolies' models doesn't allow them to charge for services provided, just look at Facebook and Google, they cannot even charge their existing users (the smart users will not pay for the value of the 'service provided') for fear of losing them. Their stock price is based on this concept of number of 'eyeballs', losing users means losing 'eyeballs' which might bring about the crash of their share prices. Users could also translate into virus afflicted (easily influenced) voters which is of some value to the unholy trinity of Wall Street Suzerains, Tech Street Monopoly Moghuls and K-Street Crony Politicians.

Creative Content Edge

In 2015 and 2016, America Exported Services worth $ 750 B globally, of this amount $125 B can be attributed to Entertainment Services. This IP Services payment is miniscule, considering how popular NBA franchise, Hollywood movies are in China, plus theoretically how big the China Market should be. How do we grow these services, and get paid for them? What is hindering the growth of IP Services as a means to grow America's economy?

First, piracy in China is the norm, all CDs, DVDs are pirated, now they download or just watch directly from the internet. Obama calls this 'Globalization'. From Chinese experts' prudent estimates, less than 10% of the Chinese movie watching populace watch the movies in cinemas or through means traceable by the IP authorities. That means the IP revenues should be easily 10 times higher from China and the Less Developed Countries, the mere enforcement of IP rights in China will close the $ 350 B trade deficit significantly, perhaps even produce a Trade Surplus with China!

Second, the restricted screenings of American films in China for fear of ideological contamination to their populace (they don't want the terrible ideas of human rights, freedom of speech, democracy to corrupt the minds of their citizens). If left to free market mechanism, the local China film industry will probably disappear in 6 months and American movies dominate the cinemas by over 85% which should easily triple or quadruple their existing market share (we are only talking about Cinemas' Screening here, not the piracy issues). We'll be able to see even more growth from resolving the Piracy issues. Perhaps the IP enforcement can be discussed together with the FX (Foreign Exchange) rates negotiation with the Chinese by our new Admin representing the American People?

The third reason has nothing to do with China or other foreign countries, it is the state of decline in diverse, sophisticated and original content from Hollywood and the Music Entertainment since the 80s. "Landscape amnesia" was used by Jared Diamond in Collapse, How societies choose to fail or succeed, to explain imperceptible changes over time. If you keep watching something as it slowly changes (creeping normalcy). If you look at the movies or music scenes of America in 1980s vs now, you will be able to see the Great Dying of Diversity! Diversity in types of Music categories (think beginning of MTVs), Diversity in movie themes, the varied talents of the various artists in all fields of expertise. This Great Dying would have been even more obvious if not for Steve Jobs bringing Animation (CGI) technologies into Hollywood (Pixar), imagine if there are no animation movies, what would the box office earnings look like? This coincides with the Monopoly Culture spreading in Hollywood too, the intolerance for Political differences will immediately lose 50% of real talents (that's how discrimination loses real talents managing only to retain the compliant mediocre). If you think most of the same actors and actresses are still there, that's because you are not looking at the real talents, real talents are behind the scenes, the great and original script writers (screenwriters that comes up with *Back to the Future*), intensely dedicated directors (Directors hungry to prove themselves, Spielberg in *Raiders of the Lost Ark*, Cameron in *The Terminator*) proud of their breakthrough genres and the excellence and unmatched quality of their final products.

Have you also noticed that the 80s and early 90s voices of Disney animation movies, likes of Great Mouse Detective, American Tail, Who Framed Roger Rabbit, etc. are from a much bigger, broader and more diverse talent pool, not merely the current actors or actresses? Which makes perfect sense, as the best and expressive voices are heard and NOT seen, as in the hey days of Radio. The Actors and actresses are 'nicer to look at' so they are there to be viewed not for their voices nor their brain prowess, so why have they now taken over the voices of the animations? Simple answer, reduction in the size of the overall pie and uneven distribution of wealth, interesting how the Ugly Monopoly Culture of Corruption works the same everywhere?

Similar to America, the 'middle class' in Hollywood has also been decimated and the Super Rich stars get paid more while the rest of talents behind the scenes gets ignored. Woody's voice became Tom Hanks, the script gets simpler and simpler, plot becomes non-existent, all 'cut and paste' from earlier ones, relying on the 'special effects' to razzle and dazzle the audience (think the latest Transformers, Super Heroes movies).

Many movie plots are not only predictable and simplistic, they are plain insulting to watch, the imbeciles doing the 'cut and paste' are so slothful, their work so sloppy, the plot isn't even coherent. Where has talents likes of Eddie Murphy, Dan Aykroyd, Steve Martin, etc. gone?

Why are 'over the hill, nice guys', nice people but mediocre actors like Matt Damon, Tom Hanks still acting in so many action movies? Where's the Pipeline of younger talent? Why's Jennifer Lawrence in practically every new movie? Compared to the 80s, the talent pipeline of young and diverse talents has dwindled to a miserly pathetic few good ones (for actor and actresses), a big ZERO for screen writers, Dedicated directors. This is the result of Monopoly and consolidation of Power in hands of few.

The P.C. One View of Uniformity kills diversity in Ideas, with Culture of Blind Compliance and Decadence, they become Closed Minded, no longer flourishing with fresh, innovative and new Ideas.

You need more examples? You just take a look at the American Music, Entertainment and Movie Industries. How many New Genre of Music has been added to the American Music scene since Techno was last introduced in mid-late 80s? this is as compared to addition of Blues, Jazz, Pop, Funk, Hip Hop, Rock, Reggae, Disco, Country, Heavy Metal, etc. in the 20s, again through the 50s – 70s

The monopoly Culture denies opportunities for the lesser known to break-out. The current Hollywood Celebrities and Music Celebrities are NO longer talented artists in search of fresh ideas with open minds, they have become, egoistic self-centered individuals who have turned themselves into Political Combatants with Closed Minds. You think they even care about the artistic value or contents of their work released these days? They are just out to reap in their huge earnings to sustain their lavish and narcissistic lifestyles.

Incumbents in Power hate Diversity of Ideas (any ideas contradictory to theirs) as new ideas can change status quo and move their cheese, just as Extremists and Radicals hates wide spread knowledge. How do we Export more Services? Using Ockham's razor to streamline the Entertainment Industry, allows talent and competition to emerge, it will also revitalize its growth and Culture of inclusiveness and real diversity Culture to grow once again. Competition is always a good thing!

> *"Many worthwhile values are involved in tourism: relaxation, the widening of one's culture and the possibility of using leisure time for spiritual pursuits. These include prayer and contemplation, and pilgrimages, which have always been part of our Catholic heritage; they also include fostering human relationships within the family and among friends… I invite all of you who are involved in tourism to uphold the dignity of your work and o be always willing to bear joyful witness to your Christian faith."*
>
> – Pope John Paul II in Monterey Peninsula, CA Sept 1987

Grow the Geo-Tourism to America Continent with Virtual, Augmented Reality Technology

We need to Export more Travel and Tourism Services, leverage VR in Ecotourism and Geo-Tourism to visit America as a continent; work with Latin Americans for win win Tourism to Latin

America too, use VR to revive the Ancient historical civilizations in America. Helping grow the economies of the various Latin American countries through tourism will increase the wealth of the Middle Working class and provide less incentive for the Drug Trade in these countries, together with lower Demand (in USA through Education), Law enforcement against Drug trafficking and increased wealth in middle class in Latin America, the profit margins in drug trade could be reduced and the problem easier to be addressed.

Rescue the snowflakes from the Piper through mutual collaboration to become Eco and Geo Tour Guides? Have them travel abroad, go overseas to see the real world, learn something of true Value to help grow all America's economies (including Latin Americas, hopefully help wean them off their economies' reliance on the drug trade), instead of being keyboard global warming warriors from their parents' basement?

Even as we had discussed Culture of Compliance, Decadence and Culture of Growth, Excellence, we need to remember that most companies' Cultures are never so distinct. They are always a blend and mixture of various Values and shaped by their respective environments experienced. We had discussed this 2 distinct Cultures in chapter 3 to focus on the stark contrast and differences between them.

Before we dive into the Best Practices and Challenges faced in Space Travel and Gaia Equilibrium, let's explore one more Culture type.

> *"We must not forget that when radium was discovered no one knew that it would prove useful in hospitals. The work was one of pure science. And this is a proof that scientific work must not be considered from the point of view of the direct usefulness of it."*
>
> – Marie Curie

What is the Culture of Innovation?

Let's define the Culture of Innovation, it should have many similarities with the Culture of Excellence and Meritocracy with a Passion for Diversity of Ideas (unlike the Quota "skin-deep diversity" of shallowness, obedience, ever Compliant to the P.C. One View). Culture of real Innovation would be inclusive of all ideas, independent thinking, intellectually curious and a-Political (any organization that is Intolerant of diverse ideas, ideologies, immediately loses 50% of talent and creativity of the population, it will be much less likely to be successful, about as competitive as the Unicorns with 'negative Cash-Flows').

The founder, leader of such successful Culture of Innovation would be passionate in his/her beliefs in what's possible, with intense personal discipline and will power to see his/her vision become a reality. As in Culture of Excellence and Meritocracy, there would be strong appreciation of personal responsibilities and accountability, with less emphasis on delivering daily operational results but more creative solutions over 'medium timeframes'.

Elaborating on concept of 'medium timeframes'. For the more matured organizations that stresses Operational Excellence; (manufacturing, supply-chain, established Sales channels, etc.) they already know what to expect of the team operationally, thus they'll focus on operational excellence, efficiency, getting the best results with minimal amount of resources spent. Analogy would be like knowing your destination and have been there a number of times, then you focus on how to get there in fastest way with least traffic congestion.

But if you have never been to a place, you might get lost (pre-GPS days, post-GPS some still get lost too), thus the focus for now, is on effectiveness (just getting there to begin with), efficiency comes later. For Creative efforts and solutions, since we do not know all the answers as we are searching for them, we focus on effectiveness [emphasis on 'thinking out of the box', being open minded, innovative] and not efficiency. But Make no mistake, we still need Accountability to deliver Results, if you still cannot find the solutions or answers after a reasonable timeframe (depends on complexity of the tasks), you should find your way to the door (to perhaps an easier task and smaller role if you had truly been trying your best).

Culture of Creativity needs its members to be able to learn and understand concepts deeply, only by internalizing pre-existing concepts deeply and stretching for new goals will New Concepts emerge. A passionate and capable individual can stretch himself/herself to accomplish a number of feats and add Great Value to humankind. A Network of groups of individuals (each group working as a team) can accomplish numerous feats exponentially greater and bring humankind to the next level higher (comparable to next Industrial Revolution).

To Expand on 'working as a team', the small team of 5-8 individuals has to believe in the possibility of the Dream (the 'stretch Goal' they came up with to begin with). Each member must bring as much 'internalized' knowledge, skills and insights to the table as possible. Each must also have the capacity to learn new concepts and think deeply, internalizing these new ideas quickly. They (the small team of action oriented intellects) must trust each other intellectually and emotionally [can only be possible after the 'storming' stage] to share their knowledge and Ideas without reservations, to openly challenge each other's ideas constructively to refine and re-refine constantly the overall concept they are all trying to build-up (with no fear of backlash from ill-will or political intentions. Some people who are less intellectually competent will take your challenge to their ideas, on emotional level and then retaliate emotionally later on totally unrelated issues). This type of alignment in ideals of intellects isn't easy to accomplish, therefore the teams cannot be too large, which is ok as we need smart people (with many diverse ideas) not More people (with the same idea).

As clarification, the Level 5 Leaders that Dare to Dream are not the same as Kings of Wishful-thinking as Elon Musk. Level 5 leaders like Steve Jobs dare to dream, they also deliver on Results; when Pixar delivers successes like Toy Story, when apple became a Great company with innovative great products like iPhone, iPads and generates great Cash-flow from real paying customers at affordable prices! Kings of Wishful thinking are like 'used car sales man' Elon Musk or 'Czar of Poverty Pimps' President Obama, they don't deliver results, their job is DONE the very minute the speech is completed or presentation ended, as far as they are concerned, their job is to make the presentation or speech (end of speech = he has crossed the finish line), the rest of what's needed to deliver the Result is too complicated and has nothing to do with them. They deemed the other factors as 'Uncontrollable' by themselves. The Level 5 leader deems all the other factors as 'Controllable' and learns to align all the necessary factors to deliver the Results for their customers or fellow country man in case of the American President.

Below is a direct quote from Steve Jobs after meeting with President Obama; the whole thing irritated Jobs.

> *"The president is very smart," Jobs told Isaacson, "but he kept explaining to us reasons why things can't get done. It infuriates me."*
>
> Steve Jobs in 2011 on his experience discussing
> jobs in America with President Obama

What Steve Jobs is experiencing Clash of Cultures, yet he was starting to see the tip of the iceberg of the 'Poverty Pimps'. The Level 5 leaders Dream Big, they understand the current capabilities and realities and the leap or stretch required to make the dream become reality. That gap or leap of faith is what the Level 5 leader takes on himself / herself to close the gap and deliver the results.

On the contrary, the used-car Sales man delivers his speech about Change, and goes play Golf, his job is done. President Obama says this himself, in Dec 2015 Interview with NPR's Steve Inskeep when asked by Steve asked why so many blame him for the lackluster Economy, Obama answered: (1) They are racists, (2) They don't think I was born in America, (3) They think I'm a Muslim, or disloyal to the country, and (4) There are always be people who don't like a president's policies. This happened on 21st Dec 2015, President Obama shows you exactly how he thinks! For those not familiar with 'controllable' vs 'uncontrollable' factors, I have attached a chart on this management concept at end of this section, elaborating on Culture of Accountability, Level 5 Leaders holding themselves Accountable and personally responsible for delivering results on stated goals. Instead we see excuses all lined up to the wazoo, blaming everyone he can think of, this is after 7 plus years on the job. Pathetic Leadership with complete lack of values.

In the Culture of Innovation, the Concept of Redundancy is critical. Redundancy in the Technology Industries refers to the excess resources expended to protect information or resources of high priorities; example when multiple servers are used in backup processes for critical transactions or information. For creativity to be possible, the stress for sheer efficiency must be set aside for the short to medium term. We can only address efficiency when we have become effective in accomplishing the Dream. Thus, in short term, it might appear as excess 'Redundancy' and inefficient in producing results. The analogy is similar to learning many new ideas and internalizing them before being able to produce breakthrough ideas or concepts (not all ideas learnt will eventually contribute towards the solution, most would not). The breakthroughs also do NOT happen right away, even as the new ideas are internalized and re-configured constantly, there might be certain 'missing pieces' before the entire picture can be clearly seen (as in building jigsaw puzzle without knowing what the final picture looks like). The missing pieces falling into place would be similar to the concept of serendipity or Conjunctures in human history. Internalizing the existing and new ideas are important as the final piece cannot click into place unless the key pieces have already been held in place (in our heads) and waiting the 'last piece' to fall in place (this last part is up to probability). If the other pieces had not been held in place, the missing piece would just come and be gone and no conjunctures would have happened, that is the function of cell membranes (for life to happen) or in the induced-fit model of enzymes, and National Identity (as in case of UK) when the Industrial Revolution took place as we'd discussed in chapter 1.

In the Culture of creativity, as much of these 'activities' and ideas are happening in the heads of the R&D engineers, Artists, Musicians, software designers, NASA's rocket scientists, etc. they could be making significant progress, breakthroughs but their managers would Not be able to tell, only the Intellect, Artist himself/herself would know. This type of situation highlights the need for Self-Discipline, personal Will Power and the Right Values of Accountability in the innovative employees themselves.

Theoretically, this type of situation in Culture of Innovation helps explain why the Unicorns, the Technology companies could be so highly valued, which would be correct in company like Apple under Steve Jobs or Amazon's early stage of growth, as the Wall Street Financial Analysts truly have no Idea how to value their real worth or the actual progress the software engineers or designers are making.

But there's more on the astronomical Valuation of the Unicorns, the FB, Amazon, Netflix, Google's valuation by Wall Street, there's a number of contributing reasons, the QEs that we'd discussed in chapter 5 started by Greenspan and taken up new level by Bernanke, Technology is the only 'growing' sector with a relatively more promising future. Some analyst might have rational reasons for high valuations as their KPIs (Key Performance Indicators) and bonuses are positively impacted. There is second reason, [we had touched on it briefly earlier], they do NOT understand the progress of what's happening in the R&D research works, the NPI (New Product Introduction) processes of these companies. Financial results is the final historical (after the fact) results, but NOT the driver [early indicator] of growth for innovative technology companies. Looking at the financial performance is like the tail wagging the dog.

Unlike other more established Industries like O&G, Defense, Manufacturing companies, etc. where the Business and Financial Model has been established and doesn't change so the Fin Analysts are happy. In the Tech world, the models are still developing as we speak so the 'one trick ponies' (low processing units) have no clue what's going on (sloth and pride prevents learning).

Due Diligence Work, to understand Valuation within Culture of Innovation

To learn new Industries and understand their start-ups, requires an open mind and eagerness to learn the new business, backed up with one's own operational experience. One's personal Operational experience provides the ability to draw analogies with new business model, to understand priorities, weightage, critical paths and 'bottle-necks' (precious limiting resources, constrains), that way when someone tries to Razzle and Dazzle you with nice sounding concepts and ideas, you can tell if certain things makes sense and what's illogical (filter out the fluff from the substance).

After you have a good understanding of the Business Operating Model, only 2 other factors are needed to assess the valuation of the company. Values of the founder and his/her track record. For track record, one needs time, what if the founder is new to the industry as startups usually are? It need not be track record of this new business, can be their previous employment, projects, studies, personal relationships could also reveal his/her Values too. Another easy data point for Values of the founder is his/her presentation about the business, if there's too much fluff, it's a bad sign. Remember to Look beyond the slick marketing and right into the heart of the value proposition. The slothful would be most content with the Investors Package prepared neatly for them, the inquisitive minds loves to understand operations and project milestones.

Back to Culture of Innovation & Creativity, we have to constantly keep in mind the concept of Potential Energy as Kinetic Energy. We can see kinetic energy in motion but potential energy is latent, we can only see it when it is released as kinetic energy, that doesn't mean we cannot understand the on-going progress in these organizations. The startup might not be delivering huge Cashflows and stellar Financial Performance (similar to Kinetic energy), but if you are deep inside its daily operations, spending time with the engineers, you can definitely feel it Potential if the operational level staff believe in the future of the company. If the potential is real and they are sincere and wishes truly to inform the public of their real progress, and not Public Relations razzle and dazzle, you will be able to tell the difference. After discussions with the CEO, we can easily sit down with the ground-level R&D engineers, managers, supervisors to design the non-financial Models and KPIs (Key Performance Indicators) for their progresses.

Management Science expertise is helpful, tools like Project schedules, process maps, project milestones, concepts of Lead time, critical paths, weightage and sequences of drivers [causation], resolving the 'bottle-necks', strong grasp of mathematics and probability. If the design engineers are too busy, they can just verbalize and communicate their ideas and up to us to design the Model and measurements, we'll then circle back and get their inputs and repeat this process a number of times till they agree on the KPIs and project milestones. Now we finally have the non-financial measurements and potential timelines for deliverables to be accomplished.

Human Nature and Organizational Behavior; a diamond in the rough or a scam?

Understandably, most people would NOT want to help others put performance measurements on themselves, they enjoy the autonomy and freedom to slack on their jobs especially if no one understands what they are doing. We need to consciously make allowance for [in respect] the autonomy of the talented designers and engineers, however the refusal to cooperate at various levels of the organizations will also provide Red Flags to the real progress being made on "new technologies".

We can understand the level of details completed or the stage of development achieved. If at high levels you already experience cover-ups and resistance to cooperate, that's a HUGE Red Flag that the entire organization is a façade. As one goes from the earth's crust towards its core, you expect the temperature to keep rising, if you go from the CEO down through VPs, Managers, group leaders and individual contributors, you would expect to get more and more details until you reach the operational transactional level where you cannot handle individual transactions but have to rely on the process maps to understand the flow and internal controls for checks and balances. If the CEO is already telling 'bulk of the story' and you don't uncover much more insights after going a couple of levels into the organization, this is again probably another scam (to feed on tax payers' subsidies) too. For every diamond in the rough, you'll probably come across 20 scams, otherwise Diamonds wouldn't be so precious right?

> *"The "Level 5" leader, an executive in whom extreme personal humility blends paradoxically with intense professional will."*
>
> Good to Great, by James C. Collins

Culture of Accountability in Culture of Innovation

Culture of Accountability and Leadership, Leaders learn to influence 'uncontrollable' into 'controllable' factors to deliver on results [they understand complex challenges and learn new skills to overcome them] and achieve the Dream (stretch goal). As one moves up in the organization, the person would also have more resources at his/her command, naturally, these leaders are also expected to have the experience, skills and insights to harness those resources made available to him/her and grow them exponentially.

If the leader doesn't know how to achieve exponential growth, he/she is Unfit to be in that position and should move aside (move over to the right slower traffic lane).

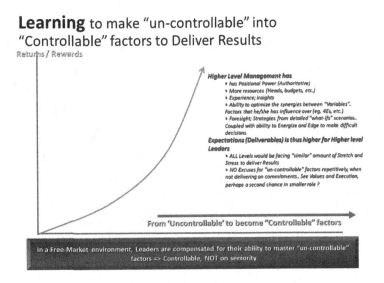

Learning to make "un-controllable" into "Controllable" factors to Deliver Results

The founder or leader of the successful start-ups should be ideally Level 5 leaders as in any organization with the Culture of Growth and Excellence.

Culture of Innovation can Never grow under the P.C. ONE View of Uniformity

As we'd discussed in chapter 8, we already have the internet "printing press" to disseminate information. We still need the breakup of the P.C. Gestapo Media and eradication of the Radical neo-fascist Activists, by promoting uniformity of ideas, they are a huge distraction away from our need to focus on innovation. We need the "schism in the Church" as the P.C. Gestapo is killing the diversity of Ideas, sprouting the Culture of Mediocrity, glorifying Ignorance and Incompetence. Poor ideas and bad concepts should be killed as early and quickly as possible so as not to waste any more resources on them.

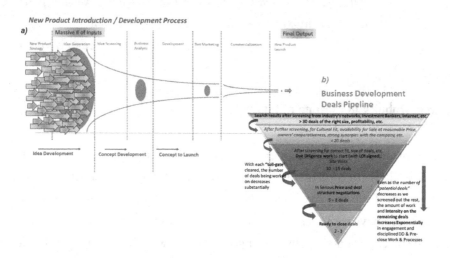

We observe the same concept at work in NPI, New Products Introduction and M&A Business Development opportunities too. You want to start off with the maximum number of opportunities or ideas, the ones that cannot work should be weeded out ASAP so that resources can be used to a) generate more opportunities and b) focus on developing the better opportunities for success. This is the same competition in Nature too. The P.C. Gestapos are TRULY Glorifying Incompetence, Ignorance and Stupidity! Sadly, by allowing nonsensical ideas and concepts to dangle around as everyone is too P.C. to say it is stupid, good and bad ideas are NOT differentiated. Good ideas are not refined, challenged and re-refined, tested and re-tested till we have a workable Model to commercialize. Ideas must be allowed to compete and the P.C. Culture is DEATH to any form of competition.

That is another reason the lower processing units love P.C. Culture because P.C. Culture protects them. In return, the P.C. Gestapo Media and Celebrities LOVE the low processing units BACK (We Love you Back), because the low processing units adore and idolizes the Celebrities (the 'one trick ponies' love praying to the Golden Calf; other humans). This is the key driver for Shallow and Shallower; symbiotic behavior, jointly degenerating the society by glorifying mediocrity in guise of diversity.

Lastly, we need Real Endeavor into New Age of Exploration (not the current amateur hour) which we will discuss in next segment. The NPI funnel of Ideas also applies to the new Technologies and Space Exploration environments too. If there's a bad idea and no one calls out the Emperor has no clothes, many of the Space X actual flight tests will end in failures. Defects should be nipped in the bud and not allowed to carry into the actual flight tests to blowup literally.

In quest for empirical evidence, we looked at the spurts in human inventions since the Industrial Revolution and see if we can identify any trends that drives inventions. One observation is that they (inventions) tend to cluster around certain periods and not evenly spread out. They stimulate each other, inventions lead to other inventions. They happen in incremental tinkering, thinking and making help spur modifications leading to newer inventions (termed the mindful hand during the Industrial Revolution). Certain events also help trigger their growth, certain amount of wealth (makes sense as you don't want your inventors living from hand to mouth) affluence in society and rapidly developing needs of the larger population. The Industrial Revolution (supported by the Age of Enlightenment) lead to a spurt of inventions. The Gilded Age in America created much underlying problems in its societies which inventions helped resolve and elevate the suffering of the common people. The two World Wars, followed by the Cold War and Space Race gave us much of the foundations of today's technologies (birth of today's internet in the 60s, Rocket science in WWII, basis and logic of computing by Turing, post WWII, technologies of Sonar and Radar were greatly refined in WWII).

Combined with the Culture of Innovation, Human Needs drive inventions, the Need to save Human Lives during the Wars, need for better Living conditions and Healthcare as human population grows exponentially. In Summary, a Culture that appreciates Sense of Responsibility, promotes Accountability, understands scarcity of Resources, has an inherent sense of crisis, one that tolerates calculated risks taking yet does not suffer fools gladly, one that expects Passion, Meritocracy and Excellence from its members [not bureaucratic blind compliance nor mediocrity].

> *"Imagination is more important than knowledge. For knowledge is limited, whereas imagination embraces the entire world, stimulating progress, giving birth to evolution. It is, strictly speaking, a real factor in scientific research. Imagination circles the world."*
>
> – Albert Einstein

> *"... Invention is often the mother of necessity, rather than vice versa."*
> - Jared Diamond in Guns, Germs and Steel

Another Perspective on Culture of Growth, Innovation and Exploration

So, which is which? Does necessity bring about invention or invention bring about necessity? In fact, both statements would be correct and Jared's statement where new inventions give rise to new uses should occur more common through human history than the other way around.

To understand Innovation and how it happens, let's review the conditions (Jared covered it in great detail in chapter 13 of Guns, Germs and Steel) that are most often associated with it. Firstly, Wealth and available resources (availability of materials, relatively more leisure time from Sedentary

Living), larger number of people in complex societies (better still a number of competing societies or groups), these all makes good sense as Innovation Culture is really a subset of Growth Culture.

'Seeding, Crystallization effect' (Genesis) and Autocatalysis of inventions is similar to ideas and concepts of sophistication building on each other as in Age of Enlightenment shared through various Intellectual Networks like *Republic of Letters, Select Societies, Poker Club, etc.

Incremental tinkering, finetuning and recombination of existing ideas/inventions are analogous to 'standing on shoulders of giants' of ideas reconfiguring and building on top of great ones. Aggregation, Grouping (Clustering) of inventions and their inventors in communities just as in the concept of Institutional Learning based on foundation of sharing, thus producing a common platform, a common collective nous. (again, similar to concept of Republic of Letters, Oyster Club, etc.) *Connectedness and interdependency of autonomous agents per the Complexity Theory resulting in adaptation [learning] of the individual agents as well as the system itself.

Ideological traits like Risk Taking, Tolerance of Diversity of Ideas, of Failures, are also observed. Protection of IP (Intellectual Property) and ability of the inventor to enjoy the fruits of his invention, is an encouragement but not a necessity. The 'Mindful Hand' (Industrial Revolution) that tinkering and making allows the thinking maker to become creative and inventive, [Manufacturing Process is synergistic with R&D process]. There is also the 'borrowing of ideas'; sharing of best practice, that allows diffusion and spread of technology. Now that we have all the pieces, what makes them come together? Conjuncture? Serendipity?

Per Aristotle, there are four causations of things to be in existence, a wine glass for example, the Material Cause is the glass it is made from, Efficient Cause is how it is made, Formal Cause is the Society's perspective (knowledge) of how it should look like and last is Telos (its intended use). Let's borrow it for our view of Innovation.

As seeding allows crystallization to happen (for snowflakes to form), the innovation process can start from any one of the four Causes. Let's start with the most intuitive, telos (Need), when coal was extracted from the ground and there was a desire to use the steam energy that was readily available there was no Formal Cause for a Steam Engine, so the 'potential inventors' then started to leverage the existing knowledge (what I would call collective nous); latest understood scientific principles, material available and engineering capability, to create the earliest version of Steam Engine from first principles, which then gradually got finetuned over time.

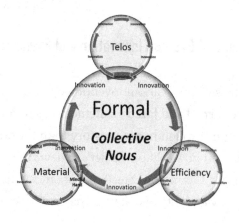

The concept of the Collective nous deserves a little more elaboration, it can be one person or an entire NASA organization or the entire human race (as $\sum$ of available thinking abilities to tap into), it also spans time of human history, as written books have made past knowledge and insights available to us through time. But only living nous can make innovation happen, not recorded or archived knowledge, why? Nous is thinking in action, it is dynamic while knowledge is usually in its static form. Nous allows the 'internalization' or 'digestion' of the 4 causes to a level that can be reconfigured and recombined to produce truly innovative solutions or even produce new Telos. Collective nous can be possible due to 'live' sharing via discussions or correspondence in Select Societies, etc. [participants living in same time periods] or "transcendence" sharing and learning through time and space [comprehensible forms of written languages], eg. Thomas Aquinas learning from Aristotle, Madison learning from David Hume, Lord Kames, etc. Formal Cause itself reside in the entire societies' collective nous and knowledge base, without which the formal cause will cease to exist and would need to be re-invented again.

Existing inventions (existing Formal cause) finding a new Telos is also a form of innovation, just like Edison's phonograph [initially marketed as voice recorder for dictation] later trademarked as gramophone (playing music), finally as the record player. Or in case of the earlier invention of sonar to spot U-boats in WW II, later refined and leveraged extensively to map ocean floors of the world.

Remember the Mindful Hand concept? During the manufacturing process (interaction between the Material and Efficient Cause into the Formal Cause), innovation can also be triggered, use of different Material, different production process can produce a new Formal Cause for same Telo; from initial Satellite Com phones in early 80s to sleek Motorola, Nokia Cell phones in mid 90s to the Smart phones of today. With the new Formal cause, additional new Telos are also discovered, the smart phones/devices now performing functions of lower end Personal Computers and providing ready web access anytime. New Material can also trigger innovation as aluminum did for human flight. New Efficiency too can trigger Innovation as in case of Henry Ford's Motor assembly lines, preceded by Philip D. Armour's meatpacking assembly lines. In summary, Material, Efficient, Formal causes can all trigger innovations that leads to new Telos causes.

Therefore, over course of human history the probability of an existing Formal cause or a new Formal cause (resulting from recombination of Material, Efficient causes) looking for new Telos would be higher than the other way around. In spite of that, Telos (User Needs) is still a key driver of innovations throughout human history and a very intense one, inventors under time pressure, with high expectations to meet. Which we now hope to leverage as we once again embark on the Space Exploration Journey envisioned by President John F Kennedy in Sept 1962.

*A Culture of Growth by Joel Mokyr

New Age of Discovery to combat Climate Change and Leading Space Explorations I:

There will be 2 parts to this segment on New Age of Discovery, as we cannot comment on individual organizations without doing in-depth Due Diligence on each of them, so in the first segment, let's discuss the Best Practices, Financing and Cultural Challenges for these Climate Change & Space Exploration organizations as a group, from independent observer's perspective. We'll also look at their organizational structures, their effectiveness in support of technology growth. We'll also compare the vertically integrated vs specialization approach and discuss each's strengths and weaknesses.

In second segment, let's discuss some of the pros and cons of the specific technologies and science behind them. Note that the second segment discusses purely the academic and concepts of the science and technology without any bias to their probability of success nor specific challenges in implementation nor their potential obstacles to progress during the execution of concept. We'll brain-storm technologies in support of Gaia Equilibrium and Space Exploration and last but not least, we'll also discuss the importance of Scientific Theories, hypothesis (*episteme*) and their role in advancing our Technical knowledge (*Techne*) [to build more advance space vehicles], after understanding our new practical experience (*praxis*) in Space Travels.

Lessons Learned / Cultural Challenges

Currently, the renewable energy industry and to a lesser degree Space exploration industry reeks heavily of P.C. Culture of Decadence. As we'd discussed in chapter 7, the renewable energy industry survives on Federal subsidies and greed of Wall Street speculators and crony capitalists' funds, therefore understandable why it would have the P.C. Culture deeply ingrained. As for Space Exploration, NASA Culture should not logically have such snowflakes' P.C. Culture, right?

Agree, NASA shouldn't have P.C. Culture, except for two events, First, President Obama's legacy of bringing 'Capitalism' to Space, asking private 'entrepreneurs' to lead space exploration, henceforth we have Space X (Elon Musk), Virgin Galactic (Sir Richard Branson), Blue Origin (Jeff Bezos) and voila you have introduced the Culture of Unicorns into Space Exploration. Second, under the Culture of Compliance, Obedience & Decadence, where the Mediocracy panders to Mediocrity, and we can see the rise of Tolerance of Incompetence and having to suffer Fools Gladly, all disguised under the shameless P.C. rhetoric of diversity, inclusiveness, etc.

So, which is A Better approach in a start-up or new Industry?

A Vertically Integrated approach as against the Differentiation, specialization approach. Steve Jobs had been a huge fan of the Vertically Integrated approach while Bill Gates has supported the differentiation and specialization approach in the Personal Computer Industry. Both are correct, in a new emerging industry or field, the vertically integrated approach would have the advantage in breakthroughs of new technologies. Once the technology has reached a certain degree of maturity, the differentiation and specialization approach would become more competitive and efficient.

I would argue that Space Exploration hasn't reached the mature stage, a vertically integrated approach [to be led by NASA] would still be the better choice for technology breakthroughs, having too many Virgin Galactic, Space X, Blue Origin, etc. might not be the fastest nor most efficient way forward. In fact, even if these start-ups do share 100% of their technology and knowledge to create a larger base (which wouldn't serve their short-term interests), we still do not know enough in these early phrases to have such silo entities and approaches, each re-inventing the wheel, each repeating the same mistakes over and again. We're wasting precious time and limited resources, try to recall the number Space X launch explosions?

As we'd discussed earlier in the NPI example, the P.C. Culture discourages competition of ideas which will prove fatal to any successful new innovations. Another weakness of the P.C. Culture is the lack of Accountability, it appears like the scientists are setting their own deadlines? Timeline for manned mission to Mars is set for after 2030s? this timeline would see the retirement of most of the more senior leaders in the organizations that can be held accountable for any delays or slipups in the mission. When President JFK announced the Moon mission in May of 1961, he also set the timeline for before end of the decade, that's less 9 years. That dream (stretch goal) was accomplished in July of 1969; 8 years after his announcement. Now after 5 decades later with all the improvement in technologies and computing powers, we can only get to Mars after 2030s? Sounds like the scientists are setting a pretty comfortable timeline for themselves and also no one to be held accountable by the time the deadline comes and goes.

International Cooperation sounds great only as a political propaganda, in reality it is a total disaster for getting anything done in efficient or effective manner. It Dilutes Accountability with different organizations working on different modules of the spacecraft or any equipment, who is ultimately responsible for all the interfaces between the various modules? You can bet there will be lots of finger pointing when the modules wouldn't work together. It also creates unnecessary bureaucracy, red tape and controversies. Just as an example, have you seen the Legal Governance debates about which countries' laws should apply in Space? These are pure mindless self-justifying job creation activities are as unnecessary and frivolous as the World Constitution. These are activities created by the same people making careers out of splitting hairs or any possible tasks with miniscule relevance conjured up solely to gouge on the Free Money (OPM, other people's money) from American Federal or International Funding. With the Funding secured, they now have too much time and resources on their hands and cooks up more mindless tasks to justify their own relevance.

Another observation (from outside perspective), most of these Renewable or Space organizations seemed to be built up around their assigned tasks. At first glance, it seems to make sense, but it is truly trying to run before one can walk. As a more effective approach, there should be matrix organizations with technologies organizations as the main focus from the start. As the technologies mature and stabilizes over time, transfer resources from technologies into the tasks organizations as the mission tasks' deadline approaches and launch date to Mars (or any other tasks) gets nearer. We'll discuss this approach again per Chart on page 367.

Generally, there seems to be large amount of uncoordinated Marketing talk (issues covered, range all over the map, without clear priorities nor focused on critical milestones). Much of the Wall Street Crony Capitalists' (as well as IT Monopolies; Facebook and google, Tesla, Amazon, etc.) money spent on talks, presentations and Boondoggles. Not much action nor discipline in testing, re-testing for results nor establishing the proof of concept. Bulk of 'virtual' action is in the marketing materials on the internet, while the only action in Space is in the Movies.

Best Practices

For best chance of success in renewable energy and Space Exploration, the organization Must be a-Political. If the organization cannot access 50% of the country's talents and ideas, they are extremely uncompetitive. Most of the current renewable energy companies will become immediate failures once Federal or Wall Street funding stops. In fact, I would argue that if the organization has P.C. Culture with left political views, it would have access to only 20-30% of the country's talents and ideas, why? In the beginning of chapter 8, we had discussed about Substance and Form, Spirit and Letter concepts?

Most of the real talent and intellects understand the Substance over form, Spirit over letter, while most of the P.C. Culture subscribers are huge fans of the form [most easily understood, paths of least resistance] as they find it much harder to work at conceptual level [the cutting edge concepts are never the Most Common mainstream ones nor most easily understood, quite the reverse].

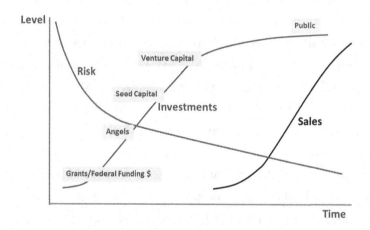

Company Financing Life Cycle

Above is a typical startup company's investment curve. Y axis is the Level of Risk, Investment, Sales while X axis is time. Using the same diagram, we can discuss the Renewable Energy & Space Program under the President Obama's 'Capitalism' in Space and the projects in the Renewable Energy Sectors. Imagine the Investment Project [blue line] represents the Renewable Energy or Space Program, it can also represent a particular New Product or New Technology. The red line represents risks associated with it. The investments start to ramp up only as the Risks of failures lowers significantly, and there's a high probability of success. If the risks are still very high, then investments should be held back till the risks are addressed adequately. This sounds logical, right? This is the simple logic why we need to weed out the weak ideas, poor concepts before investments of time and resources are poured into the best concepts and ideas with highest chances of success.

We (The organization) have to be extremely disciplined to enforce this rigor. The supporters of the bad ideas and poor concepts will never think their ideas or concepts are weak or admit that chances of failures are too high. NO, they will justify and defend their proposals tooth and nail, that why's the organization must be able to accept confrontational cultures and cultures that have the courage to Face Reality. This all sounds simple on paper, in practice, it would mean angering your colleagues and even superiors, so instead of pushing against each other within the company (colleagues that you work with on daily basis), they naturally let the "clueless investors" pick up the tab of pursuing high risks, low returns projects that always ends in failures. So, who are these 'clueless investors'? Wall Street Crony Capitalists? They are NOT that stupid.

The same chart provides the answer, Grants/Federal Funding. The most distant, with the least knowledge and with no business nor operational experience Federal Administrative apparatchiks will throw in the US Tax-payers money when the Risks in at the highest stage of the cycle. You might notice that when no other investors are even putting in a single dime, the Federal Apparatchiks comes charging in with lots of OPM (other people's money), bureaucrats with no commercial nor business expertise and with no accountability to anyone. Sadly, also with no consequences when the renewable energy or space startups fail and goes bankrupt, what happens to the loans and investments made with Tax payers monies?

As a side-bar, one might ask, if NASA takes the lead, wouldn't the tax payers be paying more? Hopefully not so, NASA has the most experience [till date] of handling Space projects, it is also the only Organization that had successfully put man on the Moon. Leading the Space efforts doesn't mean NASA manufactures all the parts, NASA can control the discipline and instill the Culture of Execution (getting things done), it can also outsource most of the heavy manufacturing work to outside contractors like Boeing, Lockheed, etc. NASA can also dictate the timelines and product specifications to its contractors which the real Free Market Capitalist companies [that thrives in Competition] will be able to fulfill (unlike the Renewable Energy Unicorns that thrives only on Federal Subsidies, Grants and Loans)

> *"...from time to time there will be some complaints that we are pushing our people too hard. I don't give a good goddamn about such complaints. I believe in the old and sound rule that an ounce of sweat will save a gallon of blood. The harder we push, the more Germans we will kill. The more Germans we kill, the fewer of our men will be killed. Pushing means fewer casualties. I want you all to remember that."*

- Gen George S. Patton

> *"The learner always begins by finding fault, but the scholar sees the positive merit in everything"*

– Georg Wilhelm Friedrich Hegel

Storming Omaha beach, Discipline and Esprit de Corps

In the real Commercial World, after the initial rounds of sending the poor concepts and weak proposals back to the drawing board, we start to narrow down the remaining ones to more rigorous testing. We start building Financial Models and also Operational Models (to understand the critical success factors), to determine if the projects are commercially viable or meets the Strategic Objectives.

There are many variations of the NPI approach, different tollgates and stages but the idea is similar to do as much Due Diligence [as many rounds of simulations], to screen out the potential failures long before investing huge resources and eventually realizing they are Failures (same concept as pilots-in-training flying many hours in the flight simulators before the actual flights).

Per the quote from Gen Patton, before we allow advancing to the Next stage, we must have many Rigorous Testing rounds before starting the down the Launch [or Commercialization] time schedules and tollgates. Not all failures during testing need to end in termination, Feedback loops help refine and build-on their concepts, "work-in-progress prototypes" to make them better and more sophisticated so as to deliver the Best final product or Idea. Project schedules is another useful tool for discussion between the engineers and project leaders, constantly missing project schedule datelines could be a red flag too [Culture of Mediocrity; 'I cannot make the dateline otherwise I might make mistakes and result would be catastrophic'].

Vertically Integrated approach is the right Strategy for Space Exploration and renewable energy endeavors. Steve Jobs has already shown us when he launched apple PCs in 70s, apple Macintosh in mid 80s and again when launching the iPhones and iPads last decade. In new emerging technologies, there are too many moving parts, too many variables that we have yet to fully comprehend and master, the vertical integrated approach allows the flexibility of tweaking different variables along different stages to meet the end objective. A piece-meal approach would not work well as we still have not figured out to get to end solution or what the end product would look like. NASA has the experience, culture and ultimately is still best hope to deliver results for America.

NASA working with US Military in testing phrase is crucial as the Culture of Accountability is bedrock of Space Exploration and breakthrough Technologies. Along the same vein, Accountability of the Leadership is most critical to the success as Culture and Values comes from the top, if you have a used-car Sales man or Poverty Pimp as the leader, the entire organization will get infested very quickly with folks of similar Values. With Culture of No Accountability, the Goals of Space Travel, colonization, terraforming would be as real as writings of the science fiction writers in the 50s and 60s, and the closest we ever get to Mars will be in Hollywood movies like Martian.

In instill discipline and bring back the Culture of Accountability, we should start exploring setting realistic but 'stretch' timelines for Space Exploration and Colonization;

- Lunar Habitation by 2020 - 22
- Manned Mission to Mars by 250 Anniversary of United States of America

Attempts into Space has to be numerous and often so that we can gain as much experience and information, there will be setbacks as Challenger, Columbia Space Shuttles and Apollo 1, we need to remember President Reagan's wrods "The future doesn't belong to the fainthearted, it belongs to the brave."

> *"We choose to go to the moon. We choose to go to the moon in this decade and do the other things, not because they are easy, but because they are hard,"*
> President John F Kennedy, September 1962

New Age of Discovery to combat Climate Change and Leading Space Explorations II:

We hope for a willingness to collaborate and work together for a better America and better World. This part is purely a technical and conceptual road-map discussion (might seemed simplistic and idealistic as we do NOT discuss the Cultural resistance, the Operational challenges as we have no detailed Due Diligence performed nor have access into the detailed specifics of the organizations).

Advancing Technology, engaging the Public in support of Space Exploration and Gaia Equilibrium

Internet News and Searches – Fair and Balance, how google and other Tech giants should step up to a higher bar, stop "burning books", killing diverse ideas and start helping human race to a richer experience and deeper understanding of existing knowledge and support the expansion of new frontiers into Space and Age of Discovery.

Deeper understanding by introducing google Insights. As the google vans went around various places around earth to take pictures of locations and help validate physical locations. In addition to the current 'most popular' answers, there should also be a number of additional Google INSIGHTS search options that offer expertise on various far-ranging topics and fields of study with inputs from various experts in their respective fields of study, also form "google Van teams" that specializes in specific subject matters, it would be similar to the Spirit behind the launch of the *Cyclopedia* in 1728 and *Encyclopedia Britannica* in 1771 ["where reason would confront falsehood with solid principles to serve as foundation for diametrically opposed truths" - Denis Diderot] where they were going after the Best and Brightest Minds and Ideas (not most common or most popular). Currently, the most common and popular answer must be right answer logic can be satisfactory but essentially flawed so we must provide an alternative option.

The Age of Enlightenment wouldn't have helped pushed human knowledge and understanding to a higher level if we used the logic of the most common and popular knowledge is the Right knowledge, this flawed logic will lead to stagnation of human knowledge acquisition and debase human wisdom and insights.

Higher Standards of Content & Experience Paid for by appreciative users

Free begets sub-standard analysis, incorrect information, mindless propagandas and irritating advertisements. We should expect the paid service providers to Deliver substantially Richer experience by leveraging Virtual Reality (VR) and better researched insights for their customers. we had touched on this opportunity for FB users to share their trips to Petra, Machu Picchu, Angkor Wat, etc. as VR or AR experiences. As they have already done for Salvador Dali's art exhibits in the museums, you can walk into many if Dali's art pieces. We'll be able to build entire ancient Rome, Jerusalem during Solomon's time in Augmented Reality too. Likewise, NASA and Google can jointly push the edge of envelope for VR experiences within the Solar Systems, on moons like Titan, Europa, Io, Triton, experience the rings of Saturn as the Voyager probes, walk on other Exo-planets VR.

We need to Imagine and Dream more with Internet's possibilities with Virtual Reality, then to make it become reality, we need good People, to understand End-users' needs, draft Process, Super-users to help push the edge of envelope with the programmers and systems analysts. Public interests and Involvement in Space Exploration will help it become a reality faster, it will also provide additional ideas and eyes to visually help the 'virtual exploration' of our Solar System.

In Commercial business software design that's much more demanding as the businesses are paying customers, the Super-users are employees who understand the business needs as well as the current software strengths and weaknesses, they can provide the insights for better software design, and provides the necessary disciplined testing phases by users.

The current challenge for google, FB, etc. is the lack of Super-Users to help constantly push the edge of the envelope for most demanding requirements; as this would also drive development costs up with no corresponding revenues. Thus, the vicious cycle of dumbing down the free users with low expectations. NASA, Space Exploration and Gaia Equilibrium projects will change all of that as there will be now a demand pull, paying customers that grade and critique the end-products and super users to aid in the development of the new advance technology.

Leveraging Artificial Intelligence, Virtual and Augmented Reality Technology to aid Space Exploration

The wide use of VR for the Solar Systems planets and moons can help the scientists with more ideas to explain certain phenomenon observed on such planets and moons. Just as amateur astronomers help spot new stars, observations in the night sky. You leverage the exponentially larger human interests and brain-power to focus on and help solve challenges faced in outer space. The VR can also become simulations before manned missions too. With so much data and information we already have on Mars and the Moon (our moon), why can't we create an entire VR version of Mars and let hundreds of thousands of interested visitors walk around Meridiani Planum, Elysium Mons or visit Viking 2 around Utopia Planitia? The demand for additional data and better experience from the public will stretch the current VR, internet technologies and also the demand for more information on Mars and other planets, etc. Once the feedback loop is established, the VR Experience in aid of Space Exploration and discovery will become an extremely positive one to further human experience and knowledge.

Artificial Intelligence also has huge promises for Deep Space Exploration; like synthetic biology it also possesses huge risks as we need to be able to address its potential for self-propagation and correspondingly containment strategy. As truly autonomous agents, how would they (A.I. units) behave individually? Even more complex question would be how would they adapt to humans or each other when the autonomous agents become connected with, become interdependent with each other? This is all assuming that the A.I. can compete with each other and humans too. Will they be able to exercise independent Imagination? If they need to compete, can they self-upgrade their programs after encountering new experiences?

When the power of the A.I. unit gets totally drained down, can it re-power itself back up? does its consciousness and learnings from last session gets lost? We can program a machine to backup itself regularly with new set of rules, to charge up its batteries before running low on power. Does an extremely well programed machine with elegantly designed set of complex rules qualify it as A.I.?

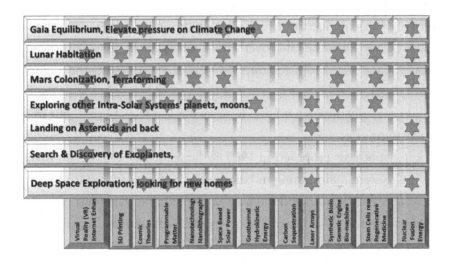

"The earth will not continue to offer its harvest, except with faithful stewardship. We cannot say we love the land and then take steps to destroy it for use by future generations."

– Pope John Paul II, Sept 1987

Gaia Equilibrium Strategy - Climate Change Projects

Earlier, we'd observed many Tasks centric organizations in the renewable energy organizations. Here we propose a matrix of Tasks with Technologies organizations, the chart above is done at a very high level, one can use the same idea and keep drilling down to an operational level. You will notice that the same technology will have many uses in various Tasks, the tasks organizations become the 'customers' or recipients of the technology organizations, similarly, each task organizations would also need different technologies to become mature and stable before they can proceed on their tasks. We've established a pull and push feedback loop.

Having members of the technology groups move into the Task groups as the Tasks get closer and technologies become more stable also enables sharing of knowledge, Institutional Learning and better understanding of possibilities in application of the technologies.

For over a decade, vast sums of Taxpayers money had been poured into renewable energy and climate change initiatives with nothing except marketing material to show for all the investments. All the funds from Department of Energy, Department of Interior, etc. needs to be accounted for. To drive culture of Accountability we need to start by being accountable to the American Public and provide total transparency to all, we need to start Auditing the existing projects, understand where the money was spent to identify potential fraud and target costs savings opportunities from wastage and unwise investments. Reality is that we cannot keep feeding the climate change pimps and their cronies. The funds have to be re-directed to start real work on real projects in NASA. This time, we ensure the US Tax Payers will be getting value for money with Return on Investments on par with other Business and Institutional Investors [as the Dutch Investors during the Age of Exploration].

There are many Geoengineering Proposals, feeding marine algae, Carbon Capture and Storage with Carbon Traps, create cloud cover with cloud injectors, increasing brightness of earth (albedo modification), putting shades and mirrors in space, even stirring the oceans, etc. We need to be cautious of the potential Dangers, as All of them would interfere with the Earth's natural balance, we still do not fully understand the numerous side effects beyond our immediate desire to lower global warming effects.

With the Gaia hypothesis proposed in 1965 by James Lovelock, we can imagine the Earth as a delicate 'living' system maintaining in balance all the forces to sustain life on the planet. If we disrupt the system and throws it off balance, we wouldn't understand enough to reverse the effects (let alone in a timely fashion). It can be compared to the human body and introducing new drugs to it, we don't really know the side effects of the drugs and how individual bodies react to the drug. The major difference here is that we can test the drug on many human subjects before FDA approval, we only have One Earth with all humans living on it.

It's for the same reason, that we discuss the following types of renewable energy; for they intervene minimally with the Earth's natural systems and leverage as much of the natural daily occurring events here. BBC Science Focus, National Geographic & Popular Science are good references.

1 - Space Based Solar Power

For a while, the low yield of the Solar panels translates into high costs of electricity generated via solar cells. The yield was in low teens in early 2000s, now it has increased to approx. 15-16% yield. For Solar farm operators, the yield drops with sand and dusk gathering on the solar panels and has to be cleaned constantly increasing maintenance costs. Connecting the solar farms onto the power grid from remote locations can also be a large initial (one time) setup costs.

The farms also cannot generate electricity at night too, reducing their productivity by at least half. Space Based Solar Power overcomes a number of these challenges but presents new ones too. As a start, it is outside Earth's atmosphere so minimal interference to Gaia's balance. The yield would increase substantially as it would be direct from sun without the earth's atmosphere filtering effects (55-60% filtered out), the solar yield can easily quadruple, combined with no downtime from earth's rotation.

The two key challenges are a) the high costs to send material into space and secondly b) remote transmission of power back to earth from the solar farms in space. If the remote transmission of power can be overcome and 3D printing help elevate some of the costs of building he solar farms in space, this mode of solar energy can be scalable and provide vast amount of new clean energy for us. The Solar panels can also act as shades to help lower Global warming too.

Japan, China and Russia are currently the biggest pursuers of this technology, Japan passed its Basic Space Law establishing Space Solar Power as their National Goal in 2008, JAXA already has a roadmap to commercialize SBSP (Space Based Solar Power).

Interestingly, USA had been testing SBSP as early as 1970s between NASA and DoE, as early as 1973 Peter Glaser was granted a US Patent for his method of transmitting power over long distances using microwaves from a very large antenna in space to an even larger one rectenna on the ground. Glaser then was a vice president at Arthur D. Little, 1974 NASA signed a contract with ADL to do more in-depth study of SBSP. They concluded that the expensive costs of putting building materials into space and lack of experience to be prohibitive. You might note that the method of power transmission was not highlighted as an obstacle. You might like to note that Nikola Tesla (who brought us A.C. Electricity, still the same means of how electricity is currently transmitted) had believed in wireless transmission of power way back in late 19th century and was ridiculed and mocked as a fool.

II - Oceanic Wind Energy

Offshore wind energy is one of the most expensive forms of renewable energy and as of 2012 was estimated around 16 cents Euro kWh, as of 2016 the 700MW Offshore Wind Farm in Borssele (Dutch) and 600MW Kriegers Flak (Denmark) are reportedly generating between 5-6 cents Euro kWh, this good news (taking the reported numbers at their face-value) would mean that Oceanic Wing Energy is becoming more commercially competitive with traditional O&G costs of electricity, costs of coal generated electricity about 2.5 cents kWh and Natural Gas about 4 cents kWh

Offshore wind speed would be faster, it doesn't compete with alternative land usage and less opposition from the residents on land whose property are affected.

The challenges would be the remote offshore sites, the weather conditions, larger wind turbines with their monopiles makes the construction and subsequent maintenance much harder than land based wind energy. European countries and UK (London Array 630MW, Greater Gabbard

504MW, Walney Wind Farm 367MW), Denmark (Anholt 400MW), Germany (BARD off-shore1 400MW), Netherlands, Belgium (Thorntonbank 325MW), etc. are clearly leading in the Offshore Wind Energy field, thanks to their government subsidies.

III - Ocean Waves (hydrokinetic)

Ocean Waves is a huge opportunity for renewable energy, EPRI [Electric Power Research Institute] estimates that total available energy from waves for USA (especially around Alaska) is about 2640 TWh/yr, of that about 1170 TWh/yr around USA continental shelf edge is recoverable and that alone translates to approx. a third of all of USA electricity usage per year (4000 TWh/yr).

TWh/yr	
West Coast	250
East Coast	160
Gulf of Mexico	60
Alaska	620
Hawaii	80
Puerto Rico	20
Total USA	**1190**

Since waves are formed by wind blowing over the surface of the ocean, as long as convection currents are circulating on earth, waves energy would be an inexhaustible source of renewable energy. Other parts of the world with abundant wave power include; western coasts of Scotland, northern Canada, southern Africa, Australia, northwestern coast of USA (as we had seen for Alaska).

There are 4 basic applications that could prove suitable for deployment on the Outer Continental Shelf (OCS): point absorbers, attenuators, overtopping devices and terminators. They all convert the kinetic energy of the waves through turbines, hydraulic pumps, electromechanical, hydro-turbines, etc. into electricity. Current costs of wave energy is estimated around 8-9 cents kWh.

You can read more about the 4 different categories of devices at

https://www.boem.gov/Ocean-Wave-Energy/

http://www.nrel.gov/gis/mhk.html

IV - Ocean Tidal (hydrokinetic)

Tidal forces are caused by the gravitational and orbital characteristics between earth and moon. They are much more predictable than solar or wind energy. In August 2011, the 254MW Sihwa Lake Tidal Power Station in South Korea became the largest in the world overtaking the 240MW

Rance Tidal Power Station in France which has been operational since 1966. The 4 Tidal power generating methods:

Tidal Stream Generator (TSG): Uses the kinetic power of moving water at certain land constrictions (for higher velocities) to power turbines, generators to produce electricity

Tidal Barrage: Makes use of the potential energy of the rising tides into basins behind the dam. With lowering tides, the potential energy is converted into mechanical energy with the water released through large turbines that converts the energy into electricity with generators

Dynamic Tidal Power (DTP): DTP is untried but promising technology that entails building long dams 30-50km out into the ocean, the tidal phase differences introduced will lead to significant water-level differential, producing strong coast-parallel oscillating tidal currents which can be found in UK, China and Korea.

Tidal Lagoon: Similar concept as Tidal barrage except circular retaining walls are built with embedded with turbines and the selected location is artificial.

There had been many US-Canadian studies for Tidal Power Plants since 50s, 60s and as late as 1977 when 3 sites were determined to be financially feasible: Shepody Bay 1550MW, Cumberline Basin 1085MW, Cobequid Bay 3800MW but were never built. United Kingdom also has good potential for Tidal Energy estimated at an annual 50 TWh. The speed of Tidal currents at Fall of Warness, off the island of Eday can reach 8 knots in spring tides, that resource alone can generate 4 TJ per year.

The biggest environment concern for Tidal Power is Marine life, fish mammals, birds will be affected by the building of the dams and barrages that will severely alter the coastal tidal flow and patterns. They can also be struck by the turbines too.

V - Ocean Currents

The Large volume of water that ocean currents carries across the world's oceans is in a constant flow as convection currents resulting from temperature differences due to solar heating of the surface waters near the equator, others due to wind, density and salinity variations.

Although the currents move slower than wind, it is 800 times denser than air. A 12 mile per hour current exerts same force as a constant 110 miles wind. In addition, the ocean currents move along great distances constantly without stop, which means we have tremendous energy potential in these ocean currents all around the world.

The gulf stream moves between 4-6 miles per hour, the Tidal stream at Fall of Warness off the island of Eday reaches 8 knots. Different design proposals for ocean current turbine and generators units.

Compared to the Wave and Tidal (the other hydrokinetic energy sources), ocean current is least mature but with Great potential. As we commercialize the Ocean Current project, equipment reliability and future maintenance would be of key concern due to the depth in ocean, remoteness and harshness of the environment to have to service the damaged equipment, either regular or forced outage would be most challenging indeed.

VI - Geothermal Energy

Geothermal energy comes from the Earth's internal heat, it can be drawn from the crust, several miles below the surface. If we get down to the magma layer, the temperature would be at 800-1000 Celsius. 500 Celsius at the outer boundary of the mantle.

How geothermal energy is being used? the underground reservoirs of steam and hot water can be used directly or to generate electricity. Direct Use, in A geothermal heat pump system, the hot water can be piped and used directly to heat buildings, offices, homes during winter, growing plants in greenhouses and melting snow on sidewalks.

To generate electricity, currently the geothermal power stations go between 200m to a mile deep to extract hot water of temperatures 182 Celsius (under pressure). Some scientists believe we can drill down into 10,000 m, that's 10km deep to extract water at 374 Celsius temperature.

The 3 types of Geothermal power plants are Dry Steam, Flash and Binary:

Dry Steam is the oldest technology, extracting steam out of ground fractures and using it directly to drive turbines.

Flash pulls the deep high pressure Hot water into cooler, low pressure water, the resulting steam drives the turbines.

In Binary, the high pressure hot water is passed by a secondary fluid with much lower boiling point than water, the vaporized fluid drives the turbine (here you get much more kinetic energy from same amount of deep hot water as more secondary fluid can be vaporized with same amount of heat, thus much more efficient in extracting the thermal energy. Most future geothermal power plants would be binary.

Geothermal is definitely the lowest costs of all renewable energy. The heat from earth is essentially free, the costs comes from building the power plant and operating it. It is always available 365 days a year. Its direct use can produce savings of 80% over fossil fuels. USA is currently the largest user of geothermal power in the world. A disadvantage is the generation of hydrogen sulfide gas and other geothermal fluids which needs to be disposed of.

VII - Nuclear Fusion Energy

At the core of our Sun, Nuclear Fusion of hydrogen nuclei into helium at 15 million degree Celsius generates all the energy that supports life on our planet. Nuclear Fusion generates 4 times as much Energy as Nuclear Fission process, it also produces nuclear waste at radioactivity much lower than that from Nuclear Fission. There would also little danger of a runaway fusion reaction as this is intrinsically not possible, any malfunction would result in a rapid shutdown of the plant. Success in Nuclear Fusion technology would immediately elevate the climate change pressures big time. It would also provide solution to the tremendous energy needs of our planet.

Acid rain, greenhouse effects would be addressed, as deuterium occurs naturally in seawater, so the availability of fuels is not an issue, nuclear Fusion could perhaps power space travel in the future too. However, there's many technical challenges of making Nuclear Fusion energy become a reality, which we will briefly discuss, there are also downsides of Fusion too. Fusion is not without radioactivity, the structural material will become radioactive during to activation during the fusion process, that material has to be treated in same fashion as the Nuclear Fission reactors after some years of operation. Secondly, the other fuel Tritium (in the D-T reaction), is radioactive. It is NOT a by-product of the Nuclear Fusion process and also exist in very small portions (a few grams) in the fusion reactors, but any leakage of the tritium is still extremely hazardous to public. As such, there is hope for a longer term solution of Deuterium-Deuterium (D-D) Fusion process.

We know Fusion is what powers the sun, under the massive gravitational force allows the fusion to happen at mere 15 million degree Celsius. Here on Earth, we'll have to achieve temperature between 100 – 200 million degrees Celsius over 10 times that in the Sun.

Alternatively, with a temperature of only 50 million degree Celsius, we must keep the Fusion process stable under intense high Pressure. Till date the only man-made device to achieve 'ignition' is the hydrogen bomb. The detonation of the first device was in 1952 codenamed Ivy Mike. 'Ignition' occurs when enough fusion reactions take place for the process to become *self-sustaining*, with fresh fuel then being added to continue the process.

Current Nuclear Fusion Technology

Tritium Hydrogen-3, Deuterium Hydrogen-2

The reaction most readily feasible is between the nuclei of the two heavy forms (isotopes) of hydrogen – deuterium (D) and tritium (T). each D-T fusion event releases 17.6 MeV (2.8×10^{-12} joule, compared to 200 MeV for a U-235 fission and 3-4 MeV for a D-D Fusion). On a mass basis, the D-T fusion reaction releases over 4 times as much energy as the uranium fission. From the D-T fusion reaction, the high energy neutrons (14 MeV) will be absorbed in a blanket containing lithium which surrounds the core. The lithium is then transformed into tritium (which fuels the reactor) and helium. The blanket must be thick enough (1 meter) to slow down the high kinetic energy neutrons. The kinetic energy gets absorbed by the blanket, it heats up, the heat energy is collected by coolant (water, helium or Li-Pb eutectic) flowing through the blanket. This heat energy is then extracted to produce electricity in the conventional way. The D-D reaction would require even higher temperatures.

The Density of Gas is much less than solid, as such, the energy density of Fusion reactions in gas is much lower than that of fission reactions in solid fuel. Since the thermonuclear fusion will always have a much lower (the heat yield per reaction is also 70 times less) power density than nuclear fission, the fusion reactor needs to be larger and more expensive than the fission reactor. The super-heated and pressurized Thermo-Nuclear Plasma needs to be confined too, the 2 main experimental approach are a) magnetic confinement and b) inertial confinement.

Magnetic confinement

This Magnetic Confinement Fusion (MCF) approach uses strong magnetic fields to contain the hot plasma at a few atmospheres pressure and heated to fusion temperature. The types of toroidal confinement systems include tokamaks, stellarators and reversed field pinch (RFP) devices.

Magnetic fields confine the plasma as electrical charges on the separated ions and electrons follow the magnetic field lines. The tokamak, Токамáк (toroidalnya kamera ee magnetnaya katushka – torus-shaped magnetic chamber) was designed in 1951 by Soviet physicists Andrei Sakharov and Igor Tamm.

Lyman Spitzer devised and began work on a stellarator in Princeton Plasma Physics Lab in 1951.

In tokamaks Токамáк, and RFP devices, the current flowing through the plasma also serves to heat it to a temperature of about 10 million degrees Celsius. Beyond that, additional heating systems are needed to achieve the temperatures necessary for fusion. In stellarators, the heating systems have to supply all the energy needed.

Currently, the main hope for Fusion Power centers on tokamak reactors and stellarators.

Inertial confinement

Inertial Confinement Fusion (ICF), a newer line of research, involves compressing a small pellet (few millimeters in diameter) containing fusion (D-T) fuels to extremely high densities using strong laser or particle beams. This heats the outer layer of the material, which explodes outwards generating an inward-moving compression front (implosion) that compresses and heats the inner layers of material. The core of the fuel may be compressed to one thousand times its liquid density, resulting in conditions where fusion can occur. The energy released then would heat the surrounding fuel, which may also undergo fusion leading to a chain reaction ('ignition') as the reaction spreads through fuel.

The History of Nuclear Fusion, Successes and Lack of

Considering that the first tokamak and stellarator were designed in 1951, 'ignition' in Nuclear Fusion was achieve in the hydrogen bomb in 1952, you might think we would have had Nuclear Fusion Power Plants by now (65 years later). Below are a few of the efforts, milestones and limited 'successes' of Nuclear Fusion Energy Research.

ITER

In 1985, Soviet Union proposed building next generation tokamak with Europe, Japan and USA, collaboration was established with auspices from International Atomic Energy Agency (IAEA). 1988-1990 initial designs drawn up for the International Thermonuclear Experimental Reactor (ITER, means path, journey in Latin). By 1998, the ITER council approved the first comprehensive design of the fusion reactor with price tag of $6 Billion. Then USA pulled out of the effort but rejoined later in 2003, when China also announced its intention to join.

By 2005, ITER announced to site the Fusion facilities at Cadarache, France. In Nov 2006, China, India, Japan, Russia, S Korea, EU and USA signed the ITER implementation agreement. Site preparation started in Jan 2007, first concrete for the buildings was poured in Dec 2013. Experiments were due to begin in 2018 but delayed till 2025. The first D-T plasma is not expected until 2035. Goal of ITER is to operate at 500MW (for at least 400s continuously) with less than 50MW of input power, achieving breakeven with a 10X gain. No electricity will be generated at ITER.

JET

In 1978, European Community (Euratom, with Sweden and Switzerland) launched the Joint European Torus (JET) project in UK. JET is the largest tokamak operating in the world today, produced its first plasma in 1983, controlled fusion power in Nov 1991. Up to 16MW Fusion power for 1s, 5MW sustained has been achieved in D-T plasma with JET. This should be a key device in setup and preparations for ITER.

KSTAR

Korean Superconducting Tokamak Reactor is at NFRI (National Fusion Research Institute) in Daejeon. Also a pilot for ITER, it produced first plasma in 2008. In 2012 achieved plasma pulse of 20s and achieved 70s in high performance operation in later 2016 setting a world record.

EAST

The Experimental Advanced Superconducting Tokamak (EAST) at China's Institute of Physical Science in Hefei, Anhui (安徽合肥) is reported to have produced hydrogen plasma at 50 million degrees Celsius for 102s.

TFTR

In USA, Tokamak Fusion Test Reactor (TFTR) operated at the Princeton Plasma Physics Laboratory (PPPL) from 1982 to 1997. It produced 10.7MW of controlled fusion power in 1994, 510 million degrees Celsius of plasma temperature in 1995 (both records then), but didn't achieve breakeven fusion energy.

ALCATOR

Since 70s, at the Massachusetts Institute of Technology (MIT), small ALCATORs (Alto Campus Torus) high magnetic field torus reactors have operated on the principle of achieving high plasma pressure as the route to long plasma confinement. Alcator C-Mod is claimed to have the highest magnetic field and highest plasma pressure of any fusion reactor, and is the largest university-based fusion reactor in the world. It operated 1993-2016. In Sept 2016 it achieved a plasma pressure of 2.05 atmospheres at a temperature of 35 million degrees Celsius. The plasma produced 300 trillion fusion reactions per second and had a central magnetic field strength of 5.7 tesla. It carried 1.4 million amps of electrical current and was heated with over 4 MW of power. The reaction occurred in a volume of approximately 1 cubic metre and the plasma lasted for two seconds.

Tokamak Energy

This is a UK private company that grew out of Culham laboratory, home to JET. http://www.tokamakenergy.co.uk/

They are developing a spherical tokamak and technology revolving around high temperature superconducting (HTS) magnets. ST25 HTS, Tokamak Energy's second reactor – demonstrated 29 hours' continuous plasma during the Royal Society Summer Science Exhibition in London in 2015, a world record. The next reactor in construction – the ST40 at Milton Park in Oxfordshire, is designed to achieve 100 million degrees C and get within a factor of ten of energy break-even conditions. To get even closer to break-even point, the plasma density, temperature and confinement time then need to be fine-tuned." The company is working with Princeton Plasma Physics Laboratory on spherical tokamaks, and with the Plasma Science and Fusion Centre at MIT on HTS magnets.

Cold Fusion, LENR

Low Energy Nuclear Reactions, Cold Fusions at room temperature is another approach in research.

You can read more about Nuclear Fusion Energy at http://www.world-nuclear.org/information-library/current-and-future-generation/nuclear-fusion-power.aspx

If you read all the history of Nuclear Fusion and the numerous challenges it faces, what would your prediction for the future of Nuclear Fusion Energy? Would the scientific and engineering obstacles prove insurmountable to us? I believe the answer lies before us if you observe the trend behind ITER & JET [too many parties, no Accountability, no results to show], as compared with TFTR, ALCATOR & Tokamak Energy [smaller group with Accountability, leverage Markets forces with competition]. With the best brains and human ingenuity in the world, we should have been able to overcome the challenges very quickly.

As in the concept of seeding for crystallization to start, we need a focused organization with Culture of Accountability consistently working on this project over time (as seed) to attract the best brains and ideas (crystallization to form). I believe with the right focus and consistent efforts of a dedicated organization, we can solve these challenges to Nuclear Fusion within a Decade.

ITER is the best example of a) lack of Culture of Accountability (too many parties involved) and b) Institutional Procrastination of Bureaucrats and Apparatchiks, comparable to the Climate-Change Pimps back home too.

Space Exploration and Discovery

Good Minds should be applied to Great Endeavors, Idle Minds create mischief. Even as we proposed for NASA, Boeing, the US Military to spearhead the efforts into Space Exploration, at some stage when certain milestones have been accomplished; habitation on Moon or Mar Colonization has become a distinct possibility, we need to allow the Free Market and Profit Motives to follow through. Only then would the Space colonization become a reality. Investors into Space Colonization Expeditions, as the Dutch Investors following on the heels of the Portuguese and Spanish, need to get their returns on investments (paybacks), mineral rights? Real Estate on Mars? Rights to Energy Sources within our Solar System? IP rights from successful ventures, rights to sell VR, AR of strange and exotic new footages of Black Holes, up close and personal view of subterranean Sea creatures of Pluto? Rights to harness Pulsars' Energy? Might still be too early since we've not landed any person on Mars as yet. But as in the Age of Exploration, the profit incentive is still a key to making Space Colonization a reality.

As we discuss Space Exploration, we can put them into four main categories, a) Intra-Solar System Exploration, b) Deep Space Searches and Discovery, c) Deep Space Travel and Exploration, d) Cosmic Theories and Hypothesis. There's abundance of Literature on Space Discovery and Exploration on Internet, so this section would be short brief highlights. Magazines like BBC Science Focus, Discover, NG, Popular Science are great reads too.

A - Near Space – Intra-Solar System

Within our Solar System, we can briefly discuss Seven Main goals a) Lunar Habitation, b) Manned Mission to Mars, c) Colonization and Terraforming Mars, d) Venus exploration, e) Asteroid Belt; 101955 Bennu, Ceres, Vesta, f) Galilean Moons, Ganymede, Io, Europa, Callisto, Saturn Rings, Titan, Enceladus, Uranus and Neptune's moons, Miranda, Ariel & Triton, g) Kuiper Belt, Pluto, Haumea, Makemake.

I - Lunar Habitation

Eugene Cernan (Apollo 17) was the last man to walk on the moon since Dec 1972, Lunar Habitation would be instrumental as a stepping stone, in getting us to Mars. It would be great place to test new technologies, excellent place to build telescope to look out into deep space as well as our Milky Way galaxy, the incoming radio waves would be free from interference as on earth. Malapert Mountain close to Moon's south pole has plenty of water ice, more forgiving climate and parts of south pole is likely to be almost always illuminated, less change in the temperatures, solar panels can absorb light 24/7 to power the lunar colony. To protect against radiation as moon has no atmosphere, nor magnetic field to shield the lunar colonists, the hope is to use 3D printing technology to create a large-scale infrastructure using the lunar soil ('regolith') to house them.

Low gravity on the moon would lead to skeleton demineralization and muscle wastage. The fundamental needs of food, oxygen and water all has to be derived from our ability to harness solar energy on the moon. The ice on moon can be melted to provide water, oxygen can also be obtained by splitting the water, indoor greenhouses can grow fresh fruits and vegetables. All these activities need energy.

The human psychological element also has to be addressed too, lessons are being learnt from trips to ISS and Mars500 project. Missions to the moon planned include Lunar Flashlight scheduled for late 2017 [now Jan 2019], it would be powered by a giant solar sail to the moon where it will search for signs of water. Another is the Resource Prospector Mission where a rover with drill and water measuring tools will measure how ice is distributed within lunar soil, if we can extract oxygen from the soil and by combining with hydrogen produce water too.

If moon can provide all these materials for space travel, it can be our re-fueling stop before heading on the Mars with much lower costs. In 2018 [now June 2020], NASA has plans to launch mission EM-1 by its SLS (Space Launch System) to send Orion space capsule (unmanned) on a 3 week test flight around the moon and manned missions between 2021-2023. If all's successful as planned, our moon will serve as launch pad to Mars.

II - Manned Mission to Mars

In 1965, NASA's Mariner 4 flew past Mars after an eight month journey, spending 25 mins and taking 21 pictures of Mars. In 1976, NASA's Viking 1 and 2 put in place rovers and orbiters that continue working and sending huge amount of information about Mars back to earth for years. By 90s, Mars Global Surveyor mapped the planet in detail and also found evidence of water. Mars Pathfinder a lander and rover was launched in Dec 1996. Mars Exploration Rover, Spirit launched in 2003 found evidence that Mars was once much wetter than it is today. It was stuck in soft soil since 2009 and NASA ended its mission 2011.

The Mars Exploration Rover, Opportunity that landed on Mats since 2004 has been making crucial findings on Mars and still active today. Mars Science Laboratory, better known as Curiosity had also started searching for signs of past life on Mars since 2012 and still active today too. In 2013, MAVEN (Mars Atmosphere and Evolution) and orbiter was launched by NASA to measure rates of change in Mars atmosphere to understand its past.

In same month of Nov in 2013, India (**ISRO**, Indian Space Research Organization) launched its Mars Orbiter Mission (MOM) with a perfect arrival in orbit around the Red planet 10 months later in Sept 2014 in the country's first attempt. MOM got into Earth's orbit minutes after launch, but waited 3 weeks before finally peeling out for Mars, as engineers at ISRO burned its engine fuel 5 times to raise its altitude gradually conserving fuel and making its final kick towards Mars much more efficient. ISRO also kept MOM simple with 1 camera and 4 other instruments for studying Mars atmosphere, the simplicity and deft flying kept the costs of their Mars mission at a fraction of the NASA's Mars missions. The ISRO's spacecraft cost $74 million, compared to the movie Gravity (starring George Clooney and Sandra Bullock, released just before MOM's launch) costed $100 million!

NASA's planned missions coming up. In 2018 [launched on 5th May 2018, Well Done NASA!], NASA's Insight Mission plans to get beneath the planet's surface taking geophysical measurements to can tell us more about Mars physical formation and the planet's subsequent physical evolution. In 2020, based on the successes and building on it, NASA hopes to send another more sophisticated rover; one of its mission would be MOXIE (Mars Oxygen ISRU Experiment) an experiment in turning Martian carbon dioxide into oxygen, if successful, someday humans might be able to breath that oxygen?

Space X missions of Hope to Mars coming soon. Space X's goal of making humans an interplanetary species, hopes to begin crewed flights to Mars by 2024, with plans to create a permanent and self-sustaining colony – population 1 million on the planet in next 50 – 100 years. The company sees thousands of regular shuttles – spaceships equipped with amenities like a movie theater – travelling between Earth and Mars every 26 months (where the 2 planets are best aligned for space travel), like a caravan of fancy giant space buses with return trips as well. 50-100 years later? Seems like Fairy Tales of Space, the EV pimp has evolved into the Climate-Change Pimp and now into the Space Pimp based on his 'one trick pony' skills of story-telling and fleecing the Wall Street's children of "Ignorance and Want" of their money.

III - Mars Colonization and Terraform Earth 2.0

A team led by Alex Rodriguez of the Planetary Science Institute in Arizona, looked at the pictures from Mars Orbiters, focused on the northern lowlands and proposed (in *Scientific Reports* paper published online in May 2016), that these could be evidence of Tsunamis on Mars some 3.5 billion years ago when an meteor splashed into an ocean of water on Mars. Alex explained that wind and glaciers couldn't have creates such geologic features, they had observed telltale signs of destruction, a washed-out coastline and rocks strewn across valleys and mountains and channels carved by water rushing back into the ocean, these observations matched with simulations already completed by another group in 2014.

Ice is another solution to protect our Explorers and colonist on Mars from Radiation by galactic cosmic rays. The hydrogen in the water molecule of H_2O is very adept at blocking radiation, just 5 cm (centimeters), about 2 inches, is able to bring gamma and UV (Ultra-Violet) rays down to safe levels. The Mars Ice Home (is a brainchild of NASA's Langley Research Center, Space Exploration Architecture and the Clouds Architecture Office) would be in the shape of a large Ice dome with living quarters and extra space inside, an icy yard of undefined open space for contemplation, relaxation, exercise, game play, others as the crew decides. Just as 3D printing using the "regolith" on moon, ice can be obtained from Mars itself, that plus an inflatable Ice Home of lightweight material would keep launch costs low. The inflatable Mars Ice Home would take

400 days to extract water from Mars surface so the assembly needs to be automatically initiated before the astronauts' arrival. A layer of trapped CO_2 (Carbon Dioxide) would also help insulate the Mars Ice Home against the Martian climate. The Ice is also see through material which would help in the aesthetics of the sunny Mars home. As a start on Mars (as on Moon), most energy source would be via Solar Energy.

In Dec 2014, Delta IV Heavy (world's most powerful rocket) propelled Orion spacecraft (Exploration Flight test-1) 3600 miles above Earth, 10X the distance of ISS (International Space Station). After 4 hours of spaceflight, Orion started its decent back to Earth reaching speeds 20,000mph and 3600°F during the re-entry. The design of Orion spacecraft came largely from the previously cancelled Constellation program, in addition, the SLS (Space Launch System) is being developed by NASA which will send Orion to Mars (currently planned for 2030s). In 2018, there's a planned unmanned Orion mission (Exploration Mission 1) to orbit the moon, testing guidance and navigation systems as well as radiation protection equipment. In 2021 [now June 2022], the first manned mission (Exploration Mission 2) proposes to send astronauts on Orion to a captured asteroid.

The journey to Mars would take 8 months, the current record in space is 340 days set by Scott Kelly (NASA Expedition 46 commander) and Mikhail "Misha" Kornienko (Russian Cosmonaut) on board the ISS from March 27th 2015 to 1st March 2016 when they landed near Zhezkazgan, Kazakhstan via the Soyuz TMA-18M capsule. Numerous physiological and psychological tests were conducted to understand the impact of space, radiation, lack of gravity, etc. on human bodies and the pace of deterioration. Currently, Orion can carry a 4 person crew for missions lasting up to 21 days as that's the amount of food and water it can carry, for the journey to Mars, the 4 person crew would need to travel in a transit vehicle with enough food and water to last the journey and plants to grow more food as needed. When they approach Mars, the crew would need to enter a lander Module (like the Apollo version), many more challenges needs to be solved before we can safely land the 88,000 lbs for a 6 person mission.

We have actually started terraforming our own Earth (intentional or unintentionally), so we know it can be done. Assuming that we get to Mars and have colonists living on Mars, the next step would be how would we start Terraforming Mars to become more Earth-like? Of the potential planets and moons in our Solar system, Mars is the best candidate for Terraforming. It has a 24 hour day, its rotation axis is almost the same angle as Earth's meaning seasons which would help plant perform photosynthesis turning CO_2 (Carbon Dioxide) into O_2 Oxygen.

First step in Mars, Global Warming, we must turn the current cold and dry weather of Mars back to warm and wet (what we believed Mars once was). We need to release gases into the atmosphere in Mars to produce the greenhouse effect to heat up the planet. Terraforming Mars would need robotic factories to dig up and pump out fluorocarbons (super greenhouse gases), as the temperature rises, the frozen CO_2 at Mars polar caps would be released into the atmosphere heating the planet above freezing (currently -76°F) to melt the ice and free liquid water on Mars. Everything we learn about Terraforming in Mars would prove to be useful in future of terraforming other extra-solar system planets. Next, we have to convert the CO_2 into O_2 Oxygen, like the great Oxygenation Event on Earth by cyanobacteria (ancestors of the photosynthesizing chloroplasts in plants cells) over 2 billion years ago. One of the many challenges on Mars is the missing carbon cycle that we have on Earth (from gas form of CO_2 to liquid form carbonic acid, to solid form of Calcium Carbonate and back into gas form again via geothermal forces).

If all the sunlight reaching Mars can be captured, theoretically, the warming process would take 10 years, realistically with the inefficiency of the greenhouse effect, it is more likely to be about 100 years. As for the Oxygenation process, the current estimate is more like 100,000 years.

Seeding Mars with Life and creating Ecosystems. Again, we might have the solution right here on Earth, 'extremophiles' living in Earth's most challenging environments show that synthetic biology could help create organisms that can live on other worlds. Tardigrades can tolerate temperatures from -458°F to 300°F, ionizing radiation and pressures 6X that in Earth's deepest oceans.

Synthetic biology involves building living machines from genetic "lego-like" blocks, Dr. Lynn Rothschild, a biologist at NASA's Ames Research Center suggested some species of bacteria would survive on the Red Planet, "I can find things that could live on the surface of Mars today" she says, "whether they're going to spread and really make it anything that we would recognize as an inhabited planet is another matter". Her lab had made several proof of concept microbes to show how synthetic biology could be used. She advises students at the Stanford and Brown University in the annual international Genetically Engineered Machine (iGEM) competition, in 2012 an iGEM team created Hell Cell, a modified version of E. coli after identifying 20 genes from extremophiles (tolerance to cold, desiccation, radiation, etc.) and inserting them into the E. coli.

We can use such techniques to have such Bio-synthesized bacteria, organisms, etc. help accelerate the Terraforming efforts on Mars. This is an extremely powerful new technology and area of research, like playing God with the bacteria and other micro-organisms would include designing life and exploiting evolution too, repeated mutation and selectively breeding organisms with traits we like could create organisms better adapted to the new environment on Mars.

Creating ecosystems to make the environment self-sustaining, the term 'planetary ecosynthesis' refers to the creation of an ecosystem on other planets (which might not necessarily end up 'earthlike'). As a start we would need to introduce the producers (photosynthetic Cyanobacteria, blue-green algae or plants) that convert light into food, herbivores then eat the producers and in turn the carnivores consume the herbivores before eventually the soil microbes and fungi decomposes the organic matter and completes the recycling process. As it is happening here on Earth, we'll need to build the same ecosystems on Mars and other elsewhere as we look ahead.

The following Intra-Solar Systems Exploration would be short introductions, you can look up more details on the Internet if you might have any interests in each particular area.

IV - Solar System Planets Exploration; Venus

As the conditions on planet Venus is so extreme with surface temperature over 800°F with sulfuric acid clouds, any machines' electronic circuits get fried in less than 127 minutes. Thus,

Jonathan Sauder (Jet propulsion Lab engineer) designed AREE (Automaton Rover for Extreme Environments) which received a NASA Innovative Advanced Concepts grant in early April 2017, consisting mostly mechanical systems.

V - Traveling to and Landing on Asteroids

September 2016, an Atlas V rocket carried a 4,650 lbs space probe Origins, Spectral Interpretation, Resource Identification, Security-Regolith Explorer (OSIRIS-REx) into space heading for a small asteroid 101955 Bennu (1/3 mile across). In Sept 2018, OSIRIS-REx will approach 101955 Bennu (believed to be carbon rich in composition similar to Allende meteorite that landed on Earth in 1969), it would spend 1 year mapping Bennu's surface, after which OSIRIS-REx will touch-down on Bennu for several seconds, eject nitrogen gas into Bennu's surface and catch the stirred up gravel and dust, then lift-off again and return to earth. OSIRIS-REx if all goes well should return to Earth in 2023 with its material from Bennu. Hayabusa2 a Japanese mission to another asteroid is expected to return on 2020.

Dwarf planet Ceres and Giant Asteroid (Proto-planet) Vesta were both visited in 2015 and 2011-2012 respectively, by NASA's Dawn Mission launched in Sept 2007. Our moon's Radius approx. 1080 miles, Ceres' radius is 300 miles & Vesta's radius is 164 miles

VI - Travel Beyond the Asteroid Belt

The Galilean Moons; Ganymede, Io, Europa (H$_2$O), Callisto

Ganymede and Titan are Jupiter's and Saturn's largest moons respectively, Europa and Enceladus both are likely to have water in either frozen form or possible water liquid ocean beneath the surface, which would make them interesting moons to explore.

Volcanic activities can be observed on Io with over 400 identified active volcanoes, probably due to gravitational forces as it gets pulled between Jupiter and the other Galilean satellites—Europa, Ganymede and Callisto.

Saturn Rings, Titan, Enceladus (H$_2$O),

Titan moon comprises of water Ice and other rocky material, its atmosphere is made up of nitrogen and minor components leading to the formation of methane and ethane clouds and nitrogen-rich organic smog. This is the interesting part about Titan, it's climate, including wind and rain, creates surface features similar to those of Earth, such as sand dunes, rivers, lakes, seas (probably of liquid methane and ethane), and deltas, and is dominated by seasonal weather patterns as on Earth. With its liquids (both surface and subsurface) and robust nitrogen atmosphere, Titan's methane cycle is analogous to Earth's water cycle, at the much lower temperature of about −179.2 °Celsius.

Uranus and Neptune's moons, Miranda, Ariel & Triton

Triton is thought to have been a dwarf planet captured from the Kuiper belt, it also has observed Geysers activities most likely liquid nitrogen.

VII - The Three largest objects in the Kuiper Belt, Pluto (H₂O), Haumea and Makemake

Pluto's Hidden Ocean. After New Horizons probe visit in July 2015, there's much talk about liquid water freezing and breaking the surface of Pluto with renewed interest in the ex-ninth planet. The impact crater, Sputnik Planum, could be sitting on top of a salty ocean.

B - Deep Space Searches and Discovery

Generations of Telescopes, Search for Exoplanets and Explaining FRBs

Search for a New Home? In 1990, the Hubble Space Telescope was placed into orbit around Earth, it is named after astronomer Edwin Hubble (1889-1953) who helped proved there were galaxies beyond Milky Way that appear to be receding from us. **Hubble Telescope** has extended human's ability to see as far as 13.4billion light years from Earth. It's position in orbit 340 miles above Earth, being outside our atmosphere allows Hubble unfiltered (nor distorted) access to more types of light and radiation to be detected, providing for much more refined measurements. Hubble's findings also allowed researchers to estimate the age of our universe at approx. 13.7 billion years, it's expected to continue service into 2018 when James Webb Space Telescope [now May 2020] is ready for launch with even larger mirror.

James Webb Space Telescope will Not be in orbit around Earth like Hubble, instead it would be heliocentric just as **Kepler Space Telescope** launched in 2009. ESA (European Space Agency) is building CHEOPS (CHaracterising ExOPlanet Satellite) for launch in 2017 [now end of 2018], as NASA is planning Transiting Exoplanet Survey Satellite (TESS) also planned for launch in 2017 [launched Apr 2018, well done NASA]. As you can tell from their names, these satellites would be looking for Exoplanets as Kepler has been doing, observing their transit (between their stars and us) and looking for biosignatures on these Exoplanets. The latest (August 2016) discovery of Exoplanet Proxima b within the habitable zone of Proxima Centauri, our closest stellar neighbor, 4.2 light years from us.

Extragalactic Signals; Fast Radio Bursts (FRBs) have been picked up by Puerto Rico's Arecibo Observatory [of Contact movie fame] since March 2016. Over 10 new bursts were observed at Arecibo over 2 months all came from same direction of deep space, each having traveled the same distance, most certainly coming from same space object. RFBs have also been detected around the world including from the Green Bank Telescope in West Virginia and the Molonglo Observatory Synthesis Telescope in Australia.

"The surface of the Earth is the shore of the cosmic ocean. On this shore, we've learned most of what we know. Recently, we've waded a little way out, maybe ankle-deep, and the water seems inviting. Some part of our being knows this is where we came from. We long to return, and we can, because the cosmos is also within us. We're made of star stuff. We are a way for the cosmos to know itself."

— Carl Sagan, Cosmos

C - Deep Space Travel and Exploration

As you can tell from last segment, Proxima Centauri our closest stellar neighbor is 4.2 light years away, which means it takes us 4.2 years to reach if we travel at speed of light. That has put Deep space travel to our nearby galaxies practical impossible even if we can travel at speed of light. The Voyager 1 spacecraft launched in 1977, only left our Solar System into interstellar space after 37 years of flight at the incredible speed of 38,000 miles per hour. If we use the Voyager 1 as a benchmark, deep space travel would look like an insurmountable challenge for humans. Recently there is a suggestion from experimental cosmologist Philip Lubin at University of California, Santa Barbara that could point us in the right direction in approaching the challenge of Deep Space Travel.

Lubin and his colleagues suggest that lasers could accelerate small probes to relativistic (near light) speeds, reaching nearby stars in a human's lifetime. "no other current technology offers a realistic path forward to relativistic flight at the moment." Lubin says. Instead of building one extremely powerful laser (a technologically challenging and expensive feat), researchers can build phased arrays comprising of large number of relatively modest laser amplifiers that can sync up to act like a single powerful laser (this approach also eliminates need for a single giant lens, instead replacing it with a phased array of smaller optics).

Currently, a 3kW ytterbium laser amplifier is about the size of a textbook (weighs 5 kilogram), eventually, scientists calculated that a 50-70 GW array 10km by 10km in earth's orbit could propel a gram size wafer-like spacecraft with a 1 meter-wide Laser-Sail, up to 25% of lightspeed after just 10 minutes of illumination! Researchers suggest this laser array could launch 40,000 relativistic wafer-size probes per year; each 'wafersat'; would be equipped with cameras, communications, power and other systems with the recent advances in nanotechnology, nanolithography, and pro-gramable matter, this doesn't sound as far-fetched as a decade ago [MIT has already reached the 'smart pebbles', 'smart sand' would be their next goal].

Lubin and his team even suggest to SETI (Search for Extraterrestrial Intelligence) to have projects looking for signs of such existing laser technologies [possibly employed by alien intelligence].

"I do not know what I may appear to the world, but to myself I seem to have been only like a boy playing on the seashore, and diverting myself in now

and then finding a smoother pebble or a prettier shell than ordinary, whilst the great ocean of truth lay all undiscovered before me."

— attributed to Isaac Newton

D - First Principles of Space Travel; Cosmic Theories and Hypothesis

Six Principles, Six Problems, Six Solutions by Stuart Clark and Richard Webb published in NewScientist, The Collection, Vol III, Issue V: Mind Expanding Ideas. In their short 8 page article, they explained the 6 Principles of 1) The speed of light is a constant, 2) the equivalence principle, 3) cosmological principle, 4) quantization, 5) uncertainty & 6) wave-particle duality. Then they introduced the resulting fields of study from these principles; Special Relativity, General Relativity, Quantum Mechanics, Quantum Field theories, entanglement, the standard model of cosmology & the standard model of particle physics. Subsequently they discussed the 6 resulting problems from the 2 standard models; namely 1) Dark matter, 2) Dark Energy, 3) inflation, 4) Force Unification, 5) Fine-tuning & 6) Measurement followed finally with the 6 solutions of 1) modified gravity, 2) supersymmetry, 3) fifth force, 4) string theories, 5) the multiverse & 6) information.

It's a great article and summation of cosmic theories. For purposes of furthering Technology, the standard model of cosmology [science] would be instrumental in helping to explain our observations of deep space phenomenon and vice versa as new discoveries raise questions about the existing models. Similarly, the standard model of particle physics would be most crucial in the prediction and achievement of Nuclear Fusion Energy (weak force), deep space travel at relativistic speeds (close to light speeds), etc. This article was concise, great summary of these complex theories and principles. It was able to discuss complex concepts (literally what the Rocket Scientists work with) at a laymen level.

The concepts in the article were not only well explained, the authors presented the facts and issues as they stand with no religious, nor philosophical bias introduced into their work.

This is refreshing as many "scientific Academia" articles are nothing more than thinly veiled attacks on the Judeo Christian American Values inherited from the Philosophies & Religious Beliefs from Western Civilizations. These "pseudo-intellects" interject many personal views and prejudices into their articles, indirectly chastising against religious beliefs and principles. These "cosmic theories conmen" exploit their miniscule knowledge and understanding (or rather lack of understanding) to brain-wash the younger generation into equating the possibilities of multiverse, dark matter, dark energy, string theories as concrete proof that the religious God does NOT exist.

This is another danger of spread of Anomic Culture which we have to be cautious against. This vein of 'scientific literature' ridiculing the values and virtues of others is dangerous for it instills arrogance in ones' own ignorance, believing we know so much when we really know so little. This ignorance of how little we know outside the comfort and protection of Earth, how fragile life is outside it's safety. The arrogant ignorance kills our ability to imagine, dulls our senses to the dangers and crises that can come our way anyday.

"As education spreads, theologies lose credence, and receive an external conformity without influence upon conduct or hope. Life and ideas become increasingly secular... The moral codes lose aura and force as its human origin is revealed, and as divine surveillance and sanctions are removed."
– Lessons of History, Will and Ariel Durant

The Greatest intellectual minds of human history through the Spring, Autumn & Warring States of Ancient China, Classical Greece, Islam's golden Age, Europe's Renaisance, Age of Enlightenment, etc. never saw any conflict between Discoveries of cutting edge Science, Philosophies nor personal Religious beliefs. Only the narow-minded and ignorant needs to operate in the Binary Mode (as the Low do), continuous new discoveries doesn't equate non-Existence of God, it merely demonstrates our own prior lack of understanding or incorrect interpetations.

"And the disciples came, and said unto him, Why speakest thou unto them in parables? .... This is why I speak to them in parables: "Though seeing, they do not see; though hearing, they do not hear or understand."
Matthew 13:10, 13 (KJV)

Just as the shallow Mainstream Media celebrities, these "cosmic theories writer conmen" don't really know much, they only know a little more than their readers or viewers. Do not be misled by these writers, confusing them with the actual inventors and geniuses that help bring the human race to a higher standard of lives through breakthrough in sciences and technologies.

A little humility goes a long way to opening one's minds. As Isaac Newton wrote in 1676, "If I have seen further, it is by standing on the shoulders of giants" [nanos gigantum humeris insidentes - Bernard of Chartres]

知不知上；不知知病。夫唯病病，是以不病。聖人不病，以其病病，是以不病。- 老子

Knowing what you do not know is a strength!

Another insight we take away from this article, it was honest in addressing the large number of gaps in our current understanding of the universe, per the 2 standard models [viewed another way, in the vast emptiness of what we know not, the little knowledge that we possess are mere specks of dust in the vastness of Space]. When you read the 6 problems and the 6 proposed solutions, Einstein's cosmological constant, fine-tuning of Higgs boson's mass, possible incompatibility of the cosmological principle with observations of accelerating expansion, yet unexplained observation of wave-particle duality, entanglement effects, etc. you'll understand how little we know, numerous contradictions, how lacking and inadequate our knowledge about many phenomena in the Cosmos or at the Quantum sub-atomic level. We're made aware of the severe limitations of human understanding, humbled by our own little insignificance and the miniscule insights we have of the universe or multiverses [1 proposed solution].

> *Aristotle's "philosophy of aspiration" – F.M. Cornford; [To be] Constantly looking forward, to what we can be rather than what we were, "the universe and everything in it is developing towards something continually better than what came before," including ourselves. To him, the world we make for ourselves continually reflects that constant striving towards improvement.*
> – Arthur Herman, The Cave and the Light

The three forms of Knowledge of *Episteme*, [Pure Theory], *Praxis*, [Practical Knowledge] and *Techne*, [Making; goal of Production] demonstrates the importance of Cosmic Theories and Hypothesis to the advancement and Development of New Space Exploration and Travel technologies. *Techne & Episteme* constantly reinforcing each other, one building on top of the other and vice versa.

> *"Reason steps in after, not before, experience; it sorts our observations into meaningful patterns and arrives at a knowledge as certain and exact as... "*
> – Aristotle

The human race needs exponentially more observations and experiences [to draw from], to help advance [compare, analyze and make meaning of] our current Cosmic Theories, for we know that observations and the theories; understanding what they mean, work hand in hand. These current number of large gaps in our understanding can only be solved with a major step up in our Space Explorations and Discoveries, exponentially larger and far more intensive from our current level. We are learning too slowly as we have too little Experience (*Praxis*)of Space to analyze. We need to increase the current efforts exponentially, get America and the World involved.

De docta ignorantia by Nicholas Of Cusa in 1440, described the Learned Man as one who is aware of his own ignorance. Only by appreciating how little we truly know, would we [the human race] understand the scale and pace of Progress we would need to make, to turn the Space Exploration and Discovery into a reality [we have a catch 22].

A significantly larger part of the human race also needs to become involved and committed to furthering Space Explorations and increasing our knowledge as a race. The human population might have increased exponentially in last century, but the amount of thinking nous at the cutting edge of discovery and innovations has shrunk since the Age of Enlightenment; the mundane part of the computations could be replaced by computers or 'smart devices', but nothing can replace the creative, passionate and ingenious human's thinking nous, ever so critical to innovative breakthroughs.

> *"The mightiest lever known to the moral world, Imagination."*
> – William Wordsworth

The nous per capital has also plummeted off the edge of a cliff due to a) the population explosion and mix, b) individual's sloth abdicating 'tedious' thinking to 'smart devices' and c) as a race, we've plateaued and now at stage of diminishing returns as we've gained significant better control over our environment on earth, [since the successes of Industrial Revolution, Enlightened Age till recent years' IT Revolution providing all the material comforts, we'd lost much of that human survival mentality].

Only by expanding into the unknown dangers of Space and experiencing real threats to our survival will we re-balance back to that Optimal level of 'Human insecurity' with its much needed sense of crisis, for survival in space. To attain the right mix of humility and sense of urgency to continue our pace of advancement for human race and bring it into the Next Transformation.

Quick Recap – Culture of Innovation and Exploration

As we started this chapter, we discussed Free Market **Competition** and how important it is to the growth of **Diverse Ideas**, to competitiveness of the American society and the ultimate survival of Human Race on Earth. We've seen how the Best in NASA solves challenges and accomplishes their goals, how they leverage Diversity in Ideas and Talents to excel in Space Exploration and Discovery. To attract the best and smartest talent, to listen and accept the best ideas, you maintain an a-Political stance, be open minded, tolerant towards different religious or philosophical beliefs.

A **Culture of Meritocracy** that appreciates the scarcity of resources, values Independent Thinking, that stresses responsibilities and delivers results, yet encourages **intellectual curiosity**, calculated risk taking. One that respects **autonomy of the talented**, that does not suffer fools gladly, is ever vigilant, with a sense of crisis, believes in personal stretch, hates complacency and bureaucracy. A Culture that promotes **Competition of talent, of ideas, rewarding talent**, one that does not pander to incompetence nor glorify mediocrity under the guise of inclusiveness or diversity.

Alignment, as we saw in the balance of 道, of the Ideological differences in GOP and Democrats both loyal to the cause of American progress and future. Loyal opposition with strong solidarity with Americans Values of **personal Accountability** and Meritocracy.

Culture of Excellence, as we'd discussed in depth in Chapter 4 about the Traditional American Values and Culture and how the Free Market Competition of Financial Capital (Real Capitalism), Human Talents and Ideas brought success and growth to America.

In this chapter, we discussed how we can bring this Culture of Excellence, Growth Culture to the World as we **Focus on the Common Goal** of solving Climate Change challenges for mankind and Space Exploration and Discovery to stimulate Growth and create Wealth for Everyone.

We understand importance of **Global Cooperation** for Space Exploration and Discovery, Climate Change Renewable Energies and Infrastructural Building, the criticality of leveraging **Global Talents** to further the Goals of Gaia Equilibrium and Space Exploration and Discoveries.

We'd discussed **Ethos** of Honor, Courage, Self-Sacrifice, Disciplined hard work and **Awful Virtues** of Self-restraint, moral rectitude, righteous anger at wrongdoers. In Conclusion, we'll discuss more about **Values** of Altruism and Future of our next Generation for America and the World. To succeed, we'll also need to understand the required **mindset of the Leadership;**

a Level 5 Leader with personal humility and most intense professional will, and that of the Inventors, Innovators, etc. "standing on the shoulders of Giants" to bring us to the next Great Transformation.

> *"There is one race of men, one race of gods, both have breath of life from a single mother (Gaia, the earth, accordingly to legend). But sundered power holds us divided, so that the one is nothing, while for the other the brazen sky is established as their sure citadel forever. Yet we have likeness, in great intelligence and strength to the immortals, though we know not what the day may bring, what course after nightfall destiny has written that we must run to the end."*

> - Pindar, Greek poet from 5th century BC on traditional Greek view of Gods and Men

Conclusion

These are the times that try men's souls

"Do not go gentle into that good night, Old age should burn and rave at close of day; Rage, rage against the dying of the light…"

- Dylan Thomas, 1914 - 1953

We must not underrate the gravity of the task which lies before us, nor the severity of the challenge we currently face, we pray to be worthy successors to those that had cometh before us and shall not be found unequal to our duties of steering our civilization; now at its crossroads, towards the right path. We can only do it together as one people, so whether you are a progressive or a patriot, let's roll up our sleeves and get to work, get Involved!

The Revelation

Remember from last chapter, Steve Job's encounter with President Obama in 2011, as recounted to us from Walter Isaacson's book? How the whole thing irritated Jobs. "The president is very smart," Jobs told Isaacson, "but he kept explaining to us reasons why things can't get done. It infuriates me." Jobs continued to press the engineering angle at the dinner, saying that at the time Apple employed 700,000 factory workers in China, plus 30,000 engineers to support those workers. It perplexed Jobs. Why couldn't those engineers be American? There wasn't a giant education barrier. They didn't need to be Ph.D.s. They could be educated in trade schools. If those engineers were Stateside, Jobs argued, then the factories could be, too. "If you could educate these engineers," he said, "then we could move more manufacturing plants here."

There's two other incidents from Steve Jobs by Walter Isaacson which I'll like to highlight. Steve would have candidates meet the top leaders, "then we'll all get together without the person and talk about whether they'll fit in," Jobs said. His goal was to be vigilant against "the bozo explosion" that leads to a company being larded with second-rate talent [*like Zuckerberg*].

*my words in italics

More on the dinner with President Obama, from Isaacson's book since we weren't present. "regardless of our political persuasions, I want you to know that we're here to do whatever you ask to help our country." Steve Jobs started the dinner conversation …. When John Chambers pushed a proposal for a repatriation tax holiday that would allow major corporations to avoid tax payments on overseas profits if they brought them back into America for domestic Investment, the President was annoyed, and so was Zuckerberg, who turned to Valarie Jarrett, sitting to his right, and whispered, "We should be talking about what's important to the country. Why is he just talking about what's good for himself?" From these series of events, recounted to us via Isaacson, we can gain a number of useful insights into Jobs, Chambers, Valerie Jarrett, Obama and lastly Zuckerberg.

Steve Jobs cares about deeply about Talent, talent makes everything work, he isn't a fan of the mindless P.C. horde, and he cares about America (Apple has a much larger International Revenue than FB, Amazon, Google, etc. but Steve understands and wants America to continue to retain the same Culture and Growth opportunities that made it possible for him to succeed)

John Chambers also cares about America, what he'd suggested (Tax holiday on profits repatriation) is perfectly reasonable and easily achievable by any political leader willing to try, albeit one without personal agenda. The vast amount of investments back in America would translate into jobs, increased efficiency and productivity for the American workforce and increased Economic Growth.

Valerie Jarrett serves her Boss' agenda well, when dinner was first suggested for President Obama to get advice from and exchange views with Jobs and a few Business leaders, she increased the number of attendance to over 20 people. Which would be a great show for publicity stunt but totally useless for any real sharing of insights nor any candid exchange of views. That didn't take place due to Jobs' health issues in 2011.

President Obama is extremely political, hates taking personal responsibilities and has NO intention to do anything for the American people. See how he gets annoyed in response to Chambers' suggestion? Damn nuisance how dare anyone add 'to-dos' on to my plate? See how he deflects Jobs' question with some political BS about Dream Act? Why does Jobs not buy his lame Politically-charged excuses? Jobs was addressing serious issues about America's broken Education Systems and sad state of America's lack of Engineering and Technical training across the entire country. And this Idiot was talking thrash about Dream Act? (way too few in numbers and totally wrong profile)

Lastly the One-trick pony Zuckerberg is truly a second-rate talent and first-rate ass-kissing sycophant. See his stupid comments about Chambers to Valerie? Trying to score points with Obama (belittling Chambers' perfectly good suggestion?) and making dim-witted comments about why Chambers isn't talking about the country? The trillions of Cash repatriated back into America is bad for investments? Bad for Job Creation? This pathetic nitwit doesn't make a single cent from selling anything of real Value to overseas buyers, all his Investors are the Wall Street Suzerains' cronies paying to dictate the rhetoric of the Social Media, obviously the Wall Street's dog will bark at whomever the masters direct it to. As comparison see Steve Job's comments about himself being too rough on people, this was back in 2011, the last year of his life:

> *"or I might say 'God, we really fucked up the engineering on this' in front of the person that's responsible. That's the ante for being in the room: You've*

got to be able to be super honest. Maybe there's a better way, a gentlemen's club where we all wear ties and speak in this Brahmin language and velvet code-words, but I don't know that way, because I am middle class from California."

- Steve Jobs

The Take Away here is simple: One who works hard, paid his dues and earns all his accomplishments in life doesn't need to tow the Politically Correct line, to conform mindlessly out of fear of rejection. There's a big difference between being polite, showing empathy, being sensitive to others and being a mindless P.C. rhetoric repeating drone.

The Missing Engineering Link

Who wants to be an engineer? The Genius of Steve Jobs, not only are Engineers the type of employment that Apple needs to help develop the company to the next higher level, they are also precisely the type of jobs needed to overcome the challenges of Climate Change and have Space Based Solar Power, Nuclear Fusion Energy, etc. become a Reality! The very type of American Jobs that will make the dreams of Lunar Habitation, Mars Colonization and Terraforming; aided by synthetic biology, or even having Laser Arrays' Powered 'wafersat' travel at relativistic speeds to Centauri Proxima made possible within our lifetimes. Studying Accounting, Finance, Law, Economics, Politics, etc. is studying about rules created by humans, Studying Relativity, Quantum Mechanics, the standard model of cosmology, dark matter, standard model of particle physics, etc. is studying the rules of God [or Nature if you prefer].

Is Steve Jobs xenophobic, talking about American Jobs? Is Steve Jobs anti-Globalism? Obviously not, we already know that this "globalist charade" is nothing more than a con by the 'globalist pimps', Steve Jobs understands that Engineers add Value, they make dreams become reality for human kind. Engineers is one of the critical piece of the puzzle to making America Great again, Design Engineers for Spaceships, Rockets, software engineers, R&D engineers, etc.

We appreciate the power of The Mindful hand, how *Techne* (productive knowledge), leverages the combination of *episteme* (theoretical knowledge) and *praxis* (practical knowledge) and "Let no one ignorant of Geometry enter here" in Plato's Academy; the value Classical Greeks placed on mathematics. For American Engineering holds the key to fulfill the 3 Conjuncture of events providing the best chances for the Human Race to launch into its next Chapter, America 'birthplace' of the Internet, now needs to A) upgrade the level of technology to next level in support of Space Exploration, B) to be able to save Diversity of Ideas by winning the Civil War against the P.C. One View of Uniformity; also currently being fought again here in America, and thirdly C) the acceleration of the Age of Discovery (Space Discovery and Exploration; also being led by NASA at this stage) and proliferation of Gaia Equilibrium Projects.

In defense of Democracy stricken with internal decay, all Americans should pitch in. whether you're an Independent, a Libertarian, a supporter of Democracy or a Liberal Progressive in the

Emotional category (as per Jared Diamond's defined Irrational Behavior), you might be surprised that a little humility goes long ways to opening Great Minds, for as Jesus answered Nicodemus; Jesus replied, "Very truly I tell you, no one can see the kingdom of God unless they are born again" John 3:3. (NIV)

Step up to the plate, standup for yourselves, Think Deeply and Understand Unemotionally, only you can allow yourself to be 'born again'. 知不知上。Willingness to learn is a great strength, the more you know, the more you will realize how little we all know and that's a good beginning. Remember the quote from Chapter 5 about the Taiping Civil War 太平天国起义 in China, that "…sometimes we do so without ever realizing that we are only gazing at our own reflection…" Focus to comprehend the substance and not be merely repeating the P.C. form. Please stop being the mouth-piece of the Activists corporations and stop thrashing your own country and the homes of your fellow citizens. Go live aboard and experience difference in culture and understand the lifestyles under other regimes before burning down yours.

Rise and Rise again, Rise above the mainstream Media P.C. Gestapo, Help save Diversity of Ideas against the P.C. Culture, provide the Rebel's Alternative voice, be a Champion of Real Liberalism, not some cronies to Top 1% Wall Street Bankers; the lackeys like Bernie, Clinton, Obama, Warren are and forever will be. Be the true professional like Ida Tarbell, see the re-birth of the Investigative Journalism, investigate the Activists Corporations and their funding, the Planned Parenthood and their trail of Blood, write about the corruption of the Clinton Foundation, do investigative journalism on the renewable energy's repeated failure over last decade, shed light on the Foreign Wealth behind the Wall Street Funds, understand and write about how the Problem Profiteers have enriched themselves, etc.

Resist the Politically Correct Mindless Hordes, become a Leader of the Loyal opposition for your country, think like Frederick Douglass who compromised to work with President Lincoln to help end slavery, like President John F Kennedy who consulted with President Eisenhower to run the country better, like Rev Martin L King Jr who also worked with the Establishment under Democratic Leadership to secure all the civil rights for the African American people, like President Nelson Mandela (Quote "you have to work with your enemy, then he becomes your partner"), who also compromised and worked with the existing establishment for peaceful transition of power to become the first President of South Africa, etc. You see the common thread, people who care about the future of their land & people, would compromise, collaborate and work together. Only extremists and radicals thrash the place or blow themselves up as they see No Future only the present.

If you are a Patriot, remember President Lincoln's Second Inaugural address, "With malice toward none, with charity for all, with firmness in the right as God gives us to see the right, let us strive on to finish the work we are in…" Let us shine light into darkness of ignorance, let us once again fight to Free the Slaves of the neo-Democrats, the Slaves of the Shame Culture, trapped by their Ignorance and Want. Let us be the Alternative Media, be the American People's Voice, defend this country against the P.C. Gestapo Media, against the Radical Fascist Activist Corporations sponsored by the Wall Street Suzerains and IT Monopolies Mughals.

We must always remember the parasites' Culture of Shame, we need to be aware of dangers of stepping forward for they will attack you like pack of wolves (like the ferocious dogs in Animal Farm, the Activists Corporations will come for you). Volunteer your service and time to the current Executive Team; help the volunteer Public Servants, they need your Ideas and Feedback, they need you to cover their backs as we make this country Great again and make the World a Better Place for all. Stand behind the current Volunteer Public Servants against the Deep State Professional Politicians, the Problem Profiteers.

Leverage the dual Strategy of Competition and Compromise. Assess which Market segment you are dealing with? Ask yourself what's their Agenda? If they are activist factions (most likely, as they are paid to be out there pushing the neo-Fascists Dem's Agendas) with rationale reason, we have to use the Competition Strategy, defend ourselves, transcend the mindless political slogans. Very seldom, we might come across 'Undifferentiated Goodness' that also wants the best for this country, in this case, we should seek collaboration and compromise if and when possible, be open minded for solutions in this case.

When we'd discussed the Culture of Decadence and how the Parasitic Virus destroys the communities that they infect, furthering their self-enrichment at the expense of their country men and women. Eventually bringing about the Collapse of the Societies, Loss of Culture and Civilization, we ask ourselves, do the parasites feel any guilt? Will virus feel any guilt when they use up all the life and energy in their afflicted hosts to replicate more virus, killing the host? The answer is obviously NO. Then, what enables a person to feel Guilt, experience Remorse?

An interesting allegory, a worker ant and a scholar went to see a sage to settle an argument. The worker ant says that there are 3 seasons in a year while the scholar insists that there are 4 seasons to a year. The Sage listened then told the worker ant, he is right about 3 seasons and sends the ant off. The scholar called the Sage a liar to which the Sage answered both of them are correct as the ant's lifespan only allowed it to experience 3 seasons. Perhaps just like the ant, the virus, parasites cannot understand the implications of their actions thus they cannot feel guilt.

But all humans should be able to feel guilt since we should be all be imbued with a conscience, we should be able to empathize with our fellow citizens and understand their pain and suffering.

> Act II, Scene II,
> *Lady Macbeth. these deeds must not be thought after these ways; so, it will make us mad.*
> *Macbeth. Methought I heard a voice cry 'sleep no more! Macbeth does murder sleep,'*
> *.......... Will all great Neptune's ocean wash this blood clean from my hand? No; this my hand will rather The multitudinous seas incarnadine, making the green one red.*
> Act V, Scene I
> *Lady Macbeth. Out, damn spot! Out, I say! .... Yet who would have thought the old man to have had so much blood in him?*

Reading Macbeth, you can experience the deep sense of helplessness, loss of sleep, loss of peace of mind and eventually loss of sanity as madness approaches, the inability to escape impending doom as it gradually envelops you, your grip on reality fades away.

Observing these self-serving, corrupt Politicians, one sure doesn't sense any guilt in their behaviors, in fact they are all cashing in their checks and favors from Wall Streets' Cronies, collecting their speech fees & monies and buying houses in Hamptons, DC, etc. Their deluded supporters might be losing their minds to stupidity, the designing politicians are definitely not losing their minds to guilt.

The Shame Culture feels no Guilt (as one needs to have internalized Values to feel Guilt), yet they can only feel Shame after being exposed for their Ugly hypocrisy, Pretentious 'Idealism', illiteracy in Numeracy and Parvenu Insecurities.

"nanos gigantum humeris insidentes"

- Bernard of Chartres

•

Who wants to be a Leader? What we expect of one

As we all write in the stream of time, I wish to be on record that I believe in the Future of this country, future of Humanity. I also believe in the threat of Climate Change (with us releasing so much carbon into the atmosphere and throwing Gaia off-balance, diminishing her ability to maintain the state of homeostasis).

We understand there's so much to do and not much time to do them. We need real Diversity of Ideas, we need the Culture of Excellence and Growth to lead these efforts. We need all able-bodies and clear thinking minds the get to work and off Welfare, if we continue to waste all these human potential and talents and allow the Welfare State to grow, the Human Race will eventually have to pay the piper as Gaia dies and we have no other place to go. For personal selfish reasons, I hope that the next Conjuncture in human history can occur within our lifetimes. So that the dreams of Mars Colonization, Space Travel at Relativistic speeds to Proxima b, etc. can be realized and be witnessed within the next 2-3 decades. For this to happen, we need Leadership and Values (following up from last chapter).

What's Leadership? Do we wait and hope for the right leader to come lead us? Do we hope for a Leader of Change? NO, Control your own destiny or someone else will. As I had learnt from an American a long time ago, anyone can be a Leader. You are the Leader! You don't need numerous followers to be a leader (the narcissistic celebrities have many followers and FB likes), you need to believe in the Cause to be a Leader. If you believe in the Cause, you have Passion, from chapter 4, we understand that Passion drives Everything, Passion drives Leadership, it drives the Free Market Competition of Financial Capital, Human Talents and Sophisticated Ideas

In last chapter, we'd discussed the mindset of Dynamic Leaders, Inventors and Innovators. This mindset is summarized best by Jim Collins's Level 5 Leaders, with their unique combination of fierce professional resolve and personal humility. Humility allows them to continuously learn new skills.

Ego is a huge driving force for learning too, but without the right Values and burden of Responsibilities (as we'd discussed in chapter 7, only Values can allow the Leader to voluntarily take on more responsibilities himself/herself), the person without right Values will 'game the system', give excuses, tell lies (sounds familiar?) behave in an egoistic way (if you watch their behavior closely) as they are off-balance. With the right Values and Huge Responsibilities, the Dynamic Leader will exhibit humility to learn new skills as they know there's much work to be done ahead and they take full responsibilities (to influence the 'uncontrollable factors' becoming controllable). What are these Values that the Leaders should have?

Values are at subconscious level, they are 'internalized' under pressure, this pressure can come from either external or internal. External pressure is reactive while internal pressure is proactively engaged. When we are young, it would be external pressure that gives us those seeds of early values (usually from our parents, friends, relatives, school environment, etc.). as we grow older, the external pressure lowers (unless you seek the intense external pressure to become part of an esteemed group or organization; like the Marines, Navy SEALs, Airforce Pilots, NASA Astronauts, etc. that's how group Values gets instilled). But just like gravity comes into existence as the planet starts to form, if you have amassed enough seeds of Values when young, and as they continue to gain mass (more values learned) they'll reach a critical point, the Values have a Gravity force of their own and starts attracting similar Values and repels dissimilar Values.

This is Internal Pressure, one can pro-actively 'internalize' new Similar Values with this Self-Driven Internal Pressure. In short, the internalized Values will attract others of similar values, energize their growth and facilitate the spread of such Values in a self-reinforcing synergistic fashion.

> *"perhaps the best way to describe their achievement, then, is to argue that they maximized the historical possibilities of their transitory moment. They were comfortable and unembarrassed in their role as a political elite, in part because their leadership role depended on their revolutionary credentials, which they had earned, not on bloodlines that they had inherited. They were unapologetic in their skepticism about unfettered democracy, because that skepticism was rooted in their recent experiences as soldiers and statesmen, and no democratic mythology had yet emerged to place them on the defensive."*
>
> – The Quartet, Joseph J Ellis

Unembarrassed and Unapologetic

To the Patriotic Leaders stepping forward for their countries, we wish to share this quote from The Quartet by Joseph J Ellis, 2015, referring to the achievements of the Founding Fathers (Washington, Hamilton, Madison, Jay, etc.)

The simple message here, if we'd earned our stripes and paid our dues in life, we need not feel embarrassed about our personal successes. Second, Democracy isn't some sacred cow (one that

Romantics and the Undifferentiated Goodness non sequiturs pray to), it is an Ideal concept that we work towards but always a WIP (work in progress), thus we should also be Unapologetic in our dealings with the greedy, ignorant & slothful; the smoldering, ever shifting gathering of factions, interests and Activists groups committed to corrupted agendas, and the mob (aka 'the People') forever vulnerable to P.C. Mainstream & Social Media's demagogues. We need to remember that righteous anger at wrong-doers is a virtue, we engage with our eyes wide open and Remember their Culture of Shame.

Values is the Key

We've discussed many Values associated with the Culture of Excellence and Growth in chapter 4 & 7. We discussed American Values of Personal accountability and responsibilities. Culture of Innovation, need to protect Diversity of Ideas, allow free competition of Ideas, free speech to challenge and constructively criticize so as to build on and refine sophisticated Ideas and concepts. Judeo Christian Values inherited from the Greek Ethos, similarly identified as Awful Virtues by Adam Smith during the Age of Enlightenment. We've deeply respect religious Values of Not judging others; He that is without sin among you, let him first cast a stone at her, Value of forgiveness not to trespass against those that trespass against us, etc. Below is another Value that I hope to discuss;

"Blessed is the Nation whose God is the Lord"

Psalm 33:12 (KJV)

What is this Value? Is it a religious Value? As the ignorant once again roll their eyes at "those that cling to their guns and religions", Yes, this quote does come from the Bible yet the Value is Universal. The Value addressed here is Altruism and it is unique to the Human Race. This quote isn't about mere "Blind puritanical Faith to God", we are NOT naïve nor blind to the liars, cheats and Pimps that exploit the American People's Trust (we know who you are), despite all these ugliness, we still choose to do the right thing for this country and its people (just because the others exploit, rape and plunder this land, doesn't mean that we should join them). Only Altruism and Love for this country translates into Alignment of Interests, for the Future of America and a Better World for Humans.

十年树木

百年树人

Altruisms is Universal and Unique to Humans, this is the version in Chinese, it takes decades for the trees to grow, but it takes centuries to cultivate a society. Another perspective, the returns (payback) of planting trees can be enjoyed in decades. The returns of investing in our Future Generations would take much longer to payback.

Since the payback (Benefits) of Investing in our next generation comes much later, Investing in Education, in teaching our young the right Values is an Altruistic Behavior* as we will probably never reap the benefits directly ourselves.

> *"Freedom is never more than one generation away from extinction. We didn't pass it to our children in the bloodstream. It must be fought for, protected, and handed on for them to do the same."*
>
> - President Ronald Reagan

> *"Woe unto the world because of offenses; for it must needs be that offenses come, but woe to the man by whom the offenses cometh. If we shall suppose that American slavery is one of those offenses which, in the providence of God, must needs come, but which having continued through His appointed time, He now wills to remove, and that He gives to both North and South this terrible war as the woe due to those by whom the offense came"*
>
> - President Abraham Lincoln in his second Inaugural address about the American Civil War

The Achilles Heel of America, our Education Systems where Values are nurtured

Per President Lincoln's quote, one asks then, what offense had caused this current Civil War again? How about not Investing personal time and effort into the Future Generation, Failing to Invest in this Country's Education for the young, not Teaching the young the right Values? As we've seen in chapter 5, the higher education system of this country has become a huge business venture dwarfing the Gaming (Casinos) Business and treating their students [snowflakes] as high-rollers clients and catering to their every wimps and fancy, in order to attract more exorbitant tuition fees so as to grow their $ 38 Billion Endowment Funds.

All these while the Public School Education systems are held hostage and manipulated by the Activists corporations of Teachers Unions whose sole aim is to get better benefits for themselves so that they send their own kids to Private schools. How did it come to this extend? Neglect and abandonment of our youth's impressionable minds, allowing the Liberal Academia conmen to subterfuge traditional Americans Values with traits like Greed and Sloth, teaching the youth to self-justify their vices by labelling Charity as their Rights.

In chapter7, we had also discussed the last technically qualified President as George H.W. Bush, with the end of Cold War in 1991, America decided to elect Bill Clinton (start of the flamboyant but technically incompetent) as President. After 24 years under 3 technically incompetents (Clinton, 43rd Bush and Obama), that's exactly 1 generation as President Ronald Reagan has warned us against. At the end of day, you always pay the Piper.

"We live in a society exquisitely dependent on science and technology, in which hardly anyone knows anything about science and technology."

- Carl Sagan

Religious Faith, Respect for all the prior generations that come before us

In the earlier chapters, we had clarified two concepts, Free Market Capitalism of Perfect Competition is the opposite of Monopoly of Wealth, Proper working of the Free Market Mechanism allows the distribution of wealth to the largest populace according to their natural abilities and willingness to work for it, countering the Monopoly of Financial Power in hands of a few.

Democracy is the opposite of Monopoly of Political Power. Democracy and Free Market Capitalism reinforces each other. If one starts moving towards Monopoly, the other tends to follow suit. The time-tested rallying cry of the revolutionaries of 'let all men be equal in what they possess' [A Misunderstood Myth of Democracy, The Stated Aim of Socialism] appeals to the sloth and greed of human. By transferring their rights to the Big Government in vain hopes of 'being equal', they allow the Monopoly of Political Power to happen, this new Monopoly of Political Power starts to intervene with the Free Market Capitalism process, start the process of Monopoly of Wealth, thereby crushing the Middle Working Class Americans between the greed and sloth of the Low (Welfare Abusers) and the Pride, Envy and Avarice of the High (Top 1% in Wealth).

Two other important Clarifications, even as we see the "globalist pimps", "pseudo intellects" [false prophets] mocks and ridicules the religious beliefs and faiths of others, they are constantly confusing themselves between the inventor, the invention and the user. We know that most modern-day technology users have ZERO idea how the Computer works, how the iPhone is built, how electricity is generated in power plants and gets to their homes. They're mere users of such inventions, yet many folks seem to think of themselves as somehow 'more advanced' [even superior] to the prior generations before them because of such inventions, forgetting that they had contributed nothing towards these inventions nor understand anything about how the inventions really work.

The users, confuse themselves with the inventors, overestimating their personal abilities. Just as the "cosmic theories writers" that tries to equate their shallow understanding of General Relativity, Quantum Mechanics, Dark Matter, etc. to be proof that God doesn't exists? Yet, this is exactly how the psychology of the insecure, egoistic 'one-trick ponies' work, just like Zuckerberg sidling up to those in power, playing on others' perception of them by associating with those, whose qualities they so desire; knowledge, wisdom, power, wealth, etc.

Similarly, many of these mediocre Liberal progressive 'academia conmen', 'pseudo intellects' tries to associate with the true pioneers of science, with no real understanding and minimal appreciation of the personal sacrifices made, hardships endured nor self-doubt and despair of countless failures experienced by likes of Galileo Galilei, Nicolaus Copernicus, Hawking, Einstein, Isaac Newton, etc. They failed to respect the process of how knowledge had been accumulated and built upon 'prior giants' hard work and efforts. How could they understand? For they are mere imposters who's never had to endure hardship nor make painful self-sacrifices, these one-trick ponies, genius Marketing con artists.

> *"Science can only ascertain what is, but not what should be, and outside of its domain value judgements of all kinds remain necessary"*
>
> – Albert Einstein

> *"And again I say unto you, It is easier for a camel to go through the eye of a needle, than for a rich man to enter into the kingdom of God."*
>
> – Matthew 19:24 (KJV)

And secondly, they also failed to appreciate how all of these greatest scientific minds never saw any conflict between their life's works of discoveries and their personal religious beliefs, in fact most of the greatest minds during the Renaissance and Age of Enlightenment are devout Christians. It is only when one is stretched to his limits, the edge of immense hardship, human endurances, challenges and uncertainty will one be more likely to experience the presence of the Creator. While those who are safe in their comfort zones of Routine, indulging in their Power and wealth, too sheltered and blinded by their eagerness to conform to and follow other fellow creations; in exchange for satisfying their short-term desires, would be unlikely to experience anything more than their dull senses would allow them.

As we'd started the book de bunking the Globalist Myth, it seems like we've discovered through the book that Ignorance and Want are indeed Global. Characteristics like Sloth, Envy, Greed, Pride all easily manifest themselves in all humans (as in the original sin), while Values like Self-sacrifice, Valor, Discipline, generosity, patience, diligence, kindness, Humility all needs to be cultivated over time with much effort expended and hardship endured.

Heading down Paths of Least resistance [which most people default towards], is a quality similar to Concept of the Original Sin in all humans, even as we all have the capacity, and the choice Not to head down those paths.

> *"Enter through the narrow gate. For wide is the gate and broad is the road that leads to destruction, and many enter through it."*
>
> Matthew 7:13 (NIV)

At this point of inflection, we hope to leave you with the Royal Society's moto "nullius in verba" (on no one's word), that Skepticism (of the Mainstream & Social Media, of the Romantic Academia and their P.C. Demagogue and Mindless M.O.B. rhetoric) can drive progress for humanity as it did during the last inflection point, when humanity stepped out of the shadows of the Dark Ages and into the light of the Enlightened Age. When Reason of the Common Sense man will triumph over the sophistries and Avarice of the P.C. One View Mainstream Media and

Activists-controlled Social Media. We look to the Renaissance of the Human Spirit, when the Torch of Enlightenment illuminates and dispels the darkness of ignorance and want.

> *"These are the times that try men's souls, The summer soldier and the sunshine patriot will, in this crisis, shrink from the service of their country; but he that stands by it now, deserves the love and thanks of man and woman."*
> - The American Crisis, Thomas Paine

Epilogue

Reflections of the Rivers of Time

Ta eis heauton; Reflecting on recent History of America and its impact on the World

"He gives to both North and South this terrible war as the woe due to those by whom the offense came", as I reflected on the words of President Lincoln, I kept asking myself what did Americans do, to deserve the present Civil War? We'd discussed a number of them, one is that the Free Spirit of Democracy still exist in America which explains the struggle between the small working Middle Class Americans against the Big State Government Monopoly of Power. In other parts of the world, the Tops-down Culture of Compliance, the Monopoly of Power has taken hold, there is minimal competition, the Main-Stream Media and Social Media has already completely dominated their minions mentally (all are now Politically Correct).

The Culture of Obedience, Conformity and Lowliness that had been ingrained in other States gradually weeds out non-compliant but potentially innovative ideas that could have contributed towards advancement of humankind. Uniformity Reigns. Their 'skin-deep' illusion of diversity exists in self-deluding you-tube videos where people of different racial descent, all enjoying each other's company, happily agreeing with each other and saying Politically Correct Slogans. In rest of the world, the process of Consolidation of Power, when faceless bureaucrats (EU) wield power behind the scenes, and their Perfect President speaks about future Socialists programs of Plenty to take care of everyone and their Pseudo-intellects discusses Globalism and why all the Jobs continue to flock into China and India. Yet if one recalls, non-Western civilizations always had the Tops Down patriarchal form of society, plus America is the poster child of Democracy, so why is the largest Democratic Republic experiencing this Civil War?

To be more specific, what steps or rather missteps did America make as a country that got it to its present conundrum? We already know that after WWII, the America's economy grew like gangbusters for following 2 decades, the devastation of most developed countries had left America as the Factory of the world then, stopping the tyranny (monopoly of power) of Nazi Germany and Imperial Japan also earned America much goodwill all around the world. It was also in 1944 at Bretton Woods Conference in New Hampshire that the World Leaders then all agreed on going on to Gold Standard.

By 1971, the world's economy essentially transacts in US$, which until then was still pegged to Gold. President Nixon in August 1971 unilaterally removed the convertibility of US$ into Gold. The World currencies were all loosely pegged to US$, while the US$ is now anchored to nothing? The first feedback loop of limited resources, supply and demand has become unhinged, as now the Feds can effectively print as much new US$ as they wish. Which is exactly what Alan Greenspan and Bernanke proceeded to do, starting in late 80s till the recent rounds of QEs from 2008 – 2014. The feedback loop of allocation of Financial Capital via the Free Market has been broken, turning the Free Market Capitalism mechanism into Crony Capitalism. The Income Inequality started to Hike up (climbing from 37% in mid-80s till it's current > 50%) and working middle-class in America shrank.

Third misstep would be taking our eyes off the ball on America's Education system; allowing the Liberal Progressives to infect the Academia, which instead of imparting values like discipline, personal responsibilities, diligence, self-restrain, honor, valor and promoting Meritocracy, now promotes paths of least resistance, glorifies Mediocrity under guise of Diversity, Inclusiveness, teaching the slothful and Greedy to justify their vices and thievery as Rights to Free Welfare, Free Healthcare, Free Education, etc. We cannot point to an exact date when this infection happened, it was probably a gradual process, nonetheless we can see its obvious effects today.

Fourth unforced Error would be the Foreign Policies overreach, to counter the Soviet threat, USA supported the Mujahideens in Afghanistan which was logical enough, however when the Soviet threat retreated by 1989, the rapid withdrawal and abandonment of America's former allies left a bad taste in their mouths, who had been armed not only with weapons but also with good planning skills and capability to raise international funds in support of their radical activities. The 1991 Gulf War was well-orchestrated with an International Alliance, the decision to withdraw from Iraq by Bush 41st was a brilliant move, leaving intact balance of power in that region, but the War had also planted the seeds of 9/11.

The Events of 9/11 triggered a number of follow on events that became extremely debilitating for America. The most obvious were the wars in Afghanistan (which was understandable since Taliban regime there help sponsored the Al Qaeda radicals) and in Iraq (which with hindsight 20/20 was more of a ploy by the neo-cons and hawks), Iraq became expensive to maintain and a drain on America's economy, adding over $ 6 Trillion dollars of Debt to the American Tax Payers. The wars were bad enough, but it was also under President Bush 43rd that 2 other significant chain of events were initiated by the Liberal Progressives, that are now paralyzing America. One is the setup and proliferation of all the Activists Corporations started by George Soros around turn of the millennium and second was the start of the Sanctuary Cities that have become the hotbed of crimes and criminals. By not understanding their obvious impacts and allowing these two cata-strophic events to transpire, President Bush 43rd made a blunder much more serious than the Iraq War of which's impact only became apparent years later.

Next Disaster to hit America, President Obama; Mr Super Showman on Steroids sell-ing Change to America which he did deliver to his credit. The QEs money printing went on hyper-drive, increasing the American Tax Payers Debts to $20T. Covering up his incompetence in Foreign Affairs and the Economy, Obama expanded the floodgates on Welfare, Healthcare,

Global Warming funds, etc. to buy Popularity, incidentally enriching his sponsors and cronies at the same time. Also, as distraction from his Economic and Foreign Policies Failures, along with accumulating favors; multi-million book deals, which he can cash in later on, he wisely panders to the Activists Groups, riling up protests and violence across America and attacks the American Law and Order by spreading demagogue about Racism, Sexism, Globalism. President Obama essentially exacerbated all the previous Presidents mistakes, intentionally or unintentionally, bringing us to the current Dark Ages of America, thankfully after 2016 Elections, we see light at the end of the tunnel and have a chance to move this country in the right direction.

How about the current dominance of the P.C. Culture, how did it arise? Is it an American Invention? In Chapter 4, we'd seen how the rise of the Liberal Progressives so call P.C. 'Values' (selectively 'cut and paste' from the Traditional American Values that suited their rhetoric omitting any real Values requiring discipline to practice) as they have no real values of their own. But how is it that for nearly quarter of century, most Americans cannot see through their lies and sophistries? Most non-Americans coming into contact with the P.C. Culture would view it as pretentious, hypocritical, at best as naïve romantics, anyone with common sense would be able to see that all the P.C. rhetoric is non-sequitur. Let's together explore a short list of why and how people get hoodwinked by the Politically Correct Subterfuges.

Why do people get blindsided by and become afflicted with the Politically Correct Virus?

Here we've highlighted 4 Behavioral Reasons:

First and more obvious one, Conformity out of fear of rejection by peers, to be ostracized by the others in the Politically Correct groups or hierarchies, personal insecurity and lack of self-confidence to stand apart from the Mainstream Media and Social Media crowd. Crowd psychology, fear of being perceived negatively and losing their so-called popularity. Perhaps also the Rational and very Real Fear of attacks by the Activists Corporations – ATLA (Assn of Trial Lawyers of America)

Next would be Lack of experience in Life to differentiate between what's realistic and what's overly idealistic. Youth, forgetfulness, lack of observation all contribute towards Lack of Experience. Logically, if you have no or few data points, it would make it harder to refute someone's statements, unless you're a P.C. neo-democrat Radical then 1 data point is all you need, the P.C. viewpoint.

Third is the natural tendency of humans to defer to those in authority or those deemed with more expertise; naively assuming the Mainstream Media or Social Media to have a certain level of Independence, Professionalism and sense of fiduciary duties to the readers or audience.

Fourthly, as we'd learned, the natural tendency of the masses to focus on the Form over the Substance, we had ended the book's Conclusion with the exhortation of "nullius in verba", on no one's word, to have a level of Skepticism towards everything one reads these days esp. if it relates to politics coming from Mainstream Media or Social Media. It helps to remember that the Mainstream Media is One Uniform view, so although there are many outlets, there is Only

ONE common view and one Perspective. Many outlets of same perspective do Not equate many different perspectives.

We'll now also attempt to go one layer deeper into how were we usually perceive issues to help avoid infection by the P.C. Virus.

Checking our Blind Spots to Protect against infection of the P.C. Virus

Most of us tend to form our perceptions subconsciously, understanding how they are formed can prevent others [the P.C. Mainstream Media Gestapo or Social Media Radicals] from shaping or distorting our perceptions to further their agendas. We have categorized 12 weaknesses in formation of Perceptions and thus areas for Improvement:

Snapshot view of history. Some people tend to have a very short timeframe view of history (instead of viewing it as a continuous flow), we had introduced this earlier as 'this is where I came in' effect. One judges whatever is presented to them at the point when one first becomes aware of certain issue, with little appreciation of what transpired before nor will happen next, like an instantaneous snapshot of point in time ignoring all the other causation and effects in the rivers of time before and after. As an example, the events leading to Arab-Israeli conflict had begun since the establishment of Palestine and Trans-Jordan in 1921 when the British were tasked by the Mandate system per Article 22 of the Covenant of the League of Nations to create a "Jewish national home" there. Prior to the British interference, that region had been under Turks rule, for over 400 hundred years, with whom the Arabs also have had no love lost. The region wasn't conflict-free before T.E. Lawrence, just that the West wasn't involved.

Yet, because many of the Mainstream Media stooges had started covering the conflict in late '60s after the 6 Day war, when Israel had already won over vast territories from the Arabs, so the Mainstream Media decided their script as championing the cause of the downtrodden stateless and homeless Palestinians, against the big bullies of Israel and America, so this similar script has persisted from 70s till today [and why not? The message is easy to sell, has wide appeal; static and simple, best of all it evokes emotions and increases viewership, minimal effort to explain; after all it's not changed since 70s]. The reality is that sad plight of the hapless Palestinians was caused not by the Israelis but by the manipulation of the other major Muslims Powers in that region [conniving not just against the Western Powers, but also against each other, multitudes of religious, sectarian, political, tribal, ideological, territorial factions]. The Arabs had decided Not to accept the separate demarcated territories proposed by UN in 1947, causing the Palestinians to remain Stateless till this day. We'd covered some of this background in chapter 6, but you get the picture [Chapter 3 of World Order by Kissinger provides more details]. There's also a tendency for one to be unduly influenced by how the issue first gets explained to them, retaining a bias that would require much more effort to clarify subsequently. Others might forget and lose track of the issues, treating each issue when they re-encounter them as their first.

There's a few other 'blindsides' related to perceptions through time [history], failure to understand past **events** (decisions made) **in their situational context** [cultural, historical, political, regional, etc.]; judging slave ownership in the 18ᵗʰ century America or lack of women's rights in Ancient Greece through 21ˢᵗ century American's viewpoint.

Another is the **time Lag Effect** [especially for major, complex policies' economic impacts or gradual societal shifts]; example like President Reagan accomplishments (we correctly judge him 3 decades later), or the visible rising affluence of African America families in 80s when the positive contributions were made by Rev Martin Luther King Jr in early - mid 60s, which started to take effect by late 60s. Over a decade later we see the cumulative effects of increased wealth when the economy picked up. The reverse holds true, the negative impacts by President Obama on African American's families beginning in 2009, racial hatred, BLM, encouraging welfare, poor economic performance, all translating over time into decline in wealth that we're seeing now, almost a decade later. Or the negative impact of Obama care; intentionally Phased-in, such that the disastrous impact hit only after he's gone. Just as the Monkey on the moving boat analogy we saw in chapter 3, many people cannot understand this time lag effect, they are not able to differentiate between the immediate effects of simple tasks (giving free welfare, free government funding) versus that of complex policies (turning around the America Economy and growing the working Middle Class of America) that would take a much longer time for their effects to come to fruition.

Devil's in the Details. The inability to get into depth of details about issues can become a limiting factor to understanding the big picture as some unfamiliar matters or issues would need the reader or audience to be able to come up to speed on complicated challenges and their causes. Examples for companies' management would be Financial or Operational data at the transactional level, the individual transactions would be so numerous we cannot possibly track and monitor them individually, thus the need to categorize and prioritize them, next to understand their causation or drivers. Once we can understand the correlation, we verify cause and effect, and finally summarize our conclusion of challenges faced, the drivers causing them and propose appropriate solutions. Weak managers cannot get into all the detailed steps explained above, so they by-pass the entire bottoms-up, fact/data-based approach with a simple popularity contest, they ask everyone for their opinions, the most popular answer is the right answer (this approach is similar to the 'leading from behind via polls' approach)

Logic and Real Knowledge extends Cross Discipline. Silo Perspective make one susceptible to being blindsided in discussions about important issues, which would naturally be complex and spans a number of fields of expertise. The artificial categorization of academia disciplines was setup only to facilitate specialization in knowledge acquisition not limit human understanding. Many people defer to subject matters experts' opinions (eg. Legal, Finance, Economics, Politics, Information Technology, etc.), forgetting everyone has some expertise in various fields and no one has all expertise in all fields. We need to also remember that no 'subject matter expertise' should ever substitute logic nor reason. Thirdly, the other parties probably have their hidden agendas, so we should not defer to their 'so called expertise' so eagerly, lastly, even if they don't have hidden agendas, their knowledge is only as good as conventional wisdom; which isn't worth much as it can be googled in a matter of seconds.

Let's try to understand the process of knowledge by the great thinkers and their purpose for doing so, as in the philosophers during China's Spring & Autumn, Warring States; 孔子 Confucius, 墨子 Mozi, 莊子Zhuang Zhou, 韩非子 HanFei Zi, 孟子 Mencius, 老子LaoTze, 荀子 Xun Kuan or Military Strategist like 孙子 Sun Tze, the Ancient Greece's philosophers like Heraclitus, Socrates, Plato, Pythagoras, Aristotle, Archimedes and all the great minds of the Age of Enlightenment shared great cumulation of knowledge that's Cross Multi disciplines' expertise.

This type of all rounded knowledge provides us the wisdom to see an issue simultaneously from multiple perspectives analogous to tri-angulating to fix a location or the thousands points of lasers to form the hologram, the same multiple perspectives allows us to see the issue more clearly than merely from a single point of reference. The ancients' aim was to bring about a better society for all humans, thus they learn about Military Strategy as war is an inevitable part of life then as now. They study philosophy to understand human's thinking processes and interactions with nature, religious knowledge to address our concerns about afterlife meanwhile incorporating ethics in both disciplines. They study Mathematics and sciences as these explain the basics of life on earth, in addition, the ability to explain and quantify observations through mathematics is powerful, as that logic allows us to pursue reason, ascending beyond pure emotions.

Economics, finances and politics (human nature, organizational behavior, social sciences) also become important as we have to manage the people towards a stable society by instituting Laws. Trade and Economics becomes necessary as Trade and Economic Wealth is the lifeblood of the society, they study Forms of government as management tool for control of the populace.

We now understand that Multiple Insights can be gleaned from different perspectives from cross disciplines' expertise while a blinkered singular perspective results when we rely solely on the 'conventional wisdom' or worse the mainstream media celebrities' narrative. Remember, there are NO Experts, only Logic and Reason, both of which you possess.

Conceptual Frameworks and First Principles. One might ask, how do we find time to learn so many disciplines? Definitely would not possible by memorizing all their forms .. Only via concepts, analogies, recognizing 'similar patterns' allows us to speed up the understanding .. Understanding their first principles and applying logic to derive the final conclusion, this similar approach can then be leveraged for different subject matters / disciplines. This is the power of learning concepts and first principles. We'd shared many similar concepts across disciplines through the book.

The EQ and IQ Gap. IQ (ability to recognize patterns, to grasp complex and abstract concepts) Vs EQ (more dynamic, 'empathy', touchy feely strengths). Most people overlap between the 2 curves (they are average on both curves) but there can be a substantial gap between the two for some people. For the society at large tends to overestimate those with high EQ but low IQ to be more able than they really are, and to underestimate the ability of those with high IQ and lower EQ. This is also a major and powerful tool / Skill often exploited by Politicians appealing to emotions (feeling) than logic (thinking). Another misperception that the 'politicians with High EQs' exploit is to 'make a grand showcase' of their presentation, touching on just small part not explaining the substantial bulk of the details and then allowing others (of lower EQ) to erroneously extrapolate their knowledge or abilities resulting in a mirage [as an example, many of the overawed investors assume because a CEO like Musk can talk a great game about the Strategy and vision for EV industry, it also means that he knows how to execute on the R&D, Manufacturing Strategies and deliver results, accomplishing the goals for Tesla's shareholders].

Error of Self Projection. Forming perceptions via Self-Projection can frequently lead to misunderstanding and misreading of critical situations. A common tool of empathy is to put yourself in the shoes of the other person. While this can be a great start to try understanding others, it also requires one not to bring in bias assumptions from your own experience as well. Instead of truly observing the other party we are addressing, we might end up, projecting ourselves into (imagining ourselves to be in) their situation. As Ada Lovelace did, she didn't think it would be possible for programming machines to think like humans (she assumed naturally humans like herself). As did other world leaders projecting incorrect image unto Obama (assuming he would deliver what he promised). A Positive Self Projection is a mistake all of us frequently make (we tend to think of people better than they are) this error in perception can Be easily exploited by others and even viewed as stupidity. On the other hand, a negative person would also self-project negativity unto their opponents which doesn't harm them much, just makes them more alert, but also insecure with endless paranoia.

Just like an arsenal with wide array of weapons, **Multiple disciplines knowledge** allows us the ability to tap into various useful skillsets and insights. Finance and Accounting allows clear understanding of all business and ability to clearly quantify profitable and non-profitable ones and from there have a bottoms-up understanding to the Marco economics. Studying economics without knowing the basics of what makes individual business profitable, is like looking at the forest from 50,000 feet without knowing how each tree functions, grasping both and reconciling the two disciplines is key to knowing whether free market is working properly.

Understanding Politics, by studying history; the Insights from Plato, Aristotle, Age of Enlightenment is as important as reading the works of Churchill, Orwell, etc. Knowing the events of the French Revolution, Russian Revolution and their subsequent history is most enlightening as all Political elite's behaviors tends to repeat themselves in history playing the same game over again. Monopoly of power through offering sophistries to the greedy, appealing to their selfishness and ignorance of the low, breaking the existing establishment and going through cycles of revolutions, anarchy and eventually back to monopoly of power.

Mathematics enables us to measure and quantify and think logically, stretching our minds with complex concepts. During the Scottish Enlightenment, Numeracy and Accounts were essential to Literacy, besides knowing to read and write. Studying Strategy teaches us to plan many steps ahead and pay close attention to all relevant details ahead of the fight to know the strengths and weaknesses of the opponent, and yet retain the flexibility to adapt and change tactics and strategy once the opponent has been engaged.

People all have personal motivations and agendas. Dealing with people from different levels in the society as well as different cultural backgrounds or societies makes one attuned to their cultural sensitivities, allows one to exercise empathy, identify with their emotions and also able to figure out their mindsets and agendas, not understanding this basic fact when absorbing information makes us easily susceptible to blindly accept whatever we are told without knowing various agendas coming at you. Most people would understand this intuitively at their workplace(?), yet when they read the social Media or watch the Mainstream Media, this simple truth seems to go out through the window.

We need to ask ourselves why are all the Political issues presented in such simplistic binary fashion (good or bad)? Can it be it logical that with the complexity of all the numerous political players (all with their personal agendas), with different ideologies and how these ideologies eventually support and shape the formation of policies. All the different resulting policies and their eventual impact (effectiveness of policies to deliver their desired results) to the society (with their varying degrees of difficulties in execution), yet the mainstream media or social media always presents the issues so simplistically as black and white binary choices? Doesn't that sound more like Entertainment 101 made Easy?

Challenge of Complex Concepts. Understanding Complex Concepts needs focus, Internalizing them needs patience and repeated practice. Many of the topics being discussed can be complex, yet we unquestioningly accept the words of the Entertainment Celebrities in Mainstream Media or snowflake writers in the Social Media? Why?

From experience, we know that unfamiliar matters or issues would need the reader or audience to be already up to speed on many underlying assumptions, (certain complex topics) in addition to understanding how others could be manipulating and exploiting them. To have an independent view, Patience and humility can help one acquire the skills of Unravelling Complexity of Ideas by themselves, together with the power of patience in exercising repeated trials and errors to internalize complex concepts. Internalizing Complex Concepts, Ideas needs Patience and also a little Humility, and Not by chanting political slogans put out in Social Media and Mass Media Cable Networks.

Following the Mainstream Media for last year, we can tell that many of the 'News' Media Celebrities struggle with both complicated and complex concepts, they struggle with Concepts whose outcome is contingent on another variable (relative), Concepts where double negatives equals a positive, concepts with Multiple Variables, moving in different direction or differing speeds, step-up differentiating concepts; examples distance, speed, acceleration (exponential vs linear). Concepts of PPP (Purchasing Power Parity), FX (Foreign Exchange) in measuring each countries' GDP (wealth). Counter intuitive Social concepts like Democracy, Capitalism, to give opportunities for work instead of giving welfare, hardship shapes character and develops virtues, how the greed of the mediocre; wishing for all to be equal ends up creating monopoly of power which will bring about Income Inequality

Dangers of Memorizing. Many people in their haste, for fear of being ridiculed or despised for not understanding the basic fundamentals of concepts, takes the shortcut of memorizing the end results (conclusions) instead of trying to internalize the concepts by repeated trial and errors by substituting [for] each example, formulae, equation with different numbers and signs (+/-) to understand the results; repeatedly in order to grasp the concept well. By Memorizing without truly understanding, they invariably start focusing on Form over Substance, people's ego and fear of being mocked for not understanding allows the sale of paths of least resistance [easiest message] by Mainstream Media, Entertainment 101 forever peddling binary messages; good v bad

Appendices

I

Apostolic Journey to the United States of America and Canada, Mass for the Rural Workers, Homily of his Holiness John Paul II in Laguna Seca, Monterey Peninsula 17th Sept 1987

> *"The earth will not continue to offer its harvest, except with faithful stewardship. We cannot say we love the land and then take steps to destroy it for use by future generations."*
>
> – Pope John Paul II, Sept 1987

Above is a quote from Pope John Paul II, back in 1987 when he visited USA and Canada, you might like to read his entire speech at the URL attached: https://w2.vatican.va/content/john-paul-ii/en/homilies/1987/documents/hf_jp-ii_hom_19870917_messa-agricoltori.html

The quote is often referenced by the environmentalists or Climate Change activists, indeed, Pope John Paul II was truly visionary, talking about environment protection 2 decades before Al Gore's Inconvenient Truth in 2006, before Gore and his cronies decided to make Global Warming his theme for fund raising after his loss to President Bush. Yet if you read the Pope's speech in its entirety, you'll truly appreciate the extent of his vision and insights into the challenges currently faced by us today! Pope John Paul II started his speech with this quote from Deuteronomy,

> *"Be careful not to forget the Lord, your God" (Deu. 8, 11) … Moses knew the tendency of the human heart to cry out to the Lord in time of need, but easily "to neglect his commandments and decrees and statutes" in the time of well-being and prosperity. He knew that God is easily forgotten."*
>
> – Pope John Paul II

He understood the type of Spiritual Malaise that sets in with peace and wealth, the type of peace with end of Cold War in 1991, the pseudo-wealth created by the Trillions printed via QEs, hundreds of millions of Americans on Social Welfare programs that Federal Government funds, taxed from the hardworking middle-class Americans, extracting approx. $ 3 Trillion per year from them annually. This Spiritual malaise causes the Problem Profiteers, snowflakes and millennials of undifferentiated Goodness, the Super-Rich anomie celebrities in entertainment media to forget virtues of hard-work, endurance, valor, fortitude, honesty, etc. instead they ridicule the values of fellow Americans and resort to the opiate of social media's activism, substituting their personal values and virtues with the empty rhetoric of social justice warriors and the politically correct slogans. The Pope also addressed the importance of Work Ethics and its impact on Values of individuals.

> *"Agricultural work is – as Pope John XXIII described it - a vocation, a God-given mission, a noble task and a contribution to civilization. God has blessed the United States with some of the richest farm land in the world. The productivity of American agriculture is a major success story. Clearly, it is a history of hard and wearying work, of courage and enterprise, and it involves the interaction of many people: growers, workers, processors, distributors and finally consumers."*
>
> – Pope John Paul II, 1987

The strengths of America highlighted by Pope John Paul II in its land, its agriculture and ecological edge over other countries might be taken for granted by some Ignorant Globalist, but the value of clean air, fresh water and abundance of high quality food produced here is Not lost on most World leaders outside America, eg. in China, Russia, etc. He highlighted the value of work, the virtues, pride and nobility that honest work brings. In his short speech of only 4 pages, the Pope also touched on potential solutions that we, as Americans can leverage to grow out of the current weak economy and help our neighbors and ourselves at the same time, a win win for all.

> *"Many worthwhile values are involved in tourism: relaxation, the widening of one's culture and the possibility of using leisure time for spiritual pursuits. These include prayer and contemplation, and pilgrimages, which have always been part of our Catholic heritage; they also include fostering human relationships within the family and among friends... I invite all of you who are involved in tourism to uphold the dignity of your work and to be always willing to bear joyful witness to your Christian faith."*
>
> – Pope John Paul II in Monterey Peninsula, CA Sept 1987

He discussed tourism, highlighted the unsustainability of continued exploitation of Earth's resources which points towards Space Exploration, Colonization. We'd touched on Space Exploration and Gaia Equilibrium in chapter 9 and also briefly on Eco-Tourism too. Let's explore a little more advantages and possibilities of Eco-Tourism to help Economic Growth around the world.

Besides large scale manufacturing, extensive Tourism is another approach to spreading and creating wealth to different parts of the world, to various developing countries in aid to their economies and plant seeds of growth for other industries; hotels, services, food and beverages, entertainment, film making and movies, internet, communications, logistics and infrastructure, exercise, outdoor sports, exploration, small scale industries to manufacture products for the tourists and later for the locals as they become more affluent. In time, these new industries will provide competition to the drug cartels as means of livelihood as the locals have many other means to earn a good living besides the drug trade. Imagine locations like Machu Picchu, Nazca lines, Iguazu Falls, etc. emulating cities like Orlando, FL, Las Vegas, NV, Niagara Falls, Buffalo, NY, etc. if they managed to achieve 20-30% of the wealth, and jobs created of the latter cities, it would be a phenomenon success. Take that and imagine the same for Angkor Wat, Cambodia, Angel Fall, Venezuela, Amazon Basin, Brazil, etc. the potential is definitely there.

Besides the obvious wealth creation, Eco-tourism, Geo-tourism or just plain tourism has many advantages. In its early stages, the wealth transfer is very efficient, it goes Direct; from the tourists directly into the hands of the more resourceful and creative locals in tourism trade, the bureaucratic government would find it difficult to siphon off or exploit, as the amount of transactions are individually very small, there's nothing to steal by the government as the value creation only happens when the service or experience happens for the tourist. Through the increased human interactions, numerous opportunities are created, opportunities for learning, for the more resourceful to be rewarded for their innovativeness and creativity. Learnings about history, geography, different cultures, languages, morals and values, even religious pilgrimages as Pope John Paul II mentioned. Opportunities to open one's Minds, learnings for the tourist, the local and volunteer Technology helper.

As we'd discussed in chapter 9, we can leverage technology to aid the growth of eco-tourism, to use all existing technologies like Virtual Reality, Augmented Reality (AR), so that the tourist can experience Ancient Greece when they're at the Acropolis in Athens, looking at sparkling new Parthenon or see the splendor of the Inca Empire when they're in Machu Picchu or Royal Courts in Cusco. Google's language translation and other related technology can also improve the experience for the tourists.

This new dimension of AR-VR assisted Eco-Tourism can be synergistic and win-win for all parties involved as we can already see the potential for technology to be pushed to a higher level with the new demand for more realistic experience, from the tourists as well as the enterprising locals who wish to expand their business. For the Technology volunteer workers to learn about foreign cultures, history, natural geography, etc. and experience the real world (eg. in Nazca, Amazon jungle, Tepuis in Venezuela, etc.), one that's outside their comfort zone of Starbucks and Apple Stores.

Our knowledge and understanding of ancient and diverse history, cultures, languages, religions, philosophies, archeology, geologies, etc. can be deepened, brought back to life, and pushed to new levels of appreciation as there's new profit incentive! Americans can help grow Economies in other American countries, drive technology improvements, reduce drug related activities in other countries and rescue our own lost millennial generation of snowflakes back from the Piper!

After Americas, Civilizations in Middle East, Asia, Africa, Eastern Europe, Russia, etc. Besides Space Exploration, Exploring the Diversity of our past history and civilizations is another frontier, made all the more real and interesting by aid of Technologies.

II

Aristotle's Nicomachean Ethics & Adam Smith's Awful Virtues

Ethos and Awful Virtues are essential to the working of Democracy and Capitalism, without the self-restraint and moderation brought about by respect for others, we'll see pure blatant exploitation of public goods, also termed "tragedy of the commons"; when Goodwill towards fellow citizens, freedom of speech, Social Welfare, healthcare, etc. gets over-exploited by the neo-democrat Liberals and P.C. Progressives; for personal gains at expense of the society.

If such abuse is not reined in and rectified, the system will breakdown and cease to function efficiently. This critical stage when breakdown occurs, is described in Complexity Theory as when the inputs extracted by the Rent-seeking politicians (together with their special interests Activists Corporations) is Greater than the outputs given back to the society. This is when the democratic society is in decline stage; the ensuing result is either anarchy or more likely a Big State Government (a lower energy society but more stable) where the power distance between the elite and common man is extremely wide, ie. when the Middle Class has been decimated.

How does Ethics and Virtues help Democracy and Capitalism? Democracy as compared to all other forms of Tops Down Government, is the most fluid with the most energy.

Other forms of Dirigiste Big-State Government are much more restrictive in ideas, free speech, etc. simply because of the threat of Ideas (which would bring judgement and criticisms of Incompetence) to those in Power, such luxury of freedom of speech is strongly discouraged (those who lived under Communism would understand). Without the profit incentive of a Free Market Capitalism, the individual naturally exercises much less initiative, less hard-work, less innovativeness (exponentially less), multiply that effect by tens, hundreds of millions of people and you can see the effect on the society. Thus, Tops down societies are much less vibrant and of lower energy state.

But when people are free to pursue their interests, exercise initiative and do as they wish as in Democratic societies with Free Market of Capitalism, there can be externality (spill-over) effects. People can start infringing on each other's interests in furthering their own (start stepping on each other's toes), That's when Ethics come into play.

Ethics and Virtues are set of transparent rules to bring about a level playing field, remember all men are created equal, as in equal opportunities. Ethics bring about a level playing field for those with abilities and potential to excel and advance their own interests without infringing on others interests. How? By advancing the entire society's interests (eg. inventing the Steam Engine, bringing AC electricity to all, etc.), by creating Value for the society such that the pie becomes bigger for all to share, they don't eat into others share of an existing pie (like the parasitic Professional Politicians, Activists Groups, Liberal P.C. Media, etc.). Ethos and Awful Virtues that applies to all, including those in Power, dovetail nicely with Democracy's message that All men should be equal in rights, empowerment and opportunities to compete for a better future for themselves!

These Big State Tops Down forms of government has various forms, the classical Greek categorized them into Monarchy, Tyranny, Aristocracy and Oligarchy. Communism or Socialism with their bureaucratic apparatchiks is merely a variation between tyranny, 'aristocracy' (nepotism) or oligarchy depending how the power is shared amongst the key players.

In chapter 3, we saw that the Liberals does NOT wish to share power with the Elected Administration, in essence, the Elite Professional Politicians refuse to hand the power back to the American people, why? One, their huge M.O.B. infrastructure is still intact (activists corporations, Mass Media, Social Media, K-Street professional politicians, problem profiteers, etc.), self-preservation is a powerful incentive and rational one. If problems get fixed by the new Elected Administration, then the Problem Profiteers would have no gravy train to ride! If the Americans can think for themselves, then the M.O.B. (brain-washing machine) infrastructure would be out of jobs too, their multi-million paychecks might be in jeopardy!

What about the *Thoughtcrime* that was committed by the American people on 8th Nov 2016? The Liberal P.C. Gestapo (including their cheerleader, the Perfect President) just cannot accept the fact that Americans are independent thinking people and didn't do as they were told to by the Mass Media, Social Media, Academia, etc. What the hell is wrong with these people? This is the Cultural part, their Ego talking! This is Irrational part, we'll cover this in more details under the Shame Culture. How about losing their wealth, could that be a motivator for not giving up Power? For their call to their snowflakes minions to RESIST? No, they are not losing their wealth, at least not yet, their multi-million Book Deals are still good for now, They Still Love their money Back. The one other reason I can think of is a rational one too. When we propose that Ethics and Virtues regulate individuals in a Democratic Society, some might have thought about the function of Laws, the legal system. In the Tyrannical Societies, there are laws too, right? How are the set of Laws different in Democratic societies Vs that of Tyrannical Regimes?

Laws are written by those in power, since in Democratic Society, the Demos (citizens) are in power, their laws are drafted to protect their rights, as the power shifts into hands of the elite in power, the laws would naturally be <u>slowly</u> amended too (as a start, interpreted differently to suit their desired outcome, then later amended all together), Activists Judges, remember them?

Ethics and Virtues are directed at the conscience of humans, it addresses the Substance, Law addresses the Form. Law comes after the fact, much later, Laws are not dreamt up in a vacuum, they are finally enacted after enough injustice have occurred till a point when the mass populace suffered enough, then the pressure on societies to put laws in place to dissuade Violence as a means of retaliation against the injustice. Laws are of much lower standard (lower bar to cross) than Ethics, usually decades behind too.

Professional Politicians can break the Ethics code easily every day, every hour without any legal consequences, in fact they must be handsomely rewarded for breaking the Ethics standard, otherwise they wouldn't be doing it. If there's no consequences for breaking the Ethics standard (like Conflict of Interests as example), then why the need to RESIST? Monopoly of Power breeds Culture of Decadence, which in turn breeds complacency, sloth, sloppiness and low standards. My guess is that the much lower Legal Standard had also been crossed numerous times, so prevalent that it cannot even pass the simplest Audit criterion. To accept unethical conduct in the political realm poisons all of society, to accept Illegal conduct by the professional politicians marks its Doom.

> *"When you see that in order to produce, you need to obtain permission from men who produce nothing - when you see money flowing to those who deal, not in goods, but in favors - when you see that men get richer by graft and pull than by work, and your laws don't protect you against them, but protect them against you - when you see corruption being rewarded and honesty becoming a self-sacrifice - you may know that your society is doomed."*
> - Ayn Rand, Atlas Shrugged (1957)

III

The World's not Flat despite its hordes of believers

"For whosoever commands the sea commands the trade; whosoever commands the trade of the world commands the riches of the world, and consequently the world itself,"

- Sir Walter Raleigh

The British Royal Navy dominated the World's oceans for about 350 years from victory over the Spanish armada in 1588 till end of WWII in 1945 when it handed over that guardian role to the US Navy. Global Trade accelerated after the Industrial revolution due in large part to the open oceans safeguarded by dominant Navies. 95% of trade crossing international borders is waterborne, so is 99.5% of inter-continental trade by weight. The last time I checked, neither the Russian Navy nor Chinese Navy are protecting the International sea lanes.

From chapter 1, we've understood that each country's leaders (if they are doing their jobs) would try to joust for best advantages for their constituents and International Trade can never be a level playing field. We've seen trading advantages secured via Foreign Exchange rates, lack of legal enforcement against Intellectual Properties infringement (stealing your copyrights), lower costs of production due to lack of Environmental Protection (EPA), tariffs, duties, lack of transparency in legal standards, State protection for domestic corporations, regional and cultural differences including varying standards from western ethics (FCPA), differences in perceptions between personal and communal wealth. Huge Trade imbalances can easily result, when your set of rules are transparent, well enforced thus facilitating foreign countries to export into USA, while another set of rules are ever-shifting, constantly under development, opaque and intentional confusing, which would effectively exclude any foreign Imports into their Domestic Markets. Yet we hear certain pseudo-intellect blathering about how the world is flat, where does such globalists myth originate from?

When Japan in the 60s and 70s grew their economy, followed by the 4 Asia Tigers in 70s and 80s, they were all exporting to America and a lesser degree to Europe. The lower production costs in these countries was understood by the Multi-National Corporations since the 60s, the economic entities (the companies) invested and build factories in these countries and leverage these lower production costs as competitive advantage over their competitors when selling their products all around the world. With the investments into these newly industrialized countries, followed by technology transfers, jobs grew, upstream and downstream industries form around these factories; suppliers, logistics, distributors, resellers, retailers, etc. economies grew and so did their middle-class in these societies. Job loss in America has impacts to their societies (like the rust belt cities) but the leaders of the economic entities are not too concerned about the social impacts, it's the job of the political leaders, not theirs. The full impact of job loss was still not felt by most Americans in the 80s. By early 90s, that equation started to change, USSR collapsed and China accelerated their integration into the international economic system (Deng personally leading it after the debacle of Tiananmen incident in '89). In mid-90s, China's economy was still very small and it looked like the rules of International Trade was going to be all western dominated, this is one point of reference for the story teller.

The more astute economic leaders investigated the potential of China's market of 1.3 Billion consumers in mid-90s and quickly understood the playing field is NOT level, and the profit pool wasn't deep; the market was too small and you cannot sell high-margins products as the consumers were too price sensitive (other words they were too poor). But they did discover that the production cost was even lower in China and the labor pool was huge, so began the rise of China as the factory of the world! This is the second data point for the story teller! China was still a very small economy then, most Americans didn't pay too much attention, neither did the economic leaders. China has 1.3 billion people (officially), that's over 4 times (most likely closer to 5 times) America's. If they do all the manufacturing for the world, America will become a giant Rust-Belt city! If China employs the similar Export Model into America and keeps its domestic Market reserved for its local players, the wealth transfer from America into China will be catastrophic for America. Over 2 decades later, both impacts are being felt today.

The economic leaders of America couldn't care less as these social impacts are not their concern, the last two political leaders (President Bush 43rd and President Obama) didn't do anything about it too, one too dumb and distracted to understand what was happening, the other too sly to take responsibility, punted it to Globalism.

In middle of last decade, the rhetoric about world is flat start to propagate, this was because China's economic rise was accelerating big time after their entry into WTO in 2002, this is the 3rd data point for the story teller, 1) common set of rules perceived from mid-90s (aka level playing field for all), 2) low costs of production in less developed countries (aka America not competitive) and 3) Rise of China, these 3 points are main thrust of the Globalist rhetoric. This line of logic would only make sense if you are a procurement agent for economic entity wishing to buy at the lowest costs for your company and you don't care about the social impacts of all your neighbors losing their jobs. This myopic view missed out on a) it was never really a level playing field as other States will NOT play by same set of rules, b) social Impacts will matter, as the middle class shrinks and economy contracts, first the quality of life will suffer, later there will be social unrests which is exactly what the China Leaders understand, that's why they protect their market from foreign companies, limit foreign imports into their economy. They clearly understand that Trade deficit will drain wealth from their country! Losing Jobs will cause social unrests in their societies! And lastly c) even for economic entities, low production costs is only a piece of the equation, Revenue from Sales is critical to generating cashflow; lifeblood of economic entities. Gaining market share in foreign markets helps increase Revenue and China's market in 2018 isn't small anymore (ask the German luxury cars manufacturers, or the French Luxury Goods producers), it is just NOT available to most American companies (ask google and FB).

In early 2018, two sleeping beauties of economic entities woke up from their 2 decade long slumber. One's a steward handpicked by Steve Jobs, the other's a one-trick pony, the founder of MS, they suddenly started commenting that China will surpass America in Technology, etc. one wonders where have these two geniuses have been in last 2 decades? Steve Jobs (leader of an economic entity, Apple) was already seeing the social impact to America and pushing on President Obama in 2011 (the political leader to do his job) so that the engineers for Apple can be hired in America and not China.

President Trump won the 2016 Election with the rallying cry of Make America Great Again! He won because, most Americans already understood that 2 decades of failing economy is killing this country. The Liberals' mocking answer was that America has always been great, now just one year later, these two progressives suddenly woke up and realized that China is catching up and probably surpassed America in some areas?

If America's renaissance continues under current Administration, this country still has many strengths, ecology and agriculture edge (China is not self-subsistent foodwise), military edge, energy edge (America is Energy independent, China is Not) and Innovative Culture Edge (Intellectually, the Chinese has many geniuses, real geniuses due to their large population size, just like India, but a Culture is more than mere intelligent individuals, it requires mutual trust, knowledge sharing, institutional learning, debates, constructive criticism, diverse views that compete but not antagonistic, dynamic leadership, etc.) Economic Trade is still advantageous to America as China is dependent on the American Market for Export but America doesn't sell much into China (Apple does).

So, all things being equal, America still has few cards left to play but only if the renaissance continues, anymore professional politicians (aka Eunuchs) chanting the Globalist Slogans and the Chinese will all be thanking their ancestors for their extra-ordinary Luck! For President Barack Obama was truly a god-sent for China, they had thought it would take them 30 – 50 years to catchup with America, The Perfect President shortened that timeframe to 10, the two sleeping beauties just confirmed it. 2008 – 2018 is exactly ten years.

IV

Ode to The Shame Culture; The Good, the Bad and the Ugly

"…Shame cultures are essentially collectivist by nature, and individual behavior in such a culture is shaped by the external opinion of others rather than internal values… In [contrast to] a guilt culture, one who knows he is guilty is expected to feel guilty and behave accordingly, even if he is the only one who knows it, because guilt is an internal motivator. Thus, shame culture, by its nature, perpetuates certain behaviors that a guilt culture does not. In a shame culture, individuals are free to engage in wrongdoing as long as no one knows they have done so."

- Psychiatrist Patricia A. Santy

We had covered many different Cultures, Culture of Decadence, of Compliance that becomes the default culture when Monopoly of Power sets in. The Anomie Culture that derides the values of others, living on the thin line of sensation between no future and no past.

The Eunuch Culture that kiss up and kick down, worships those in power and abuses the goodwill of their fellow citizens, afraid of External enemies and yet sees internal fellow citizens as their enemies (praises North Korea, Iran, ashamed to be Americans, Trump is not my president). The Snowflakes Culture that stems from Insecurity, fear of Change, micro-aggression, need for Safe Space, love their comfort zones, static environments, where dynamic situations cause traumatic experiences.

The Politically Correct Culture, birth from undifferentiated goodness but rooted in hypocrisy and pretense, herd mentality of sheep, deriving comfort and sense of accomplishments from bleating their political slogans, the non sequiturs that chants Globalists mantras with much passion but little understanding.

Yet, the one Culture that unites them all is the Culture of Decadence, more appropriately called Shame Culture because the common thread that links all that subscribe to the Shame Culture is their lack of internalized Values; which explains their lack of Guilt (see above quote).

In chapter 3, we had discussed the Sonar of Financial Wealth, (whether they are reaping in vast sums of personal wealth from their actions as 'public servants') and the Radar of Self-Sacrifice, (the painful self-sacrifices made versus the comfort of leading from behind) to detect the real agenda of the Professional Politicians.

Culture is another means to detect hidden agendas as the corrupting influence of Power will shape a common Culture which becomes telling as their behavior will betray their hidden motives and agendas, it also links them together which makes for easier tracing. Let's profile the Progressives' Shame Culture for better understanding and ease of Identification, we'll look at the Good, the Bad and the Ugly of Shame Culture.

Profiling The Shame Culture

Self Proclaimed Avant Garde Romantics

Problem Profiteers with Financial Rewards

$$$

Undifferentiated Goodness, Social Justice Warriors satisfying their Egoistic Self-Righteousness, aka chanting their Politically Correct Slogans led by the Problem Profiteers

Notice the Huge Overlap between three sub-categories, as nobody is sacrificing anything, but All within the Shame Culture are benefitting tremendously either Financially, Egoistically (Culturally), or Better still in Both

The Good

Ability to evoke strong emotions in others, appeals to emotional feelings, very High EQ, able to extract sympathy, able to either galvanize or rile up the masses, can be most political, excels in oratory skills, presentation, marketing, entertainment, acting, identifies with the masses and thus great communicator, etc.

As the true Avant Garde Romantics, Artists, Poets, Literary Geniuses; likes of William Blake, Lord Byron, J.M.W. Turner, Percy Bysshe Shelley, William Wordsworth, Mary Shelley, etc. would be the best of this Culture. Feeling is All, Live the Moment! Yet the works they produced are most admirable, pushed human race to greater heights, the level of sophistication in describing the human emotions, defining aspirations, hope, all very powerful emotions which when put to good causes can help propel our civilization in the right direction.

The Bad

Undifferentiated Goodness, focuses on form rather than substance, insecure, consensus driven, procedural regimented and inflexible, conceptually challenged, intellectually mediocre, technically untalented, 'nice person', hardworking in repetitive tasks, proud of shibboleths, Compliant 1 trick ponies. For clarifications, this are 'weaknesses' (areas of improvement) of the Shame Culture but not necessarily harmful to the society. Popularity and acceptance is highly valued, the most popular opinion outweighs getting the right solution. A large populace shares the characteristics mentioned, yet are they all part of the Shame Culture? This is where Pride and Ego turns the Bad into the Ugly.

> *"So when they continued asking him, he lifted up himself, and said unto them, He that is without sin among you, let him first cast a stone at her."*
>
> John 8:7 (KJV)

John 8:7 teaches us, not to be judgemental of others too quickly as we all have weaknesses and there's always room for improvement. If the Bad has no internal Values (as in Shame Culture), and with their intellectual sloth, close-minded insecurity they judge others quickly and harshly, starts their vicious and vindictive attacks (just watch the professional politicians on CNN, C-SPAN, NBC, etc.), then the Shame Culture has infected the Bad, turning them into the Ugly!

> *"Social consciousness… is not a summons to the activism of mass movements. Civic virtue is a mirage unless anchored in the inner virtue of each citizen…"*
>
> – William Kaufman Editor, Meditations, Marcus Aurelius

The Ugly

In chapter 3, we asked the question why are the neo-Democrats so good at lying? We now know that their Strong EQ (Emotional Intelligence) can compensate for their Intellectual weakness, it can also appeal to sympathies, strong emotions, cloaks them to appear as likeable, diligent with a nice person image. Emotions are powerful feelings, if used in a positive way, it can motivate but if leveraged for personal political agenda, it can also turn your 'average man on the street' into crazed hordes of violent looters.

The legions of the Ugly and Insecure possess Weapons of Mass Political Destruction for they are many, linked by their Shame Culture (lack of real Values because those are difficult to practise) that taps into all of human's inherent weaknesses; Guilt, Pride, Sloth, Envy, Avarice, Lust, Wrath, Hypocrisy, Pretense, etc. That's why the neo-Democrats are so good at lying, amongst many other abilities; to launch vicious, vindictive criticisms at their fellow citizens, to self-righteously judge others as sexists, racists, etc., to conceal and cloak their lack of values under guise of Political Correctness, to launch Spanish inquisition style invectives against those with *Thoughtcrimes*; views that's different from their P.C. Uniform One View. Just as the Eunuchs of Imperial courts they are also able to align themselves with external enemies (singing praises of Islamic States, Iran, North Korea, etc.) against their fellow countrymen whom they regard as their enemies (Ashamed to be Americans, racists, sexists, etc.).

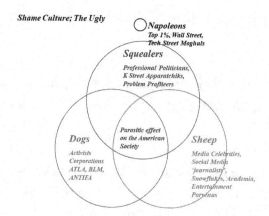

Shame Culture; The Ugly

Napoleons
*Top 1%, Wall Street,
Tech Street Moghuls*

Squealers

*Professional Politicians,
K Street Apparatchiks,
Problem Profiteers*

Dogs

*Activists
Corporations
ATLA, BLM,
ANTIFA*

*Parasitic effect
on the American
Society*

Sheep

*Media Celebrities,
Social Media
'journalists',
Snowflakes, Academia,
Entertainment
Parvénus*

See the neo-Democrats M.O.B. infrastructure. The Eunuch Culture is the epitome of Ugliness of the Shame Culture; bowing to those in Power over themselves for personal gains and selling out the entire society or country that they belong to. The Emergence of such culture is in direct correlation of the Internal Decay of a society.

V

Complexity Theory, Asibiyyah عصبيّة and the Living Company

Asabiyyah, in his masterpiece Al-Maqaddimah; an Introduction to History, Ibn-Khaldun (1332-1406), a Spanish Faylasuf, argues that it is this sense of solidarity within the group, clan that makes it strong and grow bigger, wealthier and more sophisticated. Under lax and comfortable conditions, the group loses its Asabiyyah, dissolves into factionalism and individualism, diminishing and weakening their capacity as a political unit. Other new units with strong Asabiyyah will replace it and the cycle will start all over again.

This Solidarity, Alignment is instrumental in producing the Efficient Bureaucracy in Public Service which was strong during the times of the founding fathers, also present in the Civil War years under Lincoln's administration, has been missing from the self-serving professional politicians for last two plus decades. With weak self-serving leadership, Internal Decay starts to fester very quickly. We've also the same phenomenon explained via Complexity Theory.

Complex Systems have Diverse Autonomous Agents, Connectedness, Interdependence & Adaptation (learning). They have Emergent Properties and Possible Phase Transition [when system is in a Critical Stage], critical threshold, subcritical into supercritical.

> "Inputs increase exponentially with the scale of civilization, Outputs of civilization and governments decline per unit of input when measured in terms of public goods and services provided."
>
> - Joseph A. Tainter

Rent Seeking, accumulation of wealth through non-productive means. Similar to Law of Diminishing Returns as the 'kleptocrats rulers' are Not adding Value to the society but extracting too much for value from the system for themselves and also destroying value through their incompetence, then the society naturally will offer its masses negative returns on inputs, those masses would logically opt out of society, thereby destabilizing it further. This is the Critical Threshold we are currently seeing in America after over two decades 'rent seeking' behavior by the Professional Politicians.

Without being replaced by other more efficient societies, one Solution would be to: Descale, simplify into with smaller Components, Drastically Reduce the Federal Government and transfer decision-making responsibilities and resources back to the State level or even lower if possible.

Viewed from the societies' perspective, this Esprit de Corps is a critical indicator of the health of the country, exploitation by the parasitic elements erodes and undermines the society's Alignment, leading to eventual collapse, or Civil War in this case.

VI

Liberal Imperialism, Oasis of Opportunities and the Pioneering Spirit

".. on the one hand, self-government was the fruit of civilized advancement and a goal for any people. On the other, the general welfare of a modern, complex society profited most from applying "the science of legislation," in Dugald Stewart's phrase, also means efficient bureaucracy; rule by experts and bureaucrats.

Liberal Imperialism is an enlightened, racially un-bias view of the relationship between the rulers and their subjects in various countries all around the world and asking the key question in objective manner, who can do a better job for the quality of lives for these subjects? It understands that all rulers are kleptocrats, be they local or foreign. It opens up competition between the societies asking unashamedly who can provide a better living or lifestyle for the citizens; or viewed another way, who exploits the subjects less? We can see this scenario play out with the onset of Industrial age, Western States setting up colonies all over Asia, be they British, Dutch, Portuguese, French, Spanish. In the 19th century with the Chinese Qing and Indian Mughal Empires both in decline and suffering from severe internal corruption, there was mass migration of Chinese and Indians into these colonies in search of better lives for themselves.

Simply put, the combination of Industrial Revolution, Efficient Bureaucracy and Imperial Liberalism has created enough value in these Asian Colonies (Hong Kong, Malaysia, Indonesia, Singapore, Philippines, Thailand, etc.) that compared to their home countries where corruption, misrule, strife, poverty, violent conflicts have become so rampant, the people chose to migrate to an unknown land and future! This mass migration in Asia has a parallel; where many in Europe (Old World) moved to America (New World). These new colonies in Asia, including the thirteen colonies in America represented oasis of new life & opportunities for the immigrants compared to their conditions back home, that had suffered from wars and decades of incompetent and corrupted rulers (the elite incumbents in Power, of the Old World, which the current professional politicians and their sponsors in USA are now morphing into).

Just like the Andrew Carnegies in Americas, many of the immigrant Chinese and Indians became hugely successful in their new homes which would never be possible if they had stayed back home. The qualities which contributed to their successes in new land of opportunities;

self-confidence, adaptability, courage, risk-seeking, quick on-the-feet thinking, ability to learn new skills quickly, to re-invent oneself, endure hardship, resilience, mental toughness, self-discipline, etc. these qualities are all transferable and mobile which they can bring with them (as Einstein and any top intellects during WWII, intellect is mobile), compared to those who stayed behind; who valued their existing relationships back home, treasure their power networks and status, assets such as land, lifestyles, etc. most of which are immobile which they'll have to forgo had they chose to emigrate. The same for the pioneering days, westward expansion, the same set of transferable and mobile traits serve the Pioneers well.

Now, we ask ourselves, which set of values appeals to the Professional Politicians, Wall Street and Tech Street Moguls, K Street Apparatchiks, Media and Entertainment Celebrities, etc.? The answer is self-evident as the Pigs have become the Humans in Animal Farm. (the neo-Democrats and all their cronies might be parvenus in form, but in substance they are now closer to the Power Elite in the Old World, whom our forefathers had left behind, to forge a New World with their Pioneering Spirit).

VII

Evil Axis of Parasitic Deep State Politicians, Problem Profiteers Activists Corporations, Sycophant Stooges of Social and Mass Media

The Activists Corporations are no Social Workers, they are Professional Corporate Problem Profiteers, Special Interests parasitic organizations that lobbies through various channels; direct to the Deep State Politicians and Indirect M.O.B. programming through the Social Media, Mass Media, etc. to the masses, be they 'in the know' Joneses, impressionable 'millennials' or just the plain impressionable.

Activism of Mass movements is a mere façade to serve only two purpose, as all special interests groups know, 1) to channel funds into their sponsors' coffers and 2) to provide emotional liniments to sooth the egos of the keyboard social justice warrior. True Civic Virtue need to be anchored in the inner virtues of each citizen [individual], which can only be attained via repeated practice and experiences of overcoming hardship, trials and tribulations.

The Deep State self-serving professional Politicians (aka flamboyant K Street Eunuch organizations), makes the concept of Public Service a Big Sad Joke! With their reigning Sense of Entitlement, these parasites, demoralized by the money pots of the Progressive Activists Corporations; enticed by millions in book deals, enervated by the Liberal Social and Mainstream Media such that virtues of honesty, valor, fortitude and endurance have all become pointless self-sacrifice.

After decades of indolence in DC and being Adverse to active service, the entire Federal Administration has degenerated into a useless laughing stock that specializes in spying on its own citizens and leaking States secrets.

Political Lackeys, second rate entertainment celebrities masquerading as third rate journalists, reveling in their shibboleths of grammarians, unveils their new M.O.B. maxim.

Welfare is Right
Socialism is Freedom
Ignorance is Strength
Released via the new Ministry of Truth

Reinvigorated, the Politically Correct Gestapo and their newly formed Thought Police arm, all swearing their oath to never ever allow relapse of *Thoughtcrimes* ever again!

VIII

Crony Capitalism of Wall Street seducing the Ugly Monopolies in K Street and Tech Street

Scarcity of Resources, Value derives from Scarcity. QEs torrents of liquidity decreases value of money, its dissemination via Wall Street's Financial Channels, replaces resource allocation via the Free Market with 'rules' dictated by a few Key Decision-Makers in the Too Big to Fail Banks, over time this creates a much larger Income Inequality and wounded the Middle Class of America. How exactly does this happen?

Let's trace the process step by step. Before the Fed's Trillions of QEs, resources were relatively scare, so individuals place much value in them. When making decisions on how to invest with their hard-earned money, they will do their utmost to safeguard and protect their investments, learning everything they can to ensure it generates the highest returns for themselves. When wealth is generated organically, naturally via the free market, it accumulates in the hands of individuals who have been successful in this level playing field. It tends to build up in the middle class over time. How does Free Market distribute the wealth? Over time and many countless millions and millions of transactions, the wealth gets spread per the natural abilities, hard-work, will power, ingenuity and innovativeness of individuals which is naturally endowed to them. Most importantly, because the wealth is hard-earned by the individuals, they pay extremely close attention to protect their individual interests. Yet this is only a very small part of the power of the Free Market, in addition to the hundreds of millions of extremely capable individuals protecting their own interests with perfect information, in a perfect competition Free Market, they are autonomous, highly motivated, are linked to each other (interconnected), affect each other and adapt to each other (they learn from each other's actions); summarized in Complexity Theory.

Now, we have the QEs and the funds are no longer scarce as they are artificially generated; they might be scarce to the individuals as the funds are out of their reach (yes, but they are no longer scarce to the Bank Analysts nor fund managers, they are now sitting on trillions of funds needing to be invested of OPM (other people's money). These new trillions of dollars are now in the hands of the Too-Big-To-Fail Bankers. How does the funds now get allocated? Free Market? We must remember that Hundreds of millions autonomous individual decision makers, protecting their personal interests makes up the free market. The new 'wealth' gets trapped in the Wall-Street and

Tech Street and gets allocated based on a) Financial Models built by analysts, b) presentation and Marketing skills of the Elon Musks of the world to convince the fund managers to invest in them, c) personal relations and networks of the key decision makers, and slowly over time d) cronyism, relations of who you know and Not what you know, kissing up and kicking down, nepotism will all set in. And it is because of c) and d) that the Big State Tops down Dirigiste (Centrally Planned) economies will always Underperform the Free Market. Crony Capitalism is just another form of such Dirigiste Economy.

Let's bring it closer to heart, if ten of us, each were to take $ 1000 of cash of our own money and put it on the table for a game where winner takes all. All ten will be most attentive and alert to the rules of the game (personal vested interest). Next element, if the rules were varied or if some players try to 'bend the rules' to his/her own favor, the other players will also be paying close attention (they can all adapt). Now if we ask an Analyst in Goldman Sachs to invest $ 10,000, you know what his reaction would be? They do NOT deal with such small investments, go take your money somewhere else. The point here is not the slight but the attention that individual will be paying to $ 100 million investment of OPM as compared to 100,000 investors with their individual $ 1000 investment, the amount of effort, attention and focus by the latter would Not be 100,000 times, it will be exponentially bigger as the 100,000 people will react to each other as conditions change per the minute or hour, they will also adapt if the rules change, with this 2 additional factor of react and adapt, mathematically it can be represented as $100,000^3$ (100,000 * 100,000 * 100,000) = 1000 Trillion times more focus and processing power. That is the power of Free Market

1 vs 1000 trillion minds; and you're assuming that the 1 Goldman Sachs Analyst is even remotely motivated to protect the puny (to him) $ 100 million investment of OPM. The scarcity of money has been removed as it is not longer scarce to those handling it, investing it. Yet, the common man on the street cannot reach this QE money trapped in Wall street. Because so few decision-makers are now involved; perhaps basing their decision on financial models (we assume that cronyism and personal relations hasn't set in yet), the need for perfect information; for transparency such that as much information about the companies is made available to all the small investors, has diminished drastically. With the need for perfect information diminished, the process to provide information to the individual investors becomes compromised (perfect information is another precursor for the Free Market to work efficiently). Next, we compare the adaptability of Free Market Vs the Financial Models. We hope sincerely that the Crony Capitalism hasn't reached the c) and d) stages as yet. The Banks might in earnest be relying on the Financial Models as they believe (perhaps Greenspan too) that the Wall Streets' intellects are way superior to anything the layman on the street has to offer, therefore the sophistication of the Financial Models should be superior to the Free Market [real reason is that Free Market is unpredictable to them while the Models are].

Financial Modeling based on algorithms and rules that's derived from observing the past Market trends and behavior. Going into the future, someone needs to diligently update those algorithms which cannot be possible as in real time, the market changes too quickly in split seconds, (for a Model to base its recommendation too closely on market's reaction, it will run the risks of a circular reference). To base the future on past is also dangerous. Financial Modelling may be sophisticated but it might not have the basic fundamental assumptions correct, since the analysts all have no operational working experience in the industries and have to rely on 'conventional wisdom of industry experts', assuming the experts are relaying the correct drivers and their relations forward. The industries dynamics changes with time too, usually only noticed some time after the fact.

We understand that Free Market is superior and way more sophisticated (hundreds of millions of Motivated autonomous individuals that are connected, react and adapt to each other's decisions) compared to the 'A.I.' Financial Models, but how does the Middle Income get the short end of the stick? As in any good dirigiste economy when the power aggregates in hands of the few, the effects of b), c) and d) comes into play. The Middle Class no longer control their own destiny, they don't get to play in the Free Market anymore, as only the Top 1% have the major say in the QEs allocation, perfect information also gets weakened (less transparency to the investors) as need disappears. When the market crashed, the individual investors gets decimated, the Feds bailed out the Big Banks and gives them the QE money, the individual investors gets no QEs money, they don't get to play with the big boys anymore. The allocation of the new wealth also works via different rules now, in the past, the Middle Class themselves, all together help make up the free market, leveraging their natural abilities to further their own interests, now the rules have changed, become much more simplistic but no longer transparent to the individual investors for they have been excluded from the game.

IX

Diversity of Ideas and Freedom of Speech

1st Amendment less 2nd Amendment, equals the Right to be Politically Correct (aka the Right to Kow Tow to the Flamboyant Eunuchs in Power over them), forfeiting human's unique power of Reason

> *"to disarm the people," George Mason, "was the best and most effectual way to enslave them."*

> *"Arms discourage and keep the invader and plunderer in awe, and preserve order in the world as well as property." Thomas Paine. "Horrid mischief would ensure were the law-abiding deprived of the use of them."*

Right to bear Arms wasn't an American invention, it was championed by likes of Adam Ferguson, Adam Smith, etc. during the Age of Enlightenment with the coming of the Commercial Age (Rise of Industrial Revolution and Capitalism). Why? Why did the key leaders of the Scottish Enlightenment propose the right to bear arms for the individual, as a deterrence to rise of Big State Power? And do the same conditions still apply today? The age of Scottish Enlightenment started around early 18th century, about same time as immigrants were moving to the New World. Perhaps the best way to explain it is that the rule of Democracy has not been established in any countries around the world then, the declaration came in 1776. Because there was No democratic governments, there was no distorted view of how the power lies with the people. They could see very clearly the corrupting influence of power in the ruling class, thus they see the need for he common people to protect their interests against those in power.

Here's the irony, after over 2 centuries of democratic rule in America, the naïve and impressionable actually now believes that the power lies with the people, that's putting the cart before the horse. It is precisely because the common man has no power, thus the need to educate him of his rights, the Enlightenment Movement in the 18th Century helped clarified and educate the common man of his rights, followed by the birth of the journalist profession to be the watch dog for the public (the common man) and warn of encroachment by those in Power, who wishes to abuse them of their rights. The common man is also taught to protect his/her rights with the second amendment if necessary against those in power.

If Power is naturally with the people and had always been on their side, then they wouldn't need to constantly be reminded of their rights, the need to defend them and the journalist role wouldn't exist right? Now Here's the irony, the neo pseudo-journalists had become so enriched by being the mouth-piece of those in power that they've turned around and started convincing the naïve that since the power is with the people, there's No Need to protect their rights as their rights is already guaranteed by the laws and constitution (we de-bunked this myth in appendix II).

Arms to defend our rights to what? Property rights (others cannot take what's yours), human rights (you don't want to be enslaved), but rights to free speech? Why do I need that? Why is right to free speech important to the individual and the society? We can already see that those who are always Politically Correct has no need for free speech, they already argue that they don't need their second amendment right? Right! They have no need for their 2nd amendment right to defend their 1st amendment right, they have no need to defend Free Speech as they are already saying what's Politically Correct (whatever soothes those in Power). This is really funny, but it is not a joke.

Free Speech is Not Free, in truth, it is standing against those in Power, that's why the need to defend it (with Arms if necessary). Real Free Speech is against the grain, Uphill battles, it irks those in Power as it highlights the truth, their corruption of power, their incompetence, etc.

Here's why it is no joke, the sad truth of human society is that few stand up against the grain, few stand up to Power, most people bend to Power, some kiss up to it to further their own interests, see all the Politically Correct slogans? All the Media Celebrities enriching themselves saying the same P.C. slogans day after day? Refer to appendix IV image 78, Media Sheep chanting the P.C. Slogans, Dogs tearing out the throats of the dissenting voices and the Squealers dancing from side to side wiggling their tails in the most convincing manner (professional politicians, The Perfect President?)

> "the individual considers his community only as far as it can be rendered subservient to his personal advancement and profit, human beings become weak and soft, and lose their sense of honour and courage. They must have their creature comforts, no matter what. Freedom itself becomes a commodity, to be sold to the highest bidder or seized by the strongest power."
>
> – Adam Ferguson

Freedom of Speech to Individual

What is the essence of Political Correctness? Is political correctly just chanting P.C. Slogans? Or is there more to it? Let's bring it nearer home, perhaps in a meeting setting with your boss? When he/she likes the meeting to be smooth, uneventful, no surprises, especially well-rehearsed if his/her boss is attending too, it needs to be consensus driven, no ruffling of feathers, business as usual, procedural, everything on schedule and ends on schedule. You get the picture, compare this to another meeting which is uncoordinated, with surprises on poor performance of our new product launch, candid criticism of the poor service of our staff, diverse ideas and debates as how to fix and address the issues and challenges.

To the individual, you might keep silent because you don't wish to ruffle any feathers, even when you know something is wrong and the company is in trouble, that's the essence of Political Correctness. What do you lose if you don't exercise your free speech? Not much, you might have even saved your career in short term. Maybe you might feel something in your conscience, perhaps your pride in your professionalism, your fiduciary duties to the shareholders? Really not that much to the individual in short term, the company might suffer? Too vague. Long term would be bad for everyone as the competition eats out lunch? Too long term, perhaps I can join the competition then?

That's why many choose the paths of least resistance and not against the grain, they call Politically Correct the Culture of Compliance, Culture of Uniformity, Obedience, Lowliness. The real impact of Politically Correctness is to the larger entity in longer term, the company, the society, the civilization.

Freedom of Speech to Society,

Freedom of Speech, combined with literacy (not just reading and writing, but also Numeracy, Mathematics and Accounts, for these were considered essential to Literacy during the Enlightenment Age), connected via intellectual networks like Republic of Letters, Select Societies, Poker Club, etc. all these supported by the rise in Middle Class, bringing in many sharp and able minds, brings about competition, leading to diverse and sophisticated ideas; we discussed these in chapter 4. The society is the biggest beneficiary.

Lastly, we'd also witnessed and compared the strengths of learning human societies (autonomous, competitive, adaptable but not accurate due to diverse learning capabilities) against those of Artificial Intelligence of computers (Optimal algorithm can be verified, all units are uniform always upgraded to latest and optimal algorithm, all are accurate as they are uniform). Yet the Politically Correct human societies have the weaknesses of both of the above and none of their strengths.

The Politically Correct M.O.B. rhetoric might be spreading like wildfire with the aid of the smart devices in last decade, but Chairman Mao had effectively utilized the P.C. slogans in the 60s Cultural Revolution impacting hundreds of millions of Chinese negatively for over a decade, moving the Chinese society back a generation. As far back as 200 B.C.E., over 2200 years ago, Political Correctness was already an exquisite artform summed up in the concept of 指鹿为马, the Qin Premier indicating a deer to be a horse and the entire Imperial Court was in complete agreement, those practising Free Speech then didn't do very well. Memo to the Politically Correct Liberals in America, China didn't just catchup with America (per Cook and Gates), you are 2200 years behind China (one's skill is elegant, refined and subtle while the other is clumsy and awkward).

X

Best Practice of Efficient Bureaucracy; Gold standard of Public Service

We'd looked at the Efficient Bureaucracy concept in chapter 8, this seems to be The Answer, an easy solution for the Monarchs or The People (in the case of Democracy), employ the Efficient Bureaucracy Administration to run your countries' affairs. There's been good success under the below periods of our civilization:

- America's founding fathers,
- Lincoln's team,
- British's leaders under Queen Elizabeth, intermittently for approx. 200 years till WWII,
- Japanese leaders during the Meiji restoration,
- Mamluks,
- Janissaries,
- Legalists under Qin Empire

We also documented the Culture and Characteristics of these groups:

- Strong Sense of Asabiyyah (Solidarity),
- Alignment of personal interests with that of the group,
- Esprit de Corps, A Sense of Crisis, External Threats
- No sense of Entitlement of Power
- Leaders of Convictions and Personal Belief in their destiny to shape History
- All embracing the Culture of Growth and Competition

These above strengths can even help bring about the Conjunctures of major events and trends in favor of their States; Industrial Revolution occurring in the UK and recently China's rise in last 2 decades due to State intervention. (similar to the Anna Karenina concept, when alignment of many factors are needed for a happy family)

Yet, we understand that it cannot be as easy as merely employing the right team to become the Efficient Bureaucracy Administrators as Power can and do corrupt. Joseph J. Ellis summed it up best in *The Quartet* two words, *Unembarrassed and Unapologetic, if you look at the Risks Vs Rewards Curve in chapter 3, the fine line on the curve indicates high risks and high rewards, it is easy for the public servants to fall off the curve into the area below it; that sweet spot of low risks and high rewards, when Power corrupts. Because the common people cannot check you and the Mass Media stooges would all be rushing to kiss up, staying on the fine line of razor's edge is painful, it takes integrity, values and constant sacrifice.

* perhaps that's why the Deep State GOP lost in 2008 and 2012 Elections? They were embarrassed from guilt, to be such self-serving 'Public Servants' raking in so much from the American people, while their opponents were from the Shame Culture, who feels no such Guilt, as Guilt requires some semblance of internal values.

The question now is: will the new volunteer Public Servants succeed to Make America Great again? Their heart is definitely there, can the leadership become one team?

References

World Order

Book by Henry Kissinger

Strategy

Book by B. H. Liddell Hart

The Rise and Fall of the Great Powers

Book by Paul Kennedy

The Realities Behind Diplomacy: Background Influences on British External Policy 1865-1980
  Apr 1983

by Paul M. Kennedy

To Rule the Waves: How the British Navy Shaped the Modern World

Book by Arthur L. Herman

Collapse: How societies choose to fail or succeed

Book by Jared Diamond

Guns, Germs, and Steel

Book by Jared Diamond

How the Scots Invented the Modern World

Book by Arthur L. Herman

The Quartet: Orchestrating the Second American Revolution, 1783-1789

by Joseph J. Ellis

Revolutionary Summer: The Birth of American Independence

Book by Joseph J. Ellis

The Lessons of History Feb 16, 2010

by Will Durant and Ariel Durant

In Lieu of Ideology: An Intellectual Biography of Goh Keng Swee Aug 27, 2010

by Kee Beng Ooi

Freedom's Forge: How American Business Produced Victory in World War II Jul 2, 2013

by Arthur Herman

Heroes: From Alexander the Great and Julius Caesar to Churchill and de Gaulle

Book by Paul Johnson

History Lessons: What Business and Management Can Learn from the Great Leaders of History

Book by Jonathan Gifford

Meditations

Book by Marcus Aurelius

Trumped

Book by David Stockman

The Great Deformation: The Corruption of Capitalism in America

Book by David Stockman

The Cave and the Light: Plato Versus Aristotle, and the Struggle for the Soul of Western
Civilization

by Arthur Herman

The Closing of the Western Mind

Book by Charles Freeman

The Rise and Fall of Alexandria: Birthplace of the Modern World Oct 30, 2007

by Justin Pollard and Howard Reid

The Great Transformation: The Beginning of Our Religious Traditions

Book by Karen Armstrong

A History of God

Book by Karen Armstrong

Islam: A Short History

Book by Karen Armstrong

A Culture of Growth: The Origins of the Modern Economy

Book by Joel Mokyr

A Torch Kept Lit: Great Lives of the Twentieth Century

by William F. Buckley Jr. (Author), James Rosen (Editor)

Steve Jobs Sep 15, 2015

by Walter Isaacson

The Innovators

Book by Walter Isaacson

The Innovator's Dilemma: The Revolutionary Book That Will Change the Way You Do Business
Paperback – October 4, 2011

by Clayton M. Christensen

The Innovator's Solution: Creating and Sustaining Successful Growth Hardcover – November
19, 2013

by Clayton M. Christensen

Bill O'Reilly's Legends and Lies: The Patriots May 24, 2016

by David Fisher

Narrative of the Life of Frederick Douglass, an American Slave

Book by Frederick Douglass

Churchill and Orwell: The Fight for Freedom

by Thomas E. Ricks

Bill O'Reilly's Legends and Lies: The Civil War Jun 6, 2017

by David Fisher

Broken But Unbowed: The Fight to Fix a Broken America May 17, 2016

by Greg Abbott

Currency Wars: The Making of the Next Global Crisis Aug 28, 2012

by James Rickards

The New Case for Gold Apr 5, 2016

by James Rickards

Bill O'Reilly's Legends and Lies: The Real West Apr 7, 2015

by David Fisher and Bill O'Reilly

The Human Story: Our History, from the Stone Age to Today Jul 26, 2005

by James C. Davis

The Origins of the Modern World: A Global and Environmental Narrative from the Fifteenth
    to the Twenty-First Century (World Social Change) Feb 5, 2015

by Robert B. Marks

Autumn in the Heavenly Kingdom: China, the West, and the Epic Story of the Taiping Civil War

by Stephen R. Platt

A BRIEF HISTORY OF THE ROMAN EMPIRE

By Stephen P. Kershaw

Thomas Jefferson and the Tripoli Pirates: The Forgotten War That Changed ...

Book by Brian Kilmeade and Don Yaeger

Andrew Jackson and the Miracle of New Orleans: The Battle That Shaped America's Destiny

by Brian Kilmeade and Don Yaeger

Unholy Alliance: The Agenda Iran, Russia, and Jihadists Share for Conquering the ...

Book by Jay Sekulow

Defeating Jihad: The Winnable War

Book by Sebastian Gorka

iWar: War and Peace in the Information Age Hardcover – January 3, 2017

by Bill Gertz

The Field of Fight: How We Can Win the Global War Against Radical Islam and Its Allies

Lieutenant General (Ret.) Michael T. Flynn Michael Ledeen

The Shadow Party

Book by David Horowitz and Richard Poe

Unholy Alliance: Radical Islam and the American Left

by David Horowitz

Big Agenda: President Trump S Plan to Save America

Book by David Horowitz

The Roots of Obama's Rage

Book by Dinesh D'Souza

Obama's America: Unmaking the American Dream Paperback – July 1, 2014

by Dinesh D'Souza

The Big Lie: Exposing the Nazi Roots of the American Left

by Dinesh D'Souza

Gandhi & Churchill: The Epic Rivalry that Destroyed an Empire and Forged Our Age

by Arthur Herman

Control Your Own Destiny or Someone Else Will – December 19, 1992

by Noel Tichy (Author), Stratford Sherman (Author)

The Living Company Jun 4, 2002

by Arie De Geus

Good to Great: Why Some Companies Make the Leap...and Others Don't

Book by James C. Collins

Built to Last: Successful Habits of Visionary Companies

Book by James C. Collins and Jerry I. Porras

Execution: The Discipline of Getting Things Done

by Larry Bossidy and Ram Charan

Winning the Talent Wars

by Bruce Tulgan

Get Better Or Get Beaten

by Robert Slater

Every Business Is a Growth Business: How Your Company Can Prosper Year After Year

by Ram Charan and Noel M. Tichy

Taking on the Trust: The Epic Battle of Ida Tarbell and John D. Rockefeller

Book by Steve Weinberg

After the Civil War: The Heroes, Villains, Soldiers, and Civilians Who Changed America

Book by James I. Robertson Jr.

Goh Keng Swee: A Portrait Nov 16, 2010

by Tan Siok Sun

Goh Keng Swee: A Public Career Remembered Jul 18, 2011

by Barry Desker and Chong Guan Kwa

Cop Under Fire: Moving Beyond Hashtags of Race, Crime, and Politics for a Better America

by David Clarke Jr., Nancy French (Contribution by), Sean Hannity (Foreword by)

American Commander: Serving a Country Worth Fighting For and Training the Brave Soldiers
    Who Lead the Way, Book by Ryan Zinke and Scott McEwen

The Origins of Political Order: From Prehuman Times to the French Revolution

by Francis Fukuyama

The Story of Architecture

by Jonathan Glancey

Twelve Books That Changed the World

Book by Melvyn Bragg

Mary Shelley's Frankenstein Comes to Life, NG History – Maria Pilar Queralt

How Europe won the Race to Prosperity, BBC History – Joel Mokyr

Read The Current American Civil War, a Global Perspective; we learn

- From Jared Diamond and Arie De Geus, to see human societies as living entities
- From Steve Jobs, the inverse correlation between intellectual brilliance and political correctness
- From Henry Kissinger, to view events from Multiple perspectives, understand their causes in context of various cultural backdrop, publicly visible motivations and private agendas of key players
- From Pope John Paul II, work ethics, values, America's ecological edge, wealth in its land and path forward for America and the World
- From Adam Smith, importance of awful virtues, how the free market's invisible hand works
- From Aristotle, respect Techne as productive knowledge, how the mindful hand, material, efficiency, formal and telos Cause explains the Culture of Innovation
- From traditional American Leadership Values, To Control your own destiny or someone else will, to take responsibility and be held accountable

After Reading The Current American Civil War, you'll

- Understand the current struggle between Culture of Competition and Growth against Culture of Monopoly and Decadence. Of following one's Reason against trying to be Politically Correct
- Gain Insights into the Realities behind the politics of Globalization; see that the world is not flat
- Get answers to why, after over $ 20 Trillions in National Debt, spent via QEs, etc. and $ 3 T annually in 'welfare and benefits' (more wealth than what the entire UK's working populace produces per their GDP), the America Income Inequality is at its highest in over 100 years.
- Open your eyes to the sophistries of the Problem Profiteers; evil nexus between the professional politicians and All-powerful Activist Corporations with hundreds of Billions of wealth under management
- Learn about the Shame Culture of the Anomie parvenus Reigning as Celebrities that ridicules the values of other fellow Americans
- See the binary programming of the M.O.B. (Millennial Oriented Broadcast) in action
- Follow how the flamboyant K Street Eunuch organizations, demoralized by the money pots of the Progressive Activists Corporations; enticed by millions in book deals, enervated by the Liberal Social and Mainstream Media such that honesty has become self-sacrifice, how after decades of indolence in DC and intensely adverse to active service, they've all degenerated into useless laughing stock
- Finally, comprehend why the Conjuncture of Age of Space Exploration, Competition, Freedom & Diversity of Ideas in Internet and lastly Enlightenment, awakening from the mindless indoctrination of Politically Correct, is so crucial for the Next Transformation for America and rest of the World

About the Author

Kern Lim was born and grew up in Singapore, South East Asia.

In the last quarter of century, he has lived and worked in a number of cities around the world; including Shanghai, Beijing in China, Hong Kong, Macau, Schenectady, NY, Atlanta, GA, Rochester, NY and Singapore. During this time, Kern has headed up key leadership roles in Finance, Operations Excellence, Mergers and Acquisitions with various companies in USA, China, Finland, Japan, Macau, Hong Kong and Europe, across a multitude of Industries (eg. Internet Security, nano-coating technology, Integrated Resorts, Consumer Products, Power Generation Equipment, etc.) with Companies such as General Electric Company, Hewett Packard, Eastman Kodak Company, Las Vegas Sands, etc.

In recent years, Kern has served as Independent Director on the Board, as well as Chairman of various Committees of a number of Public companies listed on the NYSE, Nasdaq, HKEx (Hong Kong Stock Exchange) and SGX (Singapore Exchange).

Kern is also a CPA (Singapore Chartered Accountant), CRMA (Certification in Risk Management Assurance of Institute of Internal Auditors, IIA Global), was Six Sigma Certified for Greenbelt, Blackbelt trained in General Electric Company, and also attended Executive Education in Stanford Graduate School of Business, International Institute of Management Development (IMD) in Lausanne, Switzerland, Kellogg Graduate School of Management (Northwestern University) in Evanston, IL and Harvard University, Graduate School of Business in Boston, MA.

Printed in the United States
By Bookmasters